CHILTON'S
REPAIR MANUAL

FORD PROBE 1989–92
All U.S. and Canadian models of Ford Probe

Sr. Vice President	Ronald A. Hoxter
Publisher and Editor-In-Chief	Kerry A. Freeman, S.A.E.
Managing Editors	Peter M. Conti, Jr. □ W. Calvin Settle, Jr., S.A.E.
Assistant Managing Editor	Nick D'Andrea
Senior Editors	Richard J. Rivele, S.A.E. □ Ron Webb
Director of Manufacturing	Mike D'Imperio
Manager of Manufacturing	John F. Butler
Editor	Michael L. Grady

CHILTON BOOK COMPANY
ONE OF THE **DIVERSIFIED PUBLISHING COMPANIES,**
A PART OF **CAPITAL CITIES/ABC, INC.**

CONTENTS

SAFETY NOTICE

Proper service and repair procedures are vital to the safe, reliable operation of all motor vehicles, as well as the safety of those performing repairs. This book outlines procedures for servicing and repairing vehicles using safe effective methods. The procedures contain many NOTES, CAUTIONS and WARNINGS which should be followed along with standard safety procedures to eliminate the possibility of personal injury or improper service which could damage the vehicle or compromise its safety.

It is important to note that repair procedures and techniques, tools and parts for servicing motor vehicles, as well as the skill and experience of the individual performing the work vary widely. It is not possible to anticipate all of the conceivable ways or conditions under which vehicles may be serviced, or to provide cautions as to all of the possible hazards that may result. Standard and accepted safety precautions and equipment should be used during cutting, grinding, chiseling, prying, or any other process that can cause material removal or projectiles.

Some procedures require the use of tools specially designed for a specific purpose. Before substituting another tool or procedure, you must be completely satisfied that neither your personal safety, nor the performance of the vehicle will be endangered.

Although the information in this guide is based on industry sources and is as complete as possible at the time of publication, the possibility exists that the manufacturer made later changes which could not be included here. While striving for total accuracy, Chilton Book Company cannot assume responsibility for any errors, changes, or omissions that may occur in the compilation of this data.

PART NUMBERS

Part numbers listed in the reference are not recommendations by Chilton for any product by brand name. They are references that can be used with interchange manuals and aftermarket supplier catalogs to locate each brand supplier's discrete part number.

SPECIAL TOOLS

Special tools are recommended by the vehicle manufacturer to perform their specific job. Use has been kept to a minimum, but where absolutely necessary, they are referred to in the text by the part number of the tool manufacturer. These tools can be purchased, under the appropriate part number, from the Owatonna Tool Company, Owatonna, MN 55060 or an equivalent tool can be purchased locally from a tool supplier or parts outlet. Before substituting any tool for the one recommended, read the SAFETY NOTICE at the top of this page.

ACKNOWLEDGEMENTS

Chilton Book Company expresses appreciation to Ford Motor Co.; Ford Parts and Service Division, Service Technical Communications Department, Dearborn, Michigan for their generous assistance.

Manufactured in the United States of America
1234567890   1098765432

Chilton's Repair Manual: Ford Probe 1989–92
ISBN 0–8019–8312–6
Library of Congress Catalog Card No. 91–058837

General Information and Maintenance

HOW TO USE THIS BOOK

Chilton's Repair Manual for the Ford Probe is intended to help you learn more about the inner workings of your vehicle and save you money on its upkeep and operation.

The first two Chapters will be the most used, since they contain maintenance and tune-up information and procedures. Studies have shown that a properly tuned and maintained car can get at least 10% better gas mileage than an out-of-tune car. The other Chapters deal with the more complex systems of your car. Operating systems from engine through brakes are covered to the extent that the average do-it-yourselfer becomes mechanically involved. It will give you detailed instructions to help you change your own brake pads and shoes, replace spark plugs, and do many more jobs that will save you money, give you personal satisfaction, and help you avoid expensive problems.

A secondary purpose of this book is a reference for owners who want to understand their car and/or their mechanics better. In this case, no tools at all are required.

Before removing any bolts, read through the entire procedure. This will give you the overall view of what tools and supplies will be required. There is nothing more frustrating than having to walk to the bus stop on Monday morning because you were short one bolt on Sunday afternoon. So read ahead and plan ahead. Each operation should be approached logically and all procedures thoroughly understood before attempting any work.

All Chapters contain adjustments, maintenance, removal and installation procedures, and repair or overhaul procedures. When repair is not considered practical, we tell you how to remove the part and then how to install the new or rebuilt replacement. In this way, you at least save the labor costs. Backyard repair of such components as the alternator is just not practical.

Two basic mechanic's rules should be mentioned here. One, whenever the left side of the car or engine is referred to, it is meant to specify the driver's side of the car. Conversely, the right side of the car means the passenger's side. Secondly, most screws and bolts are removed by turning counterclockwise, and tightened by turning clockwise.

Safety is always the most important rule. Constantly be aware of the dangers involved in working on an automobile and take the proper precautions. (See the section in this Chapter on Servicing Your Vehicle Safely and the SAFETY NOTICE on the acknowledgment page.)

Pay attention to the instructions provided. There are 3 common mistakes in mechanical work:

1. Incorrect order of assembly, disassembly or adjustment. When taking something apart or putting it together, doing things in the wrong order usually just costs you extra time; however, it CAN break something. Read the entire procedure before beginning disassembly. Do everything in the order in which the instructions say you should do it, even if you can't immediately see a reason for it. When you're taking apart something that is very intricate, you might want to draw a picture of how it looks when assembled at one point in order to make sure you get everything back in its proper position. (We will supply exploded views whenever possible). When making adjustments, especially tune-up adjustments, do them in order; often, one adjustment affects another, and you cannot expect even satisfactory results unless each adjustment is made only when it cannot be changed by any other.

2. Overtorquing (or undertorquing): While it is more common for overtorquing to cause damage, undertorquing can cause a fastener to vibrate loose causing serious damage. Especially

when dealing with aluminum parts, pay attention to torque specifications and utilize a torque wrench in assembly. If a torque figure is not available, remember that if you are using the right tool to do the job, you will probably not have to strain yourself to get a fastener tight enough. The pitch of most threads is so slight that the tension you put on the wrench will be multiplied many, many times in actual force on what you are tightening. A good example of how critical torque is can be seen in the case of spark plug installation, especially where you are putting the plug into an aluminum cylinder head. Too little torque can fail to crush the gasket, causing leakage of combustion gases and consequent overheating of the plug and engine parts. Too much torque can damage the threads or distort the plug, which changes the spark gap.

There are many commercial products available for ensuring the fasteners won't come loose, even if they are not torqued just right (a very common brand is Loctite®). If you're worried about getting something together tight enough to hold, but loose enough to avoid mechanical damage during assembly, one of these products might offer substantial insurance. Read the label on the package and make sure the product is compatible with the materials, fluids, etc. involved.

3. Crossthreading. This occurs when a part such as a bolt is screwed into a nut or casting at the wrong angle and forced. Cross threading is more likely to occur if access is difficult. It helps to clean and lubricate fasteners, and to start threading with the part to be installed going straight in. Start the bolt, spark plug, etc. with your fingers. If you encounter resistance, unscrew the part and start over again at a different angle until it can be inserted and turned several turns without much effort. Keep in mind that many parts, especially spark plugs, use tapered threads so that gentle turning will automatically bring the part you're threading to the proper angle if you don't force it or resist a change in angle. Don't put a wrench on the part until it's been turned a couple of turns by hand. If you suddenly encounter resistance, and the part has not seated fully, don't force it. Screw it back out and make sure it's clean and threading properly.

Always take your time and be patient; once you have some experience, working on your car will become an enjoyable hobby.

TOOLS AND EQUIPMENT

Naturally, without the proper tools and equipment it is impossible to properly service your vehicle. It would be impossible to catalog each tool that you would need to perform each or any operation in this book. It would also be unwise for the amateur to rush out and buy an expensive set of tools on the theory that he may need one or more of them at sometime.

The best approach is to proceed slowly, gathering together a good quality set of those tools that are used most frequently. Don't be misled by the low cost of bargain tools. It is far better to spend a little more for better quality. Forged wrenches, 6- or 12-point sockets and fine tooth ratchets are by far preferable than their less expensive counterparts. As any good mechanic can tell you, there are few worse experiences than trying to work on a car with bad tools. Your monetary savings will be far outweighed by frustration and mangled knuckles.

Begin accumulating those tools that are used most frequently; those associated with routine maintenance and tune-up.

In addition to the normal assortment of pliers and screwdrivers, you should have the following tools for routine maintenance jobs:

1. Metric and SAE wrenches, sockets and combination open end/box end wrenches in sizes from 3mm to 19mm, 1/8 in. to 3/4 in. and a spark plug socket ($^{13}/_{16}$ in. or 5/8 in. depending on plug type).

If possible, buy various length socket drive extensions. One break in this department is that the metric sockets available in the U.S. will all fit the ratchet handles and extensions you may already have (1/4 in., 3/8 in., and 1/2 in. drive).

2. Jackstands for support.
3. Oil filter wrench.
4. Oil filler spout or funnel.
5. Grease gun for chassis lubrication.
6. Hydrometer for checking the battery.
7. A container for draining oil.
8. Many rags for wiping up the inevitable mess.

In addition to the above items there are several others that are not absolutely necessary, but handy to have around. These include oil dry, a transmission funnel and the usual supply of lubricants, antifreeze and fluids, although these can be purchased as needed. This is a basic list for routine maintenance, but only your personal needs and desire can accurately determine your list of tools.

The second list of tools is for tune-ups. While the tools involved here are slightly more sophisticated, they need not be outrageously expensive. There are several inexpensive tachometers on the market that are every bit as good for the average mechanic as a $100.00 professional model. Just be sure that the meter goes to at least 1500 rpm on the scale and that it can be used on 4, 6, or 8 cylinder engines. A basic list of tune-up equipment could include:

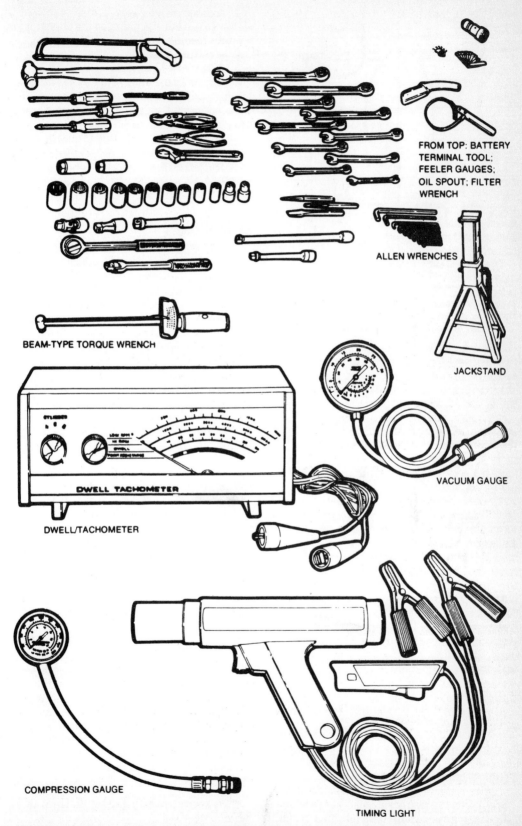

FROM TOP: BATTERY TERMINAL TOOL; FEELER GAUGES; OIL SPOUT; FILTER WRENCH

ALLEN WRENCHES

JACKSTAND

BEAM-TYPE TORQUE WRENCH

VACUUM GAUGE

DWELL TACHOMETER

DWELL/TACHOMETER

COMPRESSION GAUGE

TIMING LIGHT

The basic collection of tools and test instruments is all you need for most maintenance on your car

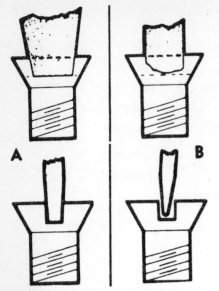

Keep screwdrivers in good shape. They should fit the slot as shown "A". If they look like those shown in "B", they need grinding or replacing

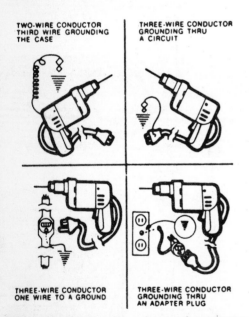

TWO-WIRE CONDUCTOR
THIRD WIRE GROUNDING
THE CASE

THREE-WIRE CONDUCTOR
GROUNDING THRU
A CIRCUIT

THREE-WIRE CONDUCTOR
ONE WIRE TO A GROUND

THREE-WIRE CONDUCTOR
GROUNDING THRU
AN ADAPTER PLUG

When using electric tools, make sure they are properly grounded

1. Tachometer.
2. Spark plug wrench.
3. Timing light (a DC light that works from the car's battery is best, although an AC light that plugs into 110V house current will suffice at some sacrifice in brightness).
4. Wire spark plug gauge/adjusting tools.

In addition to these basic tools there are several other tools and gauges you may find useful. These include:

1. A compression gauge. The screw in type is slower to use but it eliminates the possibility of a faulty reading due to escaping pressure.
2. A manifold vacuum gauge.
3. A 12V test light.
4. An induction meter. This is used for determining whether or not there is current in a wire. These are handy for use if a wire is broken somewhere in a wiring harness.

As a final note, you will probably find a torque wrench necessary for all but the most basic work. The beam type models are perfectly adequate although the newer click types are more precise.

Special Tools

NOTE: *Special tools are occasionally necessary to perform a specific job or are recommended to make the job easier. Their use has been kept to a minimum. When a special tool is indicated, it will be referred to by manufacturer's part number, and, where possible, an illustration of the tool will be provided so that an equivalent tool may be used.*

Normally, the use of special factory tools is avoided for repair procedures, since these are not readily available for the do-it-yourself mechanic. When it is possible to perform the job with more commonly available tools, it will be pointed out, but occasionally, a special tool was designed to perform a specific function and should be used. Before substituting another tool, you should be convinced that neither your safety nor the performance of the vehicle will be compromised.

Some special tools are available commercially from major tool manufacturers. Others can be purchased from your Ford dealer or from the Owatonna Tool Company, Owatonna, Minnesota 55060.

SERVICING YOUR VEHICLE SAFELY

It is virtually impossible to anticipate all of the hazards involved with automotive maintenance and service but care and common sense will prevent most accidents.

The rules of safety for mechanics range from "don't smoke around gasoline" to "use the proper tool for the job." The trick to avoiding injuries is to develop safe work habits and take every possible precaution.

Do's

● Do keep a fire extinguisher and first aid kit within easy reach.
● Do wear safety glasses or goggles when cut-

ting, drilling, grinding or prying, even if you have 20/20 vision. If you wear glasses for the sake of vision, then they should be made of hardened glass that can serve also as safety glasses, or wear safety goggles over your regular glasses.

• Do shield your eyes whenever you work around the battery. Batteries contain sulphuric acid; in case of contact with the eyes or skin, flush the area with water or a mixture of water and baking soda and get medical attention immediately.

• Do use safety stands for any under-car service. Jacks are for raising vehicles; safety stands are for making sure the vehicle stays raised until you want it to come down. Whenever the vehicle is raised, block the wheels remaining on the ground and set the parking brake.

• Do use adequate ventilation when working with any chemicals. Like carbon monoxide, the asbestos dust resulting from brake lining wear can be poisonous in sufficient quantities.

• Do disconnect the negative battery cable when working on the electrical system. The primary ignition system can contain up to 40,000 volts.

• Do follow manufacturer's directions whenever working with potentially hazardous materials. Both brake fluid and antifreeze are poisonous if taken internally.

• Do properly maintain your tools. Loose hammerheads, mushroomed punches and chisels, frayed or poorly grounded electrical cords, excessively worn screwdrivers, spread wrenches (open end), cracked sockets, slipping ratchets, or faulty droplight sockets can cause accidents.

• Do use the proper size and type of tool for the job being done.

• Do when possible, pull on a wrench handle rather than push on it, and adjust your stance to prevent a fall.

• Do be sure that adjustable wrenches are tightly adjusted on the nut or bolt and pulled so that the face is on the side of the fixed jaw.

• Do select a wrench or socket that fits the nut or bolt. The wrench or socket should sit straight, not cocked.

• Do strike squarely with a hammer. Avoid glancing blows.

• Do set the parking brake and block the drive wheels if the work requires that the engine be running.

Don'ts

• Don't run an engine in a garage or anywhere else without proper ventilation--EVER!

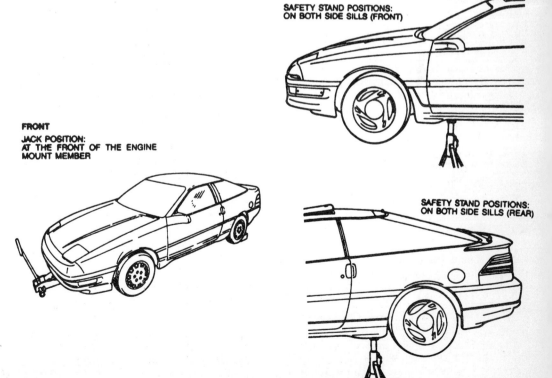

SAFETY STAND POSITIONS:
ON BOTH SIDE SILLS (FRONT)

FRONT
JACK POSITION:
AT THE FRONT OF THE ENGINE
MOUNT MEMBER

SAFETY STAND POSITIONS:
ON BOTH SIDE SILLS (REAR)

Correct positioning of jack and safety stands

Carbon monoxide is poisonous; it takes a long time to leave the human body and you can build up a deadly supply of it in your system by simply breathing in a little every day. You may not realize you are slowly poisoning yourself. Always use power vents, windows, fans or open the garage door.

• Don't work around moving parts while wearing a necktie or other loose clothing. Short sleeves are much safer than long, loose sleeves. Hard-toed shoes with neoprene soles protect your toes and give a better grip on slippery surfaces. Jewelry such as watches, fancy belt buckles, beads or body adornment of any kind is not safe working around a car. Long hair should be hidden under a hat or cap.

• Don't use pockets for toolboxes. A fall or bump can drive a screwdriver deep into your body. Even a wiping cloth hanging from the back pocket can wrap around a spinning shaft or fan.

• Don't smoke when working around gasoline, cleaning solvent or other flammable material.

• Don't smoke when working around the battery. When the battery is being charged, it gives off explosive hydrogen gas.

• Don't use gasoline to wash your hands; there are excellent soaps available. Gasoline may contain lead, and lead can enter the body through a cut, accumulating in the body until you are very ill. Gasoline also removes all the natural oils from the skin so that bone dry hands will suck up oil and grease.

• Don't service the air conditioning system unless you are equipped with the necessary tools and training. The refrigerant, R-12 is extremely cold and when exposed to the air, will instantly freeze any surface it comes in contact with, including your eyes. Although the refrigerant is normally non-toxic, R-12 becomes a deadly poisonous gas in the presence of an open flame. One good whiff of the vapors from burning refrigerant can be fatal.

HISTORY

The Probe is the product of a joint venture between the Ford Motor Company and Mazda Motor Corporation. First introduced in May of 1988 as a 1989 model, the Probe has been very successful for Ford due to its attractive aerodynamic styling and exceptional performance.

During the first model year of production, the Probe was available with a 2.2L normally aspirated 4-cylinder engine in GL and LX models, and a 2.2L turbocharged 4-cylinder engine in the GT model. For the 1990 model year, the

Probe received minor body restyling and a 3.0L V6 engine was introduced as standard equipment on the LX model. Appearance and powertrain have remained consistent through the 1992 model year.

SERIAL NUMBER IDENTIFICATION

Vehicle

The Vehicle Identification Number (VIN) is stamped on a metal plate that is riveted to the instrument panel adjacent to the windshield. It can be seen by looking through the lower corner of the windshield on the driver's side.

The VIN is a 17 digit combination of numbers and letters. The first 3 digits represent the world manufacturer identifier which is Mazda. The 4th digit indicates the type of passenger restraint system, either active or passive seat belts. The 5th digit is a Ford passenger car identifier, indicating the vehicle is imported from outside North America or is a non-Ford built passenger car sold by Ford in North America. The 6th and 7th digits indicate the body style: 20 for Probe GL, 21 for Probe LX, or 22 for Probe GT. The 8th digit is the engine code: C for the 2.2L normally aspirated engine, L for the 2.2L turbocharged engine, or U for the 3.0L V6 engine. The 9th digit is a check digit for all vehicles. The 10th digit indicates the model year: K for 1989, L for 1990, M for 1991, or N for 1992. The 11th digit is the assembly plant code, the digit 5 represents Flat Rock, Michigan. The 12th through 17th digits indicate the production sequence number.

Vehicle Certification Label

The Vehicle Certification Label is attached to the left hand door jamb below the latch striker. The upper half of the label contains the name of the manufacturer, month and year of manufacture, Gross Vehicle Weight Rating (GVWR),

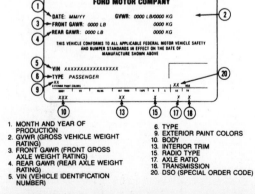

1. MONTH AND YEAR OF PRODUCTION
2. GVWR (GROSS VEHICLE WEIGHT RATING)
3. FRONT GAWR (FRONT GROSS AXLE WEIGHT RATING)
4. REAR GAWR (REAR AXLE WEIGHT RATING)
5. VIN (VEHICLE IDENTIFICATION NUMBER)
6. TYPE
9. EXTERIOR PAINT COLORS
10. BODY
13. INTERIOR TRIM
15. RADIO TYPE
17. AXLE RATIO
18. TRANSMISSION
20. DSO (SPECIAL ORDER CODE)

Sample Vehicle Certification Label

Gross Axle Weight Rating (GAWR), and the certification statement. The lower half of the label contains the VIN and a series of codes indicating exterior color, body type, interior trim type and color, radio type, axle ratio and transmission type.

Engine

The engine identification code is located in the VIN at the 8th digit. The VIN can be found on the Vehicle Certification Label and on the VIN plate attached to the instrument panel. See the Engine Identification chart for engine VIN codes.

Transaxle

The transaxle identification code is located on the lower half of the Vehicle Certification Label, which is attached to the left hand door jamb below the latch striker.

ROUTINE MAINTENANCE

Air Cleaner

The air cleaner is a paper element contained in a housing located on the left side of the engine compartment. The air filter element should be serviced according to the Maintenance Intervals Chart at the end of this Chapter.

NOTE: *Check the air filter element more often if the vehicle is operated under severe dusty conditions and replace, as necessary*

REMOVAL AND INSTALLATION

2.2L Engine

1. Disconnect the negative battery cable.
2. Disconnect the Vane Airflow Meter (VAF) electrical connector.
3. Remove the air duct clamp and the duct from the VAF meter assembly.
4. Remove the 5 air filter cover mounting screws.
5. Remove the air filter cover and the filter element.

To install:

6. Clean any dirt or other foreign material from the air filter housing.
7. Install the air filter element and the air filter cover.
8. Install and tighten the cover mounting screws.
9. Connect the air duct to the VAF meter assembly and tighten the clamp.
10. Connect the electrical connector to the VAF meter and connect the negative battery cable.

3.0L Engine

1. Loosen the clamp and disconnect the air duct from the filter housing upper cover.
2. Remove the 5 cover screws and the filter housing upper cover.
3. Remove the air filter.

To install:

4. Clean any dirt or other foreign material from the air filter housing.
5. Install the air filter element and the air filter cover.
6. Install and tighten the cover mounting screws.

ENGINE IDENTIFICATION

Year	Model	Engine Displacement Liters (cc)	Engine Series (ID/VIN)	Fuel System	No. of Cylinders	Engine Type
1989	Probe GL	2.2 (2189)	C	EFI	4	OHC
	Probe LX	2.2 (2189)	C	EFI	4	OHC
	Probe GT	2.2 (2189)	L	EFI①	4	OHC
1990	Probe GL	2.2 (2189)	C	EFI	4	OHC
	Probe LX	3.0 (2971)	U	EFI	6	OHV
	Probe GT	2.2 (2189)	L	EFI①	4	OHC
1991	Probe GL	2.2 (2189)	C	EFI	4	OHC
	Probe LX	3.0 (2971)	U	EFI	6	OHV
	Probe GT	2.2 (2189)	L	EFI①	4	OHC
1992	Probe GL	2.2 (2189)	C	EFI	4	OHC
	Probe LX	3.0 (2971)	U	EFI	6	OHV
	Probe GT	2.2 (2189)	L	EFI①	4	OHC

EFI—Electronic Fuel Injection OHV—Overhead Valve
OHC—Overhead Camshaft ① Turbocharged

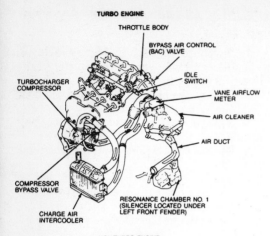

TURBO ENGINE

THROTTLE BODY

BYPASS AIR CONTROL
(BAC) VALVE

IDLE
SWITCH

VANE AIRFLOW
METER

AIR CLEANER

AIR DUCT

TURBOCHARGER
COMPRESSOR

COMPRESSOR
BYPASS VALVE

CHARGE AIR
INTERCOOLER

RESONANCE CHAMBER NO. 1
(SILENCER LOCATED UNDER
LEFT FRONT FENDER)

NON-TURBO ENGINE

THROTTLE BODY

BYPASS AIR CONTROL
(BAC) VALVE

IDLE SWITCH

VANE
AIRFLOW
METER

AIR CLEANER

AIR DUCT

RESONANCE CHAMBER NO. 2

RESONANCE CHAMBER NO. 1
(SILENCER LOCATED UNDER
LEFT FRONT FENDER)

Air intake system—2.2L engine

7. Connect the air duct to the filter housing upper cover and tighten the clamp.

Fuel Filter

The fuel filter is attached to a bracket located in the left rear of the engine compartment, next to the brake master cylinder fluid reservoir. The fuel filter should be serviced according to the Maintenance Intervals Chart at the end of this Chapter.

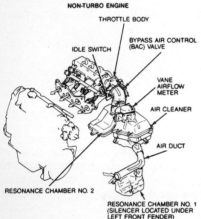

FILTER HOUSING
UPPER COVER

AIR FILTER
ELEMENT

AIR DUCT

CLAMP

AIR FILTER
HOUSING

Air cleaner assembly—3.0L engine

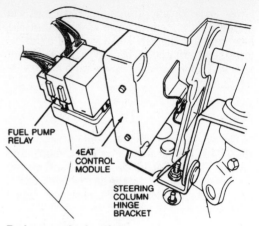

FUEL PUMP
RELAY

4EAT
CONTROL
MODULE

STEERING
COLUMN
HINGE
BRACKET

Fuel pump relay location

REMOVAL AND INSTALLATION

1. Relieve the fuel system pressure as follows:

   a. Start the engine.

   b. Disconnect the fuel pump relay from the relay box.

   c. After the engine stalls, turn the ignition switch **OFF** and reconnect the fuel pump relay to the relay box.

NOTE: *If equipped with 3.0L engine, an alternate method of relieving fuel system pressure can be used using pressure gauge tool T80L–9974–B or equivalent. Connect the tool to the fuel diagnostic valve located on the fuel supply manifold and release the fuel pressure through the drain hose into a suitable container.*

2. Disconnect the negative battery cable.

3. On 2.2L engines, remove the fuel line clamps. On 3.0L engine, remove the fuel line clips.

4. Disconnect the fuel lines from the filter and plug the ends to prevent leakage.

5. Loosen the bolt and nut and remove the fuel filter from its mounting bracket. Note the direction of the flow arrow on the filter so the replacement filter can be installed in the correct position.

To install:

6. Install the fuel filter in its mounting bracket, making sure the flow arrow is pointing in the proper direction. Tighten the bracket bolt and nut.

7. Unplug the fuel lines and connect them to the fuel filter.

8. On 2.2L engines, install the fuel line clamps. On 3.0L engine, install new fuel line clips into the fuel line connector onto the filter, assuring a positive lock.

9. Connect the negative battery cable.

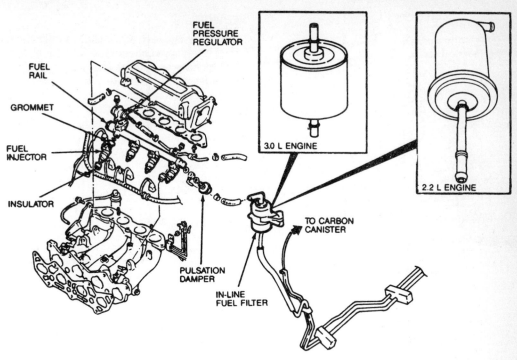

Fuel filter location

PCV Valve

The PCV valve is located in a grommet attached to the valve cover. For crankcase ventilation system testing, refer to Chapter 4.

REMOVAL AND INSTALLATION

1. Remove the PCV valve from the valve cover grommet.
2. Disconnect the hose from the PCV valve and remove it from the vehicle.

3. Check the PCV valve for deposits and clogging. If the valve rattles when shaken, it is okay. If the valve does not rattle, clean the valve with solvent until the plunger is free, or replace it.
4. Check the PCV hose and the valve cover grommet for clogging and signs of wear or deterioration. Replace, as necessary.

To install:

5. Connect the PCV hose to the PCV valve.

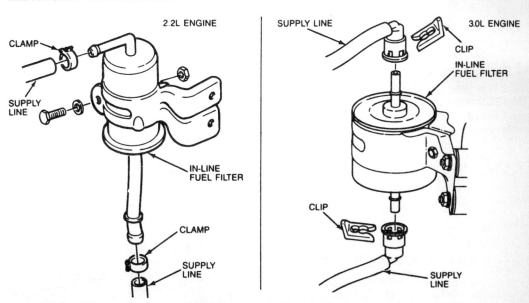

Fuel filter removal and installation

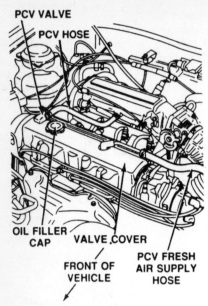

PCV VALVE

PCV HOSE

OIL FILLER CAP

VALVE COVER

FRONT OF VEHICLE

PCV FRESH AIR SUPPLY HOSE

PCV valve location—2.2L engine

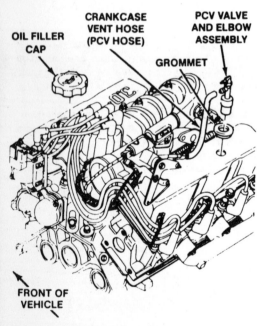

OIL FILLER CAP

CRANKCASE VENT HOSE (PCV HOSE)

PCV VALVE AND ELBOW ASSEMBLY

GROMMET

FRONT OF VEHICLE

PCV valve location—3.0L engine

6. Install the PCV valve in the valve cover grommet.

Evaporative Canister

The vapor, or carbon canister is part of the evaporative emission control system. It is located in the right rear of the engine compartment.

SERVICING

Servicing the carbon canister is only necessary if it is clogged or contains liquid fuel, indicated by odor or by excessive weight. Remove the canister and blow into the air vent in the bottom of the canister. If air passes from the fuel vapor inlet and the canister does not contain liquid fuel, it is okay. If replacement is necessary, the canister must be replaced as a unit; it cannot be disassembled. For further evaporative emission control system testing, refer to Chapter 4.

Battery

GENERAL MAINTENANCE

Corrosion of the battery terminals and cable clamps interferes with both the flow of power out of the battery and the charge flowing into the battery from the charging system. This can result in a "no start" condition. If the battery becomes completely discharged, battery life may be shortened. In some cases, a totally discharged battery may not readily accept a charge.

To reduce the need for service and to extend battery life, keep the top of the battery, the battery terminals, and the cable clamps clean and free of corrosion. Make sure the cable clamps are tightly fastened to the battery terminals. If corrosion is found, disconnect the cables and clean the clamps and terminals with a wire brush. Neutralize the corrosion with a solution of baking soda and water. After installing the cables, apply a light coating of petroleum jelly to the cable clamps and terminals to help prevent corrosion.

FLUID LEVEL (EXCEPT MAINTENANCE FREE BATTERIES)

Check the battery electrolyte level at least once a month, or more often in hot weather or

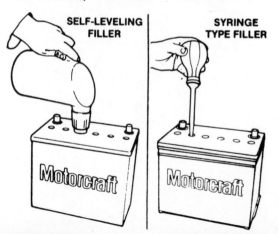

SELF-LEVELING FILLER

SYRINGE TYPE FILLER

Filling the battery

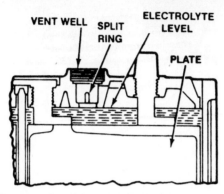

VENT WELL **SPLIT RING** **ELECTROLYTE LEVEL** **PLATE**

Cross-sectional view of typical battery

during periods of extended car operation. The level can be checked through the case on translucent polypropylene batteries; the cell caps must be removed on other models. The electrolyte level in each cell should be kept filled to the split ring inside, or the line marked on the outside of the case.

If the level is low, add only distilled water, or colorless, odorless drinking water, through the opening until the level is correct. Each cell is completely separate from the others, so each must be checked and filled individually.

If water is added in freezing weather, the car should be driven several miles to allow the water to mix with the electrolyte. Otherwise, the battery could freeze. If the battery needs water often, check the charging system.

CABLES

CAUTION: *Always remove the negative battery cable first, to avoid the possibility of grounding the car's electrical system by accident. Failure to do so could allow a spark to occur and cause the battery gases to explode, possibly resulting in personal injury.*

1. Loosen the negative battery cable nut using an adjustable or box wrench and battery pliers. The jaws on battery pliers are specially designed for gripping the cable clamp bolts.

2. Using a battery cable clamp puller, remove the negative battery cable from the battery post.

Cleaning the battery cable clamp

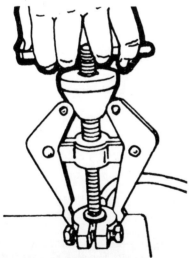

Removing the battery cable clamp

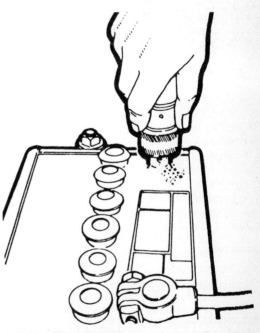

Cleaning the battery post

Cleaning side post battery terminal and cable

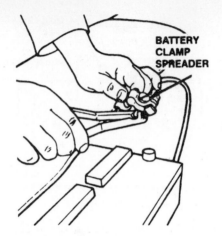

Spreading the battery cable clamp

WARNING: *Do not twist or pry the cable clamp off of the post using a screwdriver. This may crack the top of the battery or cause damage to the internal battery components and leakage at the terminals.*

3. Repeat Steps 1 and 2 to remove the positive battery cable.

4. Clean both battery posts and the cable clamps using battery cleaning tools. There are tools available for both top post and side post batteries.

5. Remove the remaining corrosion deposits from the battery and cables by flushing with a baking soda-water solution comprising 2 teaspoons of baking soda and 1 cup of water.

WARNING: *Do not allow the solution to enter the battery as this could weaken the electrolyte. Be careful not to allow the flushed deposits to come in contact with painted surfaces as paint damage may result.*

6. Follow the negative battery cable to the engine block and check the connection. If it is loose or corroded, remove the cable and clean the cable end and block with sandpaper, then reconnect the cable.

7. Follow the positive cable to the starter and clean and tighten, if necessary.

8. Apply a small amount of petroleum jelly around the base of each battery post, to help reduce the possibility of corrosion. Do not coat the battery post.

9. Install the positive battery cable on the positive battery post. It may be necessary to spread the clamp slightly using a clamp spreader tool. Do not twist the clamp in an attempt to seat it on the post. When the clamp is seated, tighten the clamp nut.

10. Repeat Step 9 to install the negative battery cable.

11. After the cables are installed, coat the top of each terminal lightly with petroleum jelly.

TESTING

Specific Gravity (Except Maintenance Free Batteries)

At least once a year, check the specific gravity of the battery using a hydrometer. The hydrometer has a squeeze bulb at one end and nozzle at the other. Battery electrolyte is sucked into the hydrometer until the float is lifted from its seat. The specific gravity is then read by noting the position of the float. If the difference between cells is 50 points (0.050) or more, the battery is bad and must be replaced.

If the difference between cells is less than 50 points (0.050) and one or more cells are less than 1.225, charge the battery for 20 minutes at 35 amps and perform the capacity test. If the battery fails, it must be replaced. If it passes, add water, if necessary, and charge the battery. If the difference between cells is less than 50 points (0.050) and all cells are above 1.225, perform the capacity test. If the battery fails, replace it.

It is not possible to check the specific gravity in this manner on sealed (maintenance free) batteries. Instead, the indicator built into the top of the case must be relied on to display any signs of battery deterioration. If the indicator is dark, the battery can be assumed to be OK. If the indicator is light, the specific gravity is low and the battery should be charged or replaced.

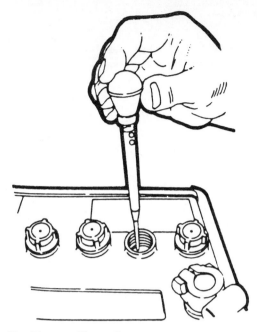

Checking specific gravity

Capacity Test

A high rate discharge battery-starter tester and a voltmeter are used for this test.

1. Turn the control knob on the tester to the **OFF** position and set the voltmeter selector switch to the 10 or 20 volt position.

2. Connect both positive test leads to the positive battery post and both negative test leads to the negative battery post. The voltmeter clips must contact the battery posts and not the high rate discharge tester clips, or actual battery terminal voltage will not be indicated.

3. Turn the load control knob on the tester until the ammeter reads approximately 3 times the ampere hour rating of the battery. For example, a 48 ampere hour battery should be tested at 150 amperes load.

4. With the ammeter reading the required load for 15 seconds, record the voltmeter reading. Do not leave the high discharge load on the battery for longer than 15 seconds.

5. If the voltmeter reading is 9.6 volts at 70°F (21°C) or more, the battery has good output capacity and will accept a charge, if necessary.

6. If the voltmeter reading is below 9.6 volts at 70°F (21°C) and the battery is fully charged, the battery is bad and must be replaced. If you are not sure about the battery's state of charge, charge the battery.

7. After the battery has been charged, repeat the capacity test. If the voltage is still less than 9.6 volts at 70°F (21°C), replace the battery. If the voltage is 9.6 or more at 70°F (21°C), the battery is good.

CHARGING

CAUTION: *Keep flame or sparks away from the battery. The battery emits explosive hydrogen gas, especially when being charged. Battery electrolyte contains sulphuric acid. If electrolyte accidently comes in contact with your skin or eyes, flush with plenty of clear water. If it lands in your eyes, get medical help immediately.*

A cold battery will not readily accept a charge, so allow the battery to warm up to approximately 40°F (5°C) before charging, if necessary. This may take 4 to 8 hours at room temperature, depending on initial temperature and battery size.

A completely discharged battery may be slow to accept a charge initially and in some cases may not accept a charge at the normal charger setting. If the battery is in this condition, charging can be initiated using the dead battery switch, on battery chargers so equipped. Follow the charger manufacturers instructions on the use of the dead battery switch.

If the battery will accept a charge, it can be charged using the automatic or manual method. If the charger is equipped with an automatic setting, the charge rate is maintained within safe limits by automatic adjustment of the voltage and current in order to prevent excessive gassing and discharge of electrolyte. It will take approximately 2 to 4 hours to charge a completely discharged battery to a usable state. A full state of charge can be obtained by charging at a low current rate of 3 to 5 amps for a few more hours.

If the charger does not have an automatic setting, the battery will have to be charged manually. Initially set the charging rate for 30 to 40 amps and charge for approximately 30 minutes or as long as there is no excessive gassing or electrolyte discharge. If there is excessive gas

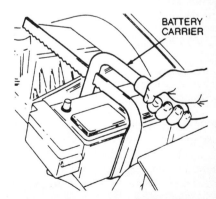

BATTERY CARRIER

Removing the battery with the battery carrier

JUMP STARTING A DEAD BATTERY

The chemical reaction in a battery produces explosive hydrogen gas. This is the safe way to jump start a dead battery, reducing the chances of an accidental spark that could cause an explosion.

Jump Starting Precautions

1. Be sure both batteries are of the same voltage.
2. Be sure both batteries are of the same polarity (have the same grounded terminal).
3. Be sure the vehicles are not touching.
4. Be sure the vent cap holes are not obstructed.
5. Do not smoke or allow sparks around the battery.
6. In cold weather, check for frozen electrolyte in the battery.
7. Do not allow electrolyte on your skin or clothing.
8. Be sure the electrolyte is not frozen.

Jump Starting Procedure

1. Determine voltages of the two batteries; they must be the same.
2. Bring the starting vehicle close (they must not touch) so that the batteries can be reached easily.
3. Turn off all accessories and both engines. Put both cars in Neutral or Park and set the handbrake.
4. Cover the cell caps with a rag—do not cover terminals.
5. If the terminals on the run-down battery are heavily corroded, clean them.
6. Identify the positive and negative posts on both batteries and connect the cables in the order shown.
7. Start the engine of the starting vehicle and run it at fast idle. Try to start the car with the dead battery. Crank it for no more than 10 seconds at a time and let it cool off for 20 seconds in between tries.
8. If it doesn't start in 3 tries, there is something else wrong.
9. Disconnect the cables in the reverse order.
10. Replace the cell covers and dispose of the rags.

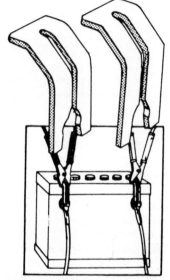

Side terminal batteries occasionally pose a problem when connecting jumper cables. There frequently isn't enough room to clamp the cables without touching sheet metal. Side terminal adaptors are available to alleviate this problem and should be removed after use.

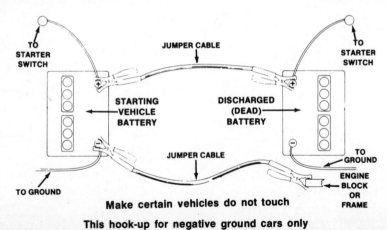

Make certain vehicles do not touch

This hook-up for negative ground cars only

emission, slow the charge rate to a level where the gassing stops. Excessive gas emission will result in non-replaceable loss of electrolyte.

REPLACEMENT

1. Disconnect the negative and then the positive battery cables from the battery.
2. Remove the battery hold-down clamps.
3. Remove the battery using a battery carrier. If a battery carrier is not available, grip the battery at opposite corners with your hands and carefully lift the battery from the tray.
. 4. Check the battery tray for corrosion or other damage. Clean the tray with a wire brush and a scraper.
5. Clean the battery and the cables.
6. Install the battery and retain with the hold-down clamps.
7. Connect the positive and then the negative battery cables.

Belts

Accessories mounted on the front of the engine are belt-driven by the crankshaft. The 2.2L engines use one V-belt to drive the alternator and another to drive the power steering pump and air conditioning compressor. The 3.0L engine uses one V-ribbed belt to drive the alternator, power steering pump and air conditioning compressor and one V-ribbed belt to drive the water pump.

The accessory drive belts should be serviced according to the Maintenance Intervals Chart at the end of this Chapter.

INSPECTION

Inspect all belts for signs of glazing or cracking. A glazed belt will be perfectly smooth from slippage, while a good belt will have a slight texture of fabric visible. Cracks will usually start at the inner edge of the belt and run outward. Replace the belt at the first sign of cracking or if glazing is severe.

ADJUSTMENT

2.2L Engines

ALTERNATOR BELT

1. Position a ruler perpendicular to the drive belt midway between the pulleys on the longest accessible belt span. Press firmly on the belt with your thumb to test the belt tension. The belt should deflect 0.24–0.31 in. (6–8mm) if it is new or 0.27–0.35 in. (7–9mm) if it is used.
2. If the belt tension is not as specified in Step 1, loosen the alternator adjustment bolt and the through bolt. Turn the alternator adjustment screw to adjust the belt tension.
3. After adjustment, tighten the through

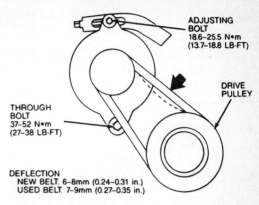

Alternator belt tension adjustment—2.2L engines

bolt to 27–38 ft. lbs. (37–52 Nm) and the adjusting bolt to 13–18 ft. lbs. (18–25 Nm).

POWER STEERING AND AIR CONDITIONING BELT

1. Position a ruler perpendicular to the drive belt midway between the pulleys on the longest accessible belt span. Press firmly on the belt with your thumb to test the belt tension. The belt should deflect 0.27–0.35 in. (7–9mm) if it is new or 0.31–0.39 in. (8–10mm) if it is used.
2. If the belt tension is not as specified in Step 1, loosen the upper and lower air conditioning compressor through bolts.
3. Using a suitable prybar against the compressor body, move the compressor until the belt tension is as specified in Step 1.
4. After adjustment, tighten the upper and lower air conditioning compressor through bolts.

3.0L Engine

The 3.0L engine uses an automatic tensioner to maintain proper belt tension. No adjustment is necessary.

REMOVAL AND INSTALLATION

2.2L Engines

1. Loosen the air conditioning compressor upper and lower through bolts. Rotate the compressor toward the engine and remove the drive belt.
2. Loosen the alternator pivot and adjuster bolts. Rotate the alternator toward the engine and remove the drive belt.
3. Inspect the drive belts for wear or damage and replace, as necessary.
To install:
4. Position the drive belts over the pulleys.
5. Adjust the belt tension as described under Adjustment.
6. Tighten the alternator and compressor mounting bolts after belt adjustment.

HOW TO SPOT WORN V-BELTS

V-Belts are vital to efficient engine operation—they drive the fan, water pump and other accessories. They require little maintenance (occasional tightening) but they will not last forever. Slipping or failure of the V-belt will lead to overheating. If your V-belt looks like any of these, it should be replaced.

Cracking or weathering

This belt has deep cracks, which cause it to flex. Too much flexing leads to heat build-up and premature failure. These cracks can be caused by using the belt on a pulley that is too small. Notched belts are available for small diameter pulleys.

Softening (grease and oil)

Oil and grease on a belt can cause the belt's rubber compounds to soften and separate from the reinforcing cords that hold the belt together. The belt will first slip, then finally fail altogether.

Glazing

Glazing is caused by a belt that is slipping. A slipping belt can cause a run-down battery, erratic power steering, overheating or poor accessory performance. The more the belt slips, the more glazing will be built up on the surface of the belt. The more the belt is glazed, the more it will slip. If the glazing is light, tighten the belt.

Worn cover

The cover of this belt is worn off and is peeling away. The reinforcing cords will begin to wear and the belt will shortly break. When the belt cover wears in spots or has a rough jagged appearance, check the pulley grooves for roughness.

Separation

This belt is on the verge of breaking and leaving you stranded. The layers of the belt are separating and the reinforcing cords are exposed. It's just a matter of time before it breaks completely.

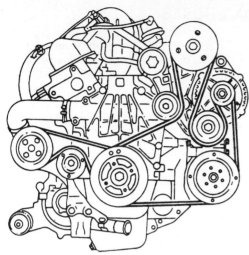

Accessory drive belt routing—3.0L engine

3.0L Engine

ALTERNATOR, POWER STEERING AND AIR CONDITIONING BELT

1. If the belt is to be reused, mark the direction of rotation on the drive belt with a crayon or marker so the belt can be reinstalled in the same position. Failure to do so may result in belt noise.

2. Remove the plastic belt shield from the power steering pump.

3. Using a ½ in. drive breaker bar or equivalent, inserted in the idler pulley tensioner, release the tension on the drive belt.

4. While releasing the belt tension, move the drive belt off of the tensioner pulley.

5. Release the tensioner and remove the belt from the engine.

6. Inspect the drive belt for wear or damage and replace, as necessary.

To install:

7. Position the drive belt on the crankshaft damper and accessory pulleys.

8. Using a ½ in. drive breaker bar or equivalent, pull the idler pulley tensioner back far enough to allow the drive belt to be positioned on the tensioner pulley.

9. Slowly release the breaker bar, allowing the idler pulley tensioner to rest against the drive belt. Remove the breaker bar from the tensioner.

10. Visually inspect the drive belt to make sure it is fully seated on all of the pulleys.

11. Install the plastic belt shield on the power steering pump.

WATER PUMP BELT

1. Remove the alternator, power steering and air conditioning belt.

2. Raise and safely support the vehicle.

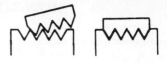

INCORRECT   CORRECT

Correct and incorrect belt positioning in the pulley grooves

3. Remove the right-hand plastic inner fender shield to gain access to the belt.

4. If the belt is to be reused, mark the direction of rotation on the drive belt with a crayon or marker so the belt can be reinstalled in the same position. Failure to do so may result in belt noise.

5. Place a wrench on the water pump pulley tensioner and turn the wrench clockwise to release the belt tension. Remove the belt.

6. Inspect the drive belt for wear or damage and replace, as necessary.

To install:

7. Place a wrench on the idler pulley tensioner and turn it counterclockwise.

8. Position the water pump belt on the pulleys.

9. Release the wrench, allowing the pulley tensioner to rest against the belt. Remove the wrench.

10. Install the plastic inner fender shield.

11. Lower the vehicle.

12. Install the alternator, power steering and air conditioning belt.

Hoses

CAUTION: *Disconnect the negative battery cable or fan motor wiring harness connector before replacing any radiator/heater hose. The fan may come on, under certain circumstances, even though the ignition is off.*

INSPECTION

Inspect the condition of the radiator and heater hoses periodically. Early spring and at the beginning of the fall or winter, when you are performing other maintenance, are good times. Make sure the engine and cooling system are cold. Visually inspect for cracking, rotting or collapsed hoses, replace as necessary. Run your hand along the length of the hose. If a weak or swollen spot is noted when squeezing the hose wall, replace the hose.

REMOVAL AND INSTALLATION

1. Remove the radiator cap.

CAUTION: *Never remove the radiator cap while the engine is running or personal injury from scalding hot coolant or steam may re-*

HOW TO SPOT BAD HOSES

Both the upper and lower radiator hoses are called upon to perform difficult jobs in an inhospitable environment. They are subject to nearly 18 psi at under hood temperatures often over 280°F., and must circulate nearly 7500 gallons of coolant an hour—3 good reasons to have good hoses.

A good test for any hose is to feel it for soft or spongy spots. Frequently these will appear as swollen areas of the hose. The most likely cause is oil soaking. This hose could burst at any time, when hot or under pressure.

Swollen hose

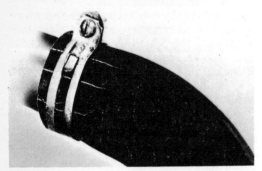

Cracked hoses can usually be seen but feel the hoses to be sure they have not hardened; a prime cause of cracking. This hose has cracked down to the reinforcing cords and could split at any of the cracks.

Cracked hose

Weakened clamps frequently are the cause of hose and cooling system failure. The connection between the pipe and hose has deteriorated enough to allow coolant to escape when the engine is hot.

Frayed hose end (due to weak clamp)

Debris, rust and scale in the cooling system can cause the inside of a hose to weaken. This can usually be felt on the outside of the hose as soft or thinner areas.

Debris in cooling system

sult. *If possible, wait until the engine has cooled to remove the radiator cap. If this is not possible, wrap a thick cloth around the radiator cap and turn it slowly to the first stop. Step back while the pressure is released from the cooling system. When you are sure all the pressure has been released, press down on the cap, still with the cloth, and turn and remove it.*

2. Position a suitable container under the radiator and open the draincock to drain the radiator.

CAUTION: *When draining the coolant, keep in mind that cats and dogs are attracted by the ethylene glycol antifreeze, and are quite likely to drink any that is left in an uncovered container or in puddles on the ground. This will prove fatal in sufficient quantity. Always drain the coolant into a sealable container. Coolant should be reused unless it is contaminated or several years old.*

3. Loosen the hose clamps at each end of the hose requiring replacement. Pull the clamps back on the hose away from the connection.

4. Twist, pull and slide the hose off the radiator, water pump, thermostat or heater connection.

NOTE: *If the hose is stuck at the connection, do not try to insert a screwdriver or other sharp tool under the hose end in an effort to free it, as the connection and/or hose may become damaged. Heater connections especially are easily damaged. If the hose is not to be reused, make a slice at the end of the hose with a single edge razor blade, perpendicular to the end of the hose. Do not cut deep so as not to damage the connection. The hose can then be peeled from the connection.*

5. Clean both hose mounting connections. Inspect the condition of the hose clamps and replace them, if necessary.

To install:

6. Coat the connection surfaces with a water resistant sealer.

7. Slide the hose clamps over the replacement hose and slide the hose ends over the connections into position.

8. Position the hose clamps. Make sure they are located beyond the raised bead of the connector, if equipped, and centered in the clamping area of the connection.

9. If the clamps are the screw type, tighten them to 22–31 inch lbs. (2.5–3.5 Nm). Do not overtighten.

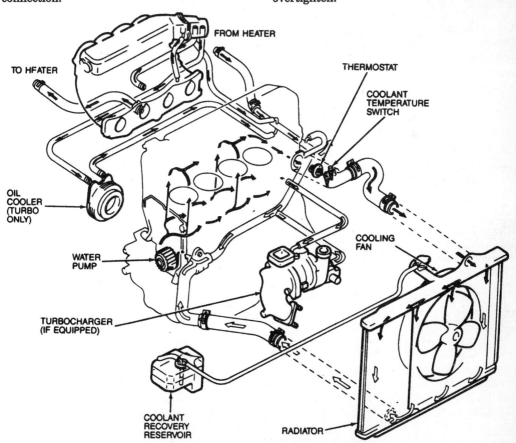

Cooling system—2.2L engine

10. Close the radiator draincock and fill the cooling system.

11. Start the engine and allow it to reach normal operating temperature. Check for leaks.

Air Conditioning System

SAFETY WARNINGS

1. Avoid contact with a charged refrigeration system, even when working on another part of the air conditioning system or vehicle. If a heavy tool comes into contact with a section of air conditioning line, it can easily cause the relatively soft material to rupture.

2. When it is necessary to apply force to a fitting which contains refrigerant, as when checking that all system couplings are securely tightened, use a wrench on both parts of the fitting involved, if possible. This will avoid putting torque on the refrigerant tubing. (It is advisable, when possible, to use tube or line wrenches when tightening these flare nut fittings.)

3. Do not attempt to discharge the system. Discharging the system should only be attempted by certified proffessional technician, using a air conditioning recycling/recovery machine.

4. Avoid applying heat to any refrigerant line or storage vessel. Charging the system should only be performed by a certified professional technician.

5. Always wear safety glasses when working around system to protect your eyes. If refrigerant contacts the eye, it is advisable in all cases to see a physician as soon as possible.

6. Frostbite from liquid refrigerant should be treated by first gradually warming the area with cool water, and then gently applying petroleum jelly. A physician should be consulted.

SYSTEM INSPECTION

Visually inspect the air conditioning system for refrigerant leaks, damaged compressor clutch, compressor drive belt tension and condition, plugged evaporator drain tube, blocked condenser fins, disconnected or broken wires, blown fuses, corroded connections and poor insulation.

A refrigerant leak will usually appear as an oily residue at the leakage point in the system. The oily residue soon picks up dust or dirt particles from the surrounding air and appears greasy. Through time, this will build up and appear to be a heavy dirt impregnated grease. Most leaks are caused by damaged or missing O-ring seals at the component connections, damaged charging valve cores or missing service gauge port caps.

The evaporator drain tube expels the condensation that accumulates in the bottom of the evaporator housing, out into the engine compartment. If the tube is obstructed, air conditioning performance can be restricted and condensation buildup can spill over onto the vehicle floor.

Any obstruction of or damage to the condenser configuration will restrict the air flow which is essential to its efficient operation. It is therefore a good rule to keep the condenser clean and in proper physical shape.

Vigorously shake the wiring harness while running the air conditioning and look for sparks (a sign of shorting) or intermittent operation (a sign of opens).

Move the refrigerant hoses and look for signs of cracks, rotted hoses or loose connections.

REFRIGERANT LEVEL CHECKS

1. Connect a manifold gauge set.

2. Run the engine at 2000 rpm.

3. Set the blower motor on high and the temperature control at cool.

4. If the compressor clutch does not engage, connect a jumper wire between the positive battery terminal and the green/black wire at the clutch connector.

5. Wait until the air conditioning system stabilizes and check the readings of the HI and LO gauges. The normal HI reading is 199–228 psi (1372–1572kpa). The normal LO reading is 19–21 psi (131–145kpa).

6. If the HI reading is 114–128 psi (786–883kpa) and the LO reading is 11.4 psi (78.6kpa), there is insufficient refrigerant in the system. The system must be leak tested and recharged with the proper amount of refrigerant.

7. If the HI reading is 284 psi (1958kpa) or more and the LO reading is 35.6 psi (245.5kpa) or more, there is excessive refrigerant in the system. Have the system recharged with the proper amount of refrigerant by a certified proffessional technician.

DISCHARGING THE SYSTEM

NOTE: *R-12 refrigerant is a chlorofluorocarbon which, when released into the atmosphere, can contribute to the depletion of the ozone layer in the upper atmosphere. Ozone filters out harmful radiation from the sun. All system discharging and recharging should only be attempted by a certified proffessional technician, using an approved R-12 Recovery/Recycling and recharging machine that meets SAE standards.*

Windshield Wipers

For maximum effectiveness and longest element life, the windshield and wiper blades should be kept clean. Dirt, tree sap, road tar and so on will cause streaking, smearing and blade deterioration if left on the glass. It is advisable to wash the windshield carefully with a commercial glass cleaner at least once a month. Wipe off the rubber blades with the wet rag afterwards. Do not attempt to move the wipers by hand; damage to the motor and drive mechanism will result.

To inspect and/or replace the wiper blades, place the wiper switch in the **LOW** speed position and the ignition switch in the **ACC** position. When the wiper blades are approximately vertical on the windshield, turn the ignition switch to **OFF**.

Examine the wiper blades. If they are found to be cracked, broken or torn, they should be replaced immediately. Replacement intervals will vary with usage, although ozone deterioration usually limits blade life to about one year. If the wiper pattern is smeared or streaked, or if the blade chatters across the glass, the elements

should be replaced. It is easiest and most sensible to replace the elements in pairs.

There are several different types of refills, and your vehicle could have any kind, since aftermarket blades and arms may not use exactly the same type refill as the original equipment.

The Anco® type uses a release button that is pushed down to allow the refill to slide out of the yoke jaws. The new refill slides back into the frame and locks in place.

Some Trico® refills are removed by locating where the metal backing strip or the refill is wider. Insert a small screwdriver blade between the frame and metal backing strip. Press down to release the refill from the retaining tab.

Other types of Trico® refills have two metal tabs which are unlocked by squeezing them together. The rubber filler can then be withdrawn from the frame jaws. A new refill is installed by inserting the refill into the front frame jaws and sliding it rearward to engage the remaining frame jaws. There are usually four jaws; be cer-

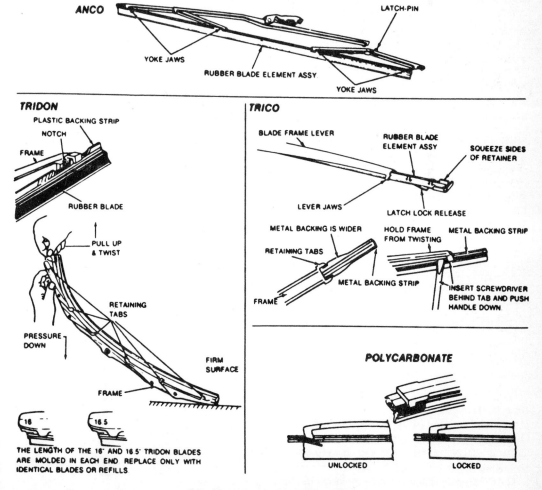

Popular types of wiper blade refills

tain when installing, that the refill is engaged in all of them. At the end of its travel, the tabs will lock into place on the front jaws of the wiper blade frame.

Another type of refill is made from polycarbonate. The refill has a simple locking device at one end which flexes downward out of the groove into which the jaws of the holder fit, allowing easy release. By sliding the new refill through all the jaws and pushing through the slight resistance when it reaches the end of its travel, the refill will lock into position.

To replace the Tridon® refill, it is necessary to remove the wiper arm or blade. This refill has a plastic backing strip with a notch about 1 in. (25mm) from the end. Hold the blade (frame) on a hard surface so the frame is tightly bowed. Grip the tip of the backing strip and pull up while twisting counterclockwise. The backing strip will snap out of the retaining tab. Do this for the remaining tabs until the refill is free of the arm. The length of these refills is molded into the end and they should be replaced with identical types.

Regardless of the type of refill used, make sure that all of the frame jaws are engaged as the refill is pushed into place and locked. If the metal blade holder and frame are allowed to touch the glass during wiper operation, the glass will be scratched.

Tires and Wheels

Inspect your tires often for signs of improper inflation and uneven wear, which may indicate a need for balancing, rotation, or wheel alignment. Check the tires frequently for cuts, stone bruises, abrasions, blisters, and for objects that may have become imbedded in the tread. More frequent inspections are recommended when rapid or extreme temperature changes occur, or where road surfaces are rough or occasionally littered with debris. Check the condition of the wheels and replace any that are bent, cracked, severely dented or have excessive runout.

The tires on your car have built-in tread wear indicators moulded into the bottom of the tread grooves. These indicators will appear as ½ in. (12.7mm) wide bands when the tread depth becomes $\frac{1}{16}$ in. (1.6mm). When the indicators appear in 2 or more adjacent grooves, it's time for new tires.

TIRE ROTATION

Your tires should be rotated at the intervals recommended in the Maintenance Interval chart at the end of this Chapter. Rotate them according to the tire rotation diagram for your vehicle. The spare should not be included in the rotation.

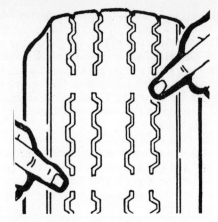

Tread wear indicators will appear when the tire is worn out

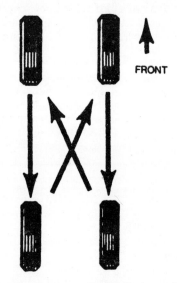

Tire rotation diagram—all 1989 Probe and 1990–92 Probe GL and LX

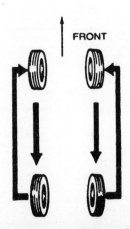

Tire rotation diagram—1990–92 Probe GT

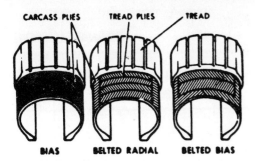

Types of tire construction

TIRE DESIGN

Your Probe comes originally equipped with radial tires. Radial tires get their name from their construction, because the carcass plies on a radial tire run at an angle of 90° to the tire bead, as opposed to a conventional bias ply tire where the carcass plies run at an angle of 90° to each another. The radial tire's construction gives the tread a great deal of rigidity and the side wall a great deal of flexibility.

When replacing your tires, use only the size, load range and construction type (radial) originally installed on the car. This information can be found on the tire pressure decal, which is located on the right door lock pillar, and is also located on the tire sidewall. The use of any other size or type may affect ride, handling, speedometer/odometer calibration, vehicle ground clearance, and tire to body clearance.

Do not mix tires of different construction (radial, bias ply or bias belted) on the same vehicle unless it is an emergency, as vehicle handling will be seriously affected with the possibility of loss of control.

TIRE INFLATION

At least once a month, check the inflation pressure on all tires, including the spare. Use an accurate tire pressure gauge. Do not trust the gauges on service station air pumps, as they are not always accurate. The inflation specifications are listed on the tire pressure decal which is located on the right door lock pillar. Check

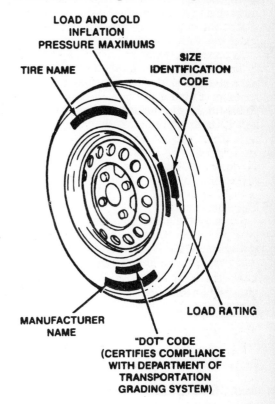

Tire information locations on a typical tire

Wheels				Tire
Size	Offset	Diameter of pitch circle	Material	Size
5½—JJ X 14			Steel	P185/70SR14
4½—J X 13			Steel	6.15–13—4PR
6—JJ X 14 (Non-Turbo) 6—JJ X 15 (Turbo)	42 mm (1.65 in.)	114.3 mm (4.5 in.)	Aluminum	P185/7HR14 P195/60VR15

Original equipment tire and wheel size chart—1989 Probe

Wheels				Tire
Size	Offset	Diameter of pitch circle	Material	Size
5½—JJ X 14 (GL/LX)			Steel	P185/70R14 (GL) P195/70R14 (LX)
6—JJ X 14 (GL) 6—JJ X 15 (Turbo)	42 mm (1.65 in.)	114.3 mm (4.5 in.)	Aluminum	P195/70R14 (GL) P205/60HR15 (LX) P205/60VR15 (GT)

Original equipment tire and wheel size chart—1990–92 Probe

and adjust inflation pressures only when the tires are cold, as pressures can increase as much as 6 psi (41kpa) due to heat.

Inflation pressures that are higher than recommended can cause a hard ride, tire bruising, carcass damage and rapid tread wear at the center of the tire. Inflation pressures that are lower than recommended can cause tire squeal, hard steering, rim dents, high temperatures and rapid wear on the outer edges of the tires. Unequal tire pressures can compromise handling and cause uneven braking.

As previously stated, radial tires have a highly flexible sidewall and this accounts for the characteristic sidewall bulge that makes the tire appear underinflated. This is normal for a radial tire, so you should not attempt to reduce this bulge by overinflating the tire.

CARE OF ALUMINUM WHEELS

Aluminum wheels are standard on the Probe GT and optional on some Probe GL and LX models. These wheels are coated to preserve their appearance.

To clean the aluminum wheels, use a mild soap and water solution and rinse thoroughly with clean water. If you want to use one of the commercially available wheel cleaners, make sure the label indicates that the cleaner is safe for coated wheels. Never use steel wool or any cleaner that contains an abrasive, or use strong detergents that contain high alkaline or caustic agents, as this will damage your wheels.

FLUIDS AND LUBRICANTS

Fuel and Engine Oil Recommendations

All Probes are equipped with a catalytic converter, necessitating the use of unleaded gasoline. The use of leaded gasoline will damage the catalytic converter. Probe GL and LX are designed to use unleaded gasoline with an octane rating of 87, which usually means regular unleaded. The Probe GT, due to its high performance turbocharged engine, is designed to use unleaded gasoline with an octane rating of 91, which usually means super unleaded.

Oil must be selected with regard to the anticipated temperatures during the period before the next oil change. Using the chart, select the oil viscosity for the lowest expected temperature and you will be assured of easy cold starting and sufficient engine protection. The oil you pour into your engine should have the designation SG marked on the container. For maximum fuel economy benefits, use an oil with the

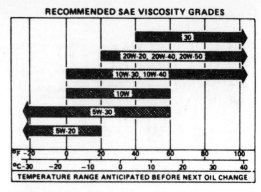

Engine oil viscosity chart

Roman Numeral II next to the words Energy Conserving in the API Service Symbol.

Engine
OIL LEVEL CHECK

Check the engine oil level every time you fill the gas tank. Make sure the oil level is between the **F** and **L** marks on the 2.2L engine or between the FULL and ADD marks on the 3.0L engine. The engine and oil must be warm and the vehicle parked on level ground to get an accurate reading. Also, allow a few minutes after turning off the engine for the oil to drain back into the pan before checking, or an inaccurate reading will result. Check the engine oil level as follows:

1. Open the hood and locate the engine oil dipstick.
2. If the engine is hot, you may want to wrap a rag around the dipstick handle before removing it.
3. Remove the dipstick and wipe it with a clean, lint-free rag, then reinsert it into the dipstick tube. Make sure it is inserted all the way or an inaccurate reading will result.
4. Pull out the dipstick and note the oil level. It should be between the marks, as stated above.
5. If the oil level is below the lower mark, replace the dipstick and add fresh oil to bring the level within the proper range. Do not overfill.
6. Recheck the oil level and close the hood.

Engine oil dipstick—3.0L engine

OIL AND FILTER CHANGE

The engine oil and oil filter should be changed at the same time, at the recommended interval on the Maintenance Intervals chart. The oil should be changed more frequently if the vehicle is being operated in very dusty areas. Before draining the oil, make sure the engine is at operating temperature. Hot oil will hold more impurities in suspension and will flow better, allowing the removal of more oil and dirt.

Used oil has been classified as a hazardous waste and must be disposed of properly. A num-ber of service stations and auto parts stores are now accepting waste oil from the public for recycling purposes. Consult with those in your area to find out what their policies are, before you drain any oil, as some will not accept oil that has been mixed with other fluids such as antifreeze or transmission fluid.

Change the oil and filter as follows:

1. Run the engine until it reaches the normal operating temperature. Raise and safely support the front of the car.

2. Slide a drain pan under the oil pan drain plug.

2.2L NON-TURBO ENGINE

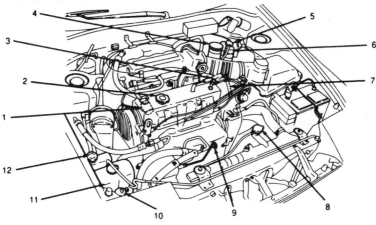

2.2L TURBO ENGINE

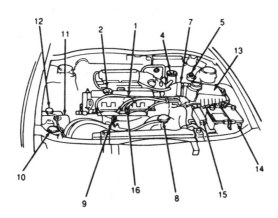

1. Oil filter	6. Fuel filter	11. Coolant reservoir
2. Engine oil filler cap	7. Automatic transaxle	12. Power steering fluid
3. Speedometer driven	fluid level dipstick	reservoir
gear (manual	8. Radiator cap	13. Air filter
transaxle fluid level	9. Engine oil level	14. Battery
check)	dipstick	15. Main fuse block
4. Brake fluid reservoir	10. Windshield washer	16. Spark plugs
5. Clutch fluid reservoir	fluid reservoir	

Engine compartment service points identification—2.2L engine

CAUTION: *The EPA warns that prolonged contact with used engine oil may cause a number of skin disorders, including cancer! You should make every effort to minimize your exposure to used engine oil. Protective gloves should be worn when changing the oil. Wash your hands and any other exposed skin areas as soon as possible after exposure to used engine oil. Soap and water, or waterless hand cleaner should be used.*

3. Wipe the drain plug and the surrounding area clean. Loosen the drain plug with a socket or box wrench, and then remove it by hand, using a rag to shield your fingers from the heat. Push in on the plug as you turn it out, so that no oil escapes until the plug is completely removed.

4. Allow the oil to drain into the pan. Be careful; if the engine is at operating temperature, the oil is hot enough to burn you.

5. Clean and install the drain plug , making sure that the gasket is still on the plug. If the gasket is missing or damaged, install a new one. Tighten the drain plug to 15 ft. lbs. (20 Nm).

6. Slide the drain pan under the oil filter. Slip an oil filter wrench onto the filter and turn it counterclockwise to loosen it. Wrap a rag around the filter and unscrew it the rest of the way. Be careful of oil running down the side of the filter.

7. Clean the oil filter adapter on the engine with a clean rag.

8. Coat the rubber gasket on the replacement filter with clean engine oil. Place the filter in position on the adapter fitting and screw it on by hand. After the rubber gasket contacts the sealing surface, turn the filter ½ turn, by hand.

9. Pull the drain pan from under the vehicle and lower the vehicle to the ground.

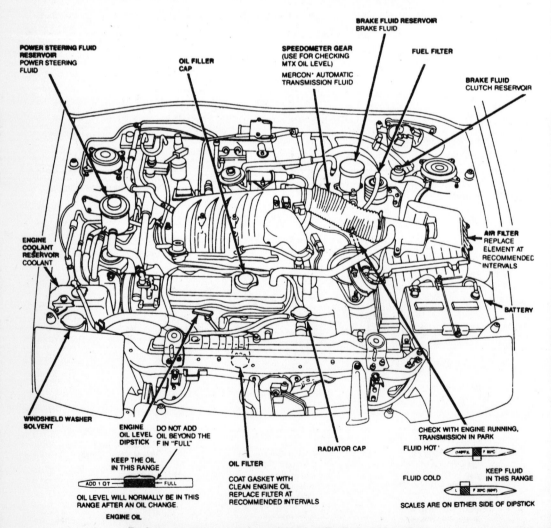

Engine compartment service points identification—3.0L engine

10. Remove the oil filler cap and fill the crankcase with the proper type and quantity of engine oil.

11. On the turbocharged engine, it is necessary to pre-lube the lubricating system before starting the engine to ensure an adequate supply of oil to the turbocharger bearings. This is done as follows:

    a. Disconnect the ignition coil electrical connector from the ignition coil.

    b. Crank the engine for approximately 20 seconds. Doing this will generate a fault code in the Self-Diagnostic portion of the Electronic Control Assembly.

    c. Reconnect the electrical connector to the ignition coil.

    d. Start the engine and run it at idle for approximately 30 seconds.

    e. Stop the engine and disconnect the negative battery cable. Depress the brake pedal for approximately 5 seconds in order to cancel the fault code.

    f. Reconnect the negative battery cable.

12. Run the engine and check for leaks. Stop the engine and check the oil level.

Manual Transaxle

FLUID RECOMMENDATIONS

Motorcraft MERCON® (DEXRON®II) automatic transmission fluid is required.

LEVEL CHECK

1. Park the car on a level surface. Apply the parking brake.

2. On vehicles equipped with a digital instrument cluster, disconnect the harness from the speed sensor assembly located on the transaxle housing.

Removing the oil pan drain plug

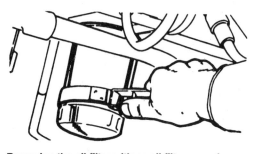

Removing the oil filter with an oil filter wrench

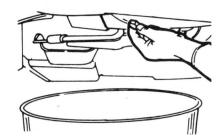

Coat the rubber gasket on the replacement filter with clean engine oil

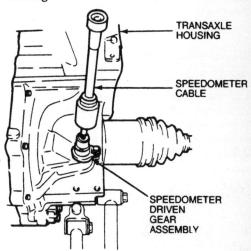

Speedometer driven gear assembly location

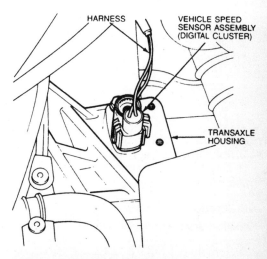

Vehicle speed sensor assembly location

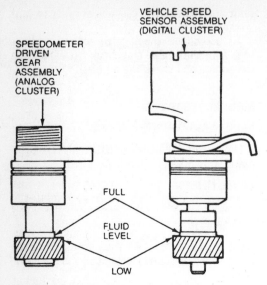

Checking the manual transaxle fluid level

3. On vehicles equipped with an analog instrument cluster, disconnect the speedometer cable from the speedometer driven gear assembly located on the transaxle housing.

4. Remove the retaining bolt and pry out the speedometer driven gear assembly or the vehicle speed sensor from the transaxle housing.

5. Check the fluid level on the speedometer driven gear assembly or the vehicle speed sensor assembly. The level should be at the full mark, just above the gear teeth.

6. If the level is low, place a funnel in the driven gear or sensor opening in the transaxle and pour in the necessary amount of fluid. Recheck the fluid level.

7. Install the speedometer driven gear or speed sensor and connect the cable or harness.

DRAIN AND REFILL

1. Raise and safely support the vehicle.

2. Slide a drain pan under the transaxle. Remove the speedometer driven gear or speed sensor on the top of the transaxle case.

3. Remove the drain plug on the bottom of the transaxle case.

4. When the fluid has been completely drained, install the drain plug and tighten to 29–43 ft. lbs. (39–59 Nm).

5. Fill the transaxle to the proper level.

6. Install the speedometer driven gear or speed sensor. Lower the vehicle.

Automatic Transaxle

FLUID RECOMMENDATIONS

Motorcraft MERCON® (DEXRON®II) automatic transmission fluid is required.

LEVEL CHECK

1. Park the car on a level surface and apply the parking brake. Run the engine to warm up the transaxle fluid.

2. Shift the transaxle through all ranges and return the lever to the **P** position.

3. Remove the dipstick and wipe it clean, then insert it firmly. Be certain that it has been pushed fully home. Remove the dipstick and check the fluid level while holding the dipstick horizontally. The level should be at or near the high mark. The dipstick has a high and low mark on both sides, which are accurate for level indications when the fluid is hot (normal operating temperature), or at other than normal operating temperature.

4. If the fluid level is below the low mark, place a funnel on the dipstick tube and add Mercon® type automatic transmission fluid, one half pint (0.23L) at a time. Check the level often between additions, being careful not to overfill the transmission.

DRAIN AND REFILL

1. Raise and safely support the vehicle.

2. Support the left-hand crossmember with a screw-type jack, or equivalent.

3. Remove the 4 bolts and 1 nut from the front of the left-hand crossmember.

4. Remove the 2 nuts and the left-hand transaxle mount through bolt from the rear of the left-hand crossmember.

5. Carefully lower the screw-type jack, allowing the crossmember to swing toward the left-hand side of the vehicle.

6. Position a drain pan under the transaxle.

7. Loosen the pan retaining bolts and drain the fluid from the transaxle.

8. When the fluid has drained to the level of the pan flange, remove the pan retaining bolts,

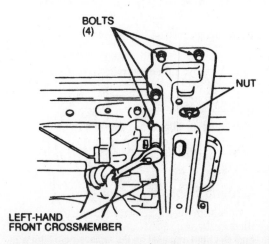

Left-hand front crossmember location

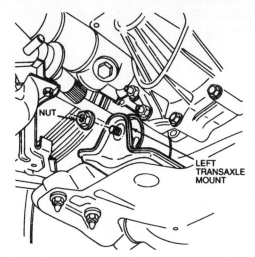

Left transaxle mount location

working from the rear, to allow it to drop and drain slowly.

9. When all the fluid has been drained, remove the pan and clean it thoroughly. Discard the pan gasket.

10. Remove and discard the transmission fluid filter and the filter-to-body gasket. The filter should not be reused or cleaned as the element material could contaminate the transaxle.

11. Install a new filter assembly using a new gasket. Tighten the retaining bolts to 69–95 inch lbs. (8–11 Nm).

12. Position a new gasket on the pan and install the pan. Tighten the pan retaining bolts to 69–95 inch lbs. (8–11 Nm).

13. Swing the left-hand crossmember into position and support it with the screw-type jack.

14. Install the 2 nuts and the left-hand transaxle mount through bolt to the rear of the left-hand crossmember. Tighten the nuts and through bolt to 49–69 ft. lbs. (67–93 Nm).

15. Install the 4 bolts and 1 nut to the front of the left-hand crossmember. Tighten the bolts to 27–40 ft. lbs. (36–54 Nm) and the nut to 55–69 ft. lbs. (79–93 Nm).

16. Remove the drain pan from under the vehicle. Remove the screw-type jack and then lower the vehicle to the ground.

17. Add approximately 7.2 qts. (6.8 liters) of fluid to the transaxle through the filler tube.

18. Run the engine and check for leaks. Check the fluid level according to the procedure described earlier.

Cooling System

Check the cooling system at the interval specified in the Maintenance Intervals chart at the end of this Chapter.

Hose clamps should be tightened, and soft or cracked hoses replaced. Damp spots, or accumulations of rust or dye near hoses, water pump or other areas, indicate areas of possible leakage. Check the radiator cap for a worn or cracked gasket. If the cap doesn't seal properly, fluid will be lost and the engine will overheat. A worn cap should be replaced with a new one.

Periodically clean any debris such as leaves, paper, insects, etc. from the radiator fins. Pick the large pieces off by hand. The smaller pieces can be washed away with water pressure from a hose.

Carefully straighten any bent radiator fins with a pair of needle nose pliers. Be careful--the fins are very soft. Don't wiggle the fins back and forth too much. Straighten them once and try not to move them again.

FLUID RECOMMENDATIONS

The recommended fluid is a 50/50 mixture of ethylene glycol antifreeze and water for year round use. Use a good quality antifreeze with water pump lubricants, rust inhibitors and other corrosion inhibitors along with acid neutralizers. Use only antifreeze that is SAFE FOR USE WITH AN ALUMINUM RADIATOR.

LEVEL CHECK

Coolant level should be checked at least once a month. With the engine cold, the coolant level should be even with the FULL mark on the coolant expansion tank.

DRAIN AND REFILL

1. Remove the radiator cap.

CAUTION: *Never remove the radiator cap while the engine is running or personal injury from scalding hot coolant or steam may result. If possible, wait until the engine has*

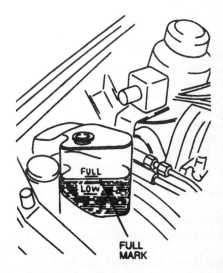

Checking the coolant level

cooled to remove the radiator cap. If this is not possible, wrap a thick cloth around the radiator cap and turn it slowly to the first stop. Step back while the pressure is released from the cooling system. When you are sure all the pressure has been released, press down on the cap, still with the cloth, and turn and remove it.

2. Position a suitable container under the radiator and open the draincock to drain the radiator.

CAUTION: *When draining the coolant, keep in mind that cats and dogs are attracted by the ethylene glycol antifreeze, and are quite likely to drink any that is left in an uncovered container or in puddles on the ground. This will prove fatal in sufficient quantity. Always drain the coolant into a sealable container.*

3. Clean the cooling system by flushing with clear water.

4. Close the radiator draincock.

5. Refill the system with a 50/50 mixture of antifreeze and water. Fill to the FULL mark on the reservoir and install the radiator cap only to the first stop.

6. Start the engine and run it at fast idle until the upper radiator hose feels warm, indicating the thermostat has opened and coolant is flowing throughout the system.

7. Stop the engine. Carefully remove the radiator cap and top off the radiator with the water/antifreeze mixture, if required.

8. Install the radiator cap securely and fill the coolant reservoir to the FULL mark.

FLUSHING AND CLEANING THE SYSTEM

Radiator and Engine Flush

1. Drain the cooling system. Remove the thermostat and reinstall the thermostat housing.

2. Disconnect the radiator overflow hose from the expansion tank and plug the end of the hose.

3. Disconnect the intake manifold outlet hose from the manifold nipple and plug both the nipple and the hose.

4. Disconnect the lower radiator hose from the radiator and position the hose to drain clear of the vehicle.

5. Connect a high pressure hose to the radiator lower hose outlet. Back flush the radiator and engine until water runs clear out of the lower radiator hose. Turn the water on and off several times to pulse the flow and help loosen sludge deposits.

WARNING: *The flushing water flow must be limited so that pressure inside the radiator does not exceed 15 psi (103.4kpa).*

6. When the system drains clear, unplug the radiator overflow hose. When water flows clear from the hose, replug it.

7. Before reconnecting the cooling system hoses, disconnect all of the hoses installed for the radiator and engine back flush procedure. The heater coolant loop must be backflushed separately to prevent loosened sediment from lodging in the heater core.

Heater Core Back Flush

1. Install and clamp a garden hose female end fitting in the heater return hose, disconnected from the bypass nipple.

2. Connect a garden hose to the hose fitting in the heater return hose and flush the heater core circuit until the drain water runs clear. Pulse the flow by turning the water on and off several times. Allow full flow for approximately 5 minutes.

3. Shut off the flushing water and remove all adapters and plugs installed for the flushing operation. Reconnect all cooling system connections and tighten the hose clamps to 22–31 inch lbs. (2.5–3.5 Nm).

4. Install the thermostat with a new housing gasket. Tighten the retaining nuts on the 2.2L engine to 14–22 ft. lbs. (19–30 Nm) or the retaining bolts on the 3.0L engine to 8–10 ft. lbs. (10–14 Nm).

5. Fill the cooling system and check for leaks.

Master Cylinder

FLUID RECOMMENDATIONS

Both the clutch and brake fluid master cylinders require brake fluid that meets or exceeds DOT 3 standards.

LEVEL CHECK

Both the clutch and brake master cylinders have translucent reservoirs which enable the fluid level to be checked without removing the reservoir cap. The clutch fluid level should at or above the step in the reservoir body. The brake fluid level should be between the MIN and MAX lines located on the side of the reservoir.

If it is necessary to add fluid, first wipe away any accumulated dirt or grease from the reservoir. Then remove the reservoir cap by twisting counter clockwise. Add fluid to the proper level. Avoid spilling brake fluid on any painted surface as it will harm the finish. Replace the reservoir cap.

Power Steering Pump

FLUID RECOMMENDATIONS

Ford power steering fluid part number E6AZ–19582–AA or equivalent, or Type F automatic transmission fluid should be used.

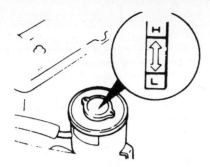

Power steering fluid reservoir—3.0L engine

LEVEL CHECK

1. Park the vehicle on level ground and apply the parking brake.

2. Run the engine until the fluid reached normal operating temperature.

3. With the engine idling, turn the steering wheel all the way to the left and right several times to get any air out of the system.

4. Return the wheels to the straight-ahead position and turn the engine off.

5. Check the power steering fluid level. Vehicles with the 2.2L engine are equipped with a see through type reservoir; make sure the fluid level is between the LOW and FULL HOT marks. Vehicles with the 3.0L engine have a dipstick type reservoir; make sure the fluid level is between the **H** and **L** marks.

6. If the fluid level is low, add small amounts of fluid until the level is correct. Do not overfill.

Chassis Greasing

The ball joints and tie rod ends on your car are sealed at the factory and cannot be lubricated.

Body Lubrication and Maintenance

At least once a year, the hood latch, auxiliary catch, door, hatchback and liftgate hinges should be lubricated with multi-purpose grease and the door and window weatherstripping should be lubricated with silicone lubricant. The body water drain holes located on the underside of each rocker panel, quarter panel and door should also be cleaned at this time.

To preserve the appearance of your car, it should be washed periodically with a mild detergent and water solution. Only wash the vehicle when the metal feels cool and the vehicle is in the shade. Rinse the entire vehicle with cold water, then wash and rinse one panel at a time, beginning with the roof and upper areas. After washing is complete, rinse the vehicle one final time and dry with a soft cloth or chamois.

Periodic waxing will remove harmful deposits from the vehicles surface and protect the finish. If the finish has dulled due to age or neglect, polishing may be necessary to restore the original gloss.

There are many specialized products available at your local auto parts store to care for the appearance of painted metal surfaces, plastic, chrome, wheels and tires as well as the interior upholstery and carpeting. Be sure to follow the manufacturers instructions before using them.

Rear Wheel Bearings

REMOVAL AND INSTALLATION

1. Raise and support the vehicle safely.

2. Remove the wheel and tire assembly and the grease cap.

3. Using a cape chisel and a hammer, raise the staked portion of the hub nut.

4. Remove and discard the hub nut.

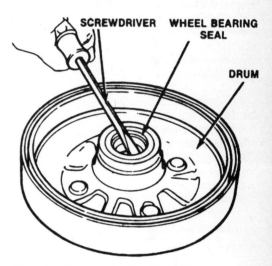

Removing the rear wheel bearing seal

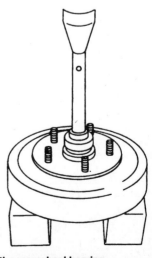

Installing the rear wheel bearing

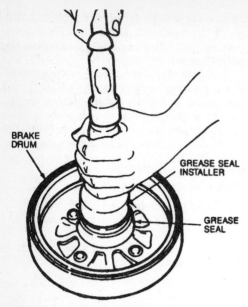

BRAKE DRUM

GREASE SEAL INSTALLER

GREASE SEAL

Installing the rear wheel bearing seal

5. Remove the brake drum or disc brake rotor assembly from the spindle. Refer to Chapter 9.

6. Using a small prybar, pry the grease seal from the brake drum or rotor and discard it.

7. Remove the snapring. Using a shop press, press the wheel bearing from the brake drum or rotor.

To install:

8. Using a shop press, press the new wheel bearing into the brake drum or rotor until it seats and install the snapring.

9. Lubricate the new seal lip with grease and install the seal, using a suitable installation tool.

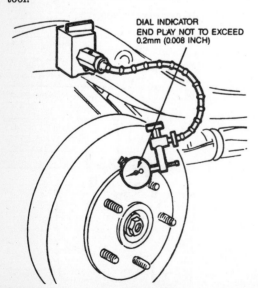

DIAL INDICATOR
END PLAY NOT TO EXCEED
0.2mm (0.008 INCH)

Checking rear wheel bearing endplay

10. Position the brake drum or rotor onto the wheel spindle.

11. Install a new locknut and tighten to 73–131 ft. lbs. (98–178 Nm).

12. Check the wheel bearing endplay as follows:

   a. Rotate the drum or rotor to make sure there is no brake drag.

   b. Install a suitable dial indicator and check the wheel bearing endplay. Endplay should not exceed 0.008 in. (0.2mm).

13. Using a dull cold chisel, stake the locknut. NOTE: *If the nut splits or cracks after staking, it must be replaced with a new nut.*

14. Install the grease cap and the wheel and tire assembly. Tighten the lug nuts to 65–87 ft. lbs. (88–118 Nm). Lower the vehicle.

TRAILER TOWING

Only the Probe GL and LX models can be used for towing. It is recommended that the Probe GT not be used for towing due to its turbocharged engine.

If you wish to tow a trailer with your car, you will have to aquire the necessary equipment from aftermarket sources as no towing packages are available from Ford.

General Recommendations

Only use the right equipment for the type of trailer you are towing. Never use a hitch that is designed to clamp to the bumper, as the bumper on your Probe is not designed to bear the load. Use only a load carrying hitch, but as this type places the tongue load of the trailer on the car's rear wheels, the load must be distributed in the trailer so that only 10–15 percent of the trailer weight is on the tongue.

Always use safety chains. Cross them under the trailer tongue and attach them to the frame, or hook retainers, not to the bumper. Be sure to leave enough slack in the chain to be able to turn corners.

Do not connect the trailer's lighting system wiring directly to your car's lighting system wiring. Obtain the proper equipment from a trailer dealer.

If you are using a rental trailer, follow the rental agency's instructions for all connections and towing procedures.

You should drive no faster than 55 mph when towing a trailer that has a 150 lb. tongue load.

Your car should be serviced more frequently when you use it for towing.

Necessary Equipment

If your car has an automatic transaxle, it is recommended that an auxiliary transmission fluid cooler be installed, if you will be towing for more than 50 miles, towing in hilly terrain or frequently towing.

Trailer and Tongue Weight Limits

Your car can tow a trailer up to a maximum of 1500 lbs. gross trailer axle weight. The maximum tongue load is 150 lbs. The trailer must also have 30 sq. ft. or less frontal area.

PUSHING AND TOWING

Manual transaxle equipped cars may be started by pushing, in the event of a dead battery. Push starting IS NOT recommended because of possible damage to the catalytic converter. If you must push start, ensure that the push car bumper doesn't override the bumper of your car. Depress the clutch pedal. Select second or third gear. Switch the ignition ON. When the car reaches a speed of approximately 10 mph, release the clutch to start the engine.

If towing is required, the vehicle should be flat-bedded, or towed with the front wheels off of the ground to prevent damage to the transaxle. If it is necessary to tow the vehicle from the rear, a wheel dolly should be placed under the front tires.

JACKING

The vehicle is supplied with a scissors jack for emergency road repairs. The scissors jack may be used to raise the car via the notches on either side at the front and rear of the doors. Do not attempt to use the jack in any other places. Always block the diagonally opposite wheel when using a jack.

When using stands, use the side members at the front or trailing axle front mounting crossmember at the back for placement points.

Whenever you plan to work under the car, you must support it on jackstands or ramps. Never use cinder blocks or stacks of wood to support the car, even if you're only going to be under it for a few minutes. Never crawl under the car when it is supported only by the tire-changing jack.

Small hydraulic, screw, or scissors jacks are satisfactory for raising the car. Drive-on trestles or ramps are also a handy and safe way to both raise and support the car. These can be bought or constructed from wood or steel. Never support the car on any suspension member or underbody panel.

CAPACITIES

Year	Model	Engine ID/VIN	Engine Displacement Liters (cc)	Engine Crankcase with Filter	Transmission (pts.)			Transfer Case (pts.)	Drive Axle		Fuel Tank (gal.)	Cooling System (qts.)
					4-Spd	5-Spd	Auto.		Front (pts.)	Rear (pts.)		
1989	Probe GL	C	2.2 (2189)	4.4	—	7.2	14.4	—	—	—	15.1	7.9
	Probe LX	C	2.2 (2189)	4.4	—	7.2	14.4	—	—	—	15.1	7.9
	Probe GT	L	2.2 (2189)	4.4	—	7.8	—	—	—	—	15.1	7.9
1990	Probe GL	C	2.2 (2189)	4.4	—	7.2	14.4	—	—	—	15.1	7.9
	Probe LX	U	3.0 (2971)	4.5	—	7.8	14.4	—	—	—	15.1	11.0
	Probe GT	L	2.2 (2189)	4.4	—	7.8	14.4	—	—	—	15.1	7.9
1991	Probe GL	C	2.2 (2189)	4.4	—	7.2	14.4	—	—	—	15.1	7.9
	Probe LX	U	3.0 (2971)	4.5	—	7.8	14.4	—	—	—	15.1	11.0
	Probe GT	L	2.2 (2189)	4.4	—	7.8	14.4	—	—	—	15.1	7.9
1992	Probe GL	C	2.2 (2189)	4.4	—	7.2	14.4	—	—	—	15.1	7.9
	Probe LX	U	3.0 (2971)	4.5	—	7.8	14.4	—	—	—	15.1	11.0
	Probe GT	L	2.2 (2189)	4.4	—	7.8	14.4	—	—	—	15.1	7.9

Follow maintenance **Schedule A** if your driving habits **MAINLY** include one or more of the following conditions:
- Short trips of less than 10 miles (16 km) when outside temperatures remain below freezing.
- Towing a trailer, or using a car-top carrier.
- Operating in severe dust conditions.
- Operating during hot weather in stop-and-go "rush hour" traffic.
- Extensive idling, such as police, taxi or door-to-door delivery service.

PERFORM AT THE MONTHS OR DISTANCES SHOWN, WHICHEVER OCCURS FIRST																				
MILES X 1000	3	6	9	12	15	18	21	24	27	30	33	36	39	42	45	48	51	54	57	60
KILOMETERS X 1000	4.8	9.6	14.4	19.2	24	28.8	33.6	38.4	43.2	48	52.8	57.6	62.4	67.2	72	76.8	81.6	86.4	91.2	96
EMISSION CONTROL SERVICE																				
Change engine oil and oil filter **every 3 months** OR 3,000 miles (whichever occurs first)	x	x	x	x	x	x	x	x	x	x	x	x	x	x	x	x	x	x	x	x
Replace spark plugs: Turbocharged					(3)					x					(3)					x
Non-turbocharged										x										x
3.0L (platinum plugs)																				x
Inspect cooling system every 12 months OR					x					x					x					x
Replace engine coolant every 36 months OR										x										x
Inspect accessory drive belts										x										x
Air cleaner element: Inspect/clean					(3)										(3)					
Replace (2)										(2)										(2)
Replace fuel filter																				x
Replace engine timing belt (1)									EVERY 60,000 MILES (96,000 km)											(1)

MILES X 1000	3	6	9	12	15	18	21	24	27	30	33	36	39	42	45	48	51	54	57	60
KILOMETERS X 1000	4.8	9.6	14.4	19.2	24	28.8	33.6	38.4	43.2	48	52.8	57.6	62.4	67.2	72	76.8	81.6	86.4	91.2	96
GENERAL MAINTENANCE																				
Inspect brake lines, connections & hoses					x					x					x					x
Inspect front and/or rear disc brakes					x					x					x					
Inspect rear drum brakes										x										x
Tighten bolts & nuts on chassis & body					x										x					
Inspect steering operation and linkage										x										x
Inspect drive shaft dust boots										x										x
Inspect exhaust system heat shield										x										x
Inspect fuel lines										(2)										x
Change automatic transaxle fluid										(4)										(4)
Rotate tires		x					x					x				x				

(1) Replacement of the timing belt is required at every 60,000 miles (96,000 km). Failure to replace the timing belt may result in damage to the engine.
(2) If operating in severe dust, more frequent intervals may be required, consult your dealer.
(3) This item not required to be performed, however, Ford recommends that you perform maintenance on this item in order to achieve best vehicle operation. Failure to perform this recommended maintenance will not invalidate the emissions warranty or manufacturer recall liability.
(4) Change automatic transaxle fluid if your driving habits frequently include one or more of the following conditions:
- Operation during hot weather (above 90°F, 32°C), carrying heavy loads and in hilly terrain.
- Towing a trailer or using a car-top carrier.
- Police, taxi or door-to-door delivery service.

Maintenance intervals chart 1

SCHEDULE B

Follow maintenance | Schedule B | if, generally, you drive your vehicle on a daily basis for more than 10 miles (16 km) and **NONE OF THE DRIVING CONDITIONS SHOWN IN SCHEDULE A APPLY TO YOUR DRIVING HABITS.**

PERFORM AT THE MONTHS OR DISTANCES SHOWN, WHICHEVER OCCURS FIRST								
MILES X 1000	7.5	15	22.5	30	37.5	45	52.5	60
KILOMETERS X 1000	12	24	36	48	60	72	84	96
EMISSION CONTROL SERVICE								
Non-Turbocharged Change engine oil and oil filter every 7,500 miles or 6 months, whichever occurs first	x	x	x	x	x	x	x	x
Turbocharged Replace engine oil and oil filter	EVERY 5,000 MILES (8 km) OR 6 MONTHS WHICHEVER OCCUR FIRST							
Replace spark plugs: Turbocharged		(3)		x		(3)		x
Non-turbocharged				x				x
3.0L (platinum plugs)								x
Inspect cooling system every 12 months OR		x		x		x		x
Replace engine coolant every 36 months OR				x				x
Inspect accessory drive belts				x				x
Replace air cleaner element (2)				(2)				(2)
Replace fuel filter								x
Replace engine timing belt (1)	EVERY 60,000 MILES (96,000 km)							(1)

	MILES X 1000	7.5	15	22.5	30	37.5	45	52.5	60
	KILOMETERS X 1000	12	24	36	48	60	72	84	96
GENERAL MAINTENANCE									
Inspect brake lines & connections			x		x		x		x
Inspect front and/or rear disc brakes			x		x		x		x
Inspect drum brakes					x				x
Tighten bolts & nuts on chassis & body			x				x		x
Inspect steering operation and linkage									
Inspect front suspension ball joints					x				x
Inspect driveshaft dust boots					x				x
Inspect exhaust system heat shield					x				x
Inspect fuel lines					(3)				x
Rotate tires		x		x		x		x	

(1) Replacement of the timing belt is required at every 60,000 miles (96,000 km). Failure to replace the timing belt may result in damage to the engine.
(2) If operating in severe dust, more frequent intervals may be required, consult your dealer.
(3) This item not required to be performed, however, Ford recommends that you perform maintenance on this item in order to achieve best vehicle operation. Failure to perform this recommended maintenance will not invalidate the emissions warranty or manufacturer recall liability.

Maintenance intervals chart 2

Engine Performance and Tune-Up

T2

TUNE-UP PROCEDURES

In order to extract the full measure of performance and economy from your engine, it is essential that it be properly tuned at regular intervals. A regular tune-up will keep your car's engine running smoothly and will prevent the annoying minor breakdowns and poor performance associated with an untuned engine. A properly tuned engine is also important to the control of tailpipe emissions.

The adjustments associated with engine

GASOLINE ENGINE TUNE-UP SPECIFICATIONS

Year	Engine ID/VIN	Engine Displacement Liters (cc)	Spark Plugs Gap (in.)	Ignition Timing (deg.)		Fuel Pump (psi)	Idle speed (rmp)		Valve Clearance	
				MT	AT		MT	AT	In.	Ex.
1989	C	2.2 (2189)	0.040	5–7 BTDC ①	5–7 BTDC ①②	64–85	725–775	725–775	Hyd.	Hyd.
	L	2.2 (2189)	0.040	8–10 BTDC	—	64–85	725–775	—	Hyd.	Hyd.
1990	C	2.2 (2189)	0.040	5–7 BTDC ①	5–7 BTDC ①②	64–85	725–775	725–775	Hyd.	Hyd.
	L	2.2 (2189)	0.040	8–10 BTDC	8–10 BTDC	64–85	725–775	725–775	Hyd.	Hyd.
	U	3.0 (2971)	0.044	10 BTDC	10 BTDC	35–40	③	③	Hyd.	Hyd.
1991	C	2.2 (2189)	0.040	5–7 BTDC ①	5–7 BTDC ①②	64–85	725–775	725–775	Hyd.	Hyd.
	L	2.2 (2189)	0.040	8–10 BTDC	8–10 BTDC	64–85	725–775	725–775	Hyd.	Hyd.
	U	3.0 (2971)	0.044	10 BTDC	10 BTDC	35–40	③	③	Hyd.	Hyd.
1992	C	2.2 (2189)	0.040	5–7 BTDC ①	5–7 BTDC ①②	64–85	725–775	725–775	Hyd.	Hyd.
	L	2.2 (2189)	0.040	8–10 BTDC	8–10 BTDC	64–85	725–775	725–775	Hyd.	Hyd.
	U	3.0 (2971)	0.044	10 BTDC	10 BTDC	35–40	③	③	Hyd.	Hyd.

BTDC—Before Top Dead Center
Hyd.—Hydraulic
① Distributor vacuum hoses disconnected and plugged
② Transaxle in park
③ Refer to underhood vehicle emission information label

tune-up should be checked every year or 12,000 miles (19,300km), whichever comes first, or more often if the vehicle is operated under severe conditions, such as trailer towing, prolonged idling, continual stop and start driving, or if starting or running problems are noticed. Refer to the Maintenance Intervals Chart in Chapter 1 for specific component replacement intervals. It is assumed that the routine maintenance described in Chapter 1 has been kept up, as this will have decided effect on the result of a tune-up. All of the applicable steps of a tune-up should be followed in order, as the result is a cumulative one.

If the specifications on the emission information label in the engine compartment disagree with the Tune-Up Specification chart in this Chapter, use the figures on the label. The label often includes changes made during the model year.

Spark Plugs

A typical spark plug consists of a metal shell surrounding a ceramic insulator. A metal electrode extends downward through the center of the insulator and protrudes a small distance. Located at the end of the plug and attached to the side of the outer metal shell is the side electrode. The side electrode bends in at a 90° angle so that its tip is even with, and parallel to, the tip of the center electrode. The distance between these two electrodes (measured in thousandths of an inch or hundreths of a millimeter) is called the spark plug gap. The spark plug in no way produces a spark but merely provides a gap across which the current can arc. The coil produces anywhere from 20,000 to 40,000 volts which travels to the distributor where it is distributed through the spark plug wires to the spark plugs. The current passes along the center electrode and jumps the gap to the side electrode, and, in do doing, ignites the air/fuel mixture in the combustion chamber.

SPARK PLUG HEAT RANGE

Spark plug heat range is the ability of the plug to dissipate heat. The longer the insulator (or the farther it extends into the engine), the hotter the plug will operate; the shorter the insulator the cooler it will operate. A plug that absorbs little heat and remains too cool will quickly accumulate deposits of oil and carbon since it is not hot enough to burn them off. This leads to plug fouling and consequently to misfiring. A plug that absorbs too much heat will have no deposits, but, due to the excessive heat, the electrodes will burn away quickly and in some instances, preignition may result. Preignition takes place when plug tips get so hot that they

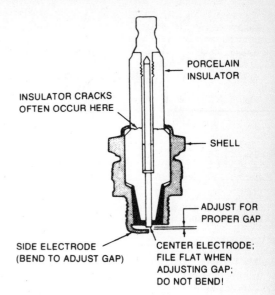

Cross section of a spark plug

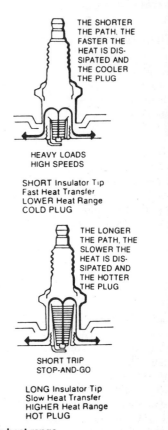

Spark plug heat range

glow sufficiently to ignite the fuel/air mixture before the actual spark occurs. This early ignition will usually cause a pinging during low speeds and heavy loads.

The general rule of thumb for choosing the correct heat range when picking a spark plug is:

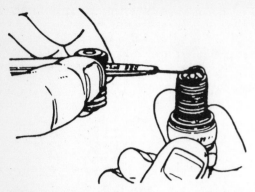

Always use a wire gauge to check the electrode gap; a flat feeler gauge may not give the proper reading

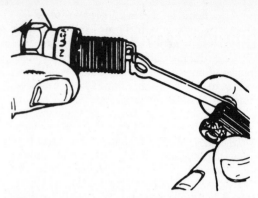

Adjust the spark plug gap by bending the side electrode

if most of your driving is long distance, high speed travel, use a colder plug; if most of your driving is stop and go, use a hotter plug. Original equipment plugs are compromise plugs, but most people never have occasion to change their plugs from the factory-recommended heat range.

REMOVAL AND INSTALLATION

Remove the spark plugs one at a time. If you remove all the spark plug wires and spark plugs at the same time, the wires may get mixed up. Take a minute before you begin and number the wires with tape. The best location for numbering is near where the wires are attached to the cap. Refer to the Firing Order diagrams for the cylinder and corresponding distributor cap numbers.

1. Grasp each wire by the rubber boot. Twist and pull the boot and wire from the spark plug. Never pull on the plug wire directly, or it may become separated from the connector inside the boot.

2. Using a spark plug socket, loosen the plugs slightly by turning counterclockwise. Wipe or blow all dirt away from around the plug base.

3. Unscrew and remove the spark plugs from the engine. Check the condition of the plugs using the Spark Plug Diagnosis chart.

4. Use a round wire feeler gauge to check the plug gap. The correct size gauge should pass through the electrode gap with a slight drag. If you're in doubt, try the next size larger and next size smaller gauges. The smaller gauge should pass through easily while the larger gauge should not pass through at all. If the gap is incorrect, use the electrode bending tool on the gauge to adjust the gap. Only the side electrode is adjustable.

To install:

5. Put a drop of penetrating oil on the base threads of the plug. Start the spark plug into the cylinder head by hand and turn until it is

snug. Tighten the plug to 11–17 ft. lbs. (15–23 Nm) on the 2.2L engine or 7–15 ft. lbs. (9–20 Nm) on the 3.0L engine.

6. Apply a small amount of silicone dielectric compound D7AZ–19A331–A or equivalent to the inside of the spark plug wire boot and connect the wire to the spark plug. If you did not number the wires, refer to the Firing Order diagrams to make sure the wires are connected properly.

Spark Plug Wires

Visually inspect the spark plug wires for burns, cuts, or breaks in the insulation. Check the spark plug boots and the nipples on the distributor cap and coil. Replace any damaged wiring. If no physical damage is obvious, the wires can be checked with an ohmmeter for excessive resistance and continuity. Resistance should be 5000Ω per 1 ft. (30.5cm) of cable. Measure the resistance with the plug wire still attached to the distributor cap.

When installing a new set of spark plug wires, replace the wires one at a time so there will be no mixup. Start by replacing the longest cable first. Install the boot firmly over the spark plug. Route the wire exactly the same as the original. Insert the nipple into the tower on the distributor cap. Repeat the process for each wire. Be sure to apply silicone dialectric compound D7AZ–19A331–A or equivalent to the spark plug wire boots and nipples prior to installation.

FIRING ORDERS

NOTE: *To avoid confusion, remove and tag the wires one at a time, for replacement.*

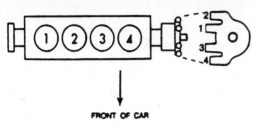

2.2L Engine
Engine Firing Order: 1-3-4-2
Distributor Rotation: Counterclockwise

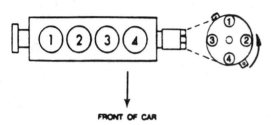

2.2L Turbocharged Engine
Engine Firing Order: 1-3-4-2
Distributor Rotation: Counterclockwise

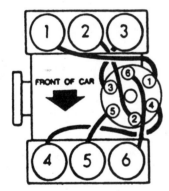

3.0L Engine
Engine Firing Order: 1-4-2-5-3-6
Distributor Rotation: Clockwise

ELECTRONIC IGNITION

Description and Operation

2.2L ENGINE

The electronic ignition on the 2.2L normally aspirated engine is a fully transistorized, high energy system. It is a conventional electronic ignition system in that it operates independent of the Electronic Control Assembly (ECA) for the most part, with both centrifugal and vacuum advance mechanisms controlling ignition advance. The ignition timing is advanced by vacuum at low speeds and by the centrifugal mechanism at higher speeds. The ECA does modify timing at altitudes above 6500 ft. to maintain proper engine performance and satisfactory exhaust emissions.

The electronic ignition on the 2.2L turbocharged engine is entirely electronic and is controlled by the ECA. The ECA sends the spark timing signal through the ignition module to the distributor based on its triggering signal from the following switches and sensors:

- Vane air flow meter
- Idle switch
- Neutral gear switch
- Clutch engage switch
- EGR valve position sensor
- Knock sensor
- Throttle position sensor
- Engine coolant temperature sensor
- Engine coolant temperature switch

Other non-electronic components in the system include the starter interlock switch, battery, distributor, spark plugs, high tension leads and ignition module. The distributor provides a signal to the ECA to indicate crankshaft top dead center by means of its cylinder TDC sensors.

Both systems operate in the same manner. When the ignition switch is turned **ON**, the power relay closes and changes the coil primary windings. When the engine is running, the ignition module grounds the negative side of the coil primary circuit which induces spark. This results in an inductive charge built up in the secondary circuit. The spark is then sent to the distributor where the rotor and distributor cap delivers it to each spark plug.

3.0L ENGINE

The 3.0L engine is equipped with the Thick Film Integrated TFI-IV electronic ignition system. In this system, the distributor is driven off the camshaft and uses no centrifugal or vacuum advance. The distributor contains the TFI ignition module and a hall effect stator assembly.

The TFI-IV module supplies voltage to the Profile Ignition Pickup (PIP) sensor, which sends the crankshaft position information to the TFI-IV module. The TFI-IV module then sends this information to the ECA, which determines the spark timing and sends and electronic signal to the TFI-IV ignition module to turn off the coil and produce the spark to fire the plug.

The operation of the distributor is accomplished through the Hall Effect stator assembly, causing the ignition coil to be switched off and on by the ECA and TFI-IV module. The vane switch is an encapsulated package consisting of a Hall sensor on one side and a permanent magnet on the other side. A rotary vane cup, made of ferrous metal, is used to trigger the signal off and on. When the window of the vane cup is between the magnet and the Hall effect device, a magnetic flux field is completed from the magnet through the Hall effect device and back to the magnet. As the vane passes through this opening, the flux lines are shunted through the vane and back to the magnet. During this time, a voltage is produced as the vane passes through the opening. When the vane clears the opening, the window edge causes the signal to go to zero volts. The signal is then used by the ECA for crankshaft position sensing and the computation of the desired spark advance based on engine demand and calibration. The voltage distribution is accomplished through a conventional rotor, cap and ignition wires.

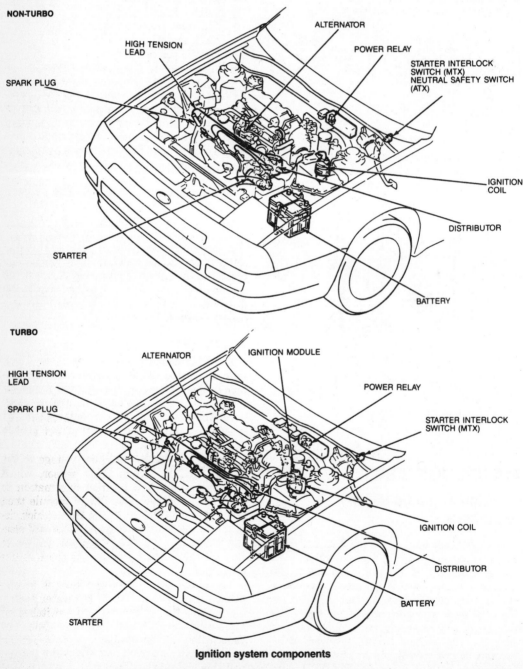

Ignition system components

Ignition system components—2.2L engines

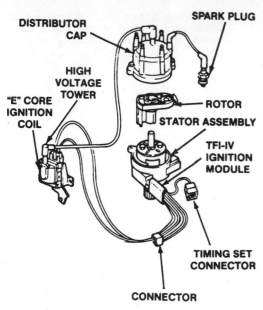

TFI-IV electronic ignition system—3.0L engine

Diagnosis and Testing

Before beginning any diagnosis and testing procedures, visually inspect the components of the ignition system and check for the following:
- Discharged battery
- Damaged or loose connections
- Damaged electrical insulation
- Poor coil, distributor and spark plug connections
- Ignition module connections
- Blown fuses
- Damaged vacuum hoses
- Damaged or worn rotor and distributor cap
- Damaged spark plugs
- Distributor cap, rotor and spark plug wires are properly seated

Check the spark plug wires and boots for signs of poor insulation that could cause cross firing. Make sure the battery is fully charged and that all accessories are off during diagnosis and testing. Make sure the idle speed is within specification.

You will need a good quality digital volt-ohmmeter, a remote starter and a spark tester for checking the ignition system. A spark tester resembles a spark plug without threads and the side electrode removed. Do not attempt to use a modified spark plug.

2.2L ENGINE

Spark Quality and Coil Wire Test

1. Connect the volt-ohmmeter to the coil and make sure that 12 volts exists at the positive terminal and 6 volts exists at the negative terminal of the coil with the ignition switch **ON**. If there is no voltage, a short or open circuit exists in the wiring harness.

2. Connect the spark tester between the coil high tension wire and ground. While cranking the engine, make sure a strong spark jumps the tester gap. If there is no spark or the spark is weak, check the ignition coil or the ignition module on the turbocharged engine for carbon tracking or other damage. Measure the resistance of the coil high tension wire; replace the wire if the resistance is greater than 5000Ω per ft. Proceed to Ignition Coil Resistance.

3. If there is a good spark at the tester in Step 2, proceed to Spark Plug Wire and Distributor Cap Resistance.

Ignition Coil Resistance Test

1. Check the resistances of the ignition coil primary, secondary and case.

2. Compare your readings with the specifications in the chart. If the ignition coil resistance

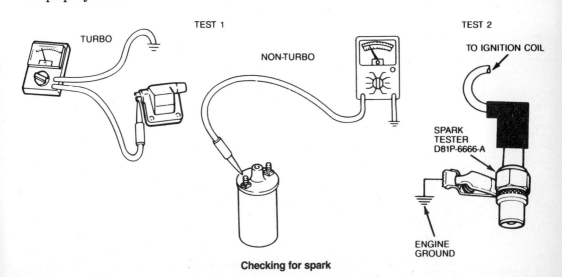

Checking for spark

is not within specifications, replace the ignition coil. If the ignition coil is within the specified limits, proceed to Spark Plug Wire and Distributor Cap Resistance.

Spark Plug Wire and Distributor Cap Resistance Test

1. Remove the distributor cap.
2. Make sure the spark plug wires are firmly seated in the cap.
3. Disconnect each spark plug wire from the spark plug and connect a volt-ohmmeter to the terminal in the distributor cap and the spark plug terminal for each wire.
4. Check the wire resistance, it should be 5000Ω per ft. (30.5cm)
5. If the resistance is not within specification, replace the wire(s) or distributor cap, as required. If the resistance is as specified, check the gap and condition of the spark plugs. If the plugs are okay, proceed to Ignition Switch Starting Circuit Test.

Ignition Switch Starting Circuit Test

1. If equipped with a manual transaxle, disconnect the interlock switch connector. If equipped with an automatic transaxle, disconnect the neutral safety switch connector.
2. Connect the digital volt-ohmmeter and check the voltage.

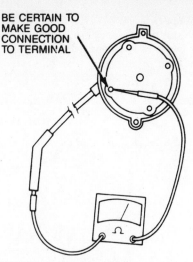

BE CERTAIN TO MAKE GOOD CONNECTION TO TERMINAL

Measuring spark plug wire resistance

3. If the voltage is as specified, proceed to the Power Relay Test. If the voltage is not as specified, replace the ignition switch, interlock switch, or neutral safety switch, as required.

Power Relay Test

1. A clicking sound should be heard at the No. 1 relay when turning the ignition on and off.

System	Resistance @ 20ºC (68ºF)	
	Turbo	Non-Turbo
Primary	0.72 to 0.88 ohm	1.04 to 1.27 ohm
Secondary	10.3 to 13.9 K ohm	7.1 to 9.7 K ohm
Case	10 M ohm min.	10 M ohm min.

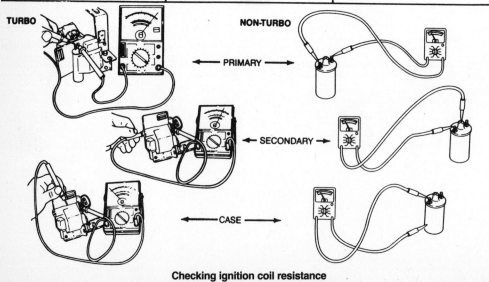

TURBO   NON-TURBO

← PRIMARY →

← SECONDARY →

← CASE →

Checking ignition coil resistance

2. Connect a volt-ohmmeter to the power relay connector terminals. There should be continuity when 12 volts and ground are connected to the other terminals.

3. If there is no continuity when power is applied, replace the power relay.

Distributor Pickup Coil Resistance Test — Non-Turbocharged Engine

1. Remove the distributor cap, rotor and cover.

2. Connect a volt-ohmmeter and check the resistance of the pickup coil.

3. The pickup coil resistance should be 900–1200Ω. If the resistance is not within specification, replace the pickup coil.

Distributor Sensor Test — Turbocharged Engine

1. Make sure the distributor wiring harness is in good condition and the connectors are making good contact.

2. Disconnect the distributor connector and check the resistance across terminals A–B, C–D, and E–F.

3. If the resistances are not within specification, replace the distributor.

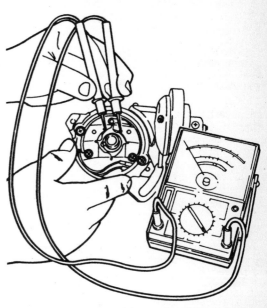

Checking distributor pickup coil resistance on 2.2L non-turbocharged engine

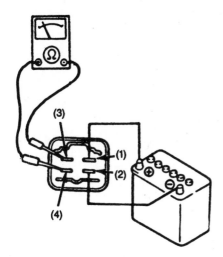

Checking the power relay

Check Conditions		10-14v Present
MTX	**ATX**	
Clutch Depressed	Transmission in N or P	Yes
Clutch Released	Transmission in Gear	No

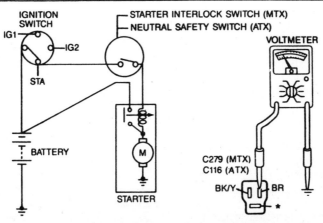

Checking the ignition switch starting circuit

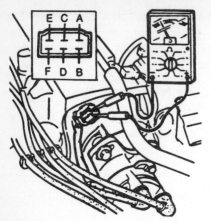

Checking the distributor sensor on 2.2L turbo-charged engine

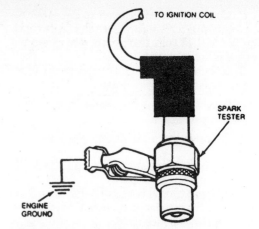

Checking for spark with the spark tester

3.0L ENGINE

Ignition Coil Secondary Voltage Test

CRANK MODE

1. Connect a spark tester between the ignition coil wire and a good engine ground.
2. Crank the engine and check for spark at the tester.
3. Turn the ignition switch **OFF**.
4. If no spark occured, check the following:
   a. Inspect the ignition coil for damage or carbon tracking.
   b. Make sure the distributor shaft is rotating when the engine is being cranked.
   c. If the ignition coil is okay and the distributor shaft rotates when the engine is cranked, proceed to the Stator Test.
5. If spark did occur, check the distributor cap and rotor for damage or carbon tracking. Proceed to the Ignition Coil Secondary Voltage Run Mode Test.

RUN MODE

1. Fully apply the parking brake. If equipped with an automatic transaxle, place the gearshift lever in **P**. If equipped with a manual transaxle, place the gearshift lever in neutral.
2. Disconnect the S terminal wire at the starter relay, then attach the remote starter switch.
3. Turn the ignition switch to the **RUN** position.
4. Using the remote starter switch, crank the engine and check for spark.
5. Turn the ignition switch **OFF**.
6. If no spark occurs, proceed to the Wiring Harness test.
7. If a spark did occur, there is no problem in the ignition system.

Wiring Harness Test

1. Push the connector tabs and separate the wiring harness connector from the ignition module. Check for dirt, corrosion or damage.
2. Check that the S terminal wire at the starter relay is disconnected.
3. Measure the battery voltage.
4. Carefully insert a small straight pin in the No. 3 terminal of the ignition module connector and measure the voltage.
NOTE: *Do not allow the straight pin to contact electrical ground while performing this test.*
5. Turn the ignition switch **OFF** and remove the straight pin.
6. Reconnect the S terminal wire at the starter relay.
7. If the results are within 90 percent of battery voltage, replace the TFI module.
8. If the results are not within 90 percent of battery voltage, check the wiring harness and connectors. Also, check for a faulty ignition switch.

Stator Test

1. Remove the distributor from the engine. Remove the TFI module from the distributor.
2. Measure the resistance between the TFI module terminals as follows:
   a. GND – PIP IN: should be greater than 5,000Ω.
   b. PIP – PIP IN: should be less than 2 kΩ.
   c. PIP PWR – TFI PWR: should be less than 200Ω.
   d. GND – IGN GND: should be less than 2Ω.
   e. PIP IN – PIP: should be less than 200Ω.
3. If the readings are within specification, replace the stator.

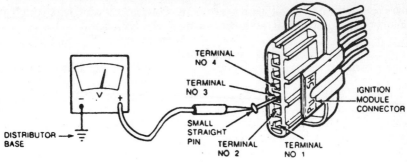

Checking the wire harness at the ignition module connector

4. If the readings are not as specified, replace the TFI module.

Coil Wire and Coil Test

1. Disconnect the ignition coil connector and check for dirt, corrosion or damage.

2. Substitute a known good coil and check for spark using the spark tester.

CAUTION: *Do not hold the coil while performing this test. Dangerous voltages may be present on the metal laminations as well as the high voltage tower.*

3. Crank the engine and check for spark.

4. Turn the ignition switch **OFF**.

5. If a spark did occur, measure the resistance of the ignition coil wire and replace it if the resistance is greater than 7 kΩ per ft. (30.5cm). If the readings are within specification, replace the ignition coil.

6. If no spark occurs, the problem is not the coil. Proceed to the EEC-IV — TFI-IV Test.

EEC-IV — TFI-IV Test

1. Disconnect the pin-in-line connector near the distributor.

2. Crank the engine.

3. Turn the ignition switch **OFF**.

4. If a spark did occur, check the PIP and ignition ground wires for continuity. If okay, the problem is not ignition.

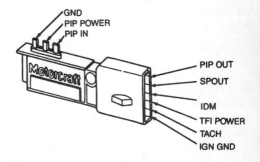

TFI-IV module terminal locations

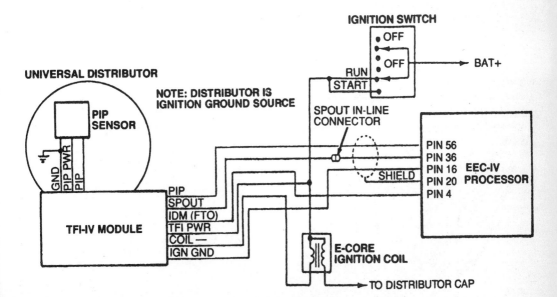

TFI-IV ignition system

5. If no spark occurs, check the voltage at the positive terminal of the ignition coil, with the ignition switch in **RUN**.

6. If the reading is not within battery voltage, check for a worn or damaged ignition switch.

7. If the reading is within battery voltage, check for faults in the wiring between the coil and TFI module terminal No. 2 or any additional wiring or components connected to that circuit.

IGNITION TIMING

NOTE: *If the information given in the following procedures differs from that on the emission information label located in the engine compartment, follow the directions given on the label. The label often reflects production running changes made during the model year.*

SETTING THE TIMING

2.2L Engine

NORMALLY ASPIRATED ENGINE

1. Apply the parking brake. If equipped with manual transaxle, place the shift lever in neutral. If equipped with automatic transaxle, place the shift lever in **P**.

2. Locate the timing marks on the crankshaft pulley and timing belt cover. You may have to crank the engine slightly to see the mark on the crankshaft pulley. If the marks are hard to see, clean them off with some degreasing cleaner and a wire brush.

3. Start the engine and allow it to come to normal operating temperature. Make sure all accessories are **OFF**.

4. Check the idle speed and adjust, if necessary.

5. Shut off the engine. Disconnect and plug the vacuum hoses at the distributor vacuum diaphragm. On 1991–92 vehicles, connect a jumper wire between the black 1-pin STI test connector, located near the left strut tower, and ground.

Timing marks location—2.2L engine

6. Connect an inductive timing light according to the manufacturers instructions.

7. Start the engine and allow the idle to stabilize.

8. Aim the timing light at the timing marks. The mark on the crankshaft pulley should align with the 6 degree BTDC mark on the timing cover scale, ± 1 degree. If the marks are aligned, proceed to Step 10. If the marks are not aligned, proceed to Step 9.

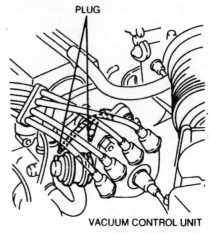

Plugging the distributor vacuum advance hoses

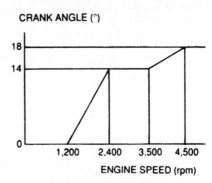

Centrifugal advance specifications

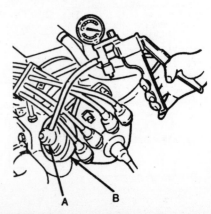

Connecting the vacuum tester

9. Loosen the distributor lock bolt just enough to turn the distributor housing. While aiming the timing light at the timing marks, turn the distributor until the marks are aligned. Tighten the distributor lock bolt to 14–19 ft. lbs. (19–25 Nm) and recheck the timing.

10. Initial timing is now set. If your timing light has the capability of checking spark advance, you can check the centrifugal advance as follows:

a. Gradually increase the engine speed.

b. Aim the timing light at the timing marks.

c. Monitor the ignition timing advance and check it against the specifications.

d. If the centrifugal advance is operating properly, proceed to Step 11. If the centrifugal advance is excessive, the governor spring is weak or broken. If the centrifugal advance is insufficient, the governor weight may be sticking.

11. If your timing light can check spark advance, you can check the vacuum advance as follows:

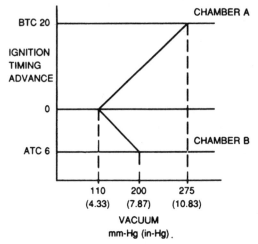

Vacuum advance specifications

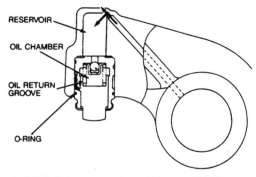

Cross sectional view of the hydraulic lash adjuster—2.2L engine

a. Connect a vacuum tester to the vacuum diaphragm.

b. Apply vacuum to chamber A and then to chamber B. The timing should advance according to the specifications.

c. If the timing does not advance as specified, replace the vacuum diaphragm.

12. Shut off the engine. Remove the timing light and the jumper wire. Remove the plugs and reconnect the vacuum hoses to the vacuum diaphragm.

TURBOCHARGED ENGINE

1. Apply the parking brake. If equipped with manual transaxle, place the shift lever in neutral. If equipped with automatic transaxle, place the shift lever in **P**.

2. Locate the timing marks on the crankshaft pulley and timing belt cover. You may have to crank the engine slightly to see the mark on the crankshaft pulley. If the marks are hard to see, clean them off with some degreasing cleaner and a wire brush.

3. Start the engine and allow it to come to normal operating temperature. Make sure all accessories are **OFF**.

4. Check the idle speed and adjust, if necessary.

5. Shut off the engine. Connect a jumper wire between the black 1-pin STI test connector, located near the left strut tower, and ground.

6. Connect an inductive timing light according to the manufacturers instructions.

7. Start the engine and allow the idle to stabilize.

8. Aim the timing light at the timing marks. The mark on the crankshaft pulley should align with the 9 degree BTDC mark on the timing cover scale, ± 1 degree. If the marks are aligned, proceed to Step 10. If the marks are not aligned, proceed to Step 9.

9. Loosen the distributor lock bolt just enough to turn the distributor housing. While aiming the timing light at the timing marks, turn the distributor until the marks are aligned. Tighten the distributor lock bolt to 14–19 ft. lbs. (19–25 Nm) and recheck the timing.

10. Shut off the engine. Remove the timing light and the jumper wire.

3.0L Engine

1. Apply the parking brake. If equipped with manual transaxle, place the shift lever in neutral. If equipped with automatic transaxle, place the shift lever in **P**.

2. Locate the timing marks on the crankshaft pulley and timing belt cover. You may have to crank the engine slightly to see the mark on the crankshaft pulley. If the marks are

hard to see, clean them off with some degreasing cleaner and a wire brush.

3. Connect a suitable inductive timing light according to the manufacturers instructions.

4. Disconnect the single wire inline spout connector, located near the distributor, by pulling the plug from the connector housing.

5. Start the engine and allow it to warm up to operating temperature. Make sure the idle speed is correct.

NOTE: *To set timing correctly, a remote starter should not be used. Use the ignition key only to start the vehicle. Disconnecting the start wire at the starter relay will cause the TFI module to revert to start mode timing after the vehicle is started. Reconnecting the start wire after the vehicle is running will not correct the timing.*

6. Aim the timing light at the timing marks. The timing should be 10 degrees BTDC. If the timing is correct, proceed to Step 8. If the timing is incorrect, proceed to Step 7.

7. Loosen the distributor hold-down bolt just enough to turn the distributor housing. While aiming the timing light at the timing marks, turn the distributor until the marks are aligned. Tighten the distributor hold-down bolt to 17–25 ft. lbs. (23–34 Nm) and recheck the timing.

8. Reconnect the single wire inline spout connector. Check the timing advance to verify the distributor is advancing beyond the initial setting.

9. Remove the inductive timing light.

VALVE LASH

The valve lash on all engines is kept in adjustment hydraulically. The 2.2L engines are equipped with hydraulic lash adjusters located in the rocker arms. The 3.0L engine is equipped with conventional hydraulic lifters located in the cylinder block.

No adjustment is possible with the lash adjusters or lifters, but they can be checked for function and clearance.

ENGINE OIL PRESSURE GAUGE

Checking the oil pressure—2.2L engine

CHECKING

2.2L Engine

1. Warm up the engine to normal operating temperature, then shut the engine off.

2. Check the condition of the engine oil. Change the oil and filter, if necessary.

3. Connect an oil pressure gauge. Start the engine and check the oil pressure. It should be 21–36 psi at 1000 rpm.

4. Stop the engine and remove the rocker arm cover. Refer to Chapter 3.

5. Push down on the hydraulic lash adjuster side of the rocker arm to make sure the hydraulic lash adjuster cannot be compressed. Use a shop rag as the rocker arm will be hot.

6. If the hydraulic lash adjuster can be compressed, it must be replaced.

3.0L Engine

This clearance check is usually only needed when the valves, valve seats and/or cylinder head gasket surface have been machined or new parts have been installed. Clearance must be checked when the lifter is completely collapsed.

1. Disconnect the negative battery cable.

2. Remove the rocker arm covers. Refer to Chapter 3.

3. Rotate the engine until the No. 1 cylinder

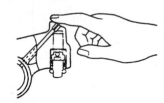

Checking the hydraulic lash adjuster—2.2L engine

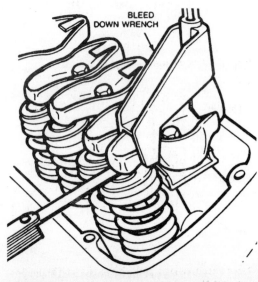

BLEED DOWN WRENCH

Checking the hydraulic lifters—3.0L engine

is at TDC of its compression stroke and check the clearance between the rocker arm and the following valves: No. 1 intake and exhaust, No. 2 exhaust, No. 3 intake, No. 4 exhaust and No. 6 intake.

4. To check the clearance, use lifter bleed down wrench T71P-6513-B or equivalent, to push down on the rocker arm and bleed the oil from the lifter.

5. Insert the appropriate thickness feeler gauge between the rocker arm and valve stem to check the clearance.

6. Rotate the crankshaft 360 degrees and check the clearance between the rocker arm and the following valves: No. 2 intake, No. 3 exhaust, No. 4 intake, No. 5 intake and exhaust and No. 6 exhaust.

7. The clearance should be 0.09–0.19 in. (2.3–4.8mm).

8. If the clearance is less than specified, shorter pushrods are available to correct the problem. If the clearance is greater than specified, longer pushrods are available.

IDLE SPEED AND MIXTURE ADJUSTMENTS

On all Probe engines, the air/fuel mixture is controlled by the Electronic Control Assembly (ECA) during all modes of operation, therefore no idle mixture adjustment is possible or necessary.

IDLE SPEED ADJUSTMENT

2.2L Engine

NOTE: *Idle speed is controlled automatically by the ECA through the Idle Speed Control (ISC) solenoid valve. Usually it is not necessary to adjust the idle speed.*

1. Check the ignition timing and adjust to specification, if necessary. Make sure the engine is in generally good condition.

2. Turn off all lights and other unnecessary electrical loads. Idle speed adjustment must be done while the radiator cooling fan is not operating.

3. Set the parking brake and place the transaxle selector lever in neutral on manual transaxle vehicles or **P** on automatic transaxle vehicles. Warm up the engine and run it for 3 minutes at 2500–3000 rpm.

4. Ground the black 1-pin test connector located near the driver's side strut tower.

5. Attach a suitable tachometer according to the manufacturer's instructions.

6. Check the idle speed. It should be 750 rpm ± 25 rpm.

7. If the idle speed is not correct, remove the blind cap from the throttle body and adjust the idle speed by turning the idle air adjust screw.

8. After adjusting the idle speed, install the blind cap, disconnect the jumper wire from the test connector and remove the tachometer from the engine.

WARNING: *Do not tamper with the adjustment screw located just to the left of the idle air adjust screw. Doing so may result in damage to the throttle body.*

3.0L Engine

The curb idle and fast idle speeds are controlled by the ECA and the idle rpm control device and cannot be adjusted. This procedure should only be attempted if there is a change in idle speed and you have eliminated the following possible causes:

● Contamination within the throttle bore.

● Contamination within the idle speed control device.

● Contaminated or defective oxygen sensor.

● Throttle sticking or binding.

● Engine not reaching operating temperature.

● Ignition timing out of specification.

● Vacuum leaks at the intake manifold, vacuum hoses, vacuum reservoirs, power brake booster, etc.

This procedure requires the use of the Ford SUPER STAR II tester, or equivalent. Refer to Chapter 4 for further information.

1. Apply the parking brake. Place the transaxle selector lever in neutral on manual transaxle vehicles or **P** on automatic transaxle vehicles.

2. Start the engine and bring to normal operating temperature. Make sure the heater and all accessories are **OFF**.

3. Make sure the throttle lever is resting on the throttle plate stop screw and the ignition timing is set to specification.

4. Make sure all engine malfunctions have been resolved.

5. Activate the Engine Running Self-Test. Refer to Chapter 4.

6. After Code 1, 11 or 111 has been displayed, quickly (within 4 seconds) unlatch and latch the STI button.

7. A single pulse code indicates the entry mode, then observe the Self-Test Output (STO) of the tester for the following:

a. A constant tone, solid light, or "STO LO" readout means the base idle rpm is within range. To exit the test, unlatch the STI button, then wait 4 seconds for reinitialization. (After 10 seconds it will exit by itself.)

b. A beeping tone, flashing light, or "STO LO" readout at 8 Hz indicates the Throttle Position (TP) sensor is out of range due to over adjustment. Adjustment may be required.

c. A beeping tone, flashing light, or "STO LO" readout at 4 Hz indicates the base idle rpm is too fast and adjustment is required.

d. A beeping tone, flashing light, or "STO LO" readout at 1 Hz indicates the base idle rpm is too slow, adjustment is required.

8. If the idle rpm is too slow, turn the throttle plate stop screw clockwise until the beeping tone, flashing light, or "STO LO" readout is constant.

9. If the idle rpm is too high, turn the throttle plate stop screw counterclockwise until the beeping tone, flashing light, or "STO LO" readout is constant.

10. Run the Key On Engine Off Self-Test and check for a TP sensor output code. Refer to Chapter 4.

11. Make sure the throttle is not stuck in the bore and the linkage is not preventing the throttle from closing.

ENGINE ELECTRICAL

Ignition Coil

REMOVAL AND INSTALLATION

2.2L Engine

NORMALLY ASPIRATED ENGINE

1. Disconnect the negative battery cable.
2. Disconnect the high tension lead from the coil by first twisting, then pulling it from the coil terminal.
3. Disconnect the distributor wiring harness from the coil. Tag the wires so they can be reinstalled in their original positions.
4. Remove the 2 mounting nuts and remove the coil and bracket assembly.
5. Loosen the clamp screw at the coil bracket and remove the coil.
6. Installation is the reverse of the removal procedure.

TURBOCHARGED ENGINE

1. Disconnect the negative battery cable.
2. Disconnect the high tension lead from the coil by first twisting, then pulling it from the coil terminal.
3. Disconnect the igniter wiring harness and remove the 2 nuts.
4. Lift the coil and igniter assembly and disconnect the coil and noise suppressor wiring harness. Tag the wires so they can be reinstalled in their original positions.
5. Slide the protective cover back and disconnect the coil wiring harness. Tag the wires so they can be reinstalled in their original positions.
6. Remove the noise suppressor. Remove the 2 screws and the ignitor module.
7. Remove the ignitor module mounting bracket and the coil.
8. Installation is the reverse of the removal procedure.

3.0L Engine

1. Disconnect the negative battery cable.
2. Disconnect the electrical connectors from

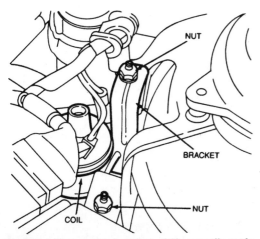

Ignition coil mounting location—2.2L normally aspirated engine

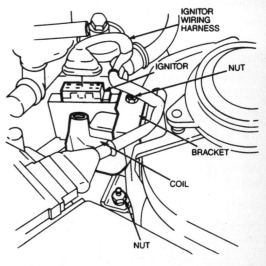

Ignition coil mounting location—2.2L turbocharged engine

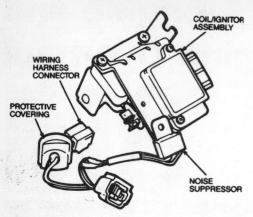

Ignition coil and ignitor assembly—2.2L turbocharged engine

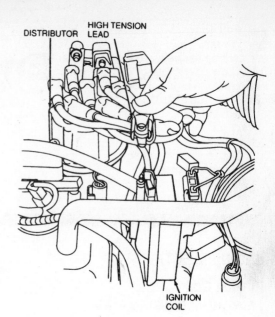

Ignition coil location—3.0L engine

the coil. Tag the wires so they can be reinstalled in their original positions.

3. Disconnect the high tension lead from the ignition coil center terminal.

4. Remove the mounting bolts and remove the ignition coil.

5. Installation is the reverse of the removal procedure.

Ignition Module

REMOVAL AND INSTALLATION

2.2L Turbocharged Engine

Refer to the Ignition Coil removal and installation procedure to remove and install the Ignition Module.

3.0L Engine

1. Disconnect the negative battery cable.

2. Remove the distributor cap and position it aside, leaving the ignition wires attached.

3. Remove the TFI-IV wiring harness connector.

4. Remove the distributor assembly. Refer to the procedure in this Chapter.

5. Remove the ignition module attaching screws.

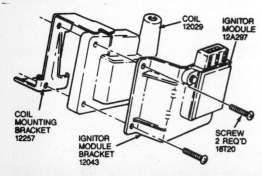

Disassembling the ignitor module from the coil

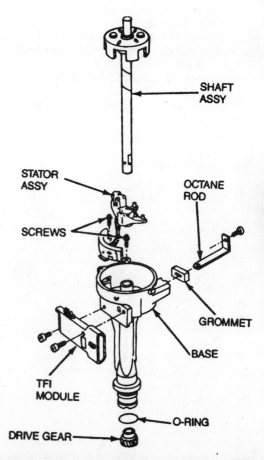

TFI-IV ignition module mounting location

6. Pull the right-hand side of the module down toward the distributor mounting flange and back up to disengage the module terminals from the connector in the distributor base. The module may be pulled toward the flange and away from the distributor.

WARNING: *Do not attempt to lift the module from the mounting surface prior to moving the entire module toward the distributor flange, as the pins will break at the distributor/module connector.*

To install:

7. Coat the metal base plate of the module with a $\frac{1}{32}$ in. (0.8mm) thick ribbon of silicone dialectric compound D7AZ–19A331–A or equivalent.

8. Place the module on the distributor base mounting surface.

9. Carefully position the module assembly toward the distributor bowl and securely engage the 3 distributor connector terminals.

10. Install the 2 module mounting screws and tighten to 15–35 inch lbs. (1.7–4.0 Nm), starting with the upper right-hand screw.

11. Install the distributor assembly. Refer to the procedure in this Chapter.

12. Connect the TFI-IV wiring harness connector and install the distributor cap.

13. Connect the negative battery cable and check the ignition timing. Refer to Chapter 2.

Distributor

REMOVAL

1. Disconnect the negative battery cable.

2. Remove the distributor cap and position it aside, leaving the ignition wires connected.

3. On the 2.2L normally aspirated engine, disconnect the vacuum hoses from the distributor diaphragm and the wiring harness at the coil. Tag the hoses and wires prior to removal so they can be reinstalled in their original locations.

4. On the 2.2L turbocharged engine, disconnect the distributor wiring harness connector located near the distributor.

5. On the 3.0L engine, disconnect the primary wiring connector from the distributor and disconnect the TFI-IV wiring harness connector at the ignition module.

6. Using a wrench on the crankshaft pulley, rotate the crankshaft to position the No. 1 piston on Top Dead Center (TDC) of the compression stroke; the crankshaft pulley mark should align with the timing plate indicator.

7. Using chalk or paint, mark the position of the distributor housing on the cylinder head on 2.2L engines or the position of the distributor housing on the cylinder block on 3.0L engine.

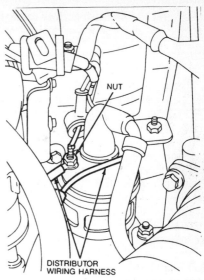

Disconnecting the distributor wiring harness connector—2.2L normally aspirated engine

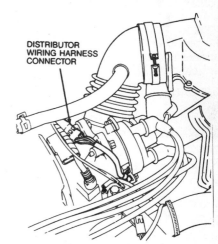

Distributor wiring harness connector location—2.2L turbocharged engine

Also mark the position of the distributor rotor in relation to the distributor housing.

8. Remove the distributor hold-down bolt(s) and remove the distributor.

9. Inspect the O-ring on the distributor housing and replace it, if it is damaged or worn.

INSTALLATION

Engine Not Rotated

1. Using engine oil, lubricate the O-ring.

2. Install the distributor, aligning the marks that were made in Step 7 of the removal procedure. Be sure to engage the drive gear with the slot in the camshaft on 2.2L engines.

3. Snug the distributor hold-down bolt(s).

4. Connect the electrical connectors and, if equipped, vacuum hoses to their original locations. Install the distributor cap.

5. Connect the negative battery cable. Start the engine and check or adjust the ignition timing. Refer to Chapter 2.

Engine Rotated

1. Using engine oil, lubricate the O-ring.

2. Disconnect the spark plug wire from the No. 1 cylinder spark plug. Remove the spark plug from the No. 1 cylinder and press a thumb over the spark plug hole.

3. Using a wrench on the crankshaft pulley, rotate the crankshaft until pressure is felt at the spark plug hole, indicating the piston is approaching TDC on the compression stroke. Continue rotating the crankshaft until the crankshaft pulley mark aligns with the timing cover indicator.

4. Place the distributor rotor in position so that it aligns with the No. 1 spark plug wire tower on the distributor cap.

5. Install the distributor. Be sure to engage the drive gear with the camshaft slot on 2.2L engines. Align the mark that was made on the distributor housing with the mark that was made on the cylinder head on 2.2L engines or cylinder block on 3.0L engine. Snug the distributor hold-down bolt(s).

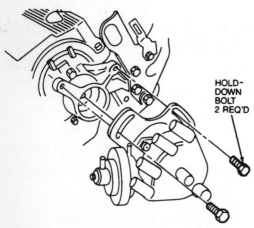

HOLD-DOWN BOLT 2 REQ'D

Distributor installation—2.2L normally aspirated engine

6. Connect the electrical connectors and, if equipped, vacuum hoses to their original locations. Install the distributor cap.

7. Install the spark plug in the No. 1 cylinder and connect the spark plug wire.

8. Connect the negative battery cable. Start the engine and check or adjust the ignition timing. Refer to Chapter 2.

Alternator

ALTERNATOR PRECAUTIONS

Several precautions must be observed with alternator equipped vehicles to avoid damage to the unit.

• If the battery is removed for any reason, make sure it is reconnected with the correct polarity. Reversing the battery connections may result in damage to the one-way rectifiers.

• When utilizing a booster battery as a starting aid, always connect the positive to positive terminals and the negative terminal from the booster battery to a good engine ground on the vehicle being started.

• Never use a fast charger as a booster to start vehicles.

• Disconnect the battery cables when charging the battery with a fast charger.

• Never attempt to polarize the alternator.

• Do not use test lights of more than 12 volts when checking diode continuity.

• Do not short across or ground any of the alternator terminals.

• The polarity of the battery, alternator and regulator must be matched and considered before making any electrical connections within the system.

• Never separate the alternator on an open circuit. Make sure all connections within the circuit are clean and tight.

• Disconnect the battery ground terminal when performing any service on electrical components.

• Disconnect the battery if arc welding is to be done on the vehicle.

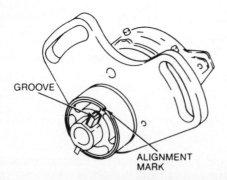

GROOVE

ALIGNMENT MARK

Distributor drive gear alignment

REMOVAL AND INSTALLATION

2.2L Engine

1. Disconnect the negative battery cable.
2. Raise and safely support the vehicle.
3. Remove the right-hand halfshaft. Refer to Chapter 7.
4. From the rear of the alternator, depress the lock tabs on the wiring terminals and pull the terminals straight off. Mark the location of the wires prior to removal so they can be reinstalled in their original positions.
5. Loosen the alternator adjustment and through bolts enough to allow the alternator to pivot. Remove the alternator drive belt.
6. Remove the alternator adjustment bracket, lock bolt and through bolt.
7. Hold the alternator to prevent it from falling and remove it through the space left by removing the halfshaft.

To install:

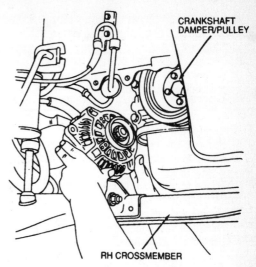

Removing the alternator—2.2L engine

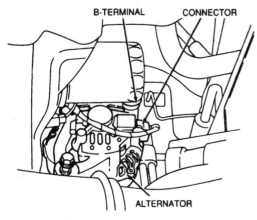

Alternator wiring connector locations—2.2L engine

8. Position the alternator and loosely install the mounting and adjustment bolts.
9. Install the drive belt and adjust the tension according to the procedure in Chapter 1. Tighten the through bolt to 27–38 ft. lbs. (37–52 Nm) and the adjusting bolt to 14–19 ft. lbs. (19–25 Nm).
10. Connect the wiring terminals at the rear of the alternator.
11. Install the right-hand halfshaft. Refer to Chapter 7.
12. Lower the vehicle. Connect the negative battery cable.

3.0L Engine

1. Disconnect the negative battery cable.
2. Remove the accessory drive belt. Refer to Chapter 1.
3. Remove and set aside the windshield washer reservoir.

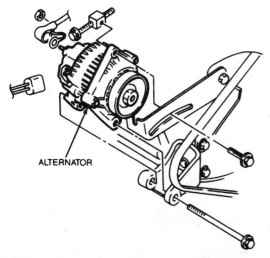

Alternator mounting exploded view—2.2L engine

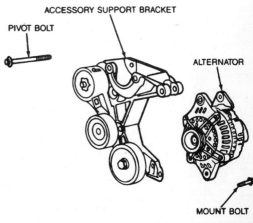

Alternator and accessory support bracket exploded view—3.0L engine

4. Remove the power steering pump reservoir return hose from the pump assembly.

5. Remove the power steering pump high pressure hose from the pump assembly.

6. Remove the upper and middle accessory support bracket mounting bolts.

7. Pull back on the idler tensioner, using a ½ in. drive breaker bar and remove the lower accessory support bracket mounting bolt.

8. Remove the mounting bolt from the side of the accessory bracket at the air conditioning compressor brace.

9. Raise the alternator/accessory support bracket to clear the engine and set aside carefully to remove the electrical connectors.

10. Disconnect the electrical connectors from the alternator. Place the alternator/accessory

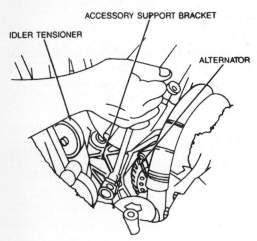

Removing the alternator/accessory support bracket assembly—3.0L engine

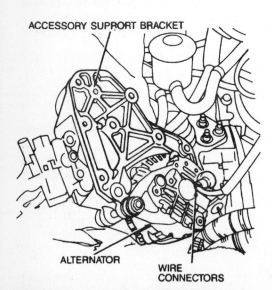

Alternator/accessory support bracket assembly—3.0L engine

support bracket on a bench for alternator removal.

11. Remove the alternator pivot bolt and remove the mounting bolt from the back side of the alternator. Remove the alternator from the accessory support bracket.

To install:

12. Position the alternator on the accessory support bracket and install the alternator pivot bolt.

13. Install the alternator mounting bolt at the rear of the alternator.

14. Position the alternator/accessory support bracket in the engine compartment and connect the electrical connectors on the back side of the alternator.

15. Position the alternator/accessory support bracket on the engine. Install the mounting bolt through the air conditioning compressor brace into the support bracket.

16. Install the middle accessory support bracket mounting bolt.

17. Pull back on the idler tensioner, using the ½ in. drive breaker bar and install the lower accessory support bracket mounting bolt.

18. Install the upper accessory support bracket mounting bolt.

19. Connect the power steering pressure and return hoses to the pump.

20. Install the accessory drive belt. Refer to Chapter 1.

21. Replace the windshield washer resevoir and connect the negative battery cable.

22. Fill and bleed the power steering system. Refer to Chapter 8.

Regulator

REMOVAL AND INSTALLATION

The electronic voltage regulator is contained within the alternator, integral with the brush holder assembly. The alternator should be removed and taken to an authorized repair facility.

Battery

REMOVAL AND INSTALLATION

1. Using a battery clamp puller and battery pliers, disconnect the negative and then the positive battery cables from the battery.

2. Remove the battery hold-down clamps.

3. Remove the battery using a battery carrier. If a battery carrier is not available, grip the battery at opposite corners with your hands and carefully lift the battery from the tray. Be careful not to spill battery acid on yourself or the vehicle.

To install:

4. Test the battery to see if it needs to be replaced or charged. Refer to Chapter 1.

5. Clean the battery cable ends and battery terminals.

6. Check the battery tray for corrosion or other damage. Clean the tray with a wire brush and a scraper.

7. Install the battery and retain with the hold-down clamps.

8. Connect the positive and then the negative battery cables to the battery.

Starter

REMOVAL AND INSTALLATION

2.2L Engine

1. Disconnect the negative battery cable. Raise and support the vehicle, safely.

2. If equipped with a manual transaxle, remove the exhaust pipe bracket.

3. Remove the transaxle-to-engine bracket and intake manifold-to-engine bracket.

ALTERNATOR SPECIFICATIONS — 2.2L ENGINE

Alternator — 2.2L		Non-Turbo	Turbo
Type		A.C.	
Output	V-A	12-70	12-70 (MTX), 12-80 (ATX)
Regulator type		Transistorized (built-in IC regulator)	
Regulated voltage	V	14.1-14.7	
Brush length	Standard	21.5 (0.846)	
mm (in)	Minimum	8.0 (0.315)	

STARTER TROUBLESHOOTING CHART

CONDITION	POSSIBLE SOURCE	ACTION
• Engine Cranks Slowly	• Undercharged battery.	• CHECK battery. CHARGE or REPLACE.
	• Loose or corroded cable connections.	• CLEAN and TIGHTEN cable connections.
	• Starter motor.	• REMOVE starter for repair.
• Engine Will Not Crank	• Undercharged battery.	• CHECK battery. CHARGE or REPLACE.
	• Ignition Switch.	• PERFORM the ignition switch check
	• Clutch Engage/Neutral Safety Switch.	• PERFORM the applicable switch check
	• Loose or corroded cable connections.	• CLEAN and TIGHTEN cable connections.
	• Faulty ignition circuit grounds.	• CHECK all ground connections.
	• Starter motor.	• REPAIR or REPLACE as required.
• Engine Will Not Crank — Starter Motor Spins	• Starter motor.	• REMOVE starter and INSPECT drive. REPLACE as required.
	• Flywheel ring gear.	• REMOVE starter and INSPECT ring gear teeth (also starter drive pinion). REPLACE as required.
• Engine Starts With Clutch Engaged (MTX) or In Shift Positions Other than PARK/NEUTRAL (ATX)	• Clutch engage/neutral safety switch.	• ADJUST or REPLACE clutch engage/neutral safety switch as required.

4. Disconnect the electrical connectors from the starter.

5. Remove the starter mounting bolts and the starter.

To install:

6. Install the starter and torque the bolts to 23–34 ft. lbs. (31–46 Nm).

7. Connect the electrical connectors to the starter.

8. Install the intake manifold-to-engine bracket and tighten the bolts to 14–22 ft. lbs. (19–30 Nm).

9. If equipped with an automatic transaxle, install the transaxle-to-engine bracket and torque the bellhousing bolt to 66–86 ft. lbs. (89–117 Nm) and the 3 other mounting bolts to 27–38 ft. lbs. (37–52 Nm).

10. If equipped with a manual transaxle, install the transaxle-to-engine bracket and connect the exhaust pipe bracket. Tighten the bracket bolts to 32–45 ft. lbs. (43–61 Nm).

11. Lower the vehicle.

12. Connect the negative battery cable and check the starter for proper operation.

3.0L Engine

1. Disconnect the negative battery cable.

2. Raise and safely support the vehicle.

3. If equipped with automatic transaxle, remove the kickdown cable routing bracket from the engine block.

4. Disconnect the wire from the starter solenoid S-terminal.

NOTE: *When disconnecting the plastic hard shell connector at the solenoid S-terminal, grasp the plastic connector, depress the plastic tab, and pull off the lead assembly. Do not pull on the lead wire or damage may result.*

5. Remove the attaching nut from the starter solenoid B-terminal and disconnect the cable from the terminal.

6. Remove the starter mounting bolts and remove the starter.

To install:

7. Position the starter and install the mounting bolts. Tighten the bolts to 15–20 ft. lbs. (20–27 Nm).

8. Connect the cable to the starter solenoid B-terminal and install the attaching nut. Tighten the nut to 80–120 inch lbs. (9–13.5 Nm).

9. Connect the wire to the starter solenoid S-terminal.

10. If necessary, install the kickdown cable routing bracket to the engine block.

11. Lower the vehicle. Connect the negative battery cable and check the starter for proper operation.

SOLENOID REPLACEMENT

1. Remove the starter according to the procedure in this Chapter.

2. Clamp the starter motor in a soft-jawed vise.

3. Remove the nut and disconnect the lead from the solenoid M-terminal.

4. Remove the solenoid retaining screws and remove the solenoid. If there are shims between the solenoid and the starter on the 2.2L engine, save them as they are used to adjust the pinion depth clearance.

5. Install the replacement solenoid and tighten the retaining screws. On the 2.2L engine, be sure to replace any shims that were removed during disassembly.

6. On the 3.0L engine, connect the solenoid M-terminal lead and tighten the nut to 80–120 inch lbs. (9–13.5 Nm).

7. On the 2.2L engine, proceed as follows:

   a. Leave the lead disconnected from the solenoid M-terminal.

   b. Connect the positive lead from a 12 volt battery to the S terminal of the solenoid and

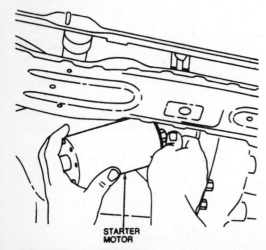

Starter removal—3.0L engine

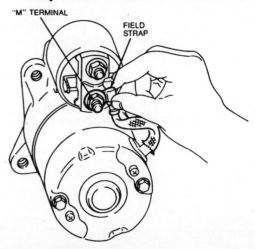

Starter solenoid M terminal location

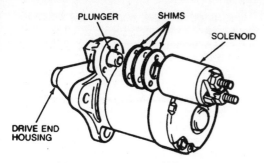

Starter solenoid shim location—2.2L engine

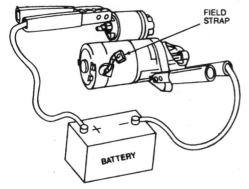

Battery connection for starter solenoid shim measurement

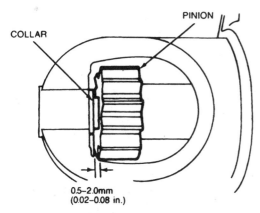

Pinion-to-collar clearance

the negative lead to the starter motor body. When the battery is connected, the solenoid should engage and kick out the pinion.

NOTE: *Do not engage the solenoid for more than 20 seconds at a time. If this test must be repeated, wait at least 3 minutes between attempts to allow the solenoid to cool.*

c. With the pinion extended, measure the clearance between the pinion and collar. The clearance should be 0.02–0.08 in. (0.5–2.0mm).

d. If the gap measurement falls outside the specified range, add or remove shims be-

tween the solenoid and drive end housing until the pinion gap is within specification.

e. Install the lead to the solenoid M-terminal and tighten the nut to 87–104 inch lbs. (10–12 Nm).

8. Install the starter according to the procedure in this Chapter.

ENGINE MECHANICAL

Description

2.2L ENGINE

The 2.2L engine has 4 cylinders situated in-line in a cast iron cylinder block. The crankshaft is supported in the cylinder block on 5 main bearing saddles. The pistons are aluminum and drive the crankshaft by way of connecting rods. The cylinder head is aluminum and contains 2 intake valves and 1 exhaust valve per cylinder. The valves are actuated by rocker arms driven directly by the camshaft, which is supported on the cylinder head on 5 camshaft saddles. The camshaft is driven off of the crankshaft by way of a cogged belt.

3.0L ENGINE

The 3.0L engine has 6 cylinders configured in a 60° V design with 3 cylinders on each bank in a cast iron cylinder block. The crankshaft is supported in the cylinder block on 4 main bearing saddles. The pistons are aluminum and drive the crankshaft by way of connecting rods. The cylinder heads are cast iron and contain 1 each intake and exhaust valve per cylinder. The

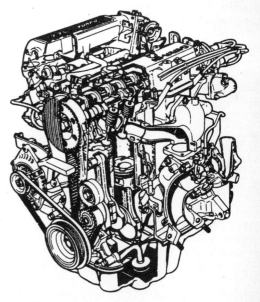

2.2L engine

valves are actuated by rocker arms which are driven by the camshaft by way of pushrods and hydraulic lifters. The camshaft and hydraulic lifters are housed in the engine block. The camshaft is driven off the crankshaft by a chain and 2 sprockets.

Engine Overhaul Tips

Most engine overhaul procedures are fairly standard. In addition to specific parts replacement procedures and complete specifications for your individual engine, this Chapter also is a guide to accepted rebuilding procedures. Examples of standard rebuilding practice are shown and should be used along with specific details concerning your particular engine.

Competent and accurate machine shop services will ensure maximum performance, reliability and engine life. In most instances it is more profitable for the do-it-yourself mechanic to remove, clean and inspect the component, buy the necessary parts and deliver these to a shop for actual machine work.

On the other hand, much of the rebuilding work (crankshaft, block, bearings, piston, rods, and other components) is still within the scope of the do-it-yourself mechanic.

TOOLS

The tools required for an engine overhaul or parts replacement will depend on the depth of your involvement. With a few exceptions, they will be the tools found in a mechanic's tool kit (see Chapter 1). More in-depth work will require any or all of the following:
- dial indicator (reading in thousandths) mounted on a universal base.
- micrometers and telescope gauges.
- jaw and screw-type pullers.
- scraper.
- valve spring compressor.
- ring groove cleaner.
- piston ring expander and compressor.
- ridge reamer.
- cylinder hone or glaze breaker.
- Plastigage®.
- engine stand.

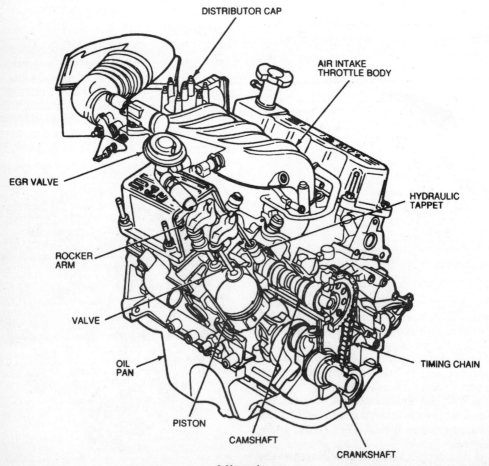

3.0L engine

The use of most of these tools is illustrated in this Chapter. Many can be rented for a one-time use from a local parts jobber or tool supply house specializing in automotive work.

Occasionally, the use of special tools is called for. See the information on Special Tools and the Safety Notice in the front of this book before substituting another tool.

INSPECTION TECHNIQUES

Procedures and specifications are given in this Chapter for inspecting, cleaning and assessing the wear limits of most major components. Other procedures such as Magnaflux® and Zyglo® can be used to locate material flaws and stress cracks. Magnaflux® is a magnetic process applicable only to ferrous materials. The Zyglo® process coats the material with a flourescent dye penetrant and can be used on any material. Check for suspected surface cracks can be more readily made using spot check dye. The dye is sprayed onto the suspected area, wiped off and area sprayed with a developer. Cracks will show up brightly.

OVERHAUL TIPS

Aluminum has become extremely popular for use in engines, due to its low weight. Observe the following precautions when handling aluminum parts:

Never hot tank aluminum parts (the caustic hot-tank solution will eat the aluminum).

Remove all aluminum parts (identification tag, etc) from engine parts prior to hot-tanking.

Always coat threads lightly with engine oil or anti-seize compounds before installation, to prevent seizure.

Never over-torque bolts or spark plugs, especially in aluminum threads. Stripped threads in any component can be repaired using any of several commercial repair kits (Heli-Coil®, Microdot®, Keenserts®, etc.)

When assembling the engine, any parts that will be in frictional contact must be prelubed to provide lubrication at initial startup. Any product specifically formulated for this purpose can be used, but engine oil is not recommended as a pre-lube.

When semi-permanent (locked, but removable) installation of bolts or nuts is desired, threads should be cleaned and coated with Loctite® or other similar, commercial nonhardening sealant.

REPAIRING DAMAGED THREADS

Several methods of repairing damaged threads are available. Heli-Coil® (shown here), Keenserts® and Microdot® are among the most widely used. All involve basically the same principle--drilling out stripped threads, tapping the

hole and installing prewound insert--making welding, plugging and oversize fasteners unnecessary.

Two types of thread repair inserts are usually supplied: a standard type for most Inch Coarse, Inch Fine, Metric Coarse and Metric Fine thread sizes and a spark plug type to fit most spark plug port sizes. Consult the individual manufacturer's catalog to determine exact applications. Typical thread repair kits will contain a selection of prewound threaded inserts, a tap (corresponding to the outside diameter threads of the insert) and an installation tool. Spark plug inserts usually differ because they require a tap equipped with pilot threads and combined reamer/tap Chapter. Most manufac-

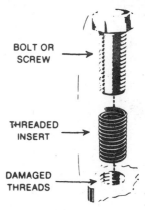

Damaged bolt hole threads can be replaced with thread repair inserts

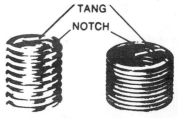

Standard thread repair insert (left), and spark plug thread insert

Drill out the damaged threads with the specified drill. Drill completely through the hole or to the bottom of a blind hole

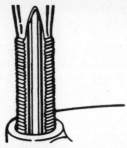

With the tap supplied, tap the hole to receive the thread insert. Keep the tap well oiled and back it out frequently to avoid clogging the threads

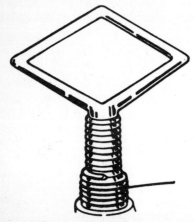

Screw the threaded insert onto the installer tool until the tang engages the slot. Screw the insert into the tapped hole until it is ¼ or ½ turn below the top surface. After installation break off the tang with a hammer and punch

turers also supply blister-packed thread repair inserts separately in addition to a master kit containing a variety of taps and inserts plus installation tools.

Before effecting a repair to a threaded hole, remove any snapped, broken or damaged bolts or studs. Penetrating oil can be used to free frozen threads; the offending item can be removed with locking pliers or with a screw or stud extractor. After the hole is clear, the thread can be repaired.

CHECKING ENGINE COMPRESSION

A noticeable lack of engine power, excessive oil consumption and/or poor fuel mileage measured over an extended period are all indicators of internal engine wear. Worn piston rings, scored or worn cylinder bores, blown head gaskets, sticking or burnt valves and worn valve seats are all possible culprits. here. A check of each cylinder's compression will help you locate the problems.

As mentioned earlier, a screw-in type com-pression gauge is more accurate than the type you simply hold against the spark plug hole, although it takes slightly longer to use. It's worth it to obtain a more accurate reading. Check engine compression as follows:

1. Warm up the engine to normal operating temperature.
2. Remove all spark plugs.
3. Disconnect the high-tension lead from the ignition coil.
4. Disconnect the cold start valve and all injector connections.
5. Screw the compression gauge into the No. 1 spark plug hole until the fitting is snug.

NOTE: *Be careful not to crossthread the plug hole. On aluminum cylinder heads use extra care, as the threads in these heads are easily ruined.*

6. Ask an assistant to depress the accelerator pedal fully. Then, while you read the compression gauge, ask the assistant to crank the engine two or three times in short bursts using the ignition switch.
7. Read the compression gauge at the end of each series of cranks, and record the highest of these readings. Repeat this procedure for each of the engine's cylinders. Compare the highest reading to the reading in each cylinder.
8. A cylinder's compression pressure is usually acceptable if it is not less than 80% of the highest reading. For example, if the highest reading is 150 psi, the lowest should be no lower than 120 psi. No cylinder should have a reading below 100 psi.
9. If a cylinder is unusually low, pour a tablespoon of clean engine oil into the cylinder through the spark plug hole and repeat the compression test. If the compression comes up after adding the oil, it appears that the cylinder's piston rings or bore are damaged or worn. If the pressure remains low, the valves may not be seating properly (a valve job is needed), or the head gasket may be blown near that cylinder. If compression in any two adjacent cylinders is low, and if the addition of oil doesn't help the compression, there is leakage past the head gasket. Oil and coolant water in the combustion chamber can result from this problem. There may be evidence of water droplets on the engine dipstick when a head gasket has blown.

Engine

REMOVAL AND INSTALLATION

CAUTION: *When draining the coolant, keep in mind that cats and dogs are attracted by the ethylene glycol antifreeze, and are quite likely to drink any that is left in an uncovered container or in puddles on the ground. This*

GENERAL ENGINE SPECIFICATIONS

Year	Engine ID/VIN	Engine Displacement Liters (cc)	Fuel System Type	Net Horsepower @ rpm	Net Torque @ rpm (ft. lbs.)	Bore × Stroke (in.)	Compression Ratio	Oil Pressure @ rpm
1989	C	2.2 (2189)	EFI	110 @ 4700	130 @ 3000	3.39 × 3.70	8.6:1	43–57 @ 3000
	L	2.2 (2189)	EFI	145 @ 4300	190 @ 3500	3.39 × 3.70	7.8:1	43–57 @ 3000
1990	C	2.2 (2189)	EFI	110 @ 4700	130 @ 3000	3.39 × 3.70	8.6:1	43–57 @ 3000
	L	2.2 (2189)	EFI	145 @ 4300	190 @ 3500	3.39 × 3.70	7.8:1	43–57 @ 3000
	U	3.0 (2971)	EFI	140 @ 4800	160 @ 3000	3.50 × 3.14	9.3:1	40–60 @ 2500
1991	C	2.2 (2189)	EFI	110 @ 4700	130 @ 3000	3.39 × 3.70	8.6:1	43–57 @ 3000
	L	2.2 (2189)	EFI	145 @ 4300	190 @ 3500	3.39 × 3.70	7.8:1	43–57 @ 3000
	U	3.0 (2971)	EFI	145 @ 4800	165 @ 3400	3.50 × 3.14	9.3:1	40–60 @ 2500
1992	C	2.2 (2189)	EFI	110 @ 4700	130 @ 3000	3.39 × 3.70	8.6:1	43–57 @ 3000
	L	2.2 (2189)	EFI	145 @ 4300	190 @ 3500	3.39 × 3.70	7.8:1	43–57 @ 3000
	U	3.0 (2971)	EFI	145 @ 4800	165 @ 3400	3.50 × 3.14	9.3:1	40–60 @ 2500

EFI—Electronic Fuel Injection

VALVE SPECIFICATIONS

Year	Engine ID/VIN	Engine Displacement Liters (cc)	Seat Angle (deg.)	Face Angle (deg.)	Spring Test Pressure (lbs. @ in.)	Spring Installed Height (in.)	Stem-to-Guide Clearance (in.) Intake	Stem-to-Guide Clearance (in.) Exhaust	Stem Diameter (in.) Intake	Stem Diameter (in.) Exhaust
1989	C	2.2 (2189)	45	45	NA	NA	0.008	0.008	0.2744–0.2750	0.2742–0.2748
	L	2.2 (2189)	45	45	NA	NA	0.008	0.008	0.2744–0.2750	0.2742–0.2748
1990	C	2.2 (2189)	45	45	NA	NA	0.008	0.008	0.2744–0.2750	0.2742–0.2748
	L	2.2 (2189)	45	45	NA	NA	0.008	0.008	0.2744–0.2750	0.2742–0.2748
	U	3.0 (2971)	45	44	180 @ 1.16	1.58	0.0010–0.0028	0.0015–0.0033	0.3126–0.3134	0.3121–0.3129
1991	C	2.2 (2189)	45	45	NA	NA	0.008	0.008	0.2744–0.2750	0.2742–0.2748
	L	2.2 (2189)	45	45	NA	NA	0.008	0.008	0.2744–0.2750	0.2742–0.2748
	U	3.0 (2971)	45	44	180 @ 1.16	1.58	0.0010–0.0028	0.0015–0.0033	0.3126–0.3134	0.3121–0.3129
1992	C	2.2 (2189)	45	45	NA	NA	0.008	0.008	0.2744–0.2750	0.2742–0.2748
	L	2.2 (2189)	45	45	NA	NA	0.008	0.008	0.2744–0.2750	0.2742–0.2748
	U	3.0 (2971)	45	44	180 @ 1.16	1.58	0.0010–0.0028	0.0015–0.0033	0.3126–0.3134	0.3121–0.3129

NA—Not available

CAMSHAFT SPECIFICATIONS

All measurements given in inches.

Year	Engine ID/VIN	Engine Displacement Liters (cc)	Journal Diameter					Elevation		Bearing Clearance	Camshaft End Play
			1	2	3	4	5	In.	Ex.		
1989	C	2.2 (2189)	1.2575–1.2585	1.2563–1.2573	1.2563–1.2573	1.2563–1.2573	1.2575–1.2585	1.620–1.630	1.640–1.650	①	0.003–0.008
	L	2.2 (2189)	1.2575–1.2585	1.2563–1.2573	1.2563–1.2573	1.2563–1.2573	1.2575–1.2585	1.620–1.630	1.640–1.650	①	0.003–0.008
1990	C	2.2 (2189)	1.2575–1.2585	1.2563–1.2573	1.2563–1.2573	1.2563–1.2573	1.2575–1.2585	1.620–1.630	1.640–1.650	①	0.003–0.008
	L	2.2 (2189)	1.2575–1.2585	1.2563–1.2573	1.2563–1.2573	1.2563–1.2573	1.2575–1.2585	1.620–1.630	1.640–1.650	①	0.003–0.008
	U	3.0 (2971)	2.0074–2.0084	2.0074–2.0084	2.0074–2.0084	2.0074–2.0084	—	0.260	0.260	0.001–0.003	0.001–0.005
1991	C	2.2 (2189)	1.2575–1.2585	1.2563–1.2573	1.2563–1.2573	1.2563–1.2573	1.2575–1.2585	1.620–1.630	1.640–1.650	①	0.003–0.008
	L	2.2 (2189)	1.2575–1.2585	1.2563–1.2573	1.2563–1.2573	1.2563–1.2573	1.2575–1.2585	1.620–1.630	1.640–1.650	①	0.003–0.008
	U	3.0 (2971)	2.0074–2.0084	2.0074–2.0084	2.0074–2.0084	2.0074–2.0084	—	0.260	0.260	0.001–0.003	0.001–0.005
1992	C	2.2 (2189)	1.2575–1.2585	1.2563–1.2573	1.2563–1.2573	1.2563–1.2573	1.2575–1.2585	1.620–1.630	1.640–1.650	①	0.003–0.008
	L	2.2 (2189)	1.2575–1.2585	1.2563–1.2573	1.2563–1.2573	1.2563–1.2573	1.2575–1.2585	1.620–1.630	1.640–1.650	①	0.003–0.008
	U	3.0 (2971)	2.0074–2.0084	2.0074–2.0084	2.0074–2.0084	2.0074–2.0084	—	0.260	0.260	0.001–0.003	0.001–0.005

① Front and rear journals—0.0014–0.0033
Center journals—0.0026–0.0045

CRANKSHAFT AND CONNECTING ROD SPECIFICATIONS

All measurements are given in inches.

Year	Engine ID/VIN	Engine Displacement Liters (cc)	Crankshaft				Connecting Rod		
			Main Brg. Journal Dia.	Main Brg. Oil Clearance	Shaft End-play	Thrust on No.	Journal Diameter	Oil Clearance	Side Clearance
1989	C	2.2 (2189)	2.3597–2.3604	①	0.0031–0.0071	3	2.0055–2.0061	0.0011–0.0026	0.004–0.0103
	L	2.2 (2189)	2.3597–2.3604	①	0.0031–0.0071	3	2.0055–2.0061	0.0011–0.0026	0.004–0.0103
1990	C	2.2 (2189)	2.3597–2.3604	①	0.0031–0.0071	3	2.0055–2.0061	0.0011–0.0026	0.004–0.0103
	L	2.2 (2189)	2.3597–2.3604	①	0.0031–0.0071	3	2.0055–2.0061	0.0011–0.0026	0.004–0.0103
	U	3.0 (2971)	2.5190–2.5198	0.0010–0.0014	0.004–0.008	3	2.1253–2.1261	0.0010–0.0014	0.006–0.014
1991	C	2.2 (2189)	2.3597–2.3604	①	0.0031–0.0071	3	2.0055–2.0061	0.0011–0.0026	0.004–0.0103
	L	2.2 (2189)	2.3597–2.3604	①	0.0031–0.0071	3	2.0055–2.0061	0.0011–0.0026	0.004–0.0103
	U	3.0 (2971)	2.5190–2.5198	0.0010–0.0014	0.004–0.008	3	2.1253–2.1261	0.0010–0.0014	0.006–0.014
1992	C	2.2 (2189)	2.3597–2.3604	①	0.0031–0.0071	3	2.0055–2.0061	0.0011–0.0026	0.004–0.0103
	L	2.2 (2189)	2.3597–2.3604	①	0.0031–0.0071	3	2.0055–2.0061	0.0011–0.0026	0.004–0.0103
	U	3.0 (2971)	2.5190–2.5198	0.0010–0.0014	0.004–0.008	3	2.1253–2.1261	0.0010–0.0014	0.006–0.014

① Nos. 1, 2, 4 and 5—0.0010–0.0017
No. 3—0.0012–0.0019

PISTON AND RING SPECIFICATIONS

All measurements are given in inches.

Year	Engine ID/VIN	Engine Displacement Liters (cc)	Piston Clearance	Ring Gap			Ring Side Clearance		
				Top Compression	Bottom Compression	Oil Control	Top Compression	Bottom Compression	Oil Control
1989	C	2.2 (2189)	0.0014–0.0030	0.008–0.014	0.006–0.012	0.012–0.035	0.001–0.003	0.001–0.003	NA
	L	2.2 (2189)	0.0014–0.0030	0.008–0.014	0.006–0.012	0.008–0.028	0.001–0.003	0.001–0.003	NA
1990	C	2.2 (2189)	0.0014–0.0030	0.008–0.014	0.006–0.012	0.012–0.035	0.001–0.003	0.001–0.003	NA
	L	2.2 (2189)	0.0014–0.0030	0.008–0.014	0.006–0.012	0.008–0.028	0.001–0.003	0.001–0.003	NA
	U	3.0 (2971)	0.0014–0.0022	0.010–0.020	0.010–0.020	0.010–0.049	0.0012–0.0031	0.0012–0.0031	NA
1991	C	2.2 (2189)	0.0014–0.0030	0.008–0.014	0.006–0.012	0.012–0.035	0.001–0.003	0.001–0.003	NA
	L	2.2 (2189)	0.0014–0.0030	0.008–0.014	0.006–0.012	0.008–0.028	0.001–0.003	0.001–0.003	NA
	U	3.0 (2971)	0.0014–0.0022	0.010–0.020	0.010–0.020	0.010–0.049	0.0012–0.0031	0.0012–0.0031	NA
1992	C	2.2 (2189)	0.0014–0.0030	0.008–0.014	0.006–0.012	0.012–0.035	0.001–0.003	0.001–0.003	NA
	L	2.2 (2189)	0.0014–0.0030	0.008–0.014	0.006–0.012	0.008–0.028	0.001–0.003	0.001–0.003	NA
	U	3.0 (2971)	0.0014–0.0022	0.010–0.020	0.010–0.020	0.010–0.049	0.0012–0.0031	0.0012–0.0031	NA

NA—Not available

TORQUE SPECIFICATIONS

All readings in ft. lbs.

Year	Engine ID/VIN	Engine Displacement Liters (cc)	Cylinder Head Bolts	Main Bearing Bolts	Rod Bearing Bolts	Crankshaft Damper Bolts	Flywheel Bolts	Manifold		Spark Plugs
								Intake	Exhaust	
1989	C	2.2 (2189)	59–64	61–65	48–51	① 108–116	71–76	14–22	16–21	11–17
	L	2.2 (2189)	59–64	61–65	48–51	① 108–116	71–76	14–22	16–21	11–17
1990	C	2.2 (2189)	59–64	61–65	48–51	① 108–116	71–76	14–22	16–21	11–17
	L	2.2 (2189)	59–64	61–65	48–51	① 108–116	71–76	14–22	16–21	11–17
	U	3.0 (2971)	②	60	23–39	92–122	54–64	③	15–22	7–15
1991	C	2.2 (2189)	59–64	61–65	48–51	① 108–116	71–76	14–22	16–21	11–17
	L	2.2 (2189)	59–64	61–65	48–51	① 108–116	71–76	14–22	16–21	11–17
	U	3.0 (2971)	④	60	25	107	54–64	③	18	7–15
1992	C	2.2 (2189)	59–64	61–65	48–51	① 108–116	71–76	14–22	16–21	11–17
	L	2.2 (2189)	59–64	61–65	48–51	① 108–116	71–76	14–22	16–21	11–17
	U	3.0 (2971)	④	60	25	107	54–64	③	18	7–15

① Figure given is for crankshaft sprocket bolt
② Tighten in 2 steps:
   Step 1: 33–41 ft. lbs.
   Step 2: 63–73 ft. lbs.
③ Tighten in 2 steps:
   Step 1: 11 ft. lbs.
   Step 2: 21 ft. lbs.
④ Tighten in 4 steps:
   Step 1: 59 ft. lbs.
   Step 2: Back off all bolts a minimum of 360°
   Step 3: 37 ft. lbs.
   Step 4: 68 ft. lbs.

will prove fatal in sufficient quantity. Always drain the coolant into a sealable container. Coolant should be reused unless it is contaminated or several years old.

2.2L Engine

1. Properly relieve the fuel system pressure and disconnect the negative battery cable.

2. Mark the hood hinge-to-hood locations and remove the hood.

3. Drain the cooling system, the engine oil, power steering fluid and, if equipped, automatic transaxle fluid into suitable containers.

4. Remove the battery, the battery carrier and the fuse holder.

5. Remove the air filter assembly and ducts. Disconnect the accelerator cable, throttle valve, and the cruise control cable, if equipped.

6. Label and disconnect the electrical connectors from the electronic fuel injection system, the ignition coil, the thermostat housing sensors, the oxygen sensor, the radiator and the cooling fan assembly.

7. If equipped with an automatic transaxle, disconnect and plug the cooler lines from the radiator. Remove the radiator cooling fan assembly and the radiator.

8. If equipped with a manual transaxle, remove the clutch release cylinder and move it aside.

9. On non-turbocharged vehicles, raise and safely support the vehicle, then remove the front exhaust pipe-to-exhaust manifold nuts, the exhaust pipe-to-catalytic converter nuts and the front exhaust pipe. Lower the vehicle.

10. Properly discharge the air conditioning system and remove the air conditioning lines from the compressor. Immediately plug the lines and the compressor openings to prevent the entrance of moisture. Disconnect the electrical connector from the compressor clutch.

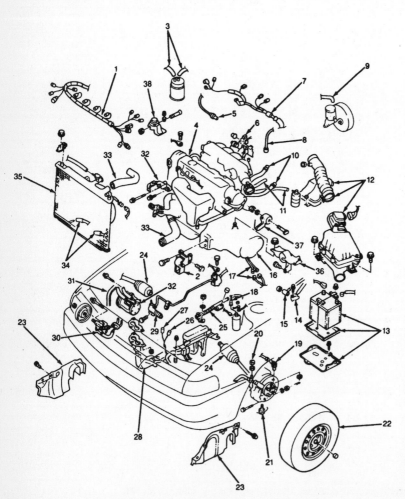

1. EFI harness
2. Engine mount No. 2
3. Canister hose
4. Engine and transaxle
5. Accelerator cable
6. 3-way solenoid assembly
7. Engine harness
8. Speedometer cable
9. Brake vacuum hose
10. Heater hose
11. Fuel hose
12. Air cleaner assembly
13. Battery and battery carrier
14. Change rod — manual transaxle
15. Extension bar — manual transaxle
16. Transaxle
17. Transaxle harness
18. High tension lead
19. Tie rod end
20. Stabilizer control rod
21. Lower arm bushing
22. Front wheel
23. Engine side cover
24. Halfshaft
25. Control cable — automatic transaxle
26. Heat gauge unit connector
27. Radiator temperature switch
28. Exhaust pipe
29. Clutch release cylinder — manual transaxle
30. Power steering pump
31. Drive belt
32. A/C compressor and bracket
33. Radiator hose
34. Transmission fluid hose — automatic transaxle
35. Radiator and cooling fan
36. Engine mount No. 4
37. Engine mount No. 1
38. Engine mount No. 3

Engine removal and installation—2.2L normally aspirated engine

11. Disconnect and plug the power steering lines from the power steering pump.

12. Disconnect the ground strap from the engine.

13. Disconnect and plug the heater hoses and the fuel lines.

14. Label and disconnect the vacuum lines from the brake booster chamber, the carbon canister, the bulkhead mounted solenoids and the distributor.

15. If equipped with an automatic transaxle, label and disconnect the electrical connectors from the transaxle.

16. Disconnect the speedometer cable from the transaxle.

17. If equipped with a turbocharger, disconnect the hoses and pipe. Cover the turbocharger with a clean rag.

18. Raise and safely support the vehicle. Remove the halfshafts from the transaxle.

19. Disconnect the shift control cable, if equipped with an automatic transaxle, or disconnect the rod, if equipped with a manual transaxle, from the transaxle. Lower the vehicle.

20. Using a suitable engine lifting device, attach it to the engine and support its weight.

21. Disconnect the engine mount bolts and remove the engine/transaxle assembly from the vehicle.

22. If neccessary, remove the transaxle-to-engine bolts and support the engine on an engine stand.

To install:

23. If the transaxle was removed from the engine, install it and torque the bolts to 66–86 ft. lbs. (89–117 Nm).

24. Lower the engine/transaxle assembly into the vehicle and secure the engine mount bolts.

25. Install the halfshafts.

NOTE: *When installing the halfshafts, hold the shafts to prevent damage to the seals,*

1. Battery and battery carrier
2. Air cleaner assembly
3. High tension lead
4. Accelerator cable
5. Throttle cable — automatic transaxle
6. Fuel hose
7. Radiator hose
8. Transmission fluid hose — automatic transaxle
9. radiator harness
10. Radiator and electric fan
11. intercooler pipe and hose
12. Heat gauge unit connector
13. Water thermo switch connector
14. Fuel injector harness
15. Engine harness
16. Brake vacuum hose
17. 3-way solenoid assembly
18. EGR solenoid assembly
19. Canister hose
20. Heater hose
21. Transaxle harness
22. Speedometer cable
23. Clutch release cylinder — manual transaxle
24. Control cable — automatic transaxle
25. Drive belt
26. A/C compressor and bracket
27. Power steering pump
28. Inner fender splash guards
29. Front wheel
30. Tie rod end
31. Stabilizer control rod
32. Lower arm bushing
33. Halfshaft
34. Change rod — manual transaxle
35. Extension bar — manual transaxle
36. Exhaust pipe
37. Engine mount No. 2
38. Engine mount No. 4
39. Engine mount No. 1
40. Engine mount No. 3

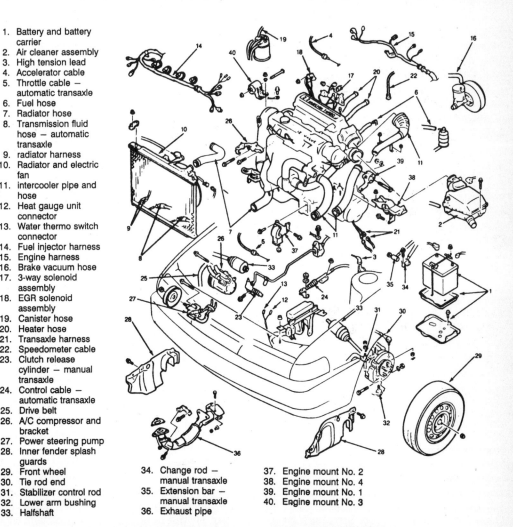

Engine removal and installation—2.2L turbocharged engine

boots and joints caused by moving the joints through angles greater than 20 degrees.

26. Depending on which transaxle the vehicle is equipped with, connect the shift control cable or rod. If equipped with a manual transaxle, install the clutch release cylinder. If equipped with an automatic transaxle, connect the electrical connectors to the transaxle.

27. Connect the speedometer cable to the transaxle and the power steering lines to the power steering pump.

28. If equipped with air conditioning, use new O-rings and connect the pressure and suction lines to the compressor. Reconnect the electrical connector to the compressor clutch.

29. Connect the engine ground strap. On non-turbocharged vehicles, install the front exhaust pipe. If equipped with a turbocharger, connect the oil pipe and hoses to the turbocharger.

30. Install the radiator and the cooling fan assembly and reconnect the electrical connectors. If equipped with an automatic transaxle, reconnect the oil cooler lines to the radiator.

31. Connect the vacuum lines to the carbon canister, the bulkhead mounted solenoids, distributor and the brake booster.

32. Connect the heater hoses to the engine and the fuel lines to the fuel system. Connect the electrical connectors to the oxygen sensor, thermostat housing sensors, the coil and the electronic fuel injection assembly.

33. Install the accelerator cable, throttle valve cable and the cruise control cable, if equipped. Install the air filter and ducts.

34. Install the battery carrier, battery and the fuse holder. Connect the battery cables.

35. Refill the cooling system. Fill the crankcase with the proper type and quantity of engine oil. If equipped, fill the automatic transaxle with the proper type and quantity of fluid. Refill the power steering reservoir and bleed the system.

36. Start the engine, allow it to reach normal operating temperatures and check for leaks. Charge the air conditioning system.

37. Install the hood, aligning the marks that were made during the removal procedure.

3.0L Engine

1. Properly relieve the fuel system pressure and disconnect the battery cables. Mark the position of the hood on its hinges and remove the hood assembly.

2. Drain the cooling system and the engine oil into suitable containers. Properly discharge the air conditioning system.

3. Remove the air cleaner assembly from the engine compartment and the vacuum valve assembly from the right side shock tower.

4. Disconnect and plug the fuel lines.

5. Remove the upper radiator hose.

6. Tag and disconnect the alternator, air conditioning compressor clutch, ignition coil and the engine coolant temperature sensor connectors.

7. Tag and disconnect the TFI module connector, injector wiring harness, air charge temperature sensor and the throttle position sensor.

8. Disconnect the oil pressure sending switch, ground straps at the intake manifold on both sides of the engine and the block heater, if equipped.

9. Disconnect the EGR sensor and the oil level sensor, located on the back side of the oil pan.

10. Tag and disconnect all vacuum lines, heater hoses and crankcase ventilation hoses.

11. Disconnect and plug the high pressure and return lines at the power steering pump.

12. Disconnect the air conditioning lines from the condenser and chassis, leaving the manifold lines attached to the compressor.

13. Disconnect the accelerator linkage, transmission throttle valve linkage and the speed control cable, if equipped.

14. Remove the battery, battery tray and the fuse box assembly.

15. Disconnect and set aside the speed control servo assembly and the transmission shift cable, if equipped with an automatic transaxle.

16. Disconnect all automatic transaxle wiring connectors and the speedometer cable on conventional (analog) cluster vehicles.

17. Disconnect the Vehicle Speed Sensor (VSS) connector on electronic cluster vehicles.

18. Disconnect and plug the cooler lines at the transaxle, if equipped with automatic transaxle.

19. Remove the clutch slave cylinder, leaving the pressure line attached, if equipped with a manual transaxle, and set it aside.

20. Remove the radiator, cooling fan and shroud.

21. Raise and safely support the vehicle. Remove the front wheel and tire assemblies.

22. Remove the lower radiator hose, the front exhaust pipe and the starter motor.

NOTE: *On vehicles with an automatic transaxle, it is advised that the torque converter nuts be removed at this time to facilitate the removal of the transaxle assembly from the engine after the engine/transaxle assembly is removed from the vehicle.*

23. Remove the shift control rod and the extension bar on manual transaxle vehicles.

24. Remove the stabilizer links and tie rod ends and disconnect the lower ball joints. Pull down on the control arms to disengage them from the spindle.

25. Remove the dynamic damper mounting bolts on the right halfshaft assembly.

26. Disengage both halfshafts by pulling outward on both side brake and spindle assemblies. In this procedure, the halfshaft assemblies are left in the chassis.

27. Install two T88C–7025–AH transaxle plugs or equivalent, into the differential side gears.

NOTE: *Failure to install the transaxle plugs may allow the differential side gears to become misaligned, making halfshaft installation difficult or impossible, without disassembling the differential.*

28. Disconnect the lower transmission mount and safely, lower the vehicle.

29. Install and position suitable engine lifting devices. Disconnect the lower front engine mount.

30. Disconnect the right side upper engine mount at the timing cover and the left side upper engine mount at the transaxle case.

31. Carefully, lift the engine and the transaxle assembly out of the vehicle.

To install:

32. Lower the engine and the transaxle assembly into the vehicle.

33. Connect and tighten the upper and lower engine mounts. Remove the engine lifting devices.

34. Remove both transaxle plugs and install the halfshafts on both sides.

35. Install the dynamic damper mounting bolts on the right side halfshaft.

36. Engage the control arms and install the lower ball joints, tie rod ends and the stabilizer links.

37. Install the shift control rod and extension bar, if equipped with a manual transaxle.

38. Replace the torque converter nuts, if equipped with an automatic transaxle.

39. Install the starter, front exhaust pipe and the lower radiator hose.

40. Replace the front tires and wheels. Safely, lower the vehicle.

41. Install the cooling fan, shroud and the radiator.

42. Install the clutch release cable with the hose attached, if equipped.

43. Reconnect the cooler lines at the transmission, if equipped.

44. Connect the Vehicle Speed Sensor (VSS) on electronic cluster vehicles.

45. Connect all automatic transmission wiring connectors and the speedometer cable on conventional (analog) cluster vehicles.

46. Install the speed control servo assembly and the transmission shift cable, if equipped.

47. Replace the battery, battery tray and the fuse box assembly.

48. Connect the accelerator linkage, transmission throttle valve linkage and the speed control cable, if equipped.

49. Connect the air conditioning lines from the condenser and chassis.

50. Install the high pressure and return lines to the power steering pump.

51. Reconnect all vacuum lines, heater hoses and crankcase ventilation hoses.

52. Reconnect the EGR sensor and the oil level sensor on the back side of the oil pan.

53. Connect the oil pressure sending switch connector, the ground straps on both sides of the engine and the block heater, if equipped.

54. Reconnect the TFI module connector, injector wiring harness, air charge temperature sensor and the throttle position sensor.

55. Install the alternator, air conditioning compressor clutch, ignition coil and the engine coolant temperature sensor.

56. Connect the fuel lines and replace the upper radiator hose.

57. Install the air cleaner assembly in the engine compartment and the vacuum valve assembly on the right side shock tower.

58. Refill the cooling system. Fill the crankcase with the proper type and quantity of engine oil. If equipped, fill the automatic transaxle with the proper type and quantity of fluid.

59. Reconnect the battery cables and install the hood assembly, aligning the marks that were made during the removal procedure.

60. Start the engine and bring to normal operating temperature. Check for any leaks.

61. Recharge the air conditioning system.

Rocker Arm (Valve) Cover

REMOVAL AND INSTALLATION

2.2L Engine

1. Disconnect the vent hose from the rocker arm cover.

2. Remove the PCV valve from the rocker arm cover.

3. Remove the spark plug wire clips.

4. Remove the rocker arm cover retaining bolts and remove the rocker arm cover and gasket.

To install:

5. Clean all old gasket material from the rocker arm cover and the cylinder head.

6. Install a new gasket onto the rocker arm cover.

7. Apply silicone sealer to the shaded area of the cylinder head.

8. Install the rocker arm cover on the cylinder head with the retaining bolts. Tighten the bolts to 52–69 inch lbs. (6–8 Nm).

9. Install the spark plug wire retaining clips

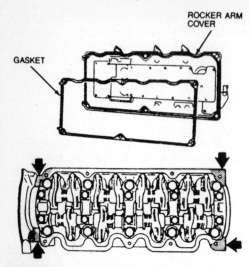

Rocker arm cover installation—2.2L engine

and install the PCV valve. Connect the vent hose to the rocker arm cover.

10. Start the engine and bring to normal operating temperature. Check for leaks.

3.0L Engine

NOTE: *The rocker arm covers on 1991–92 3.0L engines are equipped with integral (built-in) gaskets that should last the life of the car. Be sure to adhere to the instructions given in the following procedure that pertain to 1991–92 vehicles. If the integral gaskets become damaged and cannot be reused, replacement gaskets are available.*

1. Disconnect the negative battery cable.

2. Tag and disconnect the spark plug wires from the spark plugs. Remove the spark plug wire separator stand-offs from the rocker arm cover studs.

3. If the left side (front) rocker arm cover is being removed, proceed as follows:

    a. Remove the wiring harness from the rocker arm cover studs and position the harness aside.

    b. Disconnect the crankcase hose from the rocker arm cover.

4. If the right side (rear) rocker arm cover is being removed, proceed as follows:

    a. Remove the air intake throttle body assembly. Refer to Chapter 5.

    b. Remove the PCV valve.

    c. Remove the wiring harness from the rocker arm cover studs and position the harness aside.

5. On 1990 vehicles, remove the rocker arm cover retaining bolts and studs and remove the rocker arm covers. Note the position of the bolts and studs for reassembly.

6. On 1991–92 vehicles, proceed as follows:

    a. Loosen the rocker arm cover retaining bolts enough to disengage them from the cylinder head. Do not remove the retaining bolts from the rocker arm cover as they are captive to the built in gasket.

    b. Using caution, slide a sharp, thin bladed knife between the cylinder head gasket surface and the rocker arm cover gasket at the 4 RTV junctions. Cut only the RTV sealer and avoid cutting the gasket.

    c. Carefully lift the cover from the cylinder head, making sure RTV sealer is not pulling the gasket from the cover.

To install:

7. Lightly oil all bolt and stud threads before installation. Using solvent, clean the cylinder head and rocker arm cover sealing surfaces. On 1990 vehicles, remove all old gasket material and dirt. On 1991–92 vehicles, remove all silicone sealer and dirt; do not allow solvent to come in contact with the integral rocker arm gasket.

8. If the integral gasket is no longer usable on 1991–92 vehicles, it can be replaced as follows:

    a. Remove the gasket by pulling it from the rocker arm gasket channel. Note the bolt and stud locations before removing.

    b. Clean the gasket channel with a soft cloth to remove all dirt.

    c. Using a suitable solvent, clean off any remaining RTV sealer.

    d. Aligning the fastener holes, lay the new gasket onto the channel and install it with your finger.

    e. Install a gasket to each fastener by securing the fastener head with a nut driver or socket. Seat the fastener against the cover and, at the same time, roll the gasket around the fastener collar. If installed correctly, all

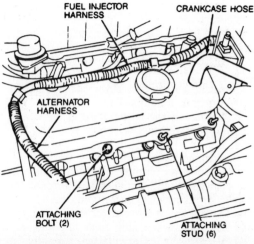

Left side (front) rocker arm cover—1990 3.0L engine

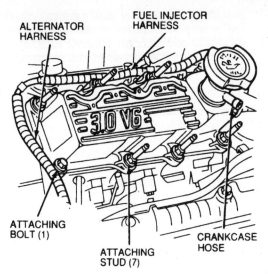

ALTERNATOR HARNESS

FUEL INJECTOR HARNESS

3.0 V6

ATTACHING BOLT (1)

ATTACHING STUD (7)

CRANKCASE HOSE

Left side (front) rocker arm cover—1991–92 3.0L engine

fasteners will be secured by the gasket and will not fall out.

f. Check the gasket for correct installation. A new gasket will lay flat to the rocker arm cover in both the channel and the fastener areas. If the gasket is installed incorrectly, there will be oil leaks.

9. On 1990 vehicles, apply a bead of silicone sealer at the cylinder head-to-intake manifold rail step (2 places per rail) and position a new gasket. Install the rocker arm cover and tighten the retaining bolts to 7–10 ft. lbs. (10–14 Nm).

10. On 1991–92 vehicles, apply a bead of silicone sealer at the cylinder head-to-intake manifold rail step (2 places per rail). Carefully position the cover on the cylinder head and install the bolts and studs. Tighten to 9 ft. lbs. (12 Nm).

NOTE: *When positioning the cover to the cylinder head, use a straight down approach to align the bolt holes. Once the cover contacts the RTV sealer, any adjustment for bolt alignment can roll the gasket from the channel, causing oil leaks.*

11. If the left side (front) rocker arm cover is being installed, proceed as follows:

a. Connect the wiring harness to the rocker arm cover studs.

b. Connect the crankcase hose to the rocker arm cover.

12. If the right side (rear) rocker arm cover is being installed, proceed as follows:

a. Connect the wiring harness to the rocker arm cover studs.

b. Install the PCV valve and connect the hoses.

c. Install the air intake throttle body assembly. Refer to Chapter 5.

13. Connect the spark plug wires to the spark plugs. Install the spark plug wire separator stand-offs to the rocker arm cover studs.

14. Connect the negative battery cable. Start the engine and bring to normal operating temperature. Check for leaks.

Rocker Arms/Shafts

REMOVAL AND INSTALLATION

2.2L Engine

1. Remove the rocker arm (valve) cover.

2. Remove the rocker arm and shaft assembly mounting bolts. Start at the ends and work toward the center of the shafts, when removing the bolts.

3. If necessary, separate the rocker arms and springs from the shafts; be sure to keep the parts in order for reinstallation purposes.

4. Clean and inspect the shafts and rocker arms for wear. Measure the difference between the rocker arm shaft outside diameter and the rocker arm inside diameter; this is the oil clearance. If the oil clearance exceeds 0.004 in. (0.10mm), replace the shaft and/or the rocker arm(s).

To install:

5. If they were disassembled, coat the rocker arm shafts and rocker arms with engine oil and assemble them with the springs. When assembling and installing on the cylinder head, note

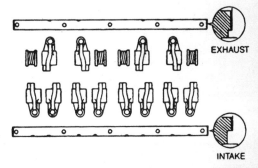

EXHAUST

INTAKE

Rocker arm shaft, rocker arm and spring positioning—2.2L engine

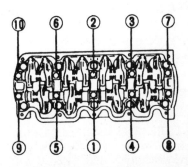

Rocker arm shaft bolt torque sequence—2.2L engine

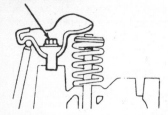

FULCRUM AND BOLT
MUST BE FULLY
SEATED AFTER
FINAL TORQUE

Rocker arm and fulcrum installation—3.0L engine

the notches at the ends of the shafts; they are different on the intake and exhaust side and cannot be interchanged.

6. Install the rocker arm/shaft assemblies onto the cylinder head and torque the rocker arm shaft-to-cylinder head bolts, in sequence, to 13–20 ft. lbs. (18–26 Nm), in 2 steps.

7. Install the rocker arm (valve) cover.

3.0L Engine

1. Remove the rocker arm (valve) cover(s).
2. Remove the rocker arm mounting bolts, fulcrums and rocker arms. Identify the position of the rocker arms and fulcrums so they may be reinstalled in their original locations.
3. Inspect the rocker arms, fulcrums and pushrod ends for wear and/or damage and replace as necessary.

To install:

4. If removed, dip each pushrod in heavy engine oil and install in its original position. If not removed, lubricate the pushrod ends with heavy engine oil.
5. Dip each rocker arm and fulcrum in heavy engine oil and install in its original position. For each rocker arm, rotate the crankshaft until the lifter rests on the base circle of the camshaft lobe, before tightening the fulcrum mounting bolts to 24 ft. lbs. (32 Nm). Make sure the fulcrum is fully seated in the cylinder head and the pushrod is fully seated in the rocker arm socket before tightening.

NOTE: *If the original valve train components are being installed, a valve clearance check is not required. If a component has been replaced, perform a valve clearance check. Refer to Chapter 2.*

6. Install the rocker arm (valve) cover(s).

Thermostat

REMOVAL AND INSTALLATION

CAUTION: *When draining the coolant, keep in mind that cats and dogs are attracted by the ethylene glycol antifreeze, and are quite likely to drink any that is left in an uncovered container or in puddles on the ground. This will prove fatal in sufficient quantity. Always drain the coolant into a sealable container. Coolant should be reused unless it is contaminated or several years old.*

2.2L Engine

1. Disconnect the negative battery cable. Drain the radiator to below the level of the thermostat.
2. Disconnect the coolant temperature switch at the thermostat housing.
3. Remove the upper radiator hose.
4. Remove the mounting nuts, thermostat housing, thermostat and gasket.

NOTE: *Do not pry the housing off.*

To install:

5. Clean the thermostat housing and the cylinder head mating surfaces.
6. Insert the thermostat into the rear cylinder head housing with the jiggle pin at the top. The spring side of the thermostat should face the housing.
7. Position a new gasket onto the studs with the seal print side facing the rear cylinder housing.
8. Install the thermostat housing and 2 nuts. Tighten the nuts to 14–22 ft. lbs. (19–30 Nm).
9. Connect the coolant temperature switch and install the upper radiator hose.
10. Fill the cooling system. Connect the negative battery cable, start the engine and check for leaks. Check the coolant level and add coolant, as necessary.

3.0L Engine

1. Disconnect the negative battery cable. Drain the cooling system.
2. Remove the radiator hose from the thermostat housing.
3. Disconnect the wiring harness bracket and remove the ground wire.
4. Remove the thermostat housing mounting bolts, the thermostat housing and the thermostat.

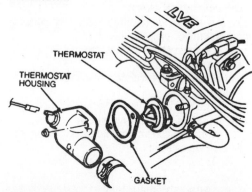

THERMOSTAT

THERMOSTAT
HOUSING

GASKET

Thermostat removal and installation—2.2L engine

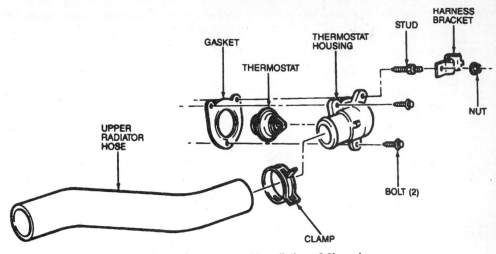

Thermostat removal and installation—3.0L engine

5. Remove the gasket and discard.

To install:

6. Clean the thermostat housing and cylinder head gasket surfaces.

7. Position the thermostat in the thermostat housing, rotating in a clockwise direction to secure in place. Align the jiggle pin with the recess located near the top of the thermostat housing.

8. Position a new gasket and install the thermostat housing. Tighten the bolts to 8–10 ft. lbs. (10–14 Nm).

9. Position the harness bracket and ground wire, then install the nut. Connect the radiator hose and install the clamp.

10. Fill the cooling system. Connect the negative battery cable, start the engine and check for leaks. Check the coolant level and add coolant, as necessary.

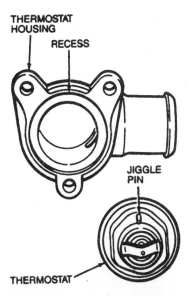

Thermostat and housing positioning—3.0L engine

Intake Manifold

REMOVAL AND INSTALLATION

CAUTION: *When draining the coolant, keep in mind that cats and dogs are attracted by the ethylene glycol antifreeze, and are quite likely to drink any that is left in an uncovered container or in puddles on the ground. This will prove fatal in sufficient quantity. Always drain the coolant into a sealable container. Coolant should be reused unless it is contaminated or several years old.*

2.2L Engine

1. Properly relieve the fuel system pressure and disconnect the negative battery cable.

2. Drain the cooling system.

3. From the bottom of the intake manifold, remove the water hose.

4. Disconnect the accelerator cables from the throttle body.

5. Remove the air duct from the throttle body.

6. Label and disconnect the vacuum lines and coolant hoses from the throttle body.

7. Tag and disconnect the electrical connectors from the throttle position sensor, the idle switch and the bypass air control valve.

8. Remove the engine lifting bracket mounting bolts from the throttle body and the engine block.

9. Disconnect the coolant line/EGR hose bracket from the throttle body and the throttle cable brackets from the intake plenum.

10. Remove the wire loom bracket. On non-turbocharged engines, remove the EGR backpressure variable transducer bracket from the right-hand side of the intake plenum. On turbocharged engines, remove the vacuum pipe

mounting bolts from the right-hand side of the intake plenum.

11. Remove the PCV hose from the intake plenum. Remove the nuts and bolts retaining the vacuum line assembly bracket at the rear of the intake plenum.

12. Label and disconnect the vacuum lines from the intake plenum.

13. Remove the plenum-to-intake manifold nuts and bolts, the plenum and the gasket.

14. Disconnect the electrical connectors from the fuel injectors. Carefully, bend the wire harness retainer brackets away from the wire har-

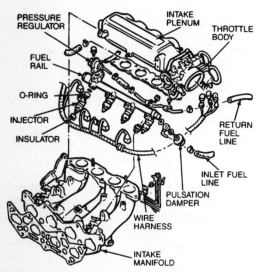

Intake manifold and plenum removal and installation—2.2L non-turbocharged engine

ness and move the harness assembly away from the intake manifold.

15. Disconnect the fuel pressure and return lines at the fuel rail.

16. Disconnect the EGR pipe from the intake manifold. Label and disconnect any electrical connectors and hoses from the intake manifold.

17. Remove the intake manifold bracket-to-manifold nuts and the bracket. Remove the intake manifold-to-cylinder head nuts/bolts, the manifold and gasket.

18. If necessary, remove the fuel rail and fuel injectors from the intake manifold.

To install:

19. Clean all gasket mating surfaces.

20. Using a new gasket, position the intake manifold on the cylinder head studs and torque the nuts/bolts to 14–22 ft. lbs. (19–30 Nm).

21. Install the intake manifold bracket-to-manifold nuts and tighten to 14–22 ft. lbs. (19–30 Nm).

22. Connect the fuel lines to the fuel rail. Connect the electrical connectors to the fuel injectors.

23. Using a new gasket, install the intake plenum onto the intake manifold and torque the nuts/bolts to 14–19 ft. lbs. (19–25 Nm).

24. Connect the vacuum lines to the intake manifold. Install the retaining bolts and nuts on the vacuum line assembly bracket to the intake plenum.

25. Install the PCV hose to the intake plenum.

26. Install the wire loom bracket and the EGR variable transducer bracket or vacuum pipe bracket to the right side of the plenum.

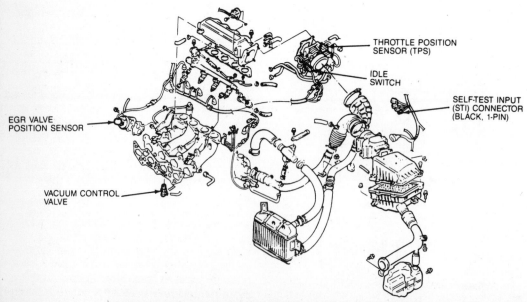

Air/fuel intake system exploded view—2.2L turbocharged engine

27. Install the throttle cable bracket, engine lifting bracket mounting bolt and coolant line/ EGR hose bracket to the intake plenum and throttle body.

28. Install the vacuum and coolant hoses to the throttle body.

29. Connect the throttle position sensor, idle switch and bypass air control valve connectors.

30. Install the air duct and the throttle cables to the throttle body.

31. Connect the EGR pipe and connect the water hose to the bottom of the intake manifold.

32. Connect the negative battery cable and fill the cooling system. Start the engine and check for leaks.

3.0L Engine

1. Properly relieve the fuel system pressure and disconnect the negative battery cable.

2. Drain the cooling system.

3. Remove the air cleaner hoses from the throttle body and rocker cover.

4. Disconnect the fuel lines from the fuel supply manifold. Cover the fuel line ends with clean shop rags to prevent dirt from entering.

5. Tag and disconnect the vacuum lines and electrical connectors from the throttle body.

6. Remove the plastic shield and the EGR supply tube from the throttle body.

7. Disconnect the throttle cable and, if equipped with automatic transaxle, the throttle valve control cable from the throttle lever.

8. Remove the fuel rail bracket bolt and the 6 throttle body mounting bolts. Remove the throttle body.

9. Disconnect the fuel injector harness stand-offs from the injector inboard rocker cover studs and each injector and remove from the engine.

10. Remove the brace from the fuel supply manifold and throttle body. Remove the fuel supply manifold and fuel injectors.

NOTE: *The intake manifold assembly can be removed with the fuel supply manifold and fuel injectors in place.*

11. Disconnect the upper radiator hose from the thermostat housing and disconnect the heater hoses.

12. Disconnect the engine coolant temperature sensor and coolant temperature sending unit connectors.

13. Tag and disconnect the spark plug wires from the spark plugs.

14. Remove the distributor cap. Mark the position of the rotor and the distributor in the engine and remove the distributor.

15. Remove the ignition coil and bracket assembly from the left side (front) cylinder head and set aside.

16. Remove the rocker arm covers.

17. Loosen the retaining bolt from the No. 3 intake valve and rotate the rocker arm fulcrum away from the valve retainer. Remove the pushrod.

18. Remove the intake manifold retaining bolts. Before attempting to remove the manifold, break the seal between the manifold and cylinder block. Place a suitable prybar between the manifold, near the thermostat, and the transaxle. Carefully pry upward to loosen the manifold.

19. Lift the intake manifold away from the engine. Place shop rags in the lifter valley to catch any dirt or gasket material. Clean all gasket mating surfaces. Be careful when scraping aluminum to prevent gouging, which may cause leak paths.

To install:

20. Lightly oil all attaching bolt and stud threads. Apply silicone sealer to the intersection of the cylinder block and cylinder head assembly at the 4 corners of the lifter valley.

21. Install the front and rear intake manifold seals. Install the intake manifold gaskets onto the cylinder heads and insert the locking tabs on the cylinder head gaskets.

NOTE: *Make sure the side of the gasket marked TO INTAKE MANIFOLD is facing away from the cylinder head.*

22. Carefully lower the intake manifold into position to prevent disturbing the silicone sealer. Install bolts No. 1, 2, 3 and 4 and snug. Install the remaining bolts and tighten, in se-

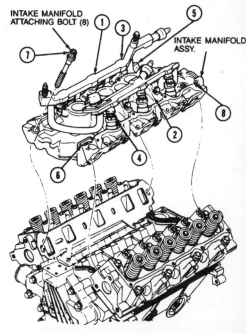

Intake manifold bolt torque sequence—3.0L engine

quence, to 11 ft. lbs. (15 Nm). Then tighten, in sequence, to 21 ft. lbs. (28 Nm).

23. Install the thermostat and housing, if removed, using a new gasket. Tighten the mounting bolts to 9 ft. lbs. (12 Nm).

24. If removed, lubricate and install new O-rings on the fuel injectors and install the fuel injectors in the fuel rail, using a light twisting-pushing motion. Install the fuel rail and injectors into the intake manifold, pushing down to seat the O-rings. While holding the fuel rail assembly in place, install the 4 retaining bolts and tighten to 7 ft. lbs. (10 Nm).

25. Install the distributor assembly, aligning the housing and rotor with the marks that were made during the removal procedure.

26. Install the No. 3 cylinder intake valve pushrod. Apply oil to the pushrod and fulcrum prior to installation. Rotate the crankshaft to place the lifter on the base circle of the camshaft and tighten the rocker arm bolt to 24 ft. lbs. (32 Nm).

27. Install the rocker arm covers and connect the fuel injector electrical harness.

28. Position a new gasket and the throttle body on the intake manifold. Install the mounting bolts and tighten to 15–22 ft. lbs. (20–30 Nm).

29. Install the fuel rail bracket bolt on the throttle body and connect the throttle cable and, if equipped, the throttle valve control cable to the throttle lever.

30. Install the MAP sensor and the EGR tube to the throttle body.

31. Connect the vacuum hoses and the electrical connectors in their original positions on the throttle body. Install the plastic shield on the throttle body.

32. Install the fuel supply manifold brace. Tighten the retaining bolts to 7 ft. lbs. (10 Nm).

33. Connect the PCV hose at the PCV valve. Connect all remaining vacuum hoses.

34. Install the EGR tube and nut, if equipped. Tighten the nuts on both ends to 37 ft. lbs. (50 Nm).

35. Connect the fuel lines to the fuel rail.

36. Install the distributor cap and connect the spark plug wires to the spark plugs. Install the wiring stand-offs to the rocker arm cover studs.

37. Install the ignition coil and bracket assembly. Tighten the mounting bolts to 35 ft. lbs. (48 Nm).

38. Connect the engine coolant temperature sensor and coolant temperature sending unit connectors.

39. Install the upper radiator and heater hoses. Fill the cooling system.

40. Change the engine oil and filter. This is necessary because engine coolant is corrosive to all engine bearing material. Replacing the engine oil after removal of a coolant carrying component guards against later failure.

41. Install the air cleaner hoses to the throttle body and rocker cover.

42. Connect the negative battery cable. Start the engine and check for coolant, oil, fuel and vacuum leaks. Check the ignition timing.

Exhaust Manifold

REMOVAL AND INSTALLATION

2.2L Engine

1. Disconnect the negative battery cable and the oxygen sensor connector.

2. Remove the turbocharger assembly, if equipped.

3. Remove the oxygen sensor from the exhaust manifold on non-turbocharged vehicles.

4. Disconnect the exhaust pipe from the ex-

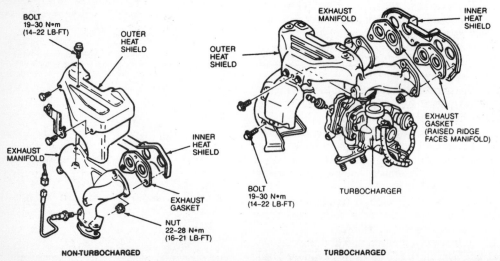

Exhaust manifold removal and installation—2.2L engine

haust manifold and remove the outer heat shield.

5. Remove the exhaust manifold-to-cylinder head bolts and the exhaust manifold, inner heat shield and gaskets.

6. Clean the mating surfaces on the exhaust manifold and the cylinder head.

To install:

7. Position the inner heat shield on the studs

8. Install the exhaust manifold gaskets with the raised edge of the gasket facing the exhaust manifold.

9. Install the exhaust manifold and tighten the bolts to 16–21 ft. lbs. (22–28 Nm).

10. Install the outer heat shield and tighten the bolts to 14–22 ft. lbs. (19–30 Nm).

11. Install the exhaust gas oxygen sensor on non-turbocharged vehicles.

12. Install the turbocharger assembly, if equipped.

13. Connect the exhaust pipe to the exhaust manifold, using a new gasket. Tighten the bolts to 26–36 ft. lbs. (34–49 Nm).

14. Connect the exhaust gas oxygen sensor wire and connect the negative battery cable.

3.0L Engine

LEFT SIDE (FRONT) MANIFOLD

1. Remove the oil dipstick tube, support bracket and heat shield retaining nuts. Carefully rotate the tube away from the manifold stud.

2. Raise and safely support the vehicle.

3. Remove the exhaust manifold-to-front exhaust pipe attaching nuts.

4. Lower the vehicle and remove the exhaust manifold attaching bolts and the manifold.

To install:

5. Clean all gasket mating surfaces. Lightly oil the bolt and stud threads.

6. Install the exhaust manifold on the cylinder head with the attaching bolts. Tighten the bolts to 18 ft. lbs. (25 Nm).

7. Raise and safely support the vehicle.

8. Connect the exhaust pipe to the manifold and tighten the attaching nuts to 20 ft. lbs. (27 Nm). Lower the vehicle.

9. Rotate the oil dipstick tube and bracket into position over the manifold stud. Install the heat shield and retaining nuts. Tighten the nuts to 13 ft. lbs. (18 Nm).

RIGHT SIDE (REAR) MANIFOLD

1. Raise and safely support the vehicle.

2. Remove the EGR supply tube from the exhaust manifold, if equipped. Use a back-up wrench on the lower fitting adapter.

3. Remove the heat shield retaining nuts and the manifold-to-exhaust pipe retaining nuts.

4. Remove the exhaust manifold retaining bolts and the manifold.

To install:

5. Clean all gasket mating surfaces. Lightly oil the bolt and stud threads.

6. Install the exhaust manifold on the cylinder head with the attaching bolts. Tighten the bolts to 15–22 ft. lbs. (20–30 Nm).

7. Connect the exhaust pipe to the manifold. Tighten the attaching nuts to 20 ft. lbs. (27 Nm).

8. Install the spark plug heat shield and retaining nuts. Tighten the nuts to 12–15 ft. lbs. (16–20 Nm).

9. Connect the EGR supply tube to the exhaust manifold. Tighten to 37 ft. lbs. (50 Nm). Lower the vehicle.

Turbocharger

REMOVAL AND INSTALLATION

Before starting the following procedure, clean the area around the turbocharger assem-

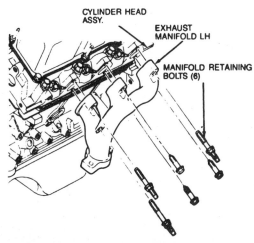

Left side (front) exhaust manifold removal and installation—3.0L engine

CYLINDER HEAD ASSY.

EXHAUST MANIFOLD LH

MANIFOLD RETAINING BOLTS (6)

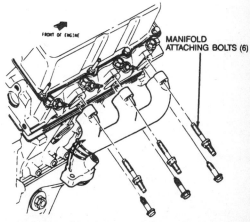

Right side (rear) exhaust manifold removal and installation—3.0L engine

FRONT OF ENGINE

MANIFOLD ATTACHING BOLTS (6)

bly with a non-caustic solution. After the turbo-charger is removed, cover the openings to prevent the entry of foreign material while it is off the engine.

During removal, be careful not to bend, nick, or in any way damage the compressor wheel blades. Damage may result in rotating assembly imbalance, and bearing and oil seal failure. Any time a turbocharger assembly has been removed, gently spin the turbine wheel before reassembly to ensure the rotating assembly does not bind.

Any time an engine bearing (main bearing, connecting rod bearing, camshaft bearing) has been damaged in a turbocharged engine, the oil and filter should be changed and the turbocharger flushed with clean engine oil to reduce the possibility of contamination.

1. Disconnect the negative battery cable.
2. Drain the cooling system.

CAUTION: *When draining the coolant, keep in mind that cats and dogs are attracted by the ethylene glycol antifreeze, and are quite likely to drink any that is left in an uncovered container or in puddles on the ground. This will prove fatal in sufficient quantity. Always drain the coolant into a sealable container. Coolant should be reused unless it is contaminated or several years old.*

3. Remove the air inlet and outlet hoses from the turbocharger assembly.

4. Remove the heat shields from the exhaust manifold and turbocharger.
5. Disconnect the oxygen sensor electrical connector and place the wire over the front of the vehicle, away from the heat shield.
6. From the top of the turbocharger, remove the oil feed line. From the lower portion of the turbocharger, remove oil return line and gasket.

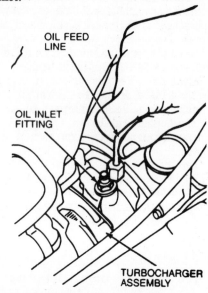

Turbo oil feed line removal and installation

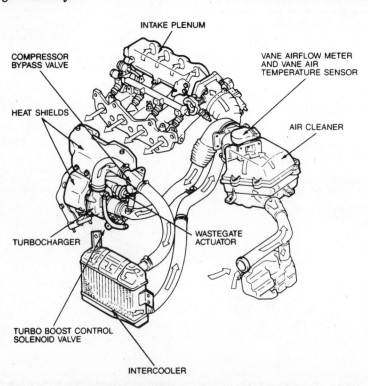

Turbocharger and intercooler location—2.2L engine

7. Disconnect the coolant inlet and outlet hoses from the turbocharger.

8. Remove the EGR tube from the exhaust manifold. Disconnect the turbo boost control solenoid valve electrical connector.

9. Remove the air tube from the turbo boost control solenoid valve at the turbocharger outlet air hose.

10. From under the turbocharger, remove the retaining bracket-to-turbocharger bolt.

11. Properly discharge the air conditioning system and remove the refrigerant line from the head of the compressor.

12. Remove the oxygen sensor from the turbocharger.

13. Disconnect the converter inlet pipe from the turbocharger joint pipe. Remove the exhaust manifold-to-cylinder head bolts, the exhaust manifold/turbocharger assembly and the gasket from the vehicle.

14. Remove the exhaust manifold-to-turbocharger nuts, the manifold and the gasket from the turbocharger. Remove the joint pipe-to-turbocharger nuts, the pipe, heat shield and the gasket from the turbocharger.

15. Clean the gasket mounting surfaces.

To install:

16. Using a new gasket, install the joint pipe and heat shield assembly on the turbocharger and torque the nuts to 27–46 ft. lbs (37–63 Nm).

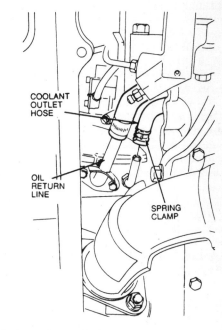

Turbo coolant outlet hose

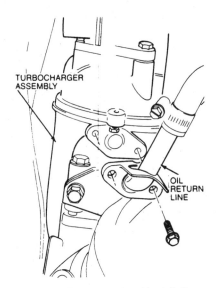

Turbo oil return line removal and installation

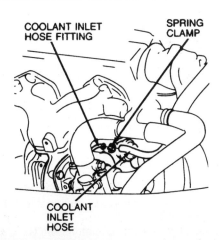

Turbo coolant inlet hose

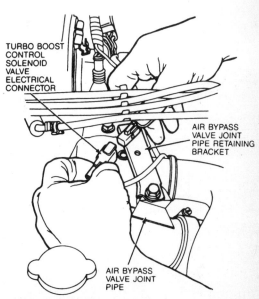

Disconnecting the turbo boost control solenoid valve electrical connector

17. Using a new gasket, install the exhaust manifold on the turbocharger and torque the nuts to 20–29 ft. lbs. (27–39 Nm).

18. Using a new gasket, position the exhaust manifold/turbocharger assembly onto the cylinder head and torque the nuts to 16–21 ft. lbs. (22–28 Nm).

19. Using a new gasket, install the converter inlet pipe to the joint pipe and torque the nuts to 26–36 ft. lbs. (34–49 Nm).

20. Install the mounting bolt to the retaining bracket under the turbocharger assembly.

21. Install the oil return line and coolant outlet hose to the turbocharger assembly.

22. Install the air tube to the turbocharger outlet air hose.

23. Connect the turbo boost control solenoid valve electrical connector.

24. Install the oxygen sensor. To ease the remaining installation procedure, leave the wiring assembly aside of the heat shield assembly.

25. Install the EGR tube onto the exhaust manifold and install the coolant inlet hose onto the turbocharger assembly.

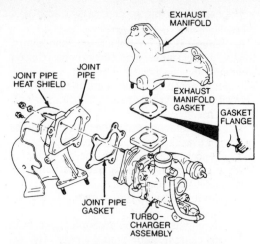

Manifold and joint pipe removal and installation

26. Pour 0.85 oz. (25ml) of engine oil in the oil inlet fitting, then install the oil feed line onto the turbocharger assembly.

27. Install the heat shields onto the exhaust manifold and turbocharger assembly.

28. Install the inlet and outlet hoses on the turbocharger compressor housing.

29. Connect the oxygen sensor electrical connector and install the wiring assembly.

30. Connect the refrigerant line to the compressor.

31. Fill the cooling system and connect the negative battery cable.

32. After replacing the turbocharger, perform the following:

    a. Disconnect the electrical connector from the ignition coil.

    b. Crank the engine for approximately 20 seconds.

    c. Reconnect the electrical connector to the ignition coil.

    d. Start the engine and operate it at idle for approximately 30 seconds.

    e. Stop the engine, disconnect the negative battery cable and depress the brake pedal for at least 5 seconds to cancel the malfunction code.

    f. Reconnect the negative battery cable.

33. Start the engine, allow it to reach normal operating temperatures and check for leaks and engine operation. Recharge the air conditioning system.

Intercooler

REMOVAL AND INSTALLATION

1. Remove the front fascia from the vehicle.

2. Remove the front bumper assembly. Refer to Chapter 10.

3. Remove all mounting nuts from the intercooler housing.

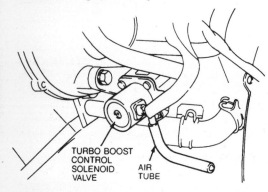

Turbo boost control solenoid valve air tube removal and installation

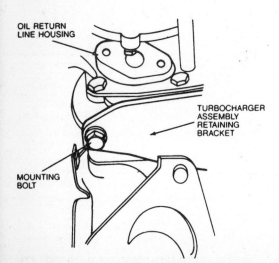

Retaining bracket mounting bolt location

4. Loosen the clamps and remove the inlet and outlet air hoses from the intercooler.

5. Remove the intercooler.

6. Installation is the reverse of the removal procedure.

Radiator

REMOVAL AND INSTALLATION

1. Disconnect the negative battery cable and the cooling fan wiring harness connectors.

2. Remove the radiator pressure cap from the filler neck.

CAUTION: *Never remove the radiator cap while the engine is running or personal injury from scalding hot coolant or steam may result. If possible, wait until the engine has cooled to remove the radiator cap. If this is not possible, wrap a thick cloth around the radiator cap and turn it slowly to the first stop. Step back while the pressure is released from the cooling system. When you are sure all the pressure has been released, press down on the cap, still with the cloth, and turn and remove it.*

3. Disconnect the overflow tube from the filler neck.

4. Drain the cooling system into a suitable container. The drain valve is located at the bottom of the radiator on the right side.

CAUTION: *When draining the coolant, keep in mind that cats and dogs are attracted by the ethylene glycol antifreeze, and are quite likely to drink any that is left in an uncovered container or in puddles on the ground. This will prove fatal in sufficient quantity. Always drain the coolant into a sealable container. Coolant should be reused unless it is contaminated or several years old.*

5. Disconnect the upper and lower radiator hoses.

6. Disconnect and plug the cooler lines at the radiator, if equipped with an automatic transaxle.

7. Disconnect the coolant temperature sensor wires, if equipped.

8. Remove the 4 bolts attaching the radiator upper tank brackets to the radiator core support.

9. Remove the radiator and the cooling fan as an assembly.

10. Remove the fan shroud mounting bolts.

11. Remove the fan and shroud assembly from the radiator.

To install:

12. Install the fan and shroud assembly. Tighten the mounting bolts to 61–87 inch lbs. (7–10 Nm).

13. Install the radiator, making sure the lower tank engages the insulators.

14. Install the upper radiator insulators and tighten the retaining bolts to 69–95 inch lbs. (8–11 Nm).

15. Unplug and connect the cooler lines, if required.

16. Reattach the wiring harness to the routing clips and install the upper and lower radiator hoses to the radiator.

17. Connect the overflow tube to the radiator and connect the cooling fan wiring connectors.

18. Close the radiator drain valve and fill the system with coolant. Install the pressure cap to the first stop only.

19. Connect the negative battery cable. Start the engine and run it at fast idle until the upper radiator hose feels warm, indicating the thermostat has opened and coolant is flowing throughout the system.

20. Stop the engine. Carefully remove the radiator cap and top off the radiator with coolant, if required.

21. Install the radiator cap securely and fill the coolant reservoir to the FULL mark.

22. Run the engine and check for leaks.

Electric Cooling Fan

REMOVAL AND INSTALLATION

1. Disconnect the negative battery cable.

2. Disconnect the cooling fan electrical connectors.

3. Remove the fan shroud-to-radiator screws and the fan/shroud assembly.

4. If removing the fan motor from the shroud, remove the fan blade-to-motor nut and washer, the fan motor-to-shroud bolts and the motor.

5. Installation is the reverse of the removal procedure. Tighten the cooling fan blade attaching nut to 69–95 inch lbs. (8–11 Nm), the motor-to-shroud screws to 23–46 inch lbs. (2.6–

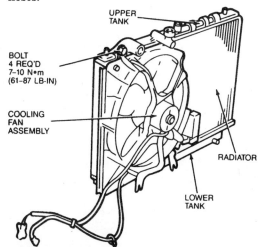

UPPER TANK

BOLT
4 REQ'D
7–10 N•m
(61–87 LB-IN)

COOLING
FAN
ASSEMBLY

RADIATOR

LOWER
TANK

Radiator/cooling fan assembly

5.2 Nm) and the shroud-to-radiator screws to 61–87 inch lbs. (7–10 Nm).

Water Pump

REMOVAL AND INSTALLATION

CAUTION: *When draining the coolant, keep in mind that cats and dogs are attracted by the ethylene glycol antifreeze, and are quite likely to drink any that is left in an uncovered container or in puddles on the ground. This will prove fatal in sufficient quantity. Always drain the coolant into a sealable container. Coolant should be reused unless it is contaminated or several years old.*

2.2L Engine

1. Disconnect the negative battery cable.
2. Drain the cooling system.
3. Remove the timing belt. Refer to the procedure in this Chapter.
4. Remove the water pump-to-engine bolts, the water pump and the O-ring. Discard the O-ring.

To install:

5. Clean the mating surfaces of the water pump and the engine block.
6. Install a new O-ring onto the water pump.
7. Install the water pump and torque the bolts 14–19 ft. lbs. (19–25 Nm).

8. Install the timing belt. Refer to the procedure in this Chapter.
9. Fill the cooling system.
10. Connect the negative battery cable, start the engine and check for leaks. Check the coolant level and add coolant, as necessary.

3.0L Engine

1. Disconnect the negative battery cable. Raise and safely support the vehicle.
2. Drain the cooling system and remove the water pump belt.

NOTE: *The accessory drive belt may be left installed and the pump belt pulled aside. The accessory drive belt must be removed however, if the water pump belt is to be replaced.*

3. Remove the upper water pump and heater hoses from the water pump.
4. Remove the lower radiator hose from the water pump steel tube.
5. Remove the steel tube brace bolt from the water pump mounting bracket.
6. Remove the water pump mounting bolts and remove the water pump.

To install:

7. Clean the mounting surfaces and install a new gasket.

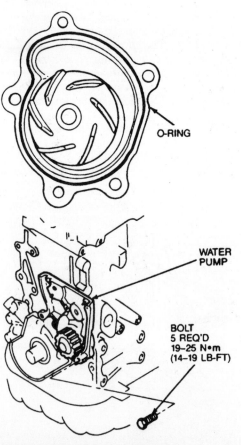

O-RING

WATER PUMP

BOLT
5 REQ'D
19–25 N•m
(14–19 LB-FT)

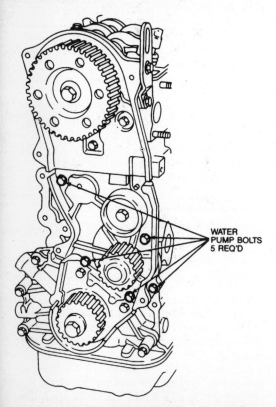

WATER PUMP BOLTS 5 REQ'D

Water pump mounting bolt locations—2.2L engine

Water pump installation—2.2L engine

8. Install the the water pump onto the mounting bracket and tighten the mounting bolts to 15–22 ft. lbs. (20–30 Nm).

9. Install the steel tube brace bolt. Install the lower radiator hose on the steel tube.

10. Install the heater and upper water pump hoses.

11. Install the water pump belt and lower the vehicle.

12. Connect the negative battery cable and fill the cooling system. Start the engine and check for leaks. Check the coolant level and add coolant, as necessary.

Cylinder Head

REMOVAL AND INSTALLATION

CAUTION: *When draining the coolant, keep in mind that cats and dogs are attracted by the ethylene glycol antifreeze, and are quite likely to drink any that is left in an uncovered container or in puddles on the ground. This will prove fatal in sufficient quantity. Always drain the coolant into a sealable container. Coolant should be reused unless it is contaminated or several years old.*

2.2L Engine

1. Disconnect the negative battery cable. Remove the drive belts.

2. Remove the crankshaft pulley as follows:

    a. Raise and safely support the vehicle.

    b. Remove the right front wheel and tire assembly.

    c. Remove the right inner fender panel.

    d. Remove the 6 bolts, pulley and baffle plate.

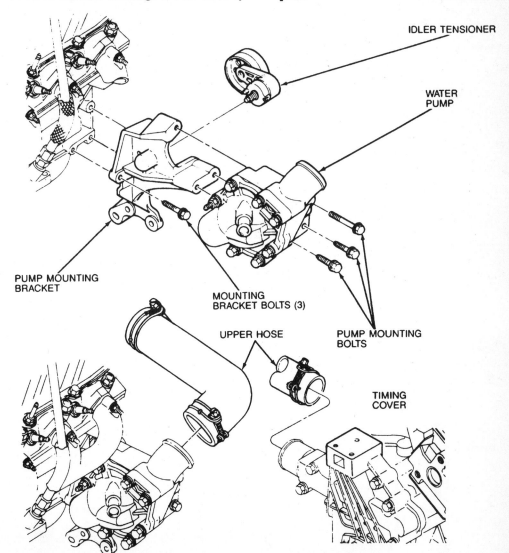

Water pump removal and installation—3.0L engine

e. Lower the vehicle.

3. Remove the timing belt covers and timing belt. Refer to the procedure in this Chapter.

4. Remove the exhaust manifold, intake manifold and the distributor.

5. Remove rocker arm cover.

6. Drain the cooling system.

7. Remove the spark plug wires and the spark plugs.

8. Tag and disconnect the electrical connectors from the thermostat housing sensors. Remove the upper radiator hose and the water bypass hose.

9. Remove the front and rear engine lifting eyes and the engine ground wire. Remove the front and rear housings and gaskets.

10. Remove the cylinder head bolts, a little at a time, in the reverse order of installation. Remove the cylinder head and discard the gasket.

11. Clean the gasket mounting surfaces.

To install:

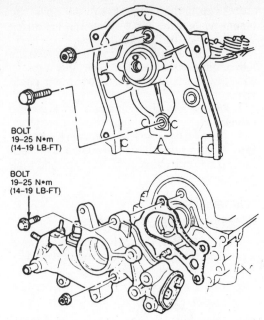

Front and rear housing removal and installation—2.2L engine

12. Position a new cylinder head gasket on the cylinder block. Install the cylinder head and torque the bolts, in sequence, to 29–32 ft. lbs. (40–42 Nm) and then again, in sequence, to 59–64 ft. lbs. (80–86 Nm).

13. Install the front and rear housings, using new gaskets, and tighten the bolts/nuts to 14–19 ft. lbs. (19–25 Nm).

14. Install the distributor and the front and rear engine lifting eyes.

15. Install the spark plugs and spark plug wires.

16. Install the intake and exhaust manifolds.

17. Install the rocker arm cover.

18. Install the timing belt and timing covers.

19. Install the crankshaft pulley and the drive belts.

20. Fill the cooling system and connect the negative battery cable.

21. Run the engine and check for any leaks. Check the ignition timing.

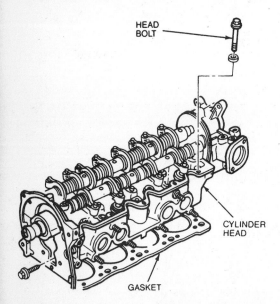

Cylinder head removal and installation—2.2L engine

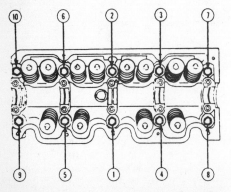

Cylinder head bolt torque sequence—2.2L engine

3.0L Engine

1. Properly relieve the fuel system pressure and disconnect the negative battery cable.

2. Drain the cooling system.

3. Remove the air cleaner hoses from the throttle body and rocker arm cover.

4. Disconnect the fuel lines from the fuel supply manifold.

5. Tag and disconnect the vacuum lines from the throttle body.

6. Tag and disconnect the air charge temper-

ature sensor, throttle position sensor and air bypass solenoid electrical connectors.

7. Remove the EGR supply tube and the MAP sensor from the throttle body.

8. Disconnect the throttle cable and, if equipped with automatic transaxle, the throttle valve control cable from the throttle lever.

9. Remove the fuel rail bracket bolt from the throttle body, remove the 6 throttle body attaching bolts and remove the throttle body.

10. Disconnect the fuel injector harness stand-offs from the inboard rocker arm cover studs and each injector and remove from the engine.

11. Disconnect the upper radiator hose and heater hoses and move them aside.

12. Disconnect the engine coolant temperature sensor and the coolant temperature sending unit connectors.

13. Mark the distributor housing to block position, then remove the distributor cap and mark the rotor position. Remove the distributor.

14. Tag and disconnect the spark plug wires from the spark plugs and remove the wires and the distributor cap.

15. Remove the ignition coil and bracket assembly from the left cylinder head and set aside.

16. If the left cylinder head is being removed, perform the following:

a. Remove the power steering protective shroud.

b. Using a ½ in. drive breaker bar, rotate the automatic belt tensioner clockwise and remove the accessory drive belt.

c. Remove the automatic belt tensioner.

d. Remove the nut and remove the power steering pulley.

e. Remove the air conditioning brace to the power steering support retaining bolts.

f. Remove the 3 power steering support retaining bolts.

g. Remove the engine oil dipstick tube attaching nut from the exhaust manifold stud. Rotate or remove the tube from the manifold.

NOTE: *The power steering support bracket may be pulled away from the engine with the alternator and power steering pump intact.*

17. Remove the spark plugs.

18. Remove the exhaust manifold(s), heat shield(s) and inlet pipe(s).

19. Remove the rocker arm covers.

20. Loosen the rocker arm fulcrum retaining bolts and remove the rocker arms, fulcrums and retaining bolts.

NOTE: *The No. 3 intake valve pushrod must be removed to allow removal of the intake manifold, regardless of which cylinder head is being removed.*

21. Remove the pushrods. Note the position of each so they may be reinstalled in their original positions.

22. Remove the intake manifold.

23. Remove the cylinder head retaining bolts and remove the cylinder head(s). Remove and discard the cylinder head gasket(s).

24. Clean all gasket mating surfaces.

To install:

25. Position new head gasket(s) on the cylinder block, using the dowel pins for alignment. Carefully position the cylinder head(s) on the block.

26. Lightly oil the threads and install the cylinder head bolts, finger tight. On 1990 vehicles, tighten the bolts, in sequence, in 2 steps; first to 37 ft. lbs. (50 Nm), and then to 68 ft. lbs. (92 Nm). On 1991–92 vehicles, tighten the bolts, in sequence, to 59 ft. lbs. (80 Nm), then back off all bolts a minimum of 1 full turn. Retighten the bolts, in sequence, in 2 steps; first to 37 ft. lbs. (50 Nm), and then to 68 ft. lbs. (92 Nm).

27. Install the intake manifold.

28. Install the distributor, aligning the marks that were made during removal.

29. Dip each pushrod in heavy engine oil, then install in their original positions.

30. For each rocker arm, rotate the crankshaft until the lifter rests on the base circle of the camshaft lobe, before tightening the fulcrum mounting bolts. Position the rocker arms over the pushrods and tighten the fulcrum mounting bolts to 24 ft. lbs. (32 Nm). Make sure the fulcrums and pushrods are fully seated before tightening.

NOTE: *If the original valve train components are being installed, a valve clearance check is not required. If a component has been replaced, perform a valve clearance check. Refer to Chapter 2.*

31. Install the exhaust manifold(s) and tighten the retaining bolts to 18 ft. lbs. (25 Nm). Install the inlet pipe retaining nuts and tighten to 20 ft. lbs. (27 Nm).

32. Install the dipstick tube into the cylinder block. Tighten the retaining nut to 13 ft. lbs. (18 Nm).

33. Install the spark plugs and tighten to 7–15 ft. lbs. (9–20 Nm).

34. Install the rocker arm covers.

35. Install the fuel injector electrical harness to the injectors and inboard rocker arm cover studs. Connect the engine harness to the main harness and secure with the retainers.

36. Install the distributor cap and connect the spark plug wires to the spark plugs.

37. Position a new gasket and the throttle body on the lower intake manifold. Install the attaching bolts and tighten to 15–22 ft. lbs. (20–30 Nm).

38. Install the fuel rail bracket bolt on the throttle body. Connect the throttle cable and, if equipped with automatic transaxle, the throttle valve control cable to the throttle lever.

39. Install the MAP sensor and the EGR supply tube to the throttle body.

40. Connect the electrical connectors for the air charge temperature sensor, throttle position sensor and air bypass solenoid.

41. Install the ignition coil and bracket. Tighten the bolts to 35 ft. lbs. (48 Nm).

42. If the left cylinder head was removed, perform the following:

    a. Install the power steering support bracket. Tighten the 3 retaining bolts to 35 ft. lbs. (48 Nm).

    b. Install the air conditioning brace to the power steering support bracket retaining bolt. Tighten the bolt to 18 ft. lbs. (25 Nm).

    c. Install the power steering pump pulley. Tighten the retaining nut to 47 ft. lbs. (64 Nm).

    d. Install the automatic belt tensioner. Tighten the retaining bolt to 35 ft. lbs. (48 Nm). Install the accessory drive belt.

    e. Install the power steering protective shroud. Tighten the 2 retaining bolts to 7 ft. lbs. (10 Nm).

43. Connect the fuel lines to the fuel supply rail.

44. Connect the upper radiator and heater hoses. Connect the vacuum lines to their original locations.

45. Change the engine oil and filter. This is necessary because engine coolant is corrosive to all engine bearing material. Replacing the engine oil after removal of a coolant carrying component guards against later failure.

46. Install the air cleaner fresh air hose to the throttle body and air cleaner. Install the closure hose to the rocker arm cover.

47. Fill the cooling system.

48. Connect the negative battery cable.

49. Start the engine and check for leaks. Check the ignition timing.

CLEANING AND INSPECTION

1. With the valves installed to protect the valve seats, remove deposits from the combustion chambers and valve heads with a scraper and drill-mounted wire brush. Be careful not to damage the cylinder head gasket surface. If the head is to be disassembled, proceed to Step 3. If the head is not to be disassembled, proceed to Step 2.

2. Remove all dirt, oil and old gasket material from the cylinder head with solvent. Clean the bolt holes and the oil passage. Be careful not to get solvent on the valve seals as the solvent may damage them. Dry the cylinder head with compressed air, if available. Check the head for cracks or other damage, and check the gasket surface for burrs, nicks and flatness. If you are in doubt about the head's serviceability, consult a reputable automotive machine shop.

3. Remove the valves, springs and retainers, then clean the valve guide bores with a valve guide cleaning tool. Remove all dirt, oil and old

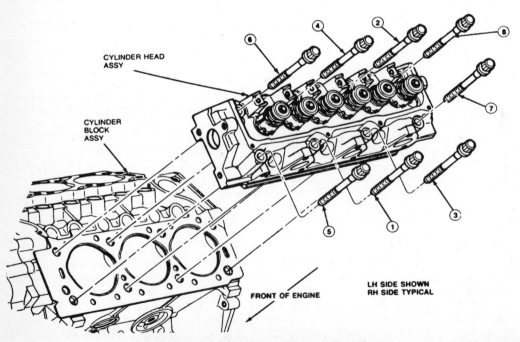

Cylinder head bolt torque sequence—3.0L engine

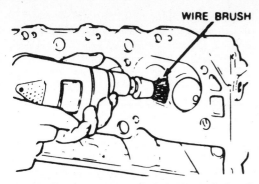

Cleaning the combustion chamber with a wire brush

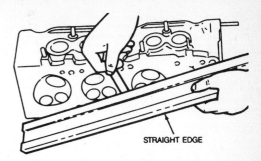

Checking cylinder head flatness

gasket material from the cylinder head with solvent. Clean the bolt holes and the oil passage.

4. Remove all deposits from the valves with a wire brush or buffing wheel.

5. Check the head for cracks in the valve seat area and ports, and check the gasket surface for burrs, nicks and flatness. If you are in doubt about the head's serviceability, consult a reputable automotive machine shop.

NOTE: *If the cylinder head was removed due to an overheating condition and a crack is suspected, do not assume that the head is not cracked because a crack is not visually found. A crack can be so small that it cannot be seen by eye, but can pass coolant when the engine is at operating temperature. Consult an automotive machine shop that has pressure testing equipment to make sure the head is not cracked.*

RESURFACING

Whenever the cylinder head is removed, check the flatness of the cylinder head gasket surface as follows:

1. Make sure all dirt and old gasket material has been cleaned from the cylinder head. Any foreign material left on the head gasket surface can cause a false measurement.

2. Place a straightedge across the gasket surface in the positions shown. Using a feeler gauge, determine the clearance at the center of the straightedge.

3. If warpage exceeds 0.006 in. (0.15mm), the cylinder head must be resurfaced. If resur-

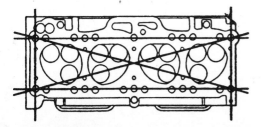

Place the straightedge in these positions to check cylinder head flatness

facing is necessary, do not plane or grind off more than 0.010 in. (0.254mm) from the original gasket surface.

Valves

REMOVAL AND INSTALLATION

1. Remove the cylinder head.

2. On the 2.2L engine, remove the rocker arms/shafts assemblies and the camshaft.

3. Block the head on its side, or install a pair of head-holding brackets made especially for valve removal.

4. Use a socket slightly larger than the valve stem and keepers, place the socket over the valve stem and gently hit the socket with a plastic hammer to break loose any varnish buildup.

5. Remove the valve keepers, retainer, and valve spring using a valve spring compressor (the locking C-clamp type is the easiest to use).

6. Place the parts from each valve in a separate container, numbered and identified for the valve and cylinder.

7. Remove and discard the valve stem oil seal, a new seal will be used at assembly time.

8. Remove the valves from the cylinder head and place, in order, through holes punched in a stiff piece of cardboard.

9. Use an electric drill and rotary wire brush to clean the intake and exhaust valve ports, combustion chamber and valve seats. In some cases, the carbon build-up will have to be chipped away. Use a blunt pointed drift for carbon chipping, being careful around valve seat areas.

10. Use a valve guide cleaning brush and safe solvent to clean the valve guides.

11. Clean the valves with a revolving wire brush. Heavy carbon deposits may be removed with blunt drift.

NOTE: *When using a wire brush to remove carbon from the cylinder head or valves, make sure the deposits are actually removed and not just burnished.*

12. Wash and clean all valve springs, keepers, retainers etc., in safe solvent. Remember to keep parts from each valve separate.

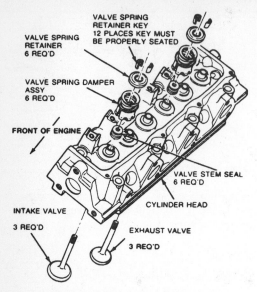

VALVE SPRING RETAINER 6 REQ'D

VALVE SPRING RETAINER KEY 12 PLACES KEY MUST BE PROPERLY SEATED

VALVE SPRING DAMPER ASSY 6 REQ'D

FRONT OF ENGINE

VALVE STEM SEAL 6 REQ'D

CYLINDER HEAD

INTAKE VALVE 3 REQ'D

EXHAUST VALVE 3 REQ'D

Valve removal and installation—3.0L engine

13. Check the cylinder head for cracks. Cracks usually start around the exhaust valve seat because it is the hottest part of the combustion chamber. If a crack is suspected but cannot be detected visually, have the area checked by pressure testing, with a dye penetrant or other method by an automotive machine shop.

14. Inspect the valves, guides, springs and seats and machine or replace parts, as necessary.

To install:

15. On the 2.2L engine, install new valve seals with valve seal installer tool T87C–6510–B or equivalent. Dip each valve in clean engine oil and install in its original location.

16. On the 3.0L engine, dip each valve in clean engine oil and install in its original location. Install new valve seals, using a ⅝ in. deep-well socket and a light mallet to seat the seal on the cylinder head and valve stem.

17. Install any required shims, the valve spring and the retainer over the valve stem. Compress the spring with the valve spring compressor and install the keepers.

18. After all the valves and springs have been assembled, take a mallet and lightly strike each valve stem tip squarely to seat the keepers.

19. On the 2.2L engine, install the camshaft and the rocker arm/shaft assemblies.

INSPECTION

1. Remove the valves from the cylinder head. Clean the valves, valve guides, valve seats and related components, as explained earlier.

2. Visually check the valves for obvious wear or damage. A burnt valve will have discolor-ation, severe galling or pitting and even cracks on one area of the valve face. Minor pits, grooves, etc. can be removed by refacing. Check the valve stems bends and for obvious wear that is indicated by a step between the part of the stem that travels in the valve guide and the part of the stem near the keeper grooves.

3. Check the valve stem-to-guide clearance. If a dial indicator is not on hand, a visual inspection can give you a fairly good idea if the guide, valve stem or both are worn. Insert the valve into the guide until the valve head is slightly away from the valve seat. Wiggle the valve sideways. A small amount of wobble is normal, excessive wobble means a worn guide and/or valve stem. If a dial indicator is on hand, mount the indicator so that gauge stem is 90° to the valve stem as close to the top of the valve guide as possible. Move the valve from the seat, and measure the valve guide-to-stem clearance by rocking the stem back and forth to actuate the dial indicator. Measure the valve stem using a micrometer and compare to specifications to determine whether stem or guide is causing excessive clearance.

4. The valve guide, if worn, must be repaired before the valve seats can be resurfaced. A new valve guide should be installed or, in some

FOR DIMENSIONS, REFER TO SPECIFICATIONS

CHECK FOR BENT STEM

DIAMETER

VALVE FACE ANGLE

1/32" MINIMUM

THIS LINE PARALLEL WITH VALVE HEAD

Critical valve dimensions

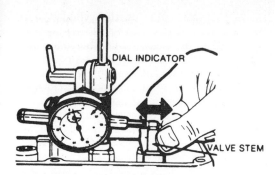

Checking valve stem-to-guide clearance

Checking valve seat concentricity

cases, knurled. Consult the automotive machine shop.

5. If the valve guide is okay, measure the valve seat concentricity using a runout gauge. Follow the manufacturers instructions. If runout is excessive, reface or replace the valve and machine or replace the valve seat.

6. Valves and seats must always be machined together. Never use a refaced valve on a valve seat that has not been machined; never use a valve that has not been refaced on a machined valve seat.

REFACING

1. Determine if the valve is usable as explained in the Inspection procedure.

2. Refer to specifications for the correct valve face machining angle. Make sure the valve refacer grinding wheels are properly dressed.

3. Reface the valve face only enough to remove the pits and grooves or correct any runout. If the edge of the valve head is less than $\frac{1}{32}$ in. (0.8mm) thick after grinding, replace the valve, as the valve will run too hot in the engine.

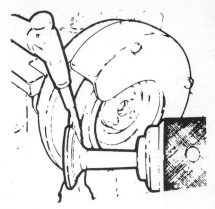

Refacing the valve face

4. Remove all grooves or score marks from the end of the valve stem, and chamfer it, as necessary. Do not remove more than 0.010 in. (0.254mm) from the end of the valve stem.

5. When the engine is reassembled, it will be necessary to check the clearance between the rocker arm pad and the valve stem tip. Refer to Chapter 2.

Valve Stem Seals

REPLACEMENT

Cylinder Heads Installed

2.2L ENGINE

1. Remove the rocker arm cover, rocker arm/shaft assemblies and camshaft. Refer to procedures in this Chapter.

2. Mount valve spring compressor bar T81P–6513–A or equivalent and angle brackets from valve spring compressor kit T88C–6565–AH on the cylinder head.

3. Turn the crankshaft until the piston of the cylinder to be worked on is at Top Dead Center (TDC).

4. Disconnect the spark plug wire and remove the spark plug on the cylinder to be worked on.

5. Thread an adapter into the spark plug hole and connect the hose from an air compressor to the adapter. The hose on many screw-in compression testers will accept a quick-disconnect fitting that an air compressor hose can be connected to. After all connections are made, turn the air on; this will keep the valve against the valve seat while the retainer is removed.

6. Using a socket slightly larger than the valve stem and keepers, place the socket over the valve stem and gently hit the socket with a plastic hammer to break loose any varnish buildup.

7. Depress the valve spring with the valve spring compressor until the valve keepers can

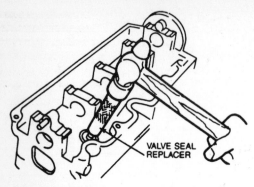

Installing the valve stem seal—2.2L engine

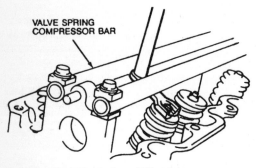

Installing the valve spring—2.2L engine

be removed. Then remove the spring seat, spring and valve seal.

NOTE: *If the air pressure has forced the piston to the bottom of the cylinder, any removal of air pressure will allow the valves to fall into the cylinder. A rubber band, tape or string wrapped around the end of the valve stem will prevent this.*

8. Install the new valve seal using replacer tool T87C–6510–B or equivalent.

9. Install the valve spring and upper spring seat.

10. Mount the valve spring compressor bar and spacers onto the front and rear camshaft bearing caps.

11. Compress the valve spring with the compressor until the keepers can be installed.

12. Release the air pressure. Install the spark plug and connect the spark plug wire.

13. Repeat the procedure for each cylinder.

14. Install the camshaft, rocker arm/shaft assemblies and rocker arm cover. Refer to the procedures in this Chapter.

3.0L ENGINE

1. Remove the rocker arm cover.

2. Turn the crankshaft until the piston of the cylinder to be worked on is at Top Dead Center (TDC). Remove the rocker arm, fulcrum and fulcrum bolt.

3. Disconnect the spark plug wire and re-

move the spark plug on the cylinder to be worked on.

4. Thread an adapter into the spark plug hole and connect the hose from an air compressor to the adapter. The hose on many screw-in compression testers will accept a quick-disconnect fitting that an air compressor hose can be connected to. After all connections are made, turn the air on; this will keep the valve against the valve seat while the retainer is removed.

5. Using a socket slightly larger than the valve stem and keepers, place the socket over the valve stem and gently hit the socket with a plastic hammer to break loose any varnish buildup.

6. Compress the valve spring using a suitable spring compressor. The type of compressor desired is common and uses the rocker arm attachment, in this case a bolt, to pivot on. The handle end of the compressor is pulled and the other end of the compressor exerts downward pressure on the valve spring. The valve keepers can then be removed.

7. Remove the valve spring, retainer and the valve stem seal.

NOTE: *If the air pressure has forced the piston to the bottom of the cylinder, any removal of air pressure will allow the valves to fall into the cylinder. A rubber band, tape or string wrapped around the end of the valve stem will prevent this.*

8. Install a new valve seal, using a ⅝ in. deep-well socket and a light mallet to seat the seal on the cylinder head and valve stem.

9. Install the valve spring and retainer. Use the compressor tool to compress the spring and install the keepers.

10. Release the air pressure. Install the spark plug and connect the spark plug wire.

11. Install the rocker arm and fulcrum. Refer to the procedure in this Chapter.

12. Repeat the procedure for each cylinder.

13. Install the rocker arm cover.

Cylinder Heads Removed

1. On the 2.2L engine, remove the rocker arms/shafts assemblies and the camshaft.

2. Block the head on its side, or install a pair of head-holding brackets made especially for valve removal.

3. Using a socket slightly larger than the valve stem and keepers, place the socket over the valve stem and gently hit the socket with a plastic hammer to break loose any varnish buildup.

4. Remove the valve keepers, retainer, and valve spring using a valve spring compressor (the locking C-clamp type is the easiest to use).

5. Place the parts from each valve in a sepa-

rate container, numbered and identified for the valve and cylinder.

6. Remove and discard the valve stem oil seal.

7. On the 2.2L engine, install new valve seals with valve seal installer tool T87C–6510–B or equivalent. Dip each valve in clean engine oil and install in its original location.

8. On the 3.0L engine, dip each valve in clean engine oil and install in its original location. Install new valve seals, using a ⅝ in. deep-well socket and a light mallet to seat the seal on the cylinder head and valve stem.

9. Install any required shims, the valve spring and the retainer over the valve stem. Compress the spring with the valve spring compressor and install the keepers.

10. After all the valves and springs have been assembled, take a mallet and lightly strike each valve stem tip squarely to seat the keepers.

11. On the 2.2L engine, install the camshaft and the rocker arm/shaft assemblies.

Valve Springs

REMOVAL AND INSTALLATION

1. Remove the cylinder head.

2. On the 2.2L engine, remove the rocker arms/shafts assemblies and the camshaft.

3. Block the head on its side, or install a pair of head-holding brackets made especially for valve service.

4. Use a socket slightly larger than the valve stem and keepers, place the socket over the valve stem and gently hit the socket with a plastic hammer to break loose any varnish buildup.

5. Remove the valve keepers, retainer, and valve spring using a valve spring compressor (the locking C-clamp type is the easiest to use). If necessary, remove the lower spring seat (2.2L engine) or any shims that may have been under the valve spring.

6. Place the parts from each valve in a separate container, numbered and identified for the valve and cylinder.

7. Inspect the valve springs for damage or wear and replace as necessary. Check the free length and/or spring pressure.

To install:

8. Install the valve spring retainer on the valve without the spring and retain it with the keepers. Pull the valve firmly against the seat.

9. Using a suitable measuring tool (calipers, or a telescope gauge with a micrometer work well), measure the distance between the cylinder head and the retainer and compare this distance with the installed height specification. Shims are available to make up the difference and are usually necessary after a valve job.

10. Install the lower spring seat (2.2L engine)

or any shims that are required under the valve spring.

11. Compress the spring using the spring compressor and install the keepers. Release the spring compressor.

12. After all the valves and springs have been assembled, take a mallet and lightly strike each valve stem tip squarely to seat the keepers.

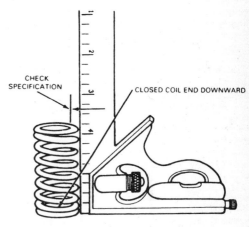

Checking the valve spring for squareness

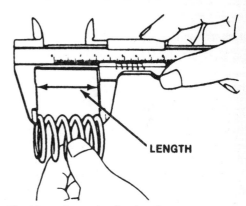

Checking valve spring free length

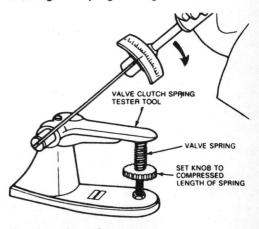

Checking valve spring pressure

13. On the 2.2L engine, install the camshaft and the rocker arm/shaft assemblies.

14. Install the cylinder head.

INSPECTION

1. Check the springs for cracks or other damage.

2. Check each spring for squareness using a steel square and a flat surface. Stand the spring and square on end on the flat surface. Slide the spring up to the square, revolve the spring slowly and observe the space between the top coil of the spring and the square. If the space exceeds 0.067 in. (1.7mm), replace the spring.

3. Measure the free length of the spring. On the 2.2L engine, the intake spring should measure 1.902–1.949 in. (48.3mm–49.5mm) and the exhaust spring should measure 1.937–1.984 in. (49.2–50.4mm). On the 3.0L engine, the free length should be approximately 1.84 in. (46.7mm).

4. On the 3.0L engine, check the springs for proper pressure at the specified spring lengths using a valve spring tester. The pressure should be (without the damper) 65 lbs. @ 1.58 in. (40mm) and 180 lbs. @ 1.16 in. (29.5mm).

Valve Seats

REMOVAL AND INSTALLATION

Valve seat replacement should be left to an automotive machine shop, due to the high degree of precision and special equipment required. Seat replacement procedures differ between the 2.2L and 3.0L engines due to their respective aluminum and cast iron construction. The following procedures can be construed as what is generally acceptable for aluminum and cast iron cylinder heads; the actual method employed should be the decision of the machinist.

The 2.2L engine uses replaceable seat inserts. These inserts can be removed by cutting them out to within a few thousandths of their outside diameter and then collapsing the remainder, or by heating the head to a high temperature and then driving the seat out. The valve seats are integral with the cylinder head on the 3.0L engine. To install a replacement seat, the old seat must be completely cut out with a special cutter tool mounted on a cylinder head machine.

To install a new seat on the 2.2L engine, the cylinder head is usually heated to a high temperature, then the seat, which is at room temperature or slightly chilled, is pressed into the head. The head is then allowed to cool and as it does, it contracts and grips the seat. On the 3.0L engine, the new seat is usually driven in with both the head and seat at room tempera-

ture. The calculated press-fit interference retains the seat in the head.

After a new seat is installed, it must be refaced.

REFACING

1. Inspect the valve guides to make sure they are usable. as described under valve inspection.

2. Make sure the grinding wheels on the refacer are properly dressed to ensure a good finish.

3. Grind the valve seats to a 45° angle, only removing enough metal to clean up the pits and grooves and correct valve seat runout.

4. After the seat has been refaced, measure the seat width using a suitable measuring tool and compare to specification.

5. If the seat is too wide, grinding wheels of 60° and 30° can be used to remove stock from the bottom and the top of the seat, respectively, and narrow the seat.

6. Once the correct seat width has been obtained, find out where the seat contacts the valve. The finished seat should contact the approximate center of the valve face.

7. Coat the seat with Prussian Blue and set the valve in place. Rotate the valve with light pressure, then remove it and check the seat contact.

8. If the blue is transferred to the center of the valve face, contact is satisfactory. If the blue is transferred to the top edge of the valve face, lower the valve seat. If the blue is transferred to the bottom edge of the valve face, raise the valve seat.

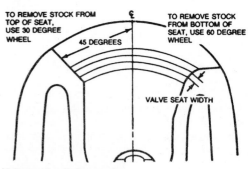

Valve seat refacing angles

Valve Guides

If the valve guides are determined to be worn during the valve inspection procedure, there are two possible repair alternatives, knurling or replacement. Either procedure can be done by a competent automotive machine shop.

If guide wear is minimal, the correct inside diameter can be restored by knurling. Knurling involves using a special tool to raise a spiral ridge on the inside of the guide while it is in-

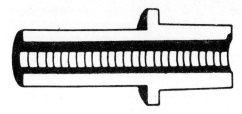

Cut-away view of a knurled valve guide

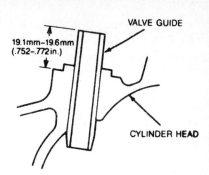

Valve guide installation dimensions

stalled in the head. This effectively reduces the inside diameter of the guide. A reamer is then usually passed through the guide to make the inside diameter smooth and uniform.

Knurling is only an alternative if there is minimum guide wear. Excessive wear can only be corrected by replacing the guide.

NOTE: *The valve seats must be refaced after guide knurling or replacement.*

REMOVAL AND INSTALLATION

2.2L Engine

1. Gradually heat the disassembled cylinder head in water to approximately 190°F (90°C).
CAUTION: *Be careful when removing and handling the head as the water and the head will be extremely hot! Wear thick, heavy, rubber gloves during this procedure.*
2. Remove the cylinder head from the water and place it on a bench. Block the head on its side, or install a pair of head-holding brackets made especially for cylinder head service.
3. Drive out the valve guide toward the camshaft side of the cylinder head using valve guide remover tool T87C–6510–A or equivalent.
4. Drive in the new guide using the same tool. Drive the guide in until 0.752–0.772 in. (19.1–19.6mm) of the guide protrudes from the top of the head.
NOTE: *Work quickly. if the head is allowed to cool, guide removal and installation will be difficult.*

VALVE GUIDE
REMOVER

Valve guide replacement—2.2L engine

3.0L Engine

The valve guide is an integral part of the cast iron cylinder head on the 3.0L engine. It can only be removed using a special cutter tool, usually mounted on a cylinder head machine. The new guide is then driven in and retained by press-fit.

Valve Lifters

REMOVAL AND INSTALLATION

CAUTION: *When draining the coolant, keep in mind that cats and dogs are attracted by the ethylene glycol antifreeze, and are quite likely to drink any that is left in an uncovered container or in puddles on the ground. This will prove fatal in sufficient quantity. Always drain the coolant into a sealable container. Coolant should be reused unless it is contaminated or several years old.*

3.0L Engine

NOTE: *Before replacing a lifter for noisy operation, make sure that the noise is not caused by improper valve-to-rocker arm clearance, worn rocker arms or pushrods.*

1. Disconnect the negative battery cable.
2. Drain the cooling system.
3. Remove the rocker arm covers, and the throttle body and intake manifold assembly.
4. Loosen each rocker arm fulcrum mounting bolt to allow the rocker arm to be lifted off the pushrod and rotated to one side.
5. Remove the pushrods, marking the location of each pushrod to ensure the proper replacement in the original position.
6. Remove the lifter(s), using a magnet. Mark the location of each lifter to ensure the proper replacement in the original position.
NOTE: *If the lifters are stuck in the bores due to excessive varnish or gum deposits, it may be necessary to use a hydraulic lifter puller or a claw-type tool to aid in removal. Rotate the lifter back and forth to loosen it from the gum or varnish that may have formed on the lifter.*

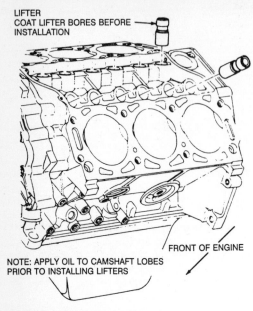

LIFTER
COAT LIFTER BORES BEFORE
INSTALLATION

FRONT OF ENGINE

NOTE: APPLY OIL TO CAMSHAFT LOBES
PRIOR TO INSTALLING LIFTERS

Valve lifter installation—3.0L engine

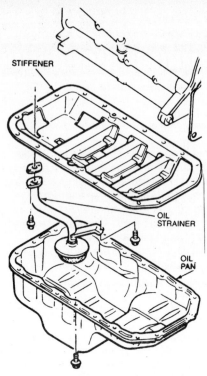

STIFFENER

OIL
STRAINER

OIL
PAN

Oil pan removal and installation—2.2L engine

To install:

7. Lubricate each lifter and bore with heavy engine oil and install the lifters into the bore. Install each lifter in the bore from which it was removed. If new lifters are being installed, check each one for free fit in the bore in which it is to be installed.

8. Lubricate each pushrod with the heavy engine oil and insert in their original position.

9. Place the rocker arms over the pushrods. For each rocker arm, rotate the crankshaft until the lifter rests on the base circle of the camshaft lobe, then position the fulcrums and tighten the mounting bolts to 24 ft. lbs. (32 Nm).

10. Lubricate all the rocker arm assemblies. NOTE: *Fulcrums must be fully seated in the cylinder head and the pushrods must be seated in the rocker arm sockets prior to tightening.*

11. Install the throttle body and intake manifold and the rocker arm covers.

12. Connect the negative battery cable.

13. Refill the cooling system and check for leaks.

Oil Pan

REMOVAL AND INSTALLATION

2.2L Engine

1. Disconnect the negative battery cable.
2. Raise and support the vehicle, safely.
3. Remove the right wheel and tire assembly and the right inner splash shield.
4. Drain the crankcase.

5. Remove the engine-to-flywheel housing support bracket, the flywheel housing dust cover bolts and cover.

6. Remove the front exhaust pipe and the exhaust pipe support bracket.

7. Remove the oil pan-to-engine bolts, the oil pan, the oil pickup tube and the stiffener.

8. Clean the gasket mounting surfaces.

To install:

9. Using silicone sealer, apply a continuous bead on both sides of the stiffener, along the inside of the bolt holes.

10. Install the stiffener, oil pump pickup tube gasket, tube and retaining bolts. Install the oil pan and gasket and tighten the mounting bolts to 69–104 inch lbs. (8–12 Nm).

11. Install the flywheel housing dust cover and tighten the bolts to 49–95 inch lbs. (8–11 Nm).

12. Install the exhaust pipe support bracket and the front exhaust pipe.

13. Install the engine-to-flywheel housing support bracket bolts into the flywheel housing and tighten to 27–38 ft. lbs. (37–52 Nm).

14. Tighten the engine-to-flywheel housing support bracket bolts at the engine block to 27–38 ft. lbs. (37–52 Nm).

15. Install the oil pan drain plug. Install the oil temperature sending unit, if equipped.

16. Install the inner fender splash shield and the wheel and tire assembly. Lower the vehicle.

17. Add engine oil to the proper level.

18. Connect the negative battery cable, start the engine and check for leaks.

3.0L Engine

1. Disconnect the negative battery cable. Raise and safely support the vehicle.

2. Drain the engine oil and remove the starter motor.

3. Remove the front and rear transaxle-to-engine braces.

4. Disconnect the low oil level sensor connector from the dash panel side of the oil pan.

5. Remove the exhaust inlet pipe from the manifolds and pull it down out of the way.

6. Drain the cooling system and remove the water pump.

7. Remove the water pump bracket and idler pulley tensioner.

8. Remove the mounting bolts and nut from the front end of the right crossmember.

9. Loosen, but do not remove the bolts and nut from the rear end of the right crossmember.

NOTE: *Allow the crossmember to drop as low as possible to allow the removal of the oil pan. If any attempt is made to remove the oil pan without lowering the crossmember first, damage to the baffle may occur. The oil pan must be pulled straight down without turning or prying it out.*

10. Remove the oil pan mounting bolts and the oil pan.

To install:

11. Apply a $\frac{1}{5}$ in. (5mm) bead of silicone sealer to the junction of the rear main bearing cap and the cylinder block and the junction of the front cover assembly and the cylinder block.

12. Position the oil pan gasket on the engine block and secure with gasket adhesive.

13. Place the oil pan on the cylinder block and tighten the mounting bolts to 9 ft. lbs. (12 Nm).

14. Lift the right crossmember into place and tighten all the nuts and bolts.

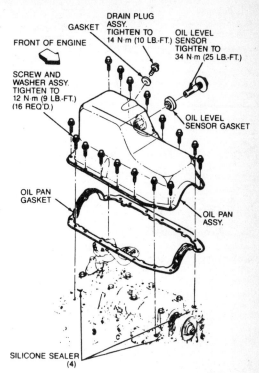

Oil pan removal and installation—3.0L engine

15. Install the water pump mounting bracket and the idler pulley tensioner.

16. Install the water pump and the exhaust inlet pipe.

17. Connect the oil level sensor and install the transaxle-to-engine braces.

18. Install the starter motor.

19. Lower the vehicle. Refill the crankcase and the cooling system.

20. Connect the negative battery cable. Run the engine and check for leaks.

Oil Pump

REMOVAL

2.2L Engine

1. Disconnect the negative battery cable. Raise and safely support the vehicle.

2. Remove the timing belt. Remove the retaining bolt and remove the crankshaft sprocket. Drain the engine oil and remove the oil pan.

3. Remove the oil pump pickup tube-to-oil pump bolts, the tube and gasket.

4. Remove the oil pump-to-cylinder block bolts, the pump and gasket.

5. If necessary, pry the oil seal from the pump and clean the seal bore.

6. Clean the gasket mounting surfaces. Inspect the pump and gears for wear.

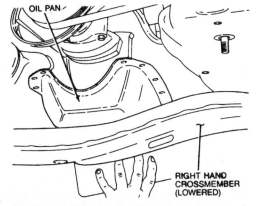

Lowering the oil pan—3.0L engine

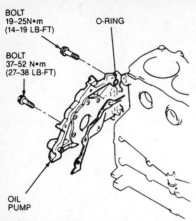

Oil pump removal and installation—2.2L engine

3.0L Engine

1. Disconnect the negative battery cable. Raise and support the vehicle, safely. Drain the engine oil.

2. Remove the oil pan and the oil pump mounting bolt.

3. Remove the oil pump and the intermediate shaft from the rear main bearing cap.

4. Pull the intermediate shaft out of the oil pump.

INSTALLATION

2.2L Engine

1. Apply a continuous bead of silicone sealer to the oil pump gasket surface.

NOTE: *Do not allow the sealer to squeeze*

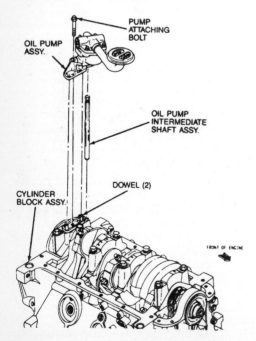

Oil pump removal and installation—3.0L engine

into the pump's outlet hole in the pump or cylinder block.

2. Install a new O-ring into the pump body.

3. Install the oil pump to the cylinder block; be careful not to cut the oil seal lip. Tighten the 8mm oil pump-to-cylinder block bolts to 14–19 ft. lbs. (19–25 Nm) and the 10mm oil pump-to-cylinder block bolts to 27–38 ft. lbs. (37–52 Nm).

4. Install the oil pump pickup tube using a new gasket.

5. Install the oil pan and the crankshaft sprocket. Tighten the crankshaft sprocket bolt to 108–116 ft. lbs. (147–157 Nm).

6. Connect the negative battery cable and refill the crankcase. Start the engine and check for leaks.

3.0L Engine

1. Insert the pump intermediate shaft into the drive hole in the pump assembly until it clicks into place.

2. Pour a small amount of clean oil into the outlet hole in the body of the oil pump.

3. Lift the oil pump assembly into place guiding the intermediate shaft through the hole in the rear main bearing cap. Seat the pump securely on the locating dowels.

4. Install the pump mounting bolt and tighten to 35 ft. lbs. (48 Nm).

5. Install the oil pan.

6. Lower the vehicle and refill the crankcase. Connect the negative battery cable, run the engine and check for leaks.

Crankshaft Damper

REMOVAL AND INSTALLATION

2.2L Engine

1. Remove the accessory drive belts. Refer to Chapter 1.

2. Raise and safely support the vehicle.

3. Remove the right front wheel and tire assembly.

4. Remove the right inner fender panel.

5. Remove the 6 bolts, damper and baffle plate.

6. Inspect the damper for damage and replace, as necessary.

To install:

7. Install the crankshaft sprocket baffle with the curved lip facing outward.

8. Install the crankshaft damper with the deep recess facing out and install the 6 bolts. Tighten the bolts to 109–152 inch lbs. (12–17 Nm).

9. Install the right inner fender panel and the wheel and tire assembly. Lower the vehicle.

10. Install the accessory drive belts. Refer to Chapter 1.

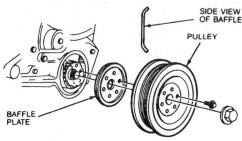

Crankshaft damper removal—2.2L engine

3.0L Engine

1. Remove the accessory drive belt. Refer to Chapter 1.

2. Raise and safely support the vehicle.

3. Remove the right front wheel and tire assembly

4. Remove the plastic inner fender shield.

5. Remove the water pump drive belt. Refer to Chapter 1.

6. Lower the vehicle.

7. Place a block of wood on the lifting pad of a floor jack. Position the pad under the oil pan and support the engine.

8. If equipped with manual transaxle, remove the right-hand engine mount from the water pump bracket.

9. Remove the 3 nuts that attach the right-hand upper engine mount to the timing cover.

10. Lower the floor jack carefully, allowing the engine to rest on the remaining mounts.

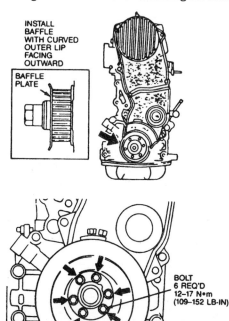

Crankshaft damper installation—2.2L engine

11. Raise and safely support the vehicle.

12. Remove the crankshaft damper retaining bolt and flat washer.

13. Using a suitable puller tool, such as damper remover T58P–6316–D or equivalent, remove the damper from the crankshaft.

14. Remove the 3 nuts and 1 bolt that attach the right-hand side of the sub-frame to the body. The sub-frame can then be pulled down slightly to provide clearance for removing the damper from the vehicle. The damper must be carefully tipped down to clear the right hand inner fender.

15. Inspect the crankshaft damper for damage. If the sealing surface is grooved, press-on sleeves are available to restore sealing ability. If a sleeve is installed, a new timing chain cover seal should also be instaled.

To install:

16. Coat the damper sealing surface with clean engine oil. Apply sealer to the damper keyway prior to installation.

17. Install the damper with a crankshaft damper installation tool, such as damper and seal installer tool T82L–6316–A or equivalent.

WARNING: *Do not drive the damper on with a hammer. This can not only damage the damper, but may also damage the crankshaft thrust bearing.*

18. Install the crankshaft damper bolt and washer and tighten to 92–122 ft. lbs. (125–165 Nm). Lower the vehicle.

19. Using the floor jack, carefully raise the engine and install the right-hand engine mount nuts. Tighten to 55–76 ft. lbs. (74–103 Nm).

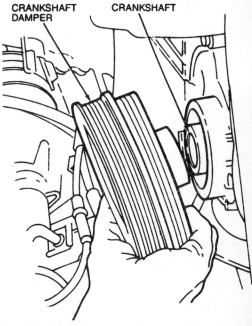

Crankshaft damper removal—3.0L engine

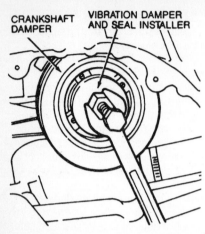

Crankshaft damper installation—3.0L engine

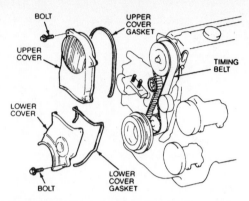

Timing belt cover removal and installation—2.2L engine

20. Install the sub-frame nuts and bolt. Tighten the bolt to 27–40 ft. lbs. (36–54 Nm) and the nuts to 69–97 ft. lbs. (93–132 Nm).

21. Lower the engine and remove the floor jack.

22. If equipped with a manual transaxle, install the right-hand engine mount to the water pump bracket.

23. Raise and safely support the vehicle.

24. Install the water pump belt. Refer to Chapter 1.

25. Install the plastic splash shield and the right-hand wheel and tire assembly. Lower the vehicle.

26. Install the accessory drive belt. Refer to Chapter 1. Install the power steering pulley shield.

Timing Belt Cover
REMOVAL AND INSTALLATION
2.2L Engine

1. Disconnect the negative battery cable.

2. Remove the accessory drive belts. Refer to Chapter 1.

3. Remove the crankshaft damper. Refer to the procedure in this Chapter.

4. Place a block of wood on the lifting pad of a floor jack. Position the pad under the oil pan and support the engine.

5. Remove the 2 nuts and dowels from the right engine mount.

6. Remove the 7 bolts that retain the timing belt covers and remove the covers and gaskets.

To install:

7. Install the lower cover gasket and the lower cover. Tighten the bolts to 61–87 inch lbs. (7–10 Nm).

8. Install the upper cover gasket and the upper cover. Tighten the bolts to 61–87 inch lbs. (7–10 Nm).

9. Position the engine mount on the engine and install the 2 nuts and dowels. Remove the floor jack.

10. Install the crankshaft damper. Refer to the procedure in this Chapter.

11. Install the accessory drive belts. Refer to Chapter 1.

12. Connect the negative battery cable.

OIL SEAL REPLACEMENT

1. Disconnect the negative battery cable. Remove the timing belt covers and timing belt.

2. If equipped with a manual transaxle, place the shift lever in **4TH** gear and firmly apply the parking brake.

3. If equipped with an automatic transaxle, remove the lower flywheel cover and install a suitable flywheel locking tool onto the flywheel ring.

4. Remove the crankshaft sprocket-to-crankshaft bolt, the sprocket and the key.

5. Using a small prybar, pry the oil seal from the engine block; be careful not to score the crankshaft or the seal seat.

To install:

6. Using an oil seal installation tool or equivalent, lubricate the seal lip with clean engine oil and drive the new seal into the engine until it seats.

7. Install the crankshaft key and sprocket. Torque the crankshaft sprocket-to-crankshaft bolt to 108–116 ft. lbs. (147–157 Nm).

8. If necessary, remove the flywheel locking tool.

9. Install the timing belt and connect the negative battery cable.

Timing Chain Cover and Seal
REMOVAL AND INSTALLATION
3.0L Engine

1. Disconnect the negative battery cable.

2. Drain the cooling system.

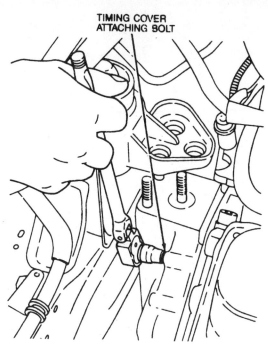

Removing the timing chain cover attaching bolts—3.0L engine

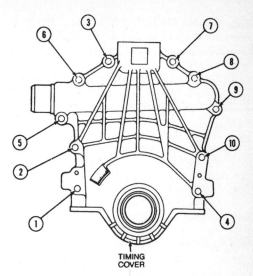

Timing chain cover bolt torque sequence—3.0L engine

3. Remove the 2 retaining bolts and remove the power steering protective shroud.

4. Remove the accessory drive belts. Refer to Chapter 1. Remove the belt tensioners.

5. Remove the crankshaft damper. Refer to the procedure in this Chapter.

6. Disconnect the water pump-to-front cover hose from the water pump connection.

NOTE: *The timing cover may be removed with the water pump hose attached.*

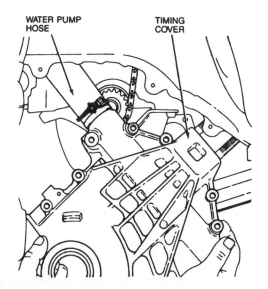

Removing the timing chain cover—3.0L engine

7. Drain the engine oil and remove the oil pan. Refer to the procedure in this Chapter.

8. Remove the 4 lowest timing cover retaining bolts and lower the vehicle.

9. Support the bottom of the engine using care to prevent damage to the crankshaft and oil pump assembly.

10. Remove the 3 nuts and 1 bolt attaching the upper engine mount to the top of the front cover.

11. Remove the 6 remaining timing cover mounting bolts.

12. Carefully insert a small prybar between the timing cover and the cylinder block. Gently pry the timing cover away from the cylinder block.

13. Carefully pull the cover over the end of the crankshaft and lower it through the bottom of the engine compartment.

To install:

14. Clean all gasket material and old silicone sealer from all gasket mating surfaces. Using a small prybar, pry the old crankshaft seal from the timing cover.

15. Lubricate the lip of a new crankshaft seal and install in the timing cover, using a seal installation tool.

16. Install a new timing cover gasket over the cylinder block dowels and install the timing cover, being careful not to damage the seal.

17. Install the 6 upper mounting bolts, finger tight. Apply pipe sealant to the threads of bolt No. 5 prior to installation (see illustration).

18. Raise and safely support the vehicle.

19. Install the 4 lower mounting bolts, finger tight. Apply pipe sealant to the threads of bolt No. 2 prior to installation (see illustration).

20. Tighten the timing cover bolts, in the sequence shown to 18 ft. lbs. (25 Nm).

21. Lower the vehicle and install the upper engine mount.

22. Raise and safely support the vehicle.

23. Install the oil pan with a new gasket. Tighten the mounting bolts to 9 ft. lbs. (12 Nm).

24. Install the crankshaft damper. Refer to the procedure in this Chapter.

25. Connect the hose from the timing cover to the water pump.

26. Lower the vehicle.

27. Install the accessory drive belt tensioners and the accessory drive belts.

28. Install the power steering protective shroud. Tighten the retaining bolts to 7 ft. lbs. (10 Nm).

29. Fill the crankcase with the proper type and quantity of engine oil. Fill the cooling system.

30. Connect the negative battery cable, start the engine and check for leaks.

Timing Belt

The timing belt should be replaced every 60,000 miles. Failure to replace the belt may result in damage to the engine.

REMOVAL AND INSTALLATION

2.2L Engine

1. Bring the engine to Top Dead Center (TDC) on the compression stroke for No. 1 piston. The notch on the crankshaft damper should align with the TDC mark on the front cover.

2. Disconnect the negative battery cable.

3. Remove the drive belts, crankshaft pulley and the timing belt covers.

4. Remove the timing belt tensioner spring and retaining bolt. Remove the idler pulley retaining bolt.

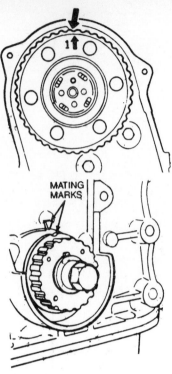

Align the camshaft and crankshaft sprocket timing marks with the marks on the cylinder head front housing and the oil pump

5. If the timing belt is to be reused, mark the direction of rotation so it can be reinstalled in the same direction.

6. Remove the timing belt.

To install:

7. Align the camshaft and crankshaft sprockets with the marks on the cylinder head and the oil pump housing, as shown.

8. Install the timing belt. If reusing the old belt, observe the direction of rotation mark made during the removal procedure.

9. Place the timing belt tensioner and spring in position. Temporarily secure the tensioner with the spring fully extended. Make sure the timing belt is installed so there is no looseness at the water pump pulley at the idler side.

10. Loosen the idler bolt. Turn the crankshaft twice in the direction of rotation; align the timing marks.

NOTE: *Always turn the crankshaft in the correct direction of rotation only. If the crankshaft is turned in the opposite direction, the timing belt may lose tension and correct belt timing may be lost.*

11. Check to see that the timing marks are correctly aligned. If they are not aligned, remove the timing belt and align the timing marks, then repeat Steps 8–11.

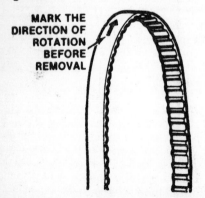

MARK THE DIRECTION OF ROTATION BEFORE REMOVAL

Mark an arrow on the old timing belt if it is to be reused

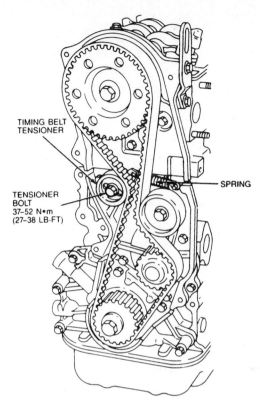

Timing belt installation—2.2L engine

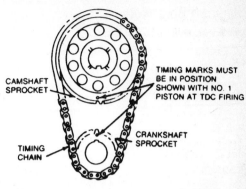

Timing chain sprocket alignment—3.0L engine

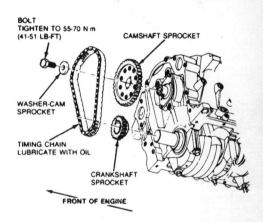

Timing chain and sprockets removal and installation

12. Tighten the tensioner bolt to 27–38 ft. lbs. (37–52 Nm).

13. Measure the belt deflection between the crankshaft and camshaft pulleys. The correct deflection should be 0.30–0.33 (7.5–8.5mm) at 22 ft. lbs. (98 Nm) of pressure. If the deflection is not correct, loosen the tensioner bolt and repeat Steps 10 and 11.

14. Install the timing belt covers, crankshaft pulley and drive belts.

15. Connect the negative battery cable.

Timing Chain

REMOVAL AND INSTALLATION

3.0L Engine

1. Disconnect the negative battery cable. Drain the cooling system and the crankcase.

2. Remove the crankshaft pulley and damper. Remove the timing cover.

3. Rotate the crankshaft until the No.1 piston is at Top Dead Center (TDC) and the timing marks are aligned.

4. Remove the camshaft sprocket retaining bolt and washer.

5. Slide the sprockets and the chain forward and remove as an assembly.

6. Clean and inspect all parts prior to installation.

To install:

7. Slide the sprockets and the chain on as as assembly with the timing marks aligned.

8. Install the camshaft retaining bolt and washer. Tighten the retaining bolt to 41–51 ft. lbs. (55–70 Nm) and lubricate the chain and sprockets with clean engine oil.

NOTE: *The camshaft retaining bolt has a drilled passage for timing chain lubrication. If damaged, do not replace with a standard bolt. Clean the oil passage with solvent prior to installation.*

9. Position the timing cover gasket onto the cylinder block alignment dowels.

10. Install the timing cover onto the cylinder block, being careful not to damage the seal.

11. Install the oil pan using a new gasket.

12. Install the crankshaft damper and pulley.

13. Refill the crankcase and the cooling system. Connect the negative battery cable.

14. Start the engine and check for any leaks. Check the ignition timing.

Camshaft Sprocket

REMOVAL AND INSTALLATION

2.2L Engine

1. Disconnect the negative battery cable. Remove the timing belt.

2. Insert a small prybar through one of the camshaft sprocket holes to keep it from turning.

3. Remove the sprocket bolt and the sprocket from the camshaft.

To install:

4. Align the dowel on the camshaft with the number 1 mark on the camshaft sprocket and install the sprocket.

5. Install the camshaft sprocket bolt. Hold the sprocket with the prybar and tighten the bolt to 35–48 ft. lbs. (47–65 Nm).

6. Install the timing belt and connect the negative battery cable.

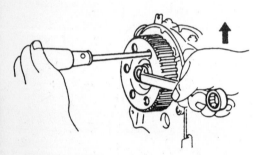

Camshaft sprocket removal and installation—2.2L engine

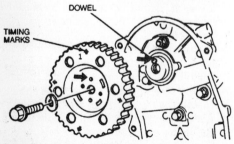

Camshaft sprocket and camshaft alignment—2.2L engine

Camshaft

REMOVAL AND INSTALLATION

2.2L Engine

1. Disconnect the negative battery cable. Drain the cooling system to a level below the thermostat housing.

2. Remove the timing belt covers, the timing belt and the camshaft sprocket.

3. Disconnect the upper radiator hose and the electrical connectors from the thermostat housing.

4. Mark the position of the distributor housing and the rotor and remove the distributor.

5. Remove the rocker arm cover and the front and rear housings. If necessary, pry out the camshaft seal from the front housing.

6. Remove the rocker arm/shaft assemblies.

7. Remove the camshaft bearing caps and the camshaft.

To install:

8. Clean all gasket mating surfaces.

9. Apply a liberal amount of clean engine oil to the camshaft journals and bearings. Install the camshaft on the cylinder head with the dowel pin facing straight up.

10. Apply silicone sealer to the cylinder head area shown. Do not let sealer come in contact with the camshaft bearings or journals.

11. Install the camshaft bearing caps with the arrows facing the front of the engine. Install the rocker arm/shaft assemblies, making sure the notches on the end of the shafts are in the correct position. Tighten the bolts, in the sequence to 13–20 ft. lbs. (18–26 Nm), in 2 equal steps.

12. Install a new gasket and the rear housing. Tighten the bolts to 14–19 ft. lbs. (19–25 Nm).

13. If the camshaft seal was removed, lubricate the lip of a new seal and install in the front housing, using a seal installation tool. Install a new gasket and the front housing. Tighten the bolts to 14–19 ft. lbs. (19–25 Nm).

14. Install the rocker arm cover, tightening the retaining bolts to 52–69 inch lbs. (6–8 Nm).

15. Install the distributor, aligning the marks that were made during the removal procedure.

16. Connect the electrical connectors and the upper radiator hose.

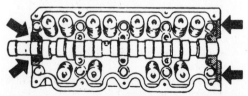

Apply sealer to the shaded areas of the cylinder head before installing the camshaft bearing caps

17. Install the camshaft sprocket, the timing belt and the timing belt covers.

18. Fill the cooling system, connect the negative battery cable and start the engine. Check the ignition timing and check for leaks.

3.0L Engine

1. Disconnect the negative battery cable. Remove the engine assembly from the vehicle and place it on a suitable workstand.

2. Remove the timing covers, rocker arm covers and the intake manifold.

3. Remove the hydraulic lifters using a magnet and keep them in order, so they may be reinstalled in their original positions. If the lifters are stuck in the bores, use a hydraulic lifter puller or equivalent, to remove them.

4. Remove the timing chain and sprockets.

5. Check the camshaft endplay as follows:

   a. Mount a dial indicator on the front of the cylinder block and rest the indicator foot on the end of the camshaft.

   b. Move the camshaft back and forth in the cylinder block and observe the dial indicator. If necessary, use a prybar to move the camshaft, but be careful not to damage the camshaft lobes or journals.

   c. If the endplay is excessive, replace the thrust plate.

6. Remove the camshaft thrust plate. Remove the camshaft by pulling it toward the front of the engine.

NOTE: *Use caution to avoid damaging the bearings, journals and lobes.*

7. Clean and inspect all parts prior to installation.

To install:

8. Lubricate the camshaft lobes and the journals with engine assembly lube. Carefully slide the camshaft through the bearings in the cylinder block.

9. Install the thrust plate and tighten the bolts to 6–8 ft. lbs. (8–12 Nm).

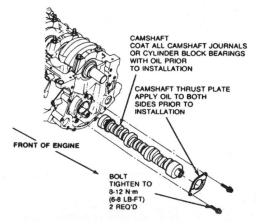

CAMSHAFT
COAT ALL CAMSHAFT JOURNALS
OR CYLINDER BLOCK BEARINGS
WITH OIL PRIOR
TO INSTALLATION

CAMSHAFT THRUST PLATE
APPLY OIL TO BOTH
SIDES PRIOR TO
INSTALLATION

FRONT OF ENGINE

BOLT
TIGHTEN TO
8-12 N·m
(6-8 LB-FT)
2 REQ'D

Camshaft installation—3.0L engine

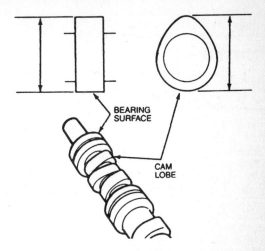

BEARING
SURFACE

CAM
LOBE

Measuring points for the camshaft journals and lobes

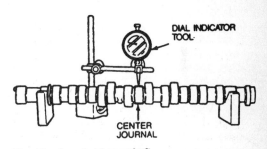

DIAL INDICATOR
TOOL

CENTER
JOURNAL

Checking for a bent camshaft

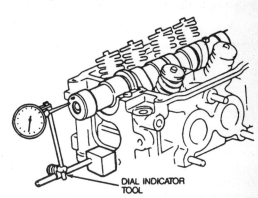

DIAL INDICATOR
TOOL

Checking camshaft endplay—2.2L engine

10. Install the timing chain and sprockets. Check the camshaft sprocket bolt for blockage of the drilled oil passages.

11. Install the timing cover and the crankshaft damper.

12. Lubricate the lifters and lifter bores with heavy engine oil and install the lifters into their original bores.

13. Install the pushrods, rocker arms, rocker covers and intake manifold.

14. Install the engine assembly and connect the negative battery cable.

15. Fill the cooling system and the crankcase. Run the engine and check for leaks.

INSPECTION

1. Clean the camshaft in solvent and allow to dry.

2. Inspect the camshaft for obvious signs of wear: scores, nicks or pits on the journals or lobes. Light scuffs or nicks can be removed with an oil stone.

3. Using a micrometer, measure the diameter of the journals and compare to specifications. Replace the camshaft if any journals are not within specification.

4. Measure the camshaft lobes across their maximum lobe height dimensions, using a micrometer. Compare your measurements with the lobe height specifications. Replace the camshaft if any lobe heights are not within specification.

5. On the 2.2L engine, mount the camshaft in V-blocks with the front and rear journals riding on the blocks. Check if the camshaft is bent using a dial indicator on the center bearing journal. The limit at the center journal is 0.0012 in. (0.03mm). Replace the camshaft if runout is excessive.

6. On the 2.2L engine, check the camshaft endplay with the camshaft laying in the cylinder on the lower bearing journals. Mount a dial indicator to the front of the cylinder head with the indicator foot resting on the end of the camshaft. Move the camshaft back and forth and observe the indicator. Compare the reading with the specification. If endplay is excessive, replace the camshaft or the cylinder head.

Camshaft Bearings

REMOVAL AND INSTALLATION

2.2L Engine

The camshaft bearings are an integral part of the cylinder head on the 2.2L engine. If the camshaft bearing surfaces are damaged, or the oil clearance is excessive and the camshaft journals are within specification, the cylinder head must be replaced. Check the camshaft oil clearance as follows:

1. Clean the camshaft journals and the bearing surface.

2. Place the camshaft in the cylinder head.

3. Position a piece of Plastigage® on the camshaft journal.

4. Install the camshaft bearing caps and rocker arm shafts. Torque the rocker arm shaft bolts to 13–20 ft. lbs. (18–26 Nm).

5. Remove the bearing caps and measure the oil clearance as shown. Compare your reading with the clearance specifications.

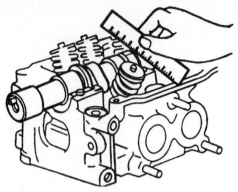

Checking camshaft bearing oil clearance—2.2L engine

6. If the clearance exceeds the maximum, remove the camshaft and measure the journal diameters. If the journal diameters are not within specification, replace the camshaft and repeat the oil clearance check. If the camshaft journal diameters are within specification, replace the cylinder head.

3.0L Engine

NOTE: *The following procedure requires the use of camshaft bearing set tool T65L–6250– A or equivalent.*

1. Remove the engine assembly and mount it on a workstand.

2. Remove the camshaft and crankshaft.

3. Using a sharp chisel or punch and hammer, cut a hole in the center of the rear bearing bore plug. Pry the plug from the bore using a prybar. Be careful not to damage the bore.

4. Select the proper size expanding collet and backup nut and assemble them on the expanding mandrel. With the expanding collet collapsed, install the collet assembly in the camshaft bearing, and tighten the backup nut on the expanding mandrel until the collet fits the camshaft bearing.

5. Assemble the puller screw and extension, if necessary, and install them on the expanding mandrel. Wrap a cloth around the threads of the puller screw to protect the bearing or journal. Tighten the puller nut against the thrust bearing and puller plate to remove the camshaft bearing. Hold the end of the puller screw to prevent it from turning.

6. Repeat Step 5 for each bearing. To remove the front bearing, install the puller from the rear of the block.

To install:

7. Position the new bearings at the bearing bores and install them with the camshaft bearing tool. Center the pulling plate and puller screw to avoid damage to the bearing. Failure to use the correct size collet can cause severe bear-

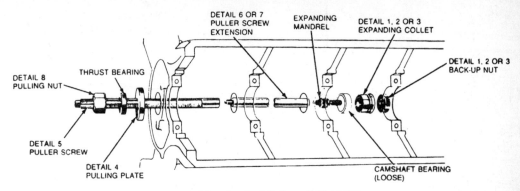

Camshaft bearing installation—3.0L engine

ing damage. Align the holes in the bearings with the oil holes in the cylinder block before pressing the bearings into place.

NOTE: *Make sure the front bearing is installed 0.020–0.035 in. (0.50–0.89mm) below the front face of the cylinder block.*

8. Test fit the camshaft to make sure it turns easily in the bearings. If the camshaft does not turn easily, check if it is bent. If the camshaft is okay, it is possible that one or more of the bearings is cocked or installed incorrectly. If the bearings are okay, check the bearing bore alignment using a straightedge and feeler gauge. If the bores are misaligned, consult an automotive machine shop for possible machining alternatives.

9. Apply a light coating of anaerobic sealer to the sealing edge of a new rear bearing bore plug. Install the plug using a suitable driver.

10. Install the camshaft and crankshaft.

11. Install the engine assembly in the vehicle.

Pistons and Connecting Rods

REMOVAL

NOTE: *Although the pistons and connecting rods can be removed from the engine (after the cylinder head and oil pan are removed) while the engine is still in the car; it is far easier to work on the engine when removed from the car, and advisable for assembly cleanliness.*

1. Remove the engine from the vehicle and mount it on a suitable workstand.

2. Remove the cylinder head(s) and the oil pan.

3. The position of each piston, connecting rod and connecting rod cap should be noted before any are removed, so they can be reinstalled in the same location.

4. Check the tops of the pistons and the sides of the connecting rods for identifying marks. In some engines, the top of the piston will be numbered to correspond with the cylinder number.

The connecting rod and connecting rod cap should have numbers stamped on them where they meet that also correspond with their cylinder number (see illustration). Refer to the firing order diagrams in Chapter 2 to see how the cylinders are numbered. If you cannot see any identifying numbers, use a number punch set and stamp in the numbers yourself.

5. Rotate the crankshaft until the piston to be removed is at the bottom of the cylinder. Check for a ridge at the top of the cylinder bore before removing the piston and connecting rod assembly, referring to the Ridge Removal and Honing procedure.

6. Loosen the connecting rod nuts until the nuts are flush with the ends of the rod bolts.

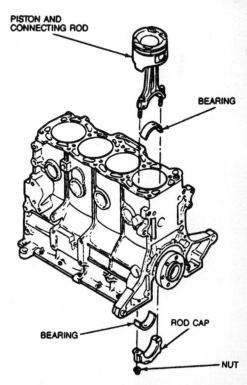

Piston and connecting rod removal—2.2L engine

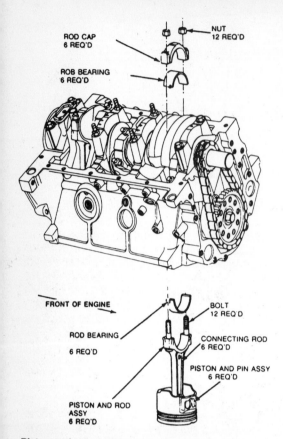

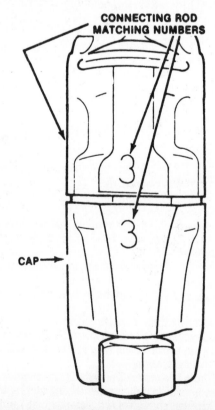

Piston and connecting rod removal—3.0L engine

3. After cleaning, inspect the piston for scuffing, scoring, cracks, pitting or excessive ring groove wear. Replace any piston that is obviously worn.

4. If the piston appears okay, measure the piston diameter using a micrometer. Measure the piston diameter in the thrust direction. On 2.2L engine, measure 0.0709 in. (18mm) below the oil ring groove. On 3.0L engine, measure in line with the centerline of the piston pin.

5. Measure the cylinder bore diameter using a bore gauge, or with a telescope gauge and micrometer. The measurement should be made in the piston thrust direction (perpendicular to the piston pin), about 2½ in. (63.5mm) below the cylinder block deck.

6. Subtract the piston diameter measurement made in Step 4 from the cylinder bore measurement made in Step 5. This is the piston-to-bore clearance. If the clearance is within specification, light finish honing is all that is necessary. If the clearance is excessive, the cylinder must be bored and the piston replaced. Consult an automotive machine shop. If the pistons are replaced, the piston rings must also be replaced.

7. If the piston-to-bore clearance is okay, check the ring groove clearance. Insert the ring that will be used in the ring groove and check

Using a hammer and a brass drift or piece of wood, lightly tap on the nuts/bolts until the connecting rod cap is loosened from the connecting rod. Remove the nuts, rod cap and lower bearing insert.

7. Slip a piece of snug fitting rubber hose over each rod bolt, to prevent the bolt threads from damaging the crankshaft during removal.

8. Using a hammer handle or piece of wood or plastic, tap the rod and piston upward in the bore until the piston rings clear the cylinder block. Remove the piston and connecting rod assembly from the top of the cylinder bore.

CLEANING AND INSPECTION

1. Remove the piston rings using a piston ring expander. Refer to the Piston Ring Replacement procedure.

2. Clean the ring grooves with a ring groove cleaner, being careful not to cut into the piston metal. Heavy carbon deposits can be cleaned from the top of the piston with a wire brush, however, do not use a wire wheel on the ring grooves or lands. Clean the oil drain holes in the ring grooves. Clean all remaining dirt, carbon and varnish from the piston with a suitable solvent and a brush; do not use a caustic solution.

Cylinder number location on connecting rods

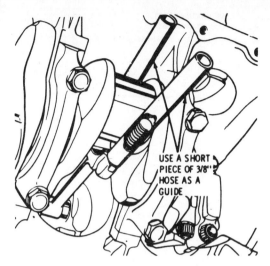

Slip pieces of rubber hose over the connecting rod bolts to protect the crankshaft during the removal procedure

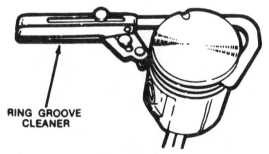

Removing the piston and connecting rod assembly

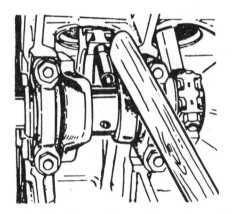

RING GROOVE CLEANER

Cleaning the piston ring grooves

the clearance with a feeler gauge, as shown. Compare your measurement with specification. Replace the piston if the ring groove clearance is not within specification.

8. Check the connecting rod for damage or obvious wear. Check for signs of fractures and check the bearing bore for out-of-round and taper.

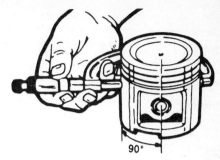

Measuring piston diameter

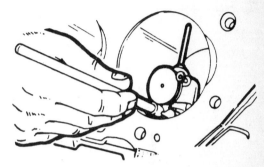

Measuring the cylinder bore diameter with a bore gauge

9. A shiny surface on the pin boss side of the piston usually indicates that the connecting rod is bent or the wrist pin hole is not in proper relation to the piston skirt and ring grooves.

10. Abnormal connecting rod bearing wear can be caused by either a bent connecting rod, an improperly machined journal, or a tapered connecting rod bore.

11. Twisted connecting rods will not create an easily identifiable wear pattern, but badly twisted rods will disturb the action of the entire piston, rings, and connecting rod assembly and may be the cause of excessive oil consumption.

12. If a connecting rod problem is suspected, consult an automotive machine shop to have the rod checked.

RIDGE REMOVAL AND HONING

1. Before the piston is removed from the cylinder, check for a ridge at the top of the cylinder bore. This ridge occurs because the piston ring does not travel all the way to the top of the bore, thereby leaving an unused portion of cylinder bore.

2. Clean away any carbon buildup at the top of the cylinder with sand paper, in order to see the extent of the ridge more clearly. If the ridge is slight, it will be safe to remove the pistons without damaging the rings or piston ring lands. If the ridge is severe, and easily catches your fingernail, it will have to be removed using a ridge reamer.

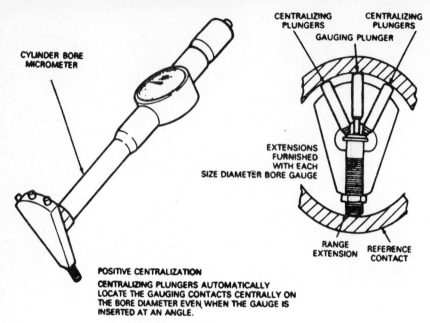

CENTRALIZING PLUNGERS

CENTRALIZING PLUNGERS

GAUGING PLUNGER

CYLINDER BORE MICROMETER

EXTENSIONS FURNISHED WITH EACH SIZE DIAMETER BORE GAUGE

RANGE EXTENSION

REFERENCE CONTACT

POSITIVE CENTRALIZATION
CENTRALIZING PLUNGERS AUTOMATICALLY LOCATE THE GAUGING CONTACTS CENTRALLY ON THE BORE DIAMETER EVEN WHEN THE GAUGE IS INSERTED AT AN ANGLE.

Typical bore gauge configuration

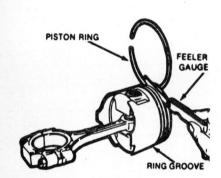

PISTON RING

FEELER GAUGE

RING GROOVE

Checking ring groove clearance

NOTE: *A severe ridge is an indication of excessive bore wear. Before removing the piston, check the cylinder bore diameter with a bore gauge, as explained in the piston and connecting rod cleaning and inspection procedure. Compare your measurement with specification. If the bore is excessively worn, the cylinder will have to be bored oversize and the piston and rings replaced.*

3. Install the ridge removal tool in the top of the cylinder bore. Carefully follow the manufacturers instructions for operation. Only remove the amount of material necessary to remove the ridge.

WARNING: *Be very careful if you are unfamiliar with operating a ridge reamer. It is very easy to remove more cylinder bore material than you want, possibly requiring a cylinder overbore and piston replacement that may not have been necessary.*

4. After the piston and connecting rod as-

sembly have been removed, check the clearances as explained in the piston and connecting rod cleaning and inspection procedure, to determine whether boring and honing or just light honing are required. If boring is necessary, consult an automotive machine shop. If light honing is all that is necessary, proceed to Step 5.

5. Honing is best done with the crankshaft removed, to prevent damage to the crankshaft and to make post-honing cleaning easier, as the honing process will scatter metal particles. However, if you do not want to remove the crankshaft, position the connecting rod journal for the cylinder being honed as far away from the bottom of the cylinder bore as possible, and wrap a shop cloth around the journal.

6. Honing can be done either with a flexible glaze breaker type hone or with a rigid hone that has honing stones and guide shoes. The flexible hone removes the least amount of metal, and is especially recommended if your piston-to-cylinder bore clearance is on the loose side. The flexible hone is useful to provide a finish on which the new piston rings will seat. A rigid hone will remove more material than the flexible hone and requires more operator skill.

7. Regardless of which type of hone you use, carefully follow the manufacturers instructions for operation.

8. The hone should be moved up and down the bore at sufficient speed to obtain a uniform finish. A rigid hone will provide a definite cross-hatch finish; operate the rigid hone at a speed to obtain a 45–65° included angle in the cross-

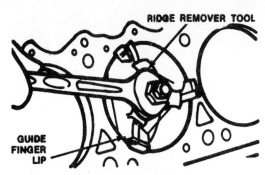

Operating a typical ridge removal tool

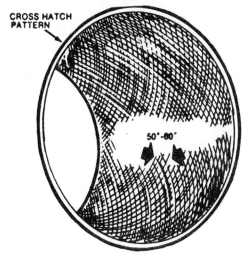

Cylinder bore cross-hatch pattern after honing

hatch. The finish marks should be clean but not sharp, free from embedded particles and torn or folded metal.

9. Periodically during the honing procedure, thoroughly clean the cylinder bore and check the piston-to-bore clearance with the piston for that cylinder.

10. After honing is completed, thoroughly wash the cylinder bores and the rest of the engine with hot water and detergent. Scrub the bores well with a stiff bristle brush and rinse thoroughly with hot water. Thorough cleaning is essential, for if any abrasive material is left in the cylinder bore, it will rapidly wear the new rings and the cylinder bore. If any abrasive material is left in the rest of the engine, it will be picked up by the oil and carried throughout the engine, damaging bearings and other parts.

11. After the bores are cleaned, wipe them down with a clean cloth coated with light engine oil, to keep them from rusting.

PISTON PIN REPLACEMENT

Both the 2.2L and 3.0L engines utilize pressed-in wrist pins, which can only be removed with a press and special fixtures. At-

tempting to remove the wrist pins with other than these special fixtures can result in damage to the piston and/or connecting rod. If a wrist pin problem is suspected (too tight, too loose, etc.) consult an automotive machine shop.

PISTON RING REPLACEMENT

1. Remove the piston rings from the piston using a piston ring expander.

2. Clean the piston ring grooves, check the piston-to-cylinder bore clearance and check the ring groove clearance as explained in the piston and connecting rod cleaning and inspection procedure.

3. After the cylinder bores have been finish honed and cleaned, check the piston ring end gap. Compress the piston rings to be used in the cylinder, one at a time, into that cylinder. Using an inverted piston, push the ring down into the cylinder bore area where normal ring wear is not encountered.

4. Measure the ring end gap with a feeler gauge and compare to specification. A gap that is too tight is more harmful than one that is too loose (If ring end gap is excessively loose, the cylinder bore is probably worn beyond specification).

5. If the ring end gap is too tight, carefully remove the ring and file the ends squarely with a fine file to obtain the proper clearance.

6. Install the rings on the piston, lowest ring first. The lowest (oil) ring is installed by hand; the top 2 (compression) rings must be installed using a piston ring expander. There is a high risk of breaking or distorting the compression rings if they are installed by hand.

7. Install the oil ring spacer in the bottom ring groove. Make sure the ends butt together and do not overlap. The ends must be on a solid portion of the piston, not over a drain hole.

8. Start the end of an oil ring rail ring into the oil ring groove above the spacer. The end gap must be approximately 1 in. (25.4mm) away from the spacer ends. Finish installing the rail ring by spiraling it the remainder of the way on. Repeat the rail installation with the

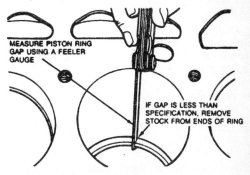

Checking piston ring end gap

A

ENDS MUST BUTT TOGETHER

SPACER GAP

Place spacer in groove with ends over solid portion of groove bottom.

B

RAIL END

SPACER GAP

Spiral remaining rail into groove below spacer. Locate rail gap approximately 1" to right of spacer ends.

C

RAIL GAP

RAIL END

SPACER GAP

With thumb holding spacer ends, spiral steel rail into groove above spacer. Locate rail gap approximately 1" to left of spacer ends.

Installing the oil ring

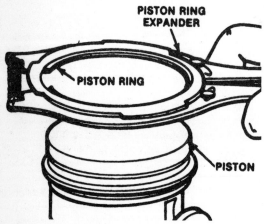

PISTON RING EXPANDER

PISTON RING

PISTON

Installing the compression ring using a ring expander

other rail ring. Its gap must be approximately 1 in. (25.4mm) on the other side of the spacer ends.

9. Install the lower compression ring in the piston ring expander with the proper side up. The piston ring packaging should contain instructions as to the directions the ring sides should face. Spread the ring with the expander and install it on the piston.

10. Repeat Step 9 to install the top compression ring. Space the compression ring gaps approximately 2 in. (50.8mm) on opposite sides of the oil ring gaps.

NOTE: *If the instructions on the ring packaging differ from this information regarding ring gap positioning, follow the ring manufacturers instructions.*

ROD BEARING REPLACEMENT

1. Inspect the rod bearings for scoring, chipping or other wear. See illustration for typical bearing wear patterns.

CRATERS OR POCKETS

FATIGUE FAILURE

BRIGHT (POLISHED) SECTIONS

IMPROPER SEATING

SCRATCHES   DIRT IMBEDDED INTO BEARING MATERIAL

SCRATCHED BY DIRT

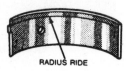

OVERLAY WIPED OUT

LACK OF OIL OR IMPROPER CLEARANCE

OVERLAY GONE FROM EDGES

HOURGLASSING

RADIUS RIDE

RADIUS RIDE

Typical plain bearing wear patterns

2. Inspect the crankshaft rod bearing journal for wear. Measure the journal diameter in several locations around the journal and compare to specification. If the crankshaft journal is scored or has deep ridges, or its diameter is below specification, the crankshaft must be removed from the engine and reground. Consult an automotive machine shop.

3. If the crankshaft journal appears usable, clean it and the rod bearing shells until they are completely free of oil. Blow any oil from the oil hole in the crankshaft.

NOTE: *The journal surfaces and bearing shells must be completely free of oil to get an accurate reading with Plastigage®.*

4. Place a strip of Plastigage® lengthwise along the bottom center of the lower bearing shell, then install the cap with the shell and torque the connecting rod nuts to specification.

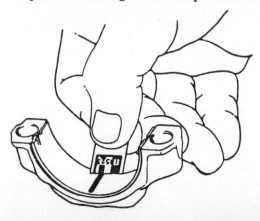

Checking rod bearing clearance using Plastigage®

Do not turn the crankshaft with the Plastigage® installed in the bearing.

5. Remove the bearing cap with the shell. The flattened Plastigage® will either be sticking to the bearing shell or the crankshaft journal.

6. Using the printed scale on the Plastigage® package, measure the flattened Plastigage® at its widest point. The number on the scale that most closely corresponds to the width of the Plastigage® indicates the bearing clearance in thousandths of an inch or hundreths of a millimeter.

7. Compare your findings with the bearing clearance specification. If the bearing clearance is excessive, the bearing must be replaced or the crankshaft must be ground and the bearing replaced.

NOTE: *If the crankshaft is still at standard size (has not been ground undersize), bearing shell sets of 0.001, (0.0254mm) 0.002 (0.050mm) and 0.003 in. (0.0762mm) over standard size are available to correct excessive bearing clearance.*

8. After clearance measuring is completed, be sure to remove the Plastigage® from the crankshaft and/or bearing shell.

9. For final bearing shell installation, make sure the connecting rod and rod cap bearing saddles are clean and free of nicks or burrs. Install the bearing shells in the connecting rod, making sure the bearing shell tangs are seated in the notches.

NOTE: *Be careful when handling any plain bearings. Your hands and the working area should be clean. Dirt is easily embedded in the bearing surface and the bearings are easily scratched or damaged.*

INSTALLATION

1. Make sure the cylinder bore and crankshaft journal are clean.

2. Position the crankshaft journal at its furthest position away from the bottom of the cylinder bore.

3. Coat the cylinder bore with light engine oil.

4. Make sure the rod bearing shells are correctly installed. Install the rubber hoses over the connecting rod bolts to protect the crankshaft during installation.

5. Make sure the piston rings are properly installed and the ring end gaps are correctly positioned. Install a piston ring compressor over the piston and rings and compress the piston rings into their grooves. Follow the ring compressor manufacturers instructions.

6. Place the piston and connecting rod assembly into the cylinder bore. Make sure the assembly is the correct one for that bore and that the piston and connecting rod are facing in the proper direction. Most pistons have an arrow or

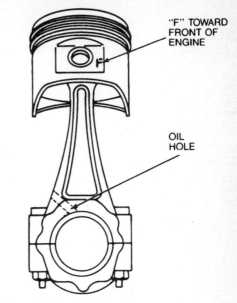

F faces the front of the engine

Piston and connecting rod positioning—2.2L engine

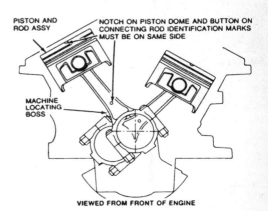

Piston and connecting rod positioning—3.0L engine

notch on the top of the piston, or the letter **F** appears somewhere on the piston to indicate "front", meaning this side should face the front of the engine.

7. Make sure the ring compressor is seated squarely on the block deck surface. If the compressor is not seated squarely, a ring could pop out from beneath the compressor and hang up on the deck surface, as the piston is tapped into the bore, possibly breaking the ring.

8. Make sure that the connecting rod is not hung up on the crankshaft counterweights and is in position to come straight on to the crankshaft.

9. Tap the piston slowly into the bore, making sure the compressor remains squarely against the block deck. When the piston is completely in the bore, remove the ring compressor.

10. Coat the crankshaft journal and the bear-

ing shells with engine assembly lube or clean engine oil. Pull the connecting rod onto the crankshaft journal. After the rod is seated, remove the rubber hoses from the rod bolts.

11. Install the rod bearing cap. Lightly oil the connecting rod bolt threads and install the rod nuts. Torque to specification.

12. After each piston and connecting rod assembly is installed, turn the crankshaft over several times and check for binding. If there is a problem and the crankshaft will not turn, or turns with great difficulty, it will be easier to find the problem (rod cap on backwards, broken

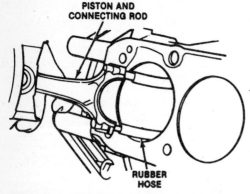

Installing the piston and connecting rod assembly—2.2L engine

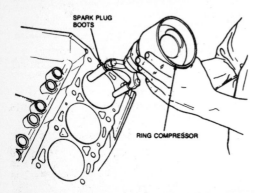

Installing the piston and connecting rod assembly—3.0L engine

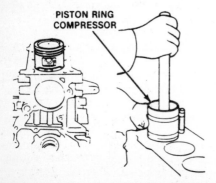

Installing the piston using the ring compressor

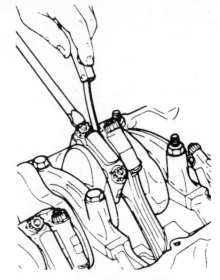

Checking connecting rod side clearance

ring, etc.) than if all the assemblies are installed.

13. Check the clearance between the sides of the connecting rods and the crankshaft using a feeler gauge. Spread the rods slightly with a screwdriver to insert the gauge. If the clearance is below the minimum specification, the connecting rod will have to be removed and machined to provide adequate clearance. If the clearance is excessive, substitute an unworn rod and recheck. If the clearance is still excessive, the crankshaft must be welded and reground, or replaced.

14. Install the oil pump (3.0L engine), oil pan and cylinder head(s).

15. Install the engine in the vehicle.

Rear Main Seal

REMOVAL AND INSTALLATION

2.2L Engine

1. Disconnect the negative battery cable.
2. Raise and safely support the vehicle.
3. Remove the transaxle assembly. Refer to Chapter 7.
4. If equipped with a manual transaxle, remove the clutch and flywheel assembly. Refer to Chapter 7.
5. If equipped with an automatic transaxle, remove the flexplate-to-crankshaft bolts, the flexplate and shim plates.
6. If necessary, remove the rear engine plate.
7. Remove the rear oil seal housing mounting bolts, the housing and the gasket.
8. Using a small prybar, pry the oil seal from the oil seal housing. Clean the gasket mounting surfaces.

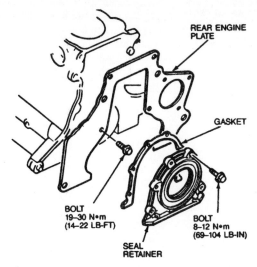

Rear main seal removal and installation—2.2L engine

To install:

9. Clean the oil seal housing. Coat the oil seal and the housing with clean engine oil.

10. Press the seal into the seal housing using a suitable installer. Make sure the hollow side of the seal is facing toward the engine.

11. Using a new gasket, install the rear oil seal housing and torque the seal housing-to-engine bolts to 69–104 inch lbs. (8–12 Nm). Trim the excess gasket material off of the housing after installation.

12. Install the rear engine plate, if removed. Tighten the bolts to 14–22 ft. lbs. (19–30 Nm).

13. Install the clutch and flywheel assembly or the flexplate, as applicable. Tighten the flywheel or flexplate bolts to 71–76 ft. lbs. (96–103 Nm).

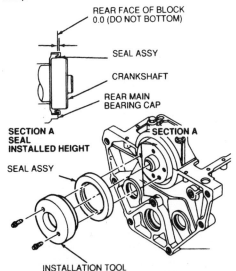

Rear main seal installation—3.0L engine

14. Install the transaxle, lower the vehicle and connect the negative battery cable.

3.0L Engine

1. Disconnect the negative battery cable.
2. Raise and safely support the vehicle.
3. Remove the transaxle assembly. Refer to Chapter 7.
4. Remove the clutch/flywheel assembly if equipped with manual transaxle or the flexplate if equipped with automatic transaxle. Refer to Chapter 7.
5. Using a sharp awl, punch a hole into the seal metal surface between the lip and the block. Use a screw and a slide hammer to pull the seal out.

To install:

6. Apply engine oil to the outer lips and inner seal edge. Using a seal installation tool, install the new rear main oil seal. Make sure the seal is seated properly.

7. Install the clutch/flywheel assembly or flexplate, as applicable. Tighten the flywheel or flexplate bolts to 54–64 ft. lbs. (73–87 Nm).

8. Install the transaxle assembly and lower the vehicle. Connect the negative battery cable.

Crankshaft and Main Bearings
REMOVAL AND INSTALLATION
2.2L Engine

1. Remove the engine assembly from the vehicle and install on a suitable workstand.
2. Remove the cylinder head, oil pan, oil pump and the flywheel.
3. Remove the piston and connecting rod assemblies. Refer to the procedure in this Chapter.
4. Remove the rear main seal housing.
5. Make sure the main bearing caps are numbered so they can be reinstalled in their original positions. Remove the bolts, then remove the bearing caps.
6. Lift the crankshaft from the cylinder block.
7. Inspect the crankshaft and bearings and repair and/or replace as necessary.

To install:

8. After cleaning, inspecting and measuring the crankshaft and checking the main bearing clearance, install the crankshaft. Apply engine assembly lube or clean engine oil to the upper bearing shells prior to installation.

9. Apply engine assembly lube or clean engine oil to the lower bearing shells, then install the main bearing caps in their original positions. Tighten the bolts to 61–65 ft. lbs. (82–88 Nm).

10. After each cap is tightened, check to see

and feel that the crankshaft can be rotated by hand. If not, remove the bearing cap and check for the source of the interference.

11. Install the rear main seal housing and the flywheel.

12. Install the piston and connecting rod assemblies.

13. Install the oil pump and the oil pan.

14. Install the cylinder head.

15. Install the engine assembly in the vehicle.

3.0L Engine

1. Remove the engine assembly from the vehicle and install on a suitable workstand.

2. Remove the accessory drive belt, water pump belt, water pump and pump mounting bracket.

3. Remove the crankshaft damper and the timing chain cover.

4. Remove the timing chain and sprockets.

5. Remove the flywheel. Remove the oil pan and the oil pump and intermediate shaft assembly.

6. Make sure all connecting rod and main bearing caps are numbered so they can be reinstalled in their original positions. Turn the crankshaft until the connecting rod from which the cap is being removed is up, then remove the cap.

7. Install snug-fitting rubber hoses over the rod bolts, to prevent damaging the crankshaft, then push the piston and connecting rod assembly up in the cylinder. Repeat this procedure for the remaining piston and connecting rod assemblies.

8. Remove the main bearing caps.

9. Lift the crankshaft from the cylinder block.

10. Inspect the crankshaft and bearings and repair and/or replace as necessary.

To install:

11. After cleaning, inspecting and measuring the crankshaft and checking the main and connecting rod bearing clearance, install the crankshaft. Apply engine assembly lube or clean engine oil to the upper main bearing shells prior to installation.

12. Apply engine assembly lube or clean engine oil to the lower bearing shells, then install the main bearing caps in their original positions. Apply RTV sealer to the rear main bearing cap parting line on the cylinder block.

13. Before tightening the main cap bolts, pry the crankshaft forward against the thrust surface of the upper thrust bearing shell. Hold the thrust bearing cap to the rear to align the thrust surfaces of both halves of the bearing. Retain the forward pressure on the crankshaft and tighten the cap bolts to 60 ft. lbs. (80 Nm).

14. Lubricate the upper connecting rod bearing shells with engine assembly lube or clean engine oil. Turn the crankshaft until the connecting rod journal is at the bottom of the stroke, then pull the piston and connecting rod assembly toward the journal until it is seated on the crankshaft.

15. Lubricate the lower connecting rod bearing shells with engine assembly lube or clean engine oil, then install the rod cap. Tighten the connecting rod nuts to specification. After all connecting rods have been installed on the crankshaft, check the connecting rod side clearance.

16. Install the timing chain, sprockets, timing cover and crankshaft damper.

17. Install a new rear main seal.

18. Clean the oil pan, oil pump and screen. Prime the oil pump by filling the inlet opening with oil and rotating the pump shaft until oil emerges from the outlet opening. Install the oil pump and intermediate shaft assembly.

19. Install the oil pan and the flywheel.

20. Install the water pump, pump mounting bracket, water pump belt and accessory drive belt.

21. Install the engine assembly in the vehicle.

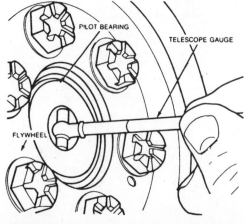

Checking the pilot bearing on vehicles with manual transaxle

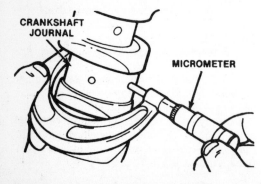

Measuring the crankshaft journal diameter

CLEANING AND INSPECTION

1. Clean the crankshaft with solvent and a brush. Clean the oil passages with a suitable brush, then blow them out with compressed air.

2. Inspect the crankshaft for obvious damage or wear. Check the main and connecting rod journals for cracks, scratches, grooves or scores. Inspect the crankshaft oil seal surface for nicks, sharp edges or burrs that could damage the oil seal or cause premature seal wear.

3. If the crankshaft passes a visual inspection, measure the main and connecting rod journals for wear, out-of-roundness or taper, using a micrometer. Measure in at least 4 places around each journal and compare your findings with the journal diameter specifications.

4. If equipped with a manual transaxle, check the fit of the clutch pilot bearing in the bore of the crankshaft. The bearing is pressed into the crankshaft and should not be loose. Inspect the inner surface of the bearing for wear or a bell-mouth condition. Check the inside diameter of the bearing for wear or damage. Check the bearing for roughness, evidence of overheating, or loss of lubricant and replace, as necessary.

5. Check journal runout using a dial indicator. Support the crankshaft in V-blocks and check the runout as shown. Compare to specifications.

6. If the crankshaft fails any inspection for wear or damage, it must be reground or replaced.

NOTE: *Due to the design of the main journal fillets, the main journals on the 3.0L engine must not be machined more than 0.010 in. (0.254mm). Further main journal refinishing may result in fatigue failure of the crankshaft.*

BEARING REPLACEMENT

1. Inspect the bearings for scoring, chipping or other wear. See illustration for typical bearing wear patterns.

2. Inspect the crankshaft journals as detailed in the Cleaning and Inspection procedure.

3. If the crankshaft journals appear usable, clean them and the bearing shells until they are completely free of oil. Blow any oil from the oil hole in the crankshaft.

NOTE: *The journal surfaces and bearing shells must be completely free of oil to get an accurate reading with Plastigage®.*

4. Place a strip of Plastigage® lengthwise along the bottom center of the lower bearing shell, then install the cap with the shell and torque the connecting rod nuts or main cap bolts to specification. Do not turn the crankshaft with the Plastigage® installed in the bearing.

5. Remove the bearing cap with the shell. The flattened Plastigage® will either be sticking to the bearing shell or the crankshaft journal.

6. Using the printed scale on the Plastigage® package, measure the flattened Plastigage® at its widest point. The number on the scale that most closely corresponds to the width of the Plastigage® indicates the bearing clearance in thousandths of an inch or hundreths of a millimeter.

7. Compare your findings with the bearing clearance specification. If the bearing clearance is excessive, the bearing must be replaced or the crankshaft must be ground and the bearing replaced.

NOTE: *If the crankshaft is still at standard size (has not been ground undersize), bearing shell sets of 0.001 in. , (0.0254mm) 0.002 in. (0.050mm) and 0.003 in. (0.0762mm) over standard size are available to correct excessive bearing clearance.*

8. After clearance measuring is completed, be sure to remove the Plastigage® from the crankshaft and/or bearing shell.

9. For final bearing shell installation, make sure the connecting rod and rod cap and/or cylinder block and main cap bearing saddles are clean and free of nicks or burrs. Install the bearing shells in the bearing saddles, making

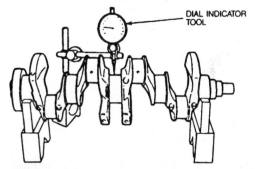

Checking crankshaft journal runout

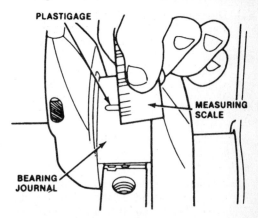

Checking main bearing clearance using Plastigage®

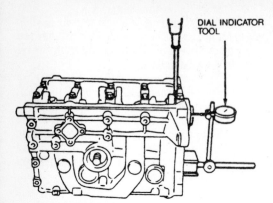

FIG. 190 Checking crankshaft endplay

Checking crankshaft endplay

sure the bearing shell tangs are seated in the notches.

NOTE: *Be careful when handling any plain bearings. Your hands and the working area should be clean. Dirt is easily embedded in the bearing surface and the bearings are easily scratched or damaged.*

10. After all of the main bearing cap bolts have been tightened, mount a dial indicator on the end of the cylinder block with the indicator foot resting on the end of the crankshaft. Move the crankshaft back and forth with a prybar, being careful not to damage the crankshaft, bearings or cylinder block, and observe the dial indicator. Check the reading against the crankshaft endplay specification. If the endplay is excessive, it can be corrected using a thicker thrust bearing or by removing the crankshaft and welding and regrinding the thrust journal.

Flywheel/Flexplate

REMOVAL AND INSTALLATION

1. Disconnect the negative battery cable.
2. Raise and safely support the vehicle.
3. Remove the transaxle assembly. Refer to Chapter 7.
4. If equipped with a manual transaxle, remove the clutch assembly. Refer to Chapter 7.
5. If equipped with manual transaxle, remove the flywheel-to-crankshaft bolts and the flywheel. If equipped with automatic transaxle, remove the flexplate-to-crankshaft bolts and the flexplate. Remove the flexplate shims, if equipped.
6. Installation is the reverse of the removal procedure. Tighten the flywheel/flexplate bolts to 71–76 ft. lbs. (96–103 Nm) on 2.2L engine or 54–64 ft. lbs. (73–87 Nm) on 3.0L engine.

EXHAUST SYSTEM

Safety Precautions

Exhaust system work can be the most dangerous type of work you can do on your car. Always observe the following precautions:

• Support the car extra securely. Not only will you often be working directly under it, but you'll frequently be using a lot of force, say, heavy hammer blows, to dislodge rusted parts. This can cause a car that's improperly supported to shift and possibly fall.

• Wear goggles. Exhaust system parts are always rusty. Metal chips can be dislodged, even when you're only turning rusted bolts. Attempting to pry pipes apart with a chisel makes the chips fly even more frequently.

• If you're using a cutting torch, keep it a great distance from either the fuel tank or lines. Stop what you're doing and feel the temperature of the fuel bearing pipes on the tank frequently. Even slight heat can expand and/or vaporize fuel, resulting in accumulated vapor, or even a liquid leak, near your torch.

• Watch where your hammer blows fall and make sure you hit squarely. You could easily tap a brake or fuel line when you hit an exhaust system part with a glancing blow. Inspect all lines and hoses in the area where you've been working.

CAUTION: *Be very careful when working on or near the catalytic converter! External temperatures can reach 1,500°F (816°C) and more, causing severe burns. Removal or installation should be performed only on a cold exhaust system.*

Special Tools

A number of special exhaust system tools can be rented from auto supply houses or local stores that rent special equipment. A common one is a tail pipe expander, designed to enable you to join pipes of identical diameter.

It may also be quite helpful to use solvents designed to loosen rusted bolts or flanges. Soaking rusted parts the night before you do the job can speed the work of freeing rusted parts considerably. Remember that these solvents are often flammable. Apply only to parts after they are cool!

INSPECTION

Once or twice a year, check the muffler(s) and pipes for signs of corrosion and damage. Check the hangers for wear, cracks or hardening. Check the heat shields for corrosion or damage. Replace components as necessary.

All vehicles are equipped with a catalytic converter, which is attached to the front exhaust pipe. The exhaust system is bolted together. Replacement parts are usually the same as the original system, with the exception of some mufflers. Splash shield removal will be required, in some cases, for removal and installation clearance.

Use only the proper size sockets or wrenches when unbolting system components. Do not tighten completely until all components are attached, aligned, and suspended. Check the system for leaks after the installation is completed.

Converter Inlet Pipe (Front Exhaust Pipe)

REMOVAL AND INSTALLATION

2.2L Engine

1. Disconnect the negative battery cable. Raise and safely the vehicle.
2. Remove the clamp securing the heat shield.
3. Remove the nuts that attach the front

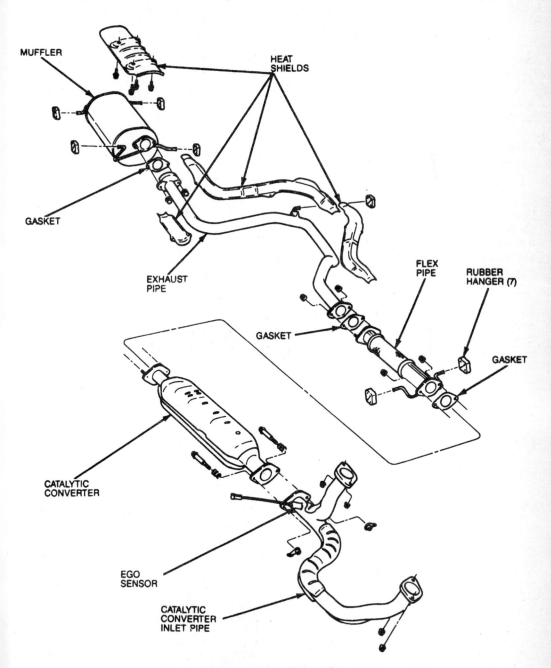

MUFFLER

HEAT SHIELDS

GASKET

EXHAUST PIPE

GASKET

FLEX PIPE

RUBBER HANGER (7)

GASKET

CATALYTIC CONVERTER

EGO SENSOR

CATALYTIC CONVERTER INLET PIPE

Exhaust system—3.0L engine

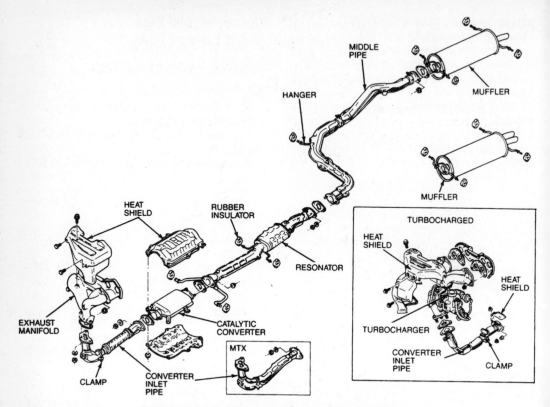

Exhaust system—2.2L engine with automatic transaxle

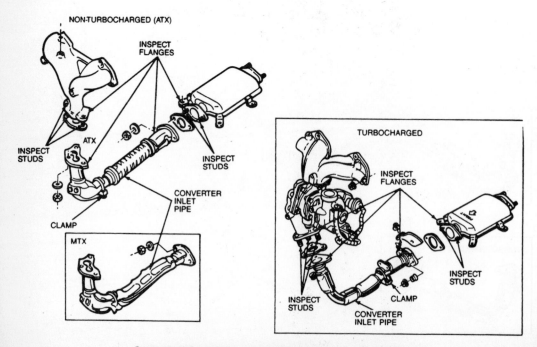

Converter inlet pipe removal and installation—2.2L engine

pipe to the exhaust manifold and to the front of the catalytic converter.

4. Push the converter rearward and remove the front pipe and mounting gaskets.

5. Inspect the mounting studs on the exhaust manifold and catalytic converter for signs of wear or deterioration and replace, as necessary.

To install:

6. Clean the exhaust manifold and converter gasket mounting flange surfaces.

7. Position a new mounting gasket on the converter flange and loosely attach the inlet pipe.

8. Position a new mounting gasket on the exhaust manifold flange and loosely install the inlet pipe.

9. Tighten all nuts and bolts, working from front to rear, making sure that there is no stress placed on the exhaust manifold.

10. Tighten the exhaust manifold to inlet pipe nuts to 26–36 ft. lbs. (34–49 Nm).

11. Tighten the inlet pipe to converter nuts to 40–59 ft. lbs. (55–80 Nm).

12. Install the heat shield clamp. Connect the negative battery cable, start the engine and check for exhaust leaks. Shut off the engine and lower the vehicle.

3.0L Engine

1. Disconnect the negative battery cable. Raise and safely support the vehicle.

2. Disconnect the Heated Exhaust Gas Oxygen (HEGO) sensor electrical connector.

3. Remove the converter-to-inlet pipe attaching bolts, nuts and springs and separate the

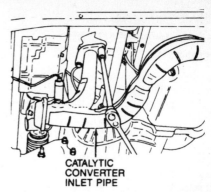

CATALYTIC CONVERTER INLET PIPE

Converter inlet pipe removal and installation—3.0L engine

converter from the inlet pipe. Remove and discard the gasket.

4. Remove the inlet pipe-to-exhaust manifold nuts and remove the inlet pipe. Remove and discard the gaskets.

To install:

5. Install new inlet pipe-to-exhaust manifold gaskets and position the pipe.

6. Grease the nuts and install the inlet pipe-to-exhaust manifold nuts.

7. Install a new gasket between the inlet pipe and the catalytic converter.

8. Install the converter-to-inlet pipe attaching bolts, nuts and springs.

9. If necessary, transfer the HEGO sensor to the new pipe, then connect the electrical connector.

10. Connect the negative battery cable, start the engine and check for exhaust leaks. Shut off the engine and lower the vehicle.

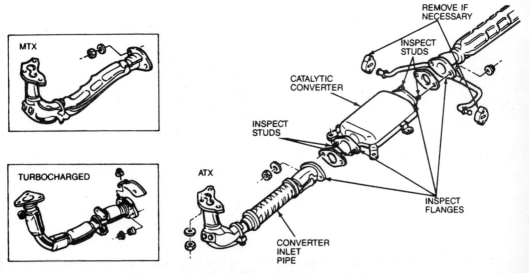

Catalytic converter removal and installation—2.2L engine

Catalytic Converter

REMOVAL AND INSTALLATION

2.2L Engine

1. Disconnect the negative battery cable. Raise and safely support the vehicle.

2. Place a support under the resonator pipe assembly.

3. Remove the mounting nuts from the front and rear of the converter.

4. Remove the front resonator pipe hanger from the mounting grommets. Push the assembly toward the rear and remove the converter.

5. Inspect the mounting studs on the converter for any signs of wear or deterioration and replace, as necessary.

To install:

6. Clean the mounting flanges. Install a front gasket to the converter and loosely install the front of the converter to the inlet pipe.

7. Install a gasket on the rear of the converter and loosely attach the resonator pipe assembly. Secure the resonator pipe assembly front mounting bracket into the mounting grommets.

8. Check the assembly for proper body clearance. Tighten the front mounting nuts to 40-59 ft. lbs. (55–80 Nm). Tighten the rear resonator pipe assembly mounting nuts to 23-34 ft. lbs. (31–46 Nm).

9. Connect the negative battery cable. Start the engine and check for exhaust leaks. Shut off the engine and lower the vehicle.

3.0L Engine

1. Disconnect the negative battery cable. Raise and safely support the vehicle.

2. Remove the converter-to-inlet pipe attaching bolts, nuts and springs. Remove and discard the gasket.

3. Remove the 2 flex pipe-to-converter nuts. Remove and discard the gasket.

4. Remove the catalytic converter. Inspect it for deterioration and restriction and replace, as necessary.

To install:

5. Position the converter and install a new gasket between the converter and the flex pipe. Grease the nuts and install the 2 flex pipe-to-converter nuts.

6. Install a new gasket between the inlet pipe and the catalytic converter. Grease the bolts and nuts and install the converter-to-inlet pipe attaching nuts, bolts and springs.

7. Connect the negative battery cable. Start the engine and check for exhaust leaks. Shut off the engine and lower the vehicle.

Resonator

REMOVAL AND INSTALLATION

2.2L Engine

1. Disconnect the negative battery cable. Raise and safely support the vehicle.

2. Support the exhaust system at the catalytic converter. Remove the front and rear resonator pipe mounting nuts.

3. Remove the resonator from the body mounting grommets. Push the assembly rearward and remove the resonator.

4. Discard the used gaskets. Inspect the mounting flanges, studs and hangers for wear or deterioration and replace, as necessary.

To install:

5. Clean the flange surfaces.

6. Install new gaskets on the flanges and loosely install the resonator assembly. Mount the brackets into the body grommets.

7. Check the body clearance and tighten the front mounting nuts to 23-34 ft. lbs. (31–46 Nm). Tighten the rear flange mounting nuts to 25-38 ft. lbs. (34–52 Nm). Remove the support at the converter.

8. Connect the negative battery cable. Start the engine and check for exhaust leaks. Shut off the engine and lower the vehicle.

Flex Pipe

REMOVAL AND INSTALLATION

3.0L Engine

1. Disconnect the negative battery cable. Raise and safely support the vehicle.

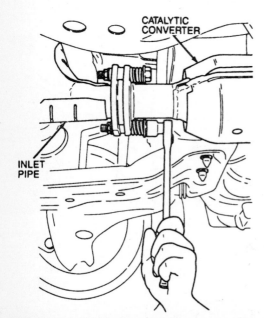

Removing the catalytic converter retaining bolts, nuts and springs—3.0L engine

CATALYTIC CONVERTER

INLET PIPE

2. Remove the 2 flex pipe-to-converter nuts. Remove and discard the gasket.

3. Remove the 2 exhaust pipe-to-flex pipe nuts.

4. Pry the rubber hangers from their mounting hooks and remove the flex pipe. Remove and discard the gasket.

To install:

5. Install a new gasket between the exhaust pipe and flex pipe. Position the flex pipe and attach the rubber hangers.

6. Grease the nuts and install the 2 exhaust pipe-to-flex pipe nuts.

7. Install a new gasket between the flex pipe and the converter. Grease the nuts and install the 2 flex pipe-to-converter nuts.

8. Connect the negative battery cable. Start the engine and check for exhaust leaks. Shut off the engine and lower the vehicle.

Exhaust (Middle) Pipe

REMOVAL AND INSTALLATION

2.2L Engine

1. Disconnect the negative battery cable. Raise and safely support the vehicle.

2. Remove the front and rear pipe mounting nuts.

3. Remove the rubber insulator from the body mount at the middle pipe. Remove the 2 front rubber insulators from the body mounts at the muffler, if necessary.

4. Remove the pipe and discard the gaskets.

5. Inspect the mounting flanges, hangers and mounts for wear or deterioration and replace, as necessary.

To install:

6. Clean the flange surfaces.

7. Install new gaskets on the flanges and loosely install the middle pipe.

8. Install the rubber insulator to the body mount at the middle pipe and the 2 insulators to the body mounts at the muffler, if removed.

9. Check the body clearance and tighten all components, beginning at the front and working toward the rear. Tighten the nuts to 25–38 ft. lbs. (34–52 Nm).

10. Connect the negative battery cable. Start the engine and check for exhaust leaks. Shut off the engine and lower the vehicle.

3.0L Engine

1. Disconnect the negative battery cable. Raise and safely support the vehicle.

2. Remove the 2 exhaust pipe-to-flex pipe nuts and the 2 exhaust pipe-to-muffler nuts.

3. Remove and discard the gaskets.

4. Pry the rubber hanger from its mounting hook and remove the exhaust pipe.

To install:

5. Clean the gasket surfaces on the flanges.

6. Install a new gasket between the exhaust pipe and the muffler. Position the exhaust pipe.

7. Grease the nuts and install the 2 exhaust pipe-to-muffler nuts.

8. Install a new gasket between the exhaust pipe and flex pipe. Grease the nuts and install the 2 exhaust pipe-to-flex pipe nuts.

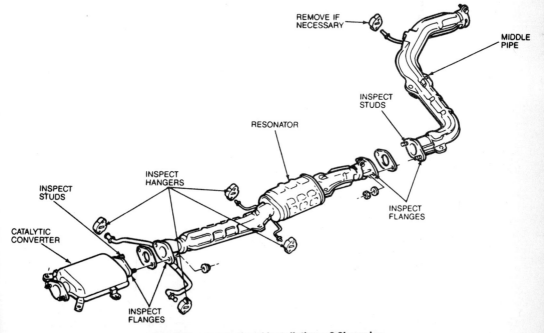

Resonator removal and installation—2.2L engine

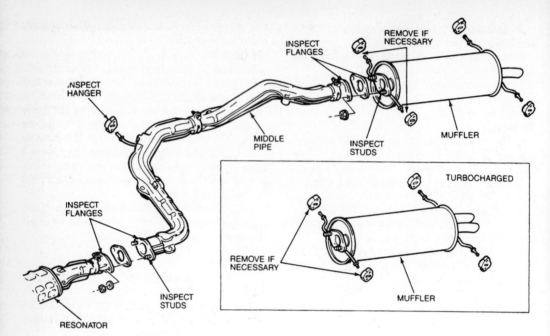

Exhaust (middle) pipe removal and installation—2.2L engine

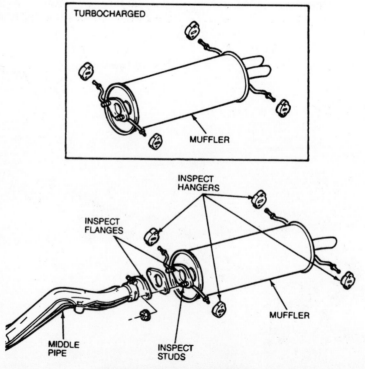

Muffler removal and installation

9. Connect the rubber hanger to its mounting hook.

10. Connect the negative battery cable. Start the engine and check for exhaust leaks. Shut off the engine and lower the vehicle.

Muffler

REMOVAL AND INSTALLATION

1. Disconnect the negative battery cable. Raise and safely support the vehicle.

2. Remove the exhaust pipe-to-muffler mounting nuts.

3. Remove the muffler from the rubber insulators and remove the muffler assembly.

4. Inspect the mounting flange and hangers for wear or deterioration and replace, as necessary.

To install:

5. Clean the flange surfaces.

6. Install a new gasket on the flange and loosely install the muffler assembly. Mount the brackets into the rubber insulators.

7. Check the body clearance and tighten the front mounting nuts to 25–38 ft. lbs. (34–52 Nm).

8. Connect the negative battery cable. Start the engine and check for exhaust leaks. Shut off the engine and lower the vehicle.

Emission Controls

AIR POLLUTION

The earth's atmosphere, at or near sea level, consists of 78% nitrogen, 21% oxygen and 1% other gases, approximately. If it were possible to remain in this state, 100% clean air would result. However, many varied causes allow other gases and particulates to mix with the clean air, causing the air to become unclean or polluted.

Certain of these pollutants are visible while others are invisible, with each having the capability of causing distress to the eyes, ears, throat, skin and respiratory system. Should these pollutants be concentrated in a specific area and under the right conditions, death could result due to the displacement or chemical change of the oxygen content in the air. These pollutants can cause much damage to the environment and to the many man made objects that are exposed to the elements.

To better understand the causes of air pollution, the pollutants can be categorized into 3 separate types, natural, industrial and automotive.

Natural Pollutants

Natural pollution has been present on earth before man appeared and is still a factor to be considered when discussing air pollution, although it causes only a small percentage of the present overall pollution problem existing in our country. It is the direct result of decaying organic matter, wind born smoke and particulates from such natural events as plains and forest fires (ignited by heat or lightning), volcanic ash, sand and dust which can spread over a large area of the countryside.

Such a phenomenon of natural pollution has been recent volcanic eruptions, with the resulting plume of smoke, steam and volcanic ash blotting out the sun's rays as it spreads and rises higher into the atmosphere, where the up-

per air currents catch and carry the smoke and ash, while condensing the steam back into water vapor. As the water vapor, smoke and ash traveled on their journey, the smoke dissipates into the atmosphere while the ash and moisture settle back to earth in a trail hundred of miles long. In many cases, lives are lost and millions of dollars of property damage result, and ironically, man can only stand by and watch it happen.

Industrial Pollution

Industrial pollution is caused primarily by industrial processes, the burning of coal, oil and natural gas, which in turn produces smoke and fumes. Because the burning fuels contain much sulfur, the principal ingredients of smoke and fumes are sulfur dioxide (SO_2) and particulate matter. This type of pollutant occurs most severely during still, damp and cool weather, such as at night. Even in its less severe form, this pollutant is not confined to just cities. Because of air movements, the pollutants move for miles over the surrounding countryside, leaving in its path a barren and unhealthy environment for all living things.

Working with Federal, State and Local mandated rules, regulations and by carefully monitoring the emissions, industries have greatly reduced the amount of pollutant emitted from their industrial sources, striving to obtain an acceptable level. Because of the mandated industrial emission clean up, many land areas and streams in and around the cities that were formerly barren of vegetation and life, have now begun to move back in the direction of nature's intended balance.

Automotive Pollutants

The third major source of air pollution is the automotive emissions. The emissions from the internal combustion engine were not an appreciable problem years ago because of the small number of registered vehicles and the nation's small highway system. However, during the early 1950's, the trend of the American people was to move from the cities to the surrounding suburbs. This caused an immediate problem in the transportation areas because the majority of the suburbs were not afforded mass transit conveniences. This lack of transportation created an attractive market for the automobile manufacturers, which resulted in a dramatic increase in the number of vehicles produced and sold, along with a marked increase in highway construction between cities and the suburbs. Multi-vehicle families emerged with much emphasis placed on the individual vehicle per family member. As the increase in vehicle ownership and usage occurred, so did the pollutant levels in and around the cities, as the suburbanites drove daily to their businesses and employment in the city and its fringe area, returning at the end of the day to their homes in the suburbs.

It was noted that a fog and smoke type haze was being formed and at times, remained in suspension over the cities and did not quickly dissipate. At first this "smog", derived from the words "smoke" and "fog", was thought to result from industrial pollution but it was determined that the automobile emissions were largely to blame. It was discovered that as normal automobile emissions were exposed to sunlight for a period of time, complex chemical reactions would take place.

It was found the smog was a photo chemical layer and was developed when certain oxides of nitrogen (NOx) and unburned hydrocarbons (HC) from the automobile emissions were exposed to sunlight and was more severe when the smog would remain stagnant over an area in which a warm layer of air would settle over the top of a cooler air mass at ground level, trapping and holding the automobile emissions, instead of the emissions being dispersed and diluted through normal air flows. This type of air stagnation was given the name "Temperature Inversion".

Temperature Inversion

In normal weather situations, the surface air is warmed by the heat radiating from the earth's surface and the sun's rays and will rise upward, into the atmosphere, to be cooled through a convection type heat expands with the cooler upper air. As the warm air rises, the surface pollutants are carried upward and dissipated into the atmosphere.

When a temperature inversion occurs, we find the higher air is no longer cooler but warmer than the surface air, causing the cooler surface air to become trapped and unable to move. This warm air blanket can extend from above ground level to a few hundred or even a few thousand feet into the air. As the surface air is trapped, so are the pollutants, causing a severe smog condition. Should this stagnant air mass extend to a few thousand feet high, enough air movement with the inversion takes place to allow the smog layer to rise above ground level but the pollutants still cannot dissipate. This inversion can remain for days over an area, with only the smog level rising or lowering from ground level to a few hundred feet high. Meanwhile, the pollutant levels increases, causing eye irritation, respirator problems, reduced visibility, plant damage and in some cases, cancer type diseases.

This inversion phenomenon was first noted in the Los Angeles, California area. The city lies in a basin type of terrain and during certain weather conditions, a cold air mass is held in the basin while a warmer air mass covers it like a lid.

Because this type of condition was first documented as prevalent in the Los Angeles area, this type of smog was named Los Angeles Smog, although it occurs in other areas where a large concentration of automobiles are used and the air remains stagnant for any length of time.

Internal Combustion Engine Pollutants

Consider the internal combustion engine as a machine in which raw materials must be placed so a finished product comes out. As in any machine operation, a certain amount of wasted material is formed. When we relate this to the internal combustion engine, we find that by putting in air and fuel, we obtain power from this mixture during the combustion process to drive the vehicle. The by-product or waste of this power is, in part, heat and exhaust gases with which we must concern ourselves.

HEAT TRANSFER

The heat from the combustion process can rise to over 4000°F (2204°C). The dissipation of this heat is controlled by a ram air effect, the use of cooling fans to cause air flow and having a liquid coolant solution surrounding the combustion area and transferring the heat of combustion through the cylinder walls and into the coolant. The coolant is then directed to a thin-finned, multi-tubed radiator, from which the excess heat is transferred to the outside air by 1 or all of the 3 heat transfer methods, conduction, convection or radiation.

The cooling of the combustion area is an important part in the control of exhaust emissions. To understand the behavior of the combustion and transfer of its heat, consider the air/fuel charge. It is ignited and the flame front burns progressively across the combustion chamber until the burning charge reaches the cylinder walls. Some of the fuel in contact with the walls is not hot enough to burn, thereby snuffing out or Quenching the combustion process. This leaves unburned fuel in the combustion chamber. This unburned fuel is then forced out of the cylinder along with the exhaust gases and into the exhaust system.

Many attempts have been made to minimize the amount of unburned fuel in the combustion chambers due to the snuffing out or "Quenching", by increasing the coolant temperature and lessening the contact area of the coolant around the combustion area. Design limitations within the combustion chambers prevent the complete burning of the air/fuel charge, so a certain amount of the unburned fuel is still expelled into the exhaust system, regardless of modifications to the engine.

EXHAUST EMISSIONS

Composition Of The Exhaust Gases

The exhaust gases emitted into the atmosphere are a combination of burned and unburned fuel. To understand the exhaust emission and its composition review some basic chemistry.

When the air/fuel mixture is introduced into the engine, we are mixing air, composed of nitrogen (78%), oxygen (21%) and other gases (1%) with the fuel, which is 100% hydrocarbons (HC), in a semi-controlled ratio. As the combustion process is accomplished, power is produced to move the vehicle while the heat of combustion is transferred to the cooling system. The exhaust gases are then composed of nitrogen, a diatomic gas (N_2), the same as was introduced in the engine, carbon dioxide (CO2), the same gas that is used in beverage carbonation and water vapor (H_2O). The nitrogen (N_2), for the most part passes through the engine unchanged, while the oxygen (O_2) reacts (burns) with the hydrocarbons (HC) and produces the carbon dioxide (CO_2) and the water vapors (H_2O). If this chemical process would be the only process to take place, the exhaust emissions would be harmless. However, during the combustion process, other pollutants are formed and are considered dangerous. These pollutants are carbon monoxide (CO), hydrocarbons (HC), oxides of nitrogen (NOx) oxides of sulfur (SOx) and engine particulates.

Lead (Pb), is considered 1 of the particulates and is present in the exhaust gases whenever leaded fuels are used. Lead (Pb) does not dissipate easily. Levels can be high along roadways when it is emitted from vehicles and can pose a health threat. Since the increased usage of unleaded gasoline and the phasing out of leaded gasoline for fuel, this pollutant is gradually diminishing. While not considered a major threat lead is still considered a dangerous pollutant.

HYDROCARBONS

Hydrocarbons (HC) are essentially unburned fuel that have not been successfully burned during the combustion process or have escaped into the atmosphere through fuel evaporation. The main sources of incomplete combustion are rich air/fuel mixtures, low engine temperatures and improper spark timing. The main sources of hydrocarbon emission through fuel evaporation come from the vehicle's fuel tank and carburetor bowl.

To reduce combustion hydrocarbon emission, engine modifications were made to minimize dead space and surface area in the combustion chamber. In addition the air/fuel mixture was made more lean through improved carburetion, fuel injection and by the addition of external controls to aid in further combustion of the hydrocarbons outside the engine. Two such methods were the addition of an air injection system, to inject fresh air into the exhaust manifolds and the installation of a catalytic converter, a unit that is able to burn traces of hydrocarbons without affecting the internal combustion process or fuel economy.

To control hydrocarbon emissions through fuel evaporation, modifications were made to the fuel tank and carburetor bowl to allow storage of the fuel vapors during periods of engine shut-down, and at specific times during engine operation, to purge and burn these same vapors by blending them with the air/fuel mixture.

CARBON MONOXIDE

Carbon monoxide is formed when not enough oxygen is present during the combustion process to convert carbon (C) to carbon dioxide (CO_2). An increase in the carbon monoxide (CO) emission is normally accompanied by an increase in the hydrocarbon (HC) emission because of the lack of oxygen to completely burn all of the fuel mixture.

Carbon monoxide (CO) also increases the rate at which the photo chemical smog is formed by speeding up the conversion of nitric oxide (NO) to nitrogen dioxide (NO_2). To accomplish this, carbon monoxide (CO) combines with oxygen (O_2) and nitrogen dioxide (NO_2) to produce carbon dioxide (CO_2) and nitrogen dioxide (NO_2). ($CO + O_2 + NO = CO_2 + NO_2$).

The dangers of carbon monoxide, which is an odorless, colorless toxic gas are many. When carbon monoxide is inhaled into the lungs and passed into the blood stream, oxygen is replaced by the carbon monoxide in the red blood cells, causing a reduction in the amount of oxygen being supplied to the many parts of the body. This lack of oxygen causes headaches, lack of coordination, reduced mental alertness and should the carbon monoxide concentration be high enough, death could result.

NITROGEN

Normally, nitrogen is an inert gas. When heated to approximately 2500°F (1371°C) through the combustion process, this gas becomes active and causes an increase in the nitric oxide (NOx) emission.

Oxides of nitrogen (NOx) are composed of approximately 97–98% nitric oxide ($NO2$). Nitric oxide is a colorless gas but when it is passed into the atmosphere, it combines with oxygen and forms nitrogen dioxide ($NO2$). The nitrogen dioxide then combines with chemically active hydrocarbons (HC) and when in the presence of sunlight, causes the formation of photo chemical smog.

OZONE

To further complicate matters, some of the nitrogen dioxide (NO_2) is broken apart by the sunlight to form nitric oxide and oxygen. (NO_2 + sunlight = NO + O). This single atom of oxygen then combines with diatomic (meaning 2 atoms) oxygen (O_2) to form ozone (O_3). Ozone is 1 of the smells associated with smog. It has a pungent and offensive odor, irritates the eyes and lung tissues, affects the growth of plant life and causes rapid deterioration of rubber products. Ozone can be formed by sunlight as well as electrical discharge into the air.

The most common discharge area on the automobile engine is the secondary ignition electrical system, especially when inferior quality spark plug cables are used. As the surge of high voltage is routed through the secondary cable, the circuit builds up an electrical field around the wire, acting upon the oxygen in the surrounding air to form the ozone. The faint glow along the cable with the engine running that may be visible on a dark night, is called the "corona discharge." It is the result of the electrical field passing from a high along the cable, to a low in the surrounding air, which forms the ozone gas. The combination of corona and ozone has been a major cause of cable deterioration. Recently, different types and better quality insulating materials have lengthened the life of the electrical cables.

Although ozone at ground level can be harmful, ozone is beneficial to the earth's inhabitants. By having a concentrated ozone layer called the 'ozonosphere', between 10 and 20 miles (16–32km) up in the atmosphere much of the ultra violet radiation from the sun's rays are absorbed and screened. If this ozone layer were not present, much of the earth's surface would be burned, dried and unfit for human life.

There is much discussion concerning the ozone layer and its density. A feeling exists that this protective layer of ozone is slowly diminishing and corrective action must be directed to this problem. Much experimenting is presently being conducted to determine if a problem exists and if so, the short and long term effects of the problem and how it can be remedied.

OXIDES OF SULFUR

Oxides of sulfur (SOx) were initially ignored in the exhaust system emissions, since the sulfur content of gasoline as a fuel is less than $\frac{1}{10}$ of 1%. Because of this small amount, it was felt that it contributed very little to the overall pollution problem. However, because of the difficulty in solving the sulfur emissions in industrial pollutions and the introduction of catalytic converter to the automobile exhaust systems, a change was mandated. The automobile exhaust system, when equipped with a catalytic converter, changes the sulfur dioxide (SO_2) into the sulfur trioxide (SO_3).

When this combines with water vapors (H_2O), a sulfuric acid mist (H_2SO_4) is formed and is a very difficult pollutant to handle and is extremely corrosive. This sulfuric acid mist that is formed, is the same mist that rises from the vents of an automobile storage battery when an active chemical reaction takes place within the battery cells.

When a large concentration of vehicles equipped with catalytic converters are operating in an area, this acid mist will rise and be distributed over a large ground area causing land, plant, crop, paints and building damage.

PARTICULATE MATTER

A certain amount of particulate matter is present in the burning of any fuel, with carbon constituting the largest percentage of the particulates. In gasoline, the remaining percentage of particulates is the burned remains of the various other compounds used in its manufacture. When a gasoline engine is in good internal condition, the particulate emissions are low but as the engine wears internally, the particulate emissions increase. By visually inspecting the tail pipe emissions, a determination can be made as to where an engine defect may exist.

An engine with light gray smoke emitting from the tail pipe normally indicates an increase in the oil consumption through burning due to internal engine wear. Black smoke would indicate a defective fuel delivery system, causing the engine to operate in a rich mode. Regardless of the color of the smoke, the internal part of the engine or the fuel delivery system should be repaired to a "like new" condition to prevent excess particulate emissions.

Diesel and turbine engines emit a darkened plume of smoke from the exhaust system because of the type of fuel used. Emission control regulations are mandated for this type of emission and more stringent measures are being used to prevent excess emission of the particulate matter. Electronic components are being introduced to control the injection of the fuel at precisely the proper time of piston travel, to achieve the optimum in fuel ignition and fuel usage. Other particulate after-burning components are being tested to achieve a cleaner particular emission.

Good grades of engine lubricating oils should be used, meeting the manufacturers specification. "Cut-rate" oils can contribute to the particulate emission problem because of their low "flash" or ignition temperature point. Such oils burn prematurely during the combustion process causing emissions of particulate matter.

The cooling system is an important factor in the reduction of particulate matter. With the cooling system operating at a temperature specified by the manufacturer, the optimum of combustion will occur. The cooling system must be maintained in the same manner as the engine oiling system, as each system is required to perform properly in order for the engine to operate efficiently for a long time.

Other Automobile Emission Sources

Before emission controls were mandated on the internal combustion engines, other sources of engine pollutants were discovered, along with the exhaust emission. It was determined the engine combustion exhaust produced 60% of the total emission pollutants, fuel evaporation from the fuel tank and carburetor vents produced 20%, with the another 20% being produced through the crankcase as a by-product of the combustion process.

CRANKCASE EMISSIONS

Crankcase emissions are made up of water, acids, unburned fuel, oil fumes and particulates. The emissions are classified as hydrocarbons (HC) and are formed by the small amount of unburned, compressed air/fuel mixture entering the crankcase from the combustion area

during the compression and power strokes, between the cylinder walls and piston rings. The head of the compression and combustion help to form the remaining crankcase emissions.

Since the first engines, crankcase emissions were allowed to go into the air through a road draft tube, mounted on the lower side of the engine block. Fresh air came in through an open oil filler cap or breather. The air passed through the crankcase mixing with blow-by gases. The motion of the vehicle and the air blowing past the open end of the road draft tube caused a low pressure area at the end of the tube. Crankcase emissions were simply drawn out of the road draft tube into the air.

To control the crankcase emission, the road draft tube was deleted. A hose and/or tubing was routed from the crankcase to the intake manifold so the blow-by emission could be burned with the air/fuel mixture. However, it was found that intake manifold vacuum, used to draw the crankcase emissions into the manifold, would vary in strength at the wrong time and not allow the proper emission flow. A regulating type valve was needed to control the flow of air through the crankcase.

Testing, showed the removal of the blow-by gases from the crankcase as quickly as possible, was most important to the longevity of the engine. Should large accumulations of blow-by gases remain and condense, dilution of the engine oil would occur to form water, soots, resins, acids and lead salts, resulting in the formation of sludge and varnishes. This condensation of the blow-by gases occur more frequently on vehicles used in numerous starting and stopping conditions, excessive idling and when the engine is not allowed to attain normal operating temperature through short runs. The crankcase purge control or PCV system will be described in detail later in this Chapter.

FUEL EVAPORATIVE EMISSIONS

Gasoline fuel is a major source of pollution, before and after it is burned in the automobile engine. From the time the fuel is refined, stored, pumped and transported, again stored until it is pumped into the fuel tank of the vehicle, the gasoline gives off unburned hydrocarbons (HC) into the atmosphere. Through redesigning of the storage areas and venting systems, the pollution factor has been diminished but not eliminated, from the refinery standpoint. However, the automobile still remained the primary source of vaporized, unburned hydrocarbon (HC) emissions.

Fuel pumped form an underground storage tank is cool but when exposed to a warner ambient temperature, will expand. Before controls were mandated, an owner would fill the fuel tank with fuel from an underground storage tank and park the vehicle for some time in warm area, such as a parking lot. As the fuel would warm, it would expand and should no provisions or area be provided for the expansion, the fuel would spill out the filler neck and onto the ground, causing hydrocarbon (HC) pollution and creating a severe fire hazard. To correct this condition, the vehicle manufacturers added overflow plumbing and/or gasoline tanks with built in expansion areas or domes.

However, this did not control the fuel vapor emission from the fuel tank and the carburetor bowl. It was determined that most of the fuel evaporation occurred when the vehicle was stationary and the engine not operating. Most vehicles carry 5–25 gallons (19–95 liters) of gasoline. Should a large concentration of vehicles be parked in one area, such as a large parking lot, excessive fuel vapor emissions would take place, increasing as the temperature increases.

To prevent the vapor emission from escaping into the atmosphere, the fuel system is designed to trap the fuel vapors while the vehicle is stationary, by sealing the fuel system from the atmosphere. A storage system is used to collect and hold the fuel vapors from the carburetor and the fuel tank when the engine is not operating. When the engine is started, the storage system is then purged of the fuel vapors, which are drawn into the engine and burned with the air/fuel mixture.

The components of the fuel evaporative system will be described in detail later in this Chapter.

CRANKCASE VENTILATION SYSTEM

Positive Crankcase Ventilation System
OPERATION

All Probe engines are equipped with the Positive Crankcase Ventilation (PCV) system. The PCV system vents crankcase gases into the engine air intake where they are burned with the fuel and air mixture. The PCV system keeps pollutants from being released into the atmosphere, and also helps to keep the engine oil clean, by ridding the crankcase of moisture and corrosive fumes. The PCV system consists of the rocker arm cover mounted PCV valve, the nipple in the air intake and the connecting hoses.

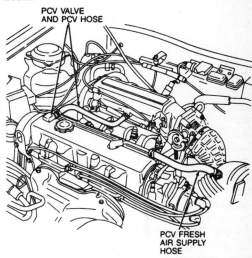

PCV valve and hoses location—2.2L engine

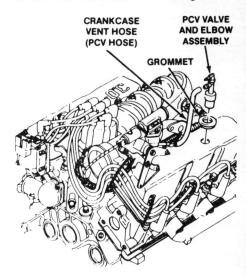

PCV valve and hose location—3.0L engine

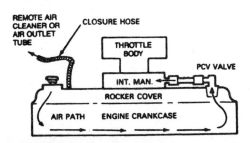

PCV system functional diagram

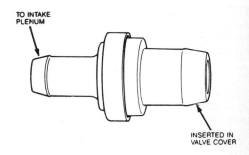

PCV valve—2.2L engine

The PCV valve regulates the amount of ventilating air and blow-by gas to the intake manifold. It also prevents backfire from traveling into the crankcase, avoiding the explosion of crankcase gases.

SERVICE

1. Visually inspect the PCV valve hose and the fresh air saupply hose and their attaching nipples or grommets for splits, cuts, damage, clogging, or restrictions. Repair or replace, as necessary.

2. If the hoses pass inspection, remove the PCV valve from the rocker arm cover. Shake the PCV valve and listen or feel for the rattle of the valve plunger within the valve body. If the valve plunger does not rattle, the PCV valve must be cleaned or replaced. If the valve plunger rattles, PCV valve is okay; reinstall it.

3. Start the engine and bring it to normal operating temperature. Remove the fresh air supply hose from the throttle body air hose nipple, and plug or cap the nipple immediately to keep the engine from stalling. Check for vacuum at the end of the supply hose using a stiff piece of paper. If the paper is retained by vacuum at the end of the hose, the PCV system is okay.

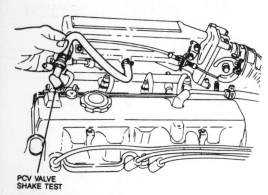

PCV VALVE
SHAKE TEST

PCV valve shake test

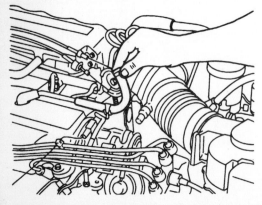

PCV system functional test

4. If the paper is not held by vacuum, check the fresh air and PCV hoses for leaks or loose connections. Also check for a loose fitting oil fill cap or loose dipstick. Correct as required until vacuum can be felt at the end of the supply hose.

NOTE: *If air pressure and oil or sludge is present at the end of the fresh air supply hose, the engine has excessive blow-by and cylinder bore or piston ring wear.*

REMOVAL AND INSTALLATION

1. Remove the PCV valve from the mounting grommet in the valve cover.

2. Disconnect the valve from the PCV hose and remove the valve from the vehicle.

3. Installation is the reverse of the removal procedure.

FUEL EVAPORATIVE EMISSION CONTROL SYSTEM

OPERATION

The evaporative emission control system prevents the escape of fuel vapors to the atmosphere under hot soak and engine off conditions by storing the vapors in a carbon canister. Then, with the engine warm and running, the system controls the purging of stored vapors from the canister to the engine, where they are efficiently burned. Evaporative emission control components consist of the carbon canister, purge valve(s), rollover/vent valve, check valve, vapor separator and the necessary lines.

Carbon Canister

The fuel vapors from the fuel tank are stored in the carbon canister until the vehicle is operated, at which time, the vapors will purge from the canister into the engine for consumption. The carbon canister contains activated carbon, which absorbs the fuel vapor. The canister is located in the engine compartment.

Purge Valves

The purge valves control the flow of fuel vapor from the carbon canister to the engine. Purge valves are either vacuum or electronically controlled. When electronically controlled, a purge valve is known as a purge solenoid. 1989 vehicles are equipped with both vacuum and electronically controlled valves. 1990–92 vehicles are equipped with purge solenoid valves only. Purging occurs when the engine is at operating temperature and off idle.

Rollover/Vent Valve

The rollover/vent valve releases excessive pressure or vacuum in the fuel tank to atmo-

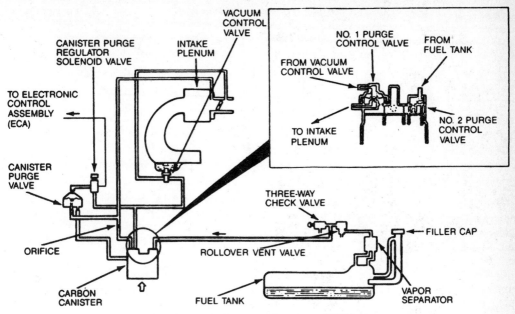

Evaporative emission control system—1989 Probe

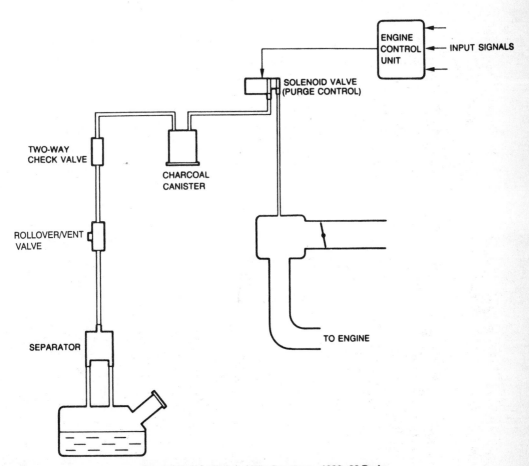

Evaporative emission control system—1990–92 Probe

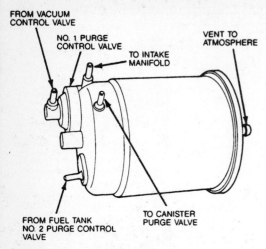

FROM VACUUM
CONTROL VALVE

NO. 1 PURGE
CONTROL VALVE

TO INTAKE
MANIFOLD

VENT TO
ATMOSPHERE

FROM FUEL TANK
NO. 2 PURGE CONTROL
VALVE

TO CANISTER
PURGE VALVE

Carbon canister—1989 Probe

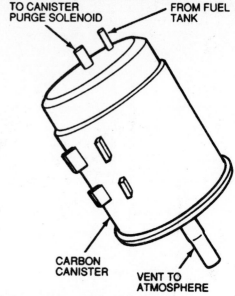

TO CANISTER
PURGE SOLENOID

FROM FUEL
TANK

CARBON
CANISTER

VENT TO
ATMOSPHERE

Carbon canister—1990–92 Probe

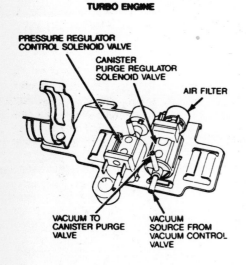

TURBO ENGINE

PRESSURE REGULATOR
CONTROL SOLENOID VALVE

CANISTER
PURGE REGULATOR
SOLENOID VALVE

AIR FILTER

VACUUM TO
CANISTER PURGE
VALVE

VACUUM
SOURCE FROM
VACUUM CONTROL
VALVE

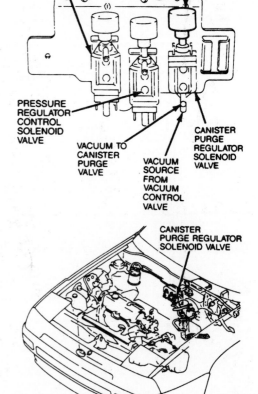

NON-TURBO ENGINE

EGR CONTROL
SOLENOID VALVE

AIR FILTER

PRESSURE
REGULATOR
CONTROL
SOLENOID
VALVE

VACUUM TO
CANISTER
PURGE
VALVE

VACUUM
SOURCE
FROM
VACUUM
CONTROL
VALVE

CANISTER
PURGE
REGULATOR
SOLENOID
VALVE

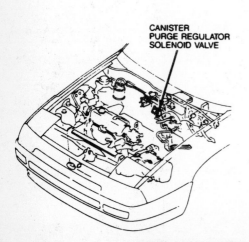

CANISTER
PURGE REGULATOR
SOLENOID VALVE

CANISTER
PURGE REGULATOR
SOLENOID VALVE

Canister purge regulator solenoid valve—1989 Probe

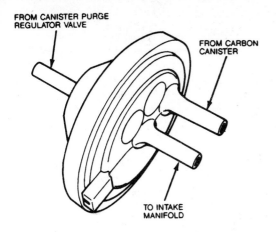

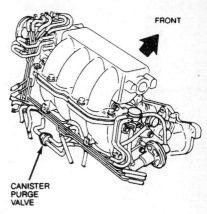

Canister purge valve—1989 Probe

sphere. In case of vehicle rollover, the valve also prevents fuel tank drainage through the evaporative hoses.

Check Valve

The check valve releases excessive pressure or vacuum in the fuel tank to atmosphere. The valve is connected in-line with the evaporative hose and rollover/vent valve. 1989 vehicles are equipped with a 3-way check valve. 1990–92 vehicles are equipped with a 2-way check valve.

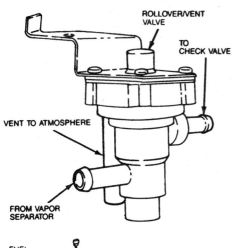

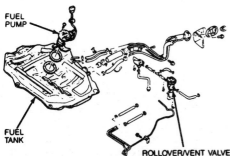

Rollover/vent valve

Vapor Separator

The vapor separator prevents fuel from flowing into the carbon canister through the fuel tank evaporative hose. The vapor separator is mounted in the rear driver's side wheel well.

SERVICE

System Inspection

1. Visually inspect the vapor and vacuum lines and connections for looseness, pinching, leakage, or other damage. If fuel line, vacuum line, or orifice blockage is suspected as the obvious cause of a malfunction, correct the cause before proceeding further.

2. Check the wiring and connectors to the solenoid, vane air flow meter (2.2L engine), speed sensor and ECA for looseness, corrosion, damage or other problems. This must be done with the engine fully warmed so as to activate the purging controls.

3. If all checks are okay, proceed to Testing.

Testing

1989 VEHICLES

1. Check the canister purge solenoid as follows:

    a. Remove the solenoid from the vehicle and connect vacuum hoses as shown.

    b. Test 1: Blow air through the valve from hose A and note whether air exits through the vent.

    c. Test 2: Apply 12 volts to one terminal of the solenoid connector and ground the other terminal. Blow air through the valve from hose A and note whether air exits at port B.

    d. If air flows freely in both tests, proceed to Step 2. If air does not flow freely in either test, replace the purge solenoid.

2. Check the canister purge valve as follows:

    a. Remove the valve from the vehicle.

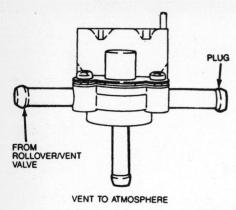

VENT TO ATMOSPHERE

3-way check valve—1989 Probe

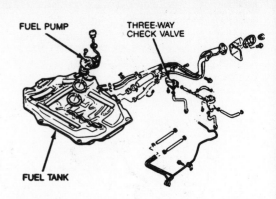

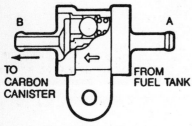

2-way check valve—1990–92 Probe

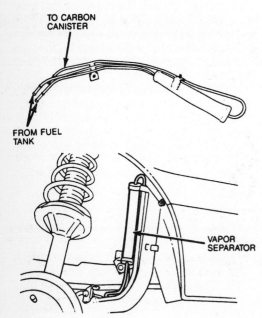

Vapor separator

b. Using a vacuum pump, apply 2.6–4.2 in. Hg of vacuum to the valve as shown.

c. Make sure that vacuum is held and air flows freely through the valve while blowing on either port A or B.

d. If the valve allows air to flow freely when the specified vacuum is applied, pro-ceed to Step 3. If the valve does not allow air to flow, it must be replaced.

3. Check the No. 1 purge control valve as follows:

a. Connect a vacuum pump.

b. With no vacuum applied, air should not flow through the valve while blowing on port A.

c. With 4.3 in. Hg of vacuum applied, make sure that vacuum is held and that air flows through the valve while blowing on port A.

d. If air does not flow in Step b, but flows in Step c, proceed to Step 4. If the valve does not function as specified, replace the carbon canister.

4. Check the No. 2 purge control valve as follows:

a. Disconnect vacuum hose B from the fuel tank line, blow on the hose and verify that air can flow.

b. If air flows through the valve at hose B, proceed to Step 5. If air does not flow through the valve at hose B, replace the carbon canister.

5. Check the vacuum control valve as follows:

a. Disconnect the vacuum hose (black with white dots) from the intake plenum and con-nect a vacuum pump to the hose.

b. Disconnect the vacuum hoses from the solenoid valve and from the No. 1 purge con-trol valve.

c. With a cold engine, less than 115°F (46°C), apply a vacuum with the vacuum pump and verify that vacuum is held.

d. With a warm engine, apply a vacuum with the vacuum pump and verify if the vacu-um is released when the valve opens. The valve opening temperature specification is 115–129°F (46–54°C), detectable as warm to the feel at the engine water outlet connection.

e. If the valve is closed when cold, and opens at the specified temperature before the engine is fully warmed up, proceed to Step 6. If the valve does not operate as specified, it must be replaced.

6. Check the 3-way check valve function as follows:

a. Remove the 3-way check valve from the vehicle.

b. Plug or cap port A, blow air into port B and verify that air exits at port C.

c. Leave port A capped or plugged. Apply a vacuum to port B, using a vacuum pump, and verify that no vacuum is held.

d. If the valve functions as specified, proceed to Step 7. If the valve does not function as specified, it must be replaced.

7. Check the rollover/vent valve as follows:

a. Remove the rollover/vent valve from the vehicle.

b. Test 1: Tee in a suitable pressure gauge to the hose normally leading to the fuel tank, cap or plug port C (Refer to illustration), and blow into port A. Verify that the valve opens at 0.78–1.00 psi.

c. Test 2: Tee in the pressure gauge at port B, cap or plug port C, and blow into port B. Verify that the valve opens at 0.14–0.71 psi.

d. With the valve mounted at 90° to horizontal or inverted 180°, attach a suitable hand held pressure tester and gauge at port A, apply 10 psi pressure and verify that pressure is held.

e. If the valve opens in a horizontal position, as specified, and holds pressure when inverted, proceed to Step 8. If the valve does not open, as specified, in the horizontal position, or does not hold pressure when inverted, it must be replaced.

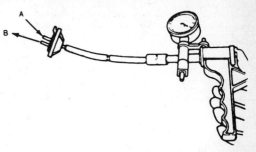

Checking the canister purge valve function—1989 Probe

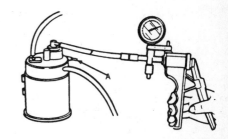

Checking the No. 1 purge control valve—1989 Probe

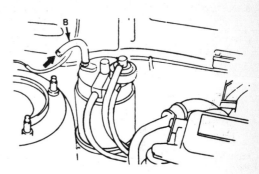

Checking the No. 2 purge control valve—1989 Probe

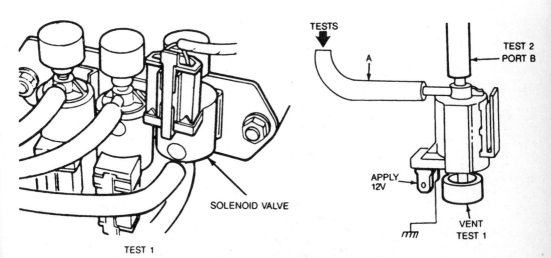

Checking the canister purge solenoid—1989 Probe

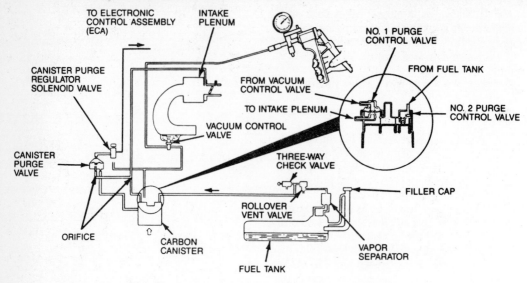

Checking the vacuum control valve function—1989 Probe

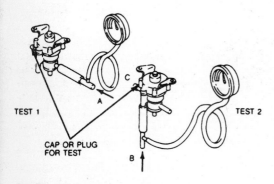

Checking the rollover/vent valve

8. Check the vapor separator for damage as follows:

a. Remove the vapor separator from the vehicle, as required.

b. Visually inspect it for mechanical damage.

c. If the separator is damaged it must be replaced. If the separator is not damaged, re-install it, if removed. System testing is completed.

1990–92 VEHICLES

1. Check the canister purge solenoid as follows:

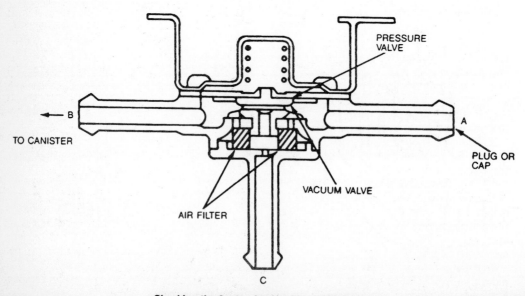

Checking the 3-way check valve—1989 Probe

a. Disconnect the vacuum hoses and the electrical connector from the solenoid valve.

b. Attach a clean test hose to port A. (Refer to illustration).

c. Blow air through the solenoid from port A and confirm that no air exits from port B.

d. Apply 12 volts to one terminal of the solenoid connector and ground the other terminal.

e. Blow air through the solenoid from port A and confirm that air exits from port B.

f. If the solenoid does not function as specified, it must be replaced.

2. Check the carbon canister for liquid fuel as follows:

a. Run the engine long enough to warm it up and purge any fuel from the carbon canister.

b. Stop the engine and remove the canister.

c. Inspect the canister for the presence of liquid fuel, indicated by odor or by excessive weight.

d. Blow into the air vent in the bottom of the canister and verify that air exits readily from the fuel vapor inlet.

e. If the carbon canister is free of liquid fuel and air passes through it easily, proceed to Step 3. If there is fuel in the canister or air does not pass through it, replace the canister.

3. Check for purge line blockage as follows:

a. Remove the purge lines (including any orifice) leading from the carbon canister to the engine intake.

b. Check each line for blockage by blowing through it. If air flows slowly, the line may contain an orifice that may be partially plugged.

c. If the line allows air to flow freely, proceed to Step 5. If air flows very slow through the line, proceed to Step 4. If air does not flow, remove the orifice, clean it thoroughly and install it in a new line, or replace the line and orifice as an assembly; proceed to Step 5.

4. Check for purge line orifice blockage as follows:

a. Remove any orifice suspected of being restricted and clean it thoroughly.

b. Reinstall it in the purge line and re-check it for resistance to air flow by blowing through the line.

c. If the line and orifice flow air more freely than when checked in Step 3, remove the orifice, replace the purge line, and reinstall the orifice, or replace the line and orifice as an assembly. The original line may contain accumulated particles.

d. If the line and orifice do not flow air more freely, proceed to Step 5.

5. Check the vapor separator as follows:

a. Visually inspect the vapor separator and its connections with the fuel tank for hose pinching, blockage, looseness, or other mechanical damage.

b. If the vapor separator and its connections are not damaged, proceed to Step 6. If the vapor separator and/or its connections are damaged, replace the vapor separator and/or repair the connecting hoses, as required.

6. Check the rollover/vent valve as follows:

a. Remove the rollover/vent valve from the vehicle.

b. Test 1: Tee in a suitable pressure gauge to the hose normally leading to the fuel tank, cap or plug port C (Refer to illustration), and blow into port A. Verify that the valve opens at 0.78–1.00 psi.

c. Test 2: Tee in the pressure gauge at port B, cap or plug port C, and blow into port B. Verify that the valve opens at 0.14–0.71 psi.

d. With the valve mounted at 90° to horizontal or inverted 180°, attach a suitable hand held pressure tester and gauge at port A, apply 10 psi pressure and verify that pressure is held.

e. If the valve opens in a horizontal position, as specified, and holds pressure when inverted, proceed to Step 7. If the valve does not open, as specified, in the horizontal position, or does not hold pressure when inverted, it must be replaced.

7. Check the 2-way check valve function as follows:

a. Visually inspect the check valve and its connections for hose pinching, blockage, looseness, or for evidence of other damage or leakage.

b. Remove the 2-way check valve.

c. Blow air through the valve from A to B (Refer to illustration) and then from B to A. Verify that air passes easily in either direction.

d. If there is no evidence of leakage, and air passes easily in either direction, the check valve is okay; system testing is completed. If the valve leaks or air will not pass easily, replace the 2-way check valve.

REMOVAL AND INSTALLATION

Carbon Canister

1. Disconnect the negative battery cable.

2. Tag and disconnect the vapor hoses from the canister.

3. Remove the canister fasteners and remove the canister.

4. Installation is the reverse of the removal procedure.

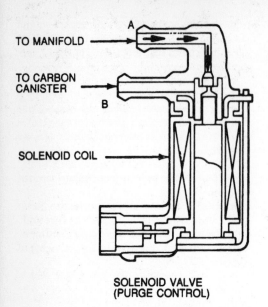
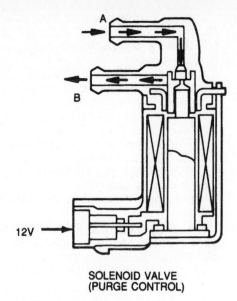

Checking the canister purge solenoid—1990–92 Probe

Purge Valve

1. Disconnect the negative battery cable.
2. Tag and disconnect the hoses from the valve.
3. Disconnect the electrical connector from the valve, if equipped.
4. Remove the valve from its mounting and remove it from the vehicle.
5. Installation is the reverse of the removal procedure.

Rollover/Vent Valve

1. Disconnect the negative battery cable.
2. Raise and safely support the vehicle.
3. Tag and disconnect the vapor hoses from the vapor valve.

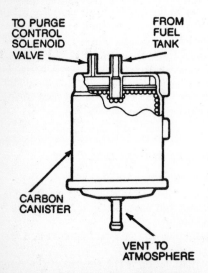

Checking the carbon canister—1990–92 Probe

4. Remove the vapor valve mounting screws and the vapor valve from the underside of the vehicle.
5. Installation is the reverse of the removal procedure.

Check Valve

1. Disconnect the negative battery cable.
2. Raise and safely support the vehicle.
3. Tag and disconnect the vapor hoses from the check valve.
4. Remove the check valve mounting screw and the check valve from the underside of the vehicle.
5. Installation is the reverse of the removal procedure.

EXHAUST EMISSION CONTROL SYSTEM

GENERAL INFORMATION

The exhaust emission control system begins at the air intake and ends at the tailpipe. The exhaust emission control system includes the exhaust gas recirculation system and exhaust catalyst, as well as the electronic controls that govern the fuel and ignition system. These components combined control engine operation for maximum engine efficiency and minimal exhaust emissions.

NOTE: *Many of the following testing procedures require the use of breakout box tool T83L–50–EEC–IV or equivalent, and either STAR tester 007–00004 or SUPER STAR II tester 007–00028 or equivalents.*

Vane Air Flow Meter

OPERATION

The Vane Air Flow (VAF) meter is mounted between the air cleaner and the throttle body assembly on vehicles with the 2.2L engine. It contains a movable vane connected to a potentiometer. As air flows through the VAF meter, the movable vane and potentiometer change position and provide an input to the ECA with vane position information. The ECA translates vane position information into the volume of air flowing into the engine.

SERVICE

Before beginning this procedure, make sure there are no air leaks between the VAF meter and the throttle body. Check the entire intake system to make sure there are no vacuum leaks. Check the PCV valve and hoses, rocker arm cover and dipstick to make sure they are seated.

1989 Vehicles

1. Visually inspect all wiring, wiring harnesses, connectors and components for evidence of overheating, insulation damage, looseness, shorting or other damage and repair, as required. If everything looks okay, go to Step 2.
2. Install the breakout box according to the manufacturers instructions, leaving the ECA disconnected. Place a voltmeter on the 20V scale and connect it between pin 18 and ground pin 20 (Refer to illusatration). If the voltage reading is 7–9 volts, go to Step 6. If the voltage reading is not 7–9 volts, go to Step 3.

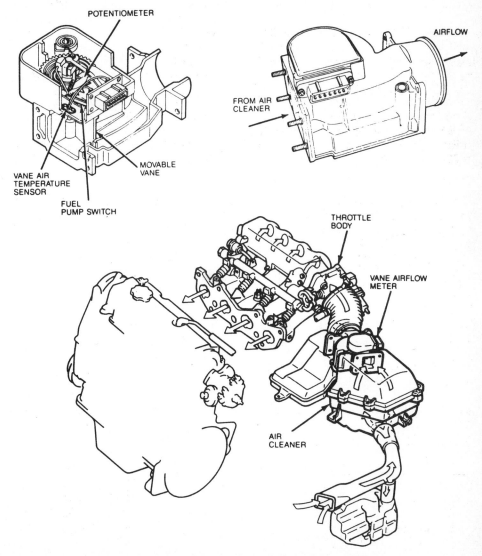

Vane air flow meter—2.2L engine

3. Turn the ignition key **ON**. Leaving the VAF meter connected, measure the voltage between VAF meter terminal E (R/W wire) and ground (do not pierce the wire). If the voltage reading is 7–9 volts, repair the open or short in the R/W wire from the VAF meter to the ECA. If the voltage reading is not 7–9 volts, go to Step 4.

4. Turn the ignition key **ON** and measure the voltage between the VAF meter terminal D (R/BK wire) and ground. If the voltage reading is above 10 volts, replace the VAF meter. If the voltage is not above 10 volts, go to Step 5.

5. Turn the ignition key **ON** and measure the voltage between relay No. 2 (R/BK wire) and ground. Do not disconnect the relay or pierce the wire. If the voltage is above 10 volts, repair the open or short in the R/BK wire from relay No. 2 to the VAF meter. If the voltage is not above 10 volts, check the vehicle power supply.

6. Turn the ignition key **OFF** and install the breakout box. Place the volt-ohmmeter on the 200Ω scale. Measure the resistance between pin 46 and pin 20 (Refer to illustration). If the resistance is below 5Ω, go to Step 7. If the resistance is not below 5Ω, check reference voltage.

7. Turn the ignition key **OFF** and install the breakout box. Place the volt-ohmmeter on the 200Ω scale. Measure the resistance between VAF meter terminal C (LG/Y wire) and pin 46.

If the resistance is below 5Ω, go to Step 8. If the resistance is not below 5Ω, repair the LG/Y wire from the VAF meter to the ECA.

8. Install the breakout box. Take voltage readings with the ignition key **ON**, then with the engine idling.

a. Measure the voltage between pin 43 and pin 20; it should be 1.7 volts with the key **ON** and 4–6 volts with the engine running.

b. Measure the voltage between pin 43 and pin 46; it should be 1.7 volts with the key **ON** and 4–6 volts with the engine running.

c. Measure the voltage between pin 20 and pin 46; it should be 0 volts with the key **ON** and 0 volts with the engine running.

d. If all voltage readings are within specification, replace the ECA. If any readings are not within specification, go to Step 9.

9. Take voltage readings with the ignition key **ON**, then with the engine idling. Leave the VAF meter connected and do not pierce the wire.

a. Measure the voltage between VAF meter terminal F (R/BK wire) and ground; it should be 1.7 volts with the key **ON** and 4–6 volts with the engine running.

b. Measure the voltage between VAF meter terminal F (R/BK wire) and terminal C (LG/Y wire); it should be 1.7 volts with the key **ON** and 4–6 volts with the engine running.

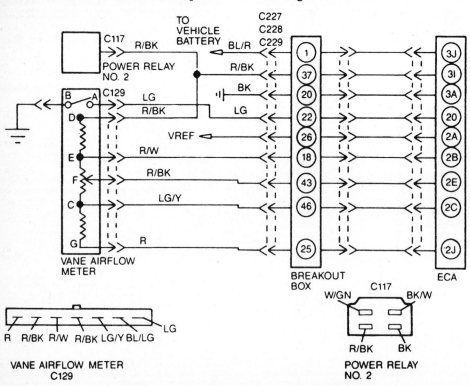

VAF meter and ACT sensor test schematic—1989 Probe

c. Measure the voltage between VAF meter terminal C (LG/Y wire) and ground; it should be 0 volts with the key **ON** and 0 volts with the engine running.

d. If all voltage readings are within specification, repair the R/BK wire from the VAF meter to the ECA. If any voltage readings are not within specification, replace the VAF meter.

1990–92 Vehicles

1. Install the breakout box tool according to the manufacturer's instructions and connect the ECA. Turn the ignition key **ON**. Using a voltmeter, measure the voltage between test pin VAF and test pin SIGRTN while moving the VAF meter air door and compare your readings with the illustration. If the voltage readings are okay, go to Step 2. If the voltage is not as specified, go to Step 3.

2. Install the breakout box tool according to the manufacturers instructions and connect the ECA. Turn the ignition key **ON**. Using a voltmeter, measure the voltage between test pin VMREF and test pin SIGRTN. If the voltage reading is between 7–9 volts, the VAF circuit is okay, replace the ECA. If the voltage reading is not between 7–9 volts, repair the VMREF wire from the VAF meter to the ECA.

3. Check the VAF signal from the VAF meter as follows:

a. Disconnect the VAF meter connector.

b. Connect jumper wires between the VMREF, SIGRTN and VPWR terminals on the harness connector and the VAF meter.

c. Turn the ignition key **ON**.

d. Using a voltmeter, measure the voltage between the VAF terminal (at the VAF meter) and the SIGRTN wire (at the harness connector).

e. Compare the voltage readings with those in the illustration while moving the VAF meter air door.

f. If the voltage readings are okay, repair the VAF wire from the VAF meter to the ECA. If the voltage readings are not okay, go to Step 4.

4. Check the VAF signal without the VMREF as follows:

a. Disconnect the VAF meter connector.

b. Using jumper wires, connect the VPWR and SIGRTN terminals between the harness connector and the VAF meter. Leave the VMREF and VAF disconnected.

c. Turn the ignition key **ON**.

d. Using a voltmeter, measure the voltage between the VAF terminal (at the VAF meter) and the SIGRTN wire (at the harness connector).

e. Compare the voltage readings with those in illustration while moving the VAF meter air door.

f. If the voltage readings are okay, repair the VMREF wire from the VAF meter to the ECA.

5. Disconnect the VAF meter connector and turn the ignition key **ON**. Using a voltmeter, measure the voltage between the VAF meter VPWR wire and the VAF meter SIGRTN wire. If the voltage reading is above 10 volts, replace the VAF meter. If the voltage reading is not above 10 volts, go to Step 6.

6. Disconnect the VAF meter connector and turn the ignition key **ON**. Using a voltmeter,

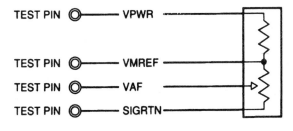

VAF meter test schematic—1990–92 Probe

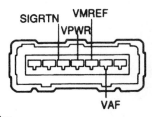

Application	Circuit	ECA Pin	BOB Pin	Wire Color
2.2L (MTX)	VAF	2O	25	R/BK
	VMREF	2J	6	R/W
	VPWR	1B	37,57	R/BK
	SIGRTN	2D	46,49	LG/Y
2.2L (ATX)	VAF	2B	25	R/BK
2.2L Turbo	VMREF	2A	6	R/W
	VPWR	1B	37,57	R/BK
	SIGRTN	3D	46,49	LG/Y

VAF meter test pin identification—1990–92 Probe

VOLTAGE (VOLTS)

GRAPH

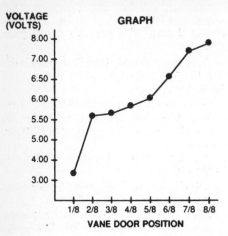

| 8.00 |
| 7.00 |
| 6.50 |
| 6.00 |
| 5.50 |
| 5.00 |
| 4.00 |
| 3.00 |

1/8 2/8 3/8 4/8 5/8 6/8 7/8 8/8

VANE DOOR POSITION

GRAPH DATA VALUES

VANE DOOR POSITION	VOLTS
1/8	3.24
2/8	5.60
3/8	5.62
4/8	5.83
5/8	6.02
6/8	6.57
7/8	7.46
8/8	7.87

Note: Voltage values may vary ± 15%.

VAF meter testing data—1990–92 Probe

measure the voltage between the VAF meter VPWR wire and ground. If the voltage reading is above 10 volts, repair the SIGRTN wire between the VAF meter and the ECA. If the voltage reading is not above 10 volts, check the vehicle power supply.

REMOVAL AND INSTALLATION

1. Disconnect the negative battery cable.
2. Disconnect the vane air flow meter electrical connector.
3. Disconnect the air duct from the air filter cover.
4. Remove the air cleaner cover attaching bolts and remove the air cleaner cover.
5. Remove the vane air flow meter attaching nuts from inside the air cleaner cover and remove the vane air flow meter.
6. Installation is the reverse of the removal procedure.

Manifold Absolute Pressure (MAP) Sensor

OPERATION

The Manifold Absolute Pressure (MAP) sensor operates as a pressure sensing disc. It does not generate a voltage, instead its output is a frequency change. The sensor changes frequency according to intake manifold vacuum; as vacuum increases sensor frequency increases. The information from the MAP sensor allows the ECA to determine what the engine load is. Its signal affects air/fuel ratio, ignition timing, EGR flow and altitude compensation. The MAP sensor is used on the 3.0L engine.

SERVICE

NOTE: *The wire color to test pin 45 is white/green. The wire color to test pin 46 is light green/yellow. The wire color to test pin 26 is light green/red.*

1. Code 22 or 126 indicates that the MAP sensor is out of Self-Test range. The correct

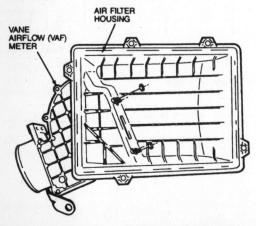

VAF meter removal and installation—2.2L engine

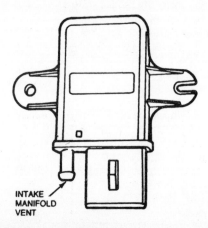

MAP sensor—3.0L engine

MAP sensor tester measurement range is 1.4–1.6 volts. Possible causes for code 22 or 126 are as follows:

MAP/BP SIG circuit open between sensor harness connector and ECA.

MAP/BP SIG circuit shorted to VREF, SIG RTN, or GND.

Damaged MAP/BP sensor.

Vacuum trapped at MAP/BP sensor.

High atmospheric pressure.

Damaged ECA.

VREF circuit open at MAP sensor.

SIG RTN circuit open at MAP sensor.

2. Check for power to the MAP sensor as follows:

a. Turn the ignition key **OFF**.

b. Disconnect the MAP sensor from the vehicle harness.

c. Connect the MAP sensor tester between the vehicle harness connector and the MAP sensor.

d. Insert the MAP sensor tester plugs into a voltmeter.

NOTE: *The green light on the tester indicates that the VREF circuit is okay, 4–6 volts. A red light, or no light, indicates the VREF is either too low or too high.*

e. Turn the ignition key **ON**. If the green light is on, proceed to Step 4. If the green light is not on, proceed to Step 3.

3. Check for power at the sensor harness connector as follows:

a. Turn the ignition key **ON**.

b. Connect the MAP sensor tester and the voltmeter as in Step 2.

c. Disconnect the MAP sensor.

d. If the green light comes on, replace the MAP sensor. If not, check the wiring harness.

4. Check the MAP sensor output as follows:

a. Measure several known good MAP sensors on available vehicles. The measured voltage will be typical for the location on the day of testing.

b. Turn the ignition key **ON**.

c. Connect the MAP sensor tester and voltmeter as in Step 2.

d. Measure the MAP sensor voltage and compare to the illustration. If the voltage is in range for the altitude, remove the MAP sensor tester and proceed to Step 5. If not, remove the tester and proceed to Step 6.

5. Check the MAP/BP SIG circuit continuity as follows:

a. Turn the ignition key **OFF** and disconnect the MAP sensor.

b. Disconnect the ECA 60 pin connector. Check for damaged or pushed out pins, corrosion, loose wires, etc. and service, as necessary.

c. Install breakout box tool T83L–50–

EEC–IV or equivalent and leave the ECA disconnected.

d. Measure the resistance between the MAP/BP SIG circuit at the MAP sensor harness connector and test pin 45 at the breakout box.

e. If the resistance is less than 5Ω, replace the ECA, remove the breakout box and reconnect the MAP sensor. If not, service the open circuit, remove the breakout box and reconnect all components.

6. Check the MAP/BP SIG circuit for shorts to VREF, SIG RTN and ground, as follows:

a. Turn the ignition key **OFF** and disconnect the MAP sensor.

b. Disconnect the ECA 60 pin connector. Check for damaged or pushed out pins, corrosion, loose wires, etc. and service, as necessary.

c. Install breakout box tool T83L–50–EEC–IV or equivalent and leave the ECA disconnected.

d. Measure the resistance between test pin 45 and test pins 26, 46, 40 and 60 at the breakout box.

e. If each resistance is greater than 10,000Ω, replace the MAP sensor, remove the breakout box and reconnect the ECA. If not, service the short circuit, remove the breakout box and reconnect all components.

7. Check MAP sensor operation as follows:

a. Turn the ignition key **OFF**.

b. Disconnect the vacuum hose from the MAP sensor and connect a vacuum pump in its place.

c. Apply 18 in. Hg of vacuum to the MAP sensor.

d. If the MAP sensor holds vacuum, proceed to Step 8. If the MAP sensor does not hold vacuum, it must be replaced.

8. If a Code 22 or 126 is obtained during the Engine Running Self-Test, attempt to eliminate the code as follows:

a. Turn the ignition key **OFF**. Plug the MAP sensor vacuum supply hose.

b. Start the engine and run it at 1500 rpm.

c. Slowly apply 15 in. Hg of vacuum to the MAP sensor.

d. While maintaining 1500 rpm, perform the Engine Running Self-Test. If Code 22 or 126 is still present, replace the MAP sensor. If not, inspect the vacuum supply hose to the MAP sensor and service, as necessary. If okay, service other Engine Running Codes.

9. A Code 72 or 129 indicates that the MAP sensor output did not change enough during the Dynamic Response Test. Possible causes are as follows:

System failed to detect partial wide-open throttle.

MAP sensor vacuum supply hose is blocked or kinked.

Damaged MAP sensor.

NOTE: *The Dynamic Response Test is used on some applications to verify operation of the TP, MAF and MAP sensors during the brief Wide-Open Throttle (WOT) performed during the Engine Running Self-Test. The signal to perform the brief WOT is a single pulse or 10 Code on the STAR tester.*

10. Rerun the Engine Running Self-Test and make sure the WOT is performed during the Dynamic Response portion of the test. If Code 72 or 129 is still present, proceed to Step 11.

11. A Code 81 or 128 indicates that MAP sensor vacuum has not changed greater than 2 in. Hg during normal vehicle operation. This could be caused by a blocked or kinked or improperly routed MAP sensor vacuum supply hose or a MAP sensor leak. Check the vacuum hoses; if they are okay, proceed to Step 12. If not, service, as necessary.

12. Check MAP sensor operation as follows:

a. Turn the ignition key **OFF**.

b. Disconnect the vacuum hose from the MAP sensor and connect a vacuum pump in its place.

c. Apply 18 in. Hg of vacuum to the MAP sensor.

d. If the MAP sensor holds vacuum, proceed to Step 13. If the MAP sensor does not hold vacuum, it must be replaced.

13. Check that vacuum to the MAP sensor decreases during Dynamic Response as follows:

a. Turn the ignition key **OFF**.

b. Tee a vacuum gauge into the intake manifold vacuum supply hose at the MAP sensor.

c. Perform the Engine Running Self-Test while observing the vacuum.

d. If the vacuum decreased by more than 10 in. Hg vacuum during the Dynamic Response test, replace the MAP sensor. If not, check for probable causes affecting engine vacuum.

14. Continuous Memory Code 22 or 126 indicates the MAP sensor was out of self-test range. The code was set during normal driving conditions. The correct range of measurement is typically 1.4–1.6 volts. Possible causes for Continuous Memory Code 22 or 126 are as follows:

Damaged MAP sensor.

Damaged wiring harness.

Damaged wiring harness connectors and/or terminals.

Unusually high/low barometric pressures.

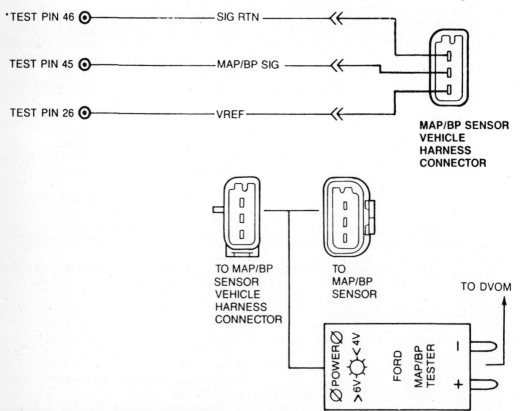

*TEST PINS LOCATED ON BREAKOUT BOX.
ALL HARNESS CONNECTORS VIEWED INTO MATING SURFACE.

MAP sensor test schematic

15. Using the Key On, Engine Off Continuous Monitor Mode, observe the volt/ohmmeter or STAR LED for indication of a fault while doing the following:

    a. Connect a vacuum pump to the MAP sensor.

    b. Slowly apply 25 in. Hg of vacuum to the MAP sensor.

    c. Slowly bleed vacuum off the MAP sensor.

    d. Lightly tap on the MAP sensor to simulate road shock.

    e. Wiggle the MAP sensor connector.

    f. If a fault is indicated, disconnect and check the connectors. If the connectors and terminals are good, replace the MAP sensor.

    g. If a fault is not indicated, proceed to Step 16.

16. While still in the Key On, Engine Off Continuous Monitor Mode, observe the volt/ohmmeter or STAR LED for a fault while grasping the wiring harness closest to the MAP sensor connector. Wiggle, shake or bend a small section of the harness while working toward the dash panel and from the dash panel to the ECA. If a fault is indicated, service as necessary.

Approximate Altitude (Ft.)	Voltage Output (±.04 Volts)
0	1.59
1000	1.56
2000	1.53
3000	1.50
4000	1.47
5000	1.44
6000	1.41
7000	1.39

MAP sensor voltage output/altitude relationship

MAP Sensor Graph

NOTE: **MAP sensor output frequency versus manifold vacuum data is based on 30.0 in-Hg barometric pressure.**

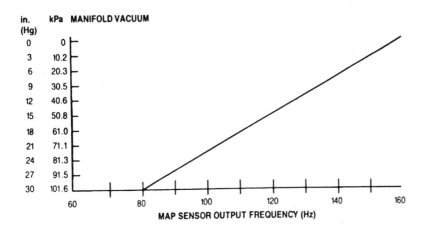

Manifold Vacuum		Frequency
in-Hg	kPa	Hz
0	0	159
3	10.2	150
6	20.3	141
9	30.5	133
12	40.6	125
15	50.8	117
18	61.0	109
21	71.1	102
24	81.3	95
27	91.5	88
30	101.6	80

MAP sensor testing data

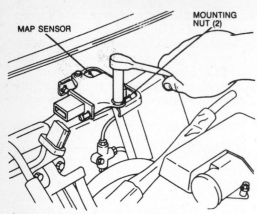

MAP sensor removal and installation

REMOVAL AND INSTALLATION

1. Disconnect the negative battery cable.
2. Disconnect the electrical connector and the vacuum line from the sensor.
3. Remove the sensor mounting nuts and remove the sensor.
4. Installation is the reverse of the removal procedure.

Temperature Sensors
OPERATION

The Air Charge Temperature (ACT) and Engine Coolant Temperature (ECT) sensors change resistance according to temperature change. ACT and ECT sensor resistance decreases as the surrounding temperature increases, providing a signal to the ECA that indicates either the temperature of the incoming air charge or engine coolant temperature. If the ACT or ECT sensor malfunctions, the lack of accurate temperature information could cause the ECA to provide output information resulting in an incorrect air/fuel ratio. This could cause poor vehicle performance and/or emission test failure.

SERVICE
2.2L Engine

ACT SENSOR

1989 Vehicles

NOTE: *The ambient temperature must be above 50°F (10°C) for this test.*
1. Visually inspect all wiring, wiring harnesses, connectors and components for evidence of overheating, insulation damage, looseness, shorting or other damage and repair, as required. If everything looks okay, go to Step 2.
2. Check sensor resistance as follows:
   a. Turn the ignition key **OFF**.

b. Install the breakout box according to the manufacturers instructions, leaving the ECA disconnected.
   c. Place the volt-ohmmeter on the 100Ω scale.
   d. Measure the resistance between test pin 25 and pin 46 (Refer to the illustration).
   e. At −4°F (−20°C), the resistance should be 13600–18400Ω. At 68°F (20°C), the resistance should be 2210–2690Ω. At 140°F (60°C), the resistance should be 493–667Ω.
   f. If the resistance reading is within specification, go to Step 2. If it is not, go to Step 6.
3. Check the sensor voltage as follows:
   a. Install the breakout box according to the manufacturers instructions.
   b. Place the volt-ohmmeter on the 10 volt scale.
   c. Turn the ignition key **ON**.
   d. Measure the voltage between pin 25 and pin 20. At 68°F (20°C), it should be 2.5 volts.
   e. Measure the voltage between pin 46 and ground pin 20. At 68°F (20°C), it should be 0 volts.
   f. If all voltage readings are within specification, replace the ECA. If they are not, go to Step 4.
NOTE: *Voltage decreases while temperature increases.*
4. Check for a short between the sensor and the ECA as follows:
   a. Turn the ignition key **OFF** and disconnect the negative battery cable.
   b. Install the breakout box according to the manufacturers instructions, leaving the ECA disconnected.
   c. Place the volt-ohmmeter on the 200Ω scale and measure the resistance between the following pins:
   >   pin 25 and pin 26
   >   pin 25 and pin 1
   >   pin 25 and pin 37
   >   pin 25 and ground pin 20
   >   pin 46 and pin 26
   >   pin 46 and pin 1
   >   pin 46 and pin 37
   d. If any resistances are below 5Ω, repair the wire(s) in question. If no resistances are below 5Ω, go to Step 5.
5. Check the signal return as follows:
   a. Turn the ignition key **OFF**.
   b. Install the breakout box according to the manufacturers instructions.
   c. Place the volt-ohmmeter on the 200Ω scale and measure the resistance between pin 46 and ground pin 20.
   d. If the resistance is below 5Ω, replace the ECA. If the resistance is not below 5Ω, check the reference voltage and signal return circuits in the sensor harness.

6. Check for opens between the sensor and the ECA as follows:

a. Turn the ignition key **OFF**.

b. Install the breakout box according to the manufacturers instructions, leaving the ECA disconnected.

c. Place the volt-ohmmeter on the 200 ohm scale and measure the resistance between pin 25 and VAF R wire pin 46 and VAF light GN/Y wire.

d. If all resistances are below 5Ω, go to Step 7. If all resistances are not below 5Ω, repair the wire(s) in question.

7. Check the sensor resistance as follows:

a. Turn the ignition key **OFF**.

b. Disconnect the sensor connector.

c. Place the volt-ohmmeter on the 10K ohm scale.

d. At 68°F (20°C), measure the resistance between the sensor terminals D and G and between terminals C and G.

e. If the resistances are between 2000–2700Ω, repair the short in the R wire. If the resistances are not between 2000–2700Ω, replace the VAF meter.

1990–92 Vehicles

1. Check the sensor input voltage as follows:

a. Install breakout box tool T83L–50–EEC–IV or equivalent and leave the ECA connected.

b. Access the temperature sensor in the VAF meter. Monitor the temperature near the sensor.

c. Turn the ignition key **ON**.

d. Measure the voltage between test pin VAT and test pin SIGRTN.

e. Compare the voltage readings to the specifications in the illustration as the temperature sensor is heated.

NOTE: *If using a hot air gun to heat the sensor, be careful not to melt any plastic or rubber components.*

f. If the voltage readings are incorrect, proceed to Step 2.

2. Check the air temperature sensor input resistance as follows:

a. Turn the ignition key **OFF**.

b. Leave the breakout box connected, but disconnect the ECA.

c. Access the temperature sensor in the VAF meter. Monitor the temperature near the sensor.

d. Measure the resistance between test pin VAT and test pin SIGRTN.

e. Compare the resistance readings to the specifications in illustration as the temperature sensor is heated.

NOTE: *If using a hot air gun to heat the sensor, be careful not to melt any plastic or rubber components.*

f. If the resistance readings are okay, proceed to Step 3. If not, proceed to Step 4.

3. Check the sensor circuit isolation as follows:

a. Turn the ignition key **OFF**.

b. Leave the breakout box connected, but disconnect the ECA.

c. Disconnect the VAF meter connector.

d. Measure the resistance between test pin VAT and all other test pins.

e. If any resistances are less than 5Ω, service the temperature sensor wire to the VAF meter. If not, replace the ECA.

4. Check temperature sensor resistance as follows:

a. Turn the ignition key **OFF**.

b. Disconnect the VAF meter connector.

c. Access the temperature sensor in the VAF meter. Monitor the temperature near the sensor.

d. Measure the resistance between the VAF meter VAT terminal and the VAF meter SIGRTN terminal (where these wires were).

e. Compare the resistance readings to the specifications in the illustration as the temperature sensor is heated.

NOTE: *If using a hot air gun to heat the sensor, be careful not to melt any plastic or rubber components.*

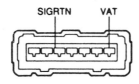

Application	Circuit	ECA Pin	BOB Pin	Wire Color
2.2L Non-Turbo (MTX)	VAT	2P	45	R
	SIGRTN	2D	46,49	LG/Y
2.2L 4EAT 2.2L Turbo	VAT	2K	45	R
	SIGRTN	3D	46,49	LG/Y

ACT sensor test pin identification—1990–92 2.2L engine

f. If the resistance readings are okay, service the VAF meter VAT and/or SIGRTN wires to the ECA. If not, replace the VAF meter.

ECT SENSOR

1989 Vehicles

1. Visually inspect all wiring, wiring harnesses, connectors and components for evidence of overheating, insulation damage, looseness, shorting or other damage and repair, as required. If everything looks okay, go to Step 2.
2. Check the ECT sensor resistance as follows:
   a. Turn the ignition key **OFF**.
   b. Install the breakout box according to the manufacturers instructions, leaving the ECA disconnected.
   c. Place the volt-ohmmeter on the 200 ohm scale and measure the resistance between pin 7 and pin 46.
   d. At −4°F (−20°C), the resistance should be 14500–17800Ω. At 68°F (20°C), the resistance should be 2200–2700Ω. At 104°F

(40°C), the resistance should be 1000–1300Ω. At 140°F (60°C), the resistance should be 500–640Ω. At 176°F (80°C), the resistance should be 280–350Ω.
   e. If all resistances are within specification, go to Step 3. If they are not, go to Step 6.
3. Check ECT sensor voltage as follows:
   a. Install the breakout box according to the manufacturers instructions.
   b. Place the volt-ohmmeter on the 20 volt scale and turn the ignition key **ON**.
   c. Measure the voltage between pin 7 and pin 46.
   d. At 68°F (20°C), the voltage should be 2.5 volts. After warming up, the voltage should be 0.3–0.6 volts.
   e. If the voltage readings are within specification, replace the ECA. If they are not, go to Step 4.
4. Check for a short between the ECT sensor and the ECA as follows:
   a. Turn the ignition key **OFF** and disconnect the negative battery cable.
   b. Install the breakout box according to the manufacturers instructions.

GRAPH

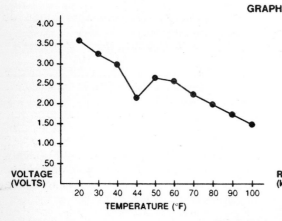
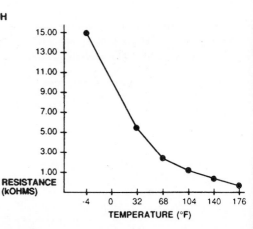

GRAPH DATA VALUES

TEMPERATURE °F	VOLTS
20	3.64
30	3.36
40	3.05
44	2.79
50	2.29
60	2.61
70	2.35
80	2.05
90	1.76
100	1.57

TEMPERATURE °F	kOHMS
-4	15
32	5.2
68	2.5
104	1.1
140	0.6
176	0.3

NOTE: Voltage and Resistance values may vary ± 15%

ACT sensor testing data—1990–92 2.2L engine

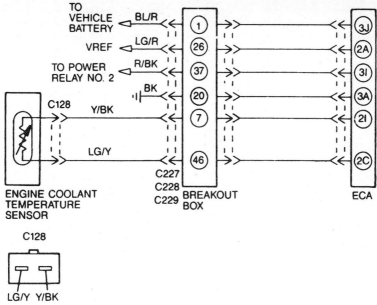

ECT sensor test schematic—1989 Probe

c. Place the volt-ohmmeter on the 200 ohm scale and measure the resistance between the following pins:

    pin 7 and pin 1
    pin 7 and pin 26
    pin 7 and pin 37
    pin 7 and pin 20
    pin 46 and pin 1
    pin 46 and pin 26
    pin 46 and pin 37

d. If any resistances are below 5Ω, repair the wire(s) in question. If any resistances are not below 5Ω, go to Step 5.

5. Check the signal return circuit as follows:

a. Turn the ignition key **OFF**.

b. Install the breakout box according to the manufacturers instructions.

c. Place the volt-ohmmeter on the 200 ohm scale and measure the resistance between pin 46 and pin 20.

d. If the resistance is below 5Ω, replace the ECA. If the resistance is not below 5Ω, check the reference voltage and signal return circuits in the sensor harness.

6. Check for an open between the ECT sensor and the ECA as follows:

a. Turn the ignition key **OFF**.

b. Install the breakout box according to the manufacturers instructions.

c. Place the volt-ohmmeter on the 200 ohm scale and measure the resistance between the ECT sensor yellow/black wire and pin 7 and between the ECT sensor light green/yellow wire and pin 46.

d. If all resistances are below 5Ω, go to

Step 7. If all resistances are not below 5Ω, repair the wire(s) in question.

7. Check the ECT sensor resistance as follows:

a. Turn the ignition key **OFF**.

b. Disconnect the ECT sensor.

c. Place the volt-ohmmeter on the 200 ohm scale and measure the resistance across the ECT sensor.

d. At −4°F (−20°C), the resistance should be 14500–17800Ω. At 68°F (20°C), the resistance should be 2200–2700Ω. At 104°F (40°C), the resistance should be 1000–1300Ω. At 140°F (60°C), the resistance should be 500–640Ω. At 176°F (80°C), the resistance should be 280–350Ω.

e. If all resistances are within specification, repair the short in the wire(s). If all resistances are not within specification, replace the ECT sensor.

1990–92 Vehicles

1. Check the ECT sensor circuit as follows:

a. Install breakout box tool T83L–50–EEC–IV or equivalent and leave the ECA disconnected.

b. Disconnect the ECT sensor.

c. Using a volt-ohmmeter, measure the continuity between test pin ECT and the ECT circuit terminal at the ECT sensor connector.

d. If there is continuity, go to Step 2. If there is no continuity, repair the ECT wire from the ECA to the ECT sensor.

2. Check the SIGRTN circuit as follows:

a. Install breakout box tool T83L–50–EEC–IV or equivalent and leave the ECA disconnected.

b. Disconnect the ECT sensor.

c. Using a volt-ohmmeter, measure the continuity between test pin SIGRTN and the SIGRTN circuit terminal at the ECT sensor connector.

d. If there is continuity, go to Step 3. If there is no continuity, repair the ECA SIGRTN wire to the ECT sensor.

3. Check ECT sensor resistance as follows:

a. Install breakout box tool T83L–50–EEC–IV or equivalent and leave the ECA connected.

b. Start the engine and bring to normal operating temperature.

c. Measure the resistance between test pins ECT and SIGRTN.

d. If the resistance is between 500–1000Ω, replace the ECA. If the resistance is not between 500–1000Ω, replace the ECT sensor.

3.0L Engine

NOTE: *The wire color to test pin 25 is yellow. The wire color to test pin 46 is light green/yellow. The wire color to test pin 7 is yellow/red.*

1. A Code 21 or 116 for the ECT or Code 24 or 114 for the ACT indicates that the corresponding sensor is out of Self-Test range. The correct range of measure is 0.3–3.7 volts. Possible causes are:

Low coolant level – ECT.

Ambient temperature below 50°F (10°C) – ACT.

Faulty harness connector.

Faulty sensor.

2. Start the engine and run it at 2000 rpm for 2 minutes. If the engine will not start, proceed to Step 5. If the engine stalls, check the idle speed control system.

3. Make sure the upper radiator hose is hot and pressurized, then rerun the Quick Test. If Codes 21, 24, 114 or 116 are present, proceed to Step 4. If they are not, service other codes. as necessary.

4. Check the VREF circuit voltage at the TP sensor as follows:

a. Turn the ignition key **OFF**.

b. Disconnect the TP sensor.

c. Turn the ignition key **ON**, but do not start the engine.

d. Using a volt-ohmmeter, measure the voltage between the VREF circuit and the SIG RTN circuit at the TP sensor vehicle harness connector.

e. If the voltage is between 4–6 volts, reconnect the TP sensor and proceed to Step 5. If not, check the vehicle battery power circuit.

5. Check the resistance of the temperature sensor with the engine off as follows:

a. Turn the ignition key **OFF**.

b. Disconnect the suspect temperature sensor.

c. Measure the resistance between the sensor signal circuit and the SIG RTN circuit at the temperature sensor.

d. If the resistance is within specification, check the ignition system if the suspect sensor is an ECT and the vehicle will not start, otherwise proceed to Step 6. If the resistance is not within specification, replace the sensor

Application	Circuit	ECA Pin	BOB Pin	Wire Color
2.2L (MTX)	ECT	2Q	7	Y/BK
	SIGRTN	2D	46,49	LG/Y
2.2L (ATX)	ECT	2E	7	Y/BK
2.2L Turbo	SIGRTN	3D	46,49	LG/Y

ECT sensor test pin identification—1990–92 2.2L engine

Coolant Temperature	ECT Sensor Resistance
-20°C (-4°F)	14.6 — 17.8 K ohms
20°C (68°F)	2.2 — 2.7 K ohms
40°C (104°F)	1.0 — 1.3 K ohms
60°C (140°F)	500 — 650 ohms
80°C (176°F)	290 — 350 ohms

ECT sensor testing data—1990–92 2.2L engine

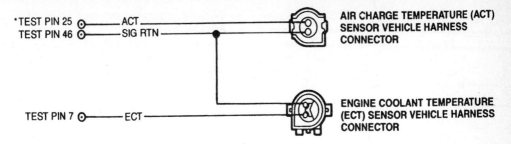

AIR CHARGE TEMPERATURE (ACT)
SENSOR VEHICLE HARNESS
CONNECTOR

TEST PIN 7 ——— ECT

ENGINE COOLANT TEMPERATURE
(ECT) SENSOR VEHICLE HARNESS
CONNECTOR

*TEST PINS LOCATED ON BREAKOUT BOX.
ALL HARNESS CONNECTORS VIEWED INTO MATING SURFACE.

ACT and ECT sensor test schematic—3.0L engine

and reconnect the vehicle harness. Rerun the Quick Test.

6. Check the resistance of the temperature sensor with the engine running as follows:

NOTE: *The engine may have cooled down. Always warm the engine before taking ECT sensor reistance measurements. Check for an open thermostat.*

a. Turn the ignition key **OFF**.

b. Disconnect the suspect temperature sensor.

c. Run the engine for 2 minutes at 2000 rpm.

d. Using a volt-ohmmeter, measure the resistance between the sensor signal circuit and the SIG RTN circuit at the temperature sensor.

e. If the resistance is within specification, replace the ECA and reconnect the vehicle harness. Rerun the Quick Test. If the resistance is not within specification, replace the sensor, reconnect the vehicle harness and rerun the Quick Test.

7. A Code 51 or 118 for the ECT or Code 54 or 113 for the ACT indicates that the corresponding sensor signal is greater than the Self-Test maximum. The maximum for ECT and ACT sensors is 4.6 volts. Possible causes are:

Open in the wiring harness.
Faulty connection.
Faulty sensor.
Faulty ECA.

8. Attempt to induce opposite Code 61 or 117, or 64 or 112, as follows:

a. Turn the ignition key **OFF**.

b. Disconnect the suspect temperature sensor.

c. Connect a jumper wire between the sensor signal circuit and SIG RTN circuit at the temperature sensor vehicle harness connector.

d. Run the Key On Engine Off Self-Test.

e. If Code, 61, 64, 112 or 117 is present, replace the sensor, remove the jumper wire and reconnect the vehicle harness. Rerun the Quick Test. If not, remove the jumper wire and proceed to Step 9.

9. Check the continuity of the sensor signal and SIG RTN circuits as follows:

a. Turn the ignition key **OFF**.

b. Disconnect the suspect temperature sensor.

c. Disconnect the ECA 60 pin connector and inspect for damaged or pushed out pins, corrosion, loose wires, etc. Repair, as necessary.

d. Install breakout box tool T83L–50–EEC–IV or equivalent, and leave the ECA disconnected.

e. Measure the resistance between the sen-

Temperature		Engine Coolant/Air Charge Temperature Sensor Values	
°F	°C	Voltage (volts)	Resistance (K ohms)
248	120	.27	1.18
230	110	.35	1.55
212	100	.46	2.07
194	90	.60	2.80
176	80	.78	3.84
158	70	1.02	5.37
140	60	1.33	7.70
122	50	1.70	10.97
104	40	2.13	16.15
86	30	2.60	24.27
68	20	3.07	27.30
50	10	3.51	58.75

ACT and ECT sensor testing data—3.0L engine

sor signal circuit at the temperature sensor vehicle harness connector and test pin 7 (ECT) or 25 (ACT) at the breakout box.

f. Measure the resistance between the SIG RTN circuit at the temperature sensor vehicle harness connector and test pin 46 at the breakout box.

g. If each resistance is less than 5Ω, replace the ECA, remove the breakout box, reconnect all components and rerun the Quick Test. If each resistance is not less than 5Ω, service the open circuits, remove the breakout box, reconnect all components and rerun the Quick Test.

10. A Code 61 or 117 for the ECT or Code 64 or 112 for the ACT indicates that the corresponding sensor's signal is less than the Self-Test minimum. The ACT and ECT sensor minimum is 0.2 volts. Possible causes are:

Grounded circuit in harness.
Faulty sensor.
Faulty ECA.
Faulty connection.

11. Attempt to induce opposite Code 51 or 118 or Code 54 or 113 as follows:

a. Turn the ignition key **OFF**.

b. Disconnect the vehicle harness from the suspect sensor. Inspect for damaged, corroded, pushed out pins or loose wires, etc. Repair as necessary.

c. Run the Key On Engine Off Self-Test.

d. If Code 51, 54, 113 or 118 is present, replace the sensor. Reconnect the harness and rerun the Quick Test. If codes are not present, proceed to Step 12.

12. Check the VREF circuit voltage at the TP sensor as follows:

a. Turn the ignition key **OFF**.

b. Disconnect the suspect temperature sensor.

c. Disconnect the TP sensor.

d. Turn the ignition key **ON**, but do not start the engine.

e. Measure the voltage between the VREF circuit and the SIG RTN circuit at the TP sensor vehicle sensor connector.

f. If the voltage is between 4–6 volts, reconnect the TP sensor and proceed to Step 13. If not, check the vehicle battery power circuit.

13. Check the temperature sensor signal circuit for short to ground as follows:

a. Turn the ignition key **OFF**.

b. Disconnect the suspect temperature sensor.

c. Disconnect the ECA 60 pin connector and inspect for damaged or pushed out pins, corrosion, loose wires, etc. Repair, as necessary.

d. Install breakout box tool T83L–50–

EEC–IV or equivalent, and leave the ECA disconnected.

e. Measure the resistance between test pin 7 (ECT) or 25 (ACT) and test pins 40, 46 and 60 at the breakout box.

f. If each resistance is greater than 10,000Ω, replace the ECA, remove the breakout box, reconnect all components and rerun the Quick Test. If each resistance is not greater than 10,000Ω, service the short circuit, remove the breakout box, reconnect all components and rerun the Quick Test.

14. Continuous Memory Codes 51 or 118 (ECT) and 54 or 113 (ACT) indicate that the sensor signal was greater than the Self-Test maximum of 4.6 volts. Continuous Memory Codes 61 or 117 (ECT) and 64 or 112 (ACT) indicate that the sensor signal was less than the Self-Test minimum of 0.2 volts. The code was generated under normal driving conditions. Possible causes are:

Faulty sensor.
Open circuit in harness.
Grounded circuit in harness.
Faulty ECA.

15. Check the sensor as follows:

a. Enter the Key On Engine Off continuous monitor mode.

b. Observe the volt-ohmmeter or STAR LED for indication of a fault while tapping on the sensor to simulate road shock.

c. Observe the volt-ohmmeter or STAR LED for indication of a fault while wiggling the sensor connector.

d. If a fault is indicated, disconnect and inspect the connectors. If they are okay, replace the sensor and clear the Continuous Memory. Rerun the Quick Test. If a fault is not indicated, proceed to Step 16.

16. While still in the Key On Engine Off continuous monitor mode, observe the volt-ohmmeter or STAR LED for fault indication while wiggling, shaking or bending small sections of the EEC-IV system vehicle harness from the sensor to the ECA. If a fault is indicated, repair as necessary, clear Continuous Memory and rerun the Quick Test. If a fault is not indicated, proceed to Step 17.

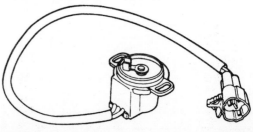

TP sensor—2.2L engines

17. Check the ECA and vehicle harness connectors for damage, loose or pushed out pins, loose or poorly crimped wires. Service as necessary.

18. A Continuous Memory Code 338 or 339 indicates a cooling system problem. Check the thermostat, water pump, radiator cap and radiator. Check for low coolant level and check for coolant leaks.

REMOVAL AND INSTALLATION

For ACT and ECT sensor removal and installation procedures, refer to Chapter 3 under Sending Units and Sensors.

Throttle Position Sensor

OPERATION

The TP sensor is a rotary potentiometer that is attached to the throttle shaft blade. It detects throttle plate opening angle and supplies the ECA with an input signal indicating throttle position. The ECA uses the TP sensor information to control fuel mixture, idle speed, spark advance and EGR flow.

SERVICE

2.2L Engine

1989 VEHICLES

1. Visually inspect all wiring, wiring harnesses, connectors and components for evidence of overheating, insulation damage, looseness, shorting or other damage and repair, as required. If everything looks okay, go to Step 2.

2. Check the VREF and SIGRTN circuits as follows:

   a. Install the breakout box according to the manufacturers instructions.

   b. Place the volt-ohmmeter on the 20 volt scale.

   c. Turn the ignition key **ON**.

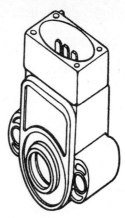

TP sensor—3.0L engine

   d. Measure the voltage between pin 26 and pin 20; it should be 4–6 volts.

   e. Measure the voltage between pin 26 and pin 46; it should be 4–6 volts.

   f. Measure the voltage between pin 20 and pin 46; it should be 4 volts.

   g. If all voltage readings are within specification, go to Step 3. If the voltage readings are not within specification, check the reference voltage and signal return circuits.

3. Check the TP sensor voltage as follows:

   a. Install the breakout box according to the manufacturers instructions.

   b. Place the volt-ohmmeter on the 20 volt scale.

   c. Turn the ignition key **ON**.

   d. Measure the voltage between pin 47 and pin 46.

   e. With the throttle closed, the reading should be 0.36–0.66 volts. With the throttle wide open, the reading should be approximately 4.3 volts.

   f. If both voltage readings are within speci-

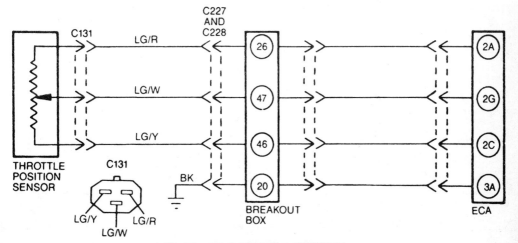

TP sensor test schematic—1989 Probe

fication, replace the ECA. If they are not, go to Step 4.

4. Check for power at the TP sensor as follows:

a. Place the volt-ohmmeter on the 20 volt scale.

b. Turn the ignition key **ON**.

c. Measure the voltage between the TP sensor LG/R wire and ground; it should be 4–6 volts.

d. Measure the voltage between the TP sensor LG/R wire and LG/Y wire; it should be 4–6 volts.

e. Measure the voltage between the TP sensor LG/Y wire and ground; it should be 0 volts.

f. If all voltage readings are within specification, go to Step 5. If they are not, repair the LG/R and/or LG/Y wire(s) from the TP sensor to the ECA.

5. Check TP sensor voltage as follows:

a. Leave the TP sensor connected.

b. Place the volt-ohmmeter on the 20 volt scale.

c. Turn the ignition key **ON**.

d. Without piercing the wire, measure the voltage between the TP sensor LG/W wire and ground.

e. With the throttle closed, the reading should be 0.36–0.66 volts. With the throttle wide open, the reading should be approximately 4.3 volts.

f. If both voltage readings are within specification, repair the open in the LG/W wire from the TP sensor to the ECA. If both voltage readings are not within specification, adjust or replace the TP sensor, as required.

1990–92 VEHICLES

1. Check throttle position input voltage as follows:

a. Install breakout box tool T83L–50–EEC–IV or equivalent, and connect the ECA.

b. Turn the ignition key **ON**.

c. Using a volt-ohmmeter, measure the re-sistance between test pin TP and test pin SIGRTN.

d. Compare voltage readings to those in the illustration as the accelerator is depressed.

e. If the voltage readings are correct, the throttle position circuit is okay, check the ECA. If not, proceed to Step 2.

2. Check the throttle position signal from the TP sensor as follows:

a. Disconnect the TP sensor connector.

b. Using jumper wires, connect the VREF and SIGRTN terminals between the harness connector and the TP sensor connector. Leave the TP wire disconnected.

c. Turn the ignition key **ON**.

d. Using a volt-ohmmeter, measure the voltage between the TP terminal and SIGRTN wire at the throttle position sensor.

e. Compare voltage readings to those in the illustration as the accelerator is depressed.

f. If the voltage readings are okay, service the throttle position sensor TP wire to the ECA. If not, proceed to Step 3.

3. Check the VREF/SIGRTN at the TP sensor as follows:

a. Disconnect the TP sensor.

b. Turn the ignition key **ON**.

c. Using a volt-ohmmeter, measure the voltage between the TP sensor VREF wire and the TP sensor SIGRTN wire, at the harness connector leading to the ECA.

d. If the voltage reading is between 4.5–5.5 volts, adjust or replace the TP sensor. If not, check reference voltage.

3.0L Engine

NOTE: *The wire color to test pin 46 is light green/yellow. The wire color to test pin 26 is light green/red. The wire color to test pin 47 is light green/black.*

1. An Engine Running Code 23 or 121 indicates that the TP sensor's rotational setting

Application	Circuit	ECA Pin	BOB Pin	Wire Color
2.2L 4EAT (MTX)	TP	2F (2M)	47	LG/BK
	VREF	2I (2K)	26	LG/R
	SIGRTN	3D (2D)	46,49	LG/Y
2.2L Turbo	TP	2F	47	LG/BK
	VREF	2I	26	LG/R
	SIGRTN	3D	46,49	LG/Y

TP sensor test pin identification—1990–92 2.2L engine

may be out of Self-Test range. Possible causes are:

> Binding throttle linkage.
> TP sensor may not be seated properly.
> Damaged TP sensor.
> Damaged ECA.

2. Check for a Code 31 or 327 in the Key On Engine Running Self-Test. If Code 31 or 327 (PFE sensor circuit voltage below Self-Test minimum) is present along with Code 23 or 121, service must be performed to eliminate Code 31 or 327. If Code 31 or 327 is not present with Code 23 or 121, proceed to Step 3.

3. Visually inspect the throttle body and throttle linkage for binding or sticking. Make sure the throttle linkage is at mechanical closed throttle. Check for binding throttle or cruise control linkage, vacuum line/wiring harness interference, etc. If the throttle moves freely and returns to the closed throttle position, proceed to Step 4. If not, service as necessary and rerun the Quick Test.

4. A Code 53 or 123 indicates that the TP sensor signal is greater than the Self-Test maximum value. Possible causes are:

> TP sensor may not be seated properly (tightened down).
> Damaged TP sensor.
> Short to power in harness.
> Damaged ECA.

5. Attempt to generate Code 63 or 122 as follows:

a. Turn the ignition key **OFF**.

b. Disconnect the TP sensor and inspect for pushed out pins, corrosion and loose wires. Service as necessary.

c. Disconnect both 4EAT module vehicle harness connectors if equipped with automatic transaxle and Stand-Alone 4EAT module.

NOTE: *To determine if the vehicle is equipped with a "Stand-Alone 4EAT" module, look for the module under the driver's side dash between the steering column and kick panel.*

d. Rerun the Key On Engine Off Self-Test. If Code 63 or 122 is present (ignore all other codes), proceed to Step 6. If not, proceed to Step 8.

6. Check VREF circuit voltage as follows:

GRAPH

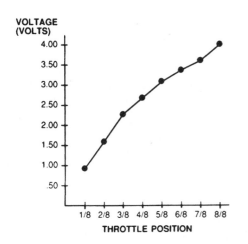

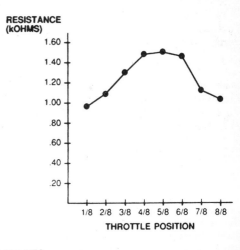

GRAPH DATA VALUES

THROTTLE POSITION	VOLTS
1/8	.998
2/8	1.60
3/8	2.37
4/8	2.74
5/8	3.15
6/8	3.43
7/8	3.60
8/8	4.02

THROTTLE POSITION	kOHMS
1/8	.989
2/8	1.104
3/8	1.278
4/8	1.462
5/8	1.480
6/8	1.459
7/8	1.144
8/8	1.072

NOTE: Voltage and Resistance values may vary ± 15%.

TP sensor testing data—1990–92 2.2L engine

a. Turn the ignition key **OFF**.

b. Disconnect the TP sensor. Disconnect both 4EAT module harness connectors, if applicable.

c. Turn the ignition key **ON**, but leave the engine off.

d. Measure the voltage between the VREF circuit and the SIG RTN circuit at the TP sensor vehicle harness connector.

e. If the voltage reading is 4–6 volts, if equipped with automatic transaxle and and Stand-Alone 4EAT, proceed to Step 7; on all other vehicles, replace the TP sensor and re-run the Quick Test.

f. If the voltage reading is not 4–6 volts, re-connect all components and check reference voltage.

7. Check for a shorted 4EAT module as follows:

NOTE: *Vehicles with automatic transaxle and Stand-Alone 4EAT module have a TP circuit input to the 4EAT module. This test is to make sure the TP circuit is not shorted inside the 4EAT module.*

a. Turn the ignition key **OFF**.

b. Reconnect the TP sensor, but leave both 4EAT module vehicle harness connectors disconnected.

c. Rerun the Key On Engine Off Self-Test.

d. If Code 53 or 123 is present (ignore all other codes), replace the TP sensor and rerun the Quick Test. If not, check for a short in the 4EAT system.

8. Check the TP circuit for shorts to power as follows:

a. Turn the ignition key **OFF** and discon-nect the TP sensor.

b. Disconnect the ECA 60 pin connector and inspect for damaged or pushed out pins, corrosion, loose wires, etc. and service as necessary.

c. Install breakout box tool T83L–50–EEC–IV or equivalent, and leave the ECA disconnected.

d. Measure the resistance between test pin 47 and test pins 26 and 57 at the breakout box.

e. If each resistance is greater than 10,000Ω, replace the ECA, remove the break-out box, reconnect the TP sensor and rerun the Quick Test. If each resistance is not greater than 10,000Ω, service the short cir-cuit, remove the breakout box, reconnect all components and rerun the Quick Test.

9. Code 63 or 122 indicates that the TP sen-sor signal is less than the Self-Test minimum value. Possible causes are:

TP sensor not seated properly (tightened down).

Damaged TP sensor.

Open harness.

Grounded harness.

Damaged ECA.

10. Attempt to generate Code 23 or 121, or Code 53 or 123 as follows:

a. Turn the ignition key **OFF**.

b. Disconnect the TP sensor and check for pushed out pins, corrosion, loose wires, etc. and service as necessary.

c. Connect a jumper wire between the VREF circuit and the TP circuit at the TP sensor vehicle harness connector.

d. Perform the Key On Engine Off Self-Test.

e. If no codes are generated, immediately remove the jumper wire and proceed to Step 14 except on vehicles with automatic transax-le and Stand-Alone 4EAT, proceed to Step 13.

f. If Code 23 or 121 or Code 53 or 123 is present (ignore all other codes), replace the TP sensor and remove the jumper wire; re-run the Quick Test. If the specified codes are not present, remove the jumper wire and pro-ceed to Step 11.

11. Check VREF circuit voltage as follows:

a. Turn the ignition key **OFF** and discon-nect the TP sensor.

b. Turn the ignition key **ON** but do not start the engine.

c. Measure the voltage between the VREF circuit and the SIG RTN circuit at the TP sensor vehicle harness connector.

d. If the voltage reading is 4–6 volts, pro-ceed to Step 12. If not, reconnect all compo-nents and check reference voltage.

12. Check TP circuit continuity as follows:

a. Turn the ignition key **OFF** and discon-nect the TP sensor.

b. Disconnect the ECA 60 pin connector and inspect for damaged or pushed out pins, corrosion, loose wires, etc. and service as necessary.

c. Install breakout box tool T83L–50–EEC–IV or equivalent, and leave the ECA disconnected.

d. Measure the resistance between the TP circuit at the TP sensor vehicle harness con-nector and test pin 47 at the breakout box.

e. If the resistance is less than 5Ω, proceed to Step 14. If not, service the open circuit, re-move the breakout box, reconnect all compo-nents and rerun the Quick Test.

13. Check for a shorted 4EAT module as follows:

NOTE: *Vehicles with automatic transaxle and Stand-Alone 4EAT module have a TP circuit input to the 4EAT module. This test is to make sure the TP circuit is not shorted in-side the 4EAT module.*

a. Turn the ignition key **OFF**.

b. Reconnect the TP sensor.

c. Disconnect both 4EAT module vehicle harness connectors if equipped with automatic transaxle and Stand-Alone 4EAT module.

NOTE: *To determine if the vehicle is equipped with a "Stand-Alone 4EAT" module, look for the module under the driver's side dash between the steering column and kick panel.*

d. Rerun the Key On Engine Off Self-Test. If Code 63 or 122 is present (ignore all other codes), disconnect the TP sensor and proceed to Step 14. If not, check for a short in the 4EAT system.

14. Check the TP circuit for shorts to ground as follows:

a. Turn the ignition key **OFF** and disconnect the TP sensor.

b. Disconnect the ECA 60 pin connector and inspect for damaged or pushed out pins, corrosion, loose wires, etc. and service as necessary.

c. Install breakout box tool T83L–50–EEC–IV or equivalent, and leave the ECA disconnected.

d. Measure the resistance between test pin 47 and test pins 40, 46 and 60 at the breakout box.

e. If each resistance is greater than 10,000Ω, replace the ECA, remove the breakout box, reconnect all components and rerun the Quick Test. If each resistance is not greater than 10,000Ω, service the short cir-

cuit, remove the breakout box, reconnect all components and rerun the Quick Test.

15. An Engine Running Code 73 or 167 indicates that the TP sensor did not exceed 25 percent of its rotation during the Dynamic Response test.

NOTE: *The Dynamic Response Test is used on some applications to verify operation of the TP, MAF and MAP sensors during the brief Wide-Open Throttle (WOT) performed during the Engine Running Self-Test. The signal to perform the brief WOT is a single pulse or 10 Code on the STAR tester.*

16. Run the Key On Engine Running Self-Test and make sure a complete WOT is performed during the Dynamic Response portion of the test. If Code 73 or 167 is still present, proceed to Step 17. If not, service other Engine Running codes as necessary, otherwise testing is completed.

17. Check TP sensor movement during the Dynamic Response test as follows:

a. Turn the ignition key **OFF**.

b. Disconnect the ECA 60 pin connector and inspect for damaged or pushed out pins, corrosion, loose wires, etc. and service as necessary.

c. Install breakout box tool T83L–50–EEC–IV or equivalent, and connect the ECA to the breakout box.

d. Connect a voltmeter to test pin 47 and test pin 46 at the breakout box.

e. Rerun the Engine Running Self-Test

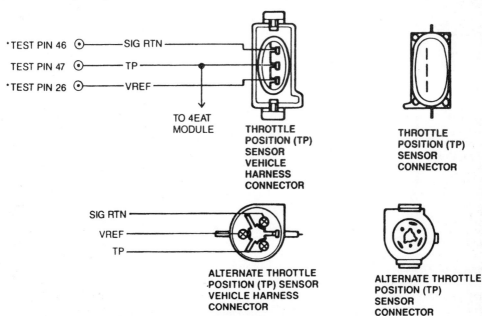

TEST PIN 46 — SIG RTN
TEST PIN 47 — TP
TEST PIN 26 — VREF

TO 4EAT MODULE

THROTTLE POSITION (TP) SENSOR VEHICLE HARNESS CONNECTOR

THROTTLE POSITION (TP) SENSOR CONNECTOR

SIG RTN
VREF
TP

ALTERNATE THROTTLE POSITION (TP) SENSOR VEHICLE HARNESS CONNECTOR

ALTERNATE THROTTLE POSITION (TP) SENSOR CONNECTOR

*TEST PINS LOCATED ON BREAKOUT BOX.
ALL HARNESS CONNECTORS VIEWED INTO MATING SURFACE.

TP sensor test schematic—3.0L engine

with a proper WOT Dynamic Response portion of the test.

f. If the voltage increases to greater than 3.5 volts during the Dynamic Response test, replace the ECA and remove the breakout box; rerun the Quick Test. If the voltage does not increase to greater than 3.5 volts, make sure the TP sensor is properly installed on the throttle body; if it is, replace the TP sensor and rerun the Quick Test.

18. Check the TP circuit under simulated road shock as follows:

a. Enter the Key On Engine Off Continuous Monitor mode.

b. Observe the volt-ohmmeter or STAR LED for an indication of a fault while: moving the throttle slowly to the WOT position, releasing the throttle slowly to the closed position and lightly tapping on the TP sensor, and wiggling the TP harness connector.

c. If the volt-ohmmeter or STAR LED indicates a fault, proceed to Step 19. If not, proceed to Step 20.

19. Measure the TP signal voltage while exercising the TP sensor as follows:

a. Turn the ignition key **OFF**.

b. Disconnect the ECA 60 pin connector and inspect for damaged or pushed out pins, corrosion, loose wires, etc. and service as necessary.

c. Install breakout box tool T83L–50–EEC–IV or equivalent, and connect the ECA to the breakout box.

d. Leave the volt-ohmmeter or STAR LED connected to the STO as in Step 18.

e. Connect a voltmeter from test pin 47 to test pin 46 at the breakout box.

f. Turn the ignition key **ON**, but do not start the engine.

g. While observing the voltmeter, repeat Step 18.

h. If the fault occurs below 4.25 volts, disconnect and inspect the connectors. If the connector and terminals are good, replace the TP sensor and clear Continuous Memory. Rerun the Quick Test.

i. If the fault does not occur below 4.25 volts, TP sensor overtravel may have caused Continuous Memory Code 53 or 123. Check the vehicle wiring harness and proceed to Step 20.

20. While still in the Key On Engine Off Continuous Monitor mode, observe the volt-ohmmeter or STAR LED for a fault indication while wiggling, shaking, or bending a small section of the EEC-IV harness while working towards the dash panel to the ECA. If a fault is indicated, service as necessary, clear Continuous Memory and rerun the Quick Test. If a fault is not indicated, proceed to Step 21.

NOTE: **The normal range of the throttle angle measurement for the Throttle Position (TP) sensor is from 0 to 85 degrees.**

TP Sensor Graph

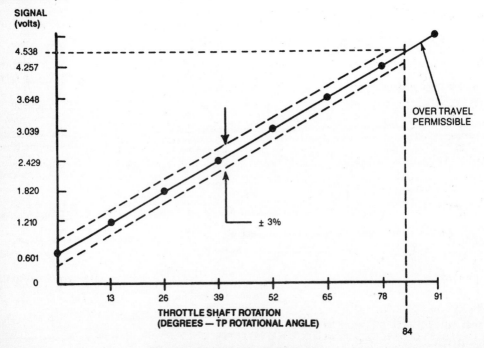

TP sensor testing data—3.0L engine

21. Check the ECA and vehicle harness connectors for damage, loose or pushed out pins, loose or poorly crimped wires. Service as necessary.

ADJUSTMENT

2.2L Engine

1. Remove the air duct from the throttle body assembly, if necessary.
2. Disconnect the TP sensor connector at the bottom of the throttle body.
3. Remove the plastic connector shield from the male side of the TP sensor connector.
4. Connect the unshielded male side TP sensor connector to the female. Make sure the wire leads are in their proper connector locations.

NOTE: *Extreme care must be taken not to accidentally ground the exposed wire leads.*

5. Turn the ignition switch to the **ON** position.
6. Make sure that both throttle valves are in the fully closed position.
7. Connect a volt-ohmmeter to the red and black wires and record the voltage reading for the red wire. It should be 4.5–5.5 volts.
8. Remove the volt-ohmmeter lead from the red wire and connect it to the white wire. Loosen, but do not completely remove the TP sensor mounting screws.
9. Turn the TP sensor to adjust the white wire voltage to the range specified for the red wire.
10. Tighten the TP sensor mounting screws

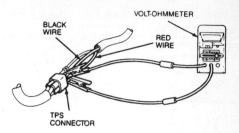
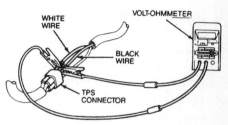

Volt-ohmmeter connections for TP sensor adjustment—2.2L engine

and recheck that the white wire voltage is within specification.

NOTE: *If the white wire voltage cannot be adjusted to specification, the TP sensor must be replaced and this procedure repeated on the new sensor.*

11. Hold the throttle valves in the fully open position. Measure the red wire voltage and record it.
12. Check that the white wire voltage is within the range of the red wire voltage recorded at full throttle.

NOTE: *If the white wire voltage cannot be adjusted to specification, the TP sensor must be replaced and this procedure repeated on the new sensor.*

13. Turn the ignition switch **OFF**.
14. Disconnect the volt-ohmmeter and replace the plastic shield on the male side TP sensor connector.
15. Reconnect the TP sensor connector.
16. Disconnect the negative battery cable and depress the brake pedal for at least 2 seconds to eliminate the ECA malfunction memory.
17. Connect the negative battery cable.

WARNING: *Do not adjust the idle switch at*

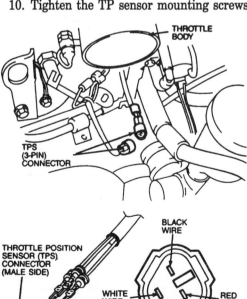

TP sensor harness connector—2.2L engine

Adjusting the TP sensor—2.2L engine

Specification: Throttle valve fully closed position

RED wire voltage (V)	WHITE wire voltage (V)	RED wire voltage (V)	WHITE wire voltage (V)
4.50–4.59	0.37–0.54	5.10–5.19	0.42–0.61
4.60–4.69	0.38–0.55	5.20–5.29	0.43–0.62
4.70–4.79	0.39–0.56	5.30–5.39	0.44–0.63
4.80–4.89	0.40–0.57	5.40–5.49	0.44–0.64
4.90–4.99	0.40–0.58	5.50	0.44–0.66
5.00–5.09	0.41–0.60		

Specification: Throttle valve fully open position

RED wire voltage (V)	WHITE wire voltage (V)	RED wire voltage (V)	WHITE wire voltage (V)
4.50–4.59	3.58–4.23	5.10–5.19	4.05–4.79
4.60–4.69	3.66–4.32	5.20–5.29	4.13–4.88
4.70–4.79	3.74–4.41	5.30–5.39	4.21–4.98
4.80–4.89	3.82–4.51	5.40–5.49	4.29–5.07
4.90–4.99	3.90–4.60	5.50	4.29–5.17
5.00–5.09	3.97–4.70		

TP sensor adjustment specifications—2.2L engine

the throttle lever. This is adjusted at the factory and should not be tampered with. Doing so may result in damage to, or the necessary replacement of, the throttle body.

3.0L Engine

The TP sensor on the 3.0L engine is not adjustable.

REMOVAL AND INSTALLATION

2.2L Engine

1. Disconnect the negative battery cable.
2. Remove the air duct from the throttle body.
3. Disconnect the electrical connector at the throttle body. Carefully bend back the TP sensor wire retaining brackets and remove the wire.
4. Remove the 2 attaching screws and remove the TP sensor from the throttle body.
To install:
5. Position the sensor onto the throttle body.
6. Install the wire into the retaining brackets and carefully bend them around the wires.
7. Install the attaching screws finger-tight.
8. Adjust the sensor as previously described.
9. Connect the electrical connector at the throttle body and install the air duct to the throttle body.
10. Connect the negative battery cable.

3.0L Engine

1. Disconnect the negative battery cable.
2. Remove the distributor protective boot.

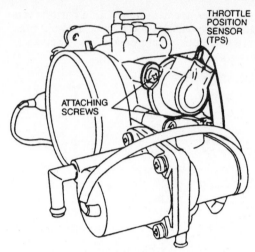

TP sensor removal and installation—2.2L engine

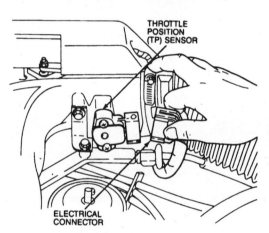

TP sensor removal and installation—3.0L engine

3. Remove the distributor cap mounting screws and position the cap and wires aside.
4. Disconnect the TP sensor electrical connector.
5. Remove the 2 TP sensor mounting screws and remove the sensor.
To install:
6. Install the TP sensor, making sure the rotary tangs on the sensor are in proper alignment and the red seal is inside the connector housing.
NOTE: *Slide the rotary tangs into position over the throttle shaft blade, then rotate the TP sensor clockwise to the installed position only. Failure to install the TP sensor this way may result in excessive idle speeds.*
7. Install the sensor retaining screws and tighten to 14 inch lbs. (1.5 Nm). This TP sensor is not adjustable.
8. Connect the TP sensor electrical connector.

9. Install the distributor cap and the protective boot.

10. Connect the negative battery cable.

Idle Speed Control System

OPERATION

The Idle Speed Control/Bypass Air (ISC/BPA) valve is used to control engine idle speed. The valve is mounted on the throttle body and allows air to bypass the throttle plates to control: cold engine fast idle, no touch start, dashpot, hot engine idle speed and engine idle load correction.

On the 3.0L engine, the valve is operated by the ECA. On the 2.2L engine, the BPA valve reacts to engine coolant temperature during cold engine conditions — below 122°F (50°C), while the ISC solenoid valve works throughout the engine rpm range and is controlled by the ECA.

SERVICE

2.2L Engine

Visually inspect the ISC/BPA valve and associated components. Check for: Loose, leaking, pinched, kinked or otherwise damaged coolant and air hoses and connections, loose fasteners or hose clamps, excessively low or high idle

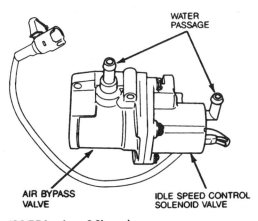

ISC/BPA valve—2.2L engine

speed when the engine is hot, hard starting when the engine is cold, poor fuel economy, engine coolant does not warm up, white smoke from the tailpipe.

Disconnect the accelerator cable and air hose at the throttle body and check that both throttle valves move smoothly when the throttle lever is moved from fully closed to fully open position. Check for contamination causing binding, bent throttle plates, loose throttle plates, or other damage.

Manipulate the coolant and air hoses to determine the extent of damage or looseness. If a component is suspected as the obvious cause of a malfunction, service the component before proceeding further. If all visual checks are okay, proceed as follows:

1. Check idle speed adjustment as follows:

   a. Ground the black, 1-pin Self-Test input connector.

   b. Turn all accessories **OFF** and warm up the engine. Note the idle speed.

   c. Run the engine until the cooling fan turns **ON**.

   d. Check the initial ignition timing and adjust, if necessary.

   e. Adjust the air adjustment screw for an idle speed of 750 ± 25 rpm, manual transaxle in neutral or automatic transaxle in **P**.

   f. Turn the engine **OFF** and allow it to cool down.

   g. After the engine has cooled, restart the engine and note the idle speed.

   h. If the engine still speeds up during warm up when the engine is started cold, check electrical connections and for vacuum leaks, check the throttle plates and linkage for binding or sticking, check the air cleaner and duct, check the VAF meter, check the ignition advance and retard functions, check the evaporative system components and check the EEC system.

   i. If the engines does not speed up during warm up when the engine is started cold, proceed to Step 2.

2. Check if the ISC/BPA valve is stuck open as follows:

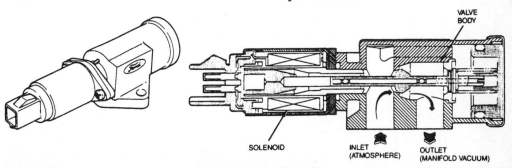

ISC/BPA valve—3.0L engine

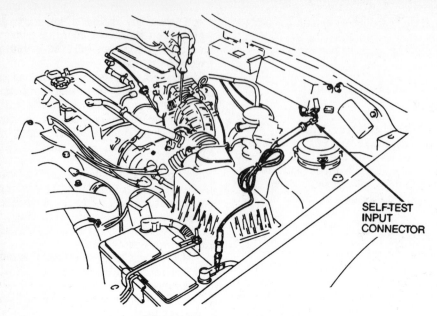

SELF-TEST
INPUT
CONNECTOR

Adjusting idle speed—2.2L engine

a. Remove the valve from the engine.

b. Connect a test hose from a hot water tap to 1 of the coolant hose nipples on the valve and circulate hot water, 130°F (56°C) minimum through the valve.

c. Blow through the valve air port A before and again after circulating the hot water, and verify whether the resistance to air flow increases when hot water is circulated. Allow enough time for the valve to respond to the water temperature change.

d. If the air flow resistance increases considerably as the valve warms up, proceed to Step 3. If there is little or no increase, replace the valve.

3. Check if the ISC/BPA valve is stuck closed as follows:

a. Remove the valve from the engine.

b. When the valve is cold, at room temperature, blow through the valve air port A and verify whether air comes out of port B.

c. If air flows freely through the valve when it is at room temperature, proceed to Step 4. If not, replace valve.

4. Check the ISC/BPA valve resistance as follows:

a. Disconnect the valve connector.

b. Connect an ohmmeter to the terminals of the valve and check the resistance.

c. If the resistance is not between 6–14Ω, replace the valve.

3.0L Engine

NOTE: *The wire color to test pin 21 is white/red. The wire color to test pin 37 and 57 is red/black.*

1. Code 12 or 412 indicates that during the Engine Running Self-Test, engine rpm could not be controlled within the Self-Test upper limit band. Possible causes are:

Open or shorted circuit.

Throttle linkage binding.

Improper idle airflow set.

Throttle body/ISC/BPA valve contamination.

Items external to Idle Speed Control system that could affect engine rpm.

Damaged ISC/BPA valve.

Damaged ECA.

2. Check for rpm drop as follows:

a. Turn the ignition key **OFF**.

b. Connect a tachometer to the engine.

c. Start the engine.

d. Disconnect the ISC/BPA harness connector.

e. If the rpm drops or the engine stalls, proceed to Step 3. If not, proceed to Step 4.

3. Check for EGR codes. If Codes 31 or 327,

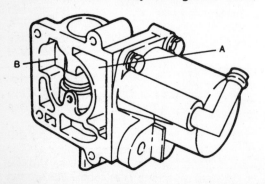

ISC/BPA valve—2.2L engine

32 or 326, 328, 33 or 332, 34 or 336, 334 or 213 are present, reconnect the ISC/BPA valve and service the appropriate system to eliminate the code(s). If not, proceed to Step 4.

4. Check for other EEC codes. If Codes 22 or 126, 41 or 172, 42 or 173, 91 or 136, or 92 or 137 are present, reconnect the ISC/BPA valve and service the appropriate system to eliminate the code(s). If not, proceed to Step 5.

5. Measure ISC/BPA valve resistance as follows:

a. Turn the ignition key **OFF**.

b. Disconnect the ISC/BPA valve.

c. Measure the ISC/BPA valve resistance.

NOTE: *Due to the diode in the solenoid, place the ohmmeter positive lead on the VPWR pin and the negative lead on the ISC pin.*

d. If the resistance is 6–13Ω, proceed to Step 6. If not, replace the ISC/BPA valve and rerun the Quick Test.

6. Check for internal short to the ISC/BPA valve case as follows:

a. Turn the ignition key **OFF**.

b. Disconnect the ISC/BPA valve.

c. Measure the resistance from either ISC/BPA valve pin to the ISC/BPA valve housing.

d. If the resistance is greater than 10,000Ω, proceed to Step 7. If not, replace the ISC/BPA valve and rerun the Quick Test.

7. Check the VPWR circuit voltage as follows:

a. Turn the ignition key **ON**, but do not start the engine.

b. Disconnect the ISC/BPA valve.

c. Measure the voltage between the VPWR circuit at the ISC/BPA valve vehicle harness connector and battery ground.

d. If the voltage is greater than 10.5 volts, proceed to Step 8. If not, service the open circuit and rerun the Quick Test.

8. Check ISC circuit continuity as follows:

a. Turn the ignition key **OFF** and disconnect the ISC/BPA valve.

b. Disconnect the ECA and inspect both 60 pin connectors for damaged or pushed out pins, corrosion, loose wires, etc. and service, as necessary.

c. Install breakout box tool T83L–50–EEC–IV or equivalent, and leave the ECA disconnected.

d. Measure the resistance between test pin 21 at the breakout box and the ISC circuit at the ISC/BPA valve vehicle harness connector.

e. If the resistance is less than 5Ω, proceed to Step 9. If not, service the open circuit, remove the breakout box and reconnect all components; rerun the Quick Test.

9. Check the ISC circuit for short to ground as follows:

a. Turn the ignition key **OFF** and disconnect the ISC/BPA valve.

b. Install breakout box tool T83L–50–EEC–IV or equivalent, and leave the ECA disconnected.

c. Measure the resistance between test pin 21 and test pins 40, 46 and 60 at the breakout box.

d. If each resistance is greater than 10,000Ω, proceed to Step 10. If not, service the short circuit, remove the breakout box and reconnect all components; rerun the Quick Test.

10. Check the ISC circuit for short to power as follows:

a. Turn the ignition key **OFF** and disconnect the ISC/BPA valve.

b. Install breakout box tool T83L–50–EEC–IV or equivalent, and leave the ECA disconnected.

c. Turn the ignition key **ON**.

d. Measure the voltage between test pin 21 at the breakout box and chassis ground.

e. If the voltage is less than 1 volt, proceed to Step 11. If not, service the short circuit, remove the breakout box and reconnect all components. Rerun the Quick Test. If code or symptom is still present, replace the ECA.

11. Check for ISC signal from the ECA as follows:

a. Turn the ignition key **OFF**.

b. Install breakout box tool T83L–50–EEC–IV or equivalent, and reconnect the ECA to the breakout box.

c. Reconnect the ISC/BPA valve.

d. Connect a volt-ohmmeter between test pin 21 and test pin 40 at the breakout box.

e. Start the engine and slowly increase engine speed to 3000 rpm.

f. If the voltage reading is 3–11.5 volts, proceed to Step 12. If not, remove the ISC/BPA valve and make sure it is not stuck open. If it is okay, replace the ECA and remove the breakout box; rerun the Quick Test.

12. Check engine idle speed. If engine idle speed appears normal, remove the ISC/BPA valve and inspect it for contamination. If there is contamination, replace the ISC/BPA valve and rerun the Quick Test.

13. If engine idle speed does not appear normal, reset the idle airflow to specification. If unable to set idle to specification, proceed to Step 14.

14. Check for problems affecting proper engine speed, such as binding throttle and/or cruise control linkage, contaminated throttle body, engine vacuum hoses and leaks around the ISC/BPA valve. If all checks out okay, re-

move the ISC/BPA valve and inspect it for contamination. If there is contamination, replace the ISC/BPA valve and rerun the Quick Test. If any of the problems exist, service as necessary, remove the breakout box and reconnect the ECA; rerun the Quick Test.

15. Code 13 or 411 indicates that during the Engine Running Self-Test, engine rpm could not be controlled within the Self-Test lower limit band. Possible causes are:

Improper idle airflow set.

Vacuum leaks.

throttle linkage binding.

Throttle plates open.

Improper ignition timing.

Throttle body/ISC solenoid contamination.

ISC circuit short to ground.

Damaged ISC solenoid.

16. If engine idle speed appears normal, remove the ISC/BPA valve and inspect it for contamination. If there is contamination, replace the ISC/BPA valve and rerun the Quick Test.

17. If engine idle speed does not appear normal, reset the idle airflow to specification. If unable to set the idle to specification, proceed to Step 18.

18. Check for conditions affecting idle as follows:

a. Check engine vacuum hoses for leaks.

b. Check throttle and/or cruise control linkage for binding.

c. Check that throttle plates are closed.

d. Check for induction system leaks. Check the ISC/BPA valve-to-throttle body gasket, EGR flange gasket, loose ISC/EGR/PCV, etc.

e. Check the throttle body for contamination.

f. Make sure the base timing is set to specification.

g. Make sure the purge solenoid(s) is not stuck open, if equipped.

h. If all of the above checks are okay, proceed to Step 19. If not, service as necessary and rerun the Quick Test.

19. Check for internal short to ISC/BPA valve case as follows:

a. Turn the ignition key **OFF** and disconnect the ISC/BPA valve.

b. Measure the resistance from either ISC/BPA valve pin to the ISC/BPA valve housing.

c. If the resistance is greater than 10,000Ω, proceed to Step 20. If not, replace the ISC/BPA valve and rerun the Quick Test.

20. Check the ISC circuit for short to ground as follows:

a. Turn the ignition key **OFF** and disconnect the ISC/BPA valve.

b. Disconnect the ECA 60 pin connector and inspect for damaged or pushed out pins, corrosion, loose wires, etc. and service as necessary.

c. Install breakout box tool T83L–50–EEC–IV or equivalent, and leave the ECA disconnected.

d. Measure the resistance between test pin 21 and test pins 40, 46 and 60 at the breakout box.

e. If all resistances are greater than 10,000Ω, proceed to Step 21. If not, service the short circuit, remove the breakout box and reconnect all components; rerun the Quick Test.

21. Check ECA output as follows:

a. Turn the ignition key **OFF**.

b. Install breakout box tool T83L–50–EEC–IV or equivalent, and reconnect the ECA to the breakout box.

c. Reconnect the ISC/BPA valve.

d. Connect a volt-ohmmeter between test pin 21 and test pin 40 at the breakout box.

e. Start the engine and slowly increse engine speed to 3000 rpm.

f. If the voltage reading is between 3–11.5 volts, remove the ISC/BPA valve and inspect for contamination. If contamination is present, replace ISC/BPA valve.

g. If voltage reading is not between 3–11.5 volts, replace ECA and remove breakout box. Rerun Quick Test.

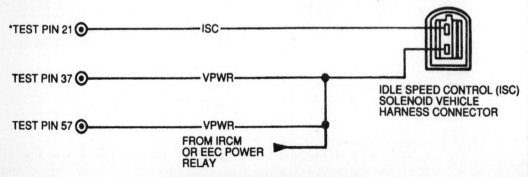

ISC/BPA valve test schematic—3.0L engine

REMOVAL AND INSTALLATION

2.2L Engine

1. Disconnect the negative battery cable and drain the cooling system.
2. Disconnect the electrical connector from the ISC/BPA valve.
3. Disconnect the hoses from the valve.
4. Remove the 4 screws and remove the valve and gasket from the throttle body.

To install:

5. Clean all gasket mating surfaces.
6. Apply sealant to both sides of a new gasket and position the valve on the throttle body. Tighten the screws.
7. Connect the hoses and the electrical connector.
8. Connect the negative battery cable. Fill the cooling system.

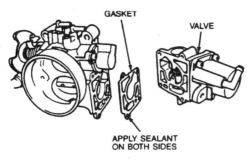

ISC/BPA valve removal and installation—2.2L engine

3.0L Engine

1. Disconnect the negative battery cable. Remove the throttle linkage cover.
2. Disconnect the ISC/BPA valve assembly connector.
3. Remove the retaining bolt and nut and remove the valve and gasket.
4. Installation is the reverse of the removal procedure. Use a new gasket and tighten the retaining bolt and nut to 71–97 inch lbs. (8–11 Nm).

NOTE: *If scraping is necessary to remove old*

gasket material, be careful not to damage the air bypass valve or the throttle body gasket surfaces or drop material into the throttle body.

Exhaust Gas Oxygen Sensor

OPERATION

The Exhaust Gas Oxygen (EGO) sensor reacts with the oxygen in the exhaust gases and sends a voltage signal to the ECA based on this reaction. A low voltage indicates too much oxygen or a lean condition while a high voltage indicates not enough oxygen or a rich condition. The ECA uses this information along with other sensor inputs to calculate air/fuel ratio.

The exhaust gas oxygen sensor is threaded into the exhaust manifold on 2.2L non-turbocharged engines, into the turbocharger on 2.2L turbocharged engines, or into the exhaust inlet pipe on 3.0L engines

SERVICE

2.2L Engine

1989 VEHICLES

1. Visually inspect all wiring, wiring harnesses, connectors and components for evidence of overheating, insulation damage, looseness, shorting or other damage and repair as necessary. If all looks okay, go to Step 2.
2. Check sensor output voltage as follows:
   a. Start the engine and bring to normal operating temperature.
   b. Disconnect the EGO sensor.
   c. Run the engine at idle.
   d. Place the volt-ohmmeter on the 5 volt scale and connect it between the EGO sensor (sensor side) and ground.
   e. Increase the engine speed to 4000–4500

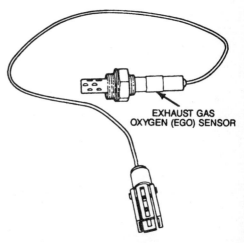

Exhaust gas oxygen sensor

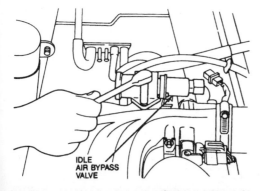

ISC/BPA valve removal and installation—3.0L engine

rpm until the volt-ohmmeter indicates approximately 0.7 volts.

f. Increase and decrease the engine speed rapidly while reading the volt-ohmmeter for EGO output voltage. With engine rpm increasing, voltage should be 0.5–1.0 volts. With engine speed decreasing, voltage should be 0–0.4 volts.

g. If the output voltage is correct, go to Step 5. If the output voltage is not correct, go to Step 3.

3. Turn the ignition key **OFF** and disconnect the sensor. Inspect the BK wire from the sensor connector for possible opens and repair as necessary. If the wire is okay, go to Step 4.

4. Check for a sensor short as follows:

a. Turn the ignition key **OFF**.

b. Place the volt-ohmmeter on the 200,000 ohm scale and connect it between the sensor connector (sensor side) and ground.

c. If the resistance is greater than 10,000Ω, replace the EGO sensor. If the resistance is not greater than 10,000Ω, repair the short in the sensor wire or replace the sensor, as required.

5. Check EGO sensor sensitivity as follows:

a. Connect the EGO sensor and start the engine.

b. Connect the SUPER STAR II adapter cable 007–00036 or equivalent, to the STO connector and ground (STI connector open). Refer to illustration.

c. Run the engine at 2500 rpm.

d. If the switch monitor light flashes 8 or more times in 10 seconds, go to Step 8. If it does not, go to Step 6.

6. Check the EGO sensor circuit as follows:

a. Turn the ignition key **OFF**.

b. Install the breakout box according to the manufacturers instructions, leaving the ECA disconnected.

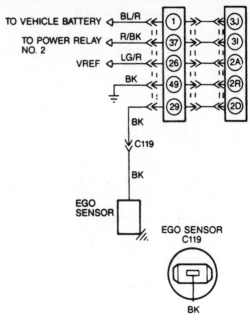

EGO sensor test schematic—1989 Probe

c. Disconnect the EGO sensor.

d. Place the volt-ohmmeter on the 200 ohm scale and measure the resistance between the EGO sensor connector (harness side) and test pin 29 at the breakout box.

e. If resistance is greater than 10Ω, repair the open circuit and reconnect the EGO sensor. If the resistance is not greater than 10Ω, go to Step 7.

7. Check the EGO sensor circuit as follows:

a. Turn the ignition key **OFF**.

b. Install the breakout box according to the manufacturers instructions, leaving the ECA disconnected.

c. Disconnect the EGO sensor.

SUPER STAR II tester adapter cable connections

d. Place the volt-ohmmeter on the 200,000Ω scale and measure the resistance between test pin 29 and test pins 1, 26, 37 and 49.

e. If any resistances are less than 10,000Ω, repair the short in the EGO sensor circuit to VPWR, VREF, KAPWR or ground, as required. If no resistances are less than 10,000Ω, replace the EGO sensor.

8. Check ECA input voltage as follows:

a. Start the engine and bring to normal operating temperature.

b. Install the breakout box according to the manufacturers instructions, and connect the ECA.

c. Place the volt-ohmmeter on the 5 volt scale and measure the voltage between test pin 29 and test pin 49 while increasing and decreasing engine speed between 1500 and 4000 rpm.

d. If the voltage changes between 0.5–1.0 volt, replace the ECA. If the voltage does not change as specified, inspect the ECA and ECA No. 2 connector for damage, looseness, corrosion or damaged pins; repair as required.

1990–92 VEHICLES

1. Check EGO sensor voltage as follows:

a. Start the engine and bring to normal operating temperature.

b. Disconnect the oxygen sensor connector.

c. Measure the voltage between the oxygen sensor wire and ground. With the engine at idle, the voltage should be 0.2–0.8 volts. When increasing engine speed, the voltage should increase. When decreasing engine speed, the voltage should decrease.

NOTE: *Voltage that remains above 0.55 volts indicates a continuously rich condition while below 0.55 volts indicates a continuously lean condition. Rich or lean conditions could be an indication of another problem.*

d. If the voltage readings are okay, go to Step 2. If the voltage readings are not as specified, replace the oxygen sensor.

2. Check EGO circuit isolation as follows:

a. Turn the ignition key **OFF**.

b. Install the breakout box to the harness connectors, leaving the ECA disconnected.

c. Disconnect the EGO sensor connector.

d. Measure the continuity between test pin EGO and the EGO sensor connector wire.

e. If there is continuity, the EGO circuit is okay — possible ECA malfunction. If there is no continuity, repair the EGO sensor EGO wire to the ECA.

3.0L Engine

1. If the EGO is always lean, slow to switch or lack of switching; fuel at adaptive limit, possible causes are:

Moisture inside the EGO sensor/harness connector resulting in a short to ground.

EGO sensor being coated with contaminants.

EGO circuit open.

EGO circuit shorted to ground.

2. Check EGO integrity as follows:

a. Turn the ignition key **OFF**.

b. Inspect the EGO harness for chaffing, burns or other indications of damage and service, as necessary.

c. Inspect the EGO sensor and connector for indication of submerging in water, oil, coolant, etc. Service as necessary.

d. Start the engine and run it at 2000 rpm for 2 minutes.

e. Turn the ignition key **OFF**.

f. Run the Engine Running Self Test.

g. If any fault codes are present, proceed to Step 3. If no fault codes are present, proceed to Step 8.

3. Check the EGO sensor as follows:

NOTE: *Vacuum/air leaks could cause Code, 41, 91, 136, 172 or 176. Check for: leaking vacuum actuator, engine sealing, EGR sys-*

EGO

EGO SENSOR
HARNESS CONNECTOR

Application	Circuit	ECA Pin	BOB Pin	Wire Color
2.2L (MTX)	EGO	2N	29	BK
2.2L (ATX) 2.2L Turbo	EGO	2C	29	BK

EGO sensor test pin identification—1990–92 2.2L engine

tem, PCV system or lead contaminated EGO sensor.

a. Turn the ignition key **OFF**.

b. Make sure the MAP sensor output voltage is in range for the vehicle's altitude.

c. Disconnect the EGO sensor from the vehicle harness.

d. Connect the volt-ohmmeter to HEGO SIGNAL at the sensor and negative battery post.

e. Disconnect and plug the line at the MAP sensor. Place the volt-ohmmeter on the 20 volt scale.

f. Start the engine and apply 10–14 in. Hg of vacuum to the MAP sensor using a vacuum pump.

g. Run the engine for 2 minutes at approximately 2000 rpm.

h. If the volt-ohmmeter indicates greater than 0.5 volts within 2 minutes, proceed to Step 4. If it does not, replace the EGO sensor, reconnect the MAP sensor vacuum line and rerun the Quick Test.

4. Check continuity of HEGO SIGNAL and HEGO GND as follows:

a. Turn the ignition key **OFF**.

b. Install breakout box tool T83L–50–EEC–IV or equivalent, and leave the ECA disconnected.

c. Disconnect the EGO sensor from the vehicle harness. Inspect both ends of the connector for damaged or pushed out pins, moisture, corrosion, loose wires, etc. Repair as necessary.

d. Measure the resistance between HEGO SIGNAL test pin at the breakout box and HEGO SIGNAL at the vehicle harness connector.

e. Measure the reistance between HEGO GND test pin at the breakout box and negative battery post.

f. If each resistance is less than 5Ω, proceed to Step 5. If each resistance is not less than 5Ω, service the open circuit, remove the breakout box, reconnect the ECA, EGO sensor and any other components that have been disconnected. Drive the vehicle 5 miles at 55 mph, then rerun the Quick Test.

5. Check the EGO circuit for short to ground as follows:

a. Turn the ignition key **OFF**.

b. Install breakout box tool T83L–50–EEC–IV or equivalent, and leave the ECA disconnected.

c. Disconnect the EGO sensor.

d. Measure the resistance between the HEGO SIGNAL test pin at the breakout box and test pins 40, 46 or 49 where applicable at the breakout box.

e. If each resistance is greater than 10,000Ω, proceed to Step 6. If not, service the short circuit, remove the breakout box, reconnect the ECA, EGO sensor and any other components that have been disconnected. Drive the vehicle 5 miles at 55 mph, then rerun the Quick Test.

6. Check the EGO sensor for short to ground as follows:

a. Turn the ignition key **OFF**.

b. Install breakout box tool T83L–50–EEC–IV or equivalent, and leave the ECA disconnected.

c. Disconnect the EGO sensor.

d. Measure the resistance between PWR GND and HEGO SIGNAL at the HEGO sensor connector.

e. If the resistance is greater than 10,000Ω, for Codes 144 or 41, 139 or 91, 171, 174, 175 or 178, proceed to Step 18. If the resistance is greater than 10,000Ω and other codes are displayed, proceed to Step 7.

f. If the resistance is not greater than 10,000Ω, replace the EGO sensor, remove the breakout box and reconnect the ECA. Drive the vehicle 5 miles at 55 mph, then rerun the Quick Test.

7. Attempt to eliminate Code 41 or 172, 91 or 136, or 176 as follows:

a. Turn the ignition key **OFF**.

b. Install breakout box tool T83L–50–EEC–IV or equivalent.

c. Disconnect and plug the MAP sensor vacuum line.

d. Connect the ECA to the breakout box.

e. Reconnect the EGO sensor.

f. Start the engine and apply 10–14 in. Hg of vacuum to the MAP sensor with a vacuum pump.

g. Run the engine for 2 minutes at approximately 2000 rpm, then allow the engine to return to idle.

h. Rerun the Engine Running Self-Test.
NOTE: *If directed here for Continuous Memory Codes the vehicle has to be driven 5 miles at 55 mph.*

i. If Code 41 or 172, 91 or 136, or 176 is still present, ignoring all other codes, remove the breakout box and reconnect the MAP sensor vacuum line. If the engine runs rough, check the ISC/BPA valve. All others, replace the ECA, drive the vehicle 5 miles at 55 mph and rerun the Quick Test.

j. If the specified codes are not present, ignoring all other codes, remove the breakout box, reconnect the ECA and MAP sensor vacuum line. The EGO sensor input is okay and the fuel delivery is okay. The problem is in an area common to all cylinders: air/vacuum leak, fuel contamination, EGR, Thermactor, MAP frequency, ignition system, etc. Repair as necessary.

8. Check the resistance of the heater element on the EGO sensor as follows:

a. Turn the ignition key **OFF**.

b. Disconnect the EGO sensor from the vehicle harness.

c. Inspect both ends of the connector for damaged or pushed out pins, moisture, corrosion, loose wires, etc. Repair as necessary.

d. Measure the resistance between the KEY PWR circuit and PWR GND circuit at the HEGO sensor connector.

e. The hot to warm resistance specification is 5–30Ω. The room temperature resistance specification is 2–5Ω.

f. If the resistance is within specification, proceed to Step 9. If the resistance is not within specification, replace the EGO sensor and rerun the Quick Test.

9. Check for power at the EGO harness connector as follows:

a. Turn the ignition key **ON**, but do not start the engine.

b. Disconnect the EGO sensor.

c. Measure the voltage between KEY POWER circuit and PWR GND circuit at the EGO vehicle harness connector.

d. If the voltage is greater than 10.5 volts, reconnect the sensor. The EGO sensor system and fuel delivery is okay. The EGO sensor may have cooled prior to the Engine Running Self-Test. If the symptom persists, the problem is in an area common to all cylinders: air/vacuum leak, fuel contamination, EGR, MAP frequency, ignition system, etc. Repair as necessary.

e. If the voltage is not greater than 10.5 volts, proceed to Step 10.

10. Check the continuity of the POWER GND circuit as follows:

a. Turn the ignition key **OFF**.

b. Disconnect the EGO sensor.

c. Measure the resistance between PWR GND circuit at the EGO vehicle harness connector and negative battery post.

d. If the resistance is less than 5Ω, service the open in the KEY PWR circuit. Reconnect the EGO sensor and rerun the Quick Test.

e. If the resistance is not less than 5Ω, service the open in the PWR GND circuit. Reconnect the EGO sensor and rerun the Quick Test.

11. Check the HEGO SIGNAL for short to power. HEGO always rich could be caused by moisture inside the HEGO harness connector resulting in a short to power or the HEGO circuit shorted to power. Proceed as follows:

a. Turn the ignition key **OFF**.

b. Disconnect the EGO sensor from the vehicle harness.

c. Inspect both ends of the connector for damaged or pushed out pins, moisture, corrosion, loose wires, etc. Repair as necessary.

d. Turn the ignition key **ON**, but do not start the engine.

e. Measure the voltage between HEGO SIG and PWR GND at the EGO vehicle harness connector.

f. If the voltage is less than 0.5 volts, proceed to Step 13. If the voltage is not less than 0.5 volts, proceed to Step 12.

12. Check for a short to power as follows:

a. Turn the ignition key **OFF**.

b. Inspect the HEGO GND and HEGO signal harness for chaffing, burns or other indications of a short to power. Repair as necessary.

c. Disconnect the ECA 60 pin connector and inspect for damaged or pushed out pins, corrosion, loose wires, etc. Repair as necessary.

d. Install breakout box tool T83L–50–EEC–IV or equivalent, and leave the ECA disconnected.

e. Disconnect the EGO sensor.

f. Measure the resistance between HEGO SIG and KEY PWR at the breakout box.

g. If the resistance is greater than 10,000Ω, replace the ECA, remove the breakout box and reconnect the EGO sensor. Drive the vehicle 5 miles at 55 mph, then rerun the Quick Test.

h. If the resistance is not greater than 10,000Ω, repair the short to power, remove the breakout box and reconnect the ECA. Drive the vehicle 5 miles at 55 mph, then rerun the Quick Test.

13. Check the EGO sensor for a short to the ignition run circuit as follows:

a. Turn the ignition key **OFF**.

b. Disconnect the EGO sensor.

c. Measure the resistance between the KEY PWR circuit and HEGO SIG circuit at the EGO sensor connector.

d. If the resistance is greater than 10,000Ω, for Codes 42 or 173, 92 or 137, 177, proceed to Step 14.

e. If the resistance is greater than 10,000Ω, for Codes 171, 174, 175, 178, proceed to Step 15.

f. If the resistance is not greater than 10,000Ω, replace the EGO sensor. Drive the vehicle 5 miles at 55 mph, then rerun the Quick Test.

14. Attempt to generate Code 41 or 172, 91 or 136, or 176 as follows:

a. Turn the ignition key **OFF**.

b. Disconnect the EGO sensor.

c. Connect a jumper wire between the HEGO SIG circuit at the EGO vehicle harness connector to the negative battery post.

d. Rerun the Engine Running Self-Test.

e. If Code 41 or 172, 91 or 136, or 176 is present, remove the jumper wire and proceed to Step 15.

f. If the specified codes are not present, remove the jumper wire and reconnect the EGO sensor. Disconnect the ECA 60 pin connector and inspect for damaged or pushed out pins, corrosion, loose wires, etc. Repair as necessary. If okay, replace the ECA. Drive the vehicle 5 miles at 55 mph, then rerun the Quick Test.

15. Check the MAP sensor for a vacuum leak as follows:

NOTE: *Due to the MAP sensor's large influence on fuel control, there is a possibility that the MAP sensor could be at fault without a Code 22 or 126. The next 2 steps will verify proper vacuum to the MAP sensor and its ability to hold vacuum.*

a. Turn the ignition key **OFF**.

b. Disconnect the vacuum line from the MAP sensor.

c. Inspect the hose for blockage, damage from wear or aging. Repair as necessary.

d. Plug the vacuum hose at the MAP side.

e. Connect a vacuum pump to the MAP sensor and apply 18 in. Hg of vacuum to the MAP sensor.

f. If the MAP sensor holds vacuum, release the vacuum and proceed to Step 16. If the MAP sensor does not hold vacuum, replace it. Reconnect the EGO sensor and drive the vehicle 5 miles at 55 mph, then rerun the Quick Test.

16. Check for loss of vacuum to the MAP sensor as follows:

a. Tee a vacuum gauge into the manifold vacuum line at the MAP sensor.

b. Start the engine and let the engine speed stabilize. Note the vacuum level.

c. Turn the ignition key **OFF**.

d. Remove the vacuum gauge and Tee and reconnect the vacuum line to the MAP sensor.

e. Tee in the vacuum gauge at a different source of intake manifold vacuum and restart the engine. Note the vacuum level.

f. If the vacuum level differs greater than 1 in. Hg, inspect the engine vacuum integrity and repair as necessary. Remove the vacuum gauge and Tee. Reconnect the EGO sensor and drive the vehicle 5 miles at 55 mph, then rerun the Quick Test.

g. If the vacuum level does not differ greater than 1 in. Hg, proceed to Step 17.

17. Check the EGO sensor as follows:

a. Turn the ignition key **OFF**.

b. Disconnect the EGO sensor.

c. Connect the volt-ohmmeter to HEGO SIGNAL at the HEGO sensor connector and to the negative battery post.

d. Place the volt-ohmmeter on the 20 volt scale.

e. Create a vacuum leak to cause the EGO sensor to go lean. Disconnect the PCV valve hose from the PCV valve.

f. Start the engine and run at approximately 2000 rpm.

g. If the volt-ohmmeter indicates less than 0.4 volts within 30 seconds, proceed to Step 18.

h. If the volt-ohmmeter does not indicate less than 0.4 volts within 30 seconds, replace the EGO sensor. Reconnect the vacuum hoses and drive the vehicle 5 miles at 55 mph. Rerun the Quick Test.

18. Check the Continuous Monitor Mode as follows:

a. Turn the ignition key **OFF**.

b. Make sure the engine is at operating temperature.

c. Start the engine and run at 2000 rpm for 2 minutes.

d. With the engine at idle, enter the Engine Running Continuous Monitor Mode.

e. Observe the volt-ohmmeter or STAR LED for indication of a fault.

f. Wiggle, shake or bend a small section of the EEC-IV harness while working from the EGO sensor to the ECA.

g. Wiggle, shake or bend a small section of the EEC-IV harness while working from the HEGO GND to the ECA

h. If a fault is indicated, isolate the fault and repair as necessary. Remove the break-

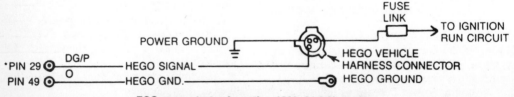

EGO sensor test schematic—1990–91 3.0L engine

out box and clear Continuous Memory. Re-run the Quick Test.

i. If a fault is not indicated, remain in the Engine Running Continuous Monitor Mode and proceed to Step 19.

19. Perform a Continuous Monitor test drive check as follows:

a. Remain in the Engine Running Continuous Monitor Mode.

b. Test drive the vehicle at 55 mph with a minimum road load for 5 miles.

c. Continue to drive on a rough road at 55 mph for 5 miles.

d. If possible, drive the vehicle through a pool of water on the road to shower the EGO sensor and/or connector.

e. If a fault is indicated, isolate the fault and repair as necessary. Remove the breakout box and clear Continuous Menory. Rerun the Quick Test.

f. If a fault is not indicated, exit the Engine Running Continuous Monitor Mode. Proceed to Step 20.

20. Check EGO switching as follows:

a. Turn the ignition key **OFF**.

b. Inspect the EEC-IV harness for proper routing and insulation; burnt, chaffed, intermittently shorted or open. Repair as necessary.

c. Disconnect the ECA 60 pin connector and inspect for damaged or pushed out pins, corrosion, loose wires, etc. Repair as necessary.

d. Install breakout box tool T83L–50–EEC–IV or equivalent, and connect the ECA to the breakout box.

e. Connect an analog voltmeter to the EGO sensor test pin and HEGO GND at the breakout box.

f. Test drive the vehicle at 55 mph with minimum road load for 5 miles.

g. Observe the voltmeter for EGO switching from 0.3–0.9 volts within 3 seconds.

h. If the EGO voltage switched, replace the EGO sensor and remove the breakout box. Reconnect the ECA and rerun the Quick Test.

REMOVAL AND INSTALLATION

2.2L Engine

NON-TURBOCHARGED ENGINE

1. Disconnect the negative battery cable.

2. Disconnect the sensor electrical connector.

3. Remove the sensor from the exhaust manifold using EGO sensor wrench T79P–9472–A or equivalent.

4. Installation is the reverse of the removal procedure.

TURBOCHARGED ENGINE

1. Disconnect the negative battery cable.

2. Disconnect the sensor electrical connector.

3. Remove the wiring harness from the spark plug wire retaining bracket and the re-

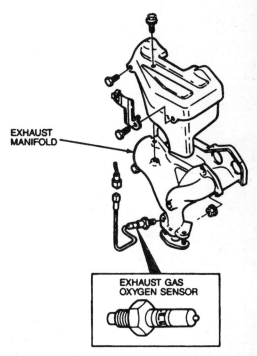

EGO sensor removal and installation—2.2L non-turbocharged engine

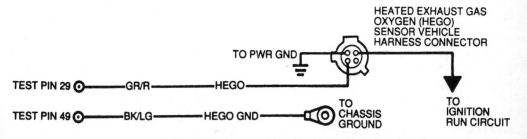

EGO sensor test schematic—1992 3.0L engine

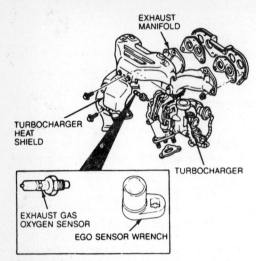

EGO sensor removal and installation—2.2L turbo-charged engine

taining bracket on the turbocharger heat shield.

4. Remove the sensor from the turbocharger using EGO sensor wrench T79P–9472–A or equivalent.

5. Installation is the reverse of the removal procedure.

3.0L Engine

1. Disconnect the negative battery cable.

2. Raise and safely support the vehicle.

3. Disconnect the sensor electrical connector.

4. Remove the sensor from the inlet pipe using EGO sensor wrench T79P–9472–A or equivalent.

5. Installation is the reverse of the removal procedure.

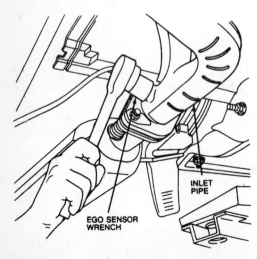

EGO sensor removal and installation—3.0L engine

Fuel Injector

OPERATION

The fuel injector nozzle is an electromechanical device which meters and atomizes the fuel delivered to the engine. The injector valve body consists of a solenoid actuated pintle or needle valve assembly that sits on a fixed size orifice. An electrical signal from the ECA activates the solenoid causing the pintle to move inward off its seat and allows fuel to flow through the orifice. The fuel supply pressure is constant; therefore, fuel flow to the engine is controlled by how long the solenoid is energized.

The fuel injectors are mounted above the individual intake ports.

SERVICE

2.2L Engine

1. Check fuel injector function as follows:

a. With the engine warmed and idling, or cranking if it does not start, and using a mechanic's stethoscope or equivalent, listen for regularly spaced operating sounds at each injector.

b. If operating sounds can be heard, proceed to Step 4. If not, proceed to Step 2.

2. Check fuel injector resistance as follows:

a. Remove the electrical connector from the injector. If necessary, remove the injector from the engine to gain access to the injector terminals.

b. Using a volt-ohmmeter, check the resistance of each injector. The resistance should be 12–16Ω on the non-turbocharged engine, and 11–15Ω on the turbocharged engine.

c. If the injector resistance is as specified, proceed to Step 3. If not, replace the faulty injectors and repeat Step 1.

3. Check the fuel injector electrical signal as follows:

a. Disconnect the injector lead and insert the continuity checker from fuel injector tester/cleaner tool 113–00001 or equivalent, into the injector lead plug.

b. Start the engine.

c. Observe whether the continuity checker blinks, indicating a completed circuit for the injector being tested.

d. Repeat the check for each injector.

e. If all the injector circuit leads show continuity, proceed to Step 4. If not, check for 12 volts at each injector lead and repair or replace leads as required.

4. Check the fuel injectors as follows:

a. Using fuel injector tester/cleaner tool 113–00001 or equivalent, clean the fuel injectors.

b. With the tester/cleaner still installed on

the fuel system, note any significant pressure loss due to injector leakage when the tester pump is turned **OFF**.

c. Check the fuel injectors individually for leakage, as required, using the injector bench fixture and the fuel injector bench testing procedure associated with the tester/cleaner and verify that each injector leakage rate is within specification − 1 drop per minute maximum.

d. If the leakage rate is not within specification, replace the faulty injectors.

3.0L Engine

1. Check fuel pressure as follows:
a. Turn the ignition key **OFF**.
b. Connect fuel pressure gauge T80L–9974–B or equivalent, to the pressure relief valve on the fuel supply manifold.
c. Make sure that manifold vacuum is connected to the fuel pressure regulator.
d. If the engine will start, run the engine and check the fuel pressure. It should be 30–45 psi.

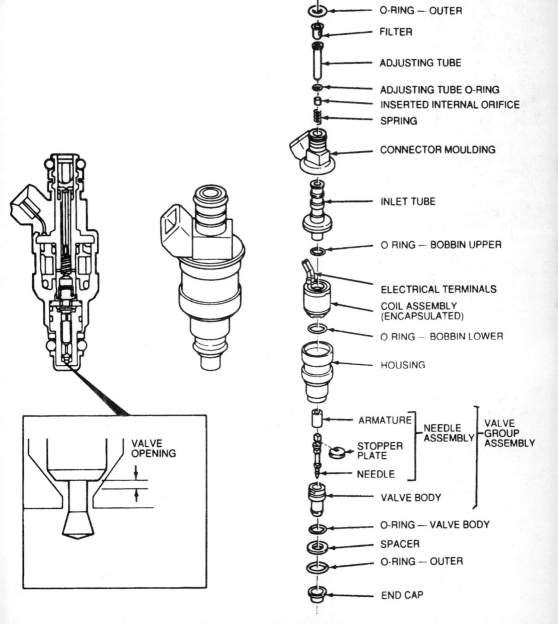

O-RING — OUTER
FILTER
ADJUSTING TUBE
ADJUSTING TUBE O-RING
INSERTED INTERNAL ORIFICE
SPRING
CONNECTOR MOULDING
INLET TUBE
O RING — BOBBIN UPPER
ELECTRICAL TERMINALS
COIL ASSEMBLY (ENCAPSULATED)
O RING — BOBBIN LOWER
HOUSING
ARMATURE | NEEDLE ASSEMBLY | VALVE GROUP ASSEMBLY
STOPPER PLATE
NEEDLE
VALVE BODY
O-RING — VALVE BODY
SPACER
O-RING — OUTER
END CAP

VALVE OPENING

Fuel injector—disassembled view

e. If the engine will not start, cycle the ignition key **ON** and **OFF** several times and check the fuel pressure. It should be 35–40 psi.

f. If the fuel pressure is within specification, proceed with testing. If it is not, check the fuel delivery system (fuel pump, fuel pump relay, pressure regulator, etc.).

2. Check the system's ability to hold fuel pressure as follows:

a. Pressurize the fuel system, as in Step 1.

b. Visually check for fuel leaking at the injector O-ring, fuel pressure regulator, and the fuel lines to the fuel charging assembly. Service as necessary.

c. Turn the ignition key **ON**, but do not start the engine.

d. Using a mechanics stethoscope, listen for leaking fuel injectors.

e. If fuel pressure remains at specification for 60 seconds and the vehicle does not start, go to Step 3.

f. If fuel pressure remains at specification for 60 seconds, for service codes or other symptoms, go to Step 4.

g. If the fuel pressure does not remain at specification, check the fuel delivery system.

3. Check fuel delivery as follows:

a. Turn the ignition key **OFF**.

b. Connect fuel pressure gauge T80L–9974–B or equivalent, to the pressure relief valve on the fuel supply manifold.

c. Pressurize the fuel system, as in Step 1.

d. Disconnect the fuel pump inertia switch, located behind the left-hand interior liftgate area trim panel.

e. Crank the engine for 5 seconds.

f. If pressure drops greater than 5 psi by the end of the 5 second crank cycle, the EEC-IV system is not the cause of the No Start condition; check other systems.

g. If pressure does not drop greater than 5 psi by the end of the 5 second crank cycle, remove the pressure gauge, reconnect the inertia switch, and go to Step 5.

4. Check cylinder balance as follows:

a. Connect a tachometer to the engine and run the engine at idle.

b. Disconnect and reconnect the injectors 1 at a time. Note the rpm drop for each injector.

NOTE: *The ISC/BPA valve will attempt to control the idle speed.*

c. If each injector produces a momentary drop in rpm, the injectors are okay. If not, proceed to Step 5.

5. Check the resistance of the injector(s) and harness as follows:

a. Turn the ignition key **OFF**.

b. Disconnect the ECA 60-pin connector. Inspect for damaged or pushed out pins, corrosion, loose wires, etc. and service, as necessary.

NOTE: *This erases Continuous Memory*

c. Install breakout box T83L–50–EEC–IV or equivalent, and leave the ECA disconnected.

d. Measure the resistance of injector bank 1 between test pin 37 and test pin 58 at the breakout box and record the resistance.

e. Measure the resistance of injector bank 2 between test pin 37 and test pin 59 at the breakout box and record the resistance.

f. The resistance should be 6.0–8.5Ω. If the resistance is within specification, proceed to Step 9. If not, proceed to Step 6.

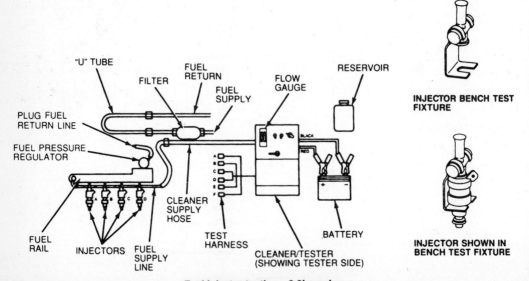

Fuel injector testing—2.2L engine

6. Check the continuity of the fuel injector harness as follows:

a. Turn the ignition key **OFF**.

b. Install breakout box T83L–50–EEC–IV or equivalent, and leave the ECA disconnected.

c. Disconnect the injector vehicle harness connector at the suspect injector.

d. Measure the resistance between test pin 37/57 at the breakout box and the VPWR pin at the injector vehicle harness connector.

e. Measure the resistance between the injector test pin(s) at the breakout box and the same injector circuit signal pin at each injector vehicle harness connector.

f. If each resistance is less than 5Ω, proceed to Step 7. If not, service the open circuit, remove the breakout box and reconnect the ECA and injectors. Drive the vehicle 5 miles at 55 mph and rerun the Quick Test.

7. Check the injector harness circuit for short to power or ground as follows:

a. Turn the ignition key **OFF**.

b. Install breakout box T83L–50–EEC–IV or equivalent, and leave the ECA disconnected.

c. Disconnect the injector vehicle harness connector at the suspect injector.

d. Measure the resistance between the injector test pin(s) and test pin 37/57, 40, 46 and 60 at the breakout box.

e. Measure the resistance between the injector test pin(s) at the breakout box and chassis ground.

f. If each resistance is greater than 10,000Ω, proceed to Step 8.

g. If each resistance is not greater than 10,000Ω, service the short circuit, remove the breakout box and reconnect the ECA and injectors. Drive the vehicle 5 miles at 55 mph and rerun the Quick Test.

8. Isolate the faulty injector circuit as follows:

a. Turn the ignition key **OFF**.

b. Install breakout box T83L–50–EEC–IV or equivalent, and leave the ECA disconnected.

c. Disconnect all the injectors on the suspect bank. Place the volt-ohmmeter on the 200 ohm scale.

d. Connect 1 injector and measure the resistance between test pin 37 and either test pin 58 or 59, as appropriate.

e. Disconnect that injector and repeat the process for each of the remaining injectors.

f. The resistance should be 13–16Ω. If each resistance is within specification, proceed to Step 9. If not, replace the injector, reconnect the ECA and the injectors; drive the vehicle 5 miles at 55 mph and rerun the Quick Test.

9. Check the injector driver signal as follows:

a. Turn the ignition key **OFF**.

b. Install breakout box T83L–50–EEC–IV or equivalent, and connect the ECA to the breakout box.

c. Connect a 12 volt test light between test pin 37 and test pin 58 at the breakout box and connect a 12 volt test light between test pin 37 and 59 at the breakout box.

d. Crank or start the engine.

e. A properly operating system will show a dim glow on the test light. If there is no light or a bright light, replace the ECA and remove the breakout box. Drive the vehicle 5 miles at 55 mph and rerun the Quick Test.

REMOVAL AND INSTALLATION

For fuel injector removal and installation procedures, refer to Chapter 5.

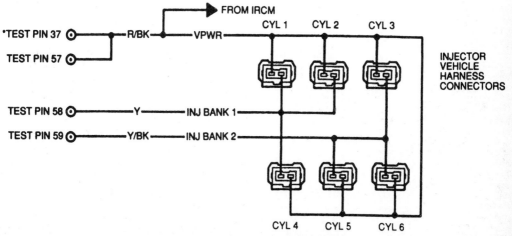

Fuel injector test schematic—3.0L engine

Barometric Pressure Sensor

OPERATION

The Barometric Pressure (BP) sensor is used on the 2.2L engine to sense changes in barometric pressure, allowing the ECA to sense the altitude at which the vehicle is operating. The signal from the BP sensor affects air/fuel ratio and idle speed. On 1989 vehicles, the BP sensor is mounted on the firewall near the main power relays. On 1990–92 vehicles, the BP sensor is contained within the ECA. If a Code 14 exists on a 1990–92 vehicle, and cannot be erased, the ECA must be replaced.

SERVICE

1989 Vehicles

1. Visually inspect all wiring, wiring harness, connectors and components for evidence of overheating, insulation damage, looseness, shorting or other damage and repair, as necessary. If all appears okay, go to Step 2.

2. Check VREF and Signal Return circuits as follows:

a. Install the breakout box according to the manufacturers instructions.

b. Place the volt-ohmmeter on the 20 volt scale.

c. Turn the ignition key **ON**.

d. Measure the voltage between pin 26 and pin 20; it should be 4–6 volts.

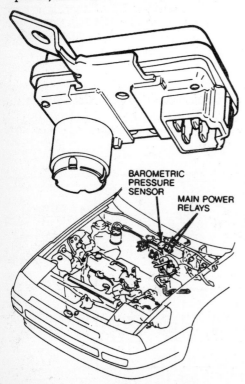

Barometric pressure sensor—1989 Probe

e. Measure the voltage between pin 26 and pin 46; it should be 4–6 volts.

f. Measure the voltage between pin 20 and pin 46; it should be 0 volts.

g. If the voltage readings are within specification, go to Step 3. If they are not, check the reference and signal return circuits.

3. Check the BP sensor voltage as follows:

a. Install the breakout box according to the manufacturers instructions.

b. Place the volt-ohmmeter on the 20 volt scale.

c. Turn the ignition key **ON**.

d. Measure the voltage between pin 45 and pin 46. At sea level, it should be 3.5–4.5 volts. At 6500 ft. above sea level, it should be 2.5–3.5 volts. When applying 30 in. Hg of vacuum to the sensor, it should be 0 volts.

e. If the voltage readings are within specification, replace the ECA. If they are not, go to Step 4.

4. Check for power at the BP sensor as follows:

a. Place the volt-ohmmeter on the 20 volt scale.

b. Turn the ignition key **ON**.

c. Measure the voltage between the BP sensor LG/R wire and ground; it should be 4–6 volts.

d. Measure the voltage between the BP sensor LG/R wire and BP sensor LG/Y wire; it should be 4–6 volts.

e. Measure the voltage between the BP sensor LG/Y wire and ground; it should be 0 volts.

f. If all voltage readings are within specification, go to Step 5. If they are not, repair the LG/R and/or LG/Y wires from the BP sensor to the ECA.

5. Check BP sensor voltage as follows:

a. Place the volt-ohmmeter on the 20 volt scale.

b. Turn the ignition key **ON**.

c. Leave the BP sensor connected and measure the voltage between the BP sensor Y wire and ground. Do not pierce the wire.

d. At sea level, the reading should be 3.5–4.5 volts. At 6500 ft. above sea level, the reading should be 2.5–3.5 volts. When applying 30 in. Hg of vacuum to the sensor, it should be 0 volts.

e. If all voltage readings are within specification, replace the BP sensor. If they are not, repair the open in the Y wire from the BP sensor to the ECA.

REMOVAL AND INSTALLATION

1. Disconnect the negative battery cable.

2. Disconnect the electrical connector from the sensor.

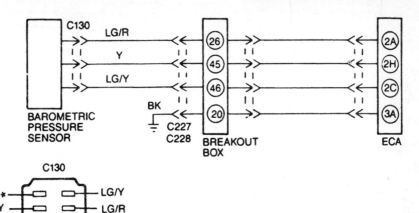

Barometric pressure sensor test schematic—1989 Probe

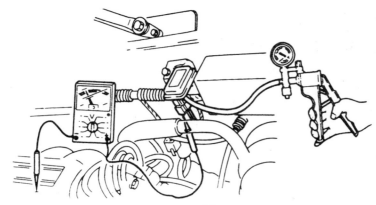

Checking the BP sensor

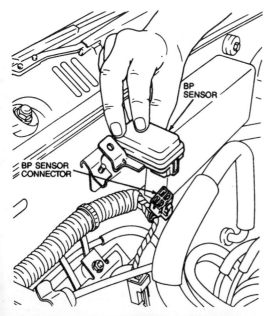

BP sensor removal and installation—1989 Probe

3. Remove the attaching nut and remove the sensor.

4. Installation is the reverse of the removal procedure.

Crankshaft Position Sensor

OPERATION

The Crankshaft Position Sensor (CPS) is used on the 2.2L turbocharged engine and is located in the distributor. The sensor detects crankshaft angle at equally spaced intervals. This information is supplied to the ECA and is used to determine engine speed (rpm). The signal from the CPS affects air/fuel ratio, injector timing, idle speed, EGR flow, fuel pressure, turbo boost pressure and ignition timing.

SERVICE

1989 Vehicles

1. Visually inspect all wiring, wiring harness, connectors and components for evidence of

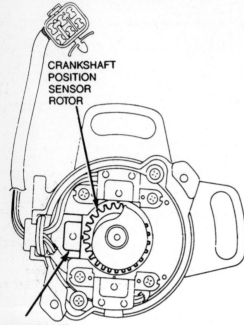

CRANKSHAFT
POSITION
SENSOR
ROTOR

CRANKSHAFT
POSITION
SENSOR
PICKUP

Crankshaft position sensor—2.2L turbocharged engine

overheating, insulation damage, looseness, shorting or other damage and repair, as necessary. If all appears okay, go to Step 2.

2. Check CPS resistance as follows:

a. Turn the ignition key **OFF**.

b. Install the breakout box according to the manufacturers instructions, leaving the ECA disconnected.

c. Place the volt-ohmmeter on the 1K ohm scale.

d. Measure the resistance between pin 42 and pin 56.

e. If the resistance is 210–260Ω, go to Step 5. If it is not, go to Step 3.

3. Check sensor resistance as follows:

a. Turn the ignition key **OFF**.

b. Disconnect the CPS sensor.

c. Place the volt-ohmmeter on the 1K ohm scale.

d. Measure the resistance between CPS terminal A and CPS terminal B.

e. If the resistance is 210–260Ω, go to Step 4. If it is not replace the CPS sensor.

4. Check for opens between the CPS and ECA as follows:

a. Turn the ignition key **OFF**.

b. Install the breakout box according to the manufacturers instructions.

c. Place the volt-ohmmeter on the 200 ohm scale.

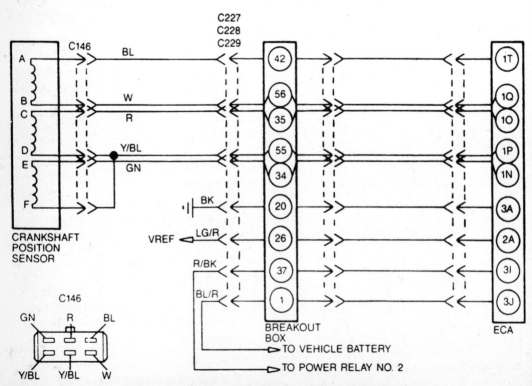

CPS and CID sensor test schematic—1989 turbocharged engine

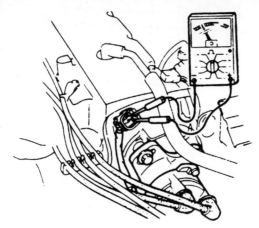

Checking the CPS or CID sensor—1989 turbo-charged engine

d. Measure the resistance between the CPS BL wire and pin 42. Measure the resistance between the CPS W wire and pin 56.

e. If all resistance readings are below 5Ω, check for shorts to the VPWR and repair as required. If all resistance readings are not below 5Ω, repair the open wire(s) in question.

5. Check CPS voltage as follows:

a. Install the breakout box according to the manufacturers instructions.

b. Place the volt-ohmmeter on the 20 volt scale.

c. Start the engine and let it idle.

d. Measure the resistance between pin 42 and ground pin 20. Measure the resistance between pin 56 and ground pin 20.

e. If all voltages are approximately 0.6–0.8 volts, replace the ECA. If they are not, go to Step 6.

6. Check if CPS voltage is shorted as follows:

a. Turn the ignition key **OFF**.

b. Install the breakout box according to the manufacturers instructions, leaving the ECA disconnected.

c. Place the volt-ohmmeter on the 200 ohm scale.

d. Measure the resistance between pin 42 and pins 1, 26, 37 and 20. Measure the resistance between pin 56 and pins 1, 26, 37 and 20.

e. If any resistance readings are below 5Ω, repair the shorted wire(s) in question. If any resistance readings are not below 5Ω, replace the ECA.

1990 Vehicles

1. Check CPS input resistance as follows:

a. Install the breakout box according to the manufacturers instructions, leaving the ECA disconnected.

b. Measure the resistance between test pins CPS and CIDREF.

c. If the resistance is 210–260Ω, go to Step 2. If it is not, go to Step 3.

2. Check CPS input voltage as follows:

a. Install the breakout box according to the manufacturers instructions, leaving the ECA disconnected.

b. Measure the voltage, while cranking the engine, between test pins CPS and CIDREF. The voltage reading should be 0.6–0.8 volts.

c. If the voltage readings are within specification, the CPS circuit is okay. If the voltage readings are not within specification, replace the CPS.

3. Check CPS resistance as follows:

a. Disconnect the distributor connector.

b. Measure the resistance between CPS terminals CPS and CIDREF.

c. If the resistance is 210–250Ω, repair the distributor CPS wire to the ECA and/or CIDREF wire. If the resistance is not within specification, replace the CPS.

1991–92 Vehicles

1. Install the breakout box according to the manufacturers instructions, leaving the ECA disconnected.

CPS

CIDREF

2.2L TURBO

DISTRIBUTOR HARNESS CONNECTOR

Application	Circuit	ECA Pin	BOB Pin	Wire Color
2.2L Turbo	CPS	3E	56, 12	BL
	CIDREF	3F	13	W

Crankshaft position sensor test pin identification—1990–92 2.2L turbocharged engine

2. Disconnect the distributor connector.

3. Measure the resistance of the CPS and CIDREF circuits between the ECA and distributor.

4. If the resistances are less than 5Ω, replace the CPS. If they are not, service the circuits in question.

REMOVAL AND INSTALLATION

The distributor assembly in the 2.2L turbocharged engine is not serviceable. If the crankshaft position sensor needs replacement, the entire distributor assembly must be replaced.

Cylinder Identification Sensors

OPERATION

The Cylinder Identification (CID) sensors are used on the 2.2L turbocharged engine and are located in the distributor. The sensors detect No. 1 and No. 4 cylinders Top Dead Center (TDC). This information is supplied to the ECA and is used to determine crankshaft position. The signal from the CID sensors affects injector timing and ignition timing.

SERVICE

1989 Vehicles

1. Visually inspect all wiring, wiring harness, connectors and components for evidence of overheating, insulation damage, looseness, shorting or other damage and repair, as necessary. If all appears okay, go to Step 2.

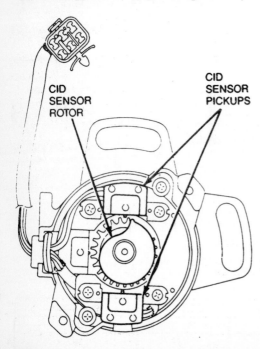

CID
SENSOR
ROTOR

CID
SENSOR
PICKUPS

Cylinder identification sensors—2.2L turbocharged engine

2. Check CID resistance as follows:

a. Turn the ignition key **OFF**.

b. Install the breakout box according to the manufacturers instructions, leaving the ECA disconnected.

c. Place the volt-ohmmeter on the 1K ohm scale.

d. Measure the resistance between pin 34 and pin 55; it should be 210–260Ω.

e. Measure the resistance between pin 35 and pin 55; it should be 210–260Ω.

f. Measure the resistance between pin 34 and pin 35; it should be 420–520Ω.

g. If all resistance readings are within specification, go to Step 5. If they are not, go to Step 3.

3. Check CID sensor resistance as follows:

a. Turn the ignition key **OFF**.

b. Disconnect the CID sensor.

c. Place the volt-ohmmeter on the 1K ohm scale.

d. Measure the resistance between CID terminal C and CID terminal D. Measure the resistance between CID terminal E and CID terminal F.

e. If both resistances readings are 210–260Ω, go to Step 4. If they are not, replace the CID sensor.

4. Check for opens between the CID and ECA as follows:

a. Turn the ignition key **OFF**.

b. Install the breakout box according to the manufacturers instructions.

c. Place the volt-ohmmeter on the 200 ohm scale.

d. Measure the resistance between the CID R wire and pin 35. Measure the resistance between the CID Y/BL wire and pin 55. Measure the resistance between the CID GN wire and pin 34.

e. If all resistance readings are below 5Ω, check for short(s) to the VPWR and repair, as necessary. If all resistance readings are not below 5Ω, service the open wire(s) in question.

5. Check CID voltage as follows:

a. Install the breakout box according to the manufacturers instructions.

b. Place the volt-ohmmeter on the 20 volt scale.

c. Start the engine and let it idle.

d. Measure the voltage between pin 34 and ground pin 20. Measure the voltage between pin 35 and ground pin 20. Measure the voltage between pin 55 and ground pin 20.

e. If all voltages are approximately 0.6-0.8 volts, replace the ECA. If they are not, go to Step 6.

6. Check if CID voltage is shorted as follows:

a. Turn the ignition key **OFF**.

b. Install the breakout box according to the manufacturers instructions, leaving the ECA disconnected.

c. Place the volt-ohmmeter on the 200 ohm scale.

d. Measure the resistance between pin 34 and pins 1, 26, 37 and 20. Measure the resistance between pin 35 and pins 1, 26, 37 and 20. Measure the resistance between pin 55 and pins 1, 26, 37 and 20.

e. If any resistances are below 5Ω, service the shorted wire(s) in question. If any resistances are not below 5Ω, replace the ECA.

1990–92 Vehicles

1. Check CID input resistance as follows:

a. Install the breakout box according to the manufacturers instructions, leaving the ECA disconnected.

b. Measure the resistance between test pin CID 1 and test pin CIDREF.

c. Measure the resistance between test pin CID 2 and test pin CIDREF.

d. If the resistance readings are between 210–260Ω, the CID circuits are okay. If the resistance readings are other than specified, go to Step 2.

2. Check CID sensor resistance as follows:

a. Disconnect the distributor connector.

b. Measure the resistance between the CID 1 wire and the CIDREF wire.

c. Measure the resistance between the CID 2 wire and the CIDREF wire.

d. If the resistance readings are between 210–260Ω, service the CID 1 or CID 2 wire and/or CIDREF wire to the ECA.

e. If the resistance readings are other than specified, replace the CID 1 or CID 2 sensor.

REMOVAL AND INSTALLATION

The distributor assembly in the 2.2L turbocharged engine is not serviceable. If a CID sensor needs replacement, the entire distributor assembly must be replaced.

Knock Control System

OPERATION

A knock control system is used on the 2.2L turbocharged engine, consisting of a knock sensor and knock control unit. The knock sensor is an electronic device capable of measuring vibration and converting the vibration signal to an electrical output that measures the engine knock. The voltage signal generated by the knock sensor is sent to the knock control unit, which determines whether the signal from the knock sensor is preignition or other vibration. A signal is sent to the ECA and spark timing is retarded according to the intensity of the knock.

The knock sensor is threaded in the engine block near the oil pressure switch. The knock control unit is mounted on the firewall.

SERVICE

1989 Vehicles

1. Visually inspect all wiring, wiring harness, connectors and components for evidence of overheating, insulation damage, looseness, shorting or other damage and repair, as necessary. If all appears okay, go to Step 2.

2. Check knock control unit voltage as follows:

a. Install the breakout box according to the manufacturers instructions.

b. Place the volt-ohmmeter on the 20 volt scale.

c. Turn the ignition key **ON**.

d. Measure the voltage between pin 23 and ground pin 20.

e. Tap on the engine lifting eye lightly with a 4 oz. hammer while increasing and decreasing engine rpm between 2500–4000 rpm.

f. If the voltage is 3.3–5.0 volts normally and decreases during tapping, go to Step 8. If not, go to Step 3.

3. Check knock control unit power as follows:

CID2

CID1
CIDREF

DISTRIBUTOR HARNESS CONNECTOR

Application	Circuit	ECA Pin	BOB Pin	Wire Color
2.2L Turbo	CID2	3H	30	R
	CIDREF	3F	13	W
	CID1	3G	28	GN

CID sensor test pin identification—1990–92 2.2L turbocharged engine

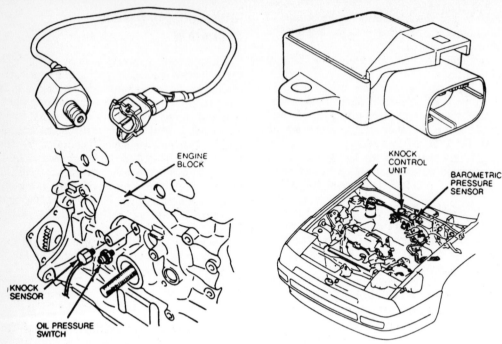

Knock sensor and knock control unit—2.2L turbocharged engine

a. Place the volt-ohmmeter on the 20 volt scale.

b. Turn the ignition key **ON**.

c. Measure the voltage between the knock control unit R/BK wire and ground.

d. If the reading is above 10 volts, go to Step 5. If it is not, go to Step 4.

4. Check relay No. 2 for power as follows:

a. Place the volt-ohmmeter on the 20 volt scale.

b. Turn the ignition key **ON**.

c. Measure the voltage between power relay No. 2 (R/BK wire) and ground, with the relay connected. Do not pierce the wire.

d. If the voltage is above 10 volts, repair the R/BK wire from relay No. 2 to the knock control unit. If the voltage is not above 10 volts, check the battery and related wiring.

5. Check the knock control unit ground as follows:

a. Place the volt-ohmmeter on the 200 ohm scale.

b. Turn the ignition key **ON**.

c. Measure the resistance between the knock control unit BK/LG wire and ground.

d. If the resistance is above 5Ω, repair the BK wire. If it is not, go to Step 6.

6. Check voltage at knock control unit terminal C as follows:

a. Place the volt-ohmmeter on the 20 volt scale.

b. Turn the ignition key **ON**.

c. Measure the voltage between the knock control unit R/Y wire and ground, with the knock control unit connected. Do not pierce the wire.

d. Tap on the engine lifting eye lightly with a 4 oz. hammer while increasing and decreasing engine rpm between 2500–4000 rpm.

e. If the voltage is 3.3–5.0 volts normally and decreases during tapping, repair the open or short to ground or short to the VPWR of the R/Y wire from the knock control unit to the ECA. If the voltage is not as specified, go to Step 7.

7. Check knock sensor voltage as follows:

a. Disconnect the knock sensor.

b. Place the volt-ohmmeter on the 1 volt AC scale.

c. Measure the voltage between the knock sensor Y/BL wire and the knock sensor BK wire.

d. Tap on the engine lifting eye with a 4 oz. hammer.

e. If the voltage reading is 0 volts normally and approximately 0.030 volts during tapping, replace the knock control unit. If the voltage reading is not as specified, replace the knock sensor.

8. Check knock control unit voltage at the STO as follows:

a. Install the breakout box according to the manufacturers instructions.

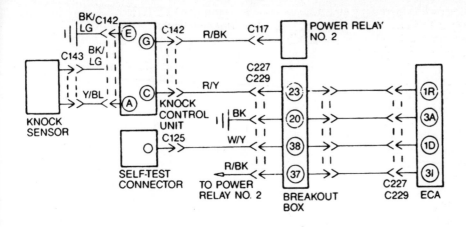

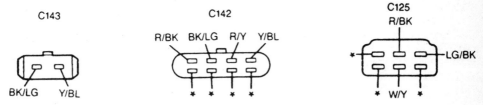

C143   C142   C125
R/BK

R/BK   BK/LG   R/Y   Y/BL

BK/LG   Y/BL   * * * *   LG/BK   * W/Y *

Knock control system test schematic—1989 turbocharged engine

b. Ground the STI connector.

c. Place the volt-ohmmeter on the 20 volt scale.

d. Make sure all accessories are **OFF**. Turn the ignition key **ON**.

e. Measure the voltage between pin 37 and pin 38.

f. Tap on the engine lifting eye with a 4 oz. hammer.

g. If the voltage reading is 0 volts normally and approximately 10 volts during tapping, the knock control system is okay. If the volt-age reading is not as specified, replace the ECA.

1990–92 Vehicles

1. Check knock control input voltage as follows:

a. Install the breakout box according to the manufacturers instructions.

b. Measure the voltage between test pin KC and ground.

c. Tap on the engine lifting eye lightly with

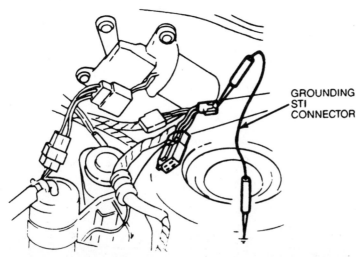

Checking knock control unit voltage at the STO—1989 turbocharged engine

a 4 oz. hammer while increasing and decreasing engine rpm between 2500–4000 rpm.

d. If the voltage is 3.3–5.0 volts normally and decreases during tapping, the knock control circuit is okay. If the voltage is not as specified, go to Step 2.

NOTE: *Quicker and harder tapping will cause voltage to be decreased more than slower and softer taps.*

2. Check the knock control signal from the knock control unit as follows:

a. Disconnect the knock control unit connector.

b. Install jumper wires between the harness connector and knock control unit VPWR, GND and KS wires. Leave the KC wire disconnected.

c. Measure the voltage between the knock control unit KC terminal (where the KC wire was) and ground.

d. Tap on the engine lifting eye lightly with a 4 oz. hammer while increasing and decreasing engine rpm between 2500–4000 rpm.

e. If the voltage reading is 6.6–10 volts normally and decreased while tapping, repair the knock control unit KC wire to the ECA. If the voltage reading is not as specified, go to Step 3.

3. Check the VPWR circuit at the knock control unit as follows:

a. Disconnect the knock control unit connector.

b. Measure the voltage between the knock control unit VPWR wire and ground.

c. Turn the ignition key **ON**.

d. If the voltage reading is above 10 volts, go to Step 4. If it is not, check the vehicle power circuit.

4. Check the ground at the knock control unit as follows:

a. Disconnect the knock control unit connector.

b. Measure the voltage between the knock control unit VPWR wire and knock control unit GND wire.

c. Turn the ignition key **ON**.

d. If the voltage reading is above 10 volts, go to Step 5. If it is not, repair the knock control unit GND wire.

5. Check the knock sensor signal at the knock control unit as follows:

a. Disconnect the knock control unit connector.

b. Place the volt-ohmmeter on the AC scale.

c. Measure the AC voltage between the knock control unit KS wire and ground.

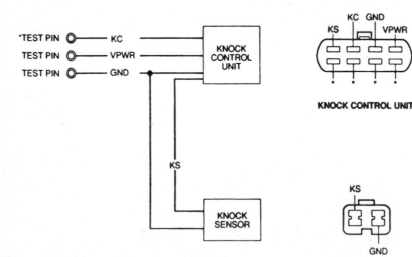

*TEST PINS ARE SPECIFIED IN THE CHART.
ALL HARNESS CONNECTORS ARE VIEWED INTO MATING SURFACE.

KNOCK SENSOR
HARNESS CONNECTORS

Application	Circuit	ECA Pin	BOB Pin	Wire Color
2.2L Turbo	KC	2M	24	R/Y
	VPWR	1B	37,57	R/BK
	GND	3C	16	BK/LG
	KS	NA	NA	Y/BL

Knock control system test schematic—1990–92 2.2L turbocharged engine

d. Tap on the engine lifting eye lightly with a 4 oz. hammer.

e. If AC voltage is above 0.030 volts while tapping, replace the knock control unit. If the voltage is not as specified, go to Step 6.

6. Check the signal at the knock sensor as follows:

a. Disconnect the knock control unit connector.

b. Place the volt-ohmmeter on the AC scale.

c. Measure the AC voltage between the knock sensor KS wire and GND wire.

d. Tap on the engine lifting eye lightly with a 4 oz. hammer.

e. If AC voltage is above 0.030 volts while tapping, repair the knock sensor KS wire to the knock control unit. If the voltage is not as specified, replace the knock sensor.

REMOVAL AND INSTALLATION

Knock Sensor

For knock sensor removal and installation procedures, refer to Chapter 3 under Sending Units and Sensors.

Knock Control Unit

1. Disconnect the negative battery cable.
2. Remove the attaching screws and nuts from the control unit housing at the retaining bracket.
3. Disconnect the electrical connector from the knock control unit and remove it from the vehicle.
4. Installation is the reverse of the removal procedure.

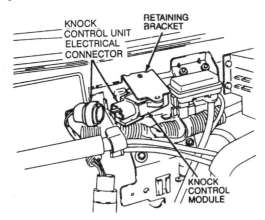

Knock control unit removal and installation

Exhaust Gas Recirculation System

OPERATION

The Exhaust Gas Recirculation (EGR) system is designed to reintroduce exhaust gas into the combustion cycle, thereby lowering combustion temperatures and reducing the formation of nitrous oxide (NOx).

2.2L Engines

The 2.2L non-turbocharged engine is equipped with the Back pressure Variable Transducer (BVT) EGR system. The 2.2L turbocharged engine is equipped with the Control/Vent Solenoids (CVS) system. Both systems share the following operation characteristics:

The amount of exhaust gas recirculated varies from zero with a cold engine to a fixed flow rate with a hot engine, intermediate load, and 1500 rpm minimum engine speed. The flow rate increases steadily as coolant temperature rises past 158°F (70°C) on non-turbocharged engines, and 104°F (40°C) on turbocharged engines. Both non-turbocharged and turbocharged engines are equipped with a control solenoid, triggered by the ECA and sensor system. The ECA and its sensors will disable the EGR (by closing the EGR valve) at zero throttle opening, full throttle, low coolant temperature, transaxle in neutral, low engine speed (less than 1500 rpm) or in the event of a component malfunction. To disable the EGR, the ECA cuts off the vacuum to the EGR valve by either closing the EGR control solenoid (non-turbocharged engines), or by opening the EGR vent solenoid (turbocharged engines).

BVT SYSTEM

On the non-turbocharged engine, the EGR is on only when the ECA and sensor system open the EGR control solenoid, allowing vacuum to close the EGR back pressure variable transducer valve and to open the EGR valve. The transducer valve closes under moderate levels of exhaust back pressure and intake vacuum, when sufficient engine speed and load are reached. Under these conditions, the valve closes and shuts off the venting of ported vacuum, which is high enough to open the EGR valve when it is not being vented.

CVS SYSTEM

On the turbocharged engine, vacuum to open the EGR valve is too low during average driving, so a vacuum reservoir with an integral check valve is used to collect vacuum during deceleration, and to store it for use during average driving when the EGR must be used. When the ECA and its sensors shut off the EGR, it vents the vacuum acting on the EGR valve by opening the vent solenoid valve, which is packaged together with the EGR control solenoid as a unit.

3.0L Engine

The 3.0L engine is equipped with the Pressure Feedback Electronic (PFE) EGR system.

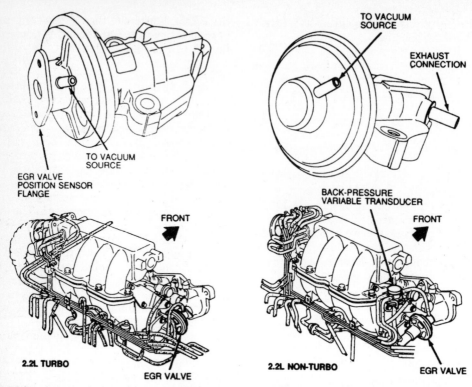

2.2L TURBO

2.2L NON-TURBO

EGR valves—2.2L engines

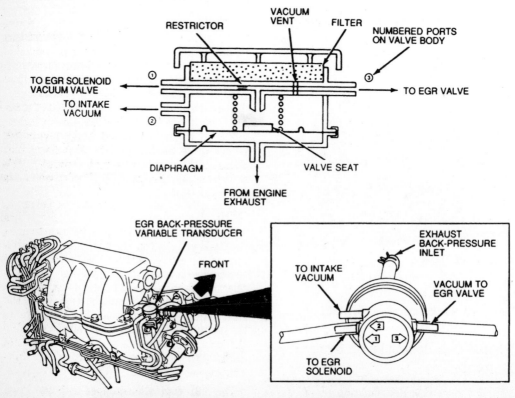

EGR back-pressure variable transducer—2.2L non-turbocharged engine

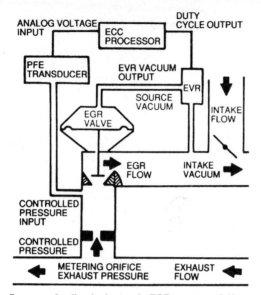

Pressure feedback electronic EGR system—3.0L engine

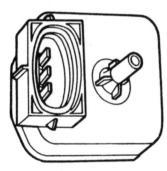

Pressure feedback electronic EGR transducer—3.0L engine

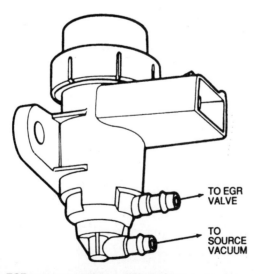

EGR vacuum regulator—3.0L engine

The PFE is a subsonic closed loop EGR system that controls EGR flow rate by monitoring the pressure drop across a remotely located sharp-edged orifice. The system uses a pressure transducer as the feedback device and controlled pressure is varied by valve modulation using vacuum output of the EGR Vacuum Regulator (EVR) solenoid. With the PFE system, the EGR valve only serves as a pressure regulator rather than a flow metering device.

SERVICE

2.2L Engine

NON-TURBOCHARGED ENGINE

1. Check the EGR back-pressure variable transducer function as follows:

   a. Remove the transducer from the vehicle.

   b. Connect a vacuum pump to port No. 3 (Refer to illustrations).

   c. Block the No. 1 port.

   d. Blow into the exhaust gas port while applying vacuum with the pump. Verify that vacuum is held.

   e. Release the exhaust gas port and verify that vacuum is not held.

   f. If the transducer functions as specified, go to Step 2. If it does not, it must be replaced.

2. Check the EGR vacuum regulator solenoid function as follows:

   a. Disconnect the vacuum hoses and electrical lines from the EGR vacuum regulator solenoid.

   b. Blow through the (black/blue stripe) vacuum hose at A and verify that air flows from port B (Refer to illustrations).

   c. Apply 12 volts and ground to the connections as shown.

   d. Blow through vacuum nipple A and verify that air flows from the air filter.

   e. If the solenoid functions correctly, go to Step 3. If it does not function as specified, the solenoid must be replaced.

3. Check EGR valve function as follows:

   a. Manually move the valve diaphragm

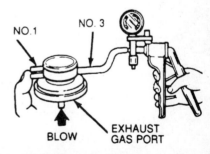

Testing the EGR back-pressure variable transducer—2.2L non-turbocharged engine

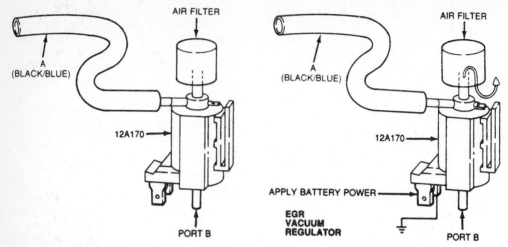

Testing the EGR vacuum regulator solenoid—2.2L non-turbocharged engine

with a finger and verify that the valve moves freely, and that spring resistance is present.

b. Start the engine and bring to normal operating temperature.

c. Connect a vacuum tester as shown.

d. Let the engine idle and apply 1.6–2.4 in. Hg of vacuum with the tester.

e. Verify that the engine runs roughly with the specified vacuum applied, and that the engine stalls if higher vacuum is applied.

f. If the valve functions properly, the system is okay. If the valve does not function as specified, it must be replaced.

NOTE: *If equipped with an EGR valve position sensor, refer to the testing procedure to confirm the condition of the sensor.*

TURBOCHARGED ENGINE

1. Check EGR control solenoid valve function as follows:

a. Disconnect the vacuum hoses and electrical lines from the control solenoid valve.

b. Blow through the vacuum hose at A and verify that air does not flow (Refer to illustrations, as applicable).

c. Apply 12 volts and ground to the connections as shown.

d. Blow through the vacuum hose at A and verify that air flows.

e. If the valve functions properly, go to Step 2. If it does not, replace the valve.

2. Check EGR vent solenoid valve function as follows:

a. Disconnect the vacuum hoses and electrical lines from the vent solenoid valve.

b. Blow through the vent hose at B and verify that air flows (Refer to illustrations, as applicable).

c. Apply 12 volts and ground to the connections as shown.

d. Blow through the vent hose at B and verify that air does not flow.

e. If the valve functions properly, go to Step 3. If it does not, replace the valve.

3. Check EGR valve function as follows:

a. Manually move the valve diaphragm with a finger and verify that the valve moves freely, and that spring resistance is present.

b. Start the engine and bring to normal operating temperature.

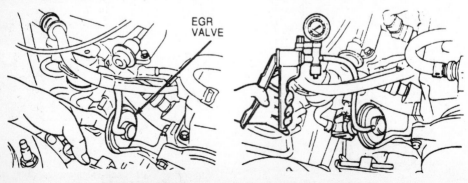

Testing the EGR valve—2.2L non-turbocharged engine

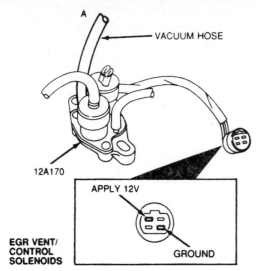

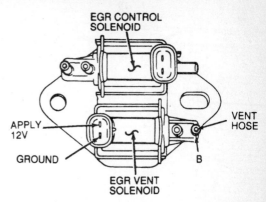

Testing the EGR vent solenoid valve—1992 2.2L turbocharged engine

**EGR VENT/
CONTROL
SOLENOIDS**

Testing the EGR control solenoid valve—1989–91 2.2L turbocharged engine

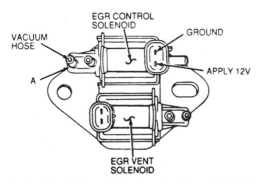

Testing the EGR control solenoid valve—1992 2.2L turbocharged engine

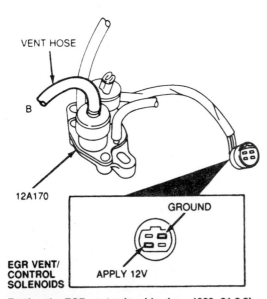

**EGR VENT/
CONTROL
SOLENOIDS**

Testing the EGR vent solenoid valve—1989–91 2.2L turbocharged engine

c. Connect a vacuum tester as shown.

d. Let the engine idle and apply 1.6–2.4 in. Hg of vacuum with the tester.

e. Verify that the engine runs roughly with the specified vacuum applied, and that the engine stalls if higher vacuum is applied.

f. If the valve functions properly, go to Step 4. If the valve does not function as specified, it must be replaced.

NOTE: *If equipped with an EGR valve position sensor, refer to the testing procedure to confirm the condition of the sensor.*

4. Check vacuum reservoir function as follows:

a. Remove the vacuum reservoir.

b. Attach a vacuum tester as shown.

c. Apply a vacuum at A and verify that vacuum is not held.

d. Apply a vacuum at B and verify that vacuum is held.

e. If the reservoir functions properly, the system is okay. If it does not, replace the reservoir.

EGR VALVE POSITION (EVP) SENSOR

1989 Vehicles

1. Visually inspect all wiring, wiring harness, connectors and components for evidence of overheating, insulation damage, looseness, shorting or other damage and repair, as necessary. If all appears okay, go to Step 2.

2. Check the VREF and Signal Return circuits as follows:

a. Install the breakout box according to the manufacturers instructions.

b. Place the volt-ohmmeter on the 20 volt scale and turn the ignition key **ON**.

c. Measure the voltage between pin 26 and pin 20; it should be 4–6 volts.

d. Measure the voltage between pin 26 and pin 46; it should be 4–6 volts.

e. Measure the voltage between pin 20 and pin 46; it should be 0 volts.

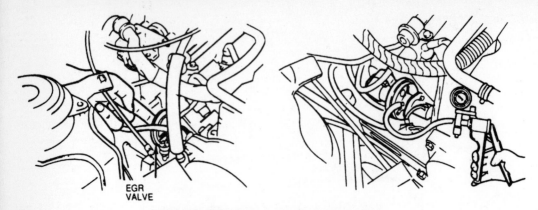

EGR
VALVE

Testing the EGR valve—2.2L turbocharged engine

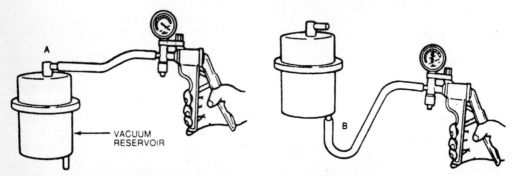

VACUUM
RESERVOIR

A

B

Testing the vacuum reservoir—2.2L turbocharged engine

f. If all voltage readings are within specification, go to Step 3. If they are not, check the reference voltage and signal return circuits.

3. Check EVP voltage as follows:

a. Install the breakout box according to the manufacturers instructions.

b. Place the volt-ohmmeter on the 20 volt scale.

c. Disconnect the vacuum hose from the EVP and connect a vacuum pump in its place.

d. Turn the ignition key **ON**.

e. Measure the voltage between pin 27 and

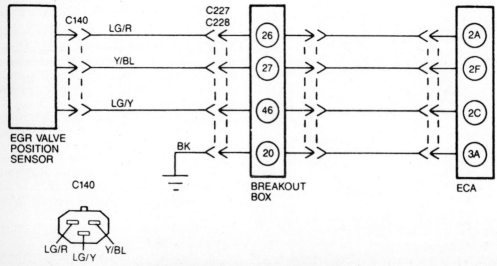

EVP sensor test schematic—1989 vehicles

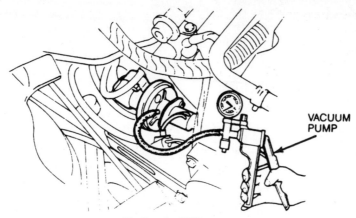

Testing the EVP sensor

pin 46 with no vacuum applied; it should be 0.25–0.95 volts.

f. Measure the voltage between pin 27 and pin 46 with 4.7 in. Hg of vacuum applied; it should be approximately 4 volts.

g. If both voltage readings are within specification, replace the ECA. If the voltage readings are not within specification, go to Step 4.

4. Check for power at the EVP sensor as follows:

a. Place the volt-ohmmeter on the 20 volt scale and turn the ignition key **ON**.

b. Measure the voltage between the EVP LG/R wire and ground; it should be 4–6 volts.

c. Measure the voltage between the EVP LG/R wire and EVP LG/Y wire; it should be 4–6 volts.

d. Measure the voltage between the EVP LG/Y wire and ground; it should be 0 volts.

e. If all voltage readings are within specification, go to Step 5. If all voltage readings are not within specification, repair the LG/R and/or the LG/Y wire(s) from the EVP to the ECA.

5. Check EVP sensor voltage as follows:

a. Disconnect the vacuum hose from the EVP and connect a vacuum pump in its place. Leave the electrical connector connected to the sensor.

b. Place the volt-ohmmeter on the 20 volt scale and turn the ignition key **ON**.

c. Measure the voltage between the EVP Y/BL wire and ground with no vacuum applied. Do not pierce the wire.

d. Measure the voltage between the EVP Y/BL wire and ground with 4.7 in. Hg of vacuum applied. Do not pierce the wire.

e. If both voltage readings are within specification, repair the open in the Y/BL wire from the EVP sensor to the ECA. If the voltage readings are not within specification, replace the EVP sensor.

1990–92 Vehicles

1. Check EVP input voltage as follows:

a. Install the breakout box according to the manufacturers instructions, and connect the ECA.

*TEST PINS ARE SPECIFIED IN THE CHART.
ALL HARNESS CONNECTORS ARE VIEWED INTO MATING SURFACE.

Application	Circuit	ECA Pin	BOB Pin	Wire Color
2.2L (MTX)	EVP	2L	27	Y/BL
	VREF	2K	26	LG/R
	SIGTRN	2D	46,49	LG/Y
2.2L (ATX),	EVP	2J	27	Y/BL
2.2L Turbo	VREF	2I	26	LG/R
	SIGTRN	3D	46,49	LG/Y

EVP sensor test schematic—1990–92 2.2L engines

b. Connect a vacuum pump to the EGR valve vacuum port.

c. Measure the voltage between EVP test pin 27 and SIGRTN test pins 46 and 49.

d. Turn the ignition key **ON**.

e. Compare the voltage readings to the data in the illustration as vacuum is increased.

f. If the voltage readings are okay, the EVP circuit is functioning correctly. If the voltage readings are not as specified, go to Step 2.

2. Check EVP sensor voltage as follows:

a. Disconnect the EVP sensor connector.

b. Using jumper wires, connect the VREF and SIGRTN pins between the harness connector and the EVP sensor connector. Leave the EVP wire disconnected.

c. Connect a vacuum pump to the EGR valve vacuum port.

d. Measure the voltage between the EVP sensor EVP terminal and the SIGRTN wire.

e. Turn the ignition key **ON**.

f. Compare the voltage readings to the data in the illustration as the vacuum is increased.

g. If the voltage readings are okay, repair the EVP sensor EVP wire to the ECA. If the voltage readings are not as specified, go to Step 3.

3. Check the VREF/SIGRTN circuit to the EVP sensor as follows:

a. Disconnect the EVP sensor connector.

b. Measure the voltage between the EVP sensor VREF wire and EVP sensor SIGRTN wire (at the harness connector leading to the ECA).

c. Turn the ignition key **ON**.

d. If the voltage reading is 4.5–5.5 volts, replace the EVP sensor. If the voltage reading is not 4.5–5.5 volts, check reference voltage.

3.0L Engine

1. Check system integrity as follows:

a. Check the vacuum hoses and connections for looseness, pinching, leakage, splitting, blockage and proper routing.

b. Inspect the EGR valve for loose attaching bolts or damaged flange gasket.

c. If the system appears to be in good condition and the vacuum hoses are properly routed, go to Step 2. If any problems are evident, repair as necessary.

2. Check EGR vacuum at idle as follows:

a. Start the engine and bring to normal operating temperature.

b. With the engine running at idle, disconnect the EGR vacuum supply at the EGR valve and check for a vacuum signal.

NOTE: *The EVR solenoid has a constant internal leak. You may notice a small vacuum signal. This signal should be less than 1 in. Hg of vacuum at idle.*

c. If the EGR vacuum signal is less than 1 in. Hg of vacuum at idle, go to Step 3. If the EGR vacuum signal is not as specified, reconnect the EGR vacuum hose. Inspect the EVR solenoid for leakage and run the Quick Test.

3. Check EGR valve function as follows:

a. Install a suitable tachometer according to the manufacturers instructions.

b. Disconnect the ISC/BPA valve electrical connector.

GRAPH

INCHES OF HG	VOLTS
0"	0.867
1"	0.893
2"	0.923
3"	1.434
4"	1.84
5"	2.09
6"	3.86
7"	4.93
8"	4.93

GRAPH DATA VALUES

Note: Voltage values may change ± 15%.

EVP sensor testing data—1990–92 2.2L engines

c. Disconnect and plug the vacuum supply hose from the EGR valve nipple.

d. Start the engine, let it idle with the transaxle in neutral (make sure the parking brake is applied) and observe the idle speed. If necessary, adjust the idle speed (Refer to Chapter 2).

e. Slowly apply 5–10 in. Hg of vacuum to the EGR valve nipple using a hand vacuum pump.

f. If the idle speed drops more than 100 rpm with vacuum applied, and returns to normal (± 25 rpm) after the vacuum is removed, the EGR valve is okay. Reconnect the EGR valve vacuum supply hose and reconnect the ISC/BPA valve connector.

g. If the idle speed does not change and return as indicated in Step 3f, inspect the EGR valve for blockage or contamination. Clean or replace the valve, as required.

REMOVAL AND INSTALLATION

EGR Valve

1. Disconnect the negative battery cable.
2. Disconnect the vacuum line from the EGR valve.
3. If equipped, disconnect the electrical connector and remove the EVP sensor.
4. Remove the mounting bolts and remove the EGR valve.
5. Installation is the reverse of the removal procedure. Be sure to remove all old gasket material before installation. Use a new gasket during installation.

Pressure Feedback Electronic Transducer

3.0L ENGINE

1. Disconnect the negative battery cable.
2. Disconnect the electrical connector and the pressure input line(s) from the transducer.
3. Remove the transducer.
4. Installation is the reverse of the removal procedure.

EGR Vacuum Regulator

3.0L ENGINE

1. Disconnect the negative battery cable.
2. Disconnect the electrical connector and the vacuum lines from the regulator.
3. Remove the regulator mounting bolts and remove the regulator.
4. Installation is the reverse of the removal procedure.

Back-pressure Variable Transducer

2.2L NON-TURBOCHARGED ENGINE

1. Tag and disconnect the vacuum lines and inlet line from the transducer.
2. Remove the transducer from its mount.

3. Installation is the reverse of the removal procedure.

EGR Solenoid Valves

2.2L ENGINES

1. Disconnect the negative battery cable.
2. Disconnect the electrical connector from the solenoid valve.
3. Tag and disconnect the vacuum hoses from the solenoid valve.
4. Remove the solenoid vacuum valve from its mounting.
5. Installation is the reverse of the removal procedure.

EGR Valve Position Sensor

2.2L ENGINES

1. Disconnect the negative battery cable.
2. Disconnect the electrical connector from the EVP sensor.
3. Remove the mounting bolts and remove the EVP sensor.
4. Installation is the reverse of the removal procedure.

Exhaust Catalyst System

OPERATION

Engine exhaust consists mainly of Nitrogen (N_2), however, it also contains Carbon Monoxide (CO), Carbon Dioxide (CO_2), Water Vapor (H_2O), Oxygen (O_2), Nitrogen Oxides (NOx) and Hydrogen, as well as various, unburned Hydrocarbons (HC). Three of these exhaust components, CO, NOx and HC, are major air pollutants, so their emission to the atmosphere has to be controlled.

The 3-way catalytic converter, mounted in the engine exhaust system, works as a gas reactor to convert and reduce the pollutant levels to within legally prescribed limits.

The catalyst metals are thinly coated onto and supported by a honeycomb shaped high temperature ceramic, mounted inside the converter shell. The result is a highly effective converter design having minimum restriction to exhaust gas flow.

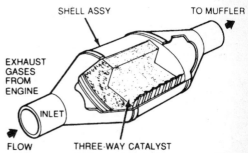

Cut-away view of the catalytic converter

REMOVAL AND INSTALLATION

For catalytic converter removal and installation procedures, refer to Chapter 3.

Emission Warning Lamps

All vehicles are equipped with a Malfunction Indicator Light (MIL) which appears on the instrument panel as the words **CHECK ENGINE**. This light should come on briefly when the ignition key is turned **ON** but should turn off when the engine is started. If the light stays on after the engine is started or if it comes on at any time during engine operation, a problem in the electronic engine control system is indicated; refer to the Self-Diagnostic System.

There are also 2 different service interval reminder systems, the Vehicle Maintenance Monitor or System Scanner. The Vehicle Maintenance Monitor is available only on vehicles with an analog instrument cluster. It will indicate a service interval check on a module located on the front center portion of the headliner, just above the rear view mirror. The System Scanner is found on vehicles with electronic instrument clusters. It will indicate a service interval check on a display, located in the lower left corner of the instrument cluster.

RESETTING

To reset the service interval light on vehicles equipped with the Vehicle Maintenance Monitor, insert a small pointed instrument into the service interval cancel switch. Depress the switch once.

To cancel the service check message on the System Scanner, press the **SERV** button on the keyboard, located to the right of the instrument cluster, and hold until 3 tones are sounded.

SELF-DIAGNOSTIC SYSTEM

General Information

All Probes have self-diagnostic capabilities. The ECA monitors all input and output functions within the electronic engine control sys-

ANALOG

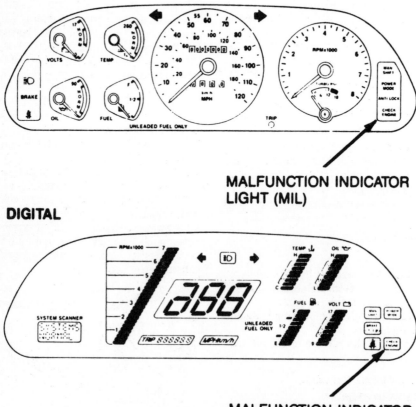

MALFUNCTION INDICATOR LIGHT (MIL)

DIGITAL

MALFUNCTION INDICATOR LIGHT (MIL)

Malfunction indicator light locations

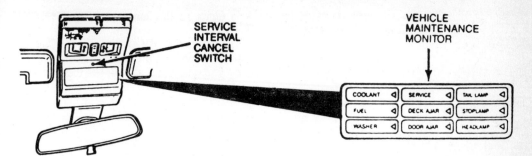

Vehicle Maintenance Monitor service interval cancel switch location

tem. If a malfunction is detected, the information will be stored in the ECA memory in the form of a 2 or 3 digit code. These codes can be accessed using the Quick Test procedure. The Quick Test procedure is slightly different for the 2.2L engines, which use the Electronic Engine Control (EEC) system, and the 3.0L engine, which uses the Electronic Engine Control-IV (EEC-IV) system.

2.2L ENGINES

The Quick Test procedure is divided into 3 sections, the Key On Engine Off (KOEO) and Key On Engine Running (KOER) Self-Tests and the Switch Monitor test. Codes can be obtained from the KOEO and KOER tests using a scan tool, such as the Ford SUPER STAR II tester, an analog voltmeter or the dashboard Malfunction Indicator Light (MIL).

If using the scan tool, codes will be output and displayed as numbers, such as the number 23. If codes are being read through the dashboard MIL, the codes will be displayed as groups of flashes separated by pauses. A Code 23 would be shown as 2 flashes, a pause, and then 3 flashes. A longer pause will occur between codes. If codes are being read on an analog voltmeter, the needle sweeps indicate the

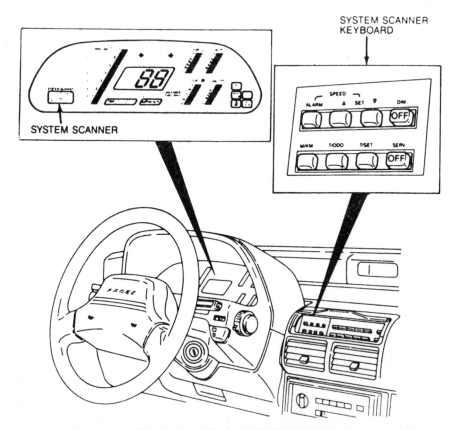

System scanner display and keyboard location

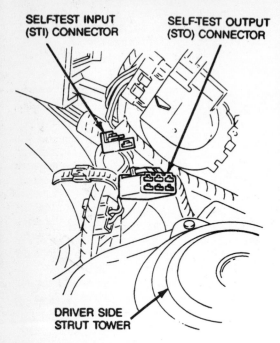

Diagnostic connector location

code digits in the same manner as the MIL flashes.

Unlike the EEC-IV system, the EEC system does not broadcast a PASS designator or code. If no fault codes are stored, the display screen on the scanner will remain blank. Also, the EEC system does not operate switches or sensors during KOEO or KOER testing.

The EEC diagnostic connector, or Self-Test Output (STO) connector is located at the left rear corner of the engine compartment. The Self-Test Input (STI) connector is separate from the main diagnostic connector.

Key On Engine Off Self-Test

1. Make sure the scan tool is OFF and connect it to the self-test connectors (Refer to illustration). Switch the scan tool to the MECS position. Make sure the adapter ground cable is connected to the negative battery cable.

2. Make sure the scan tool button is ON or latched down.

3. Turn the ignition switch **ON** but do not start the engine, then turn the scan tool ON.

4. Once energized, the tester should display

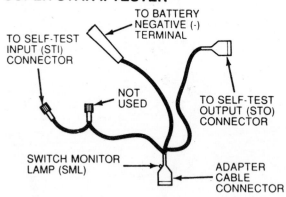

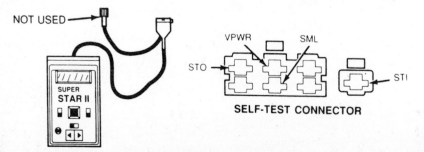

Scan tool connections—2.2L engine

888 and beep for 2 seconds. Release the test button and **00** should appear, signifying the tool is ready to read codes.

5. Re-engage the test button.
6. KOEO codes will be transmitted.
7. Record all codes displayed.
8. After all codes are received, release the test button to review all the codes retained in tester memory.
9. Make sure all codes displayed are recorded. Clear the ECA memory and perform the KOEO test again. This will isolate hard faults from intermittents. Any hard faults will cause the code(s) to be repeated in the 2nd test. An intermittent which is not now present will not set a new code.
10. Record all codes from the 2nd test. After repairs are made on hard fault items, the intermittents must be recreated by tapping suspect sensors, wiggling wires or connectors or reproducing circumstances on a test drive.

NOTE: *For both KOEO and KOER tests, the message STO LO always displayed on the screen indicates that the system cannot initiate the Self-Test. The message STI LO displayed with an otherwise blank screen indicates PASS or No Codes Stored.*

Key On Engine Running Self-Test

1. Make sure the self-test button is released or de-activated on the SUPER STAR II tester and that the tester is properly connected.
2. Start the engine and run it at 2000 rpm for 2 minutes. This will warm up the oxygen sensor.
3. Turn the ignition switch **OFF**.
4. Turn the ignition switch **ON** for 10 seconds but do not start the engine.

5. Start the engine and run it at idle.
6. Activate or latch the self-test button on the scan tool.
7. All relevant codes will be displayed and should be recorded.

Reading Codes With Analog Voltmeter

In the absence of a scan tool, an analog voltmeter may be used to obtain codes. Set the meter range to read DC 0–20 volts. Connect the positive lead of the meter to the STO pin in the diagnostic connector and connect the negative lead of the meter to the negative battery terminal or a good engine ground.

Follow the directions for performing the KOEO and KOER tests. To activate the tests, use a jumper wire to connect the STI connector to ground. The codes will be transmitted as groups of needle sweeps.

Reading Codes With MIL

The MIL on the dashboard may also be used to obtain codes. Follow the directions for performing the KOEO and KOER tests. To activate the tests, use a jumper wire to connect the STI connector to ground.

Codes are transmitted as flashes with a pause between the digits. A Code 32 would be sent as 3 flashes, a pause, followed by 2 flashes. A slightly longer pause divides codes from each other. Be ready to count and record the codes; the only way to repeat a code is to re-cycle the system.

Switch Monitor Tests

This test mode allows the operator to check the input signal from individual switches to the ECA. All switches to be tested must be OFF at

1 NEEDLE PULSE (SWEEP) + 1 NEEDLE PULSE (SWEEP) = 2 NEEDLE PULSES (SWEEPS) FOR 1ST DIGIT

16-SECOND PULSE BETWEEN DIGITS

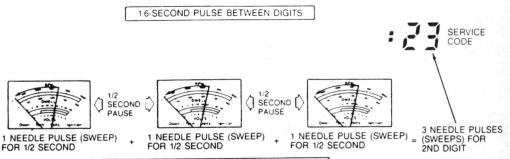

: **23** SERVICE CODE

1 NEEDLE PULSE (SWEEP) FOR 1/2 SECOND + 1/2 SECOND PAUSE + 1 NEEDLE PULSE (SWEEP) FOR 1/2 SECOND + 1/2 SECOND PAUSE + 1 NEEDLE PULSE (SWEEP) FOR 1/2 SECOND = 3 NEEDLE PULSES (SWEEPS) FOR 2ND DIGIT

4-SECOND PAUSE BETWEEN SERVICE CODES, WHEN MORE THAN ONE CODE IS INDICATED

Code display patterns on an analog voltmeter

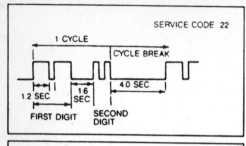

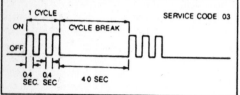

Examples of MIL code output patterns

the time the test begins; if one switch is on, it will affect the testing of another. The test must begin with the engine cool. The tests may be performed with either the SUPER STAR II tester or an analog voltmeter. When using the scan tool, the small LED on the adapter cable will light to show that the ECA has received the switch signal. If the voltmeter is used, the voltage will change when the switch is engaged or disengaged.

1. The engine must be off and cooled. Place the transaxle in Park or Neutral.

2. Turn all accessories **OFF**.

3. If using the SUPER STAR II, connect it properly. If using an analog voltmeter, use a jumper wire to ground the STI terminal. Connect the positive voltmeter lead to the SML terminal of the diagnostic connector and connect the negative lead to a good engine ground.

4. Turn the ignition switch **ON**. Engage the center button on the SUPER STAR II. Most switches can be exercised without starting the engine.

5. Operate each switch according to the test chart and note the response either on the LED or the volt scale. Remember that an improper response means the ECA did not see the switch operation; check circuitry and connectors before assuming the switch is faulty.

6. Turn the ignition switch **OFF** when testing is complete.

Clearing Codes

Codes stored within the ECA memory must be erased when repairs are completed. Also, erasing codes during diagnosis can separate hard faults from intermittents. To erase stored codes, disconnect the negative battery cable, then depress the brake pedal for at least 10 seconds. Reconnect the battery cable and recheck

the system for any remaining or newly set codes.

3.0L ENGINE

The Quick Test procedure is divided into 2 sections, the Key On Engine Off (KOEO) and Key On Engine Running (KOER) Self-Tests. Codes can be obtained from each test using a scan tool, such as the Ford STAR or SUPER STAR II tester, an analog voltmeter, or the dashboard Malfunction Indicator Light (MIL).

If using the scan tool, codes will be output and displayed as numbers, such as the number 116. If codes are being read through the dashboard MIL, the codes will be displayed as groups of flashes separated by pauses. A Code 116 would be shown as a flash, a pause, a flash, another pause, followed by 6 flashes. A longer pause will occur between codes. If codes are being read on an analog voltmeter, the needle sweeps indicate the code digits in the same manner as the MIL flashes.

Key On Engine Off Self-Test

1. Connect the scan tool to the self-test connectors. Make sure the test button is unlatched or up.

2. Set the SUPER STAR II tester switch to the EEC-IV position.

3. Start the engine and run it until normal operating temperature is reached.

4. Turn the engine **OFF** for 10 seconds.

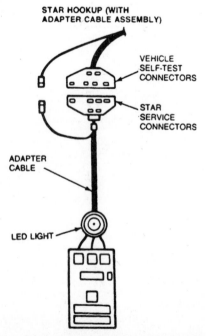

STAR or SUPER STAR II tester connection—3.0L engine

5. Turn on the power to the tester. Activate the test button to the test position.

6. Turn the ignition switch **ON**, but do not start the engine.

7. The KOEO codes will be transmitted. Six to nine seconds after the last KOEO code, a single separator pulse will be transmitted. Six to nine seconds after this pulse, the codes from the Continuous Memory will be transmitted.

8. Record all codes displayed. Do not depress the throttle during the test.

NOTE: *The STAR tester cannot be used to read 3-digit codes. If the STAR tester is used, the display will be blank. The SUPER STAR II tester or equivalent, must be used to read 3-digit codes.*

Key On Engine Running Self-Test

1. Make sure the self-test button is released or de-activated on the SUPER STAR II tester.

2. Start the engine and run it at 2000 rpm for 2 minutes to warm the oxygen sensor.

3. Turn the ignition switch **OFF** for 10 seconds.

4. Depress the test button to the test position, then restart the engine.

5. An engine identification code will be transmitted only on vehicles with 2-digit codes. This is a single digit number representing ½ the number of cylinders in a gasoline engine. On the STAR tester, this number may appear with a zero, i.e., 30 = 3. The code is used to confirm that the correct processor is installed and that the Self-Test has begun.

6. If the vehicle is equipped with a Brake On/Off (BOO) switch, the brake pedal must be depressed and released after the ID code is transmitted.

7. If the vehicle is equipped with a power steering pressure switch, the steering wheel must be turned at least ½ turn within 2 seconds after the engine ID code is transmitted.

8. Certain vehicles will display a Dynamic Response code 6–20 seconds after the engine ID code. This will appear as 1 pulse on a meter or as a 10 on the STAR tester. When this code appears, briefly take the engine to WOT. This allows the system to test the TP sensor, MAF and MAP sensors. For 3-digit code applications, the Dynamic Response indicator will light on the SUPER STAR II tester but no Dynamic Response code will be displayed.

9. All relevant codes will be displayed and should be recorded. These codes refer only to faults present during this test cycle. Codes stored in Continuous Memory are not displayed in this test mode.

10. Do not depress the throttle during testing unless a dynamic response code is displayed.

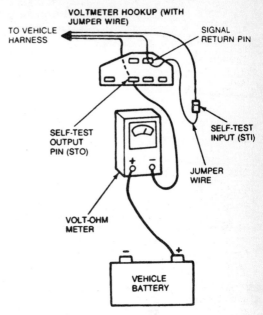

Analog voltmeter connection—3.0L engine

Reading Codes With Analog Voltmeter

In the absence of a scan tool, an analog voltmeter may be used to obtain codes. Set the meter range to read DC 0–15 volts. Connect the positive lead of the meter to the positive battery terminal and connect the negative lead of the meter to the self-test output pin of the diagnostic connector.

Follow the directions for performing the KOEO and KOER tests. To activate the tests, use a jumper wire to connect the signal return pin on the diagnostic connector to the self-test input connector. The self-test input line is the separate wire and connector near the diagnostic connector.

Codes will be transmitted as groups of needle sweeps. The Continuous Memory codes are separated from the KOEO codes by 6 seconds, a single sweep and another 6 second delay.

Reading Codes With MIL

The MIL on the dashboard may also be used to obtain codes. Follow the directions for performing the KOEO and KOER tests. To activate the tests, use a jumper wire to connect the signal return pin on the diagnostic connector to the self-test input connector. The self-test input line is the separate wire and connector with or near the diagnostic connector.

Codes are transmitted as flashes with a pause between the digits. A Code 332 would be sent as 3 flashes, a pause, 3 flashes and another pause, followed by 2 flashes. A slightly longer pause divides codes from each other. Be ready to count and record the codes; the only way to repeat a code is to re-cycle the system. The Continuous Memory codes are separated from the KOEO codes by 6 seconds, single flash and another 6 second delay.

Clearing Codes
CONTINUOUS MEMORY CODES

These codes are retained in memory for 80 warm-up cycles. To clear the codes for the purpose of testing or confirming repair, perform the KOEO test. When codes begin to be displayed, de-activate the test by either disconnecting the jumper wire or releasing the test button on the scan tool. Stopping the test during code transmission will erase the Continuous Memory. Do not disconnect the negative battery cable to clear these codes as the Keep Alive Memory (KAM) will be cleared.

KEEP ALIVE MEMORY (KAM)

The KAM contains the adaptive factors used by the ECA to compensate for component tolerances and wear. It should not be routinely cleared during diagnosis. If an emissions related part is replaced during repair, the KAM must be cleared. Failure the clear the KAM may cause driveability problems since the correction factor for the old component will be applied to the new component.

To clear the KAM, disconnect the negative battery cable for at least 5 minutes. After the memory is cleared and the battery reconnected, the vehicle must be driven at least 10 miles so the ECA can relearn the needed correction factors. The distance to be driven depends on the engine and vehicle, but all drives should include steady-throttle cruise on open roads. Certain driveability problems may be noted during the drive because the adaptive factors are not yet functioning.

Fuel System

5

GASOLINE FUEL INJECTION SYSTEM

Description of System

The electronic fuel injection system on your Probe consists of two subsystems, the fuel delivery system and the electronic control system. The fuel delivery system supplies fuel to the fuel injectors at a specified pressure. The electronic control system regulates the flow of fuel from the injectors into the engine.

The fuel delivery system consists of an electric fuel pump, fuel filters, fuel supply manifold, fuel pressure regulator and fuel injectors. The electric fuel pump, mounted in the fuel tank, draws fuel through a filter screen attached to the fuel pump/sending unit assembly. Fuel is pumped to the engine compartment, through another filter, and into the fuel supply manifold. The fuel supply manifold supplies fuel directly to the injectors. A constant fuel pressure drop is maintained across the injector nozzles by the fuel pressure regulator. The pressure regulator is mounted on the fuel supply manifold, downstream from the fuel injectors. Excess fuel supplied by the fuel pump is relieved by the regulator and returned to the fuel tank through the fuel return line. The fuel injectors spray a metered quantity of fuel into the intake air stream when they are energized. The quantity of fuel is determined by the electronic control system.

The electronic control system consists of the Electronic Control Assembly (ECA) and the engine sensors and switches that provide input to the ECA. On the 2.2L engines, the Vane Air Flow (VAF) meter monitors the amount of air flow into the engine, measures air temperature, controls the electric fuel pump and supplies this information to the ECA. On the 3.0L engine, air entering the engine is measured by the Speed, Manifold Absolute Pressure (MAP), and Air Charge Temperature (ACT) sensors and provides this information to the ECA. On all engines, information is also supplied to the ECA regarding engine coolant temperature, engine speed, and exhaust gas oxygen content. Based on the input information, the ECA computes the required fuel flow rate and determines the needed injector pulse width, then outputs a command to the fuel injector to meter the exact quantity of fuel.

On the 2.2L turbocharged engine, exhaust gas energy is used to pressurize the intake air, thereby supplying more than the normal amount of air into the combustion chamber. This engine has sensors and provides input to the ECA exclusive to this type of induction, otherwise the fuel injection system on the turbocharged engine operates the same as the normally aspirated engines.

Relieving Fuel System Pressure

1. Start the engine.
2. Disconnect the fuel pump relay, located under the dash on the driver's side.
3. After the engine stalls, turn **OFF** the ignition key.
4. Reconnect the fuel pump relay.

NOTE: *On the 3.0L engine, an alternate method of relieving fuel system pressure can be used using pressure gauge tool T80L-9974-B or equivalent. Connect the tool to the fuel diagnostic valve located on the fuel supply manifold and release the fuel pressure through the drain hose into a suitable container.*

Electric Fuel Pump

REMOVAL AND INSTALLATION

1. Relieve the fuel pressure and disconnect the negative battery cable.

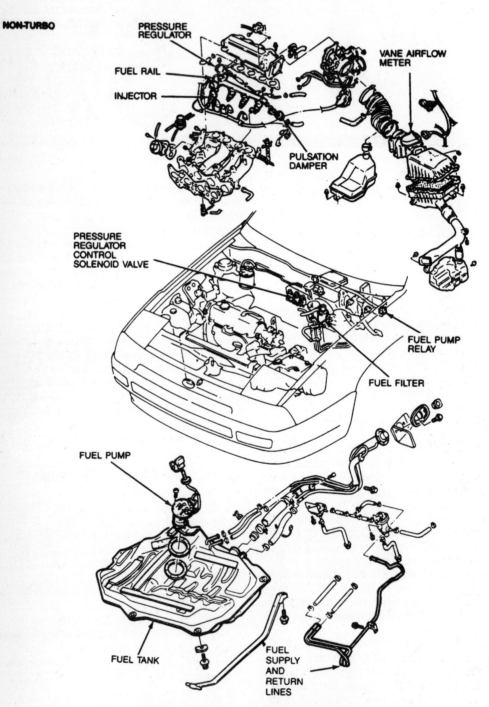

NON-TURBO

PRESSURE REGULATOR

FUEL RAIL

INJECTOR

VANE AIRFLOW METER

PULSATION DAMPER

PRESSURE REGULATOR CONTROL SOLENOID VALVE

FUEL PUMP RELAY

FUEL FILTER

FUEL PUMP

FUEL TANK

FUEL SUPPLY AND RETURN LINES

Fuel system—2.2L non-turbocharged engine

CHILTON'S
FUEL ECONOMY & TUNE-UP TIPS

55 WAYS TO IMPROVE FUEL ECONOMY

Tune-up • Spark Plug Diagnosis • Emission Controls

Fuel System • Cooling System • Tires and Wheels

General Maintenance

CHILTON'S FUEL ECONOMY & TUNE-UP TIPS

Fuel economy is important to everyone, no matter what kind of vehicle you drive. The maintenance-minded motorist can save both money and fuel using these tips and the periodic maintenance and tune-up procedures in this Repair and Tune-Up Guide.

There are more than 130,000,000 cars and trucks registered for private use in the United States. Each travels an average of 10-12,000 miles per year, and, and in total they consume close to 70 billion gallons of fuel each year. This represents nearly ⅔ of the oil imported by the United States each year. The Federal government's goal is to reduce consumption 10% by 1985. A variety of methods are either already in use or under serious consideration, and they all affect you driving and the cars you will drive. In addition to "down-sizing", the auto industry is using or investigating the use of electronic fuel delivery, electronic engine controls and alternative engines for use in smaller and lighter vehicles, among other alternatives to meet the federally mandated Corporate Average Fuel Economy (CAFE) of 27.5 mpg by 1985. The government, for its part, is considering rationing, mandatory driving curtailments and tax increases on motor vehicle fuel in an effort to reduce consumption. The government's goal of a 10% reduction could be realized — and further government regulation avoided — if every private vehicle could use just 1 less gallon of fuel per week.

How Much Can You Save?

Tests have proven that almost anyone can make at least a 10% reduction in fuel consumption through regular maintenance and tune-ups. When a major manufacturer of spark plugs sur-

TUNE-UP

1. Check the cylinder compression to be sure the engine will really benefit from a tune-up and that it is capable of producing good fuel economy. A tune-up will be wasted on an engine in poor mechanical condition.

2. Replace spark plugs regularly. New spark plugs alone can increase fuel economy 3%.

3. Be sure the spark plugs are the correct type (heat range) for your vehicle. See the Tune-Up Specifications.

Heat range refers to the spark plug's ability to conduct heat away from the firing end. It must conduct the heat away in an even pattern to avoid becoming a source of pre-ignition, yet it must also operate hot enough to burn off conductive deposits that could cause misfiring.

The heat range is usually indicated by a number on the spark plug, part of the manufacturer's designation for each individual spark plug. The numbers in bold-face indicate the heat range in each manufacturer's identification system.

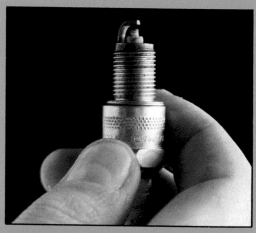

Periodically, check the spark plugs to be sure they are firing efficiently. They are excellent indicators of the internal condition of your engine.

Manufacturer	Typical Designation
AC	R **45** TS
Bosch (old)	WA **145** T30
Bosch (new)	HR **8** Y
Champion	RBL **15** Y
Fram/Autolite	4**15**
Mopar	P-**62** PR
Motorcraft	BRF-**42**
NGK	BP **5** ES-15
Nippondenso	W **16** EP
Prestolite	14GR **5** 2A

On AC, Bosch (new), Champion, Fram/Autolite, Mopar, Motorcraft and Prestolite, a higher number indicates a hotter plug. On Bosch (old), NGK and Nippondenso, a higher number indicates a colder plug.

4. Make sure the spark plugs are properly gapped. See the Tune-Up Specifications in this book.

5. Be sure the spark plugs are firing efficiently. The illustrations on the next 2 pages show you how to "read" the firing end of the spark plug.

6. Check the ignition timing and set it to specifications. Tests show that almost all cars have incorrect ignition timing by more than 2°.

veyed over 6,000 cars nationwide, they found that a tune-up, on cars that needed one, increased fuel economy over 11%. Replacing worn plugs alone, accounted for a 3% increase. The same test also revealed that 8 out of every 10 vehicles will have some maintenance deficiency that will directly affect fuel economy, emissions or performance. Most of this mileage-robbing neglect could be prevented with regular maintenance.

Modern engines require that all of the functioning systems operate properly for maximum efficiency. A malfunction anywhere wastes fuel. You can keep your vehicle running as efficiently and economically as possible, by being aware of your vehicle's operating and performance characteristics. If your vehicle suddenly develops performance or fuel economy problems it could be due to one or more of the following:

PROBLEM	POSSIBLE CAUSE
Engine Idles Rough	Ignition timing, idle mixture, vacuum leak or something amiss in the emission control system.
Hesitates on Acceleration	Dirty carburetor or fuel filter, improper accelerator pump setting, ignition timing or fouled spark plugs.
Starts Hard or Fails to Start	Worn spark plugs, improperly set automatic choke, ice (or water) in fuel system.
Stalls Frequently	Automatic choke improperly adjusted and possible dirty air filter or fuel filter.
Performs Sluggishly	Worn spark plugs, dirty fuel or air filter, ignition timing or automatic choke out of adjustment.

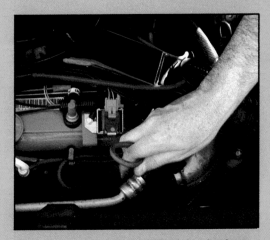

Check spark plug wires on conventional point type ignition for cracks by bending them in a loop around your finger.

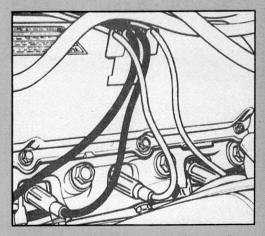

Be sure that spark plug wires leading to adjacent cylinders do not run too close together. (Photo courtesy Champion Spark Plug Co.)

7. If your vehicle does not have electronic ignition, check the points, rotor and cap as specified.

8. Check the spark plug wires (used with conventional point-type ignitions) for cracks and burned or broken insulation by bending them in a loop around your finger. Cracked wires decrease fuel efficiency by failing to deliver full voltage to the spark plugs. One misfiring spark plug can cost you as much as 2 mpg.

9. Check the routing of the plug wires. Misfiring can be the result of spark plug leads to adjacent cylinders running parallel to each other and too close together. One wire tends to pick up voltage from the other causing it to fire "out of time".

10. Check all electrical and ignition circuits for voltage drop and resistance.

11. Check the distributor mechanical and/or vacuum advance mechanisms for proper functioning. The vacuum advance can be checked by twisting the distributor plate in the opposite direction of rotation. It should spring back when released.

12. Check and adjust the valve clearance on engines with mechanical lifters. The clearance should be slightly loose rather than too tight.

SPARK PLUG DIAGNOSIS

Normal

APPEARANCE: This plug is typical of one oper-ating normally. The insulator nose varies from a light tan to grayish color with slight electrode wear. The presence of slight deposits is normal on used plugs and will have no adverse effect on engine performance. The spark plug heat range is correct for the engine and the engine is running normally.

CAUSE: Properly running engine.

RECOMMENDATION: Before reinstalling this plug, the electrodes should be cleaned and filed square. Set the gap to specifications. If the plug has been in service for more than 10-12,000 miles, the entire set should probably be re-placed with a fresh set of the same heat range.

Oil Deposits

APPEARANCE: The firing end of the plug is covered with a wet, oily coating.

CAUSE: The problem is poor oil control. On high mileage engines, oil is leaking past the rings or valve guides into the combustion chamber. A common cause is also a plugged PCV valve, and a ruptured fuel pump diaphragm can also cause this condition. Oil fouled plugs such as these are often found in new or recently over-hauled engines, before normal oil control is achieved, and can be cleaned and reinstalled.

RECOMMENDATION: A hotter spark plug may temporarily relieve the problem, but the engine is probably in need of work.

Incorrect Heat Range

APPEARANCE: The effects of high temperature on a spark plug are indicated by clean white, often blistered insulator. This can also be ac-companied by excessive wear of the electrode, and the absence of deposits.

CAUSE: Check for the correct spark plug heat range. A plug which is too hot for the engine can result in overheating. A car operated mostly at high speeds can require a colder plug. Also check ignition timing, cooling system level, fuel mixture and leaking intake manifold.

RECOMMENDATION: If all ignition and engine adjustments are known to be correct, and no other malfunction exists, install spark plugs one heat range colder.

Photos Courtesy Fram Corporation

Carbon Deposits

APPEARANCE: Carbon fouling is easily identi-fied by the presence of dry, soft, black, sooty deposits.

CAUSE: Changing the heat range can often lead to carbon fouling, as can prolonged slow, stop-and-start driving. If the heat range is cor-rect, carbon fouling can be attributed to a rich fuel mixture, sticking choke, clogged air cleaner, worn breaker points, retarded timing or low compression. If only one or two plugs are carbon fouled, check for corroded or cracked wires on the affected plugs. Also look for cracks in the distributor cap between the towers of affected cylinders.

RECOMMENDATION: After the problem is cor-rected, these plugs can be cleaned and rein-stalled if not worn severely.

MMT Fouled

APPEARANCE: Spark plugs fouled by MMT (Methycyclopentadienyl Maganese Tricarbonyl) have reddish, rusty appearance on the insulator and side electrode.

CAUSE: MMT is an anti-knock additive in gasoline used to replace lead. During the combustion process, the MMT leaves a reddish deposit on the insulator and side electrode.

RECOMMENDATION: No engine malfunction is indicated and the deposits will not affect plug performance any more than lead deposits (see Ash Deposits). MMT fouled plugs can be cleaned, regapped and reinstalled.

High Speed Glazing

APPEARANCE: Glazing appears as shiny coating on the plug, either yellow or tan in color.

CAUSE: During hard, fast acceleration, plug temperatures rise suddenly. Deposits from normal combustion have no chance to fluff-off; instead, they melt on the insulator forming an electrically conductive coating which causes misfiring.

RECOMMENDATION: Glazed plugs are not easily cleaned. They should be replaced with a fresh set of plugs of the correct heat range. If the condition recurs, using plugs with a heat range one step colder may cure the problem.

Ash (Lead) Deposits

APPEARANCE: Ash deposits are characterized by light brown or white colored deposits crusted on the side or center electrodes. In some cases it may give the plug a rusty appearance.

CAUSE: Ash deposits are normally derived from oil or fuel additives burned during normal combustion. Normally they are harmless, though excessive amounts can cause misfiring. If deposits are excessive in short mileage, the valve guides may be worn.

RECOMMENDATION: Ash-fouled plugs can be cleaned, gapped and reinstalled.

Detonation

APPEARANCE: Detonation is usually characterized by a broken plug insulator.

CAUSE: A portion of the fuel charge will begin to burn spontaneously, from the increased heat following ignition. The explosion that results applies extreme pressure to engine components, frequently damaging spark plugs and pistons.

Detonation can result by over-advanced ignition timing, inferior gasoline (low octane) lean air/fuel mixture, poor carburetion, engine lugging or an increase in compression ratio due to combustion chamber deposits or engine modification.

RECOMMENDATION: Replace the plugs after correcting the problem.

Photos Courtesy Champion Spark Plug Co.

EMISSION CONTROLS

13. Be aware of the general condition of the emission control system. It contributes to reduced pollution and should be serviced regularly to maintain efficient engine operation.

14. Check all vacuum lines for dried, cracked or brittle conditions. Something as simple as a leaking vacuum hose can cause poor performance and loss of economy.

15. Avoid tampering with the emission control system. Attempting to improve fuel econ-

FUEL SYSTEM

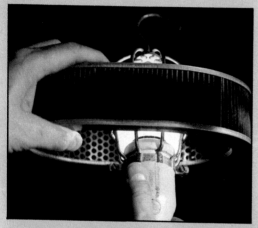

Check the air filter with a light behind it. If you can see light through the filter it can be reused.

Extremely clogged filters should be discarded and replaced with a new one.

18. Replace the air filter regularly. A dirty air filter richens the air/fuel mixture and can increase fuel consumption as much as 10%. Tests show that ⅓ of all vehicles have air filters in need of replacement.

19. Replace the fuel filter at least as often as recommended.

20. Set the idle speed and carburetor mixture to specifications.

21. Check the automatic choke. A sticking or malfunctioning choke wastes gas.

22. During the summer months, adjust the automatic choke for a leaner mixture which will produce faster engine warm-ups.

COOLING SYSTEM

29. Be sure all accessory drive belts are in good condition. Check for cracks or wear.

30. Adjust all accessory drive belts to proper tension.

31. Check all hoses for swollen areas, worn spots, or loose clamps.

32. Check coolant level in the radiator or expansion tank.

33. Be sure the thermostat is operating properly. A stuck thermostat delays engine warm-up and a cold engine uses nearly twice as much fuel as a warm engine.

34. Drain and replace the engine coolant at least as often as recommended. Rust and scale

TIRES & WHEELS

38. Check the tire pressure often with a pencil type gauge. Tests by a major tire manufacturer show that 90% of all vehicles have at least 1 tire improperly inflated. Better mileage can be achieved by over-inflating tires, but never exceed the maximum inflation pressure on the side of the tire.

39. If possible, install radial tires. Radial tires deliver as much as ½ mpg more than bias belted tires.

40. Avoid installing super-wide tires. They only create extra rolling resistance and decrease fuel mileage. Stick to the manufacturer's recommendations.

41. Have the wheels properly balanced.

omy by tampering with emission controls is more likely to worsen fuel economy than improve it. Emission control changes on modern engines are not readily reversible.

16. Clean (or replace) the EGR valve and lines as recommended.

17. Be sure that all vacuum lines and hoses are reconnected properly after working under the hood. An unconnected or misrouted vacuum line can wreak havoc with engine performance.

23. Check for fuel leaks at the carburetor, fuel pump, fuel lines and fuel tank. Be sure all lines and connections are tight.

24. Periodically check the tightness of the carburetor and intake manifold attaching nuts and bolts. These are a common place for vacuum leaks to occur.

25. Clean the carburetor periodically and lubricate the linkage.

26. The condition of the tailpipe can be an excellent indicator of proper engine combustion. After a long drive at highway speeds, the inside of the tailpipe should be a light grey in color. Black or soot on the insides indicates an overly rich mixture.

27. Check the fuel pump pressure. The fuel pump may be supplying more fuel than the engine needs.

28. Use the proper grade of gasoline for your engine. Don't try to compensate for knocking or "pinging" by advancing the ignition timing. This practice will only increase plug temperature and the chances of detonation or pre-ignition with relatively little performance gain.

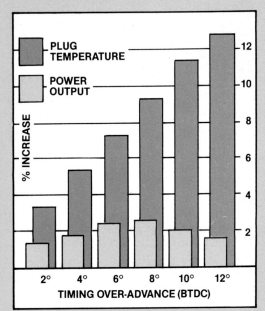

Increasing ignition timing past the specified setting results in a drastic increase in spark plug temperature with increased chance of detonation or preignition. Performance increase is considerably less. (Photo courtesy Champion Spark Plug Co.)

that form in the engine should be flushed out to allow the engine to operate at peak efficiency.

35. Clean the radiator of debris that can decrease cooling efficiency.

36. Install a flex-type or electric cooling fan, if you don't have a clutch type fan. Flex fans use curved plastic blades to push more air at low speeds when more cooling is needed; at high speeds the blades flatten out for less resistance. Electric fans only run when the engine temperature reaches a predetermined level.

37. Check the radiator cap for a worn or cracked gasket. If the cap does not seal properly, the cooling system will not function properly.

42. Be sure the front end is correctly aligned. A misaligned front end actually has wheels going in differed directions. The increased drag can reduce fuel economy by .3 mpg.

43. Correctly adjust the wheel bearings. Wheel bearings that are adjusted too tight increase rolling resistance.

Check tire pressures regularly with a reliable pocket type gauge. Be sure to check the pressure on a cold tire.

GENERAL MAINTENANCE

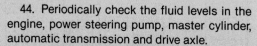

Check the fluid levels (particularly engine oil) on a regular basis. Be sure to check the oil for grit, water or other contamination.

A vacuum gauge is another excellent indicator of internal engine condition and can also be installed in the dash as a mileage indicator.

44. Periodically check the fluid levels in the engine, power steering pump, master cylinder, automatic transmission and drive axle.

45. Change the oil at the recommended interval and change the filter at every oil change. Dirty oil is thick and causes extra friction between moving parts, cutting efficiency and increasing wear. A worn engine requires more frequent tune-ups and gets progressively worse fuel economy. In general, use the lightest viscosity oil for the driving conditions you will encounter.

46. Use the recommended viscosity fluids in the transmission and axle.

47. Be sure the battery is fully charged for fast starts. A slow starting engine wastes fuel.

48. Be sure battery terminals are clean and tight.

49. Check the battery electrolyte level and add distilled water if necessary.

50. Check the exhaust system for crushed pipes, blockages and leaks.

51. Adjust the brakes. Dragging brakes or brakes that are not releasing create increased drag on the engine.

52. Install a vacuum gauge or miles-per-gallon gauge. These gauges visually indicate engine vacuum in the intake manifold. High vacuum = good mileage and low vacuum = poorer mileage. The gauge can also be an excellent indicator of internal engine conditions.

53. Be sure the clutch is properly adjusted. A slipping clutch wastes fuel.

54. Check and periodically lubricate the heat control valve in the exhaust manifold. A sticking or inoperative valve prevents engine warm-up and wastes gas.

55. Keep accurate records to check fuel economy over a period of time. A sudden drop in fuel economy may signal a need for tune-up or other maintenance.

TURBO

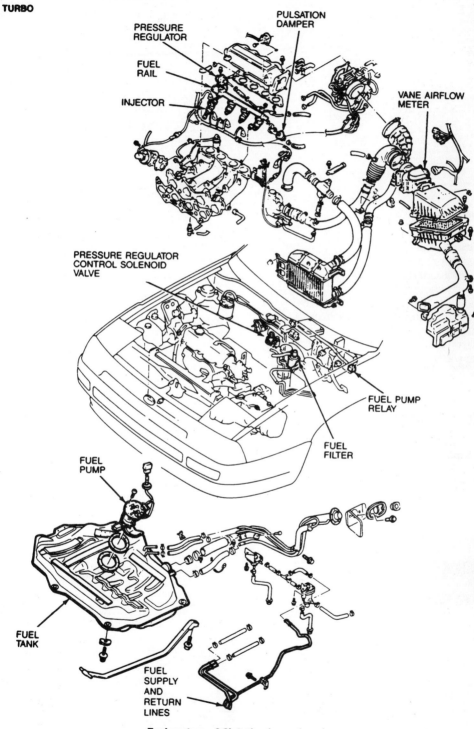

Fuel system—2.2L turbocharged engine

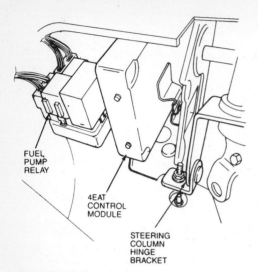

Fuel pump relay location

2. Depress the clips on each end of the rear seat cushion and remove the cushion.

3. Disconnect the electrical connector from the fuel pump/sending unit.

4. Remove the attaching screws from the fuel pump/sending unit access cover and remove the cover.

5. Disconnect the fuel supply and return hoses from the fuel pump/sending unit.

6. Remove the attaching screws and the fuel pump/sending unit from the fuel tank.

7. Disconnect the sending unit electrical connector, remove the sending unit attaching nuts and remove the sending unit from the fuel pump assembly.

To install:

8. Attach the sending unit to the fuel pump assembly and install the nuts. Connect the sending unit electrical connector.

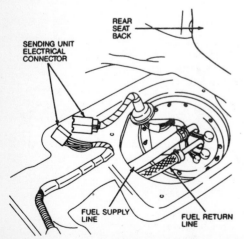

Fuel pump/sending unit assembly location, shown with access cover removed

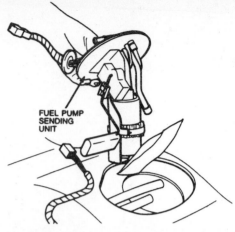

Fuel pump/sending unit assembly removal and installation

9. Install the fuel pump/sending unit into the fuel tank and install the mounting screws.

10. Connect the fuel supply and return lines.

11. Install the access cover and the mounting screws.

12. Connect the sending unit electrical connector.

13. Position the rear seat cushion over the floor, making sure to align the retaining pins with the clips. Push down firmly until the 2 retaining pins are locked into the rear seat retaining clips.

14. Connect the negative battery cable, start the engine and check for proper system operation and for fuel leaks.

TESTING

1. Relieve the pressure in the fuel system, then disconnect the negative battery cable.

2. Install a suitable fuel pressure gauge between the fuel filter and the fuel rail.

3. On 2.2L engines, connect a jumper wire between the **BK** and **LG** terminals of the fuel pump test connector. On the 3.0L engine, ground the fuel pump lead of the self-test connector through a jumper wire at the **FP** lead.

4. Connect the negative battery cable, turn the ignition key **ON** and check the fuel pump pressure. The pressure should be 64–85 psi. on the 2.2L engines or 35–40 psi. on the 3.0L engine.

5. If there is no fuel pressure, remove the fuel tank cap and try to hear if the fuel pump is operating. If the pump sounds like it's running, check for a restriction in the fuel line. If the pump is not running, check for power to the pump and check the pump motor ground. If there is no power to the pump, check all electrical connections and check the fuel pump relay.

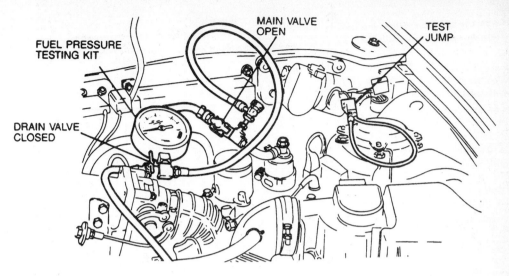

Fuel pressure testing—2.2L engine

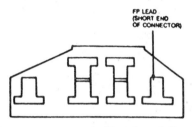

Self-Test connector terminal location—3.0L engine

6. If fuel pressure is low, check for a restriction in the fuel line or clogged fuel filters.

7. Remove the jumper wire, relieve the fuel system pressure and disconnect the negative battery cable.

8. Remove the fuel pressure gauge and reconnect the fuel line.

9. Connect the negative battery cable.

Fuel Injectors

REMOVAL AND INSTALLATION

2.2L Engine

1. Relieve the fuel system pressure.

2. Disconnect the negative battery cable and drain the cooling system.

3. Remove the accelerator cables and the air duct from the throttle body.

4. Mark all vacuum and coolant hoses for ease of reassembly and remove the hoses from the throttle body.

5. Disconnect the throttle position sensor, idle switch and air bypass valve connectors.

6. Remove the engine lifting bracket mounting bolt and coolant line/EGR hose retaining bracket from the throttle body.

7. Remove the throttle cable retaining brackets and wire loom bracket from the right side of the intake plenum.

8. On the turbocharged 2.2L engine, disconnect the vacuum pipe mounting bolts from the right side of the intake plenum. On non-turbocharged 2.2L engines, remove the EGR backpressure variable transducer bracket from the right side of the intake plenum.

9. Remove the PCV hose from the intake plenum.

10. Remove the retaining nuts and bolts from the vacuum line assembly bracket at the rear of the intake plenum.

11. Mark all vacuum lines for ease of reassembly and remove the lines from the intake plenum.

12. Remove the intake plenum retaining bolts and nuts and remove the intake plenum and gasket.

NOTE: *After removing the intake plenum,*

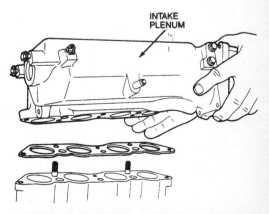

Intake plenum removal and installation—2.2L engine

cover the intake manifold ports with a clean cloth to prevent dust and dirt from entering.

13. Remove the electrical connectors from the fuel injectors. On non-turbocharged engines with automatic transmissions, remove the electrical connector from the engine coolant temperature switch.

14. Carefully bend the wire harness retainer brackets away from the wire harness and move the harness assembly away from the intake manifold.

15. Remove the fuel supply line from the pulsation damper.

16. Remove the fuel return line bracket from the intake manifold and remove the clamp and return fuel line at the bracket.

17. Remove the attaching bolts, spacers, insulators and the fuel rail with the injectors, pressure regulator and pulsation damper attached.

18. Remove the fuel injectors, grommets and O-rings from the fuel rail. Remove the O-rings from the fuel injectors.

To install:

19. Position the insulators and fuel injectors into the intake manifold. Position the grommets and new O-rings onto the fuel injectors. Apply a small amount of engine oil to the O-rings during installation.

20. Position the spacers and the fuel rail on the injectors. Install the attaching bolts to the fuel rail and tighten to 14–19 ft. lbs. (19–25 Nm).

21. Connect the electrical connectors to the fuel injectors. Connect the connector to the engine coolant temperature switch, if removed.

22. Install the fuel return line bracket onto the intake manifold and install the return fuel line at the bracket. Secure with the clamp.

23. Install the fuel supply line onto the pulsation damper and secure with the clamp.

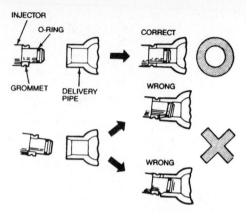

Injector grommet and O-ring installation—2.2L engine

24. Remove all old gasket material from the intake plenum and intake manifold.

25. Install a new gasket and position the intake plenum onto the intake manifold. Install the attaching bolts and nuts and tighten to 14–19 ft. lbs. (19–25 Nm).

26. Connect the vacuum lines and install the retaining bolts on the vacuum line assembly bracket to the intake manifold.

27. Install the PCV hose and the wire loom bracket mounting bolts.

28. On non-turbocharged engines, install the EGR back-pressure variable transducer bracket to the right side of the intake. On turbocharged engines, install the vacuum pipe mounting bolts.

29. Install the throttle cable retaining brackets on the front of the intake plenum.

30. Install the engine lifting bracket mounting bolt and coolant line/EGR hose retaining bracket to the throttle body.

31. Install all vacuum and coolant hoses to the throttle body. Connect the throttle position sensor, idle switch and air bypass valve connectors.

32. Install the air duct and the accelerator cables to the throttle body. Check the adjustment of the accelerator cable.

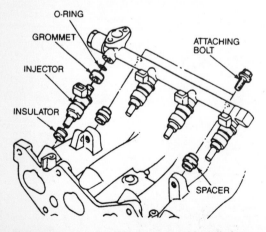

Fuel injector and fuel rail removal and installation—2.2L engine

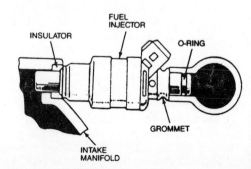

Fuel injector installation—2.2L engine

33. Install the wire harness into the retainer brackets and carefully bend the brackets toward the wire harness.

34. Connect the negative battery cable and properly fill and bleed the cooling system.

35. Turn the ignition switch **ON** to pressurize the fuel system. Check for fuel leaks and correct as necessary before starting the engine.

3.0L Engine

1. Relieve the fuel system pressure.

2. Disconnect the negative battery cable.

3. Remove the air cleaner tube and plastic shield from the throttle body.

4. Remove the EGR supply tube and disconnect all the vacuum hoses from the air intake throttle body. Tag the hoses prior to removal for ease of installation.

5. Disconnect the air charge temperature sensor, idle speed control solenoid and throttle position sensor.

6. Remove the manifold absolute pressure sensor from the throttle body.

7. Disconnect the throttle cable and the throttle valve control cable, if equipped with an automatic transaxle, from the throttle lever.

8. Remove the fuel rail bracket bolt from the throttle body.

9. Remove the 6 air intake throttle body mounting bolts and lift off the throttle body.

10. Disconnect the fuel supply and return lines. Refer to the Spring Lock Coupling Connect and Disconnect Procedure chart.

11. Disconnect the fuel injector wiring harness.

12. Disconnect the vacuum line from the fuel pressure regulator.

13. Remove the 4 fuel injector manifold mounting bolts.

14. Disengage the fuel rail assembly by lifting and gently rocking the rail.

15. Remove the injectors by lifting while gently rocking side to side.

NOTE: *Handle the injectors and rail assembly with extreme care to prevent damage to the sealing areas and metering orifices.*

To install:

16. Inspect the injector O-rings for wear or damage. Install new O-rings, if required.

17. Lubricate new O-rings with a light grade oil and install 2 on each injector.

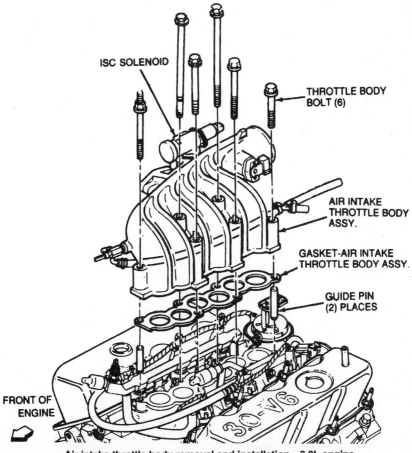

ISC SOLENOID

THROTTLE BODY BOLT (6)

AIR INTAKE THROTTLE BODY ASSY.

GASKET-AIR INTAKE THROTTLE BODY ASSY.

GUIDE PIN (2) PLACES

FRONT OF ENGINE

3.0 V6

Air intake throttle body removal and installation—3.0L engine

18. Make sure the injector cups are free of contamination or damage.

19. Install the injectors in the fuel rail using a light twisting-pushing motion.

20. Install the rail assembly and the injectors carefully into the lower intake manifold, one side at a time.

21. Push down on the fuel rail to make sure the O-rings are seated.

22. Install the retaining bolts and tighten to 7 ft. lbs. (10 Nm) while holding the fuel rail in place.

23. Connect the fuel supply and return lines. Refer to the Spring Lock Coupling Connect and Disconnect Procedure chart.

24. Before connecting the fuel injector harness, connect the negative battery cable and turn the key to the **ON** position. This will pressurize the fuel system.

25. Check for leaks where the injector is installed into the intake manifold and fuel rail; correct as necessary.

26. Turn the ignition key **OFF** and disconnect the negative battery cable.

27. Connect the fuel injector wiring harness.

28. Position the air intake throttle body and gasket on the lower intake manifold.

NOTE: *Lightly oil all bolt threads before installation.*

29. Install the mounting bolts and tighten to 15–22 ft. lbs. (20–30 Nm).

30. Install the fuel rail bracket on the throttle body and tighten securely.

31. Install the throttle cable and throttle valve control cable, if equipped with an automatic transaxle, on the throttle lever.

32. Install the manifold absolute pressure sensor on the throttle body.

33. Connect the throttle position sensor, idle speed control solenoid and the air charge temperature sensor.

34. Connect all vacuum hoses to the air intake throttle body.

35. Install the EGR supply tube. Install the plastic shield on the throttle body.

36. Install the air cleaner tube onto the throttle body and connect the negative battery cable.

Fuel Charging Assembly
REMOVAL AND INSTALLATION
2.2L Engine

1. Properly relieve the fuel system pressure and disconnect the negative battery cable.

2. Drain the cooling system.

3. From the bottom of the intake manifold, remove the water hose.

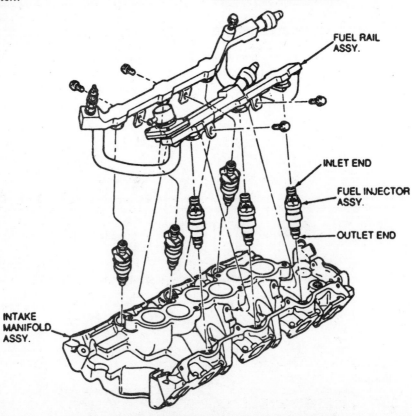

Fuel rail and injector removal and installation—3.0L engine

4. Disconnect the accelerator cables from the throttle body.

5. Remove the air duct from the throttle body.

6. Label and disconnect the vacuum lines and coolant hoses from the throttle body.

7. Tag and disconnect the electrical connectors from the throttle position sensor, the idle switch and the bypass air control valve.

8. Remove the engine lifting bracket mounting bolts from the throttle body and the engine block.

9. Disconnect the coolant line/EGR hose bracket from the throttle body and the throttle cable brackets from the intake plenum.

10. Remove the wire loom bracket. On non-turbocharged engines, remove the EGR backpressure variable transducer bracket from the right-hand side of the intake plenum. On turbocharged engines, remove the vacuum pipe mounting bolts from the right-hand side of the intake plenum.

11. Remove the PCV hose from the intake plenum. Remove the nuts and bolts retaining the vacuum line assembly bracket at the rear of the intake plenum.

12. Label and disconnect the vacuum lines from the intake plenum.

13. Remove the plenum-to-intake manifold nuts and bolts, the plenum and the gasket.

14. Disconnect the electrical connectors from the fuel injectors. Carefully, bend the wire harness retainer brackets away from the wire harness and move the harness assembly away from the intake manifold.

15. Disconnect the fuel pressure and return lines at the fuel rail.

16. Disconnect the EGR pipe from the intake manifold. Label and disconnect any electrical connectors and hoses from the intake manifold.

17. Remove the intake manifold bracket-to-manifold nuts and the bracket. Remove the intake manifold-to-cylinder head nuts/bolts, the manifold and gasket.

18. If necessary, remove the fuel rail and fuel injectors from the intake manifold.

To install:

19. Clean all gasket mating surfaces.

20. Using a new gasket, position the intake manifold on the cylinder head studs and torque the nuts/bolts to 14–22 ft. lbs. (19–30 Nm).

21. Install the intake manifold bracket-to-manifold nuts and tighten to 14–22 ft. lbs. (19–30 Nm).

22. Connect the fuel lines to the fuel rail. Connect the electrical connectors to the fuel injectors.

23. Using a new gasket, install the intake plenum onto the intake manifold and torque the nuts/bolts to 14–19 ft. lbs. (19–25 Nm).

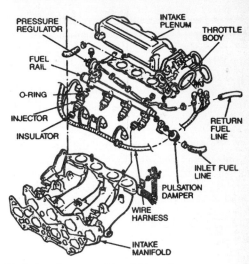

Fuel charging assembly—2.2L engine

24. Connect the vacuum lines to the intake manifold. Install the retaining bolts and nuts on the vacuum line assembly bracket to the intake plenum.

25. Install the PCV hose to the intake plenum.

26. Install the wire loom bracket and the EGR variable transducer bracket or vacuum pipe bracket to the right side of the plenum.

27. Install the throttle cable bracket, engine lifting bracket mounting bolt and coolant line/EGR hose bracket to the intake plenum and throttle body.

28. Install the vacuum and coolant hoses to the throttle body.

29. Connect the throttle position sensor, idle switch and bypass air control valve connectors.

30. Install the air duct and the throttle cables to the throttle body.

31. Connect the EGR pipe and connect the water hose to the bottom of the intake manifold.

32. Connect the negative battery cable and fill the cooling system. Start the engine and check for leaks.

3.0L Engine

1. Properly relieve the fuel system pressure and disconnect the negative battery cable.

2. Drain the cooling system.

3. Remove the air cleaner hoses from the throttle body and rocker cover.

4. Disconnect the fuel lines from the fuel supply manifold. Cover the fuel line ends with clean shop rags to prevent dirt from entering.

5. Tag and disconnect the vacuum lines and electrical connectors from the throttle body.

6. Remove the plastic shield and the EGR supply tube from the throttle body.

7. Disconnect the throttle cable and, if

equipped with automatic transaxle, the throttle valve control cable from the throttle lever.

8. Remove the fuel rail bracket bolt and the 6 throttle body mounting bolts. Remove the throttle body.

9. Disconnect the fuel injector harness stand-offs from the injector inboard rocker cover studs and each injector and remove from the engine.

10. Remove the brace from the fuel supply manifold and throttle body. Remove the fuel supply manifold and fuel injectors.

NOTE: *The intake manifold assembly can be removed with the fuel supply manifold and fuel injectors in place.*

11. Disconnect the upper radiator hose from the thermostat housing and disconnect the heater hoses.

12. Disconnect the engine coolant temperature sensor and coolant temperature sending unit connectors.

13. Tag and disconnect the spark plug wires from the spark plugs.

14. Remove the distributor cap. Mark the position of the rotor and the distributor in the engine and remove the distributor.

15. Remove the ignition coil and bracket assembly from the left side (front) cylinder head and set aside.

16. Remove the rocker arm covers.

17. Loosen the retaining bolt from the No. 3 intake valve rocker arm and rotate the rocker arm fulcrum away from the valve retainer. Remove the pushrod.

18. Remove the intake manifold retaining bolts. Before attempting to remove the manifold, break the seal between the manifold and cylinder block. Place a suitable prybar between the manifold, near the thermostat, and the transaxle. Carefully pry upward to loosen the manifold.

19. Lift the intake manifold away from the engine. Place shop rags in the lifter valley to catch any dirt or gasket material. Clean all gasket mating surfaces. Be careful when scraping aluminum to prevent gouging, which may cause leak paths.

To install:

20. Lightly oil all attaching bolt and stud threads. Apply silicone sealer to the intersection of the cylinder block and cylinder head assembly at the 4 corners of the lifter valley.

21. Install the front and rear intake manifold seals. Install the intake manifold gaskets onto the cylinder heads and insert the locking tabs on the cylinder head gaskets.

NOTE: *Make sure the side of the gasket marked TO INTAKE MANIFOLD is facing away from the cylinder head.*

22. Carefully lower the intake manifold into position to prevent disturbing the silicone sealer. Install bolts No. 1, 2, 3 and 4 and snug. In-

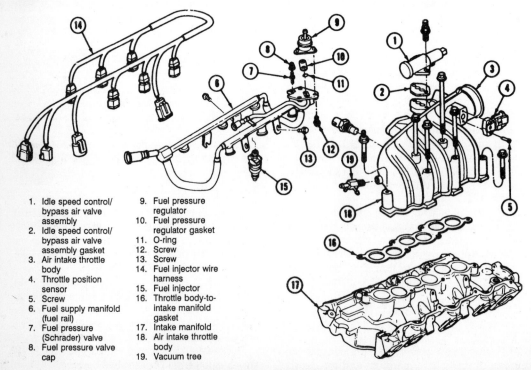

1. Idle speed control/ bypass air valve assembly
2. Idle speed control/ bypass air valve assembly gasket
3. Air intake throttle body
4. Throttle position sensor
5. Screw
6. Fuel supply manifold (fuel rail)
7. Fuel pressure (Schrader) valve
8. Fuel pressure valve cap
9. Fuel pressure regulator
10. Fuel pressure regulator gasket
11. O-ring
12. Screw
13. Screw
14. Fuel injector wire harness
15. Fuel injector
16. Throttle body-to-intake manifold gasket
17. Intake manifold
18. Air intake throttle body
19. Vacuum tree

Fuel charging assembly—3.0L engine

stall the remaining bolts and tighten, in sequence, to 11 ft. lbs. (15 Nm). Then tighten, in sequence, to 21 ft. lbs. (28 Nm).

23. Install the thermostat and housing, if removed, using a new gasket. Tighten the mounting bolts to 9 ft. lbs. (12 Nm).

24. If removed, lubricate and install new O-rings on the fuel injectors and install the fuel injectors in the fuel rail, using a light twisting-pushing motion. Install the fuel rail and injectors into the intake manifold, pushing down to seat the O-rings. While holding the fuel rail assembly in place, install the 4 retaining bolts and tighten to 7 ft. lbs. (10 Nm).

25. Install the No. 3 cylinder intake valve pushrod. Apply oil to the pushrod and fulcrum prior to installation. Rotate the crankshaft to place the lifter on the base circle of the camshaft and tighten the rocker arm bolt to 24 ft. lbs. (32 Nm).

26. Install the rocker arm covers and connect the fuel injector electrical harness.

27. Position a new gasket and the throttle body on the intake manifold. Install the mounting bolts and tighten to 15–22 ft. lbs. (20–30 Nm).

28. Install the fuel rail bracket bolt on the throttle body and connect the throttle cable and, if equipped, the throttle valve control cable to the throttle lever.

29. Install the MAP sensor and the EGR tube to the throttle body.

30. Connect the vacuum hoses and the electrical connectors in their original positions on the throttle body. Install the plastic shield on the throttle body.

31. Install the fuel supply manifold brace. Tighten the retaining bolts to 7 ft. lbs. (10 Nm).

32. Connect the PCV hose at the PCV valve. Connect all remaining vacuum hoses.

33. Install the EGR tube and nut, if equipped. Tighten the nuts on both ends to 37 ft. lbs. (50 Nm).

34. Connect the fuel lines to the fuel rail.

35. Install the distributor assembly, aligning the housing and rotor with the marks that were made during the removal procedure. Install the distributor cap and connect the spark plug wires to the spark plugs. Install the wiring stand-offs to the rocker arm cover studs.

36. Install the ignition coil and bracket assembly. Tighten the mounting bolts to 35 ft. lbs. (48 Nm).

37. Connect the engine coolant temperature sensor and coolant temperature sending unit connectors.

38. Install the upper radiator and heater hoses. Fill the cooling system.

39. Change the engine oil and filter. This is necessary because engine coolant is corrosive to all engine bearing material. Replacing the engine oil after removal of a coolant carrying component guards against later failure.

40. Install the air cleaner hoses to the throttle body and rocker cover.

41. Connect the negative battery cable. Start the engine and check for coolant, oil, fuel and vacuum leaks. Check the ignition timing.

Fuel Pressure Regulator

REMOVAL AND INSTALLATION

2.2L Engine

1. Relieve the fuel system pressure.

2. Disconnect the negative battery cable and drain the cooling system.

3. Remove the accelerator cables and the air duct from the throttle body.

4. Mark all vacuum and coolant hoses for ease of reassembly and remove the hoses from the throttle body.

5. Disconnect the throttle position sensor, idle switch and air bypass valve connectors.

6. Remove the engine lifting bracket mounting bolt and coolant line/EGR hose retaining bracket from the throttle body.

7. Remove the throttle cable retaining brackets and wire loom bracket from the right side of the intake plenum.

8. On the turbocharged 2.2L engine, disconnect the vacuum pipe mounting bolts from the right side of the intake plenum. On non-turbocharged 2.2L engines, remove the EGR backpressure variable transducer bracket from the right side of the intake plenum.

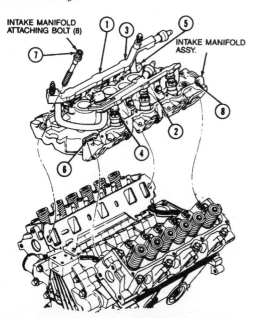

INTAKE MANIFOLD ATTACHING BOLT (8)

INTAKE MANIFOLD ASSY.

Intake manifold bolt torque sequence—3.0L engine

9. Remove the PCV hose from the intake plenum.

10. Remove the retaining nuts and bolts from the vacuum line assembly bracket at the rear of the intake plenum.

11. Mark all vacuum lines for ease of reassembly and remove the lines from the intake plenum.

12. Remove the intake plenum retaining bolts and nuts and remove the intake plenum and gasket.

NOTE: *After removing the intake plenum, cover the intake manifold ports with a clean cloth to prevent dust and dirt from entering.*

13. Disconnect the fuel return hose.

14. Disconnect the vacuum line from the pressure regulator.

15. Remove the attaching bolts and remove the pressure regulator from the fuel rail. Remove the O-ring from the pressure regulator.

To install:

16. Install a new O-ring on the pressure regulator. Install the pressure regulator on the fuel rail and tighten the attaching bolts to 69–95 inch lbs. (8–11 Nm).

17. Connect the vacuum line to the pressure regulator and connect the fuel return hose.

18. Remove all old gasket material from the intake plenum and intake manifold.

19. Install a new gasket and position the intake plenum onto the intake manifold. Install the attaching bolts and nuts and tighten to 14–19 ft. lbs. (19–25 Nm).

20. Connect the vacuum lines and install the retaining bolts on the vacuum line assembly bracket to the intake manifold.

21. Install the PCV hose and the wire loom bracket mounting bolts.

22. On non-turbocharged engines, install the EGR back-pressure variable transducer bracket to the right side of the intake. On turbocharged engines, install the vacuum pipe mounting bolts.

23. Install the throttle cable retaining brackets on the front of the intake plenum.

24. Install the engine lifting bracket mounting bolt and coolant line/EGR hose retaining bracket to the throttle body.

25. Install all vacuum and coolant hoses to the throttle body. Connect the throttle position sensor, idle switch and air bypass valve connectors.

26. Install the air duct and the accelerator cables to the throttle body. Check the adjustment of the accelerator cable.

27. Install the wire harness into the retainer brackets and carefully bend the brackets toward the wire harness.

28. Connect the negative battery cable and properly fill and bleed the cooling system.

29. Turn the ignition switch **ON** to pressurize the fuel system. Check for fuel leaks and correct as necessary before starting the engine.

3.0L Engine

1. Relieve the fuel system pressure and disconnect the negative battery cable.

2. Position the engine wiring harness so it is clear of the work area.

3. Disconnect the vacuum hose from the pressure regulator.

4. Remove the 3 pressure regulator mounting screws.

5. Remove the pressure regulator and remove the O-ring and gasket.

To install:

6. Clean the gasket mating surfaces.

7. Install a new gasket and O-ring on the pressure regulator.

8. Install the pressure regulator on the fuel rail and tighten the mounting screws.

9. Connect the vacuum hose to the pressure regulator and restore the engine wiring harness to its original position.

10. Connect the negative battery cable. Turn

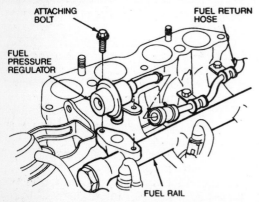

Fuel pressure regulator removal and installation—2.2L engine

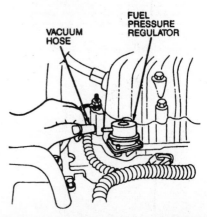

Fuel pressure regulator removal and installation—3.0L engine

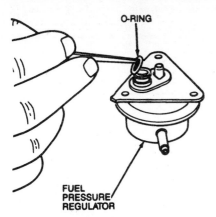

Removing the O-ring from the fuel pressure regulator—3.0L engine

the ignition key **ON** to pressurize the fuel system. Check for fuel leaks and correct as necessary before starting the engine.

Fuel Pressure Relief Valve

REMOVAL AND INSTALLATION

3.0L Engine

1. Relieve the fuel system pressure and disconnect the negative battery cable.
2. Remove the cap from the relief valve.
3. Using an open-end wrench or suitable deep-well socket, remove the pressure relief valve from the fuel rail.
4. Installation is the reverse of the removal procedure. Tighten the valve to 66 inch lbs. (7.75 Nm).

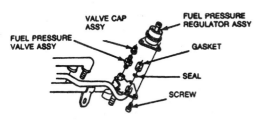

Fuel pressure relief valve location—3.0L engine

Fuel Tank

REMOVAL AND INSTALLATION

1. Relieve the fuel system pressure.
2. Disconnect the negative battery cable.
3. Depress the clips on each end of the rear seat cushion and remove the cushion.
4. Disconnect the sending unit electrical connector, remove the 4 attaching screws and the sending unit access cover.
5. Disconnect the fuel supply and return lines from the sending unit.

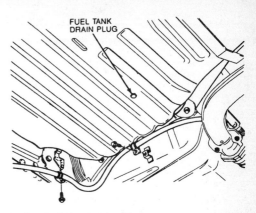

Fuel tank drain plug location

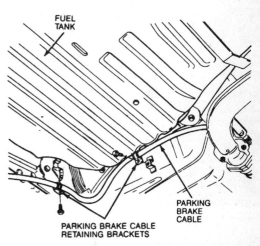

Removing the parking brake cable retaining brackets

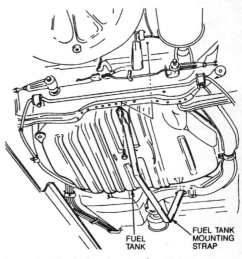

Removing the fuel tank mounting straps

6. Raise and safely support the vehicle.
7. Position a suitable container under the fuel tank drain plug. Remove the plug and drain the fuel tank.

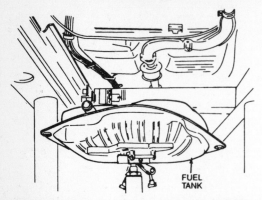

Support the fuel tank during removal and installation

8. Disconnect the vapor hoses and fuel filler neck hose at the fuel filler neck assembly.

9. Remove the 2 parking brake cable retaining brackets from the chassis to gain access to the fuel tank.

10. Remove the fuel tank mounting strap.

11. Support the fuel tank, remove the 3 attaching bolts and brackets and remove the fuel tank.

To install:

12. Position the fuel tank and install the 3 attaching bolts and brackets. Tighten the bolts to 16–22 ft. lbs. (22–30 Nm).

13. Install the fuel tank mounting strap. Tighten the mounting bolt to 32–45 ft. lbs. (43–61 Nm).

14. Install the 2 parking brake cable retaining brackets to the chassis.

15. Connect the fuel tank filler neck hose and the 3 vapor hoses to the fuel tank filler neck assembly.

16. Install the fuel tank drain plug and tighten to 9–13 ft. lbs. (12–18 Nm).

17. Lower the vehicle and connect the fuel supply and return hoses to the sending unit.

18. Install the sending unit access cover with the 4 attaching screws. Reconnect the sending unit electrical connector.

19. Position the rear seat cushion over the floor, making sure to align the retaining pins with the clips. Push down firmly until the 2 retaining pins are locked into the rear seat retaining clips.

20. Fill the fuel tank with fuel and check for leaks.

21. Connect the negative battery cable.

SENDING UNIT REPLACEMENT

1. Relieve the fuel pressure and disconnect the negative battery cable.

2. Depress the clips on each end of the rear seat cushion and remove the cushion.

3. Disconnect the electrical connector from the fuel pump/sending unit.

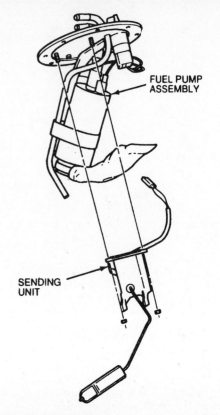

Fuel tank sending unit

4. Remove the attaching screws from the fuel pump/sending unit access cover and remove the cover.

5. Disconnect the fuel supply and return hoses from the fuel pump/sending unit.

6. Remove the attaching screws and the fuel pump/sending unit from the fuel tank.

7. Disconnect the sending unit electrical connector, remove the sending unit attaching nuts and remove the sending unit from the fuel pump assembly.

To install:

8. Attach the sending unit to the fuel pump assembly and install the nuts. Connect the sending unit electrical connector.

9. Install the fuel pump/sending unit into the fuel tank and install the mounting screws.

10. Connect the fuel supply and return lines.

11. Install the access cover and the mounting screws.

12. Connect the sending unit electrical connector.

13. Position the rear seat cushion over the floor, making sure to align the retaining pins with the clips. Push down firmly until the 2 retaining pins are locked into the rear seat retaining clips.

14. Connect the negative battery cable, start the engine and check for proper system operation and for fuel leaks.

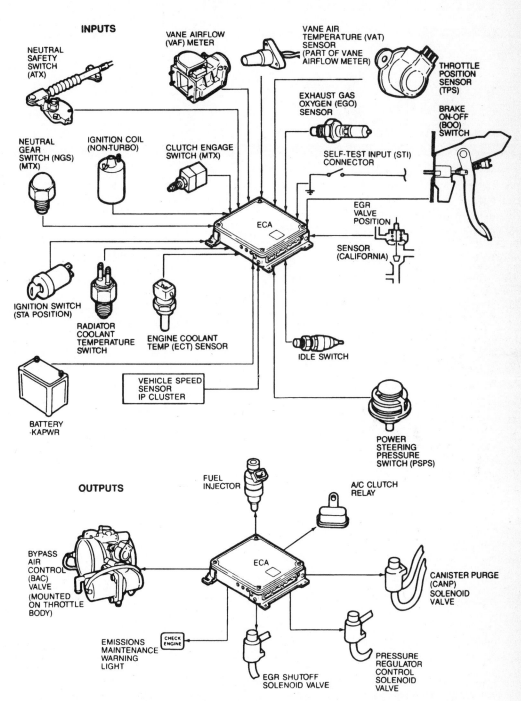

INPUTS

NEUTRAL
SAFETY
SWITCH
(ATX)

VANE AIRFLOW
(VAF) METER

VANE AIR
TEMPERATURE (VAT)
SENSOR
(PART OF VANE
AIRFLOW METER)

THROTTLE
POSITION
SENSOR
(TPS)

EXHAUST GAS
OXYGEN (EGO)
SENSOR

BRAKE
ON-OFF
(BOO)
SWITCH

NEUTRAL
GEAR
SWITCH (NGS)
(MTX)

IGNITION COIL
(NON-TURBO)

CLUTCH ENGAGE
SWITCH (MTX)

SELF-TEST INPUT (STI)
CONNECTOR

ECA

EGR
VALVE
POSITION

SENSOR
(CALIFORNIA)

IGNITION SWITCH
(STA POSITION)

RADIATOR
COOLANT
TEMPERATURE
SWITCH

ENGINE COOLANT
TEMP (ECT) SENSOR

IDLE SWITCH

VEHICLE SPEED
SENSOR
IP CLUSTER

BATTERY
-KAPWR

POWER
STEERING
PRESSURE
SWITCH (PSPS)

FUEL
INJECTOR

A/C CLUTCH
RELAY

OUTPUTS

BYPASS
AIR
CONTROL
(BAC)
VALVE
(MOUNTED
ON THROTTLE
BODY)

ECA

CANISTER PURGE
(CANP)
SOLENOID
VALVE

EMISSIONS
MAINTENANCE
WARNING
LIGHT

CHECK
ENGINE

EGR SHUTOFF
SOLENOID VALVE

PRESSURE
REGULATOR
CONTROL
SOLENOID
VALVE

Electronic control system input and output devices—2.2L non-turbocharged engine

Chassis Electrical

UNDERSTANDING AND TROUBLESHOOTING ELECTRICAL SYSTEMS

With the rate at which both import and domestic manufacturers are incorporating electronic control systems into their production lines, it won't be long before every new vehicle is equipped with one or more on-board computer. These electronic components (with no moving parts) should theoretically last the life of the vehicle, provided nothing external happens to damage the circuits or memory chips.

While it is true that electronic components should never wear out, in the real world malfunctions do occur. It is also true that any computer-based system is extremely sensitive to electrical voltages and cannot tolerate careless or haphazard testing or service procedures. An inexperienced individual can literally do major damage looking for a minor problem by using the wrong kind of test equipment or connecting test leads or connectors with the ignition switch **ON**. When selecting test equipment, make sure the manufacturers instructions state that the tester is compatible with whatever type of electronic control system is being serviced. Read all instructions carefully and double check all test points before installing probes or making any test connections.

The following section outlines basic diagnosis techniques for dealing with computerized automotive control systems. Along with a general explanation of the various types of test equipment available to aid in servicing modern electronic automotive systems, basic repair techniques for wiring harnesses and connectors is given. Read the basic information before attempting any repairs or testing on any computerized system, to provide the background of information necessary to avoid the most common and obvious mistakes that can cost both time and money. Although the replacement and testing procedures are simple in themselves, the systems are not, and unless one has a thorough understanding of all components and their function within a particular computerized control system, the logical test sequence these systems demand cannot be followed. Minor malfunctions can make a big difference, so it is important to know how each component affects the operation of the overall electronic system to find the ultimate cause of a problem without replacing good components unnecessarily. It is not enough to use the correct test equipment; the test equipment must be used correctly.

Safety Precautions

CAUTION: *Whenever working on or around any computer based microprocessor control system, always observe these general precautions to prevent the possibility of personal injury or damage to electronic components.*

● Never install or remove battery cables with the key ON or the engine running. Jumper cables should be connected with the key OFF to avoid power surges that can damage electronic control units. Engines equipped with computer controlled systems should avoid both giving and getting jump starts due to the possibility of serious damage to components from arcing in the engine compartment when connections are made with the ignition ON.

● Always remove the battery cables before charging the battery. Never use a high output charger on an installed battery or attempt to use any type of "hot shot" (24 volt) starting aid.

● Exercise care when inserting test probes into connectors to insure good connections without damaging the connector or spreading the pins. Always probe connectors from the rear (wire) side, NOT the pin side, to avoid accidental shorting of terminals during test procedures.

• Never remove or attach wiring harness connectors with the ignition switch ON, especially to an electronic control unit.

• Do not drop any components during service procedures and never apply 12 volts directly to any component (like a solenoid or relay) unless instructed specifically to do so. Some component electrical windings are designed to safely handle only 4 or 5 volts and can be destroyed in seconds if 12 volts are applied directly to the connector.

• Remove the electronic control unit if the vehicle is to be placed in an environment where temperatures exceed approximately 176°F (80°C), such as a paint spray booth or when arc or gas welding near the control unit location in the car.

ORGANIZED TROUBLESHOOTING

When diagnosing a specific problem, organized troubleshooting is a must. The complexity of a modern automobile demands that you approach any problem in a logical, organized manner. There are certain troubleshooting techniques that are standard:

1. Establish when the problem occurs. Does the problem appear only under certain conditions? Were there any noises, odors, or other unusual symptoms?

2. Isolate the problem area. To do this, make some simple tests and observations; then eliminate the systems that are working properly. Check for obvious problems such as broken wires, dirty connections or split or disconnected vacuum hoses. Always check the obvious before assuming something complicated is the cause.

3. Test for problems systematically to determine the cause once the problem area is isolated. Are all the components functioning properly? Is there power going to electrical switches and motors? Is there vacuum at vacuum switches and/or actuators? Is there a mechanical problem such as bent linkage or loose mounting screws? Doing careful, systematic checks will often turn up most causes on the first inspection without wasting time checking components that have little or no relationship to the problem.

4. Test all repairs after the work is done to make sure that the problem is fixed. Some causes can be traced to more than one component, so a careful verification of repair work is important to pick up additional malfunctions that may cause a problem to reappear or a different problem to arise. A blown fuse, for example, is a simple problem that may require more than another fuse to repair. If you don't look for a problem that caused a fuse to blow, for example, a shorted wire may go undetected.

Experience has shown that most problems tend to be the result of a fairly simple and obvious cause, such as loose or corroded connectors or air leaks in the intake system; making careful inspection of components during testing essential to quick and accurate troubleshooting. Special, hand held computerized testers designed specifically for diagnosing the EEC-IV system are available from a variety of aftermarket sources, as well as from the vehicle manufacturer, but care should be taken that any test equipment being used is designed to diagnose that particular computer controlled system accurately without damaging the control unit (ECU) or components being tested.

NOTE: *Pinpointing the exact cause of trouble in an electrical system can sometimes only be accomplished by the use of special test equipment. The following describes commonly used test equipment and explains how to put it to best use in diagnosis. In addition to the information covered below, the manufacturer's instructions booklet provided with the tester should be read and clearly understood before attempting any test procedures.*

TEST EQUIPMENT

Jumper Wires

Jumper wires are simple, yet extremely valuable, pieces of test equipment. Jumper wires are merely wires that are used to bypass sections of a circuit. The simplest type of jumper wire is merely a length of multistrand wire with an alligator clip at each end. Jumper wires are usually fabricated from lengths of standard automotive wire and whatever type of connector (alligator clip, spade connector or pin connector) that is required for the particular vehicle being tested. The well equipped tool box will have several different styles of jumper wires in several different lengths. Some jumper wires are made with three or more terminals coming from a common splice for special purpose testing. In cramped, hard-to-reach areas it is advisable to have insulated boots over the jumper wire terminals in order to prevent accidental grounding, sparks, and possible fire, especially when testing fuel system components.

Jumper wires are used primarily to locate open electrical circuits, on either the ground (-) side of the circuit or on the hot (+) side. If an electrical component fails to operate, connect the jumper wire between the component and a good ground. If the component operates only with the jumper installed, the ground circuit is open. If the ground circuit is good, but the component does not operate, the circuit between the power feed and component is open. You can sometimes connect the jumper wire directly from the battery to the hot terminal of the component, but first make sure the component uses 12 volts in operation. Some electrical components, such as fuel injectors, are designed to operate on about 4 volts and running 12 volts directly to the injector terminals can burn out the wiring. By inserting an inline fuseholder between a set of test leads, a fused jumper wire can be used for bypassing open circuits. Use a 5 amp fuse to provide protection against voltage spikes. When in doubt, use a voltmeter to check the voltage input to the component and measure how much voltage is being applied normally. By moving the jumper wire successively back from the lamp toward the power source, you can isolate the area of the circuit where the open is located. When the component stops functioning, or the power is cut off, the open is in the segment of wire between the jumper and the point previously tested.

CAUTION: *Never use jumpers made from wire that is of lighter gauge than used in the circuit under test. If the jumper wire is of too small gauge, it may overheat and possibly melt. Never use jumpers to bypass high resistance loads (such as motors) in a circuit. Bypassing resistances, in effect, creates a short circuit which may, in turn, cause damage and fire. Never use a jumper for anything other than temporary bypassing of components in a circuit.*

12 Volt Test Light

The 12 volt test light is used to check circuits and components while electrical current is flowing through them. It is used for voltage and ground tests. Twelve volt test lights come in different styles but all have three main parts; a ground clip, a probe, and a light. The most commonly used 12 volt test lights have pick-type probes. To use a 12 volt test light, connect the ground clip to a good ground and probe wherever necessary with the pick. The pick should be sharp so that it can penetrate wire insulation to make contact with the wire, without making a large hole in the insulation. The wrap-around light is handy in hard to reach areas or where it is difficult to support a wire to push a probe pick into it. To use the wrap around light, hook the wire to probed with the hook and pull the trigger. A small pick will be forced through the wire insulation into the wire core.

CAUTION: *Do not use a test light to probe electronic ignition spark plug or coil wires. Never use a pick-type test light to probe wiring on computer controlled systems unless specifically instructed to do so. Any wire insulation that is pierced by the test light probe should be taped and sealed with silicone after testing.*

Like the jumper wire, the 12 volt test light is

used to isolate opens in circuits. But, whereas the jumper wire is used to bypass the open to operate the load, the 12 volt test light is used to locate the presence of voltage in a circuit. If the test light glows, you know that there is power up to that point; if the 12 volt test light does not glow when its probe is inserted into the wire or connector, you know that there is an open circuit (no power). Move the test light in successive steps back toward the power source until the light in the handle does glow. When it does glow, the open is between the probe and point previously probed.

NOTE: *The test light does not detect that 12 volts (or any particular amount of voltage) is present; it only detects that some voltage is present. It is advisable before using the test light to touch its terminals across the battery posts to make sure the light is operating properly.*

Self-Powered Test Light

The self-powered test light usually contains a 1.5 volt penlight battery. One type of self-powered test light is similar in design to the 12 volt test light. This type has both the battery and the light in the handle and pick-type probe tip. The second type has the light toward the open tip, so that the light illuminates the contact point. The self-powered test light is dual purpose piece of test equipment. It can be used to test for either open or short circuits when power is isolated from the circuit (continuity test). A powered test light should not be used on any computer controlled system or component unless specifically instructed to do so. Many engine sensors can be destroyed by even this small amount of voltage applied directly to the terminals.

Open Circuit Testing

To use the self-powered test light to check for open circuits, first isolate the circuit from the vehicle's 12 volt power source by disconnecting the battery or wiring harness connector. Connect the test light ground clip to a good ground and probe sections of the circuit sequentially with the test light. (start from either end of the circuit). If the light is out, the open is between the probe and the circuit ground. If the light is on, the open is between the probe and end of the circuit toward the power source.

Short Circuit Testing

By isolating the circuit both from power and from ground, and using a self-powered test light, you can check for shorts to ground in the circuit. Isolate the circuit from power and ground. Connect the test light ground clip to a good ground and probe any easy-to-reach test point in the circuit. If the light comes on, there is a short somewhere in the circuit. To isolate the short, probe a test point at either end of the isolated circuit (the light should be on). Leave the test light probe connected and open connectors, switches, remove parts, etc., sequentially, until the light goes out. When the light goes out, the short is between the last circuit component opened and the previous circuit opened.

NOTE: *The 1.5 volt battery in the test light does not provide much current. A weak battery may not provide enough power to illuminate the test light even when a complete circuit is made (especially if there are high resistances in the circuit). Always make sure that the test battery is strong. To check the battery, briefly touch the ground clip to the probe; if the light glows brightly the battery is strong enough for testing. Never use a self-powered test light to perform checks for opens or shorts when power is applied to the electrical system under test. The 12 volt vehicle power will quickly burn out the 1.5 volt light bulb in the test light.*

Voltmeter

A voltmeter is used to measure voltage at any point in a circuit, or to measure the voltage drop across any part of a circuit. It can also be used to check continuity in a wire or circuit by indicating current flow from one end to the other. Voltmeters usually have various scales on the meter dial and a selector switch to allow the selection of different voltages. The voltmeter has a positive and a negative lead. To avoid damage to the meter, always connect the negative lead to the negative (-) side of circuit (to ground or nearest the ground side of the circuit) and connect the positive lead to the positive (+) side of the circuit (to the power source or the nearest power source). Note that the negative voltmeter lead will always be black and that the positive voltmeter will always be some color other than black (usually red). Depending on how the voltmeter is connected into the circuit, it has several uses.

A voltmeter can be connected either in parallel or in series with a circuit and it has a very high resistance to current flow. When connected in parallel, only a small amount of current will flow through the voltmeter current path; the rest will flow through the normal circuit current path and the circuit will work normally. When the voltmeter is connected in series with a circuit, only a small amount of current can flow through the circuit. The circuit will not work properly, but the voltmeter reading will show if the circuit is complete or not.

Available Voltage Measurement

Set the voltmeter selector switch to the 20V position and connect the meter negative lead to the negative post of the battery. Connect the positive meter lead to the positive post of the battery and turn the ignition switch ON to provide a load. Read the voltage on the meter or digital display. A well charged battery should register over 12 volts. If the meter reads below 11.5 volts, the battery power may be insufficient to operate the electrical system properly. This test determines voltage available from the battery and should be the first step in any electrical trouble diagnosis procedure. Many electrical problems, especially on computer controlled systems, can be caused by a low state of charge in the battery. Excessive corrosion at the battery cable terminals can cause a poor contact that will prevent proper charging and full battery current flow.

Normal battery voltage is 12 volts when fully charged. When the battery is supplying current to one or more circuits it is said to be "under load". When everything is off the electrical system is under a "no-load" condition. A fully charged battery may show about 12.5 volts at no load; will drop to 12 volts under medium load; and will drop even lower under heavy load. If the battery is partially discharged the voltage decrease under heavy load may be excessive, even though the battery shows 12 volts or more at no load. When allowed to discharge further, the battery's available voltage under load will decrease more severely. For this reason, it is important that the battery be fully charged during all testing procedures to avoid errors in diagnosis and incorrect test results.

Voltage Drop

When current flows through a resistance, the voltage beyond the resistance is reduced (the larger the current, the greater the reduction in voltage). When no current is flowing, there is no voltage drop because there is no current flow. All points in the circuit which are connected to the power source are at the same voltage as the power source. The total voltage drop always equals the total source voltage. In a long circuit with many connectors, a series of small, unwanted voltage drops due to corrosion at the connectors can add up to a total loss of voltage which impairs the operation of the normal loads in the circuit.

INDIRECT COMPUTATION OF VOLTAGE DROPS

1. Set the voltmeter selector switch to the 20 volt position.
2. Connect the meter negative lead to a good ground.

3. Probe all resistances in the circuit with the positive meter lead.

4. Operate the circuit in all modes and observe the voltage readings.

DIRECT MEASUREMENT OF VOLTAGE DROPS

1. Set the voltmeter switch to the 20 volt position.

2. Connect the voltmeter negative lead to the ground side of the resistance load to be measured.

3. Connect the positive lead to the positive side of the resistance or load to be measured.

4. Read the voltage drop directly on the 20 volt scale.

Too high a voltage indicates too high a resistance. If, for example, a blower motor runs too slowly, you can determine if there is too high a resistance in the resistor pack. By taking voltage drop readings in all parts of the circuit, you can isolate the problem. Too low a voltage drop indicates too low a resistance. If, for example, a blower motor runs too fast in the MED and/or LOW position, the problem can be isolated in the resistor pack by taking voltage drop readings in all parts of the circuit to locate a possibly shorted resistor. The maximum allowable voltage drop under load is critical, especially if there is more than one high resistance problem in a circuit because all voltage drops are cumulative. A small drop is normal due to the resistance of the conductors.

HIGH RESISTANCE TESTING

1. Set the voltmeter selector switch to the 4 volt position.

2. Connect the voltmeter positive lead to the positive post of the battery.

3. Turn on the headlights and heater blower to provide a load.

4. Probe various points in the circuit with the negative voltmeter lead.

5. Read the voltage drop on the 4 volt scale. Some average maximum allowable voltage drops are:

FUSE PANEL – 7 volts
IGNITION SWITCH – 5volts
HEADLIGHT SWITCH – 7 volts
IGNITION COIL (+) – 5 volts
ANY OTHER LOAD – 1.3 volts
NOTE: *Voltage drops are all measured while a load is operating; without current flow, there will be no voltage drop.*

Ohmmeter

The ohmmeter is designed to read resistance (ohms) in a circuit or component. Although there are several different styles of ohmmeters, all will usually have a selector switch which permits the measurement of different ranges of resistance (usually the selector switch allows the multiplication of the meter reading by 10, 100, 1000, and 10,000). A calibration knob allows the meter to be set at zero for accurate measurement. Since all ohmmeters are powered by an internal battery (usually 9 volts), the ohmmeter can be used as a self-powered test light. When the ohmmeter is connected, current from the ohmmeter flows through the circuit or component being tested. Since the ohmmeter's internal resistance and voltage are known values, the amount of current flow through the meter depends on the resistance of the circuit or component being tested.

The ohmmeter can be used to perform continuity test for opens or shorts (either by observation of the meter needle or as a self-powered test light), and to read actual resistance in a circuit. It should be noted that the ohmmeter is used to check the resistance of a component or wire while there is no voltage applied to the circuit. Current flow from an outside voltage source (such as the vehicle battery) can damage the ohmmeter, so the circuit or component should be isolated from the vehicle electrical system before any testing is done. Since the ohmmeter uses its own voltage source, either lead can be connected to any test point.

NOTE: *When checking diodes or other solid state components, the ohmmeter leads can only be connected one way in order to measure current flow in a single direction. Make sure the positive (+) and negative (-) terminal connections are as described in the test procedures to verify the one-way diode operation.*

In using the meter for making continuity checks, do not be concerned with the actual resistance readings. Zero resistance, or any resistance readings, indicate continuity in the circuit. Infinite resistance indicates an open in the circuit. A high resistance reading where there should be none indicates a problem in the circuit. Checks for short circuits are made in the same manner as checks for open circuits except that the circuit must be isolated from both power and normal ground. Infinite resistance indicates no continuity to ground, while zero resistance indicates a dead short to ground.

RESISTANCE MEASUREMENT

The batteries in an ohmmeter will weaken with age and temperature, so the ohmmeter must be calibrated or "zeroed" before taking measurements. To zero the meter, place the selector switch in its lowest range and touch the two ohmmeter leads together. Turn the calibration knob until the meter needle is exactly on zero.

NOTE: *All analog (needle) type ohmmeters*

must be zeroed before use, but some digital ohmmeter models are automatically calibrated when the switch is turned on. Self-calibrating digital ohmmeters do not have an adjusting knob, but its a good idea to check for a zero readout before use by touching the leads together. All computer controlled systems require the use of a digital ohmmeter with at least 10 megohms impedance for testing. Before any test procedures are attempted, make sure the ohmmeter used is compatible with the electrical system or damage to the on-board computer could result.

To measure resistance, first isolate the circuit from the vehicle power source by disconnecting the battery cables or the harness connector. Make sure the key is OFF when disconnecting any components or the battery. Where necessary, also isolate at least one side of the circuit to be checked to avoid reading parallel resistances. Parallel circuit resistances will always give a lower reading than the actual resistance of either of the branches. When measuring the resistance of parallel circuits, the total resistance will always be lower than the smallest resistance in the circuit. Connect the meter leads to both sides of the circuit (wire or component) and read the actual measured ohms on the meter scale. Make sure the selector switch is set to the proper ohm scale for the circuit being tested to avoid misreading the ohmmeter test value.

CAUTION: *Never use an ohmmeter with power applied to the circuit. Like the self-powered test light, the ohmmeter is designed to operate on its own power supply. The normal 12 volt automotive electrical system current could damage the meter.*

Ammeters

An ammeter measures the amount of current flowing through a circuit in units called amperes or amps. Amperes are units of electron flow which indicate how fast the electrons are flowing through the circuit. Since Ohms Law dictates that current flow in a circuit is equal to the circuit voltage divided by the total circuit resistance, increasing voltage also increases the current level (amps). Likewise, any decrease in resistance will increase the amps in a circuit. At normal operating voltage, most circuits have a characteristic amount of amperes, called "current draw" which can be measured using an ammeter. By referring to a specified current draw rating, measuring the amperes, and comparing the two values, one can determine what is happening within the circuit to aid in diagnosis. An open circuit, for example, will not allow any current to flow so the ammeter reading will be zero. More current flows

through a heavily loaded circuit or when the charging system is operating.

An ammeter is always connected in series with the circuit being tested. All of the current that normally flows through the circuit must also flow through the ammeter; if there is any other path for the current to follow, the ammeter reading will not be accurate. The ammeter itself has very little resistance to current flow and therefore will not affect the circuit, but it will measure current draw only when the circuit is closed and electricity is flowing. Excessive current draw can blow fuses and drain the battery, while a reduced current draw can cause motors to run slowly, lights to dim and other components to not operate properly. The ammeter can help diagnose these conditions by locating the cause of the high or low reading.

Multimeters

Different combinations of test meters can be built into a single unit designed for specific tests. Some of the more common combination test devices are known as Volt/Amp testers, Tach/Dwell meters, or Digital Multimeters. The Volt/Amp tester is used for charging system, starting system or battery tests and consists of a voltmeter, an ammeter and a variable resistance carbon pile. The voltmeter will usually have at least two ranges for use with 6, 12 and 24 volt systems. The ammeter also has more than one range for testing various levels of battery loads and starter current draw and the carbon pile can be adjusted to offer different amounts of resistance. The Volt/Amp tester has heavy leads to carry large amounts of current and many later models have an inductive ammeter pickup that clamps around the wire to simplify test connections. On some models, the ammeter also has a zero-center scale to allow testing of charging and starting systems without switching leads or polarity. A digital multimeter is a voltmeter, ammeter and ohmmeter combined in an instrument which gives a digital readout. These are often used when testing solid state circuits because of their high input impedance (usually 10 megohms or more).

The tach/dwell meter combines a tachometer and a dwell (cam angle) meter and is a specialized kind of voltmeter. The tachometer scale is marked to show engine speed in rpm and the dwell scale is marked to show degrees of distributor shaft rotation. In most electronic ignition systems, dwell is determined by the control unit, but the dwell meter can also be used to check the duty cycle (operation) of some electronic engine control systems. Some tach/dwell meters are powered by an internal battery, while others take their power from the car battery in use. The battery powered testers usually require calibration much like an ohmmeter before testing.

Special Test Equipment

A variety of diagnostic tools are available to help troubleshoot and repair computerized engine control systems. The most sophisticated of these devices are the console type engine analyzers that usually occupy a garage service bay, but there are several types of aftermarket electronic testers available that will allow quick circuit tests of the engine control system by plugging directly into a special connector located in the engine compartment or under the dashboard. Several tool and equipment manufacturers offer simple, hand held testers that measure various circuit voltage levels on command to check all system components for proper operation. Although these testers usually cost about $300-$500, consider that the average computer control unit (or ECM) can cost just as much and the money saved by not replacing perfectly good sensors or components in an attempt to correct a problem could justify the purchase price of a special diagnostic tester the first time it's used.

These computerized testers can allow quick and easy test measurements while the engine is operating or while the car is being driven. In addition, the on-board computer memory can be read to access any stored trouble codes; in effect allowing the computer to tell you where it hurts and aid trouble diagnosis by pinpointing exactly which circuit or component is malfunctioning. In the same manner, repairs can be tested to make sure the problem has been corrected. The biggest advantage these special testers have is their relatively easy hookups that minimize or eliminate the chances of making the wrong connections and getting false voltage readings or damaging the computer accidentally.

NOTE: *It should be remembered that these testers check voltage levels in circuits; they don't detect mechanical problems or failed components if the circuit voltage falls within the preprogrammed limits stored in the tester PROM unit. Also, most of the hand held testes are designed to work only on one or two systems made by a specific manufacturer.*

A variety of aftermarket testers are available to help diagnose different computerized control systems. Owatonna Tool Company (OTC), for example, markets a device called the OTC Monitor which plugs directly into the diagnostic connector. The OTC tester makes diagnosis a simple matter of pressing the correct buttons and, by changing the internal PROM or inserting a different diagnosis cartridge, it will work on any model from full size to subcompact, over a wide range of years. An adapter is supplied with the tester to allow connection to all types of diagnostic connectors, regardless of the number of pin terminals used. By inserting an updated cartridge into the OTC tester, it can be easily updated to diagnose any new modifications of computerized control systems.

Wiring Harnesses

The average automobile contains about ½ mile of wiring, with hundreds of individual connections. To protect the many wires from damage and to keep them from becoming a confusing tangle, they are organized into bundles, enclosed in plastic or taped together and called wire harnesses. Different wiring harnesses serve different parts of the vehicle. Individual wires are color coded to help trace them through a harness where sections are hidden from view.

A loose or corroded connection or a replacement wire that is too small for the circuit will add extra resistance and an additional voltage drop to the circuit. A ten percent voltage drop can result in slow or erratic motor operation, for example, even though the circuit is complete. Automotive wiring or circuit conductors can be in any one of three forms:

1. Single strand wire
2. Multistrand wire
3. Printed circuitry

Single strand wire has a solid metal core and is usually used inside such components as alternators, motors, relays and other devices. Multistrand wire has a core made of many small strands of wire twisted together into a single conductor. Most of the wiring in an automotive electrical system is made up of multistrand wire, either as a single conductor or grouped together in a harness. All wiring is color coded on the insulator, either as a solid color or as a colored wire with an identification stripe. A printed circuit is a thin film of copper or other conductor that is printed on an insulator backing. Occasionally, a printed circuit is sandwiched between two sheets of plastic for more protection and flexibility. A complete printed circuit, consisting of conductors, insulating material and connectors for lamps or other components is called a printed circuit board. Printed circuitry is used in place of individual wires or harnesses in places where space is limited, such as behind instrument panels.

Wire Gauge

Since computer controlled automotive electrical systems are very sensitive to changes in resistance, the selection of properly sized wires is critical when systems are repaired. The wire gauge number is an expression of the cross section area of the conductor. The most common system for expressing wire size is the American Wire Gauge (AWG) system.

Wire cross section area is measured in circular mils. A mil is $\frac{1}{1000}$ in. (0.001 in.); a circular mil is the area of a circle one mil in diameter. For example, a conductor $\frac{1}{4}$ in. in diameter is 0.250 in. or 250 mils. The circular mil cross section area of the wire is 250 squared (250^2)or 62,500 circular mils. Imported car models usually use metric wire gauge designations, which is simply the cross section area of the conductor in square millimeters (mm^2).

Gauge numbers are assigned to conductors of various cross section areas. As gauge number increases, area decreases and the conductor becomes smaller. A 5 gauge conductor is smaller than a 1 gauge conductor and a 10 gauge is smaller than a 5 gauge. As the cross section area of a conductor decreases, resistance increases and so does the gauge number. A conductor with a higher gauge number will carry less current than a conductor with a lower gauge number.

NOTE: *Gauge wire size refers to the size of the conductor, not the size of the complete wire. It is possible to have two wires of the same gauge with different diameters because one may have thicker insulation than the other.*

12 volt automotive electrical systems generally use 10, 12, 14, 16 and 18 gauge wire. Main power distribution circuits and larger accessories usually use 10 and 12 gauge wire. Battery cables are usually 4 or 6 gauge, although 1 and 2 gauge wires are occasionally used. Wire length must also be considered when making repairs to a circuit. As conductor length increases, so does resistance. An 18 gauge wire, for example, can carry a 10 amp load for 10 feet without excessive voltage drop; however if a 15 foot wire is required for the same 10 amp load, it must be a 16 gauge wire.

An electrical schematic shows the electrical current paths when a circuit is operating properly. It is essential to understand how a circuit works before trying to fiure out why it doesn't. Schematics break the entire electrical system down into individual circuits and show only one particular circuit. In a schematic, no attempt is made to represent wiring and components as they physically appear on the vehicle; switches and other components are shown as simply as possible. Face views of harness connectors show the cavity or terminal locations in all multi-pin connectors to help locate test points.

If you need to backprobe a connector while it is on the component, the order of the terminals must be mentally reversed. The wire color code can help in this situation, as well as a keyway, lock tab or other reference mark.

NOTE: *Wiring diagrams are not included in this book. As vehicles have become more complex and available with longer option lists, wiring diagrams have grown in size and complexity. It has become almost impossible to provide a readable reproduction of a wiring diagram in a book this size. Information on ordering wiring diagrams from the vehicle manufacturer can be found in the owner's manual.*

WIRING REPAIR

Soldering is a quick, efficient method of joining metals permanently. Everyone who has the occasion to make wiring repairs should know how to solder. Electrical connections that are soldered are far less likely to come apart and will conduct electricity much better than connections that are only "pig-tailed" together. The most popular (and preferred) method of soldering is with an electrical soldering gun. Soldering irons are available in many sizes and wattage ratings. Irons with higher wattage ratings deliver higher temperatures and recover lost heat faster. A small soldering iron rated for no more than 50 watts is recommended, especially on electrical systems where excess heat can damage the components being soldered.

There are three ingredients necessary for successful soldering; proper flux, good solder and sufficient heat. A soldering flux is necessary to clean the metal of tarnish, prepare it for soldering and to enable the solder to spread into tiny crevices. When soldering, always use a resin flux or resin core solder which is non-corrosive and will not attract moisture once the job is finished. Other types of flux (acid core) will leave a residue that will attract moisture and cause the wires to corrode. Tin is a unique metal with a low melting point. In a molten state, it dissolves and alloys easily with many metals. Solder is made by mixing tin with lead. The most common proportions are 40/60, 50/50 and 60/40, with the percentage of tin listed first. Low priced solders usually contain less tin, making them very difficult for a beginner to use because more heat is required to melt the solder. A common solder is 40/60 which is well suited for all-around general use, but 60/40 melts easier, has more tin for a better joint and is preferred for electrical work.

Soldering Techniques

Successful soldering requires that the metals to be joined be heated to a temperature that will melt the solder—usually 360-460°F (182-238°C). Contrary to popular belief, the purpose of the soldering iron is not to melt the solder itself, but to heat the parts being soldered to a temperature high enough to melt the solder when it is touched to the work. Melting flux-cored solder on the soldering iron will usually destroy the effectiveness of the flux.

NOTE: *Soldering tips are made of copper for good heat conductivity, but must be "tinned" regularly for quick transference of heat to the project and to prevent the solder from sticking to the iron. To "tin" the iron, simply heat it and touch the flux-cored solder to the tip; the solder will flow over the hot tip. Wipe the excess off with a clean rag, but be careful as the iron will be hot.*

After some use, the tip may become pitted. If so, simply dress the tip smooth with a smooth file and "tin" the tip again. An old saying holds that "metals well cleaned are half soldered." Flux-cored solder will remove oxides but rust, bits of insulation and oil or grease must be removed with a wire brush or emery cloth. For maximum strength in soldered parts, the joint must start off clean and tight. Weak joints will result in gaps too wide for the solder to bridge.

If a separate soldering flux is used, it should be brushed or swabbed on only those areas that are to be soldered. Most solders contain a core of flux and separate fluxing is unnecessary. Hold the work to be soldered firmly. It is best to solder on a wooden board, because a metal vise will only rob the piece to be soldered of heat and make it difficult to melt the solder. Hold the soldering tip with the broadest face against the work to be soldered. Apply solder under the tip close to the work, using enough solder to give a heavy film between the iron and the piece being soldered, while moving slowly and making sure the solder melts properly. Keep the work level or the solder will run to the lowest part and favor the thicker parts, because these require more heat to melt the solder. If the soldering tip overheats (the solder coating on the face of the tip burns up), it should be retinned. Once the soldering is completed, let the soldered joint stand until cool. Tape and seal all soldered wire splices after the repair has cooled.

Wire Harness and Connectors

The on-board computer (ECA) wire harness electrically connects the control unit to the various solenoids, switches and sensors used by the control system. Most connectors in the engine compartment or otherwise exposed to the elements are protected against moisture and dirt which could create oxidation and deposits on the terminals. This protection is important because of the very low voltage and current levels used by the computer and sensors. All connectors have a lock which secures the male and female terminals together, with a secondary lock holding the seal and terminal into the connec-

tor. Both terminal locks must be released when disconnecting ECA connectors.

These special connectors are weather-proof and all repairs require the use of a special terminal and the tool required to service it. This tool is used to remove the pin and sleeve terminals. If removal is attempted with an ordinary pick, there is a good chance that the terminal will be bent or deformed. Unlike standard blade type terminals, these terminals cannot be straightened once they are bent. Make certain that the connectors are properly seated and all of the sealing rings in place when connecting leads. On some models, a hinge-type flap provides a backup or secondary locking feature for the terminals. Most secondary locks are used to improve the connector reliability by retaining the terminals if the small terminal lock tangs are not positioned properly.

Molded-on connectors require complete replacement of the connection. This means splicing a new connector assembly into the harness. All splices in on-board computer systems should be soldered to insure proper contact. Use care when probing the connections or replacing terminals in them as it is possible to short between opposite terminals. If this happens to the wrong terminal pair, it is possible to damage certain components. Always use jumper wires between connectors for circuit checking and never probe through weather-proof seals.

Open circuits are often difficult to locate by sight because corrosion or terminal misalignment are hidden by the connectors. Merely wiggling a connector on a sensor or in the wiring harness may correct the open circuit condition. This should always be considered when an open circuit or a failed sensor is indicated. Intermittent problems may also be caused by oxidized or loose connections. When using a circuit tester for diagnosis, always probe connections from the wire side. Be careful not to damage sealed connectors with test probes.

All wiring harnesses should be replaced with identical parts, using the same gauge wire and connectors. When signal wires are spliced into a harness, use wire with high temperature insulation only. With the low voltage and current levels found in the system, it is important that the best possible connection at all wire splices be made by soldering the splices together. It is seldom necessary to replace a complete harness. If replacement is necessary, pay close attention to insure proper harness routing. Secure the harness with suitable plastic wire clamps to prevent vibrations from causing the harness to wear in spots or contact any hot components.

NOTE: *Weatherproof connectors cannot be replaced with standard connectors. Instruc-*

tions are provided with replacement connector and terminal packages. *Some wire harnesses have mounting indicators (usually pieces of colored tape) to mark where the harness is to be secured.*

In making wiring repairs, it's important that you always replace damaged wires with wires that are the same gauge as the wire being replaced. The heavier the wire, the smaller the gauge number. Wires are color-coded to aid in identification and whenever possible the same color coded wire should be used for replacement. A wire stripping and crimping tool is necessary to install solderless terminal connectors. Test all crimps by pulling on the wires; it should not be possible to pull the wires out of a good crimp.

Wires which are open, exposed or otherwise damaged are repaired by simple splicing. Where possible, if the wiring harness is accessible and the damaged place in the wire can be located, it is best to open the harness and check for all possible damage. In an inaccessible harness, the wire must be bypassed with a new insert, usually taped to the outside of the old harness.

When replacing fusible links, be sure to use fusible link wire, NOT ordinary automotive wire. Make sure the fusible segment is of the same gauge and construction as the one being replaced and double the stripped end when crimping the terminal connector for a good contact. The melted (open) fusible link segment of the wiring harness should be cut off as close to the harness as possible, then a new segment spliced in as described. In the case of a damaged fusible link that feeds two harness wires, the harness connections should be replaced with two fusible link wires so that each circuit will have its own separate protection.

NOTE: *Most of the problems caused in the wiring harness are due to bad ground connections. Always check all vehicle ground connections for corrosion or looseness before performing any power feed checks to eliminate the chance of a bad ground affecting the circuit.*

Repairing Hard Shell Connectors

Unlike molded connectors, the terminal contacts in hard shell connectors can be replaced. Weatherproof hard-shell connectors with the leads molded into the shell have non-replaceable terminal ends. Replacement usually involves the use of a special terminal removal tool that depress the locking tangs (barbs) on the connector terminal and allow the connector to be removed from the rear of the shell. The connector shell should be replaced if it shows any evidence of burning, melting, cracks, or breaks.

Replace individual terminals that are burnt, corroded, distorted or loose.

NOTE: *The insulation crimp must be tight to prevent the insulation from sliding back on the wire when the wire is pulled. The insulation must be visibly compressed under the crimp tabs, and the ends of the crimp should be turned in for a firm grip on the insulation.*

The wire crimp must be made with all wire strands inside the crimp. The terminal must be fully compressed on the wire strands with the ends of the crimp tabs turned in to make a firm grip on the wire. Check all connections with an ohmmeter to insure a good contact. There should be no measurable resistance between the wire and the terminal when connected.

Mechanical Test Equipment

Vacuum Gauge

Most gauges are graduated in inches of mercury (in.Hg), although a device called a manometer reads vacuum in inches of water (in. H_2O). The normal vacuum reading usually varies between 18 and 22 in.Hg at sea level. To test engine vacuum, the vacuum gauge must be connected to a source of manifold vacuum. Many engines have a plug in the intake manifold which can be removed and replaced with an adapter fitting. Connect the vacuum gauge to the fitting with a suitable rubber hose or, if no manifold plug is available, connect the vacuum gauge to any device using manifold vacuum, such as EGR valves, etc. The vacuum gauge can be used to determine if enough vacuum is reaching a component to allow its actuation.

Hand Vacuum Pump

Small, hand-held vacuum pumps come in a variety of designs. Most have a built-in vacuum gauge and allow the component to be tested without removing it from the vehicle. Operate the pump lever or plunger to apply the correct amount of vacuum required for the test specified in the diagnosis routines. The level of vacuum in inches of Mercury (in.Hg) is indicated on the pump gauge. For some testing, an additional vacuum gauge may be necessary.

Intake manifold vacuum is used to operate various systems and devices on late model vehicles. To correctly diagnose and solve problems in vacuum control systems, a vacuum source is necessary for testing. In some cases, vacuum can be taken from the intake manifold when the engine is running, but vacuum is normally provided by a hand vacuum pump. These hand vacuum pumps have a built-in vacuum gauge that allow testing while the device is still attached to the component. For some tests, an additional vacuum gauge may be necessary.

HEATER

Blower Motor

REMOVAL AND INSTALLATION

1. Disconnect the negative battery cable.
2. Remove the sound deadening panel from the passenger side.
3. Remove the glove box assembly and the brace.
4. Remove the cooling hose from the blower motor assembly.
5. Disconnect the electrical connector from the blower motor.
6. Remove the 3 blower motor-to-blower motor housing screws and blower motor.
7. If necessary, remove the blower wheel-to-blower motor clip and the wheel.
8. To install, reverse the removal procedure and check the blower motor operation.

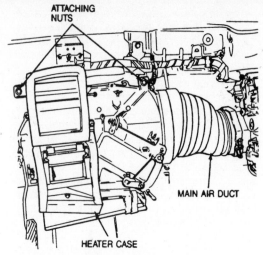

Heater case—non-air conditioned vehicle

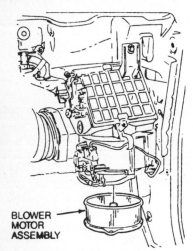

Blower motor removal and installation

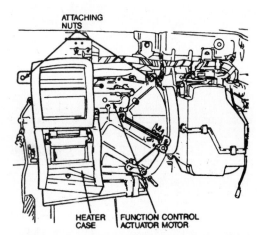

Heater case—automatic temperature control equipped vehicles

Heater Core

REMOVAL AND INSTALLATION

1. Disconnect the negative battery cable. Drain the cooling system into a suitable container.
2. Remove the instrument panel assembly. Refer to Chapter 10.
3. Disconnect the heater hoses from the heater core extension tubes and cap the extension tubes to prevent spilling coolant into the passenger compartment.
4. On non-air conditioned vehicles, remove the main air duct from the vehicle.
5. If equipped with air conditioning, remove the evaporator casing from the vehicle. Refer to the Evaporator Core removal and installation procedure in this Chapter.
6. Remove the 3 heater case mounting nuts.

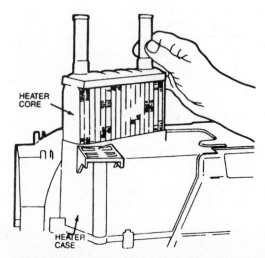

Removing the heater core from the heater case

7. If equipped with automatic temperature control, disconnect the electrical connectors from the function control and temperature blend actuator motors.

8. Remove the heater case by pulling it straight out, being careful not to damage the extension tubes.

9. Remove the 2 screws attaching the heater core tube braces to the heater case and remove the tube braces. Remove the heater core by pulling it straight out.

To install:

10. Install the heater core in the heater case. Install the heater core tube braces and secure them with the screws.

11. Position the heater case onto its mounting studs, being careful not to damage the heater core extension tubes. Install the 3 mounting nuts.

12. If equipped with automatic temperature control, connect the electrical connectors to the actuator motors.

13. Install the main air duct or evaporator case into the vehicle, as required.

14. Make sure the rubber grommets for the extension tubes are still in place in the engine side of the bulkhead.

15. Uncap the extension tubes and connect the heater hoses. Secure them with the clamps.

16. Install the instrument panel.

17. Fill the cooling system and connect the negative battery cable. Check the operation of the heater system and check for leaks.

Control Cables

REMOVAL AND INSTALLATION

1. Disconnect the negative battery cable.

2. Remove the control panel assembly. Refer to the procedure in this Chapter.

3. Remove the applicable housing brace and remove the cable.

To install:

4. Insert the cable end into the hole of the control lever.

5. Position the cable housing into its seat.

6. Install the cable housing brace.

7. Install the control panel assembly.

8. Check the operation of the control cable.

ADJUSTMENT

Function Selector Cable

1. Position the function selector lever in the **DEFROST** position.

2. Remove the driver's side sound deadening panel.

3. Release the cable located on the left side of the heater case from the cable housing brace.

4. With the cable end on the door lever pin, push the door lever down to its extreme stop.

5. Secure the cable into the cable housing brace.

6. Install the driver's side sound deadening panel.

Excessive air bleed out of the instrument panel registers when the heater control is in the floor mode may be caused by a misadjusted function selector cable at the mode cam on the heater assembly. To adjust the cable, proceed as follows:

1. Disconnect the function selector cable from the cable clip on the heater assembly.

2. Adjust the mode cam on the heater assembly to the **PANEL** position.

3. Adjust the control assembly lever to the **PANEL** position.

4. Connect the function selector cable to the cable clip.

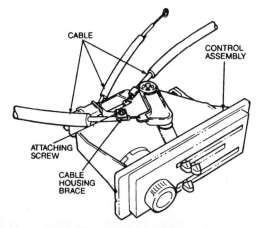

Control cable removal and installation

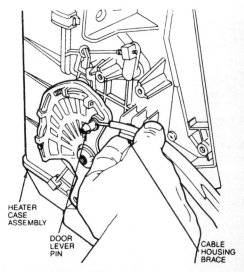

Function selector cable adjustment

Temperature Control Cable

1. Position the temperature control lever in the **MAX-WARM** position.
2. Remove the passenger's side sound deadening panel.
3. Remove the cable located on the right side of the heater case from the cable housing brace.
4. With the cable end on the door lever pin, push the door lever down to its extreme stop.
5. Secure the cable into the cable housing brace.
6. Check the temperature control lever for proper operation.
7. Install the passenger's side sound deadening panel.

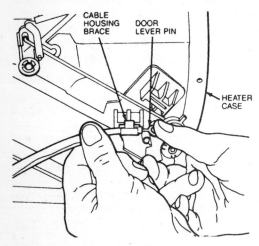

Temperature control cable adjustment

REC/FRESH Control Cable

1. Position the REC/FRESH control lever in the fresh air position.
2. Remove the passenger's side sound deadening panel.

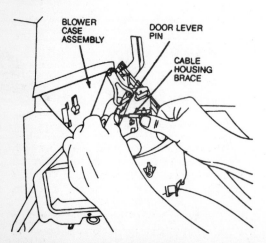

REC/FRESH control cable adjustment

3. Remove the cable located on the left side of the blower case from the cable housing brace.
4. With the cable end on the door lever pin, push the door lever forward to its extreme stop.
5. Secure the cable into the cable housing brace.
6. Check the air door control lever for proper operation.
7. Install the passenger's side sound deadening panel.

Control Panel

REMOVAL AND INSTALLATION

1. Disconnect the negative battery cable.
2. Remove the bezel cover from the control assembly face.
3. Remove the 4 attaching screws from the control assembly housing.
4. Remove the passenger and driver side sound deadening panels.
5. Remove the REC/FRESH control cable at the REC/FRESH selector door assembly.
6. Disconnect the blower switch electrical connector and the control assembly illumination electrical connector.
7. Remove the temperature control cable from the temperature blend door assembly at the right-hand side of the heater case.
8. Remove the function selector cable from the function control door assembly at the left-hand side of the heater case.
9. Remove the control assembly and control cables as an assembly.

NOTE: *While removing the control panel assembly, notice how the cables are routed for proper installation*

To install:

10. Position the control panel assembly into the instrument panel while routing the control cables as noted during removal.

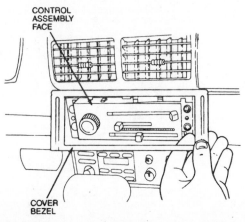

Removing the cover bezel from the heater control panel

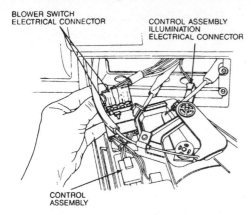

BLOWER SWITCH
ELECTRICAL CONNECTOR

CONTROL ASSEMBLY
ILLUMINATION
ELECTRICAL CONNECTOR

CONTROL
ASSEMBLY

Heater control panel removal and installation

11. Connect the blower switch and control assembly illumination electrical connectors.

12. Secure the control assembly with the 4 attaching screws.

13. Install the plastic bezel cover onto the face of the control assembly.

14. Install and adjust all control cables to their respective control and selector door assemblies and adjust the cables. Refer to the procedures in this Chapter.

15. Install both sound deadening panels.

16. Connect the negative battery cable. Check for proper control assembly operation.

Blower Switch

REMOVAL AND INSTALLATION

Manual Air Conditioning

1. Disconnect the negative battery cable.

2. Remove the control assembly from the vehicle. Refer to the procedure in this Chapter.

3. Remove the blower switch knob by pulling it straight off of the blower switch shaft.

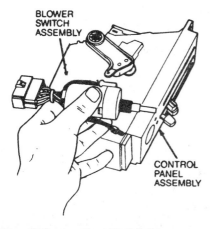

BLOWER
SWITCH
ASSEMBLY

CONTROL
PANEL
ASSEMBLY

Blower switch removal and installation

4. Remove the attaching nut from the blower switch shaft.

5. Remove the male side blower switch connector from the control assembly housing.

6. Remove the blower switch assembly from the control assembly.

7. Installation is the reverse of the removal procedure.

AIR CONDITIONER

NOTE: *Refer to Chapter 1 for discharging, charging, etc. of the air conditioning system.*

Compressor

REMOVAL AND INSTALLATION

2.2L Engine

NOTE: *The suction accumulator/drier and orifice tube (liquid line) should also be replaced whenever the compressor is replaced.*

1. Disconnect the negative battery cable. Refer to Chapter 1 for properly evacuating the air conditioning system.

2. Remove the suction and discharge manifold assembly from the compressor.

3. Remove the 2 attaching bolts at the upper compressor mounting bracket from the compressor to engine mounting bracket.

4. Remove the belt tension adjusting bolt from the belt tension fitting.

5. Remove the attaching nut from the compressor at the upper compressor mounting bracket.

6. Remove the upper through bolt from the compressor and remove the upper compressor mounting bracket.

7. Disconnect the clutch field coil electrical connector.

8. Remove the lower through bolt from the compressor at the chassis-to-compressor mounting bracket.

9. Remove the compressor, front compressor mounting bracket and rear compressor mounting bracket as an assembly.

10. Remove the through bolt from the compressor at the rear compressor mounting bracket and remove the rear bracket, spacer and front bracket from the compressor.

To install:

NOTE: *A service replacement compressor should be emptied of any oil it contains from the factory. Add 3.3 oz. (100 ml) of Motorcraft YN-2 refrigerant oil, or equivalent. This will maintain the total system oil charge within the specified limits.*

11. Position the rear compressor mounting bracket, front mounting bracket and spacer to the compressor and install the through bolt.

12. Position the compressor and bracket assembly into the vehicle and install the through bolt into the chassis-to-compressor mounting bracket.

13. Connect the clutch field coil electrical connector.

14. Position the upper compressor mounting bracket onto the compressor and install the upper through bolt.

15. Install the attaching bolts at the upper compressor mounting bracket into the compressor-to-engine mounting bracket.

16. Install the belt tension fitting into the upper compressor mounting bracket and install the attaching nut. Install the belt tension adjusting bolt.

17. Install the suction and discharge manifold hose assembly.

18. Adjust the belt tension to specification.

19. Have the system leak tested, evacuated and charged by a certified technician. Check the operation of the system.

3.0L Engine

NOTE: *The suction accumulator/drier and orifice tube (liquid line) should also be replaced whenever the compressor is replaced.*

1. Disconnect the negative battery cable. Have the system properly discharged by a certified technician.

2. Remove the alternator/accessory support bracket (Refer to Chapter 3) and disconnect the clutch field coil electrical connector.

3. Remove the 4 compressor mounting bolts.

NOTE: *Remove the brace with the 2 upper mounting bolts.*

4. Lift the compressor, with the air conditioning hoses still attached, from the engine compartment and set it down carefully on the radiator core support.

5. Remove the 4 hose manifold bolts and pull the hose assemblies aside. Remove the compressor.

To install:

NOTE: *A service replacement compressor should be emptied of any oil it contains from the factory. Add 3.3 oz. (100 ml) of Motorcraft YN-9 refrigerant oil, or equivalent. This will maintain the total system oil charge within the specified limits.*

6. Position the hose assemblies on the compressor and install the manifold attaching bolts.

7. Position the compressor assembly on the mounting bracket and install the 4 mounting bolts and brace.

8. Connect the clutch field coil electrical connector and install the alternator/accessory support bracket.

9. Connect the negative battery cable and properly evacuate and recharge the system.

Evaporator Core
REMOVAL AND INSTALLATION

1. Disconnect the negative battery cable.

2. Have a certified technician properly discharge the refrigerant from the air conditioning system.

3. Remove the carbon canister.

4. Disconnect the air conditioning lines from the evaporator (Refer to the Sping Lock Cou-

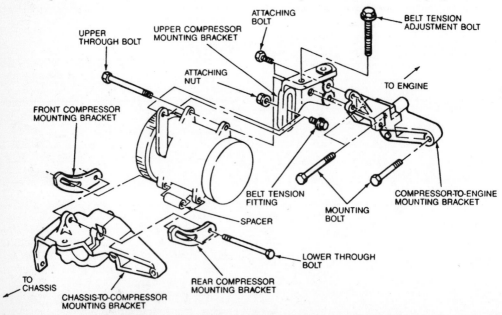

Air conditioning compressor removal and installation—2.2L engine

pling Connect and Disconnect Chart). Plug the lines to prevent dirt and moisture from entering the system.

5. Remove the instrument panel. Refer to Chapter 10.

6. Disconnect the electrical connectors from the air conditioning relays at the top of the evaporator case.

7. Remove the air duct bands and remove the drain hose.

8. Remove the evaporator case attaching nuts and carefully remove the case from the vehicle.

9. Remove the foam seals at the inlet and outlet of the evaporator by peeling them away from the evaporator case.

10. Remove the 7 retaining clips from the housing, separate the case halves and remove the evaporator.

To install:

NOTE: *Add 0.845–1.014 oz. (25–30 ml) of clean refrigerant oil (Motorcraft YN-2 or equivalent, for the 2.2L engine or Motorcraft YN-9 or equivalent, for the 3.0L engine) to a new replacement evaporator core to maintain total system refrigerant oil requirements.*

11. Install the evaporator core into the evaporator case.

12. Assemble the case halves with the 7 retaining clips and install the foam seals.

13. Carefully position the evaporator case into the vehicle and install the attaching nuts.

14. Install the drain hose to the evaporator case.

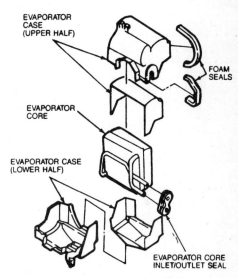

Evaporator core removal and installation

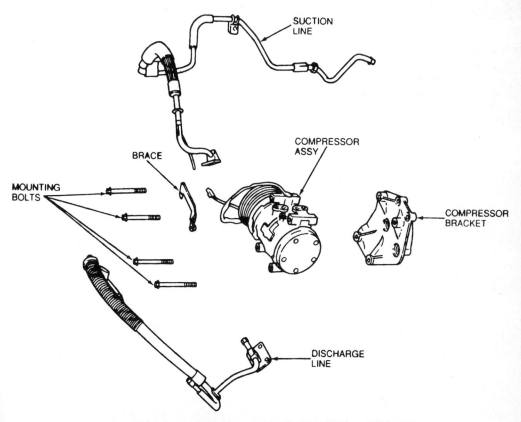

Air conditioning compressor removal and installation—3.0L engine

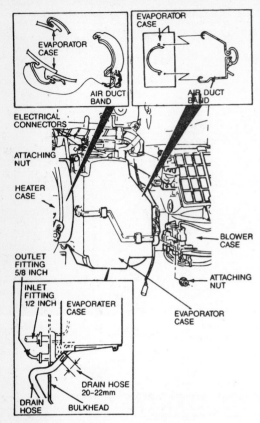

Evaporator case removal and installation

15. Install and secure the air duct bands and connect the electrical connectors.

16. Install the instrument panel into the vehicle.

17. Unplug the liquid line and install it into the evaporator inlet by performing the spring-lock coupling connect procedure.

18. Unplug the suction line and install it into the evaporator outlet by performing the spring-lock coupling connect procedure.

19. Install the carbon canister and connect the negative battery cable.

20. Leak test, evacuate and recharge the air conditioning system. Check the system for proper operation.

Control Panel
REMOVAL AND INSTALLATION
Manual Air Conditioning

For removal and installation of the control panel, and control cable adjustment, refer to the procedures under HEATER, in this Chapter.

Automatic Temperature Control

1. Disconnect the negative battery cable.

2. Remove the bezel cover from the control assembly face.

3. Remove the 4 attaching screws from the control assembly housing.

4. Disconnect the 2 electrical connectors from the control assembly and remove the assembly.

5. Installation is the reverse of the removal procedure. Check the control assembly for proper operation.

Blower Switch
REMOVAL AND INSTALLATION
Manual Air Conditioning

1. Disconnect the negative battery cable.

2. Remove the control assembly from the vehicle. Refer to the procedure in this Chapter.

3. Remove the A/C push-button knob by pulling it straight off the blower switch shaft.

4. Remove the blower switch knob by pulling it straight off the blower switch shaft.

5. Remove the attaching nut from the blower switch shaft.

6. Remove the A/C indicator light from the blower switch housing.

7. Remove the male side blower switch connector from the control assembly housing.

8. Remove the blower switch assembly from the control assembly.

9. Installation is the reverse of the removal procedure. Check the blower switch for proper operation.

Automatic Temperature Control

The blower switch is not serviceable. If it is determined that the switch is malfunctioning, the entire control assembly must be replaced.

Refrigerant Lines
QUICK-CONNECT COUPLINGS

The refrigerant lines on your Probe are connected to the various air conditioning system components (except compressor) with spring lock couplings. These couplings require the use of special tools to connect and disconnect them, as shown in the Spring Lock Coupling Procedure chart. Do not attempt to disconnect a refrigerant line using any other type of tool, or the line may be damaged.

ENTERTAINMENT SYSTEMS

Radio, Tape Player and Compact Disc

REMOVAL AND INSTALLATION

NOTE: *The following procedure applies to all Probe radio options.*

1. Disconnect the negative battery cable.
2. Remove the ash tray.
3. Remove the selector trim panel on vehicles equipped with an automatic transaxle. Remove the gear shift and boot trim panel on vehicles equipped with a manual transaxle.
4. Remove the cigar lighter assembly and disconnect the cigar lighter connector.

SPRING LOCK COUPLING CONNECT AND DISCONNECT PROCEDURE

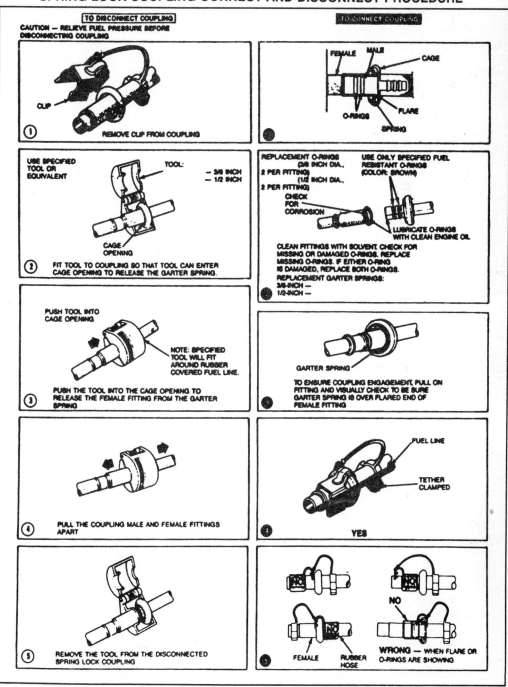

5. Disconnect the cigar lighter lamp by twisting the socket and removing.

6. Remove the 2 radio mounting screws. Insert 2 radio removal tools T87P–19061–A or equivalent, into the face plate holes until the tension of the clips is felt.

NOTE: *The first time the radio is removed requires the flashing in the bezel facing to be broken, which requires extra force.*

7. Flex outward on both sides of the radio simultaneously and pull the radio from the instrument panel, using the tools as handles.

8. Disconnect the electrical connectors and antenna cable from the radio.

To install:

9. Connect the electrical connectors and antenna cable into the radio.

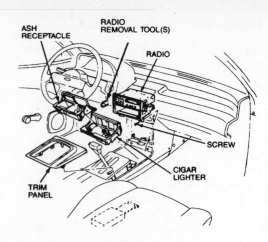

Radio removal and installation

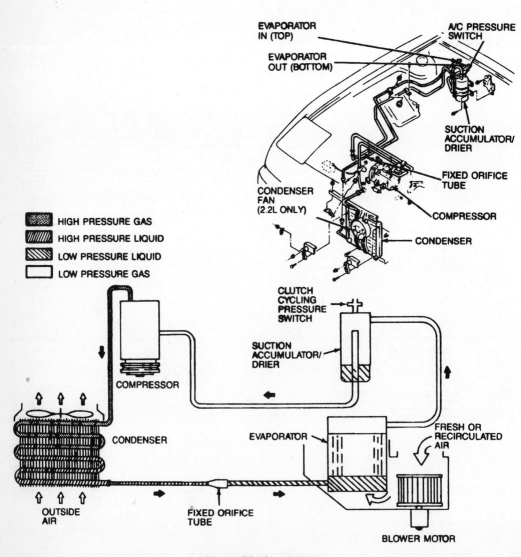

Air conditioning system

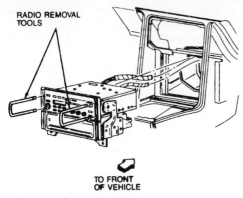

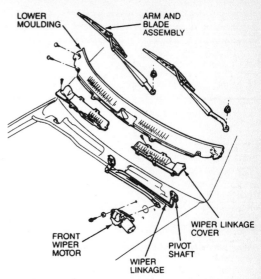

Windshield wiper system components

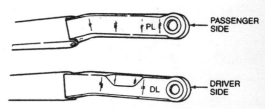

Windshield wiper arm position identification

Positioning of the radio removal tools

10. Install the radio and the 2 attaching screws.
11. Connect the cigar lighter lamp to the cigar lighter assembly.
12. Connect the cigar lighter connector to the cigar lighter assembly and install the cigar lighter assembly.
13. Install the selector trim panel, or gearshift and boot trim panel, as required.
14. Install the ash tray.
15. Connect the negative battery cable.

WINDSHIELD WIPERS AND WASHERS

Windshield Wiper Blade and Arm

NOTE: *The windshield wipers on your Probe can operate in either a summer or winter mode, which allows the wiper blades to rest either on the windshield, or below it. The summer/winter mode electrical connector is located on the interior fuse panel. The wiper blades will rest below the windshield when the electrical connector is plugged into the socket marked SUMMER. The wiper blades will rest on the windshield when the electrical connector is plugged into the socket marked WINTER. In the summer mode, the blades may be lifted off the moulding by placing the arms on the wiper lift brackets.*

REMOVAL AND INSTALLATION

1. Unscrew the retaining nut and remove the arm and blade assembly from the pivot shaft.
2. Remove the wiper blade from the wiper arm. Refer to Chapter 1.
To install:
3. Install the wiper blade on the wiper arm.
4. Turn the wiper switch **ON** and allow the motor to move the pivot shafts through 3–4 cycles. Turn the wiper switch **OFF**.
5. Install the arm and blade assembly so the

tip of the wiper blade is 0.79–1.18 in. (20–30mm) from the bottom of the windshield.
NOTE: *The driver's side wiper arm is marked "DL". The passenger's side wiper arm is marked "PL".*
6. Install the retaining nut and tighten to 7–10 ft. lbs. (10–14 Nm).
7. Cycle the wipers several times and re-torque the retaining nut.
NOTE: *Make sure the windshield wiper arm is horizontal to the pivot shaft so the pivot shaft splines are fully seated in the wiper arm.*

Rear Window Wiper Blade and Arm
REMOVAL AND INSTALLATION

1. Lift the cover and remove the retaining nut.
2. Remove the arm and blade assembly.
3. Remove the wiper blade from the wiper arm. Refer to Chapter 1.
To install:
4. Install the wiper blade on the wiper arm.
5. Turn the wiper switch **ON** and allow the motor to move the pivot shafts through 3–4 cycles. Turn the wiper switch **OFF**.

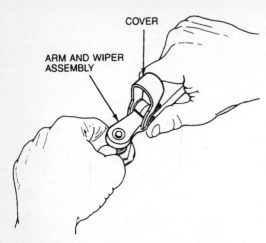

Rear wiper arm and blade assembly removal and installation

6. Install the arm and blade assembly so the tip of the wiper blade is 0.79–1.18 in. (20–30mm) from the bottom of the rear window.
7. Install and tighten the retaining nut.

Windshield Wiper Motor

REMOVAL AND INSTALLATION

1. Disconnect the negative battery cable.
2. Remove the windshield wiper arm and blades assemblies. Refer to the procedure in this Chapter.
3. Disconnect the hose from the wiper washer jet nozzle.
4. Remove the lower cowl molding.
5. Remove the wiper linkage cover.
6. Disconnect the wiper linkage by pulling off the wiper motor output arm. Disconnect the electrical connectors.
7. Remove the wiper motor mounting bolts and remove the wiper motor.
To install:
8. Install the wiper motor and mounting bolts.
9. Connect the electrical connectors.
10. Attach the wiper linkage to the motor output arm.
11. Install the wiper linkage cover and the lower molding.
12. Connect the washer nozzles and connect the negative battery cable.
13. Install the wiper arm and blade assemblies.

Rear Window Wiper Motor

REMOVAL AND INSTALLATION

1. Disconnect the negative battery cable.
2. Remove the arm and blade assembly. Refer to the procedure in this Chapter.

3. Remove the boot, nut, and the mount from the rear wiper motor pivot.
4. Remove the liftgate interior trim panel. Refer to Chapter 10.
5. Disconnect the wiper motor electrical connector.
6. Remove the rear wiper motor mounting bolts, and remove the motor.
To install:
7. Install the rear wiper motor and attaching bolts. Make sure the ground wire is connected tightly.
8. Connect the motor electrical connector.
9. Install the liftgate trim panel.
10. Install the mount, nut and boot to the motor pivot shaft.

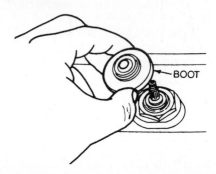

Removing the boot from the rear window wiper motor pivot shaft

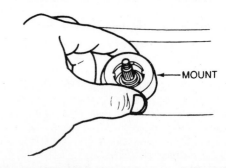

Removing the mount from the rear window wiper motor pivot shaft

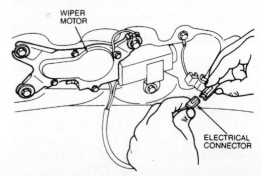

Rear window wiper motor removal and installation

11. Connect the negative battery cable. Install the rear wiper arm and blade assembly.

Interval Wiper Module
REMOVAL AND INSTALLATION

1. Disconnect the negative battery cable.
2. Remove the lower left-hand sound deadening panel and carefully lower to the floor.
3. Depress the tab on the interval wiper module and pull the module from the junction block.
4. Installation is the reverse of the removal procedure.

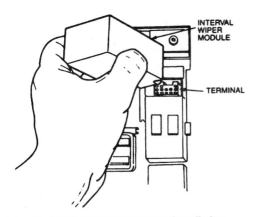

Interval wiper module removal and installation

Wiper Linkage
REMOVAL AND INSTALLATION

1. Remove the arm and blade assemblies. Refer to the procedure in this Chapter.
2. Remove the lower moulding and wiper linkage cover.
3. Disconnect the wiper linkage by pulling it off of the wiper motor output arm.
4. Remove the pivot shaft retaining caps and remove the pivot shafts and wiper linkage.
5. Installation is the reverse of the removal procedure.

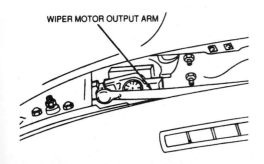

Wiper linkage removal and installation

Windshield Washer Fluid Reservoir
REMOVAL AND INSTALLATION

1. Disconnect the negative battery cable.
2. Remove the radiator coolant reservoir.
3. Remove the washer reservoir retaining bolts.
4. Disconnect the electrical connector and the hose from the washer reservoir.
5. Remove the washer reservoir assembly.
6. Installation is the reverse of the removal procedure.

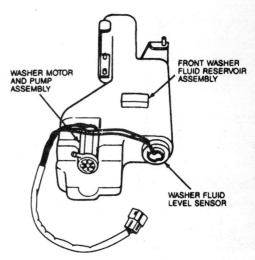

Windshield washer reservoir and pump motor assembly

Windshield Washer Motor
REMOVAL AND INSTALLATION

1. Disconnect the negative battery cable.
2. Remove the windshield washer fluid reservoir, as previously described.
3. Pry off the washer motor and pump assembly.
4. Installation is the reverse of the removal procedure.

Rear Window Washer Reservoir
REMOVAL AND INSTALLATION

1. Disconnect the negative battery cable.
2. Remove the left-hand lower trunk side trim panel. Refer to Chapter 10.
3. Remove the refill cap and disengage the support. Remove the support from the refill hose.
4. Disconnect the electrical connector and remove the hose.
5. Remove the rear washer reservoir.
6. Installation is the reverse of the removal procedure.

Rear window washer reservoir

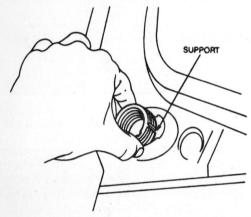

Removing the support from the rear window washer reservoir

Rear Window Washer Motor

REMOVAL AND INSTALLATION

1. Disconnect the negative battery cable.
2. Remove the rear window washer reservoir, as previously described.
3. Pry off the motor and pump assembly.
4. Installation is the reverse of the removal procedure.

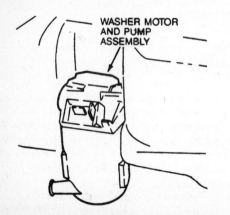

Rear window washer pump motor

INSTRUMENTS AND SWITCHES

Instrument Cluster

REMOVAL AND INSTALLATION

1. Disconnect the negative battery cable.
2. Remove the instrument cluster module as follows:

   a. Remove the steering wheel. Refer to Chapter 8.

   b. Remove the 2 column cover screws and remove the cover.

   c. Remove the 9 cluster module mounting screws.

   d. Carefully pull the cluster module outward and disconnect the 7 electrical connectors from the cover.

   e. Remove the ignition switch illumination bulb and remove the cluster module.

3. Loosen the 2 cover hinge screws and remove the 6 upper cluster cover screws. Remove the cover.

NOTE: *During removal, be careful not to rip the rubber seal that joins the upper and lower portions of the cluster cover panels.*

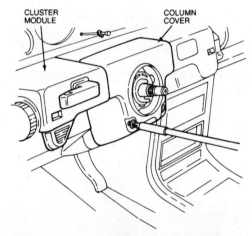

Steering column cover removal and installation

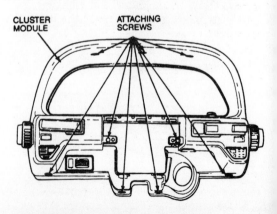

Cluster module attaching screw locations

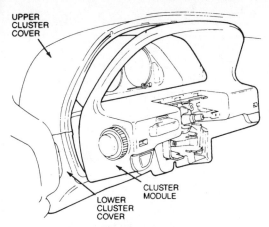

Cluster module removal and installation

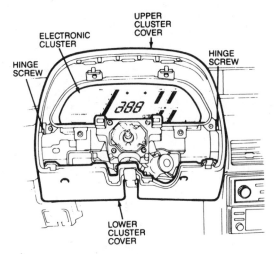

Cluster cover removal and installation

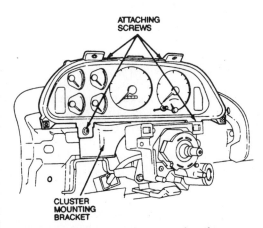

Instrument cluster mounting screw locations—analog cluster

4. Remove the lower cluster cover panel and remove the 4 cluster mounting screws.

5. Disconnect the electrical connectors from the back of the cluster. If equipped with analog

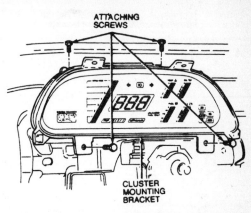

Instrument cluster mounting screw locations—electronic cluster

instrument cluster, disconnect the speedometer cable.

6. Remove the cluster from the vehicle.

To install:

7. Position the cluster onto the cluster mounting bracket and connect the electrical connectors. If equipped with analog instrument cluster, connect the speedometer cable.

8. Install the 4 cluster mounting screws and install the lower cluster cover.

NOTE: *During installation, be careful not to rip the rubber seal that joins the upper and lower portions of the cluster cover panels.*

9. Position the upper cluster cover and install the attaching screws.

10. Tighten the 2 cover hinge screws.

11. Install the instrument cluster module as follows:

   a. Connect the 7 electrical connectors.

   b. Install the ignition illumination bulb into the cluster module.

   c. Position the cluster module and install the 9 attaching screws.

   d. Install the column cover and the steering wheel.

12. Connect the negative battery cable. Check all gauges, speedometer and tachometer for proper operation.

Speedometer

REMOVAL AND INSTALLATION

Electronic Instrument Cluster

The speedometer is not serviceable. If the speedometer malfunctions, the entire instrument cluster must be replaced. Refer to the Instrument Cluster removal and installation procedure in this Chapter.

Analog Instrument Cluster

1. Remove the instrument cluster. Refer to the procedure in this Chapter.

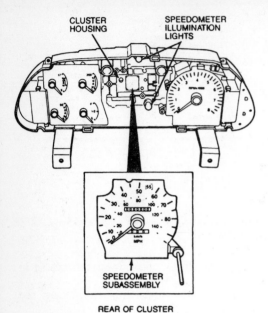

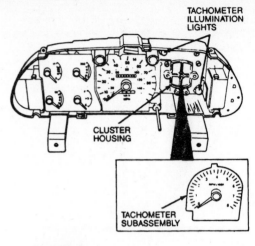

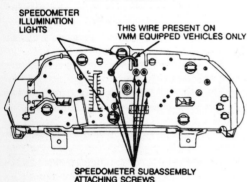

Speedometer removal and installation—analog instrument cluster

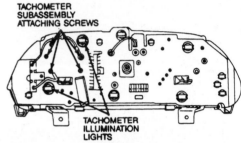

Tachometer removal and installation—analog instrument cluster

2. Remove the cluster lens.
3. Remove the attaching screws and the speedometer.
4. Installation is the reverse of the removal procedure.

Tachometer
REMOVAL AND INSTALLATION
Electronic Instrument Cluster

The tachometer is not serviceable. If the tachometer malfunctions, the entire instrument cluster must be replaced. Refer to the Instrument Cluster removal and installation procedure in this Chapter.

Analog Instrument Cluster

1. Remove the instrument cluster. Refer to the procedure in this Chapter.
2. Remove the cluster lens.

3. Remove the attaching screws and the tachometer.
4. Installation is the reverse of the removal procedure.

Speedometer Cable
REMOVAL AND INSTALLATION

1. Disconnect the negative battery cable.
2. Remove the upper and lower instrument cluster cover panels. (Do not remove the instrument cluster).
3. Reach behind the instrument cluster, depress the lock tab and pull the speedometer cable out of the instrument cluster.
4. Open the hood and locate the speedometer cable connector. Unscrew the connector and separate the upper and lower cables.
5. Slide the rubber dust boot back from the

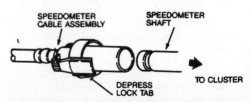

Speedometer cable-to-speedometer connection

lower cable-to-transaxle connector. Unscrew the speedometer cable from the speedometer driven gear on the transaxle.

6. Remove the rubber grommet from the firewall and slide the grommet down the cable. Gently pry the retaining ring from the firewall and pull the speedometer cable out through the firewall.

To install:

7. Insert the upper speedometer cable through the firewall into the lower instrument panel.

8. Install the retaining ring and grommet into the firewall.

9. Connect the lower speedometer cable to the speedometer driven gear. Slide the boot into position.

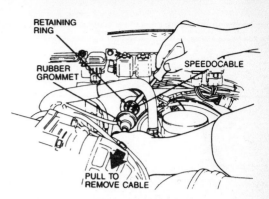

Grommet and retaining ring removal

10. Join both cables and tighten the connector.

11. Connect the upper speedometer cable to the rear of the speedometer. Make sure the locking tab is secured onto the back of the speedometer head.

12. Install the upper and lower instrument cluster covers.

13. Connect the negative battery cable. Check speedometer operation.

Oil Pressure Gauge

REMOVAL AND INSTALLATION

Electronic Instrument Cluster

The oil pressure gauge is built integrally into the electronic cluster. If the gauge malfunctions, the entire instrument cluster must be replaced. Refer to the Instrument Cluster removal and installation procedure in this Chapter.

Analog Instrument Cluster

The oil pressure gauge is integral with the fuel gauge subassembly. If the gauge malfunctions, the subassembly must be replaced. Refer to the Fuel Gauge removal and installation procedure in this Chapter.

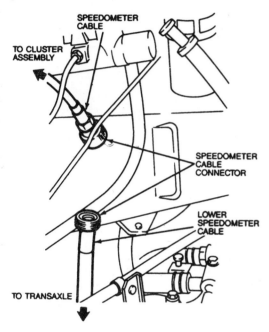

Upper and lower speedometer cable connectors

Fuel Gauge

REMOVAL AND INSTALLATION

Electronic Instrument Cluster

The fuel gauge is built integrally into the electronic cluster. If the gauge malfunctions, the entire instrument cluster must be replaced. Refer to the Instrument Cluster removal and installation procedure in this Chapter.

Analog Instrument Cluster

1. Remove the instrument cluster. Refer to the procedure in this Chapter.

2. Remove the lens assembly.

3. Remove the attaching screws from the gauge subassembly and remove the subassembly.

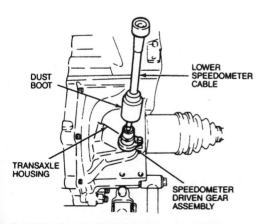

Speedometer cable-to-speedometer driven gear connection

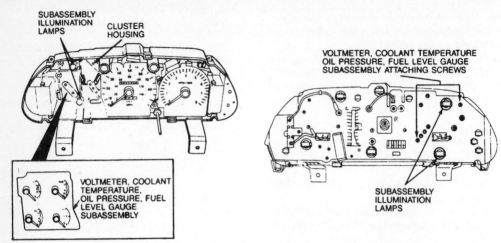

Fuel gauge subassembly removal and installation—analog instrument cluster

4. Installation is the reverse of the removal procedure.

Temperature Gauge
REMOVAL AND INSTALLATION
Electronic Instrument Cluster

The temperature gauge is built integrally into the electronic cluster. If the gauge malfunctions, the entire instrument cluster must be replaced. Refer to the Instrument Cluster removal and installation procedure in this Chapter.

Analog Instrument Cluster

The temperature gauge is integral with the fuel gauge subassembly. If the gauge malfunctions, the subassembly must be replaced. Refer to the Fuel Gauge removal and installation procedure in this Chapter.

Printed Circuit Board
REMOVAL AND INSTALLATION

1. Remove the instrument cluster. Refer to the procedure in this Chapter.
2. Disassemble the cluster.

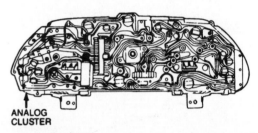

Instrument cluster circuit board—2.2L non-turbocharged engine

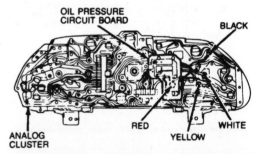

Instrument cluster circuit board—2.2L turbocharged engine with manual transaxle

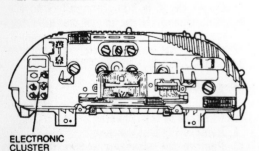

Instrument cluster circuit board—3.0L engine with electronic cluster

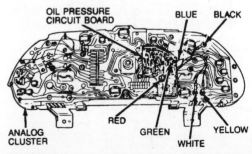

Instrument cluster circuit board—2.2L turbocharged engine with automatic transaxle

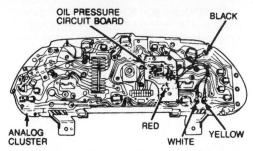

OIL PRESSURE
CIRCUIT BOARD

BLACK

ANALOG
CLUSTER

RED

WHITE YELLOW

Instrument cluster circuit board—3.0L engine with analog cluster

3. When replacing the main circuit board or the oil pressure circuit board, refer to the illustrations for proper attaching wire color designations.

4. Installation is the reverse of the removal procedure.

Voltmeter

REMOVAL AND INSTALLATION

Electronic Instrument Cluster

The voltmeter is built integrally into the electronic cluster. If the gauge malfunctions, the entire instrument cluster must be replaced. Refer to the Instrument Cluster removal and installation procedure in this Chapter.

Analog Instrument Cluster

The voltmeter is integral with the fuel gauge subassembly. If the gauge malfunctions, the subassembly must be replaced. Refer to the Fuel Gauge removal and installation procedure in this Chapter.

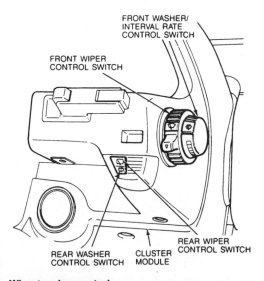

FRONT WASHER/
INTERVAL RATE
CONTROL SWITCH

FRONT WIPER
CONTROL SWITCH

REAR WASHER
CONTROL SWITCH

CLUSTER
MODULE

REAR WIPER
CONTROL SWITCH

Wiper/washer controls

Windshield Wiper Switch

REMOVAL AND INSTALLATION

1. Disconnect the negative battery cable.
2. Remove the instrument cluster module as follows:
   a. Remove the steering wheel.
   b. Remove the 2 column cover screws and remove the cover.
   c. Remove the 9 cluster module mounting screws.
   d. Carefully pull the cluster module outward and disconnect the 7 electrical connectors from the cover.
   e. Remove the ignition switch illumination bulb and remove the cluster module.

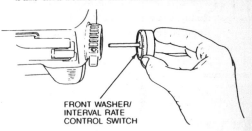

FRONT WASHER/
INTERVAL RATE
CONTROL SWITCH

Windshield washer/interval rate control switch removal and installation

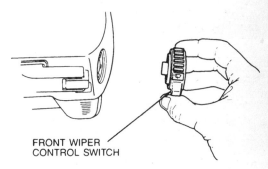

FRONT WIPER
CONTROL SWITCH

Windshield wiper control switch knob removal and installation

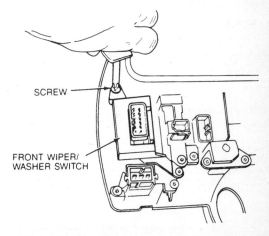

SCREW

FRONT WIPER/
WASHER SWITCH

Windshield wiper switch removal and installation

3. Gently, pull the washer/interval rate control switch knob and wiper control switch knob from the windshield wiper switch.

4. From the rear of the instrument cluster module cover, remove the windshield wiper switch housing screws and the switch.

5. Installation is the reverse of the removal procedure. Check windshield wiper switch operation.

Rear Window Wiper Switch

REMOVAL AND INSTALLATION

1. Disconnect the negative battery cable.

2. Remove the instrument cluster module as follows:

    a. Remove the steering wheel.

    b. Remove the 2 column cover screws and remove the cover.

    c. Remove the 9 cluster module mounting screws.

    d. Carefully pull the cluster module outward and disconnect the 7 electrical connectors from the cover.

    e. Remove the ignition switch illumination bulb and remove the cluster module.

3. Remove the windshield wiper switch. Refer to the procedure in this Chapter.

4. Remove the retaining screws and remove the rear wiper control switch button by releasing the tangs.

5. Remove the rear wiper/washer switch.

6. Installation is the reverse of the removal procedure.

Headlight Switch

REMOVAL AND INSTALLATION

1. Disconnect the negative battery cable.

2. Remove the turn signal switch. Refer to the procedure in this Chapter.

2. Gently, pull the rotary knob from the headlight switch.

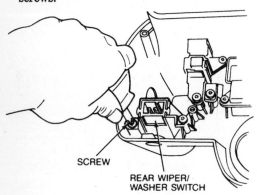

SCREW

REAR WIPER/
WASHER SWITCH

Rear window wiper switch removal and installation

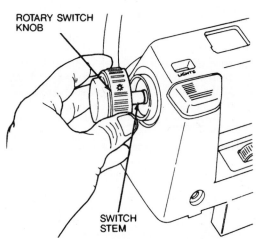

ROTARY SWITCH
KNOB

SWITCH
STEM

Headlight switch knob removal and installation

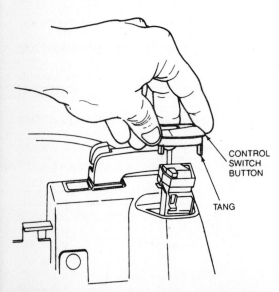

CONTROL
SWITCH
BUTTON

TANG

Rear window wiper switch button removal and installation

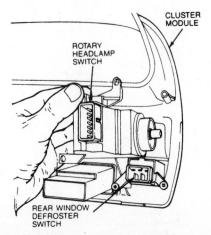

CLUSTER
MODULE

ROTARY
HEADLAMP
SWITCH

REAR WINDOW
DEFROSTER
SWITCH

Headlight switch removal and installation

3. From the rear of the instrument cluster module cover, remove the rotary switch housing screws and the switch.

4. Installation is the reverse of the removal procedure. Check headlight switch operation.

Turn Signal Switch
REMOVAL AND INSTALLATION

1. Disconnect the negative battery cable.
2. Remove the steering wheel. Refer to Chapter 8.
3. Remove the center cover mounting screws and the cover.
4. Remove cluster module mounting screws, pull the cluster module away from the dash and disconnect the electrical connectors. Remove the cluster module.
5. Remove the turn signal lever-to-turn signal switch screw and the lever.
6. From the rear of the instrument cluster module, remove the turn signal switch screws and the switch.

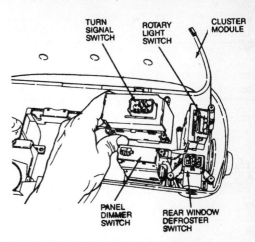

Turn signal switch removal and installation

7. Installation is the reverse of the removal procedure. Check turn signal switch operation.

Clock
REMOVAL AND INSTALLATION

The clock is built into the electronic radios. If the clock malfunctions, the radio must be repaired or replaced.

Ignition Switch
REMOVAL AND INSTALLATION
1989 Vehicles

1. Disconnect the negative battery cable.
2. Remove the lower instrument cluster cover as follows:
    a. Remove the steering wheel. Refer to Chapter 8.
    b. Remove the 2 column cover screws and the cover.
    c. Remove the 9 cluster module mounting screws.
    d. Carefully pull the cluster module outward and disconnect the electrical connectors.
    e. Remove the ignition switch illumination bulb and remove the cluster module.
    f. Loosen the 2 cover hinge screws and the 6 upper cluster cover screws. Remove the cover.
    g. Remove the lower cluster cover panel.
3. Remove the lap duct and the defrost duct.
4. Remove the mounting nuts from the hinge bracket.
5. Remove the steering column upper mounting bolts/nuts and allow the steering column to hang down.
6. Remove the screw securing the ignition switch to the ignition switch housing.
7. Disconnect the 4 ignition switch snap con-

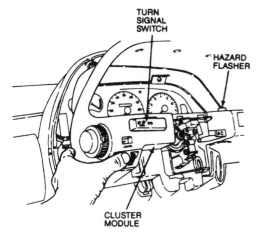

Cluster module removal and installation

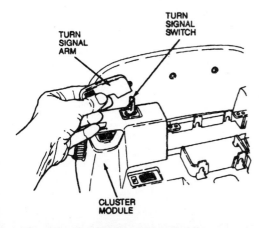

Turn signal arm removal and installation

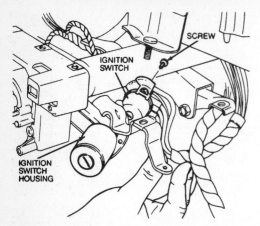

Ignition switch removal and installation—1989 Probe

nectors located to the left of the steering column.

8. Remove the protective loomin from the ignition switch wires.

9. Note the position of each wire in the 4-terminal connector for installation reference. Disconnect the 2 wires (green wire and red wire/orange tracer) of the key-in warning buzzer at the 4-terminal connector by disengaging the tang with a paperclip or other suitable tool.

To install:

10. Connect the 2 wires of the key-in warning buzzer to the 4-terminal connector as follows:

    a. Align the flat side of the wire end with the grooved portion of the connector.

    b. Push the wire into the connector until the locking tang engages the end of the wire.

11. Install the protective looming around the ignition switch wires.

12. Connect the 4 snap electrical connectors of the ignition switch to their mating connectors, pushing together until the locking tangs are in place.

13. Install the ignition switch into the switch housing and secure it with the screw.

14. Raise the steering column into position. Install the upper bracket bolts and tighten to 12–17 ft. lbs. (16–23 Nm).

15. Install the cluster support nuts and tighten to 6.5–10 ft. lbs. (8.8–14 Nm). Install the hinge bracket nuts and tighten to 12–17 ft. lbs. (16–23 Nm).

16. Install the lap duct and defroster duct.

17. Install the lower cluster cover panel and the cluster cover.

18. Install the ignition switch illumination bulb. Connect the electrical connectors and install the cluster module with the attaching screws.

19. Install the column cover and the steering wheel.

20. Connect the negative battery cable and check ignition switch operation.

1990 Vehicles

1. Disconnect the negative battery cable.

2. Remove the lower instrument cluster cover as follows:

    a. Remove the steering wheel.

    b. Remove the 2 column cover screws and the cover.

    c. Remove the 9 cluster module mounting screws.

    d. Carefully pull the cluster module outward and disconnect the electrical connectors.

    e. Remove the ignition switch illumination bulb and remove the cluster module.

    f. Loosen the 2 cover hinge screws and the 6 upper cluster cover screws. Remove the cover.

    g. Remove the lower cluster cover panel.

3. Loosen the shift cable nut retaining nut and allow the cable to hang down.

4. Remove the ignition switch mounting screw.

5. Disconnect the ignition switch wire connectors located to the left of the steering column.

6. Remove the protective looming from the ignition wires, note the position of each wire in the 4 terminal protector for replacing.

7. Disconnect the key-in warning buzzer wires (green wire and red wire/orange tracer) by disengaging the tang with a paper clip or other suitable tool.

8. Remove the ignition switch.

To install:

9. Connect the 2 wires of the key-in warning buzzer to the 4-terminal connector as follows:

    a. Align the flat side of the wire end with the grooved portion of the connector.

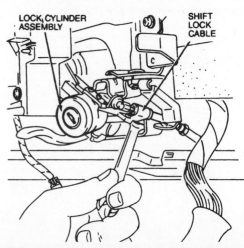

Ignition switch removal and installation—1990 Probe

b. Push the wire into the connector until the locking tang engages the end of the wire.

10. Install the protective looming around the ignition switch wires.

11. Connect the 4 snap electrical connectors of the ignition switch to their mating connectors, pushing together until the locking tangs are in place.

12. Install the ignition switch into the switch housing and secure it with the screw.

13. Position the shift lock cable and install the retaining nut.

14. Install the lower cluster cover panel and the cluster cover.

15. Install the ignition switch illumination bulb. Connect the electrical connectors and install the cluster module with the attaching screws.

16. Install the column cover and the steering wheel.

17. Connect the negative battery cable and check ignition switch operation.

1991–92 Vehicles

1. Disconnect the negative battery cable.

2. Remove the lower instrument cluster cover as follows:

a. Remove the steering wheel.

b. Remove the 2 column cover screws and the cover.

c. Remove the 9 cluster module mounting screws.

d. Carefully pull the cluster module outward and disconnect the electrical connectors.

e. Remove the ignition switch illumination bulb and remove the cluster module.

f. Loosen the 2 cover hinge screws and the 6 upper cluster cover screws. Remove the cover.

g. Remove the lower cluster cover panel.

3. If equipped with automatic transaxle, remove the shift-lock cable attaching bolt and disconnect the cable from the lock cylinder housing.

4. Remove the steering column lower panel and lower plate.

5. Remove the side register duct.

6. If equipped, remove the tilt lever through-bolt, tilt lever and attaching nuts. Remove the tilt lever housing attaching bolts and spring.

7. Disconnect the ignition switch electrical connectors and remove the ignition switch retaining screw.

8. Remove the retainers from the lock cylinder electrical connector and disconnect the connector from the lock cylinder housing.

9. Remove the ignition switch from the lock cylinder housing.

To install:

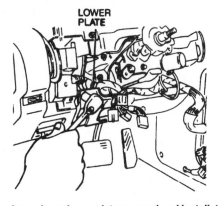

Steering column lower plate removal and installation

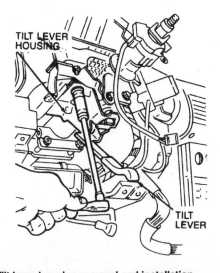

Tilt lever housing removal and installation

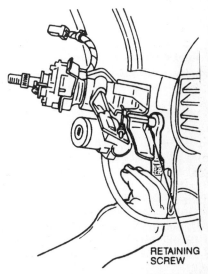

Ignition switch retaining screw removal and installation

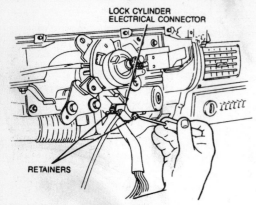

LOCK CYLINDER
ELECTRICAL CONNECTOR

RETAINERS

Lock cylinder electrical connector retainers removal and installation

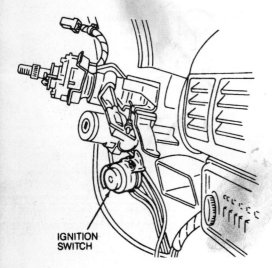

IGNITION
SWITCH

Ignition switch removal and installation

10. Install the electrical connector into the lock cylinder housing.

11. Install the electrical connector retainers onto the lock cylinder housing and connector.

12. Install the ignition switch into the lock cylinder housing and install the retaining screw.

13. Connect all other ignition switch electrical connectors.

14. If necessary, install the tilt lever housing attaching bolts and spring, and the tilt lever, through bolt, and attaching nuts.

15. Install the side register duct. Install the steering column lower plate and lower panel.

16. If equipped with automatic transaxle, connect the shift-lock cable to the lock cylinder housing and install the bracket attaching bolt.

17. Install the lower cluster cover panel and the cluster cover.

18. Install the ignition switch illumination bulb. Connect the electrical connectors and in-stall the cluster module with the attaching screws.

19. Install the column cover and the steering wheel.

20. Connect the negative battery cable and check ignition switch operation.

LIGHTING

Headlights

REMOVAL AND INSTALLATION

CAUTION: *The halogen headlight contains pressurized gas. It may shatter if the glass envelope is scratched or dropped. Handle the headlight carefully. Keep the headlight out of the reach of children.*

1. Extend the headlights and set the headlight rotary switch in the 4th position. The headlights should remain in the extended position with all lights extinguished.

NOTE: *If the power headlight door system becomes inoperative, your Probe is equipped with a manual retractor system that allows you to raise the headlights manually. To raise the headlights, reach up under the front fascia, remove the cap from the retractor handle, and turn the handle.*

2. Disconnect the negative battery cable.

3. Remove the attaching screws from the plastic bezel and remove the bezel from the headlight housing.

4. Remove the screws from the retaining collar and remove the retaining collar.

5. Pull the headlight out from the mounting bracket and disconnect the electrical connector at the back of the headlight.

To install:

6. Connect the electrical connector to the headlight and position the headlight against the mounting bracket.

7. Install the retaining collar and secure the collar and headlight with the screws.

8. Install the plastic bezel.

9. Connect the negative battery cable.

10. Turn the headlights **ON** and check if headlight aim has changed. Adjust if necessary, then turn the headlights **OFF**.

Signal and Marker Lights

REMOVAL AND INSTALLATION

Front Turn Signal and Parking Lights

1. Remove the attaching screws and partially remove the front parking light lens.

2. Remove the bulb socket and rubber gasket from the lens assembly by turning it in a counterclockwise direction.

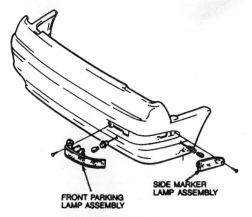

Front turn signal/parking light and front side marker light removal and installation

3. Remove the bulb from the socket by carefully pushing it in to clear the socket slots and twisting it counterclockwise.

4. Installation is the reverse of the removal procedure.

Front Side Marker Lights

1. Remove the attaching screws and partially remove the front side marker light lens.

2. Remove the bulb socket and rubber gasket from the lens by turning it in a clockwise direction.

3. Remove the bulb from the socket by carefully pushing it in to clear the socket slots and twisting it counterclockwise.

4. Installation is the reverse of the removal procedure.

Rear Turn Signal, Brake and Parking Lights

BULBS

1. Remove the plastic fasteners securing the trunk end trim panel and remove the panel (Refer to Chapter 10). Remove the right side upper trunk side garnish to gain access to the far right side bulb.

2. Carefully remove the desired socket wiring from its respective retaining clip and turn it counterclockwise to remove the socket.

3. Carefully push the bulb in far enough to clear the socket slots, turn it counterclockwise and remove.

4. Installation is the reverse of the removal procedure.

LENS

1. Remove the trunk end trim panel. Refer to Chapter 10.

2. Remove the upper trunk side garnish and lower trunk side trim from the side of the vehicle that needs to be removed.

3. Disconnect the rear light electrical connector.

4. Remove the attaching nuts from the light assembly.

5. Remove the light assembly and rubber gaskets from the vehicle. The light bulb sockets remain with the light housing during removal.

6. Installation is the reverse of the removal procedure.

High Mount Brake Light

BULB

1. Remove the service window cover from the lower liftgate trim panel.

2. Disconnect the high mount brake light electrical connector.

3. Turn the service arm counterclockwise and remove the bulb/socket assembly.

4. Remove the bulb from the socket by pulling it straight out.

5. Installation is the reverse of the removal procedure.

HOUSING

1. Remove the liftgate side trim panels and the lower liftgate trim panel. Refer to Chapter 10.

2. Remove the attaching nuts from the light

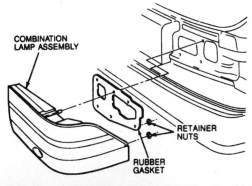

Rear turn signal, brake and parking light assembly removal and installation

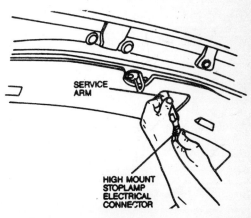

High mount brake light bulb removal and installation

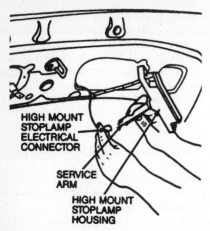

High mount brake light housing removal and installation

housing and carefully push in on the housing assembly.

3. Remove the housing and gasket assembly through the passenger side of the lift gate.

4. Disconnect the electrical connector.

5. Turn the service arm counterclockwise and remove the bulb/socket assembly.

6. Installation is the reverse of the removal procedure.

License Plate Lights

1. Loosen, but do not completely remove the attaching screws on the light lens. Remove the license plate lens assembly.

2. Remove the bulb by pulling it straight down and away from the socket.

3. Installation is the reverse of the removal procedure.

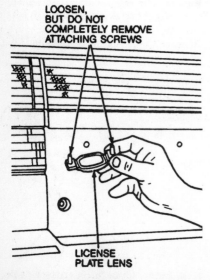

License plate light lens removal

Fog Lights
REMOVAL AND INSTALLATION

1. Disconnect the negative battery cable.

2. Remove the mounting nut from the fog light mounting bracket.

3. Remove the fog light housing and bracket as an assembly through the front fascia of the vehicle.

4. Remove the attaching screws from the fog light lens retaining brackets at the housing. Carefully remove the lens assembly from the housing, then disconnect the electrical connectors.

5. Remove the wire retaining rubber grommet from the housing and remove the wire harness from the housing.

6. Remove the mounting nut from the mounting bracket and remove the bracket from the fog light housing.

7. Remove the bulb as follows:

a. Carefully remove the rubber grommet from the lens assembly.

b. Release the bulb retaining bracket by pushing in on the release tabs and pulling up.

c. Remove the bulb assembly from the housing by pulling it straight out of the lens.

8. Installation is the reverse of the removal procedure. Make sure the bulb is correctly piloted into the lens assembly.

CAUTION: *The halogen fog light bulb con-*

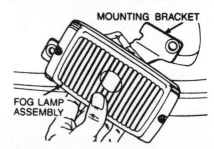

Fog light housing and bracket assembly removal and installation

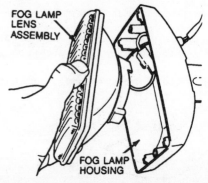

Separating the fog light lens assembly from the fog light housing

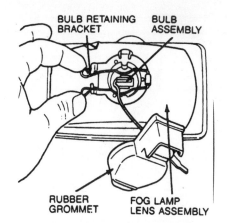

Releasing the fog light bulb retaining bracket

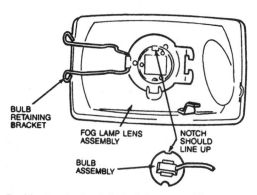

Positioning the fog light bulb for assembly

tains gas under pressure. The bulb may shatter if the glass envelope is scratched or the bulb is dropped. Handle the bulb carefully. Grasp the bulb only by its base. Avoid touching the glass envelope. Keep the bulb out of the reach of children.

TRAILER WIRING

Wiring the car for towing is fairly easy. There are a number of good wiring kits available and these should be used, rather than trying to design your own. All trailers will need brake lights and turn signals as well as tail lights and side marker lights. Most states require extra marker lights for overly wide trailers. Also, most states have recently required back-up lights for trailers, and most trailer manufacturers have been building trailers with back-up lights for several years.

Additionally, some Class I, most Class II and just about all Class III trailers will have electric brakes.

Add to this number an accessories wire, to operate trailer internal equipment or to charge the trailer's battery, and you can have as many as seven wires in the harness.

Determine the equipment on your trailer and buy the wiring kit necessary. The kit will contain all the wires needed, plus a plug adapter set which included the female plug, mounted on the bumper or hitch, and the male plug, wired into, or plugged into the trailer harness.

When installing the kit, follow the manufacturer's instructions. The color coding of the wires is standard throughout the industry.

One point to note, some domestic vehicles, and most imported vehicles, have separate turn signals. On most domestic vehicles, the brake lights and rear turn signals operate with the same bulb. For those vehicles with separate turn signals, you can purchase an isolation unit so that the brake lights won't blink whenever the turn signals are operated, or, you can go to your local electronics supply house and buy four diodes to wire in series with the brake and turn signal bulbs. Diodes will isolate the brake and turn signals. The choice is yours. The isolation units are simple and quick to install, but far more expensive than the diodes. The diodes, however, require more work to install properly, since they require the cutting of each bulb's wire and soldering in place of the diode.

One final point, the best kits are those with a spring loaded cover on the vehicle mounted socket. This cover prevents dirt and moisture from corroding the terminals. Never let the vehicle socket hang loosely. Always mount it securely to the bumper or hitch.

CIRCUIT PROTECTION

Fuses

The main fuse block is located inside the left side of the engine compartment near the battery. There is also an interior fuse panel located just above the left side kick panel.

REPLACEMENT

Main Fuse Block

EXCEPT 80 OR 100 AMP FUSE

1. Disconnect the negative battery cable.
2. Unhook the lock tab from the main fuse block cover and open the cover.
3. Pull the 10, 15, 30, 40, or 60 amp fuse from the main fuse holder.
4. Installation is the reverse of the removal procedure.

80 OR 100 AMP FUSE

1. Disconnect the negative battery cable.
2. Remove the mounting nuts from the main

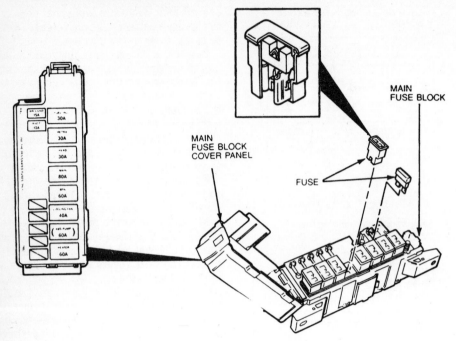

Fuse mounting—main fuse block

fuse block retaining bracket and slide the bracket off the mounting studs.

3. Unhook the lock tab from the main fuse block cover and open the cover.

4. Open the access cover on the left-hand side of the main fuse block.

5. Remove the bolts and terminal wire fastened to the right-hand side of the 80 or 100 amp fuse.

6. Remove the 80 or 100 amp fuse by pulling it straight out of the main fuse holder.

7. Installation is the reverse of the removal procedure.

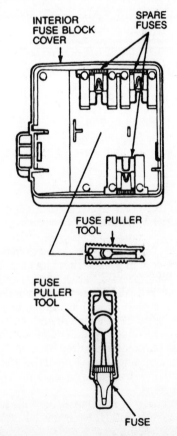

Interior fuse panel cover and fuse puller tool

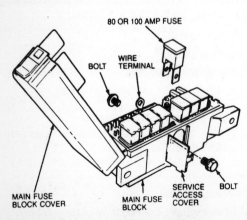

80 or 100 amp fuse removal and installation

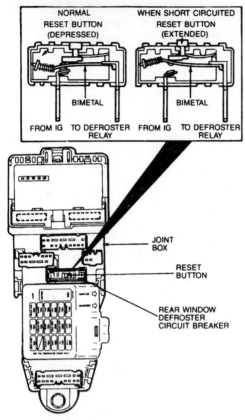

Rear window defroster circuit breaker location

Interior Fuse Panel

The interior fuses simply unplug from the fuse panel. Use the fuse puller tool provided with your car to remove fuses from the panel. The tool is located on the back of the interior fuse panel cover.

Circuit Breaker

A bimetal circuit breaker is located in the joint box, which is just above the interior fuse panel. This circuit breaker protects the rear window defrost circuit and is the plug-in type.

Relays

The main relay box is located on the upper left-hand side of the firewall (bulkhead). There is also a relay box mounted inside the vehicle under the left side of the instrument panel.

REPLACEMENT

1. Disconnect the negative battery cable.
2. If replacing a relay at the main relay box, disconnect the electrical connector and slide the relay from its mounting bracket.
3. If replacing a relay at the interior relay box, simply unplug the relay.
4. Installation is the reverse of the removal procedure.

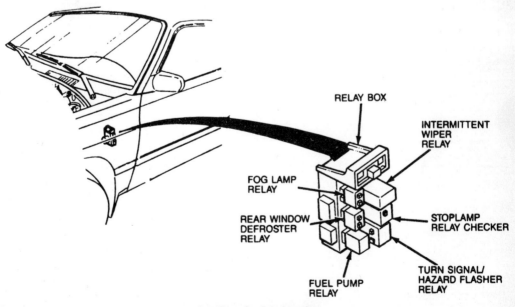

Interior relay box location

MAIN FUSE BLOCK FUSES
1989–90 VEHICLES

Fuse	Affect These Circuits
HEAD 30A (Main)	Headlight
BTN 60A (Main)	Front Fog Lamps, Glove Compartment Lamp, Parking Lamps, Front and Rear Marker Lamps, Tail Lamps, License Lamps, Illumination Lamps, Cargo Lamp, Stoplamps, High Mount Stop Lamp, Horn, Power Antenna, Turn and Hazard Flasher Lamps, Power Seat, Power Door Locks, 4EAT System, Sound Warning System, Heating and Air Conditioning (Electronic Control)
MAIN 80A (Main)	Charging System, Remote Control Mirror, Audio System, Cigar Lighter, Air Conditioner, Programmed Ride Control System, Front Wiper and Washer, Rear Wiper and Washer, Backup Lamps, Cruise Control System, Meter and Warning Lights, Electronically Controlled Power Steering System, Emission and Fuel Control System, Rear Window Defroster, Power Window, Ignition System, Vehicle Maintenance Monitor (VMM), System Scanner (Electronic Cluster)
RETRA 30A (Main)	Headlamp Retractors
ABS PUMP 60A (Main)	ABS Control System
FUEL INJ. 30A (Main)	Emission and fuel injection
AIR COND 15A (Main)	Air Conditioning Compressor, Magnetic Clutch Control System
AUDIO 10A (Main)	Audio System
COOLING FAN 40A (Main)	Cooling Fan System
HEATER 60A (Main)	Heater Control System

The fuses are color-coded by amp rating

Fuse Value Amps	Color Code
30	Pink
40	Green
60	Yellow
80	Black

MAIN FUSE BLOCK FUSES
1991–92 VEHICLES

Main Fuse Panel			
Fuse	Amps	Wire Color	Circuit Protected
Fuel Inj.	30A	BR	Electronic Engine Controls, Charging System, Meter & Warning System
Retra.	30A	BK/W	Headlamp Retractors
Head	30A	R	Headlamps
Main	80A (GL) 100A (GT/LX)	BK	All Circuits (except Starter Motor/Relay)
BTN	60A	W/R	Door Lock, Stop, Hazard, Room, Belt, Cigar, Power Seat & Tail Fuses
Cooling Fan	40A	BK/R	Cooling System, Charging System & Electronic Engine Controls
ABS Pump	60A (GT/LX)	BL/R	Anti-lock Brake System
Heater	40A	BL	Heating, AC & Programmed Ride Control System
St. Sign (Start Signal)	15A (GL/GT)	BK/PK	ECA, Fuel Pump Relay
Fog	15A (GT)	R/W	Fog Lamps
Wiper	20A	BK/R	Front Wiper/Washer
Air Cond./ Fuel Pump	20A	GN	Heating, Air Conditioner & Electronic Engine Controls
Audio	15A	GN/W	Radio, Hood, Lamp & Remote Control Mirrors

Amps	Color Code
15	Light Blue
20	Yellow
30	Pink
40	Green
60	Yellow
80	Black
100	Blue

INTERIOR FUSE PANEL FUSES
1989–90 VEHICLES

Fuse	Affect These Circuits
POWER SEAT 30A	Power Seats
POWER WIND 30A	Power Windows
TAIL 15A	Glove Compartment Lamp, Parking Lamps, Side Marker Lamps, Tail Lamps, License Lamps, Rear Side Marker Lamps, Illumination Lamps
ROOM 10A	Sound Warning System, 4EAT Control System, Luggage Compartment Lamp, Audio, Illumination, Power Antenna, Engine Control System, VMM System
EIC 10A	Instrument Cluster, VMM System
REAR WIPER 15A	Rear Wiper and Washer
RADIO 15A	Remote Control Mirrors, Audio/Power Antenna (Up/Down Action when Radio is Turned On/Off)
FOG 15A	Front Fog Lights
METER 15A	Backup Lamps, Power Antenna, Sound Warning System, Rear Window Defroster, 4EAT Control System, Cruise Control System, Cooling Fan Control System
DOOR LOCK 30A	Power Door Locks
COOLING FAN 20A	Cooling Fan Control System (Add Fan Relay No. 1)
WIPER 20A	Front Wiper and Washer
CIGAR 15A	Cigar Lighter
HAZARD 10A	Turn Signal and Hazard Flasher Lamps
TURN 10A	Power Steering Control (Electronically Controlled), ABS Control System, Turn Signal and Hazard Flasher Lamps
STOP 20A	Brake Lamps, High Mount Brake Lamp, Horns
ENGINE 15A	Main Relay No. 1 and No. 2, Fuel Pump Relay, Electronic Control Unit, Ignition Relay
MONITOR 7.5A	VMM System
DEFOG 30A Circuit Breaker	Rear Window Defroster

The fuses are color-coded by amp rating

Fuse Value Amps	Color Code
7.5	Amber
10	Red
15	Light Blue
20	Yellow
30	Light Green

INTERIOR FUSE PANEL FUSES
1991–92 VEHICLES

Fuse	Amps	Circuits Protected
1. Radio	15A	Radio, Warning/Chime, Power Antenna & Front Wiper/Washer
2. Power Window	30A	Power Window
3. Engine	15A	Fuel Pump Relay, Cooling Fan System, AC-Heating & Meter/Warning & ECA
4. Meter	15A	Shift-lock Control System, ECA, Meter/Warning Passive Restraint System, Backup Lamp, Rear Window Defroster, Heater/AC System, Programmed Ride Control, Speed Control, Radio & 4EAT System
5. Power Seat	30A	Sound Warning, Power Seat & Power Door Lock
6. Monitor	7.5A	Meter/Warning
7. Turn	10A	Turn/Hazard, ABS Control System & Power Steering Control System
9. Tail	15A	Headlamps, Illumination Lamps, Tail/License/Side Marker & Parking Lamps
10. Belt	30A	Passive Restraint System
11. Cigar	15A	Meter/Warning & Cigar Lighter
12. Rear Wiper	15A	Liftgate Wiper & Washer
13. Door Lock	20A	Power Door Lock
14. Stop	20A	ECA, Stoplamps, Speed Control, Horn & 4EAT
15. Hazard	15A	Turn/Hazard
16. Room	10A	Shift-lock Control, ECA, Meter/Warning, Luggage Compartment Lamp, Sound Warning, Power Antenna, Audio System, Illuminated Entry & Interior Lighting
17. Engine 2	15A	HEGO
18. Cooling Fan	15A	Meter/Warning (Display), DRL & Heater/AC
19. Defog (C.B.)	30A	Rear Window Defroster

Fuse Value Amps	Color Code
4	Pink
5	Tan
7.5	Brown
10	Red
15	Light Blue
20	Yellow
25	Natural
30	Light Green

RELAY LOCATIONS

RELAY AND UNIT	LOCATION	NUMBER
Turn Signal/Hazard Flasher Relay	Under dash panel	—
Stop and Tail Lamp Checker Relay	Under dash panel	—
Intermittent Wiper Relay	Under dash panel	—
Fuel Pump Relay	Under dash panel	—
Rear Defroster Relay	Under dash panel	—
Fog Lamp Relay	Under dash panel	—
EFI Main Relay	On the bulkhead	I
EFI Main Relay	On the bulkhead	II
Cooling Fan Relay No. 1*	On the bulkhead	III
Horn Relay	On the bulkhead	—
Cooling Fan Relay No. 2	On the bulkhead	—

*Cooling Fan Relay No. 1 is only for models equipped with 4EAT

Drive Train

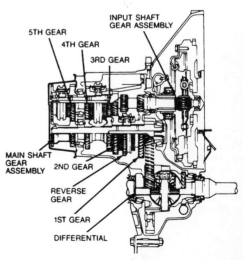

UNDER-STANDING THE MANUAL TRANSMISSION

Because of the way an internal combustion engine breathes, it can produce torque, or twisting force, only within a narrow speed range. Most modern engines must turn betwen 2500 and 3500 rpm to produce their peak torque. By 4500 rpm they are producing so little torque that continued increases in engine speed produce no power increases.

The torque peak on overhead camshaft engines is, generally, much higher, but much narrower.

The manual transmission and clutch are employed to vary the relationship between engine speed and the speed of the wheels so that adequate engine power can be produced under all circumstances. The clutch allows engine torque to be applied to the transmission input shaft gradually, due to mechanical slippage. The car can, consequently, be started smoothly from a full stop.

The transmission changes the ratio between the rotating speeds of the engine and the wheels by the use of gears. 4-speed or 5-speed transmissions are most common. The gear ratios allow full engine power to be applied to the wheels during acceleration at low speeds and at highway/passing speeds.

The transmission contains a mainshaft which passes all the way through the transmission, from the clutch to the differential. This shaft is separated at one point, so that front and rear portions can turn at different speeds.

Power is transmitted by a countershaft in the lower gears and reverse. The gears of the countershaft mesh with gears on the mainshaft, allowing power to be carried from one to the other. All the countershaft gears are integral with that shaft, while several of the mainshaft gears can either rotate independently of the shaft or

be locked to it. Shifting from one gear to the next causes one of the gears to be freed from rotating with the shaft and locks another to it. Gears are locked and unlocked by internal dog clutches which slide between the center of the gear and the shaft. The forward gears usually employ synchronizers; friction members which smoothly bring gear and shaft to the same speed before the toothed dog clutches are engaged.

MANUAL TRANSAXLE

General Information

There are two types of 5-speed manual transaxles used in the Probe. One type is for the 2.2L turbocharged and 3.0L engines and has special design features which enable it to handle the higher torque output of these engines. The other type is used only with the 2.2L non-turbocharged engine.

Cut-away view of the manual transaxle—2.2L non-turbocharged engine

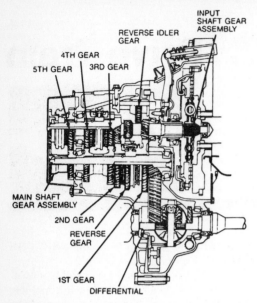

Cut-away view of the manual transaxle—2.2L turbo-charged and 3.0L engines

Both types have reverse gear synchromesh shifting and the 5th/reverse clutch hub assembly on the input shaft. The helical cut forward gears are in constant mesh with the corresponding gears on the opposing shaft. The forward gears are selected by means of a synchronizer mechanism. 3rd, 4th and 5th gears are mounted on the input shaft. First, 2nd and reverse gears are mounted on the main shaft. The reverse gears have straight cut teeth and are engaged through the reverse idler gear by means of a synchronizer mechanism.

The transaxle used with the 2.2L turbocharged and 3.0L engines has 3 separate shift rods for 1st/2nd, 3rd/4th and 5th/reverse, and uses needle bearings to reduce the sliding resistance of the forward gears.

Back-up Light Switch

REMOVAL & INSTALLATION

1. Disconnect the negative battery cable.
2. Raise and safely support the vehicle.
3. Drain the transaxle fluid. Refer to Chapter 1.
4. Disconnect the back-up light switch electrical connector.
5. Remove the back-up light switch and discard the gasket.

To install:

6. Install the back-up light switch using a new gasket. Tighten the switch to 15–21 ft. lbs. (20–29 Nm).
7. Connect the back-up light switch electrical connector.

8. Fill the transaxle with fluid to the proper level. Refer to Chapter 1.
9. Lower the vehicle and connect the negative battery cable. Check for proper operation.

Transaxle

REMOVAL & INSTALLATION

1. Disconnect the battery cables, negative cable first. Remove the battery and the battery tray.
2. Disconnect the main fuse block and disconnect the coil wire from the distributor. Disconnect and mark the wiring assembly, as necessary.
3. Disconnect the electrical connector from the air flow meter and remove the air cleaner assembly.
4. On 2.2L non-turbocharged engine, remove the resonance chamber and bracket. On 2.2L turbocharged engine, remove the throttle body-to-intercooler air hose and the air cleaner-to-turbocharger air hose.
5. Disconnect the speedometer cable (analog cluster) or cluster harness (electronic cluster).
6. If equipped with the 3.0L engine, drain the engine coolant and close the drain valve. Remove the upper radiator hose.
7. Disconnect both ground wires from the transaxle. Raise and safely support the vehicle.
8. Remove the front wheel and tire assemblies and the splash shields. Drain the transaxle.
9. Remove the slave cylinder and move it aside.
10. Remove the tie rod ends-to-steering knuckle cotter pins and nuts. Disconnect the tie rod ends from the steering knuckle.
11. Remove the stabilizer link assemblies from the lower control arm.
12. Remove the lower control ball joint-to-steering knuckle nut/bolt. Using a prybar, pry the lower control arm downward to separate the ball joint from the steering knuckle.
13. Remove the right-hand joint shaft bracket.

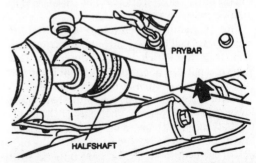

Using a prybar to remove the halfshaft from the transaxle

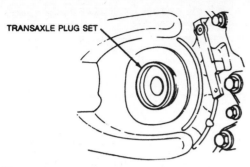

Transaxle plug positioning

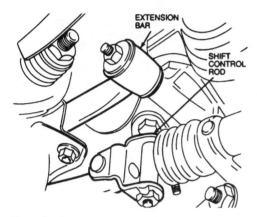

Extension bar and shift control rod

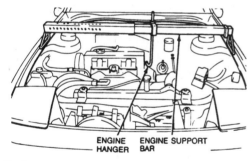

Engine support bar positioning

14. Position a prybar between the halfshaft and transaxle case; pry the halfshafts from the transaxle and suspend them on a wire.

15. Install 2 transaxle plugs, T88C–7025–AH or equivalent, between the differential side gears to keep the gears from becoming mispositioned.

16. Remove the gusset plate-to-transaxle bolts on 2.2L engine. Disconnect the extension bar and shift control rod.

17. Remove the front exhaust pipe on the 3.0L engine.

18. Remove the flywheel inspection plate on the 2.2L engine.

19. Remove the starter motor and the access brackets.

20. Attach engine support bar D87L–6000–A or equivalent to the engine and support its weight.

21. Remove the center transaxle mount and bracket, the left transaxle mount and the right transaxle mount-to-frame nut and bolt.

22. Remove the crossmember and the left-hand side lower arm as an assembly.

23. Attach and secure a suitable jack to the transaxle.

24. Remove the transaxle-to-engine bolts, lower the transaxle and remove it from the vehicle.

To install:

25. Apply a small amount of grease to the input shaft splines.

26. Raise and position the transaxle. Install the transaxle-to-engine bolts and torque to 66–86 ft. lbs. (89–117 Nm).

27. Install the center transaxle mount and bracket and torque the bolts to 27–40 ft. lbs. (36–54 Nm) and the nuts to 47–66 ft. lbs. (64–89 Nm).

NOTE: *Do not install the nut that braces the throttle air inlet hose bracket.*

28. Install the left transaxle mount and torque the left transaxle-to-mount bolts on the 2.2L non-turbocharged engine to 27–38 ft. lbs. (37–52 Nm) or on the 2.2L turbocharged engine and 3.0L engine to 49–69 ft. lbs. (67–93 Nm). Torque the mount-to-bracket nut and bolt to 49–69 ft. lbs. (67–93 Nm).

29. Install the crossmember and the left side lower arm as an assembly. Tighten the bolts to 27–40 ft. lbs. (36–54 Nm) and the nuts to 55–69 ft. lbs. (75–93 Nm).

30. Install the right transaxle mount bolt and nut and tighten to 63–86 ft. lbs. (85–117 Nm).

31. Install the starter motor and access brackets.

32. Install the flywheel inspection cover on

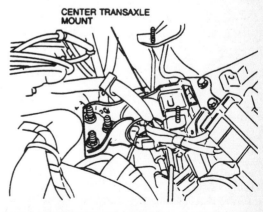

Center transaxle mount location

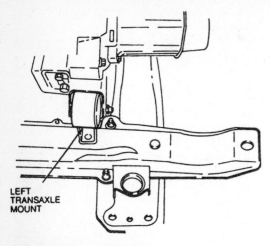

Left transaxle mount location

2.2L engine. Tighten the bolts to 69–95 inch lbs. (8–11 Nm).

33. Connect the extension rod and control rod. Install the front exhaust pipe on 3.0L engine.

34. Install the slave cylinder and tighten the bolts to 14–19 ft. lbs. (19–26 Nm).

35. Install the gusset plate-to-transaxle bolts on the 2.2L engine and tighten to 27–38 ft. lbs. (37–52 Nm).

36. On the end of each halfshaft, install a new circlip. This must be done whenever halfshafts are serviced.

37. Remove the transaxle plugs and install the halfshaft until the clips snap into place. Attach the lower arm ball joints to the knuckles.

38. Install and torque the tie rod end-to-steering knuckle nut to 22–33 ft. lbs. (29–44 Nm) and install a new cotter pin. Tighten the lower control arm ball joint-to-steering knuckle nut and bolt to 32–40 ft. lbs. (43–54 Nm).

39. Install the stabilizer link assembly-to-lower control arm. Turn the upper nuts (on each

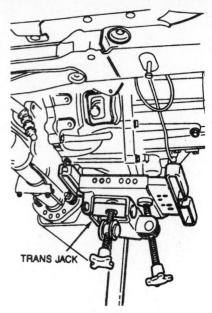

Supporting the transaxle with a jack

assembly) until 0.79 in. (20mm) of bolt thread can be measured above the nuts.

40. Install the splash shields and the front wheel and tire assemblies; torque the lug nuts to 65–87 ft. lbs. (88–118 Nm). Lower the vehicle.

41. Connect the ground wires to the transaxle case and tighten to 69–95 inch lbs. (8–11 Nm).

42. On the 2.2L non-turbocharged engine, install the resonance chamber and bracket; torque to 69–95 inch lbs. (8–11 Nm). On turbocharged engines, install the throttle body-to-intercooler air hose and torque the bracket-to-mount nut to 47–66 ft. lbs. (64–89 Nm).

43. On 3.0L engine, install the upper radiator hose and fill the cooling system.

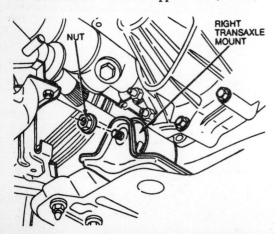

Right transaxle mount nut removal and installation

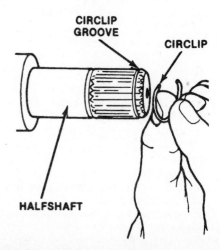

Installing a new circlip on the halfshaft

44. Install the air cleaner assembly and tighten to 69–95 inch lbs. (8–11 Nm).

45. Connect the electrical connector to the air flow meter. Connect the previously marked wiring assembly, if disconnected.

46. Reconnect the main fuse block and connect the coil wire to the distributor.

47. Remove the engine support bracket.

48. Connect the speedometer cable or harness, as applicable.

49. Install the battery tray, battery and connect the battery cables.

50. Refill the transaxle assembly. Connect the negative battery cable, start the engine and check for leaks.

Halfshafts

REMOVAL & INSTALLATION

1. Disconnect the negative battery cable. Raise and safely support the vehicle.

2. Remove the front wheel and tire assembly and the necessary inner fender splash guards.

3. Remove the stabilizer link assembly from the lower control arm.

4. Using a cape chisel and a hammer, raise the staked portion of the hub nut.

5. Using an assistant to depress the brake pedal, loosen, do not remove, the hub nut.

6. Remove the lower control arm ball joint clamp bolt. Using a prybar, pry the lower control arm downward to separate the ball joint from the steering knuckle.

NOTE: *If removing the right halfshaft, remove the dynamic damper from the cylinder block.*

7. Separate the halfshaft from the transaxle as follows:

a. Pull outward on the steering knuckle/brake assembly to separate the halfshaft from the transaxle. To prevent damage to the transaxle oil seal, do not pull the halfshaft all the way out of the transaxle. Apply only enough force to loosen the shaft from the differential side gear.

b. If the halfshafts are difficult to remove, a pry bar can be used to loosen it from the dif-

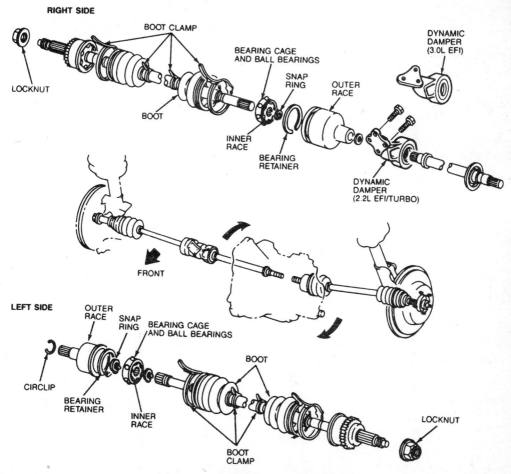

Halfshaft assemblies—manual transaxle

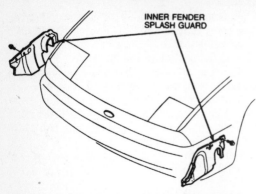

Inner fender splash guard removal and installation

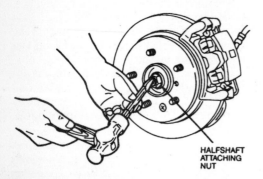

Raising the staked portion of the halfshaft attaching nut

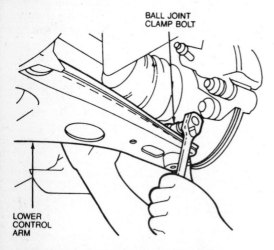

Ball joint clamp bolt removal and installation

ferential side gear. Insert the bar between the halfshaft and the transaxle case. Lightly tap on the end of the bar until the halfshaft loosens from the differential side gear.

WARNING: *Be extremely careful. Make sure the prybar does not damage the transaxle case, transaxle oil seal, CV-joint or CV-joint boot.*

8. Remove and discard the hub nut. Pull the halfshaft out of the wheel hub.

NOTE: *If the halfshaft binds in the hub splines, use a plastic hammer to tap it out or a wheel puller to press it out. Never use a metal hammer.*

9. Support the halfshaft and slide it out of the transaxle. Be careful not to damage the transaxle oil seal.

10. Install differential plug T87C–7025–C or equivalent into the halfshaft openings of the transaxle case; this will keep the differential side gears from becoming mispositioned.

To install:

11. On the end of each halfshaft, install a new circlip. Start 1 end of the clip in the groove and work the clip over the stub shaft end and into

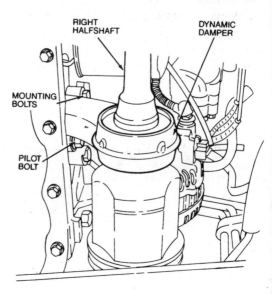

Dynamic damper location

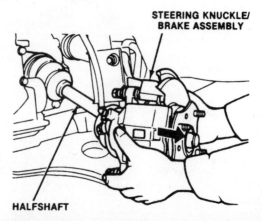

Pulling outward on the steering knuckle/brake assembly to separate the halfshaft from the transaxle

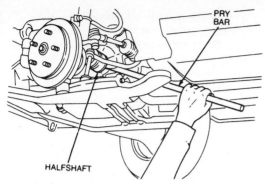

Using a prybar to separate the halfshaft from the transaxle

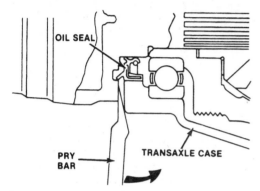

Correct positioning of the pyrbar between the half-shaft and transaxle case

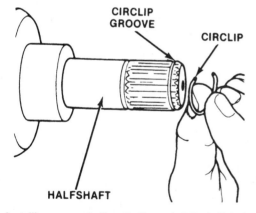

Installing a new circlip onto the end of the halfshaft

the groove. This will prevent over-expanding the clip.

12. Remove the transaxle plugs and inspect the transaxle oil seals. If they show any signs of wear or damage, they must be replaced.

13. Lubricate the halfshaft splines with a suitable grease, align the splines with the differential side gears and push the halfshaft into the differential. Make sure the circlip gap is positioned at the top of the splines. When it seats

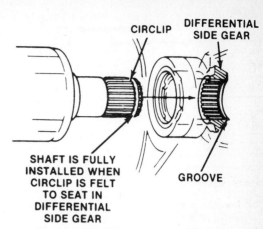

Installing the halfshaft into the differential

properly, the circlip can be felt as it snaps into the differential side gear groove.

14. Position the halfshaft through the wheel hub and install a new attaching nut. Do not tighten the nut at this time.

NOTE: *If installing the right halfshaft, install the dynamic damper and tighten the mounting bolts to 31–46 ft. lbs. (42–62 Nm).*

15. Position the lower control arm ball joint into the steering knuckle and install the clamp bolt/nut. Tighten the nut to 32–40 ft. lbs. (43–54 Nm).

16. Install the stabilizer link assemblies. Turn the nuts until 0.79 in. (20mm) of bolt thread can be measured from the upper nut.

17. Install the splash shields.

18. Tighten the halfshaft attaching nut to 116–174 ft. lbs. (157–235 Nm). Stake the nut using a suitable chisel with a rounded cutting edge.

NOTE: *If the nut splits or cracks after staking, it must be replaced with a new nut.*

19. Install the wheel and tire assembly and lower the vehicle.

CLUTCH

CAUTION: *The clutch driven disc contains asbestos, which has been determined to be a cancer causing agent. Never clean clutch surfaces with compressed air! Avoid inhaling any dust from any clutch surface! When cleaning clutch surfaces, use a commercially available brake cleaning fluid.*

The purpose of the clutch is to disconnect and connect engine power at the transmission. A car at rest requires a lot of engine torque to get all that weight moving. An internal combustion engine does not develop a high starting torque (unlike steam engines), so it must be allowed to

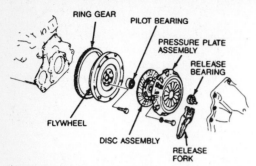

Clutch assembly components

operate without any load until it builds up enough torque to move the car. Torque increases with engine rpm. The clutch allows the engine to build up torque by physically disconnecting the engine from the transmission, relieving the engine of any load or resistance. The transfer of engine power to the transmission (the load) must be smooth and gradual; if it weren't, drive line components would wear out or break quickly. This gradual power transfer is made possible by gradually releasing the clutch pedal. The clutch disc and pressure plate are the connecting link between the engine and transmission. When the clutch pedal is released, the disc and plate contact each other (clutch engagement), physically joining the engine and transmission. When the pedal is pushed in, the disc and plate separate (the clutch is disengaged), disconnecting the engine from the transmission.

The Probe clutch is a single plate, dry friction disc with a diaphragm-style spring pressure plate. The clutch disc has a splined hub which attaches the disc to the input shaft. The disc has friction material where it contacts the flywheel and pressure plate. Torsion springs on the disc help absorb engine torque pulses. The pressure plate applies pressure to the clutch disc, holding it tight against the surface of the flywheel. The diaphragm spring is located between two fulcrum rings riveted to the clutch cover. The clutch operating mechanism consists of a release bearing, fork and cylinder. The release fork and slave cylinder transfer pedal motion to the release bearing. In the engaged position, the diaphragm spring holds the pressure plate against the clutch disc, so engine torque is transmitted to the input shaft. When the clutch pedal is depressed, the release bearing pushes the diaphragm spring center toward the flywheel. The diaphragm spring pivots the fulcrum, relieving the load on the pressure plate. Steel spring straps riveted to the clutch cover lift the pressure plate from the clutch disc, disengaging the engine drive from the transaxle and enabling the gears to be changed.

The hydraulic clutch control system consists of a fluid reservoir, master cylinder, slave cylinder and pressure line. The clutch master cylinder and reservoir are mounted on the firewall

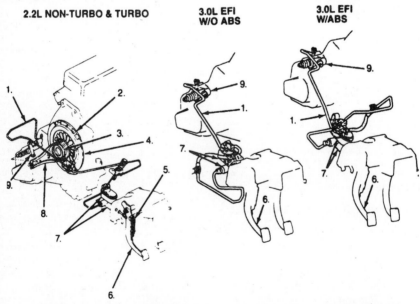

2.2L NON-TURBO & TURBO   **3.0L EFI W/O ABS**   **3.0L EFI W/ABS**

1. Pressure line	4. Disc assembly	7. Clutch master cylinder and reservoir	8. Release fork
2. Pressure plate assembly	5. Spring		9. Slave cylinder
3. Release bearing	6. Clutch pedal		

Clutch hydraulic system

(bulkhead). Fluid level is checked at the reservoir.

The clutch master cylinder converts mechanical clutch pedal movement into hydraulic fluid movement. The fluid pressure is transmitted down the pressure line to the slave cylinder. The slave cylinder is mounted on the transaxle. It converts the hydraulic fluid movement to mechanical movement, allowing the release fork and bearing to engage and disengage the clutch.

Adjustments

PEDAL HEIGHT

1. To determine if the pedal height requires an adjustment, measure the distance from the bulkhead to the upper center of the pedal pad. The distance should be 8.524–8.720 in. (216.5–221.5mm).

2. To adjust, remove the lower dash panel and the air ducts.

3. Loosen the locknut and turn the stopper bolt until the pedal height is within specification.

4. Tighten the locknut.

5. Install the ducts and the lower dash panel.

PEDAL FREE PLAY

1. To determine if the pedal free play needs adjustment, measure the free play. The free play should be 0.20–0.51 in. (5–13mm).

2. To adjust, remove the lower dash panel and the air ducts.

3. Loosen the locknut and turn the pushrod until the pedal play is within specification.

4. Measure the distance from the floor to the center of the pedal pad when the pedal is fully depressed. The distance should be 2.7 in. (68mm) or more.

5. Tighten the locknut and install the lower dash panel and the air ducts.

Driven Disc and Pressure Plate
REMOVAL & INSTALLATION

1. Disconnect the negative battery cable. Raise and safely support the vehicle.

2. Remove the transaxle assembly. Refer to the procedure in this Chapter.

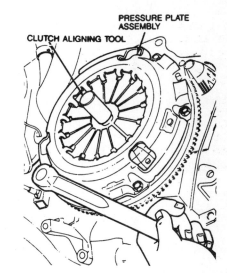

Pressure plate removal and installation

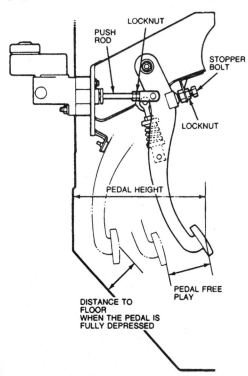

Clutch pedal height and free play

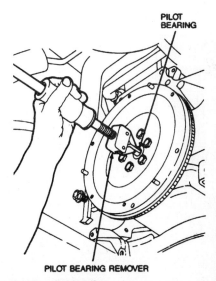

Removing the pilot bearing

3. Position a suitable clutch alignment tool through the pressure plate, clutch disc and into the pilot bearing; this will keep the assembly from dropping when the bolts are removed.

4. Use a suitable tool to keep the flywheel from turning. Remove the pressure plate-to-flywheel bolts, a little at a time, evenly, to relieve the spring pressure.

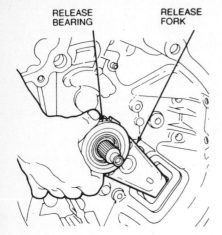

Release bearing and fork removal and installation

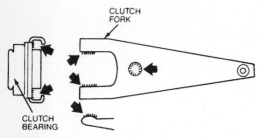

Lubricate these areas on the release bearing and fork

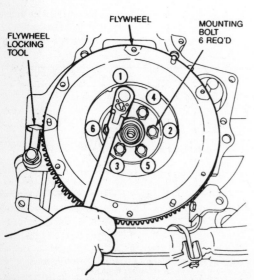

Flywheel bolt torque sequence

5. Remove the pressure plate, clutch disc and alignment tool.

6. Inspect the pressure plate and clutch disc for wear and/or damage and replace, as necessary.

7. Inspect the pilot bearing for excessive wear or scoring. Remove it, using a suitable puller, only if replacement is necessary.

8. Inspect the flywheel for scoring, cracks, worn or broken teeth, or other damage. Remove the flywheel if machining or replacement is necessary. Use care when removing the last bolt to prevent dropping the flywheel.

9. Remove the release bearing and fork. Inspect them for wear or damage and replace, as necessary

To install:

10. Apply clutch grease to the release bearing and release fork in the areas as shown in the illustration.

11. Install the release fork and bearing.

12. If removed, install the flywheel. Make sure the crankshaft flange and flywheel mating surfaces are clean. Tighten the flywheel bolts, in sequence, to 71–76 ft. lbs. (96–103 Nm) on

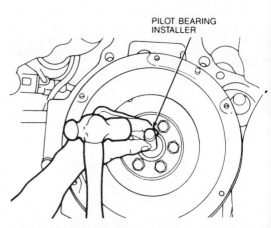

Installing the pilot bearing

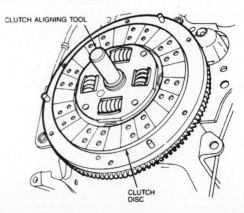

Proper positioning of the clutch disc

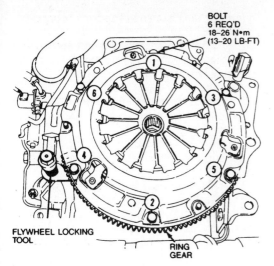

Pressure plate bolt torque sequence

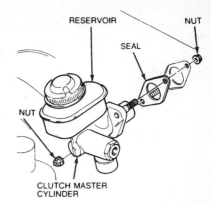

Clutch master cylinder removal and installation

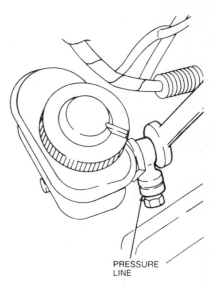

Disconnecting the pressure line from the master cylinder

2.2L engines or 54–64 ft. lbs. (73–87 Nm) on the 3.0L engine.

13. If removed, install a new pilot bearing using a suitable installation tool. When installed, the pilot bearing should be 0.150–0.165 in. (3.8–4.2mm) below the surface of the crankshaft flange.

14. Apply a small amount of clutch grease to the clutch disc and input shaft splines. Do not let grease get on the clutch face.

15. Install the clutch disc and alignment tool. Make sure the disc is facing the direction shown.

16. Install the pressure plate to the flywheel. Install the pressure plate-to-flywheel bolts and torque, evenly, a little at a time, to 13–20 ft. lbs. (18–26 Nm) in the proper sequence.

17. Install the transaxle assembly and lower the vehicle.

18. Connect the negative battery cable. Check for proper clutch operation.

Master Cylinder
REMOVAL & INSTALLATION

WARNING: *Clutch master cylinder fluid will damage painted surfaces, so be sure to use a container or rags to collect it. If any fluid gets on a painted surface, wipe it off immediately with a rag.*

1. Disconnect the negative battery cable. Remove the ABS relay box, if equipped.

2. Disconnect the pressure line to the cylinder, using the proper wrench.

3. Remove the mounting nuts and remove the clutch master cylinder.
To install:

4. Install the clutch master cylinder and

tighten the mounting nuts to 14–19 ft. lbs. (19–26 Nm).

5. Connect the pressure line and tighten the nut securely.

6. Install the ABS relay box, if equipped.

7. Bleed the air from the clutch system. Follow the procedure in this Chapter.

8. Connect the negative battery cable and check for proper operation.

OVERHAUL

1. While overhauling the master cylinder, work in a clean area and keep all components as clean as possible.

2. Press down on the piston and cup assembly with a suitable tool and remove the retaining snapring.

3. Remove the piston and cup assembly by blowing compressed air through the pressure line passage. Place a rag over the bore opening

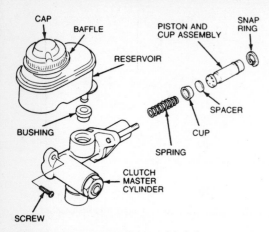

Clutch master cylinder disassembled view

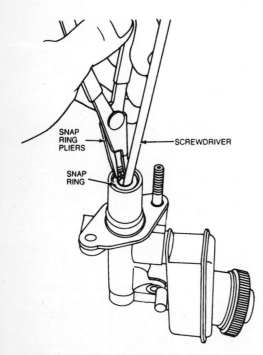

Snapring removal and installation

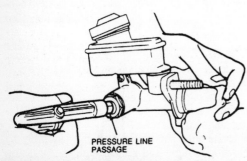

Piston and cup assembly removal

to prevent the piston and cup from being ejected too fast.

4. Remove the spacer, cup and spring. Remove the reservoir attaching screw, the reservoir and mounting bushing. Remove the cap and baffle.

5. Clean and inspect all components. If the cylinder bore is pitted, replace the complete cylinder.

6. Install a new bushing and the reservoir, baffle and cap. Install the reservoir attaching screw.

7. Apply clean fluid to the cylinder bore and cups. Install the spring, new cup, spacer and new piston and cup assembly into the bore. Press the piston and cup assembly into the bore with a suitable tool and install the snapring.

Slave Cylinder
REMOVAL & INSTALLATION

1. Disconnect the negative battery cable.
2. Disconnect the pressure line at the slave cylinder. Plug the pressure line to prevent leaking.
3. Remove the slave cylinder mounting bolts and remove the slave cylinder.

To install:

4. Install the slave cylinder and tighten the mounting bolts to 12–17 ft. lbs. (16–23 Nm).
5. Connect the pressure line and tighten the nut to 10–16 ft. lbs. (13–22 Nm).
6. Connect the negative battery cable.
7. Bleed the air from the clutch system. Follow the procedure in this Chapter.
8. Check for proper operation.

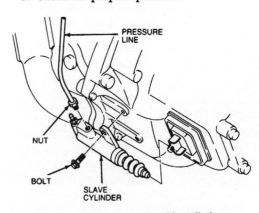

Clutch slave cylinder removal and installation

OVERHAUL

1. Pull off the push rod and boot.
2. Remove the piston and cup assembly by blowing compressed air through the pressure line passage. Place a rag over the bore opening

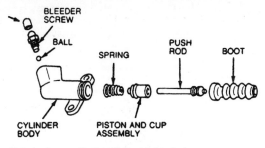

Clutch slave cylinder disassembled view

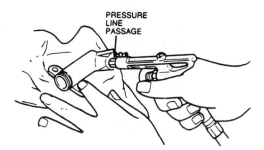

Piston and cup assembly removal

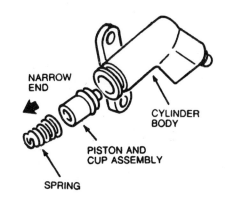

Proper positioning of the spring

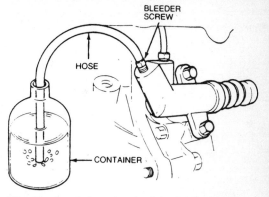

Bleeding the air from the clutch hydraulic system

2. Place the other end of the hose in a container.

3. Slowly, pump the clutch pedal several times.

4. With the clutch pedal depressed, loosen the bleeder screw to release the fluid and air.

5. Tighten the bleeder screw. Repeat this procedure until there are no air bubbles in the fluid in the container.

AUTOMATIC TRANSAXLE

General Information

The 4EAT Electronically Controlled Automatic Transaxle is installed in the Probe. It features a combination of electronic and mechanical systems for controlling forward gear shifting and torque converter lockup, for quietness and economy. A manual switch is provided to allow the transaxle to be manually shifted while driving on steep, slippery, or dangerous roads.

The 4EAT has a single compact combination-type planetary gear with 4-speed capability. It also features a variable-capacity oil pump which provides a constant oil quantity at and above a medium speed, and reduces the power losses resulting from pumping more oil than necessary at higher speeds.

The electronic system controls the transmission shifting in forward speeds and torque converter lockup by means of solenoid operated valves. When energized, the solenoid valves actuate the clutches and bands to control shifting in the planetary gear. Shift timing and lockup are regulated by the 4EAT control unit in programmed logic and in response to various input sensors and switches.

Fluid Pan

For automatic transaxle fluid pan removal and installation, and filter service procedures,

to prevent the piston and cup from being ejected too fast.

3. Remove the spring, bleeder cap and screw, and the ball.

4. Clean and inspect all components. If the cylinder bore is pitted, replace the complete cylinder.

5. Install the ball, bleeder screw and cap. Install the spring with the narrow end facing the piston and cup assembly, as shown.

6. Install a new piston and cup assembly. Install the pushrod and boot.

HYDRAULIC SYSTEM BLEEDING

NOTE: *The fluid in the master cylinder reservoir must be maintained at the ¾ level or higher during air bleeding.*

1. Remove the bleeder cap from the slave cylinder and attach a hose to the bleeder screw.

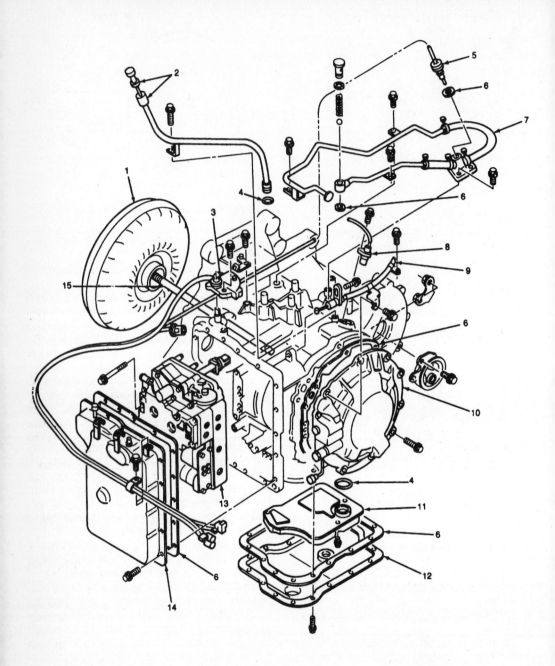

1. Converter assembly
2. Dipstick tube
3. Neutral safety switch
4. O-ring
5. Transaxle oil
   temperature switch
6. Gasket
7. Hose assembly
8. Pulse signal
   generator
9. Kickdown cable
10. Front oil pump
    assembly
11. Oil strainer
12. Oil pan
13. Valve body
14. Valve body cover
15. Oil pump driveshaft

4EAT automatic transaxle

refer to the automatic transaxle drain and refill procedure, in Chapter 1.

Adjustments

2–4 BAND

1. Raise and safely support the vehicle.
2. Remove the lower transaxle fluid pan. Refer to Chapter 1.
3. Loosen the locknut and tighten the piston stem to 78–95 inch lbs. (9–11 Nm).
4. Loosen the piston stem 2 turns.
5. Hold the piston stem and tighten the locknut to 18–29 ft. lbs. (25–39 Nm).
6. Install the fluid pan.
7. Lower the vehicle and fill the transaxle with the proper type and quantity of fluid.
8. Check for proper transaxle operation.

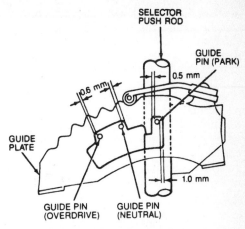

Guide plate and guide pin clearance

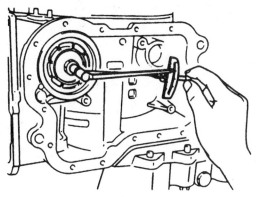

Adjusting the 2-4 band

SHIFT CABLE

1. Disconnect the negative battery cable. Shift the gear selector to the **P** detent.
2. Remove the selector knob mounting screws and remove the selector knob.
3. Remove the selector trim piece and the 4

position indicator mounting screws. Disconnect the illumination bulb.

4. Disconnect the shift control switch and programmed ride control switch wiring harnesses.
5. Remove the position indicator.
NOTE: *Make sure the detent spring roller is in the P detent.*
6. Loosen nuts **A** and **B**. The loosen the shift control cable attaching trunnion bolt.
7. Turn the transaxle-mounted shift lever clockwise to put the transaxle in the **P** position.
8. Tighten nut **A** by hand until it contacts the spacer, then an additional ½ turn.
9. Tighten the trunnion bolt to 67–96 inch lbs. (8–11 Nm). Tighten nut **B** to 67–96 inch lbs. (8–11 Nm).
10. Lightly, press the selector pushrod and make sure the guide plate and guide pin clearances are within specification.
11. Check that the guide plate and guide pin clearances are within the specifications when the selector lever is shifted to **N** and **D**.
12. Connect the illumination bulb.
13. Connect the shift control switch and the programmed ride control switch wiring harnesses.
14. Install the position indicator and tighten the mounting screws.
15. Install the selector trim piece and position the selector knob. Tighten the knob screws.
16. Connect the negative battery cable.

KICKDOWN CABLE

1. From the left front wheel well, remove the splash shield.
2. At the transaxle, remove the square head plug, marked **L**, and install an adapter and a suitable pressure gauge in the hole.
3. Rotate the kickdown cable locknuts to the furthest point from the throttle cam to loosen the cable all the way.

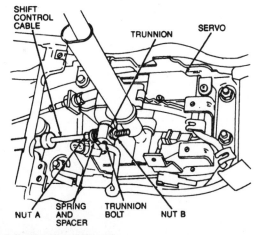

Adjusting the shift cable

4. Place the transaxle into the **P** position and warm the engine; the idle speed should be 750 ± 25 rpm.

5. Rotate the locknuts toward the throttle cam until the line pressure exceeds 63–66 psi, rotate the locknuts away from the throttle cam until the line pressure is 63–66 psi and tighten the locknuts.

6. Turn the engine **OFF**, install the square head plug and torque to 43–87 inch lbs. (5–10 Nm).

7. When installing a new kickdown cable, fully open the throttle valve, crimp the pin with

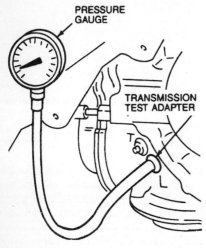

Pressure gauge connection for kickdown cable adjustment

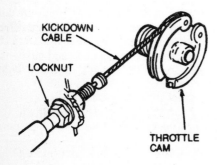

Kickdown cable adjustment

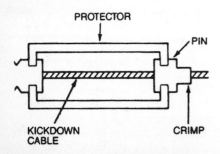

Crimping the pin on a new kickdown cable

the protector installed as shown. Remove the protector.

Neutral Safety Switch

NOTE: *The neutral safety switch incorporates the function of the back-up light switch.*

REMOVAL & INSTALLATION

1. Disconnect the negative battery cable.
2. On turbocharged vehicles, remove the intercooler inlet and outlet hoses.
3. Remove the shift cable and the shift cable bracket retaining nut.
4. Remove the 2 bolts retaining the switch to the case.
5. Disconnect the neutral safety switch electrical connector and then remove the switch from the vehicle.

To install:

6. Turn the manual shaft to the **N** position.
7. Install the neutral safety switch and loosely tighten the bolts. Connect the electrical connector.
8. Remove the screw from the switch and insert a 0.079 in. (2.0mm) pin. Move the neutral safety switch until the pin engages the switch alignment hole.
9. Tighten the switch mounting bolts to 69–95 inch lbs. (8–11 Nm), remove the pin and install the screw.
10. Install the shift cable bracket nut and connect the shift cable.
11. On turbocharged vehicles, install the intercooler inlet and outlet hoses.
12. Connect the negative battery cable.

ADJUSTMENT

1. Unplug the 3-pronged neutral safety switch connector, located under the battery tray. Connect an ohmmeter between terminals **A** and **B**.

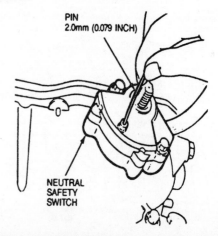

Neutral safety switch adjustment

2. With the transaxle selector lever in **P** or **N**, there should be continuity between the terminals.

3. If continuity does not exist, adjust the switch as follows:

 a. On turbocharged vehicles, remove the intercooler inlet and outlet hoses.

 b. Turn the manual shaft to the **N** position and loosen the switch mounting bolts.

 c. Remove the screw from the switch and insert a 0.079 in. (2.0mm) pin.

 d. Move the neutral safety switch until the pin engages the switch alignment hole.

 e. Tighten the switch mounting bolts to 69–95 inch lbs. (8–11 Nm), remove the pin and install the screw.

 f. On turbocharged vehicles, install the intercooler inlet and outlet hoses.

4. Retest continuity with the transaxle selector lever in **P** or **N**. If continuity does not exist, replace the neutral safety switch.

Transaxle

REMOVAL & INSTALLATION

2.2L Engine

1. Disconnect the battery cables (negative cable first). Remove the battery and the battery tray.

2. Disconnect the main fuse block and disconnect the coil wire from the distributor.

3. Disconnect the electrical connector from the air flow meter and remove the air cleaner assembly.

4. Remove the resonance chamber and bracket.

5. Disconnect the speedometer cable (analog cluster) or harness (electronic cluster).

6. Disconnect the transaxle electrical con-

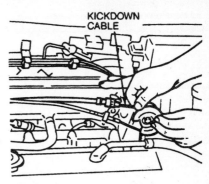
Disconnecting the kickdown cable

nectors and separate the harness from the transaxle clips.

7. Disconnect both ground wires, the range selector cable and the kickdown cable from the transaxle. Raise and safely support the vehicle.

8. Remove the front wheel and tire assemblies and the splash shields. Drain the transaxle fluid.

9. Disconnect and plug the oil cooler hoses from the transaxle. Insert plugs to prevent fluid leakage.

10. Remove the tie rod ends-to-steering knuckle cotter pins and nuts. Disconnect the tie rod ends from the steering knuckle.

11. Remove the stabilizer link assemblies from the lower control arm.

12. Remove the lower control ball joint-to-steering knuckle nut/bolt. Using a prybar, pry the lower control arm downward to separate the ball joint from the steering knuckle.

13. Remove the right-hand halfshaft bracket.

14. Position a prybar between the halfshaft and transaxle case; pry the halfshafts from the transaxle.

15. Install 2 transaxle plugs, T88C–7025–AH

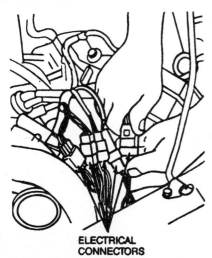
Disconnecting the transaxle electrical connectors

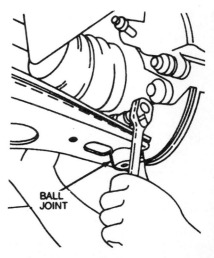
Removing the bolt and nut from the lower ball joint

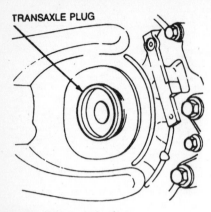

Positioning the transaxle plugs

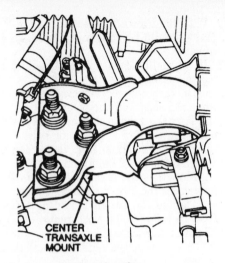

Center transaxle mount location

or equivalent, into the halfshaft openings of the transaxle case; this will keep the differential side gears from becoming mispositioned.

16. Remove the gusset plate-to-transaxle bolts.

17. Remove the torque converter-to-transaxle cover, the starter and the access brackets.

18. Using paint or chalk, matchmark the torque converter-to-flexplate position and remove the mounting nuts.

19. Mount engine support bar D87L–6000–A or equivalent, to the engine and support its weight.

20. Remove the center transaxle mount and bracket, the left transaxle mount and the nut and bolt attaching the right-hand transaxle mount to the frame.

21. Remove the crossmember and the left lower arm as an assembly.

22. Position a suitable jack under the transaxle and secure the transaxle to the jack.

23. Position a prybar between the torque converter and flexplate; pry the torque converter studs off of the flexplate.

24. Remove the transaxle-to-engine bolts, lower the transaxle and remove it from the vehicle.

To install:

25. Raise and position the transaxle, align the torque converter-to-flexplate matchmark and studs. Install the transaxle-to-engine bolts and torque to 66–86 ft. lbs. (89–117 Nm).

26. Install the center transaxle mount and bracket and torque the bolts to 27–40 ft. lbs. (36–54 Nm) and the nuts to 47–66 ft. lbs. (64–89 Nm).

27. Install the left transaxle mount. Tighten the transaxle-to-mount nut to 63–86 ft. lbs. (85–117 Nm). Tighten the mount-to-bracket bolt and nut to 49–69 ft. lbs. (67–93 Nm).

28. Install the crossmember and left lower arm as an assembly. Tighten the bolts to 27–40 ft. lbs. (36–54 Nm) and the nuts to 55–69 ft. lbs. (75–93 Nm).

29. Install the right transaxle mount bolt and nut. Tighten to 63–86 ft. lbs. (85–117 Nm).

30. Install the starter motor and access brackets.

31. Install the torque converter nuts and tighten to 32–45 ft. lbs. (43–61 Nm).

32. Install the torque converter cover and tighten the bolts to 69–95 inch lbs. (8–11 Nm).

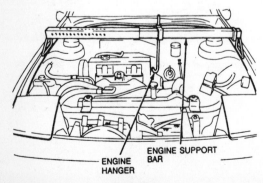

Engine support bar installation

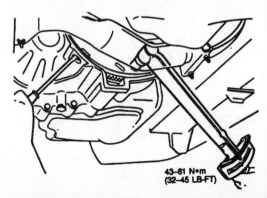

Torquing the torque converter mounting nuts

33. Install the gusset plate-to-tranaxle bolts and tighten to 27–38 ft. lbs. (37–52 Nm).

34. On the end of each halfshaft, install a new circlip.

35. Remove the transaxle plugs and install the halfshaft until the circlips snap into place.

36. Attach the lower ball joints to the steering knuckle.

37. Install the tie rods and tighten to 22–33 ft. lbs. (29–44 Nm). Install new cotter pins.

38. Install the bolts and nuts to the lower arm ball joints and tighten to 32–40 ft. lbs. (43–54 Nm).

39. Install the stabilizer link assembly-to-lower control arm. Turn the upper nuts (on each assembly) until 0.79 inch (20mm) of bolt thread can be measured above the nuts.

40. Install the oil cooler hoses to the transaxle.

41. Install the splash shields and the front wheel and tire assemblies; torque the lug nuts to 65–87 ft. lbs. (88–118 Nm).

42. Connect and adjust the kickdown cable. Connect the range selector cable and torque the bolt to 33–47 ft. lbs. (44–64 Nm).

43. Install the resonance chamber and bracket; torque to 69–95 inch lbs. (8–11 Nm).

44. Connect the electrical connectors and attach the harness to the transaxle clips. Connect the gound wires.

45. Connect the speedometer cable or harness, as necessary.

46. Install the air filter assembly and connect the air flow meter connector

47. Connect the center distributor terminal lead and main fuse block.

48. Install the battery carrier and the battery. Connect the battery cables.

49. Remove the engine support bracket.

50. Refill the transaxle and check for leaks and proper operation.

3.0L Engine

1. Disconnect the battery cables and remove the battery and battery tray.

2. Disconnect the main fuse block.

3. Disconnect the air cleaner hose from the air cleaner, remove the bolt/nut/washer assemblies and remove the air cleaner.

4. Remove the cruise control actuator mounting bolts and nut and move the assembly aside.

5. Disconnect the speed sensor or speedometer cable from the transaxle.

6. Move the pinch clamps on the transaxle cooler lines aside, then disconnect and plug the lines at the radiator.

7. Disconnect the transaxle electrical connectors, then disconnect the harness from the routing brackets.

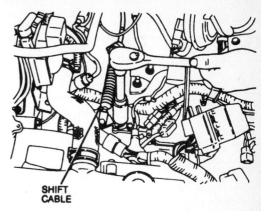

SHIFT CABLE

Disconnecting the shift cable from the transaxle

8. Disconnect the shift cable from the transaxle and routing bracket. Remove the transaxle wiring harness bracket and disconnect the 2 ground straps from the transaxle.

9. Disconnect the kickdown cable from the cable bracket and the throttle cam.

10. Install engine support bar D88L–6000–A or equivalent to support the engine and transaxle. Remove all accessible transaxle-to-engine bolts from the top of the engine compartment and remove the transaxle upper mount nuts.

11. Raise and safely support the vehicle.

12. Remove the front wheel and tire assemblies and the inner fender splash shields. Drain the transaxle fluid.

13. Disconnect the stabilizer links from the lower control arms and the bolts/nuts from the ball joints. Separate the ball joints from the steering knuckles by prying downward on the lower control arm while pushing inward on the rotor.

14. Remove the mounting bolts from the right halfshaft dynamic damper. Remove the halfshafts by inserting a prybar between the shaft and transaxle case and prying out.

15. Install transaxle plugs T88C–7025–AH or

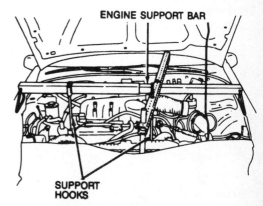

ENGINE SUPPORT BAR

SUPPORT HOOKS

Engine support bar installation

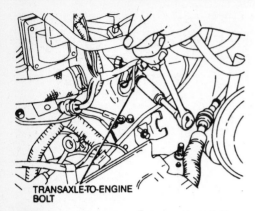

Transaxle-to-engine bolt removal and installation

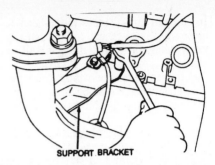

Transaxle support bracket removal and installation

equivalent, in the transaxle to prevent the differential side gears from moving out of position.

16. Remove the starter and bracket and the transaxle support bracket.

17. Remove the torque converter inspection plate. Matchmark the converter and the flexplate and remove the attaching nuts. Use a prybar to move the converter away from the flexplate, disengaging the converter studs.

18. Position a transmission jack under the transaxle. Remove the rear lower mount bolts and the front lower mount through-bolt. Remove the left front crossmember and lower control arm as an assembly.

19. Remove the remaining transaxle-to-engine bolts and lower the transaxle from the vehicle.

To install:

20. Raise the transaxle into position, aligning the matchmark and the torque converter studs with the flexplate. Install the transaxle-to-engine lower bolts and tighten to 66–86 ft. lbs. (89–117 Nm).

21. Install the left front crossmember and lower control arm assembly. Tighten the bolts to 27–40 ft. lbs. (36–54 Nm) and the nut to 55–69 ft. lbs. (75–93 Nm).

22. Install the front lower mount through bolt and tighten to 66–86 ft. lbs. (85–117 Nm).

Install the rear lower mount bolts and tighten to 49–69 ft. lbs. (67–93 Nm).

23. Install the torque converter attaching nuts and tighten to 32–45 ft. lbs. (43–61 Nm). Install the inspection plate and mounting bolt.

24. Install the transaxle support bracket and the starter motor and bracket.

25. Install a new circlip on the end of each halfshaft. Remove the transaxle plugs and install the halfshaft, making sure the clips lock in place.

26. Install the mounting bolts to the right halfshaft dynamic damper. Tighten to 31–46 ft. lbs. (42–62 Nm).

27. Attach the ball joints to the steering knuckles. Install the bolts and nuts and tighten to 27–40 ft. lbs. (36–54 Nm).

28. Install the stabilizer link assemblies. Turn the nuts until 0.79 in. (20mm) of bolt thread can be measured from the upper nut.

29. Install the splash guards and the wheel and tire assemblies. Tighten the lug nuts to 65–87 ft. lbs. (88–118 Nm). Lower the vehicle.

30. Install the upper mount nuts and tighten to 47–66 ft. lbs. (64–89 Nm). Install the remaining transaxle-to-engine bolts and tighten to 66–86 ft. lbs. (89–117 Nm).

31. Remove the engine support bar.

32. Connect the kickdown cable to the throttle cam and the cable bracket. Tighten the adjusting nuts.

33. Connect the ground straps and install the wiring harness bracket.

34. Connect the shift cable to the routing

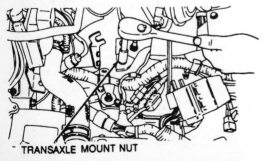

Transaxle upper mount nut removal and installation

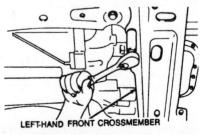

Left-hand front crossmember and lower control arm removal and installation

bracket and the transaxle. Install the attaching nut and tighten to 33–47 ft. lbs. (44–64 Nm).

35. Connect the transaxle electrical connectors, then connect the harness routing brackets to the transaxle.

36. Unplug the transaxle cooler lines and connect them to the radiator. Install the pinch clamps.

37. Connect the speed sensor or speedometer cable to the transaxle.

38. Position the cruise control actuator and install the mounting bolts and nut.

39. Position the air cleaner assembly and install the bolt/nut/washer assemblies. Connect the air cleaner hose and install the clamp.

40. Connect the main fuse block.

41. Install the battery tray and battery. Connect the battery cables.

42. Refill the transaxle and check for leaks and proper operation. Adjust the kickdown cable.

Halfshafts

REMOVAL & INSTALLATION

1. Disconnect the negative battery cable. Raise and safely support the vehicle.

2. Remove the front wheel and tire assembly and the necessary inner fender splash guards.

3. Remove the stabilizer link assembly from the lower control arm.

4. Using a cape chisel and a hammer, raise the staked portion of the hub nut.

5. Using an assistant to depress the brake pedal, loosen, do not remove, the hub nut.

6. Remove the lower control arm ball joint clamp bolt. Using a prybar, pry the lower control arm downward to separate the ball joint from the steering knuckle.

NOTE: *If removing the right halfshaft, remove the dynamic damper from the cylinder block.*

7. Separate the halfshaft from the transaxle as follows:

   a. On the right side, insert a prybar between the transaxle case and the halfshaft. Lightly tap on the end of the bar until the halfshaft loosens from the differential side gear.

   b. On the left side, pull on the spindle to remove the halfshaft from the differential side gear.

WARNING: *Be extremely careful. Make sure the prybar does not damage the transaxle*

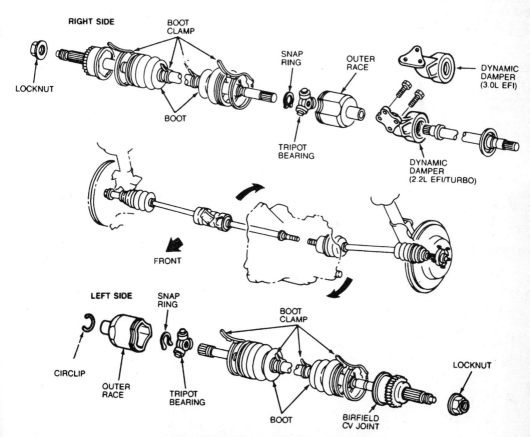

Halfshaft assemblies—automatic transaxle

case, *transaxle oil seal, CV-joint or CV-joint boot.*

8. Remove and discard the hub nut. Pull the halfshaft out of the wheel hub.

NOTE: *If the halfshaft binds in the hub splines, use a plastic hammer to tap it out or a wheel puller to press it out. Never use a metal hammer.*

9. Support the halfshaft and slide it out of the transaxle. Be careful not to damage the transaxle oil seal.

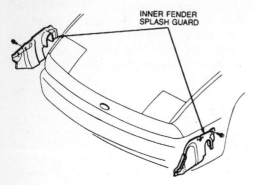

Inner fender splash guard removal and installation

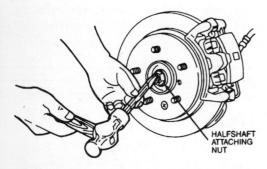

Raising the staked portion of the halfshaft attaching nut

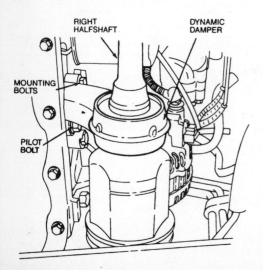

Dynamic damper location

10. Install differential plug T87C–7025–C or equivalent into the halfshaft openings of the transaxle case; this will keep the differential side gears from becoming mispositioned.

To install:

11. On the end of each halfshaft, install a new circlip. Start 1 end of the clip in the groove and work the clip over the stub shaft end and into the groove. This will prevent over-expanding the clip.

12. Remove the transaxle plugs and inspect the transaxle oil seals. If they show any signs of wear or damage, they must be replaced.

13. Lubricate the halfshaft splines with a suitable grease, align the splines with the differential side gears and push the halfshaft into the differential. Make sure the circlip gap is positioned at the top of the splines. When it seats properly, the circlip can be felt as it snaps into the differential side gear groove.

14. Position the halfshaft through the wheel hub and install a new attaching nut. Do not tighten the nut at this time.

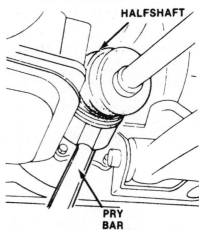

Separating the halfshaft from the transaxle case with a prybar

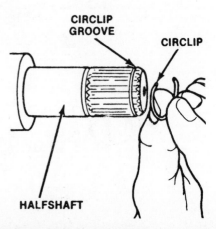

Install a new circlip on the halfshaft

NOTE: *If installing the right halfshaft, install the dynamic damper and tighten the*

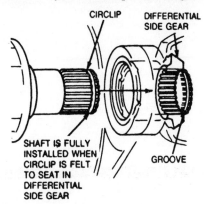

Installing the halfshaft into the differential

mounting bolts to 31–46 ft. lbs. (42–62 Nm).

15. Position the lower control arm ball joint into the steering knuckle and install the clamp bolt/nut. Tighten the nut to 32–40 ft. lbs. (43–54 Nm).

16. Install the stabilizer link assemblies. Turn the nuts until 0.79 in. (20mm) of bolt thread can be measured from the upper nut.

17. Install the splash shields.

18. Tighten the halfshaft attaching nut to 116–174 ft. lbs. (157–235 Nm). Stake the nut using a suitable chisel with a rounded cutting edge.

NOTE: *If the nut splits or cracks after staking, it must be replaced with a new nut.*

19. Install the wheel and tire assembly and lower the vehicle.

Suspension and Steering

8

WHEELS

Wheels

REMOVAL AND INSTALLATION

1. Apply the parking brake and block the opposite wheel.

2. If equipped with automatic transaxle, place the selector lever in **P**. If equipped with manual transaxle, place the transaxle in reverse.

3. If equipped, remove the wheel cover.

4. Break loose the lug nuts.

NOTE: *The aluminum wheels are available with anti-theft wheel lug nuts. The key for these lug nuts should be attached to the lug wrench, stowed with the spare tire. To remove or install the anti-theft wheel lug nut, insert the key into the slot of the lug nut, place the lug nut wrench on the key, and while applying pressure on the key, remove or install the lug nut. Make sure the key is held square to the nut; if it is on an angle, the key or lug nut may become damaged. DO NOT use a power impact wrench on the lug nut key.*

5. Raise the vehicle until the tire is clear of the ground.

6. Remove the lug nuts and the tire and wheel assembly.

To install:

7. Make sure the wheel and brake drum or hub mating surfaces, and the wheel lug studs, are clean and free of all foreign material.

8. Position the wheel on the hub or drum and hand-tighten the lug nuts. Tighten all the lug nuts, in a criss-cross pattern, until they are snug.

9. Lower the vehicle. Tighten the lug nuts, in a criss-cross pattern, to 65–87 ft. lbs. (88–118 Nm). Always use a torque wrench to final tighten the lug nuts, to prevent warping the disc brake rotors or brake drums, and to prevent stretching the wheel studs.

INSPECTION

Check the wheels for any damage. They must be replaced if they are bent, dented, heavily rusted, have elongated bolt holes, or have excessive lateral or radial runout. Wheels with excessive runout may cause a high-speed vehicle vibration.

Replacement wheels must be of the same load capacity, diameter, width, offset and mounting configuration as the original wheels. Using the wrong wheels may affect wheel bearing life, ground and tire clearance, or speedometer and odometer calibrations.

Wheel Lug Studs

REPLACEMENT

1. Remove the hub or hub/drum assembly from the vehicle. Refer to procedures in this Chapter.

2. Remove the stud using a press or drive the stud from the hub using a hammer and drift.

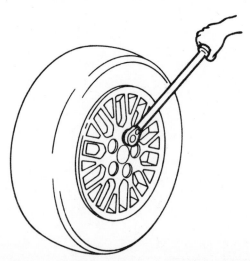

Always use a torque wrench to final tighten the lug nuts

Make sure the hub or hub/drum assembly is properly supported.

3. Line up the serrations on the replacement stud with the serrations in the hub.

4. Install the stud using a press or drive the stud in using a hammer and drift. Make sure the hub or hub/drum assembly is properly supported.

5. Install the hub or hub/drum assembly.

FRONT SUSPENSION

The front suspension consists of MacPherson struts and a single wishbone lower control arm. Strut towers located in the wheel wells locate the upper ends of the MacPherson struts. If the vehicle is equipped with Programmed Ride Control (PRC), the PRC actuator bolts to the top of the strut mounting block which houses a rubber mounted strut bearing. The upper end of the coil spring rides in a heavy rubber spring seat. A forged steering knuckle bolts to the shock absorber. If the vehicle is not equipped with PRC, the struts used are the conventional non-adjustable type and cannot be interchanged with the PRC type. Also, PRC actua-

tors will be absent from the strut mounting block.

The lower ball joint is pressed into the control arm and is attached to the steering knuckle. The wide stance control arms are supported by rubber bushings at each end. Body lean on turns is controlled by a hollow stabilizer bar that connects to both lower control arms.

The front wheels are attached to the front hub and rotor assemblies. The front hub and rotor assemblies are supported by 1-piece roller bearings mounted in the steering knuckle. The wheel bearing is pressed into the steering knuckle. The hub assembly is pressed into the wheel bearing during assembly.

The Progrmmed Ride Control feature allows for the selection of sport, normal and soft combinations of damping control from the front and rear shock absorbers. The PRC switch, located in the center console, lets the driver select either the manual or both automatic control modes of the PRC suspension.

Selecting SOFT will provide soft damping at all times and under all conditions. Selecting NORM or SPORT will engage the Automatic Adjusting Suspension feature, which provides combinations of hard or very hard damping de-

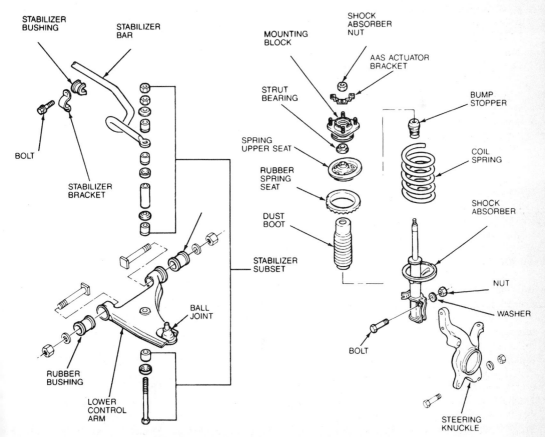

Front suspension components—disassembled view

pendent upon sensor inputs for vehicle speed, acceleration, braking and cornering. This helps to control vehicle roll, pitch and dive and provides improved handling at high speed.

MacPherson Struts

REMOVAL AND INSTALLATION

1. Raise and support the vehicle, safely.
2. Remove the wheel and tire assembly.
3. Remove the rubber cap from the strut mounting block. If equipped, disconnect the programmed ride control module connector.
4. At the inside of the strut mounting block and chassis strut tower, place an alignment mark.
5. If equipped, remove the programmed ride control actuator.
6. If equipped with anti-lock brakes, disconnect the electrical harness and remove the bracket.
7. Remove the brake caliper from the caliper anchor bracket. Suspend the caliper with mechanics wire; do not disconnect the brake hose. Remove the caliper anchor bracket.
8. Remove the U-clip from the brake line hose and slide it out of the strut bracket.
9. Remove the strut-to-steering knuckle bolts.

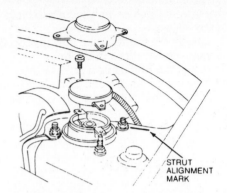

Matchmark the inside of the strut mounting block and chassis strut tower

10. Remove the vane airflow meter assembly and remove the ignition coil bracket from the strut tower.
11. Remove the strut-to-chassis nuts and remove the strut from the vehicle.

To install:

12. Install the strut in the shock tower. Align the marks that were made during removal and torque the strut-to-chassis nuts to 34–46 ft. lbs. (46–63 Nm).
13. Install the vane airflow meter assembly and the ignition coil bracket.

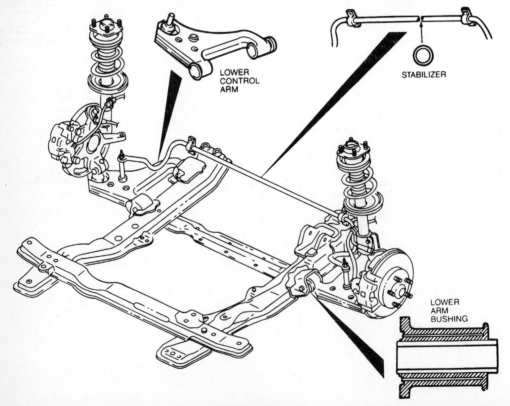

Front suspension

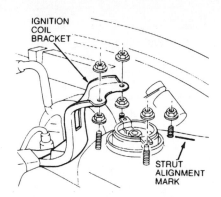

Ignition coil bracket removal and installation

14. If equipped, install the programmed ride control actuator and the connector.

15. Install the rubber cap on the strut tower.

16. Align the strut to the steering knuckle and torque the nuts/bolts to 69–86 ft. lbs. (93–117 Nm).

17. Install the caliper anchor bracket and caliper. Connect the brake hose to its bracket on the strut.

18. Install the anti-lock brake system bracket and harness, if equipped.

19. Install the wheel and tire assembly. Tighten the lug nuts to 65–87 ft. lbs. (88–118 Nm). Lower the vehicle.

OVERHAUL

1. Place the strut assembly in a suitable vise. Loosen, but do not remove the shock absorber nut.

2. Remove the strut assembly from the vice and compress the spring, using Macpherson strut spring compressor D85P–7178–A or equivalent.

3. Remove the shock absorber nut.

4. Gradually release the spring compressor. Be careful not to strip the threads on the shock absorber as the spring expands.

5. Remove the programmed ride control actuator bracket, if equipped, strut mounting block, upper rubber spring seat, dust boot, bump stopper and the coil spring from the shock absorber.

To install:

6. Install the coil spring, bump stopper, dust boot and the upper spring seat on the shock absorber.

7. Install the strut mounting block and the programmed ride control actuator bracket, if equipped, making sure the notch on the mounting block is 180 degrees from the knuckle mounting bracket on the shock absorber.

8. Compress the spring with the compressor tool and install the shock absorber nut. Tighten the nut to 47–69 ft. lbs. (64–84 Nm).

9. Gradually release the compressor tool and remove from the strut assembly.

Lower Ball Joint

INSPECTION

Raise and safely support the vehicle until the front wheel is clear of the floor. Try to rock the wheel up and down. If any play is felt, have an assistant rock the wheel while observing the

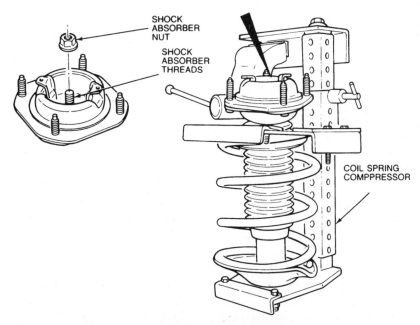

Compressing the coil spring

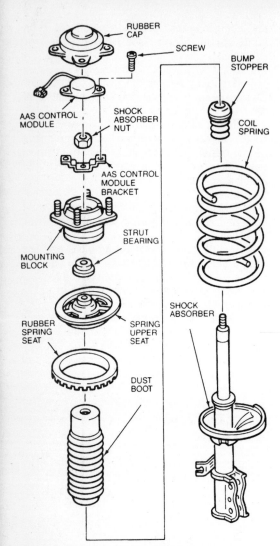

MacPherson strut—disassembled view

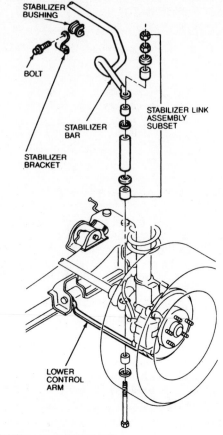

Stabilizer bar components

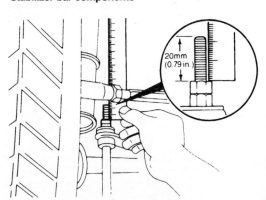

Measuring the exposed thread length

lower ball joint. If any movement is seen between the steering knuckle and control arm, the ball joint is bad. If not, any wheel play indicates wheel bearing wear.

REMOVAL AND INSTALLATION

The lower ball joint is an integral part of the lower control arm. If the ball joint needs replacement, the entire lower arm must be replaced.

Stabilizer Bar

REMOVAL AND INSTALLATION

1. Raise and safely support the vehicle.
2. Remove the wheel and tire assemblies.
3. Remove the stabilizer bar link assembly mounting bolts from the lower control arm.
4. Remove the mounting bolt from the stabilizer bar bushing. Remove the stabilizer bar.

To install:

5. Install the stabilizer bar link assembly mounting bolts at the control arm. Hand tighten only.
6. Install the stabilizer bar bushing. Tighten the bushing bolt to 27–40 ft. lbs. (36–54 Nm).
7. Tighten the link nut until 0.79 in. (20mm) of thread remains above the nut.
8. Install the wheel and tire assemblies. Tighten the lug nuts to 65–87 ft. lbs. (88–118 Nm). Lower the vehicle.

Lower Control Arm

REMOVAL AND INSTALLATION

1. Raise and safely support the vehicle. Remove the wheel and tire assembly.

2. Remove the brake caliper and support it with mechanics wire from the coil spring.

3. Remove the stabilizer link assembly from the lower control arm.

4. Remove the ball-joint clamp bolt from the steering knuckle. Using a prybar, pry downward to separate the ball joint from the steering knuckle.

5. If equipped, remove the harmonic damper from the chassis sub-frame; the damper is located on the left side of the vehicle.

6. Remove the lower control arm-to-chassis mounting bolts and nuts and remove the lower control arm.

To install:

7. Install the control arm and tighten the mounting bolts to 69–93 ft. lbs. (93–127 Nm).

8. Install the harmonic damper, if equipped.

9. Install the ball joint stud into the steering knuckle and tighten the clamp bolt to 32–40 ft. lbs. (43–54 Nm).

10. Install the stabilizer bar link assembly. Refer to the procedure in this Chapter.

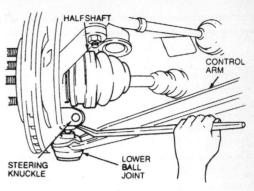

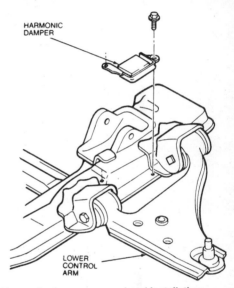

Separating the ball joint from the steering knuckle

Harmonic damper removal and installation

11. Install the brake caliper.

12. Install the wheel and tire assembly. Tighten the lug nuts to 65–87 ft. lbs. (88–118 Nm). Lower the vehicle.

Steering Knuckle

REMOVAL AND INSTALLATION

1. Raise and safely support the vehicle. Remove the front wheel and tire assembly.

2. Using a small cape chisel and a hammer, raise the staked portion of the hub nut.

3. Have an assistant apply the brakes and remove the hub nut. Discard the hub nut; it must not be reused.

4. Remove the stabilizer bar-to-control arm, bolt, nut, washers and bushings.

5. At the tie rod end, remove the cotter pin and nut. Using a suitable tie rod end separator tool or equivalent, separate the tie rod end from the steering knuckle.

6. Remove the caliper and anchor bracket

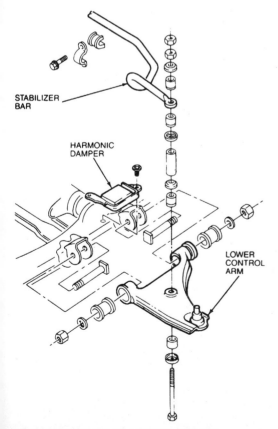

Lower control arm removal and installation

and support the caliper assembly from the coil spring with mechanics wire.

7. Remove the disc brake rotor.

8. Remove the lower control arm ball joint clamp bolt and nut. Using a prybar, pry the lower control arm downward and separate the ball joint from the steering knuckle.

9. Remove the steering knuckle-to-strut attaching bolts.

10. Slide the steering knuckle/hub assembly out of the strut bracket and off the end of the halfshaft, being careful not to damage the grease seals. Should the wheel hub bind on the halfshaft splines, use a plastic hammer to jar it free.

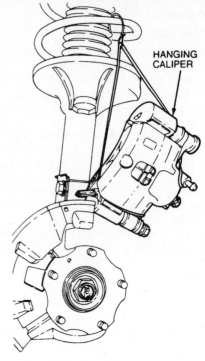

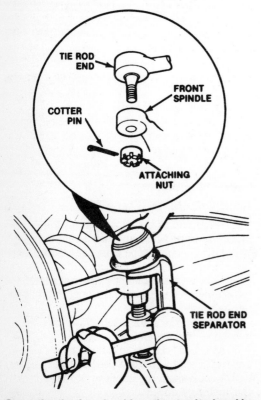

Raising the staked portion of the halfshaft nut

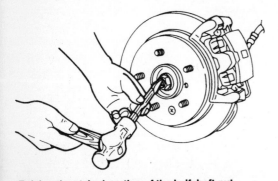

Separating the tie rod end from the steering knuckle

Support the disc brake caliper

NOTE: *Never use a metal faced hammer to separate the halfshaft from the wheel hub. Damage to the CV-joint internal components will result. If the halfshaft splines are rusted to the hub, it may be necessary to use a 2-jawed hub puller to separate them.*

To install:

11. Grease the halfshaft splines. Slide the steering knuckle/hub assembly onto the halfshaft and position it into the strut bracket. Torque the strut-to-steering knuckle bolts/nuts to 69–86 ft. lbs. (93–117 Nm).

12. Push the lower control arm ball joint into the steering knuckle and torque the clamp bolt to 32–40 ft. lbs. (43–54 Nm).

13. Install the disc brake rotor.

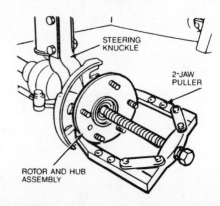

Using a puller to separate the halfshaft from the hub

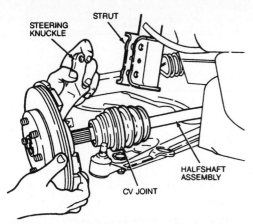

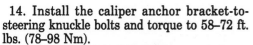

Steering knuckle/hub assembly removal and installation

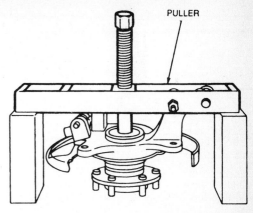

Removing the hub assembly from the steering knuckle

14. Install the caliper anchor bracket-to-steering knuckle bolts and torque to 58–72 ft. lbs. (78–98 Nm).

15. Using a new hub nut, have an assistant apply the brakes and torque the nut to 116–174 ft. lbs. (157–235 Nm). Using a rounded edge cold chisel, stake the hub nut.

NOTE: *If the nut splits or cracks after staking, it must be replaced with a new nut.*

16. Connect the tie rod end to the steering knuckle, torque the nut to 22–33 ft. lbs. (29–44 Nm) and install a new cotter pin.

NOTE: *Should the slots of the nut not align with the cotter pin hole, tighten the nut for proper alignment. Never loosen the nut.*

17. Connect the stabilizer bar to the lower control arm and tighten the nut until 0.79 in. (20mm) of the bolt threads are exposed beyond the nut.

18. Install the wheel and tire assembly and torque the lug nuts to 65–87 ft. lbs. (88–118 Nm).

19. Lower the vehicle.

Front Hub and Bearing

REPLACEMENT

1. Remove the steering knuckle/hub assembly. Refer to the procedure in this Chapter.

2. Remove the bearing grease seal using a small prybar. Discard the seal.

3. Remove the hub assembly from the steering knuckle using knuckle puller T87C–1104–A or equivalent.

NOTE: *If the inner race remains on the hub, grind a section of the inner bearing race to approximately 0.0197 in. (0.5mm) and use a chisel to remove the race.*

4. Remove the snapring from the steering knuckle.

5. Remove the wheel bearing from the steer-

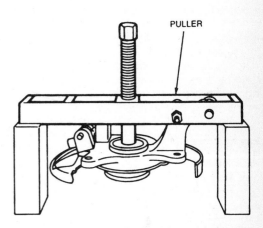

Removing the wheel bearing from the steering knuckle

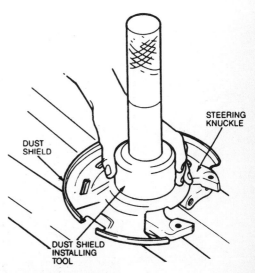

Installing the dust shield

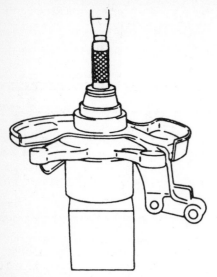

Installing the wheel bearing into the steering knuckle

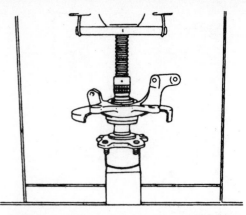

Installing the hub assembly into the steering knuckle

ing knuckle using knuckle puller T87C–1104–A or equivalent.

6. Leave the disc brake duct shield on the steering knuckle, unless it is damaged. The shield is pressed onto the knuckle and is difficult to remove without damage.

7. Inspect the hub and steering knuckle for cracks, wear and scoring. Replace, as necessary.

8. If removed, install the dust shield using installation tool T87C–1175–B or equivalent.

9. Using a press, install the wheel bearing into the steering knuckle, then install the snapring.

10. Lubricate the lip of a new grease seal with grease, then install the seal into the knuckle, using a suitable seal installer.

11. Install the hub assembly into the steering knuckle using a press and suitable fixtures.

12. Install the steering knuckle/hub assembly on the vehicle.

Front End Alignment
CASTER

Front caster adjustment is not a separate procedure on the Probe. Front caster should fall within specification when the front camber is adjusted. Make sure the tires are correctly and uniformly inflated and any abnormal loads are removed from the vehicle. If the caster is not within specification after the camber is adjusted, and the control arms, stabilizer and bushings are in good condition, check the vehicle body for distortion at suspension mounting points due to collision damage, curb or pothole impacts, improper hoisting, etc. Usually, front wheel drive cars are not sensitive to caster differences from side to side that are less than 1 degree.

CAMBER

Camber is always set before any other adjustments. Camber can cause both pull and tire wear if it is not set correctly.

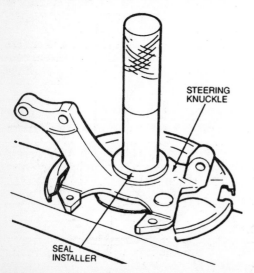

STEERING
KNUCKLE

SEAL
INSTALLER

Installing a new grease seal

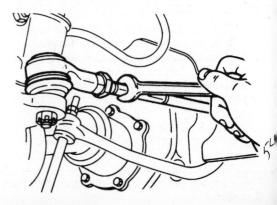

Adjusting the toe

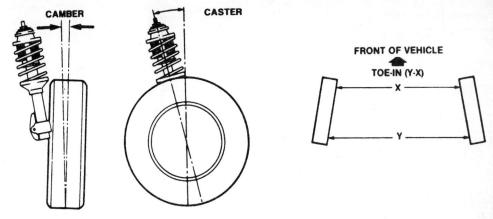

Camber, caster and toe

The top mounting studs on the front struts are offset to allow camber adjustment. Camber adjustment is done by removing the stud nuts, lowering the strut and rotating it to one of three positions. Each of these positions provides a different camber and caster angle combination to facilitate front end alignment.

TOE

Toe is the difference in distance between the front edge of the front tires and the rear edge of the front tires (The difference between X and Y axis. An incorrect toe setting can affect steering feel and cause excessive tire wear.

The toe setting is adjusted by loosening the locknut on each tie rod end and turning the rod until the toe is within specification. The tie rods must be turned in or out an equal amount on each side to keep the steering wheel centered.

REAR SUSPENSION

The rear suspension is fully independent utilizing rear MacPherson struts at each wheel. If the vehicle is equipped with Programmed Ride Control (PRC), the rear strut towers locate the PRC actuators and the strut assemblies. A forged rear spindle bolts to the shock absorber, double rear lateral links, and a single trailing arm. It is these components and a rear crossmember that make up the rear suspension.

If the vehicle is not equipped with PRC, the struts used are the conventional non-adjustable type and cannot be interchanged with the PRC struts. The PRC actuators will not be on the strut mounting block. Both the lateral links and the trailing arm have rubber bushings at each end. The lateral links are attached to the rear subframe and the spindle with a common bolt and nut assembly at each end. The trailing arm bolts to the shock absorber and a bracket on the floor pan. Never try to straighten a damaged rear suspension component. Always replace with a new part.

Lateral links, trailing arms, and spindles are normally replaced only if damaged. If a suspension part has been damaged, have the underbody dimensions checked. If the underbody dimensions are not correct, the body will have to be straightened before installing new suspension parts.

The rear wheels and brake drum/rotors are supported on a 1-piece, non-serviceable, non-adjustable bearing. The inner race rides on the

FRONT WHEEL ALIGNMENT SPECIFICATIONS

Year	Model	Caster Range (deg.)	Caster Preferred Setting (deg.)	Camber Range (deg.)	Camber Preferred Setting (deg.)	Toe-in (in.)	Steering Axis Inclination (deg.)
1989	Probe	$^{15}/_{32}$P–1$^{31}/_{32}$P	1$^7/_{32}$P	$^7/_{16}$N–1$^{1}/_{16}$P	$^5/_{16}$P	$^1/_8$P	12$^{25}/_{32}$
1990	Probe	1$^{1}/_{16}$P–2$^3/_{16}$P	1$^7/_{16}$P	1N–$^1/_2$P	$^1/_4$N	$^1/_8$P	12$^{25}/_{32}$
1991	Probe	$^{15}/_{16}$P–2$^7/_{16}$P	1$^{11}/_{16}$P	1N–$^1/_2$P	$^1/_4$N	$^1/_8$P	12$^{25}/_{32}$
1992	Probe	$^{15}/_{16}$P–2$^7/_{16}$P	1$^{11}/_{16}$P	1N–$^1/_2$P	$^1/_4$N	$^1/_8$P	12$^{25}/_{32}$

N—Negative
P—Positive

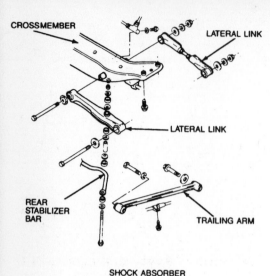

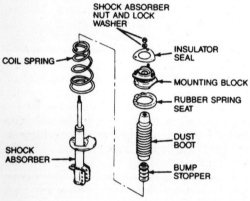

Rear suspension components—disassembled view

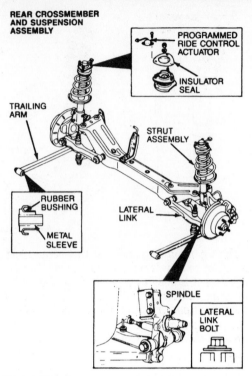

Rear suspension

spindle, which is bolted to the rear strut and control arms. The bearing outer race is press-fit into the hub. A staked nut on the outer side and a retaining ring on the inner side hold the bearing and hub in position on the spindle.

MacPherson Strut

REMOVAL AND INSTALLATION

1. Raise and support the vehicle, safely. Remove the wheel and tire assembly.

2. Remove the upper trunk side garnish and lower trunk side trim to gain access to the strut assembly.

3. If equipped with programmed ride control, disconnect the programmed ride control module connector and removed the module.

4. If equipped with anti-lock brakes, remove the anti-lock brake harness and remove the bracket.

5. If equipped with drum brakes, remove the drum and backing plate assembly. If equipped with rear disc brakes, remove the rear disc

brake caliper and rotor assembly. Refer to Chapter 9.

6. Remove the brake line U-clip from the strut housing.

7. Loosen, but do not completely remove, the trailing arm bolt. Remove the spindle-to-strut bolts.

8. From inside the vehicle, remove the strut-to-chassis nuts. Remove the strut assembly.

To install:

9. Position the strut into the strut tower and torque the strut-to-chassis nuts to 34–46 ft. lbs. (46–63 Nm).

10. If equipped with programmed ride control, install the module and reconnect the connector.

11. Install the lower trunk side trim and the upper trunk side garnish.

12. Install the spindle-to-strut mounting bolts and tighten to 69–86 ft. lbs. (93–117 Nm). Tighten the trailing arm mounting bolt to 64–86 ft. lbs. (86–117 Nm).

13. Install the brake drum and backing plate or the caliper and rotor assembly, as applicable. Install the brake line U-clip onto the strut.

14. If equipped, install the ABS brake harness and bracket.

15. Install the wheel and tire assembly and tighten the lug nuts to 65–87 ft. lbs. (88–118 Nm). Lower the vehicle.

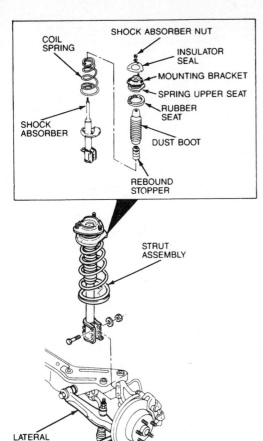

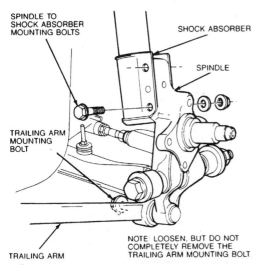

MacPherson strut components

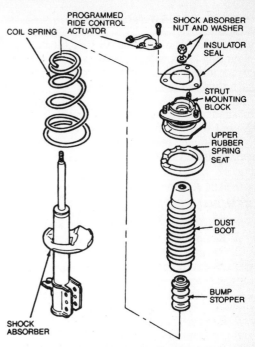

MacPherson strut—disassembled view

2. Remove the strut assembly from the vice and compress the spring, using spring compressor 086–00029 or equivalent.

3. Remove the shock absorber nut.

4. Gradually release the spring compressor. Be careful not to strip the threads on the shock absorber as the spring expands.

5. Remove the strut mounting block, upper rubber spring seat, dust boot, bump stopper and the coil spring from the shock absorber.

To install:

6. Install the coil spring, bump stopper, dust

Removing the strut from the spindle

OVERHAUL

1. Mount the strut assembly in a suitable vise and loosen, but do not completely remove the shock absorber nut.

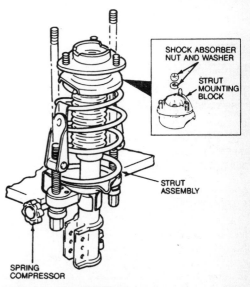

Compressing the coil spring

boot and the upper spring seat on the shock absorber.

7. Install the strut mounting block. The mounting block will not seat on the shock absorber unless the notches on the block line up with those on the shock absorber.

8. Compress the spring with the compressor tool and install the shock absorber nut. Tighten the nut to 47–69 ft. lbs. (64–84 Nm).

9. Gradually release the compressor tool and remove from the strut assembly.

Control Arms

REMOVAL AND INSTALLATION

1. Raise and support the vehicle, safely.
2. Remove the tire and wheel assembly.
3. Remove the brake drum and the backing plate assembly or the rear brake caliper and rotor assembly, if equipped.
4. Loosen, but do not completely remove, the spindle to strut assembly mounting bolts.
5. Remove the common lateral link arm bolt and nut from the spindle.
6. Remove the trailing arm mounting bolt at the spindle and the spindle to strut assembly mounting bolts.
7. Remove the spindle from the strut assembly.
8. Remove the rear stabilizer bar. Refer to the procedure in this Chapter.
9. Remove the nut from the common lateral link mounting bolt at the rear crossmember and remove the rear lateral link.

NOTE: *Because of lack of clearance between the fuel tank and the common lateral link mounting bolt, the bolt and the front lateral link cannot be removed at this time.*

10. Remove the parking brake mounting bolts from the trailing arm assembly.

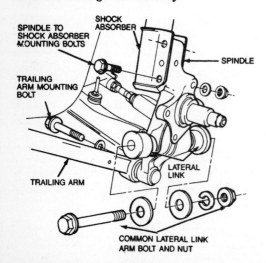

Spindle removal and installation

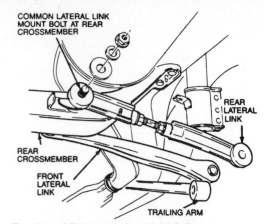

Rear lateral link removal and installation

11. Remove the trailing arm mounting bolt and the trailing arm.

12. Remove the exhaust mounting bolts and the brake line retaining bracket from the rear crossmember. Remove the mounting bolts from the end of the crossmember.

13. Remove the rear crossmember and front lateral link as an assembly. Remove the common lateral link mounting bolt from the rear crossmember and remove the front lateral link from the crossmember.

To install:

14. Position the front lateral link on the crossmember and install the common lateral link mounting bolt.

15. Install the crossmember into the vehicle and install the mounting bolts, exhaust mounting bolts and the brake line retaining bracket bolt to the crossmember.

16. Tighten the crossmember mounting bolts to 27–40 ft. lbs. (36–54 Nm) and the brake line retaining bracket bolt to 13–20 ft. lbs. (18–26 Nm).

17. Position the trailing arm into the body mounting bracket and tighten the mounting bolt to 49–69 ft. lbs. (63–93 Nm).

18. Install the parking brake cable mounting bolts to the trailing arm.

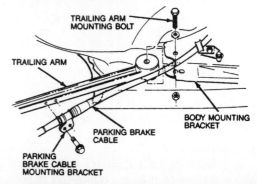

Trailing arm removal and installation

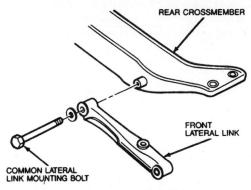

Front lateral link removal and installation

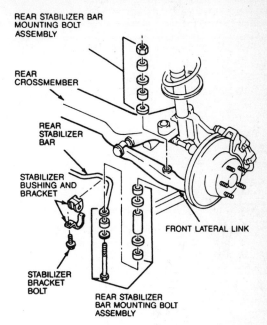

Stabilizer bar components

19. Position the rear lateral link onto the common lateral link mounting bolt at the rear crossmember and install the nut to the bolt. Tighten the mounting bolt and nut at the rear crossmember to 64–86 ft. lbs. (86–117 Nm).

20. Install the rear stabilizer bar assembly.

21. Place the spindle onto the strut assembly mounting bracket and tighten the mounting bolts to 69–86 ft. lbs. (93–117 Nm).

22. Install the common lateral link arm bolt and nut through the spindle and tighten to 64–86 ft. lbs. (86–117 Nm).

23. Install the trailing arm mounting bolt and tighten to 64–86 ft. lbs. (86–117 Nm).

24. Install the brake drum and backing plate assembly or the brake caliper and rotor assembly, as applicable.

25. Install the wheel and tire assembly and tighten the lug nuts to 65–87 ft. lbs. (88–118 Nm). Lower the vehicle.

Stabilizer Bar

REMOVAL AND INSTALLATION

1. Raise and safely support the vehicle.

2. Remove the mounting bolt assembly from the front lateral link.

3. Remove the stabilizer bushing and bracket from the rear crossmember.

4. Installation is the reverse of the removal procedure. Tighten the stabilizer bracket bolt to 27–40 ft. lbs. (36–54 Nm) and the stabilizer bar mounting bolt to 12–17 ft. lbs. (16–23 Nm).

Rear Wheel Bearings

REPLACEMENT

1. Raise and support the vehicle, safely.

2. Remove the wheel and tire assembly and the grease cap.

3. Using a cape chisel and a hammer, raise the staked portion of the hub nut.

4. Remove and discard the hub nut.

5. Remove the brake drum or disc brake rotor assembly from the spindle.

6. Using a small prybar, pry the grease seal from the brake drum or rotor and discard it.

7. Remove the snapring. Using a shop press, press the wheel bearing from the brake drum or rotor.

To install:

8. Using a shop press, press the new wheel bearing into the brake drum or rotor until it seats and install the snapring.

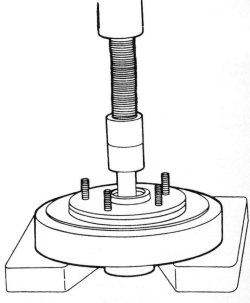

Removing the rear wheel bearing

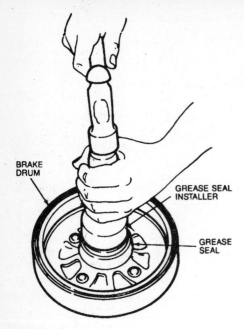

Installing a new grease seal

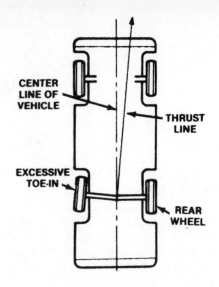

NOTE: THE THRUST LINE IS THE PATH BOTH REAR WHEELS TAKE AS THEY ROLL DOWN THE ROAD.

Rear wheel thrust line

9. Lubricate the new seal lip with grease and install the seal, using a suitable installation tool.

10. Position the brake drum or rotor onto the wheel spindle.

11. Install a new locknut and tighten to 73–131 ft. lbs. (98–178 Nm).

12. Using a dull cold chisel, stake the locknut. NOTE: *If the nut splits or cracks after staking, it must be replaced with a new nut.*

13. Install the grease cap and the wheel and tire assembly. Tighten the lug nuts to 65–87 ft. lbs. (88–118 Nm). Lower the vehicle.

Rear End Alignment

Rear end alignment should be checked whenever the front end is aligned. If the rear toe and tracking are not set correctly, accelerated tire wear may occur. The thrust line of the rear wheels may also be affected. The thrust line is the path the rear wheels take as they roll down the road. Ideally, the thrust line should align perfectly with the center line of the vehicle. If the thrust line is not correct, the vehicle will slightly understeer in one direction and oversteer in the other. It will also affect wheel centering.

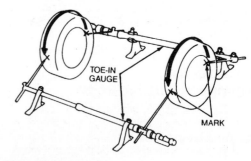

Measuring rear toe-in

REAR WHEEL ALIGNMENT SPECIFICATIONS

| Year | Model | Caster | | Camber | | Toe-in (in.) | Steering Axis Inclination (deg.) |
		Range (deg.)	Preferred Setting (deg.)	Range (deg.)	Preferred Setting (deg.)		
1989	Probe	—	—	$1/4$N–$1\,1/4$P	$1/2$P	0	—
1990	Probe	—	—	$1\,3/16$N–$5/16$P	$7/16$N	$1/8$P	—
1991	Probe	—	—	$1\,3/16$N–$5/16$P	$7/16$N	$1/8$P	—
1992	Probe	—	—	$1\,3/16$N–$5/16$P	$7/16$N	$1/8$P	—

N—Negative
P—Positive

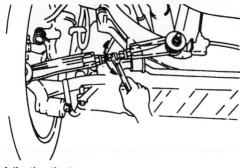

Adjusting the toe

Rear toe-in should be adjusted prior to setting the front alignment angles. Adjustment is made by loosening the jam nuts on each rear lateral link and turning the rods in or out until the toe is within specification. The rods must be turned an equal amount on each side.

STEERING

There are 2 different kinds of steering systems used on the Probe, the standard power steering system and the electronic Variable Assist Power Steering (VAPS) system.

The standard power steering system consists of a rack and pinion steering gear, a belt driven pump, and the necessary interconnecting hydraulic lines.

The non-electronically controlled power rack and pinion steering gear has an integral valving and power assist system. The valve body is an integral part of the steering gear housing. The pressure line and return line from the pump attach at the valve body. A rotary valve directs high pressure hydraulic fluid through external oil lines to the correct side of the rack piston.

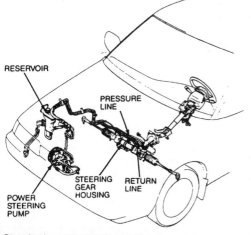

Standard power steering system

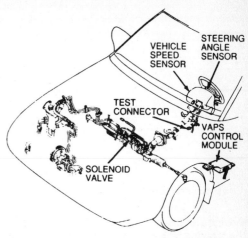

Variable Assist Power Steering (VAPS) system

A spring loaded pressure pad assembly is used to keep the rack in constant contact with the pinion. Rubber boots at each end of the rack seal out dust, dirt and contaminants. The steering gear housing is mounted on bulkhead with a rubber bushing and mounting bracket at each end. The mounting brackets are attached to the bulkhead with three bolts at each bracket.

The Variable Assist Power Steering (VAPS) feature automatically adjusts power steering pressure. VAPS provides light steering effort during low speed and parking maneuvers and higher steering effort at higher speeds for improved road feel. The VAPS system consists of the VAPS control unit, steering angle sensor, vehicle speed sensor, solenoid valve, test connector, and inter-connecting wiring.

The Variable Assist Power Steering System is completely automatic, with no driver operated controls. The system continuously monitors steering wheel angle and vehicle speed to determine when to adjust steering system pressure. The system opens a solenoid valve to provide full power assist at vehicle speeds less than 6.2 mph or when the steering wheel is turned more than 45° to the right or left. The system reduces power assist under other conditions.

The VAPS Control Unit has a special feature which should be noted before performing any VAPS diagnostic procedures. A slide switch located on the VAPS Control Unit allows for 10 percent harder steering effort or a 10 percent lighter steering effort from normal production setting. Note the position of this switch before proceeding with diagnostics.

Steering Wheel

REMOVAL AND INSTALLATION

1. Disconnect the negative battery cable.
2. Remove the steering wheel horn pad by re-

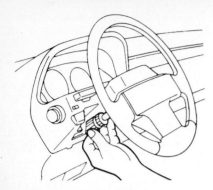

Horn pad removal and installation

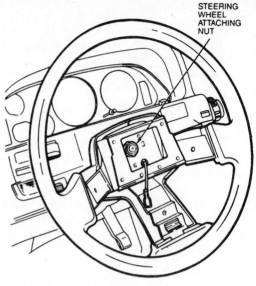

STEERING
WHEEL
ATTACHING
NUT

moving the mounting screws from the rear of the steering wheel. Disconnect the wiring from the horn pad.

3. Remove the steering wheel mounting nut. Place matchmarks on the steering wheel and the shaft for installation alignment.

4. Use a steering wheel puller and remove the steering wheel.

WARNING: *Do not subject the steering shaft to severe impact in the axial direction when removing or installing the steering wheel.*

To install:

5. Align the matchmarks and place the steering wheel on the steering column shaft.

6. Install the steering wheel mounting nut and tighten to 29–36 ft. lbs. (39–49 Nm).

7. Connect the horn wire and install the horn pad. Connect the negative battery cable.

Turn Signal Cancel Switch
REMOVAL AND INSTALLATION

1. Disconnect the negative battery cable.
2. Remove the steering wheel.
3. Remove the 2 retaining screws and remove the column cover.
4. Remove the 9 attaching screws from the instrument cover.
5. Carefully, pull the instrument cover outward and disconnect the electrical connectors. Remove the ignition illumination bulb and remove the cover.
6. Remove the lower panel, lap duct and defrost duct.
7. Disconnect the turn signal cancel switch electrical connectors and remove the switch from the column.

To install:

8. Position the switch on the column and connect the electrical connectors.
9. Install the lower panel, lap duct and defrost duct.
10. Connect the electrical connectors and install the ignition illumination bulb.

Remove the steering wheel mounting nut

11. Position the instrument cover and install the 9 attaching screws.
12. Position the column cover and install the 2 retaining screws.
13. Install the steering wheel and connect the negative battery cable.

Ignition Lock Cylinder
REMOVAL AND INSTALLATION

1. Remove the ignition switch. Refer to the procedure in Chapter 6.
2. Remove the lock cylinder assembly mounting screws and remove the lock cylinder assembly.
3. Installation is the reverse of the removal procedure. Check for proper operation.

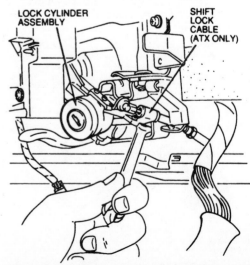

LOCK CYLINDER
ASSEMBLY

SHIFT
LOCK
CABLE
(ATX ONLY)

Ignition lock cylinder removal and installation

Steering Column

REMOVAL AND INSTALLATION

1. Disconnect the negative battery cable.
2. Remove the steering wheel.
3. Remove the column cover screws and the cover.
4. Remove the 9 attaching screws from the instrument cover. Carefully, pull the cover outward and disconnect the electrical connectors from the cover. Remove the ignition illumination bulb and the instrument cover.
5. Loosen the 2 instrument cluster cover-to-hinge screws, remove the 6 instrument cluster cover-to-dash screws and the instrument cluster cover.
6. Remove the lower panel, the lap duct and the defrost duct.

7. Disconnect the electrical connectors from the ignition switch and turn signal cancel switch.
8. Remove the upper U-joint cinch bolt from the lower end of the steering shaft.
9. Remove the mounting nuts from the hinge bracket.
10. Remove the 4 cluster support nuts and the 2 nuts and 4 bolts from the upper steering column brackets. Remove the steering shaft assembly.
11. At the steering rack, lift the boot from the intermediate shaft U-joint and remove the lower U-joint cinch bolt.
12. Remove the 4 intermediate shaft dust cover assembly nuts, the intermediate shaft and the dust cover assembly.

To install:

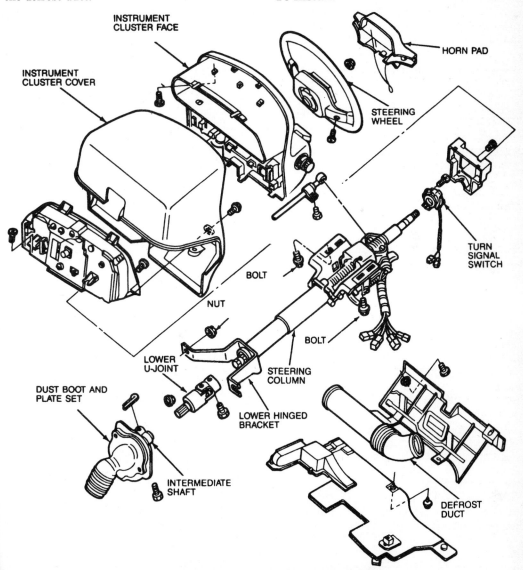

Steering column and related components

13. Using an assistant to support the intermediate shaft and dust cover assembly, guide the lower U-joint onto the steering rack pinion.

14. Install the lower intermediate shaft U-joint cinch bolt and torque it to 13–20 ft. lbs. (18–26 Nm). Install the dust cover nuts.

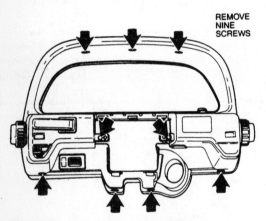

Steering column cover removal and installation

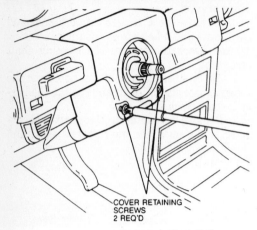

Instrument cover removal and installation

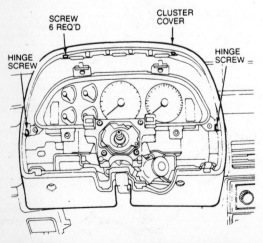

Instrument cluster cover removal and installation

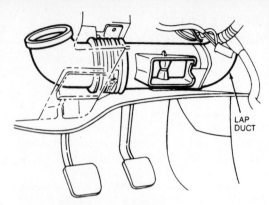

Air duct removal and installation

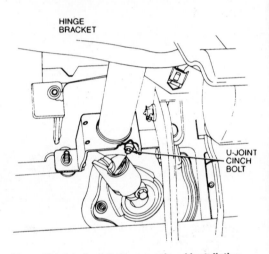

Upper U-joint cinch bolt removal and installation

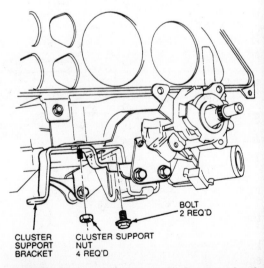

Steering column bracket nuts and bolts removal and installation

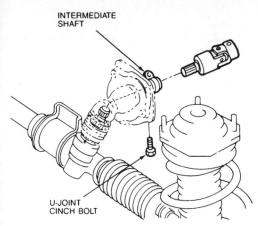

Lower U-joint cinch bolt removal and installation

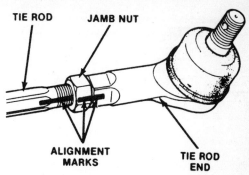

Paint alignment marks on the tie rod end, jam nut and tie rod before removal

15. Using an assistant to support the steering column, guide the column into the upper intermediate U-joint. Do not install the cinch bolt at this time.

16. Install the hinge bracket nuts, but do not tighten at this time.

17. Install the upper cinch bolt into the intermediate U-joint and tighten to 13–20 ft. lbs. (18–26 Nm).

18. Install the upper column bracket bolts. Tighten the hinge bracket nuts to 12–17 ft. lbs. (16–23 Nm) and the upper bracket bolts to 6.5–10 ft. lbs. (8.8–14 Nm).

19. Install the cluster support nuts and tighten to 6.5–10 ft. lbs. (8.8–14 Nm).

20. Connect the electrical connectors at the ignition switch and turn signal cancel switch.

21. Install the lap duct and the defrost duct. Install the lower panel.

22. Position the instrument cluster cover and install the attaching screws. Tighten the 2 cover hinge screws.

23. Connect the electrical connectors and install the ignition illumination bulb into the instrument cover and install the cover.

24. Install the column cover and the steering wheel. Connect the negative battery cable.

Steering Linkage
REMOVAL AND INSTALLATION
Tie Rod Ends

1. Raise and safely support the vehicle. Remove the wheel and tire assembly.

2. Remove the cotter pin and the nut from the tie rod end stud.

3. Separate the tie rod end from the steering knuckle using separator tool T85M–3395–A or equivalent. If the tie rod end does not separate easily, give the steering knuckle a sharp blow with a brass hammer or drift to shock the taper.

4. Paint or mark an alignment stripe on the tie rod end, jam nut, and tie rod.

5. Loosen the jam nut and remove the tie rod end.

To install:

6. Thread the jam nut and tie rod end onto the tie rod.

7. Align the marks made during removal and tighten the jam nut to 51–72 ft. lbs. (69–98 Nm).

8. Install the tie rod end in the steering knuckle. Install the nut and tighten to 22–33 ft. lbs. (29–44 Nm).

9. Install a new cotter pin. If the slots in the nut do not align with the hole in the tie rod end stud, tighten the nut for proper alignment; never loosen the nut.

10. Install the wheel and tire assembly and lower the vehicle. Check the front end alignment.

Power Rack and Pinion
ADJUSTMENT
Rack Yoke Preload

NOTE: *Readjusting the rack yoke preload will seldom cure hard steering or poor steering wheel return following a turn. First check for damage such as would be caused by hitting a curb. Then check for tight universal joints in the steering column and for tight or binding suspension parts.*

STANDARD POWER STEERING

1. Disconnect the negative battery cable. Remove the steering rack assembly from the vehicle and place it in a holding fixture.

2. Using pinion torque adapter tool T88C–3504–BH or equivalent, and an inch pound torque wrench, check the pinion turning torque; it should be 89–124 inch lbs. (10–14 Nm).

3. If the torque is not to specifications, loosen the locknut.

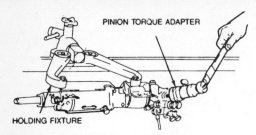

Measuring steering gear pinion torque

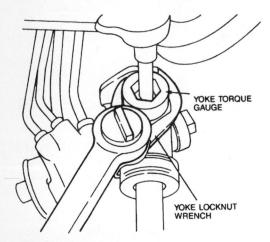

Adjusting the rack yoke preload

4. Using yoke torque gauge tool T88C–3504–AH or equivalent, torque the adjusting cover to 7.2 ft. lbs. (9.8 Nm), loosen the cover, retorque to 3.6 ft. lbs. (4.9 Nm) and loosen the cover 45 degrees.

5. Using yoke locknut wrench tool T88C–3504–KH or equivalent, torque the locknut to 36–43 ft. lbs. (49–59 Nm).

6. Install the steering rack assembly. Refill the power steering reservoir. Start the engine and bleed the system. Test drive and check the steering operation.

ELECTRONIC POWER STEERING

1. Disconnect the negative battery cable. Remove the steering rack assembly from the vehicle and place it in a holding fixture.

2. Using pinion torque adapter tool T88C–3504–BH or equivalent, and an inch pound torque wrench, check the pinion turning torque; it should be 89–124 inch lbs. (10–14 Nm).

3. If the torque is not to specifications, loosen the locknut.

4. Using yoke torque gauge tool T88C–3504–AH or equivalent, torque the adjusting cover to 39–48 inch lbs. (4.5–5.5 Nm), then loosen it 35 degrees.

5. Using yoke locknut wrench tool T88C–3504–KH or equivalent, torque the locknut to 29–36 ft. lbs. (40–50 Nm).

6. Install the steering assembly. Refill the power steering reservoir. Connect the negative battery cable.

7. Start the engine and bleed the system. Test drive and check the steering operation.

REMOVAL AND INSTALLATION

Standard Power Steering

1. Disconnect the negative battery cable.

2. Raise and safely support the vehicle. Remove the front wheel and tire assemblies.

3. Remove the cotter pins and nuts from the tie rod end studs. Separate the tie rod ends from the steering knuckles using separator tool T85M–3395–A or equivalent.

NOTE: *If the tie rod end does not separate easily, give the steering knuckle a sharp blow with a brass hammer or drift to shock the taper.*

4. From both sides of the vehicle, remove the lower inner fender plastic splash shield.

5. At the steering assembly, pull back the steering column dust boot, turn the steering shaft until the clamp bolt is accessible and lock the steering column. Using paint, matchmark the steering column pinion shaft-to-intermediate shaft lower universal joint location.

6. Remove the clamp bolt from the intermediate shaft lower universal joint.

7. Disconnect and plug both hydraulic lines at the steering gear. Position the lines aside.

8. Remove the 6 steering gear-to-chassis bolts and lower the steering gear until it rests on the crossmember. Slide the steering gear toward the right side until the left tie rod clears the left lower control arm, then carefully slide the steering gear to the left and remove from the vehicle.

To install:

9. Move the steering gear into position through the right side lower inner fender well opening, until the pinion shaft is just below the intermediate shaft universal joint.

10. Raise the steering gear into position, align the pinion shaft-to-intermediate universal joint matchmark and install the steering gear-to-chassis bolts. Torque the bolts to 27–40 ft. lbs. (36–54 Nm).

11. Install the pinion shaft-to-intermediate universal joint clamp bolt and torque to 13–20 ft. lbs. (18–26 Nm).

12. Connect the hydraulic lines to the steering gear. Tighten the large hydraulic line to 25–33 ft. lbs. (34–44 Nm) and the small hydraulic line to 18–22 ft. lbs. (25–29 Nm).

13. Connect the tie rod ends to the steering knuckles. Install the attaching nuts and tighten to 22–33 ft. lbs. (29–44 Nm), then install new cotter pins.

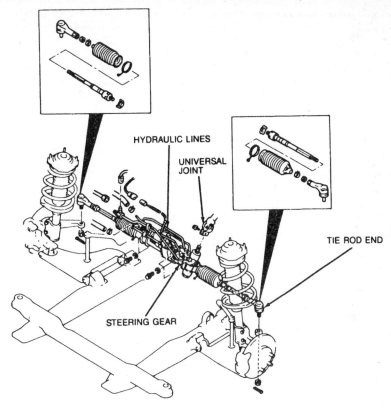

HYDRAULIC LINES

UNIVERSAL JOINT

TIE ROD END

STEERING GEAR

Steering gear removal and installation

14. Install the splash shields.

15. Install the wheel and tire assemblies.

16. Lower the vehicle. Refill the power steering reservoir. Start the engine, bleed the power steering system and check for leaks.

Electronic Power Steering

1. Disconnect the negative battery cable.

2. Raise and safely support the vehicle. Remove the front wheel and tire assemblies.

3. Remove the cotter pins and nuts from the tie rod end studs. Separate the tie rod ends from the steering knuckles using separator tool T85M–3395–A or equivalent.

NOTE: *If the tie rod end does not separate easily, give the steering knuckle a sharp blow with a brass hammer or drift to shock the taper.*

4. From both sides of the vehicle, remove the lower inner fender plastic dust shields.

5. At the steering assembly, pull back the steering column dust boot, turn the steering shaft until the clamp bolt is accessible and lock the steering column. Using paint, matchmark the steering column pinion shaft-to-intermediate shaft lower universal joint location.

6. Remove the clamp bolt from the intermediate shaft lower universal joint.

7. Disconnect the electrical connector from the solenoid valve and the power steering pressure switch.

8. Disconnect and plug the hydraulic lines at the steering gear; discard both copper washers from each fitting and position the lines aside.

9. Remove the steering gear-to-chassis bolts and lower the steering gear until it clears the bulkhead. Slide the steering gear toward the right side until the left tie rod clears the left lower control arm, then carefully slide it to the left and remove from the vehicle.

To install:

10. Slide the steering gear into position through the right side lower inner fender well opening, until the pinion shaft is just below the intermediate shaft universal joint.

11. Raise the steering gear into position, align the pinion shaft-to-intermediate universal joint matchmark and install the steering gear-to-chassis bolts. Torque the bolts to 27–40 ft. lbs. (36–54 Nm).

12. Install the pinion shaft-to-intermediate universal joint clamp bolt and torque to 13–20 ft. lbs. (18–26 Nm).

13. Using new copper washers, connect the hydraulic lines to the steering gear. Connect the electrical connectors to the solenoid valve and the power steering pressure switch.

14. Connect the tie rod ends to the steering

knuckles. Install the attaching nuts and tighten to 22–33 ft. lbs. (29–44 Nm), then install new cotter pins.

15. Install the front wheel and tire assemblies. Lower the vehicle.

16. Refill the power steering reservoir. Start the engine, bleed the power steering system and check for leaks.

Power Steering Pump

REMOVAL AND INSTALLATION

2.2L Engine

1. Disconnect the negative battery cable.

2. At the right fender, remove the inner fender splash shield.

3. Loosen the power steering pump and remove the drive belt.

4. Disconnect and plug the pressure and return hoses from the pump

5. Remove the pump-to-bracket bolts and the pump; if necessary, remove the drive pulley from the pump.

To install:

6. Position the pump on the bracket and torque the bolts to 27–34 ft. lbs. (31–46 Nm).

7. Connect the pressure and return hoses to the pump.

8. Install the drive belt. Refill the power steering reservoir. Connect the negative battery cable, start the engine and bleed the system.

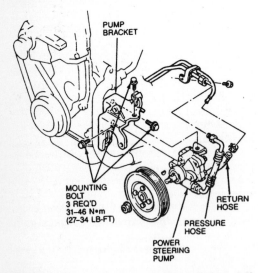

Power steering pump removal and installation—2.2L engine

3.0L Engine

1. Disconnect the negative battery cable.

2. Remove the washer reservoir and place aside.

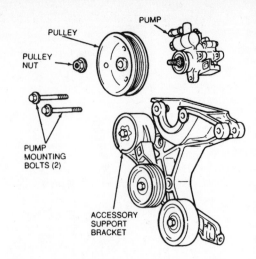

Power steering pump, pulley and accessory support bracket—3.0L engine

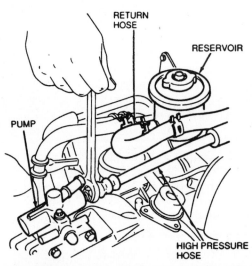

Disconnecting the high-pressure hose at the power steering pump—3.0L engine

3. Remove the plastic shield and the accessory drive belt.

4. Remove the drive pulley from the pump.

5. Disconnect and plug both power steering hoses at the pump.

6. Remove the pump mounting bolts and lift the pump from the accessory support bracket.

To install:

7. Position the pump on the accessory support bracket.

8. Install the pump mounting bolts and tighten to 15–22 ft. lbs. (20–30 Nm).

9. Install the drive pulley and replace both power steering hoses.

10. Install the drive belt and the plastic shield. Install the washer reservoir and connect the negative battery cable.

11. Fill the pump reservoir and bleed the system.

BLEEDING

1. Raise and support the vehicle, safely.

2. Disconnect the coil wire. Refill the power steering pump reservoir to the specified level.

3. Crank the engine. Check and refill the reservoir.

4. Crank the engine and rotate the steering wheel from lock-to-lock.

NOTE: *The front wheels must be off the ground during lock-to-lock rotation of the steering wheel.*

5. Check and refill the power steering pump reservoir.

6. Connect the coil wire, start the engine and allow it to run for several minutes.

7. Rotate the steering wheel from lock-to-lock several times, until the air bubbles are eliminated from the fluid.

8. Turn the engine **OFF**. Check and/or refill the reservoir.

9. Disconnect the negative battery cable, depress the brake pedal for at least 5 seconds and reconnect the negative battery cable.

Brakes

BRAKE SYSTEM

Operation

The hydraulic brake system on the Probe is a diagonally split system with a dual master cylinder. The left front and right rear are on one brake circuit while the right front and left rear are on another brake circuit.

A dual proportioning valve regulates hydraulic pressure in the brake circuit. When the brake pedal is applied, full brake circuit pressure passes through the proportioning valve to the rear brake circuit until the valves's split point is reached. Above the split point, the proportioning valve begins to reduce hydraulic pressure to the rear brake circuit, creating a balanced braking condition between the front and rear wheels while maintaining balanced hydraulic pressure at each rear wheel. Double walled steel tubing extends from the master cylinder pressure fitting to the rear cylinders and front calipers. Flexible hoses make the final connections between the body mounted brake tubes and the suspension mounted brake assemblies.

When the brake pedal is depressed, it moves a piston mounted in the bottom of the master cylinder. The movement of this piston creates hydraulic pressure in the master cylinder. This pressure is carried to the wheel cylinders or calipers by the brake lines.

When the hydraulic pressure reaches the wheels, after the pedal has been depressed, it enters the wheel cylinders or calipers. Here it comes into contact with a piston or pistons. The hydraulic pressure causes the piston(s) to move, which moves the brake shoes or pads (disc brakes), causing them to come into contact with the drums or rotors (disc brakes). Friction between the brake shoes and the drums causes the car to slow down. There is a relationship between the amount of pressure that is applied to the brake pedal and the amount of force which moves the brake shoes against the drums. Therefore, the harder the brake pedal is depressed, the quicker the car should stop.

Since a hydraulic system operates on fluids, air is a natural enemy. Air in the system retards the passage of hydraulic pressure from the master cylinder to the wheels. Anytime a hydraulic component below the master cylinder is opened or removed, the system must be bled (of air) to ensure proper operation.

The wheel cylinders used with drum brakes are composed of a cylinder with a polished inside bore, which is mounted on the brake shoe backing plate, two boots, two pistons, two cups, a spring, and a bleeder screw. When hydraulic pressure enters the wheel cylinder, it contacts the two cylinder cups. The cups seal the cylinder and prevent fluid from leaking out. The hydraulic pressure forces the cups outward. The cups in turn force the pistons outward. The pistons contact the brake shoes and the hydraulic pressure in the wheel cylinders overcomes the pressure of the brake springs, causing the shoes to contact the brake drum. When the brake pedal is released, the brake shoe return springs pull the brake shoes away from the drum. This forces the pistons back toward the center of the wheel cylinder. Wheel cylinders can fail in two ways; they can leak or lock up. Leaking wheel cylinders are caused either by defective cups or irregularities in the wheel cylinder bore. Frozen wheel cylinders are caused by foreign matter getting into the cylinders and preventing the pistons from sliding freely.

The calipers used with the disc brakes contain a piston, piston seal, piston dust boot, and bleeder screw. When hydraulic pressure enters the caliper, the piston is forced outward causing the disc brake pad to come into contact with the rotor. When the brakes are applied, the piston seal, mounted on the caliper housing, becomes slightly distorted in the direction of the rotor. When the brakes are released, the piston seal moves back to its normal position and, at the same time, pulls the piston back away from the brake pad. This allows the brake pads to move away from the rotor. Calipers can fail in three ways, two of these being caused by defective piston seals. When a piston seal becomes worn, it can allow brake fluid to leak out to contaminate the pad and rotor. If a piston seal becomes weak, it can fail to pull the piston away from the brake shoe when the brakes are released, allowing the brake pad to drag on the rotor when the car is being driven. If foreign material enters the caliper housing, it can prevent the piston from sliding freely, causing the brakes to stick on the rotor.

Clean, high-quality brake fluid, meeting DOT 3 specs, is essential to the proper operation of the brake system. Always buy the highest quality brake fluid available. If the brake fluid should become contaminated, it should be drained and flushed, and the master cylinder filled with new fluid. Never reuse brake fluid. Any brake fluid that is removed from the brake system should be discarded.

Since the hydraulic system is sealed, there must be a leak somewhere in the system if the master cylinder is repeatedly low on fluid.

BRAKE OPERATING SYSTEM

Adjustments
DRUM BRAKES

The Probe features a self-adjuster mechanism that is built into the parking brake strut, and compensates for normal brake lining wear.

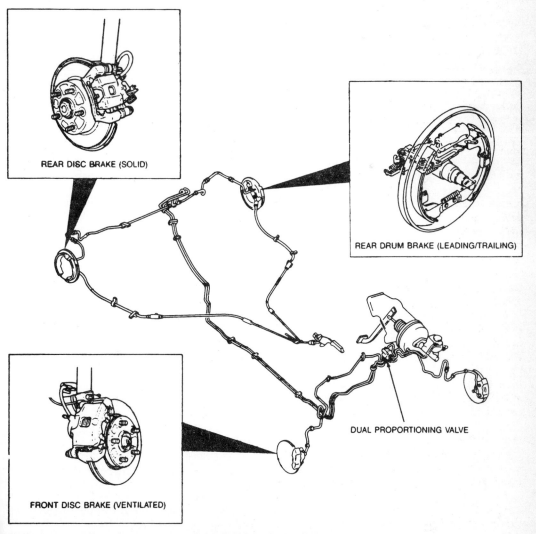

REAR DISC BRAKE (SOLID)

REAR DRUM BRAKE (LEADING/TRAILING)

DUAL PROPORTIONING VALVE

FRONT DISC BRAKE (VENTILATED)

Hydraulic brake system

No external adjustment is necessary or possible.

BRAKE PEDAL

Pedal Height

1. Check the distance from the center of the pedal pad to the floor. The distance should be 8.74–8.94 in. (222–227mm).

2. If adjustment is necessary, disconnect the stoplight switch electrical connector and loosen the switch locknut.

3. Rotate the switch until the pedal height is within specification.

4. Tighten the locknut and connect the electrical connector.

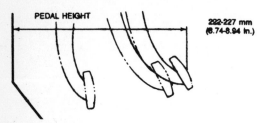

Brake pedal height dimension

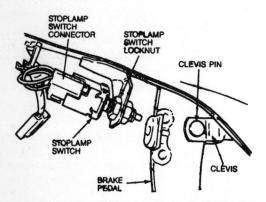

Adjust the brake pedal height with the stoplight switch

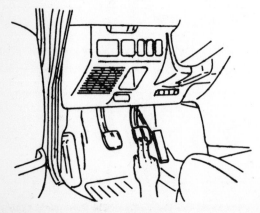

Checking the brake pedal free play

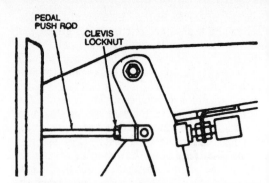

Adjust the brake pedal free play at the brake pedal pushrod

Pedal Free Play

1. If equipped with power brakes, depress the brake pedal a few times in order to eliminate the vacuum in the power booster.

2. Gently depress the pedal by hand and check the brake free play (the distance the pedal travels until the valve plunger contacts the stopper plate and resistance is felt). The free play should be 0.16–0.28 in. (4–7mm).

3. If adjustment is necessary, loosen the clevis locknut on the brake pedal pushrod.

4. Turn the clevis until the free play is within specification.

5. Tighten the clevis locknut.

Stoplight Switch

REMOVAL AND INSTALLATION

1. Disconnect the negative battery cable.

2. Disconnect the electrical connector at the switch.

3. Remove the switch locknut and remove the switch.

4. Installation is the reverse of the removal procedure. Adjust the brake pedal height.

Brake Pedal

REMOVAL AND INSTALLATION

1. Remove the spring clip and clevis pin from the brake pedal.

2. Remove the nut, lockwasher and washer from the pedal bolt.

3. Slide the pedal all the way to the left and remove the spacer.

4. Tilt the pedal to the left and remove the pedal assembly.

5. Remove the pedal bolt from the pedal bracket and remove the return spring and bushings from the pedal.

To install:

6. Apply white lithium grease to the pedal bushings and clevis pin.

7. Install the pedal bushings in the pedal.

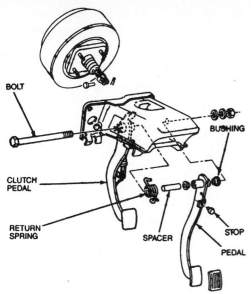

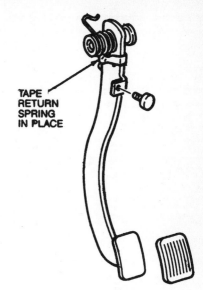

Brake pedal removal and installation—manual transaxle

Hold the return spring in place with tape

Master Cylinder

REMOVAL AND INSTALLATION

1. Disconnect the negative battery cable.
2. Disconnect the electrical connector from the fluid level sensor.
3. Disconnect the brake lines from the master cylinder. On vehicles with anti-lock brakes, the brake lines are retained with banjo bolts.
4. Cap the brake lines and the master cylinder ports.
5. Remove the mounting nuts and, if equipped, remove the clutch pipe bracket.
6. Remove the master cylinder.

To install:

7. Check, and if necessary, adjust the power brake booster pushrod. Refer to the procedure in this Chapter.
8. Position the master cylinder on the power

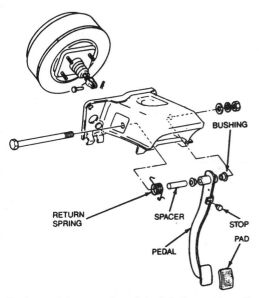

Brake pedal removal and installation—automatic transaxle

8. Position the return spring on the pedal and use a piece of tape to hold the spring in place.
9. Install the pedal bolt in the pedal bracket, pedal and spacer.
10. Install the washer, lockwasher and nut on the pedal bolt.
11. Position the clevis on the brake pedal, then install the clevis pin in the clevis and brake pedal. Install the spring clip on the clevis pin.
12. Adjust the brake pedal height and free play.

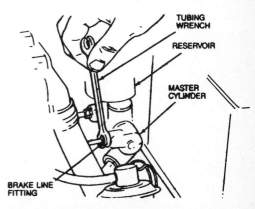

Disconnect the brake lines from the master cylinder—except vehicles with ABS

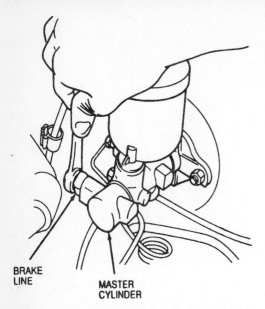

BRAKE
LINE   MASTER
                    CYLINDER

Banjo bolt removal and installation—vehicles with ABS

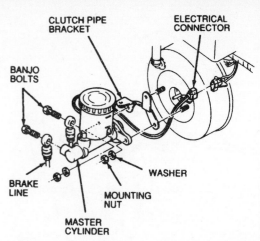

Master cylinder removal and installation—vehicles with ABS

brake booster studs. Install the clutch pipe bracket, if equipped.

9. Install the master cylinder mounting nuts and tighten to 8–12 ft. lbs. (10–16 Nm).

10. Connect short lengths of brake line to the master cylinder that point back into the reservoir. Position the ends of the lines so they will be submerged in brake fluid.

11. Fill the master cylinder reservoir with DOT-3 brake fluid and cover the reservoir with a shop towel. Slowly pump the brake pedal until clear fluid comes out of both temporary brake lines.

CAUTION: *Do not allow brake fluid to spill on the vehicle's finish; it will remove the*

paint. In case of a spill, flush the area with water.

12. Remove the temporary brake lines and connect the brake lines to the master cylinder. On vehicles without anti-lock brakes, tighten the brake line nuts to 10–16 ft. lbs. (13–22 Nm). On vehicles with anti-lock brakes, tighten the banjo bolts to 16–22 ft. lbs. (22–29 Nm).

13. Connect the fluid level sensor electrical connector.

14. Fill the master cylinder reservoir to the proper level and bleed the brake system.

OVERHAUL

Except 1992 Vehicles with Anti-lock Brakes

DISASSEMBLY

1. Check the continuity of the fluid level switch using a volt-ohmmeter. When the reservoir is full, the switch should be open.

2. Push down on the fluid level sensor float. The switch contacts should be closed when the float is pushed down.

3. If the fluid level switch is defective, it should be replaced.

4. Mount the master cylinder in a soft-jawed

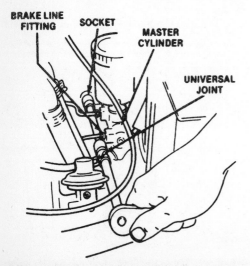

Master cylinder mounting nut removal

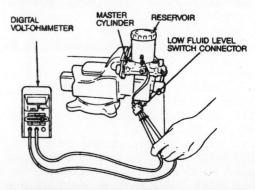

Checking the low fluid level switch

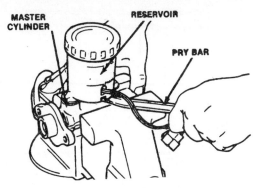

Removing the master cylinder reservoir

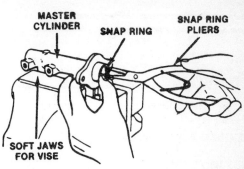

Removing the master cylinder snapring

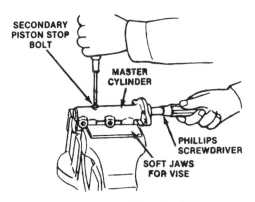

Removing the secondary piston stop bolt

vise and remove the reservoir retaining screw.

5. Gently pry up on the reservoir with a small prybar and remove it from the master cylinder.

6. Push in on the primary piston and remove the secondary piston stop bolt.

7. Use snapring pliers to remove the master cylinder snapring.

8. Position a cardboard box filled with clean shop towels in front of the master cylinder bore. Apply a small amount of compressed air to the master cylinder port to push out the pistons, and catch the pistons in the box. Use the least amount of air necessary to drive out the pistons.

9. Remove the reservoir grommets from the master cylinder.

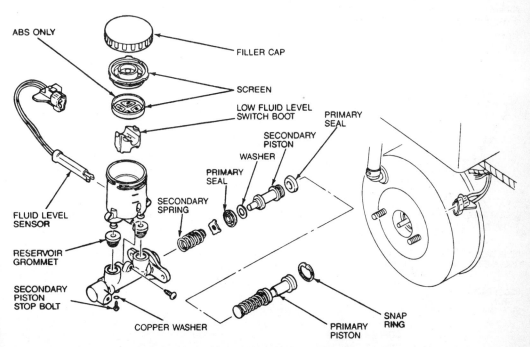

Master cylinder disassembled view—1989–91 vehicles

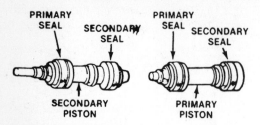

Master cylinder pistons and seals

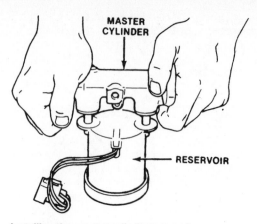

Installing the master cylinder reservoir

ASSEMBLY

1. Clean the master cylinder housing with brake cleaner. Make sure no residue remains.

2. Inspect the housing bore for wear, scoring, corrosion or other damage. Replace the entire master cylinder if the bore is not serviceable.

3. Lubricate the housing bore with clean brake fluid. Clean the master cylinder pistons with brake cleaner and install new seals. Some master cylinder rebuidling kits come with new pistons.

4. Lubricate the master cylinder pistons with clean brake fluid and install the pistons in the master cylinder housing. Install the snapring.

5. Push in on the primary piston and install the secondary piston stop bolt.

6. Install the reservoir grommets in the master cylinder housing and lubricate then with clean brake fluid.

7. Place the reservoir upside down on a clean work bench and press the master cylinder down over the reservoir. Install the reservoir retainer screw.

8. Install the master cylinder.

1992 Vehicles with Anti-lock Brakes

DISASSEMBLY

1. Mount the master cylinder in a soft-jawed vice. Remove the fluid level sensor and remove the reservoir retaining screw.

2. Gently pry up on the reservoir with a small prybar and remove it from the master cylinder.

3. Remove the reservoir mounting bushings.

4. Remove the stop pin and O-ring.

6. Push the primary piston in fully with a rod and use snapring pliers to remove the master cylinder snapring.

7. Remove the spacer, piston guide assembly, stopper and primary piston assembly.

8. Position a cardboard box filled with clean shop towels in front of the master cylinder bore. Apply a small amount of compressed air to the

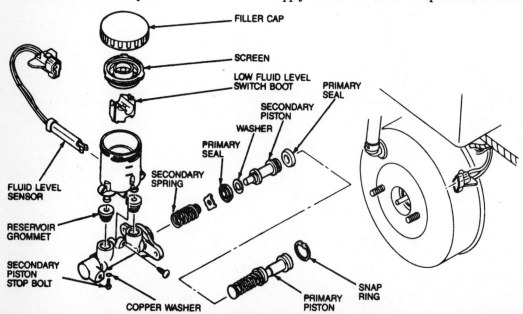

Master cylinder disassembled view—1992 non-ABS vehicles

master cylinder port to push out the secondary piston, and catch the piston in the box. Use the least amount of air necessary to drive out the piston.

9. Remove the O-ring.

ASSEMBLY

1. Clean the master cylinder housing with brake cleaner. Make sure no residue remains.

2. Inspect the housing bore for wear, scoring, corrosion or other damage. Replace the entire master cylinder if the bore is not serviceable.

3. Lubricate a new O-ring with clean brake fluid and install on the master cylinder.

4. Install new seals on the secondary piston assembly and install the assembly into the master cylinder with the piston hole facing the stop pin.

5. Install a new O-ring on the stop pin. Install the stop pin in the master cylinder and tighten.

6. Push and release the piston to make sure it is held by the stop pin.

7. Lubricate the stopper and piston guide assembly with clean brake fluid. Slowly and evenly insert the primary piston assembly, stopper, and piston guide assembly into the cylinder.

NOTE: *If the piston guide assembly does not install easily, use a suitable pipe or socket to tap it into position.*

8. Install the spacer and the snapring.

9. Lubricate the reservoir bushings with clean brake fluid and install them in the master cylinder.

10. Place the reservoir upside down on a clean work bench and press the master cylinder down over the reservoir. Install the reservoir retainer screw.

11. Install the fluid level sensor and install the master cylinder on the vehicle.

Power Brake Booster

The power brake booster reduces the effort required to push the brake pedal and apply the brakes. Power assist occurs due to a pressure differential within the brake booster.

When the engine is running and the brakes are not applied, there is engine vacuum on both sides of the booster diaphragm. When the brake pedal is pressed, the input rod assembly moves forward inside the valve body until the vacuum port closes. At this point there is still vacuum on each side of the diaphragm. As the input rod assembly continues to move forward, an atmospheric port is opened and atmospheric pressure enters the rear half of the brake booster. The engine vacuum on the front side of the diaphragm and atmospheric pressure on the back side of the diaphragm assist the input rod in pushing the diaphragm plate forward and the master cylinder pushrod against the master cylinder piston.

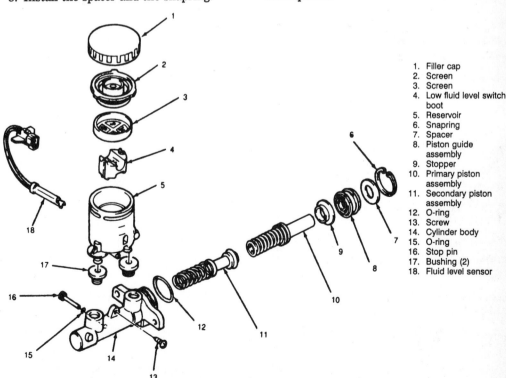

1. Filler cap
2. Screen
3. Screen
4. Low fluid level switch boot
5. Reservoir
6. Snapring
7. Spacer
8. Piston guide assembly
9. Stopper
10. Primary piston assembly
11. Secondary piston assembly
12. O-ring
13. Screw
14. Cylinder body
15. O-ring
16. Stop pin
17. Bushing (2)
18. Fluid level sensor

Master cylinder disassembled view—1992 vehicles with ABS

When the brake pedal is held in this position, the diaphragm momentarily continues to move forward, compressing the outer edges of the reaction disc. This causes the center of the disc to press the input rod back and close the vacuum port or atmospheric port, depending on whether the brake pedal is released or depressed further.

The vacuum hose from the engine contains an internal check valve that closes when the engine is shut off, trapping engine vacuum in the booster. This reserve vacuum allows several assisted brake applications with the engine off.

REMOVAL AND INSTALLATION

1. Remove the master cylinder. Refer to the procedure in this Chapter.
2. Disconnect the hose connecting the intake manifold to the power brake booster.
3. Working under the instrument panel, remove the spring clip in the brake pedal clevis pin. Remove the clevis pin and brake pedal pushrod from the brake pedal.
4. Remove the 4 attaching nuts that hold the booster to the bulkhead and remove the power brake booster.

To install:

5. Have an assistant position the power brake booster on the bulkhead so the 4 retaining studs protrude through the bulkhead into the passenger compartment.

6. Working under the instrument panel, install the 4 booster retaining nuts.
7. Apply lithium grease to the clevis pin and install it through the brake pedal pushrod and the brake pedal.
8. Install the clevis pin spring clip in the clevis pin.
9. Connect the hose connecting the power brake booster to the intake manifold. Because there is a check valve located in the center of the hose, make sure the arrow on the hose points toward the engine.
10. Check the power brake booster pushrod length and adjust, if necessary. Refer to the procedure in this Chapter.
11. Install the master cylinder.

POWER BRAKE BOOSTER PUSHROD ADJUSTMENT

Except 1992 Vehicles with Anti-lock Brakes
WITH ADJUSTMENT GAUGE

1. Install adjustment gauge T87C–2500–A or equivalent on the end of the master cylinder.
2. Measure the depth of the pushrod socket in the master cylinder.
3. Apply 19.7 in. Hg of vacuum to the booster using a hand vacuum pump.
4. Invert gauge T87C–2500–A or equivalent onto the booster.
5. Check the clearance between the end of

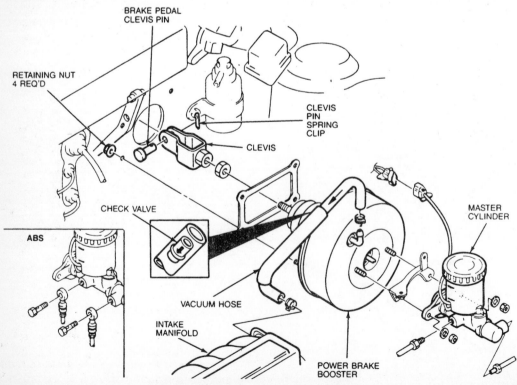

Power brake booster removal and installation

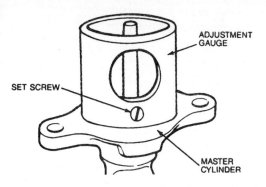

Measuring the depth of the master cylinder pushrod socket

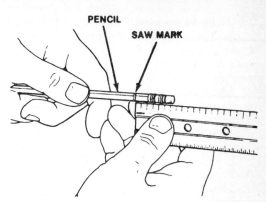

Measure the length of the pencil to the saw mark

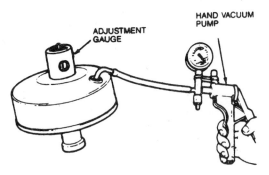

Checking the clearance between the end of the gauge and the pushrod

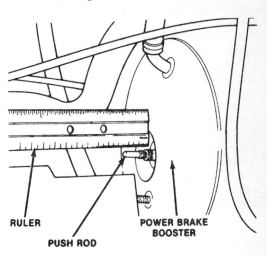

RULER

PUSH ROD

POWER BRAKE BOOSTER

Measure the pushrod protrusion

the gauge and the master cylinder pushrod. There should be no clearance between the gauge and the pushrod.

6. If adjustment is necessary, loosen the pushrod locknut and adjust the clearance.

WITHOUT ADJUSTMENT GAUGE

1. If adjustment gauge T87C–2500–A is not available, a pencil can be used instead.

2. Insert the pencil in the pushrod socket and mark it with a hacksaw blade.

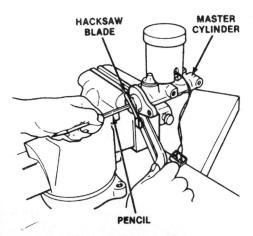

Mark the pencil with a hacksaw blade

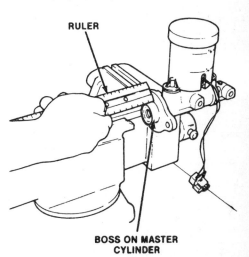

Measure the master cylinder boss

3. Measure the length of the pencil to the saw mark with a ruler.

4. Using a ruler, measure how far the master cylinder pushrod protrudes out of the booster.

5. Measure the master cylinder boss with a

ruler. Subtract the length of the boss from the length of the pencil. The difference in length between the master cylinder pushrod and the corrected pencil length is equal to the pushrod clearance.

6. Adjust the pushrod length to get the correct clearance. It should be 0.025 in. (1mm) shorter than the pushrod socket when using this method.

1992 Vehicles with Anti-lock Brakes

1. Remove the master cylinder.

2. Loosen the brass holding screw on master cylinder gauge T92C–2500–A or equivalent and retract the gauge rod. Attach the gauge to the booster and tighten the retaining nuts to 87–140 inch lbs. (10–16 Nm).

3. Start the engine and let it idle for approximately 15 seconds.

4. Push lightly on the end of the gauge rod until it just contacts the power brake pushrod. Tighten the brass holding screw to secure the gauge rod in place.

5. Remove the master cylinder gauge from the booster and turn the engine **OFF**.

NOTE: *Be very careful not to disturb the gauge rod setting when removing the gauge from the booster. If the setting is changed*

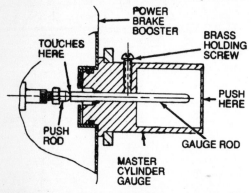

Master cylinder gauge attached to the power brake booster

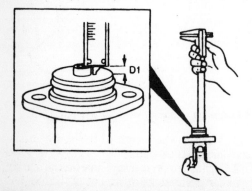

Measure the height of the master cylinder gauge rod

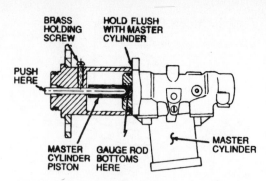

Master cylinder gauge attached to the master cylinder

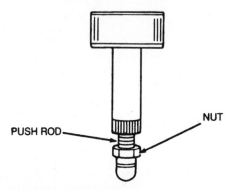

Power brake booster pushrod

during removal, a faulty measurement will be recorded and may cause unnecessary pushrod adjustment.

6. Using a depth gauge, measure and record the height of the master cylinder gauge rod. This measurement will be called "D1".

7. Loosen the master cylinder gauge brass holding screw and place the gauge on the master cylinder.

8. Push lightly on the end of the gauge rod, until it just bottoms in the master cylinder piston. Tighten the brass screw.

9. Remove the master cylinder gauge from the master cylinder.

NOTE: *Be very careful not to disturb the gauge rod setting when removing the gauge from the master cylinder. If the setting is changed during removal, a faulty measurement will be recorded and may cause unnecessary pushrod adjustment.*

10. Using a depth gauge, measure and record the height of the gauge rod, as in Step 6. This measurement will be called "D2".

11. Subtract D1 from D2. Adjust the power brake pushrod nut to lengthen or shorten the booster pushrod the amount equal to the difference between D1 and D2. If measurement D1 is larger than D2, the pushrod must be lengthened. If measurement D2 is larger than D1, the pushrod must be shortened.

Proportioning Valve
REMOVAL AND INSTALLATION

1. Remove the 2 bolts from the fuel filter bracket and position the fuel filter aside.

2. If necessary, remove the master cylinder and hydraulic actuation assembly on vehicles with anti-lock brakes, to gain access to the proportioning valve.

3. Using a tubing wrench, loosen all of the brake lines connected to the proportioning valve and the brake lines at the master cylinder.

4. Remove the brake lines between the proportioning valve and the master cylinder.

5. Disconnect all the brake lines connected to the proportioning valve and remove the valve.

To install:

6. Position the valve on the bulkhead and loosely install one of the attaching bolts.

7. Loosely install the brake lines between the master cylinder and the proportioning valve and loosely install the 6 brake lines into the valve.

8. Install the other attaching bolt into the valve and tighten both bolts to 14–17 ft. lbs. (19–23 Nm).

9. Tighten all the brake lines to 10–16 ft. lbs. (13–22 Nm).

10. If removed, install the hydraulic actuation assembly and the master cylinder.

11. Bleed the brakes. Bleed the lines at the proportioning valve first and then at the wheels.

Brake Hoses and Lines
REMOVAL AND INSTALLATION

Brake Hose

1. Raise and safely support the vehicle.

2. Remove the wheel and tire assembly.

3. Loosen the brake line fitting at the body support bracket, then remove the retainer clip from the bracket and hose.

4. At the other end of the hose, loosen the brake line fitting or remove the banjo bolt, as necessary. Discard the copper washers that seal the banjo fitting.

5. Remove the retainer clip that secures the brake hose to the strut, and remove the brake hose.

To install:

6. Install 2 new copper washers and loosely install the banjo bolt, or loosely install the brake line fitting, as necessary.

7. At the other end of the hose, loosely install the brake line fitting at the body support bracket.

8. Install the retainer clips at both support brackets.

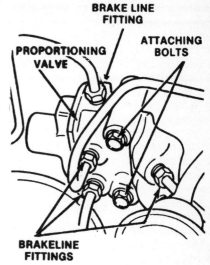

Proportioning valve removal and installation

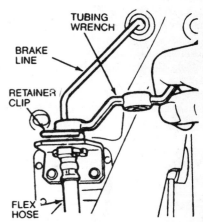

Loosening the brake line fitting from the brake hose at the body support bracket

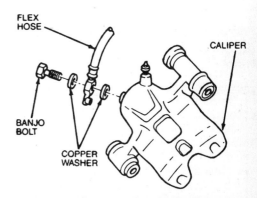

Brake hose attachment at the brake caliper

9. Tighten the brake line fitting(s) to 10–16 ft. lbs. (13–22 Nm) and, if necessary, tighten the banjo bolt to 16–22 ft. lbs. (22–29 Nm).

10. Bleed the brake system.

11. Install the wheel and tire assembly and lower the vehicle.

Brake Line

1. Raise and safely support the vehicle.
2. Remove the necessary components to gain access to the brake line.
3. Disconnect the brake line fittings at each end of the line to be replaced.
4. Disconnect the brake line from any retaining clips and remove the line from the vehicle.

To install:

5. Try to obtain a replacement line that is the same length as the line that was removed. If the line is longer, you will have to cut it and flare the end.
6. Use a suitable tubing bender to make the necessary bends in the line. Work slowly and carefully; try to make the bends look as close as possible to those on the line being replaced.

NOTE: *When bending the brake line, be careful not to kink or crack the line. If the brake line becomes kinked or cracked, it must be replaced.*

7. Before installing the brake line, flush it with brake cleaner to remove any dirt or foreign material.
8. Install the line into the vehicle. Be sure to attach the line to the retaining clips, as necessary. Make sure the replacement brake line does not contact any components that could rub the line and cause a leak.
9. Connect the brake line fittings and tighten to 10–16 ft. lbs. (13–22 Nm).
10. Bleed the brake system.
11. Install any removed components and lower the vehicle.

BRAKE LINE FLARING

Use only brake line tubing approved for automotive use; never use copper tubing. Whenever possible, try to work with brake lines that are already cut to the length needed. These lines are available at most auto parts stores and have machine made flares, the quality of which is hard to duplicate with most of the available inexpensive flaring kits.

When the brakes are applied, there is a great amount of pressure developed in the hydraulic system. An improperly formed flare can leak with resultant loss of stopping power. If you have never formed a double-flare, take time to familiarize yourself with the flaring kit; practice forming double-flares on scrap tubing until you are satisfied with the results.

The following procedure applies to most commercially available double-flaring kits. If these instructions differ in any way from those in your kit, follow the instructions in the kit.

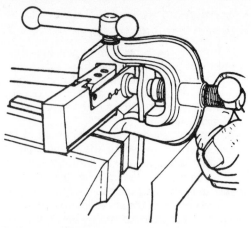

Flaring the brake line

1. Cut the brake line to the necessary length using a tubing cutter.
2. Square the end of the tube with a file and chamfer the edges.
3. Insert the tube into the proper size hole in the bar until the end of the tube sticks out the thickness of the single flare adapter. Tighten the bar wing nuts tightly so the tube cannot move.
4. Place the single flare adapter into the tube and slide the bar into the yoke.
5. Position the yoke screw over the single flare adapter and tighten it until the bar is locked in the yoke. Continue tightening the yoke screw until the adapter bottoms on the bar. This should form the single flare.

NOTE: *Make sure the tube is not forced out of the hole in the bar during the single flare operation. If it is, the single flare will not be formed properly and the procedure must be repeated from Step 1.*

6. Loosen the yoke screw and remove the single flare adapter.
7. Position the yoke screw over the tube and tighten until the taper contacts the single flare and the bar is locked in the yoke. Continue tightening to form the double flare.

NOTE: *Make sure the tube is not forced out of the hole in the bar during the double flare operation. If it is, the double flare will not be*

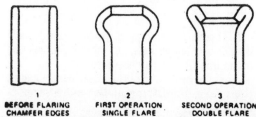

1	2	3
BEFORE FLARING CHAMFER EDGES	FIRST OPERATION SINGLE FLARE	SECOND OPERATION DOUBLE FLARE

Brake line flaring sequence

formed properly and the procedure must be repeated from Step 1.

8. Loosen the screw and remove the bar from the yoke. Remove the tube from the bar.

9. Check the flare for cracks or uneven flaring. If the flare is not perfect, cut it off and begin again at Step 1.

Bleeding
SYSTEM PRIMING

When a new master cylinder has been installed, or the brake system emptied or partially emptied, fluid may not flow from the bleeder screws during normal bleeding. It may be necessary to prime the system using the following procedure:

1. Disconnect the brake lines from the master cylinder.

2. Install short brake lines in the master cylinder ports and position them that they point back into the reservoir and the ends of the lines are submerged in brake fluid.

3. Fill the reservoir with clean DOT-3 brake fluid and cover the reservoir with a shop towel.

4. Slowly pump the brake pedal until clear, bubble-free fluid comes out of both temporary brake lines.

CAUTION: *Do not allow brake fluid to spill on the vehicle's finish; it will remove the paint. In case of a spill, flush the area with water.*

5. Remove the short brake lines and reconnect the vehicle brake lines to the master cylinder.

6. Bleed each brake line at the master cylinder as follows:

a. Have an assistant slowly pump the brake pedal 10 times and then hold firm pressure on the pedal.

b. Position a shop towel under the rear most brake line fitting. Open the fitting with atubing wrench until a stream of brake fluid comes out. Have the assistant maintain pressure on the brake pedal until the brake line fitting is tightened.

c. Repeat Steps a and b until clear, bubble-free fluid comes out from around the tubing fitting.

d. Repeat the operation on the front brake line fitting.

7. If any of the brake lines, calipers, or wheel cylinders have been removed, it may be helpful to prime the system by gravity bleeding. This should be done after the master cylinder is primed and bled. To prime the system:

a. Fill the master cylinder with clean DOT-3 brake fluid.

b. Loosen both wheel cylinder bleeder

screws, if equipped, and leave them open until clear brake fluid flows out. Frequently check the master cylinder reservoir to make sure it does not run dry.

c. Tighten the wheel cylinder bleeder screws.

d. One at a time, loosen the caliper bleeder screws and leave them open until clear fluid flows out. Frequently check the master cylinder reservoir to make sure it does not run dry.

e. Tighten the bleeder screws.

8. After the master cylinder has been primed, the lines bled at the master cylinder, and the brake system primed, proceed with normal brake system bleeding.

MANUAL BLEEDING

1. Clean all dirt from the master cylinder filler cap.

2. If the master cylinder is known or suspected of having air in the bore, it must be bled before any of the wheel cylinders and/or calipers are bled. Refer to the System Priming procedure.

3. Bleed the wheel cylinders and/or calipers as follows:

a. Begin at the rear bleeder screw.

NOTE: *The brake system on your Probe is diagonally split. If bleeding is begun at the right rear wheel, bleed the left front caliper next, followed by the left rear and right front. If bleeding is begun at the left rear wheel, bleed the right front caliper next, followed by the right rear and left front.*

b. Attach a drain hose to the bleeder screw. The end of the hose should fit snugly around the end of the bleeder screw.

c. Place the other end of the hose in a container partially filled with clean brake fluid.

d. Have an assistant slowly pump the brake pedal 5–10 times and maintain pressure on the pedal after the last stroke.

e. Loosen the bleeder screw approximately ¾ turn. Make sure your assistant keeps constant pressure on the pedal until the pedal drops all the way down and the bleeder screw is closed again. If the pedal pressure is released, air will be drawn back into the system.

f. Tighten the bleeder screw.

g. Repeat this operation until the fluid is clear and air bubbles no longer appear in the container.

h. Repeat these steps at the other wheel cylinder and calipers.

NOTE: *Never reuse the brake fluid expelled from the bleeder screws during the bleeding operation.*

4. After the bleeding procedure is completed,

make sure the fluid level is correct in the master cylinder reservoir.

FRONT DISC BRAKES

CAUTION: *Brake pads contain asbestos, which has been determined to be a cancer-causing agent. Never clean brake surfaces with compressed air! Avoid inhaling any dust from any brake surface! When cleaning brake surfaces, use a commercially available brake cleaning fluid.*

Brake Pads

REMOVAL AND INSTALLATION

1. Remove approximately ⅔ of the brake fluid from the master cylinder reservoir.
2. Raise and safely support the vehicle.
3. Remove the wheel and tire assembly.
4. If necessary, clean the brake assembly with brake cleaner and allow to dry.
5. Remove the caliper mounting bolt. Pivot the caliper upward on the fixed guide pin and secure it out of the way.

WARNING: *Do not allow the caliper to hang by the brake hose.*

6. Tag the anti-rattle shims so they can be reinstalled in their original position.
7. Remove the brake pads and retaining clips from the caliper anchor.
8. Inspect the disc brake rotor and machine or replace, as necessary.

To install:

9. Install the retaining clips.
10. Install the brake pads into the caliper anchor. The pad with the wear indicator is the inboard pad.
11. Install the anti-rattle shims in their original position.
12. Compress the caliper piston into its bore using pliers or another suitable tool.
13. Pivot the caliper down over the brake pads and install the caliper mounting bolt. Tighten the bolt to 23–30 ft. lbs. (31–34 Nm).
14. Install the wheel and tire assembly. Tighten the lug nuts to 65–87 ft. lbs. (80–118 Nm).

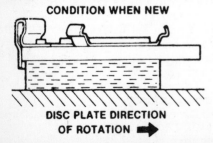

CONDITION WHEN NEW

DISC PLATE DIRECTION OF ROTATION ➡

Brake pad wear indicator-to-brake rotor relationship

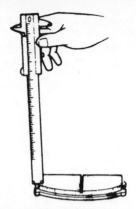

Checking the brake pad thickness

15. Lower the vehicle. Pump the brake pedal several times to position the caliper piston.
16. Check the fluid level in the master cylinder reservoir.

INSPECTION

When the pads are removed from the caliper, inspect them for oil or grease contamination, abnormal wear or cracking, and for deterioration or damage due to heat. Check the thickness of the pads. The minimum allowable thickness is 0.12 in. (3mm).

The brake pads are equipped with a wear indicator that will make a squealing noise when the pads are worn. This alerts you to the need for brake service before any rotor damage occurs.

Brake Caliper

REMOVAL AND INSTALLATION

1. Raise and safely support the vehicle.
2. Remove the wheel and tire assembly.
3. Remove the banjo bolt attaching the brake hose to the caliper, and discard the 2 sealing washers. Plug the hose to prevent fluid leakage.
4. Remove the caliper mounting bolt and pivot the caliper upward and off the brake pads.
5. Slide the caliper from the guide pin and remove from the vehicle.

To install:

6. Remove the guide pin bushing dust boots and push out the caliper guide pin bushing.
7. Lubricate the guide pin bushings with high temperature grease and install them in the caliper. Install the guide pin bushing dust boots.
8. Slide the caliper onto the guide pin and pivot the caliper down onto the brake pads. To provide the necessary clearance, it may be necessary to pull slightly outward on the caliper.
9. Install the caliper mounting bolt and tighten to 23–30 ft. lbs. (31–41 Nm).

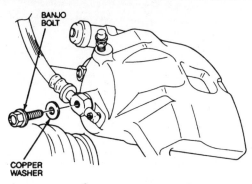

Disconnect the brake hose from the caliper

pressure can force the piston out of the caliper bore with enough force to cause personal injury. Never attempt to catch the piston by hand as it comes out of the bore.

NOTE: *Do not attempt to pry the piston from the bore.*

4. Remove and discard the dust boot and piston seal. A plastic or wooden pick can be used to remove the seal; a metal tool can scratch or nick the seal groove resulting in a possible leak.

10. Install 2 new copper washers and the banjo bolt on the brake hose banjo fitting.

11. Position the brake hose on the caliper and install the banjo bolt. Tighten the bolt to 16–22 ft. lbs. (22–29 Nm).

12. Bleed the brakes.

13. Install the wheel and tire assembly and tighten the lug nuts to 65–87 ft. lbs. (80–118 Nm). Lower the vehicle.

OVERHAUL

Disassembly

1. Disconnect the brake hose from the caliper. Open the bleeder screw and allow the brake fluid to drain from the caliper through the brake hose fitting. Remove the caliper assembly.

2. Remove the caliper guide bushing and dust boots and remove the snapring.

3. Position a block of wood or a roll of shop towels between the piston and the caliper. Apply air pressure through the brake hose fitting to remove the piston from the caliper.

CAUTION: *Apply only enough air pressure to ease the piston out of the caliper. Excessive*

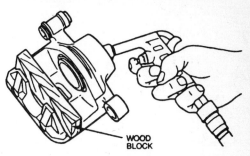

Removing the caliper piston

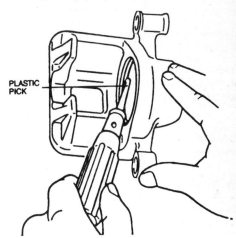

Removing the caliper piston seal

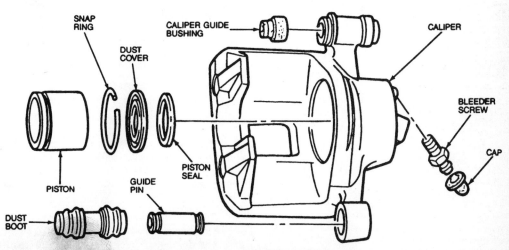

Front disc brake caliper disassembled view

Assembly

1. Clean the caliper housing and piston with brake cleaner. Inspect the housing and piston for pitting, scuffing, or other damage and replace as necessary.

2. Lubricate a new piston seal with clean brake fluid and install the seal in the caliper groove. Make sure the seal is not twisted and that it is firmly seated in the caliper bore.

3. Lubricate the caliper bore and piston with clean brake fluid.

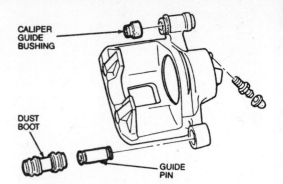

Installing the caliper guide bushing, guide pin and dust boot

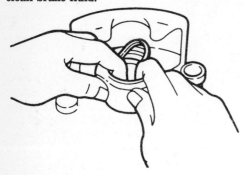

Installing a new piston seal in the caliper bore

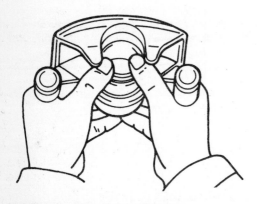

Installing the piston in the caliper bore

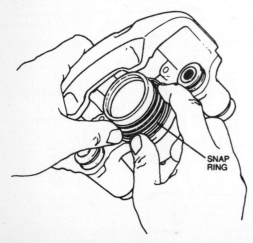

Installing the dust boot snapring

4. Install the dust boot on the piston and slide the dust boot into its groove.

5. Install the piston in the caliper bore and push it down into the bottom of the bore using a gentle, rocking motion.

6. Slide the dust boot over the boss on the caliper bore and install the snapring.

7. Install the caliper guide bushing, dust boot and guide pin.

8. Install the caliper on the vehicle.

9. After the brakes have been bled, with the car in neutral, spin the rotor to make sure the brakes are not dragging.

Disc Brake Rotor

REMOVAL AND INSTALLATION

1. Raise and safely support the vehicle.

2. Remove the wheel and tire assembly.

3. Remove the caliper anchor bracket bolts and remove the anchor bracket and caliper as an assembly. Support the caliper assembly from the coil spring with mechanics wire or string; do not disconnect the brake hose.

WARNING: *Do not let the caliper assembly hang by the brake hose.*

4. Remove the disc brake rotor. Handle the rotor with care, to prevent nicking or scratching the rotor surface.

To install:

5. Attach the disc brake rotor to the hub.

6. Install the caliper anchor bracket and tighten the bolts to 58–72 ft. lbs. (78–98 Nm).

7. Install the wheel and tire assembly. Tighten the lug nuts to 65–87 ft. lbs. (80–118 Nm).

8. Lower the vehicle. Apply the brake pedal several times to make sure the caliper piston is positioned.

INSPECTION

Check the disc brake rotor for scoring, cracks or other damage. Check the minimum thickness, parallelism and rotor runout.

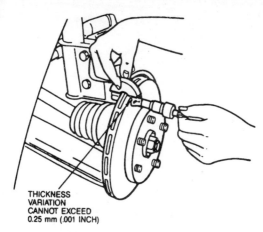

THICKNESS
VARIATION
CANNOT EXCEED
0.25 mm (.001 INCH)

Checking disc brake rotor thickness and parallelism

Check the disc brake rotor thickness using a micrometer or calipers. The brake rotor minimum thickness is 0.860 in. (22mm). This is the thickness at which point the rotor becomes unsafe to use and must be discarded. The minimum thickness that the rotor can be machined to is 0.890 in. (22.7mm), as this thickness allows room for rotor wear after it has been machined and returned to service.

Measure the rotor thickness in several places to check parallelism. The thickness variation must not vary more than 0.001 in. (0.025mm). If the thickness variation exceeds specification, machine the rotor if it is not below the minimum thickness specification for machining. If the thickness variation is still excessive after machining, the rotor must be replaced.

Check the rotor for runout using a dial indicator. Install a few lugnuts to hold the rotor against the hub while checking. Mount the dial indicator on the strut and position the indicator foot on the outermost diameter of the contact surface of the disc pads. Make sure there is no wheel bearing free play. Rotor runout must not

exceed 0.004 in. (0.1mm). If the rotor runout exceeds specification, machine the rotor if it is not below the minimum thickness specification for machining. If the rotor runout is still excessive after machining, the rotor must be replaced.

The disc brake rotor must be machined while it is bolted to the hub. The rotor and hub are mounted as an assembly on the rotor lathe, and then the rotor is turned. Machining the rotor separately, without the hub, may cause rotor runout.

REAR DRUM BRAKES

CAUTION: *Brake shoes contain asbestos, which has been determined to be a cancer causing agent. Never clean the brake surfaces with compressed air! Avoid inhaling any dust from any brake surface! When cleaning brake surfaces, use a commercially available cleaning fluid.*

Brake Drum
REMOVAL AND INSTALLATION

1. Raise and safely support the vehicle.
2. Remove the wheel and tire assembly and remove the grease cap.
3. Carefully raise the staked portion of the attaching nut using a suitable chisel.
4. Remove and discard the hub nut. Remove the brake drum/bearing assembly.
To install:
5. Position the brake drum/bearing assembly on the spindle and install a new locknut. Tighten the locknut to 73–131 ft. lbs. (98–178 Nm).
6. Stake the attaching nut using a suitable chisel with a rounded cutting edge.
NOTE: *If the nut splits or cracks after staking, it must be replaced with a new nut.*

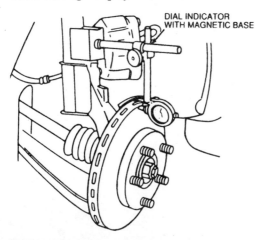

DIAL INDICATOR
WITH MAGNETIC BASE

Checking disc brake rotor runout

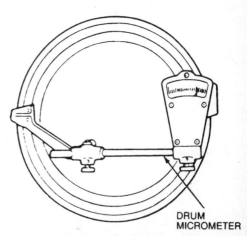

DRUM
MICROMETER

Measuring the drum brake diameter

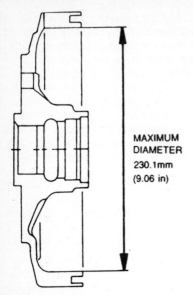

MAXIMUM
DIAMETER
230.1mm
(9.06 in)

Drum brake maximum diameter

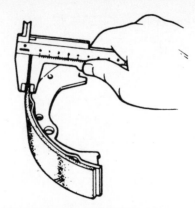

Measuring brake shoe lining thickness

drum and at the bottom of the deepest groove, to determine if the drum can be machined or must be replaced.

If the braking surface diameter is worn in excess of the maximum diameter, 9.06 in. (230.1mm), the drum must be replaced.

7. Install the grease cap and the wheel and tire assembly. Tighten the lug nuts to 65–87 ft. lbs. (88–118 Nm).

8. Lower the vehicle.

INSPECTION

Clean all grease, brake fluid, and other contaminants from the brake drum using brake cleaner. Visually check the drum for scroring, cracks, or other damage.

Measure the diameter of the drum using a suitable micrometer. Measure the diameter at various points around the circumference of the

Brake Shoes
INSPECTION

Inspect the brake shoes for peeling, cracking, or exremely uneven wear on the lining. Check the lining thickness using calipers. If the brake lining is less than 0.040 in. (1mm), the shoes must be replaced. The shoes must also be replaced if the linings are contaminated with brake fluid or grease.

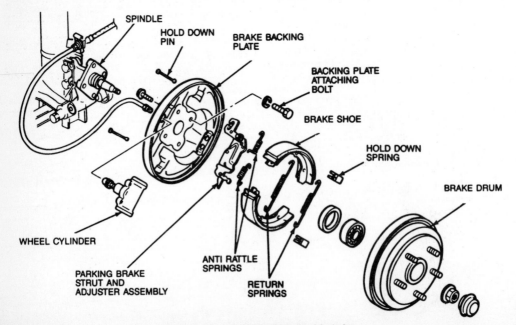

Drum brake assembly disassembled view

REMOVAL AND INSTALLATION

1. Raise and safely support the vehicle.
2. Remove the wheel and tire assembly and the brake drum. Clean the brake assembly using brake cleaner.
3. Remove the brake shoe return springs and anti-rattle spring.
4. Remove the brake shoe hold-down springs. Push the hold-down spring inward using a screwdriver, and twist the hold-down pin using needlenose pliers until the head of the pin aligns with the slot in the spring. Release the spring and pin.
5. Remove the front and rear brake shoes from the parking brake strut.

NOTE: *Unless they are broken or worn, leave the parking brake strut, adjuster mechanism and the adjuster spring in place.*

To install:
6. Inspect the anti-rattle and return springs for separated or twisted coils, twisted, bent or damaged shanks or discoloration. Discoloration indicates brake overheating; overheated springs lose some of their tension and should be replaced.
7. Using high temperature grease, lubricate the 6 shoe contact pads and the adjuster mechanism.

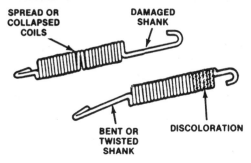

Check the ant-rattle and return springs for damage

NOTE: *If new shoes are being installed, the brake drums should always be resurfaced. This removes glazing, ensures an equal friction surface from side-to-side, and corrects out of round and bell mouth conditions.*

8. Position the rear brake shoe in the parking brake strut and install the rear hold-down pin and spring.
9. Position the front brake shoe against the parking brake strut and backing plate and install the hold-down pin and spring.
10. Install the brake shoe return springs.
11. Insert a small prybar between the knurled quadrant and the parking brake strut; twist the prybar until the quadrant just touches the backing plate.
12. Install the brake drum, and wheel and tire assembly. Lower the vehicle.
13. Firmly apply the brakes 2–3 times to adjust the rear brakes.

Wheel Cylinder

REMOVAL AND INSTALLATION

1. Raise and safely support the vehicle. Remove the wheel and tire assembly.
2. Remove the brake drum and the brake shoes.
3. Using a tubing wrench, disconnect the brake line from the wheel cylinder.
4. Remove the wheel cylinder-to-backing plate bolts and the wheel cylinder.

To install:
5. Install the wheel cylinder and loosely install the mounting bolts.
6. Connect the brake line to the wheel cylinder and tighten the fitting, using a tubing wrench.
7. Tighten the wheel cylinder mounting bolts to 7–9 ft. lbs. (10–13 Nm).
8. Install the brake shoes and the brake drum.
9. Bleed the brakes.

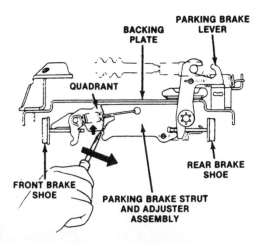

Positioning the self-adjuster mechanism

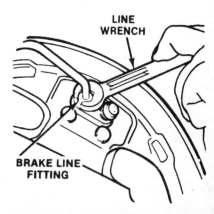

Disconnecting the brake line from the wheel cylinder

10. Install the wheel and tire assembly and lower the vehicle.

Brake Backing Plate

REMOVAL AND INSTALLATION

1. Raise and safely support the vehicle.
2. Remove the wheel and tire assembly.
3. Remove the brake drum and the brake shoes.
4. Remove the parking brake return spring using needlenose pliers. Be careful not to over-extend the spring.
5. Remove the parking brake cable attaching bolts and remove the cable from the backing plate.
6. Disconnect the parking brake cable from the parking brake lever.
7. Disconnect the brake line fitting from the wheel cylinder using a tubing wrench.
8. Remove the wheel cylinder attaching bolts and remove the wheel cylinder.
9. Remove the backing plate attaching bolts and remove the backing plate from the spindle.

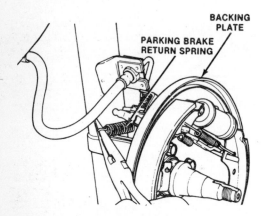

Removing the parking brake return spring

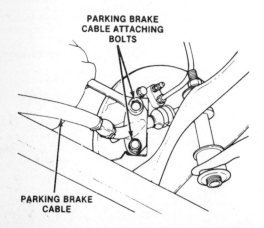

Removing the parking brake cable from the backing plate

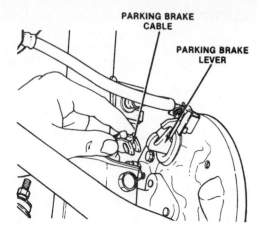

Disconnecting the parking brake cable from the parking brake lever

To install:

10. Install the backing plate on the spindle with the attaching bolts. Tighten the bolts to 31–47 ft. lbs. (45–67 Nm).
11. Position the wheel cylinder on the backing plate, install the bolts and tighten to 7–9 ft. lbs. (10–13 Nm).
12. Connect the brake line to the wheel cylinder and tighten the fitting to 10–16 ft. lbs. (13–22 Nm).
13. Install the parking brake lever in the backing plate. Lubricate the pin on the parking brake strut with high temperature grease.
14. Install the brake shoes.
15. Connect the parking brake cable to the parking brake lever. Install the cable-to-backing plate bolts and tighten securely.
16. Install the parking brake return spring.
17. Install the brake drum and the wheel and tire assembly. Lower the vehicle.
18. Firmly apply the brakes 2–3 times to adjust the rear brakes.

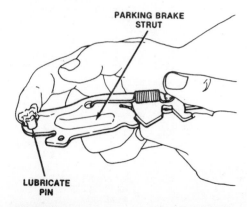

Lubricate the parking brake strut pin with high temperature grease

REAR DISC BRAKES

CAUTION: *Brake pads contain asbestos, which has been determined to be a cancer causing agent. Never clean brake surfaces with compressed air! Avoid inhaling any dust from any brake surface! When cleaning brake surfaces, use a commercially available cleaning fluid.*

Brake Pads

REMOVAL AND INSTALLATION

WARNING: *The rear brake system is subjected to high hydraulic pressure. Do not apply the brake pedal once the caliper has been removed from the anchor bracket.*

1. Remove approximately ⅔ of the brake fluid from the master cylinder reservoir.
2. Raise and safely support the vehicle.
3. Remove the wheel and tire assembly.
4. Loosen the parking brake cable housing adjusting nut. Remove the cable housing from the bracket and the parking brake lever.
5. Remove the caliper mounting bolt and pivot the caliper to clear the brake shoes. If necessary, pry the caliper outward. Remove the caliper and support it from the strut with mechanics wire.

WARNING: *Do not let the caliper hang by the brake hose.*

6. Remove the V-spring from the disc brake pads. Remove the disc brake pads, anti-rattle shims and retaining clips.

NOTE: *If the disc brake pads and anti-rattle shims are to be reused, they must be installed in their original positions.*

7. Inspect the disc brake rotor and machine or replace, as necessary.

To install:

8. Install the retaining clips. Position the anti-rattle shims on the disc brake pads and install the pads into the caliper anchor bracket.

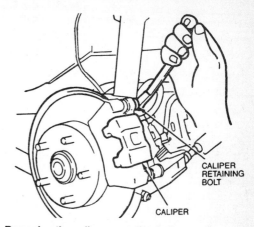
Removing the caliper mounting bolt

NOTE: *If the disc brake pads and anti-rattle shims are being reused, they must be installed in their original positions.*

9. Install the V-spring into the disc brake pads.
10. If new disc brake pads are being installed, the caliper piston must be compressed into the caliper bore to allow the caliper to fit over the pads. Use brake piston turning tool T75P-2588-B or equivalent, to rotate the caliper piston clockwise and screw the piston fully into the bore.
11. Lubricate the guide pin bushings with high temperature grease and install the caliper onto the guide pin. Pivot the caliper over the disc brake pads.
12. Install the caliper mounting bolt and tighten to 12–17 ft. lbs. (16–24 Nm).
13. Install the parking brake cable into the parking brake lever and bracket. Adjust the cable so there is no clearance between the cable end and the parking brake lever. Tighten the parking brake cable locknut to 14–21 ft. lbs. (20–28 Nm).

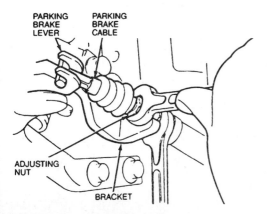
Removing the parking brake cable

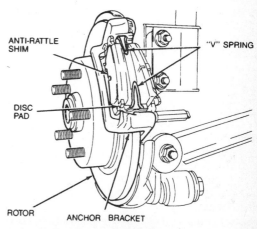
Rear disc brake pads installation

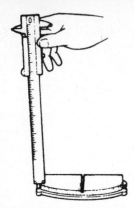

Checking disc brake pad thickness

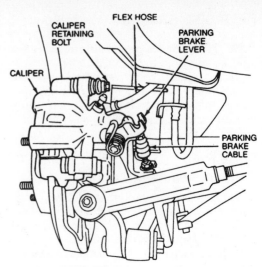

Rear disc brake caliper

14. Install the wheel and tire assembly and lower the vehicle.

15. Pump the brake pedal several times to position the caliper piston. Check the fluid level in the master cylinder reservoir and add clean brake fluid, if necessary.

INSPECTION

When the pads are removed from the caliper, inspect them for oil or grease contamination, abnormal wear or cracking, and for deterioration or damage due to heat. Check the thickness of the pads. The minimum allowable thickness is 0.04 in. (1mm).

The brake pads are equipped with a wear indicator that will make a squealing noise when the pads are worn. This alerts you to the need for brake service before any rotor damage occurs.

Brake Caliper

REMOVAL AND INSTALLATION

1. Raise and safely support the vehicle. Remove the wheel and tire assembly.

2. Loosen the parking brake cable housing adjustment nut. Remove the cable housing from the bracket and the parking brake lever.

3. Remove the banjo bolt mounting the brake hose to the caliper.

4. Remove and discard the copper washers from the banjo fitting.

5. Remove the caliper mounting bolt.

6. Pivot the caliper off the brake pads and slide the caliper off the guide pin.

7. Remove the disc pads and the caliper guide pin from the anchor bracket.

8. Remove the bolts from the anchor bracket and remove the anchor bracket.

To install:

9. Install the anchor bracket and tighten the mounting bolts to 33–49 ft. lbs. (45–67 Nm).

10. Install the caliper guide pin and the brake pads and shims.

11. Lubricate the guide pin bushings with high temperature grease. Install the caliper onto the guide pin and pivot the caliper over the brake pads. Tighten the mounting bolt to 12–17 ft. lbs. (16–24 Nm).

12. Install new copper washers and the banjo bolt mounting the brake hose to the caliper. Tighten the banjo bolt to 16–20 ft. lbs. (22–26 Nm).

13. Position the parking brake cable into the parking brake lever and bracket.

14. Adjust the parking brake cable so there is no clearance between the cable end and the parking brake lever. Tighten the parking brake cable locknut to 12–17 ft. lbs. (16–22 Nm).

15. Bleed the brakes.

16. Install the wheel and tire assembly and lower the vehicle.

OVERHAUL

Disassembly

1. Remove the disc brake caliper from the vehicle.

2. Open the bleeder screw and drain the brake fluid from the caliper through the brake hose fitting. After draining, close the bleeder screw.

3. Remove the caliper guide bushing and dust boots.

4. Use a small prybar to pry the retaining spring off the dust boot. Discard the dust boot.

5. Using brake piston turning tool T75P-2588–B or equivalent, rotate the caliper piston counterclockwise and remove the piston from the adjuster spindle.

6. Use a plastic or wooden pick to remove the piston seal from the caliper, then discard the

seal. Do not use a metal tool to remove the seal, as it may scratch or nick the seal groove, resulting in a possible leak.

7. Remove the stopper retaining snapring.

8. Remove the adjusting spindle, stopper and connecting link. Separate the adjuster spindle and the stopper.

9. Remove and discard the O-ring from the adjuster spindle.

10. Remove the parking brake return spring and the operating lever nut and lockwasher.

11. Mark the relationship between the operating lever and the shaft, then remove the lever from the shaft.

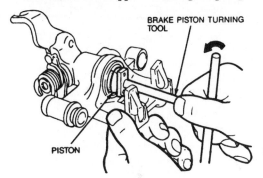

Removing the piston from the caliper

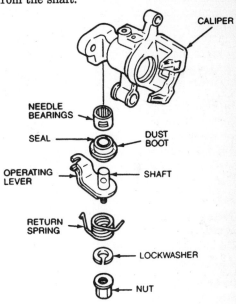

Removing the return spring, operating lever, seal and needle bearing

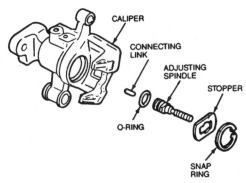

Removing the adjusting spindle, stopper and connecting link

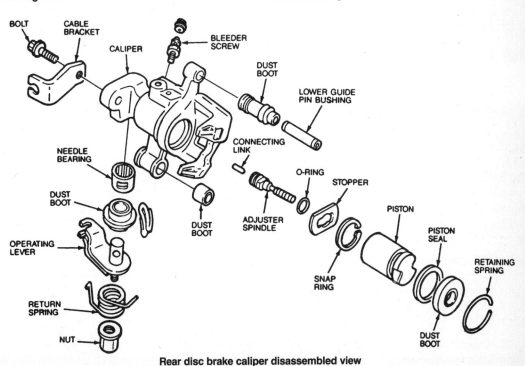

Rear disc brake caliper disassembled view

12. Remove the seal, shaft and needle bearing from the caliper housing.

Assembly

1. Clean the caliper and all parts to be reused with brake cleaner.

2. Inspect the caliper bore, piston seal groove and piston for cuts, deep scratches and pitting. Inspect the upper guide pin and lower guide pin bushing for wear and the upper guide pin and lower guide pin bushing dust boots for damage and poor sealing. Replace parts as necessary.

3. Apply the grease supplied in the rebuilding kit to the points shown.

4. Align the opening in the bearing with the bore in the caliper housing, then install the needle bearing.

5. Install the operating shaft into the caliper housing. Align the marks made during removal and install the operating lever.

6. Install the lockwasher and nut. Install the connecting link into the operating shaft.

7. Install the O-ring onto the adjuster spindle. Position the stopper onto the adjuster spindle so the pins will align with the caliper housing.

8. Install the adjuster spindle and the stopper into the caliper.

9. Install the stopper retaining snapring. Make sure the operating lever and adjuster spindle move freely.

10. Install the parking brake return spring.

11. Install the square-cut O-ring into the piston bore.

12. Using brake piston turning tool T75P-2588–B or equivalent, rotate the piston clockwise to install it onto the adjuster spindle. Screw the piston in fully. Align the grooves in the piston with the opening in the caliper.

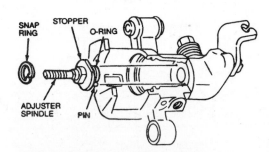

Installing the connecting link into the operating shaft

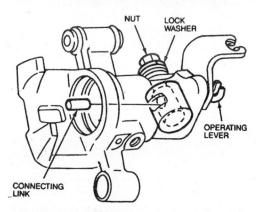

Installing the adjuster spindle and stopper

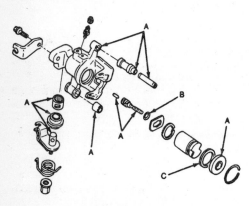

A—ORANGE COLORED GREASE
B—WHITE COLORED GREASE
C—RED COLORED GREASE

Apply grease to these points

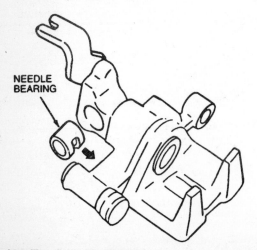

Installing the needle bearing

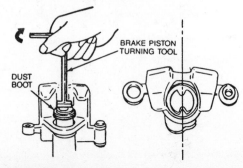

Installing the caliper piston

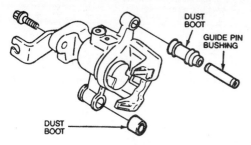

Installing the guide pin bushing and dust boots

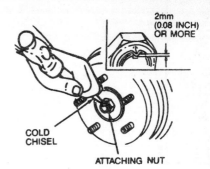

Staking the wheel bearing nut

13. Install a new piston seal in the caliper. Install the dust boot and retaining spring.

14. Install the upper guide pin dust boot and lower guide pin bushing dust boot. Install the upper guide pin and lower guide pin bushing.

15. Install the caliper onto the vehicle.

Disc Brake Rotor

REMOVAL AND INSTALLATION

1. Raise and safely support the vehicle.

2. Remove the wheel and tire assembly.

3. Remove the 2 anchor bracket bolts and remove the caliper and anchor bracket assembly. Do not disconnect the brake hose from the caliper. Support the caliper with mechanics wire from the coil spring.

WARNING: *Do not let the caliper hang by the brake hose.*

4. Remove the grease cap. Unstake the wheel bearing nut, using a cape chisel. Remove the nut and washer and discard the nut.

5. Remove the disc brake rotor. If equipped, remove the anti-lock brake signal ring from the rotor.

To install:

6. If equipped, install the anti-lock brake signal ring onto the rotor hub.

7. Install the rotor on the spindle.

8. Install the washer and a new nut. Tighten the nut to 73–131 ft. lbs. (98–178 Nm).

9. Stake the nut using a chisel with a rounded cutting edge. If the nut splits or cracks after staking, it must be replaced with a new nut.

10. Install the grease cap.

11. Install the caliper and anchor bracket assembly. Tighten the anchor bracket bolts to 33–49 ft. lbs. (45–67 Nm).

12. Install the wheel and tire assembly. Tighten the lug nuts to 65–87 ft. lbs. (80–118 Nm). Lower the vehicle.

INSPECTION

Check the disc brake rotor for scoring, cracks or other damage. Check the minimum thickness, parallelism and rotor runout.

Check the disc brake rotor thickness using a micrometer or calipers. The brake rotor minimum thickness is 0.315 in. (8mm). This is the thickness at which point the rotor becomes unsafe to use and must be discarded. The minimum thickness that the rotor can be machined to is 0.345 in. (8.762mm), as this thickness allows room for rotor wear after it has been machined and returned to service.

Measure the rotor thickness in several places to check parallelism. The thickness variation must not vary more than 0.001 in. (0.025mm). If the thickness variation exceeds specification, machine the rotor if it is not below the minimum thickness specification for machining. If

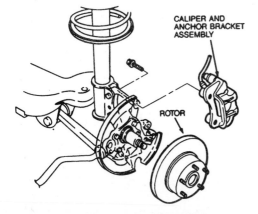

Rear disc brake rotor removal and installation

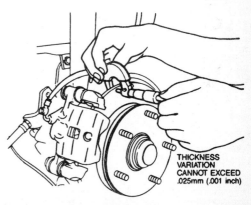

Checking disc brake rotor thickness and parallelism

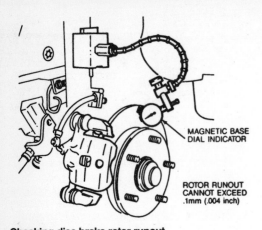

Checking disc brake rotor runout

the thickness variation is still excessive after machining, the rotor must be replaced.

Check the rotor for runout using a dial indicator. Mount the dial indicator on the strut and position the indicator foot on the outermost diameter of the contact surface of the disc pads. Make sure there is no wheel bearing free play. Rotor runout must not exceed 0.004 in. (0.1mm). If the rotor runout exceeds specification, machine the rotor if it is not below the minimum thickness specification for machining. If the rotor runout is still excessive after machining, the rotor must be replaced.

The disc brake rotor must be machined while it is bolted to the hub. The rotor and hub are mounted as an assembly on the rotor lathe, and then the rotor is turned. Machining the rotor separately, without the hub, may cause rotor runout.

PARKING BRAKE

Cables

REMOVAL AND INSTALLATION

1. Raise and safely support the vehicle.
2. Using a pair of needlenose pliers, remove the parking brake return spring from each backing plate; be careful not to overextend the spring.
3. If equipped with drum brakes, remove the attaching bolts from the parking brake cable housing and pull it away from the backing plate. Disconnect the cables from the backing plate parking brake levers.
4. If equipped with disc brakes, loosen the locknut and remove the parking brake cable from the lever.
5. Unbolt the cable housing clamps from the trailing arms and the body.

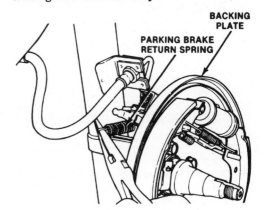

Removing the parking brake return spring at the backing plate

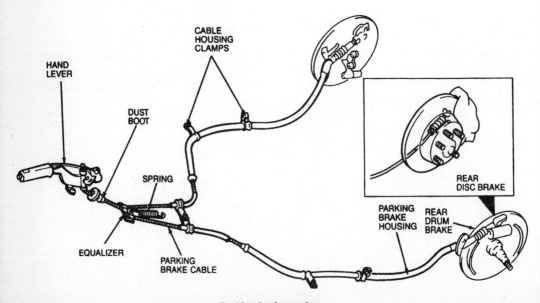

Parking brake system

6. Disconnect the parking brake return spring from the parking brake equalizer.

7. Disconnect the parking brake cable from the equalizer and remove the cable from the vehicle.

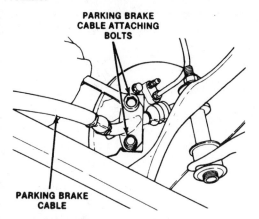

Removing the parking brake cable attaching bolts—drum brake vehicles

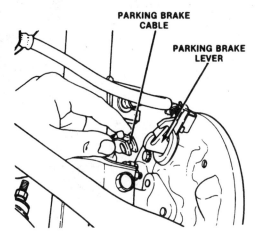

Disconnecting the parking brake cable from the parking brake lever—drum brake vehicles

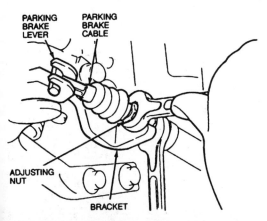

Disconnecting the parking brake cable from the parking brake lever—disc brake vehicles

8. Inspect the parking brake cable for free movement in the cable housing. If the cable does not move freely, lubricate or replace the cable assembly, as necessary.

To install:

9. Install the 2 cable ends in the parking brake equalizer. Apply multi-purpose grease to the cable clamps and the brake cable.

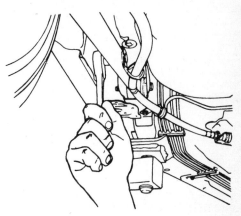

Removing the cable housing clamp from the trailing arm

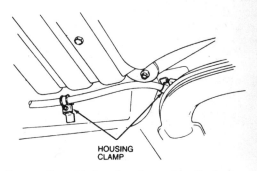

Remove the cable housing clamps from the body

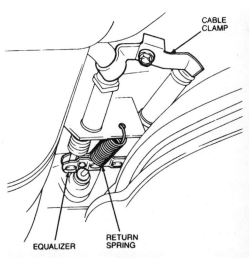

Remove the cable from the equalizer

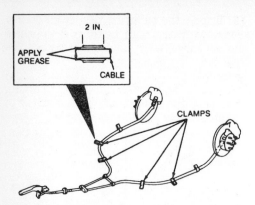

Apply multi-purpose grease to the cable and cable clamps

10. Install the cable housing clamps on the body and the trailing arms.

11. Connect the cables to the backing plate parking brake levers.

NOTE: *On rear disc brakes, there must be no clearance between the cable end and the lever.*

12. If equipped with drum brakes, position the parking brake cable against the backing plate and install the attaching bolts.

13. If equipped with disc brakes, tighten the locknut to 12–17 ft. lbs. (16–22 Nm).

14. Lower the vehicle and adjust the parking brake.

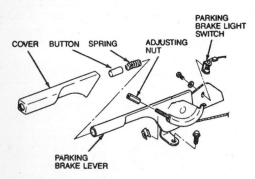

Parking brake lever assembly

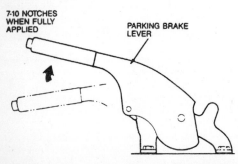

The parking brake should be fully set when the lever is raised 7–10 notches

ADJUSTMENT

1. Remove the center console attaching screws and the console.

2. Turn the parking brake adjusting nut until the brakes are fully applied when the parking brake lever is lifted 7–10 notches.

3. Reinstall the center console.

Parking Brake Lever

REMOVAL AND INSTALLATION

1. Remove the attaching screws from the floor console and remove the console.

2. Remove the attaching screws from the parking brake warning light switch, located on the parking brake lever. Remove the switch from the lever.

3. Remove the locknut from the parking brake adjusting nut using a 10mm wrench.

4. Remove the 2 attaching bolts from the parking brake lever and remove the parking brake lever.

5. Raise and safely support the vehicle.

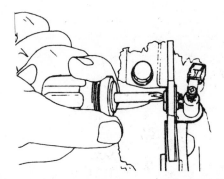

Parking brake warning light switch removal and installation

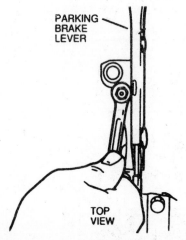

Removing the locknut from the parking brake adjusting nut

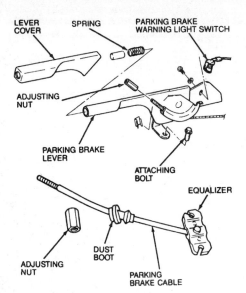

Parking brake lever, cable and related components

6. Working under the vehicle, disconnect the parking brake return spring from the parking brake equalizer. Remove the equalizer and cable from the tunnel access plate.

To install:

7. Working under the vehicle, install the equalizer, cable, and cable boot into the access plate.

8. Lower the vehicle.

9. Working inside the vehicle, install the equalizer cable into the parking brake lever. Loosely install the cable adjusting nut.

10. Position the parking brake lever on the tunnel and install the 2 attaching bolts.

11. Position the parking brake warning light switch on the parking brake lever and install the attaching screws.

12. Raise and safely support the vehicle.

13. Working under the vehicle, install the 2 parking brake cables in the equalizer. Install the parking brake return spring at the equalizer.

14. Lower the vehicle and adjust the parking brake.

15. Install the console.

ANTI-LOCK BRAKE SYSTEM

Description and Operation

The Anti-lock Brake System (ABS) releases and applies brake fluid pressure to the brake calipers during special braking conditions. ABS does not function under normal braking conditions, nor does it affect front to rear brake proportioning. When one or more wheels begins to lock up, ABS automatically senses the condition and activates the pressure control function.

The ABS control module is located under the driver's seat. Through its preprogramming, the control module decides which wheel(s) need brake pressure modulation. Once the decision is made, the control module sends the appropriate signals to the solenoid valves located in the hydraulic actuation assembly. The solenoid valves modulate fluid pressure through the flow control valves, resulting in reduced pressure at the caliper(s) to prevent further lockup.

The anti-lock brake system consists of all standard brake system components as well as the following components:
- Control module
- Hydraulic actuation assembly
- ABS relay
- Speed sensors
- Wheel sensor rotors

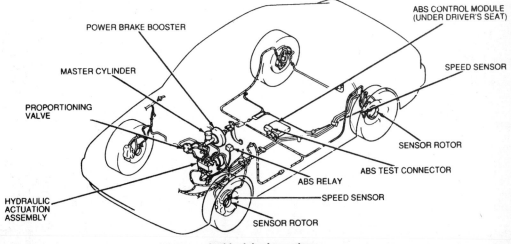

Anti-lock brake system

Troubleshooting

VISUAL INSPECTION

Check for problems in other areas that may affect ABS operation, such as suspension and steering components, tire condition and air pressure, wheel bearings, and brake components that are common to all brake systems. If all systems and components are OK, visually inspect for the following:

- Blown fuses
- Blown ABS warning bulb
- Shorted wires
- Poor connections
- Corroded connectors
- Poor insulation

NOTE: Connector pinout is shown looking into harness side of connectors.

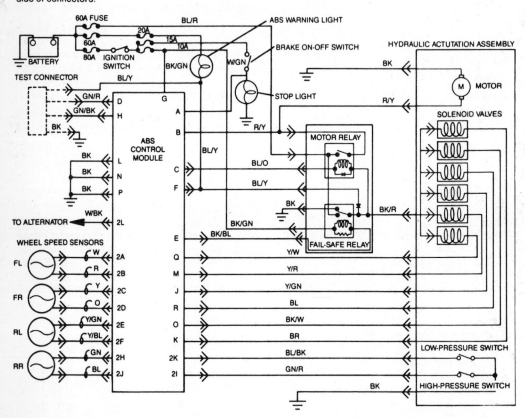

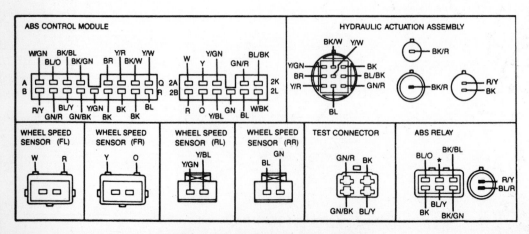

ABS electrical schematic—1989–91 Probe

- Damaged wheel speed sensors
- Damaged wheel speed sensor rotors
- Damaged ABS relay(s)
- Damaged hydraulic actuation assembly
- Damaged stoplight switch
- Damaged ABS control module
- Insufficient ABS hydraulic fluid
- Damaged brake lines

Perform any necessary service and refer to the ABS Symptom Chart.

QUICK TEST

The Quick Test is divided into two specialized tests: the Key On-Engine Running Test and the Continuous Test. Before performing either test, inspect the ABS warning light to make sure that indeed a fault has been detected by the ABS control module, or if the system is operating normally. When the ABS is operating normally, the ABS warning light will illuminate

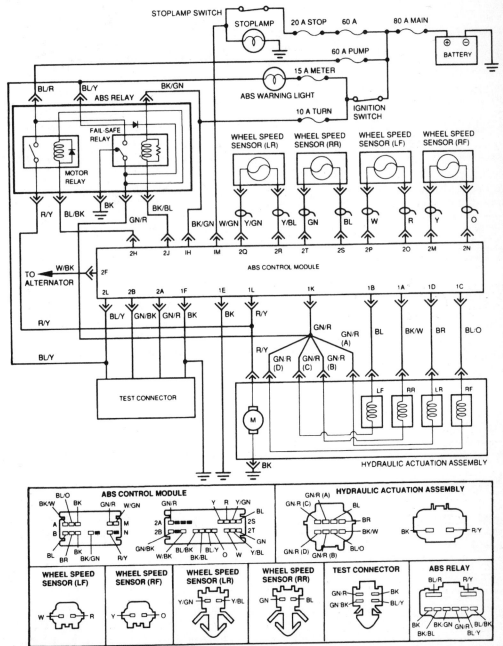

NOTE: Connector pinout is shown looking into harness side of connectors.

ABS electrical schematic—1992 Probe

during Key On-Engine Off and go off after the engine starts.

If the ABS warning light stays on after the engine starts, this indicates a present failure. Any time the ABS warning light flashes, this indicates either a present or past (intermittent) failure. All failure codes are stored in the ABS control module until they are erased. Codes are retrieved by identifying voltage fluctuations of a voltmeter connected to the ABS test connector.

Key On Engine Running Test

When activated, this test checks the ABS control module and system circuitry by testing its integrity and processing capability. The test also verifies that the various sensors and actuators are connected and operating properly. Code patterns will be indicated through the ABS test connector, and the ABS warning light will indicate the type of failure.

Continuous Test

This test is used to diagnose intermittent failures in the ABS. It is the same as the Key On-Engine Running Test, but also lets you attempt to recreate the intermittent failure by tapping, moving, and wiggling the harness and/or suspected sensor. If the voltmeter indicates a fault, the corresponding code pattern will be indicated. Now, with the knowledge of the affected circuits, a close check of the harness and associated connectors can be made.

NOTE: *Remember to keep your eyes on the volt-ohmmeter and ABS warning light for any change which will indicate where the intermittent is located.*

Any time a repair is made, erase ABS control module memory and repeat the Quick Test to make sure the repair was effective. If all phases of the Quick Test result in a pass, the problem is most likely non-electronic related and is with the standard brake system.

VEHICLE PREPARATION

1. Apply the parking brake.
2. If equipped with automatic transaxle, place the selector lever in **P**. If equipped with manual transaxle, place the transmission in neutral.
3. Block the drive wheels.
4. Turn OFF all electrical loads: radio, lights, blower fan, etc.

ABS WARNING LIGHT INDICATION

1. Turn the ignition key **ON**, but do not start the engine.
2. Observe the ABS warning light.
3. If the light is illuminated, operation is normal; proceed to Step 7.

BK	Black	N	Natural
BL	Blue	O	Orange
BR	Brown	PK	Pink
DB	Dark Blue	P	Purple
DG	Dark Green	R	Red
GY	Gray	T	Tan
GN	Green	W	White
LB	Light Blue	Y	Yellow
LG	Light Green		

Wire colors and their abbreviations

4. If the light is not illuminated, check the ABS warning light circuit 15 amp fuse and bulb. If the fuse and bulb are OK, go to Pinpoint Test Q1 on 1989–91 vehicles or Pinpoint Test WL on 1992 vehicles.

5. If the light is flashing, go to Step 7 on 1989–91 vehicles. If the light is flashing on 1992 vehicles, verify that the test connector is not jumped or shorted to ground between the GN/BK and B/K wires.

6. On 1992 vehicles, if the light illuminates for 1½ seconds and goes out before the engine starts, go to Pinpoint Test A1.

7. Start the engine.

8. Drive the vehicle, if necessary. Certain ABS faults require that the vehicle be driven in order for the warning light to come ON. Other faults will cause the light to turn ON each time the engine is started.

9. Observe the ABS warning light.

10. If the light is not illuminated on 1989–91 vehicles, this is normal operation. If an ABS symptom exists, or the light was flashing with the key **ON**, but the engine not running, perform Pinpoint Test Q. If no ABS symptoms exist and the light was illuminated with the key **ON**, but the engine not running, the ABS is operating normally.

11. If the light is not illuminated on 1992 vehicles, this is normal operation. If ABS symptoms exist, there may be an intermittent problem; go to Equipment Hookup. If no ABS symptoms exist and the light was illuminated with the key **ON**, but the engine not running, the ABS is operating normally.

12. If the light is illuminated, there is system failure; go to Equipment Hookup.

13. If the light is flashing on 1989–91 vehicles, a present or intermittent failure is indicated; go to Equipment Hookup.

EQUIPMENT HOOKUP

1. Verify that a failure has been detected in the ABS. An illuminated or flashing ABS warning light in the Key On-Engine Running mode indicates a failure. On 1992 vehicles, if the ABS warning light is not illuminated in the Key On-

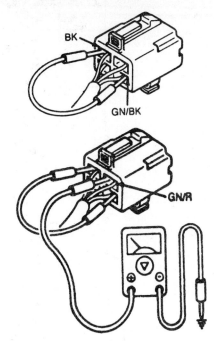

Connecting the jumper wire and volt-ohmmeter

Engine Running mode, but symptoms exist, it may indicate a past or intermittent problem.

2. Turn the ignition key **OFF**.

3. Remove the driver's seat to gain access to the ABS control module.

4. Connect a jumper wire at the test connector from the GN/BK to BK terminals.

5. Connect an analog volt-ohmmeter between the GN/R terminal and engine ground.

6. Set the volt-ohmmeter on a DC voltage range to read 0–20 volts.

7. Go to Service Code Retrieval.

SERVICE CODE RETRIEVAL

1. Make sure the ABS warning light illuminated, prior to the equipment hookup, with the key **ON**, but the engine OFF (and on 1989–91 vehicles, illuminated or flashed with the key **ON** and the engine running) before continuing.

2. On 1989–91 vehicles, start the engine. On 1992 vehicles, turn the ignition key **ON**.

3. Observe the ABS warning light.

4. A service code is represented as a pulsing or sweeping movement of the volt-ohmmeter's needle across the dial face. Codes will be repeated after all memory codes have been displayed once.

5. On 1989–91 vehicles, proceed as follows:

a. If the ABS warning light flashes once every 10 seconds, record the service codes and refer to Code Identification Chart A.

b. If the ABS warning light is illuminated constantly, record the service codes and refer to Code Identification Chart B.

c. If the ABS warning light flashes more than once every 10 seconds, this indicates past or intermittent faults. Record the service codes before erasing each fault (refer to Code Identification Chart B). Follow the Clearing Memory Codes procedure, then go to the Continuous Test.

6. On 1992 vehicles, proceed as follows:

a. If the ABS warning light flashes briefly, then goes out, the ABS is OK. Check for non-ABS related symptoms.

b. If the ABS warning light is illuminated constantly, record the service codes. Follow the Clearing Memory Codes procedure to erase the fault codes from memory, then re-attempt service code retrieval and record all recreated service codes; refer to the Code Identification Chart. Service the recreated service codes, as necessary. If the problem still exists, or if no codes were recreated, go to the Continuous Test.

c. If the ABS warning light flashes, this indicates past or intermittent faults. Record the service codes, then follow the Clearing Memory Codes procedure to erase fault codes from memory. Go to the Continuous Test.

CONTINUOUS TEST

1. Connect the jumper wire and volt-ohmmeter, as in Equipment Hookup.

2. On 1989–91 vehicles, start the engine. On 1992 vehicles, turn the ignition key **ON**.

3. Tap, move, and wiggle the suspect sensor and/or harness, working with short sections from the sensor to the dash panel and to the ABS control module. On 1989–91 vehicles, it is necessary to drive the vehicle each time this is done to recreate the intermittent failure and to allow the control module to sense and record the service code. On 1992 vehicles, drive the vehicle if necessary.

4. Keep your eyes on the ABS warning light and volt-ohmmeter for any indication.

NOTE: *On 1992 vehicles, with the key ON, any fault recreated during the Continuous Test will illuminate the warning light constantly. If the key is turned OFF, then back ON without clearing codes from memory, the warning light will flash along with the volt-ohmmeter, indicating a past or intermittent fault.*

5. On 1989–91 vehicles, proceed as follows:

a. If the ABS warning light flashes more than once every 10 seconds, record the service codes and refer to Code Identification Chart B.

b. If the ABS warning light flashes once every 10 seconds, record the service codes and refer to Code Identification Chart A. Service only the codes recreated in this test step.

c. If the ABS warning light is illuminated constantly, record the service codes and refer to Code Identification Chart B. Service only the codes recreated in this test step.

d. If the ABS warning light is illuminated, but no service code is indicated on the volt-ohmmeter, this is normal operation. If an intermittent fault cannot be recreated, turn the ignition key **OFF**, disconnect the suspect sensor and the control unit from the harness very carefully. Visually inspect all terminals for corrosion, bad crimps, improperly seated terminals, etc. Reconnect the harness connectors and re-attempt the Continuous Test.

6. On 1992 vehicles, proceed as follows:

a. If the ABS warning light is illuminated constantly, record the service codes and refer to the Code Identification Chart. Service only the codes recreated in this test step.

b. If the ABS warning light is not illuminated, this is normal operation. If an intermittent fault cannot be recreated, turn the ignition key **OFF**, disconnect the suspect sensor and the control unit from the harness very carefully. Visually inspect all terminals for corrosion, bad crimps, improperly seated terminals, etc. Reconnect the harness connectors and re-attempt the Continuous Test.

CLEARING MEMORY CODES

1989–91 Vehicles

1. Connect the A (GN/R) and B (GN/BK) terminals with a jumper wire.
2. Turn the ignition switch **ON**.
3. Check that the ABS warning light is illuminated, and wait 1–2 seconds.
4. Turn the ignition switch **OFF**.
5. Disconnect the jumper wire from terminal a (GN/R).
6. Start the engine and wait for the warning light to go OFF.
7. Turn the ignition switch **OFF** after 30 seconds.
8. Remove the jumper wire.

NOTE: *One failure condition is erased each time Steps 1–7 are taken. Since the memory can store up to 32 failures, repeat the procedure if the warning light flashes after repairs have been made. Repeat the steps until all memories have been cancelled. The memory in the control unit is not cancelled when the battery is disconnected.*

1992 Vehicles

1. Connect the B (GN/BK) and C (BK) terminals at the test connector with a jumper wire.

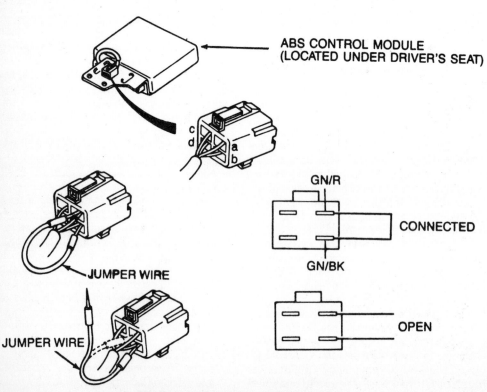

Clearing memory codes—1989–91 vehicles

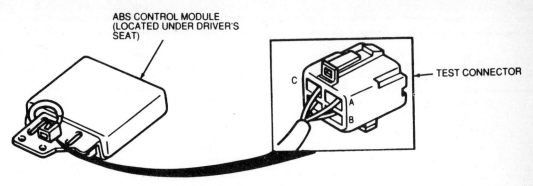

ABS CONTROL MODULE
(LOCATED UNDER DRIVER'S
SEAT)

TEST CONNECTOR

Clearing memory codes—1992 vehicles

2. Turn the ignition switch **ON**.

3. Output the service codes using the volt-ohmmeter.

4. After the first code is repeated, depress the brake pedal 10 times at intervals of less than 1 second.

5. Turn the ignition switch **OFF**.

6. Disconnect the jumper wire from the terminals at the test connector.

PINPOINT TESTS

Do not run any Pinpoint Tests unless instructed to do so by the Quick Test. Each Pinpoint Test assumes that a fault has been detected in the system with direction to enter a specific repair procedure. Doing any Pinpoint Test without direction from the Quick Test may produce incorrect results and replacement of good components.

Do not replace any parts unless the test results indicate they should be replaced.

When more than one service code is received, always start service with the first code received.

Do not measure voltage or resistance at the processor or connect any test lights to it, unless otherwise specified.

Isolate both ends of a circuit, and turn the key **OFF** whenever checking for shorts or continuity, unless otherwise specified.

Disconnect solenoids and switches from the harness before measuring for continuity, resistance, or energizing by way of a 12-volt source.

When using the Pinpoint Tests, follow each step in order, starting from the first step in the appropriate test. Follow each step until the fault is found.

After completing any repairs to the ABS, make sure that all components are properly reconnected and repeat the Quick Test.

An open is defined as any resistance reading greater than 5 ohms, unless otherwise specified. A short is defined as any resistance reading less than 10,000 ohms to ground, unless otherwise specified.

Control Module
REMOVAL AND INSTALLATION

1. Remove the driver's seat. Refer to Chapter 10.

2. Detach the ABS test connector by squeezing its lock tabs.

3. Remove the module mounting bolts, noting the location of the ground wire.

4. Disconnect the electrical connectors and remove the control module.

5. Installation is the reverse of the removal procedure.

Speed Sensors
REMOVAL AND INSTALLATION

Front

1. Disconnect the negative battery cable. Raise and safely support the vehicle.

2. Remove the front wheel and tire assembly.

3. Remove the retaining bolts and the speed sensor from steering knuckle.

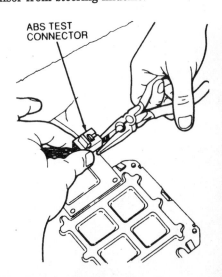

ABS TEST
CONNECTOR

Disconnecting the ABS test connector

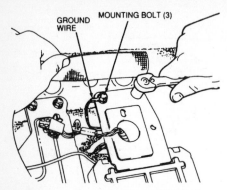

Removing the control module mounting bolts

4. Remove the routing bracket from the strut assembly.

5. Remove the routing bracket from the inner fender well and disconnect the wiring harness.

6. Remove the speed sensor.

NOTE: *The left and right speed sensors are not interchangeable. L or R is indicated on the bracket.*

To install:

7. Route the sensor wiring harness in the vehicle and connect the wiring harness.

8. Install the routing bracket onto the inner fender well.

9. Install the routing bracket onto the strut assembly. Tighten the bolt to 12–17 ft. lbs. (16–23 Nm).

10. Install the speed sensor into the knuckle and tighten the bolts to 12–17 ft. lbs. (16–23 Nm).

11. Make sure the wiring harness will clear all suspension components.

12. Install the wheel and tire assembly and lower the vehicle. Connect the negative battery cable.

Rear

1. Disconnect the negative battery cable. Raise and safely support the vehicle.

2. Remove the wheel and tire assembly.

3. Remove the retaining bolt and the speed sensor from the knuckle.

4. Remove the routing bracket from the strut assembly.

5. Remove the routing bracket from the inner fender well.

6. Remove the interior panels as neccessary to gain access to the wiring harness.

7. Disconnect the wiring harness and remove the speed sensor.

NOTE: *The left and right speed sensors are not interchangeable. L or R is indicated on the bracket.*

To install:

8. Route the sensor wiring harness in the vehicle and connect the wiring harness.

9. Install the routing bracket onto the inner fender well.

10. Install the routing bracket onto the strut

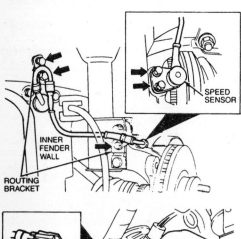

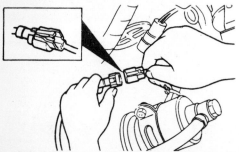

Front speed sensor removal and installation

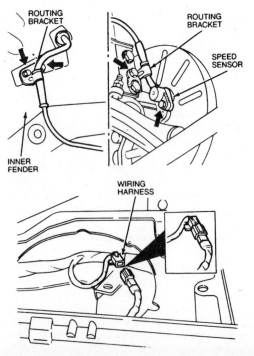

Rear speed sensor removal and installation

assembly. Tighten the nut to 12–17 ft. lbs. (16–23 Nm).

11. Install the speed sensor into the knuckle and tighten the bolt to 12–17 ft. lbs. (16–23 Nm).

12. Make sure the wiring harness will clear all suspension components.

13. Install any interior panels that were removed.

14. Install the wheel and tire assembly and lower the vehicle. Connect the negative battery cable.

Hydraulic Actuation Unit

REMOVAL AND INSTALLATION

1989–91 Vehicles

1. Disconnect the negative battery cable.

2. Remove the fuel filter and air filter assemblies.

3. Remove the coil and disconnect the wiring harness from the bottom of the coil and the fuel filter mounting bracket.

4. Remove the coil and fuel filter mounting bracket. Disconnect the 3 electrical connectors.

5. Remove the banjo bolts and copper washers from the brake lines at the hydraulic actuation unit. Disconnect the brake lines between the master cylinder and the hydraulic actuation unit.

NOTE: *Note the routing of the brake lines to ensure proper installation.*

6. Remove the routing clip from the brake lines. Using a 6 in. (153mm) extension and a 6-point, 10mm crowfoot wrench, disconnect the 4 brake lines at the hydraulic actuation unit.

NOTE: *Note the location of each brake line to ensure proper installation.*

7. Remove the mounting nuts, lockwashers and washers. Lift the hydraulic actuation unit from the mounting bracket and remove the mounting bushings from the actuation assem-

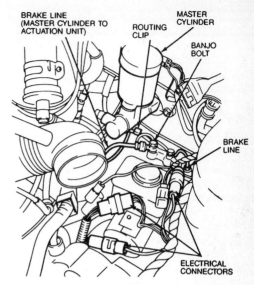

Brake line and electrical connector locations

bly. If neccessary, remove the mounting bracket.

To install:

8. Install the mounting bracket, bushings and the hydraulic actuation unit. Tighten the mounting nuts to 14–19 ft. lbs. (19–25 Nm).

9. Connect the 3 electrical connectors, making sure the connectors lock in place.

10. Using a 6 in. (153mm) extension and a 6-point, 10mm crowfoot wrench, install 4 brake lines to the actuation assembly. Tighten to 10–16 ft. lbs. (13–22 Nm).

11. Position the 2 brake lines between the actuation assembly and the master cylinder. Install the banjo bolts with new copper washers and tighten the banjo bolts to 16–22 ft. lbs. (22–29 Nm).

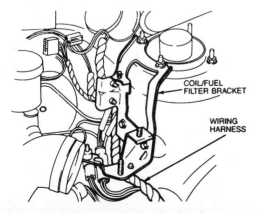

Coil and fuel filter mounting bracket location

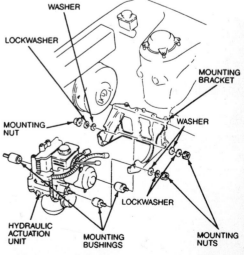

Hydraulic actuation unit removal and installation—1989–91 vehicles

12. Install the coil and fuel filter mounting bracket. Tighten the nuts to 34–46 ft. lbs. (56–63 Nm). Connect the wire harness to the bottom of the coil and fuel filter mounting bracket.

13. Install the coil, air filter and fuel filter assemblies.

14. Fill and bleed the brake system. Connect the negative battery cable.

1992 Vehicles

1. Disconnect the negative battery cable.

2. Remove the air cleaner assembly.

3. Disconnect the electrical connectors at the ignition coil.

4. Remove the 2 mounting nuts at the coil and module bracket and remove the coil and module bracket.

5. Remove the 4 mounting nuts at the fuel filter bracket and move the filter and bracket aside.

6. Disconnect the 2 electrical connectors leading to the hydraulic actuation unit.

7. Disconnect the brake lines from the hydraulic actuation unit. Remove the brake lines necessary for actuation unit removal.

8. Remove the mounting nuts and remove the hydraulic actuation unit.

To install:

9. Install the hydraulic actuation unit and tighten the nuts to 14–19 ft. lbs. (19–25 Nm).

10. Connect the brake lines and tighten to 10–16 ft. lbs. (13–22 Nm).

11. Connect the electrical connectors leading to the actuation unit.

12. Position the fuel filter and bracket and tighten the mounting nuts.

13. Install the ignition coil and module bracket. Tighten the mounting nuts.

14. Connect the electrical connectors at the ignition coil.

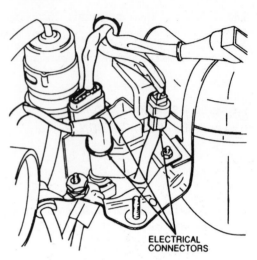

Disconnect the electrical connectors at the ignition coil

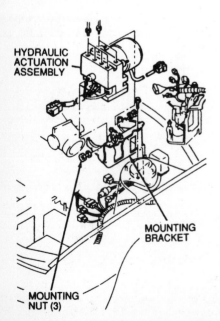

Hydraulic actuation unit removal and installation—1992 vehicles

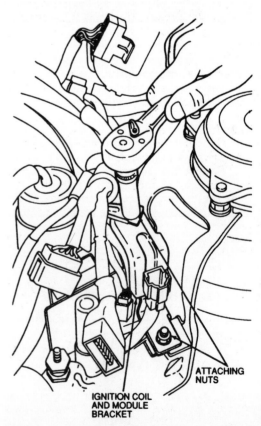

Ignition coil and module bracket removal and installation

15. Install the air cleaner assembly.

16. Fill and bleed the brake system. Connect the negative battery cable.

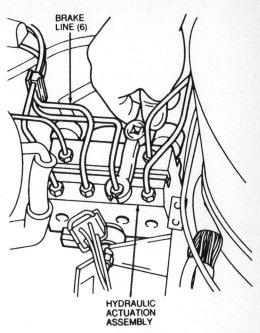

Disconnect the brake lines from the hydraulic actuation unit

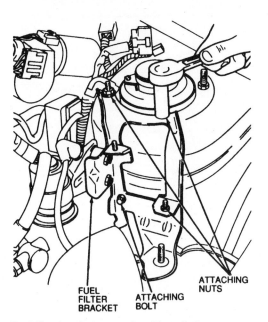

Fuel filter bracket removal and installation

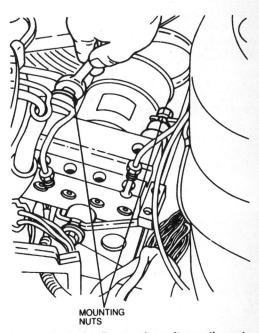

Remove the hydraulic actuation unit mounting nuts

Wheel Sensor Rotors

REMOVAL AND INSTALLATION

Front

1. Raise and safely support the vehicle. Remove the wheel and tire assembly.

2. Remove the halfshaft assembly. Refer to Chapter 7.

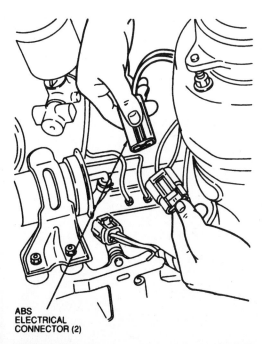

Disconnect the electric connectors to the hydraulic actuation unit

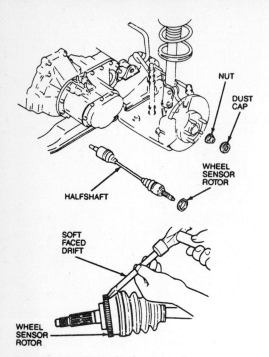

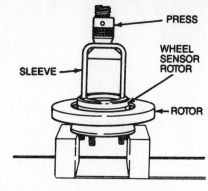

Pressing on the rear wheel sensor rotor

Removing the front wheel sensor rotor

3. Using a soft-faced drift, tap the sensor rotor from the outboard CV-joint.

To install:

4. Position the sensor rotor on the CV-joint with the chamfered edge facing the halfshaft.

5. Using a soft-faced drift, tap the sensor rotor onto the outboard CV-joint.

6. Install the halfshaft assembly.

7. Install the wheel and tire assembly and lower the vehicle.

Rear

1. Raise and safely support the vehicle.

2. Remove the wheel and tire assembly.

3. Remove the caliper and anchor bracket, without disconnecting the brake hose. Support

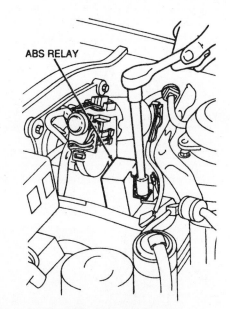

Removing the ABS relay mounting nut

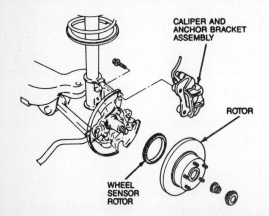

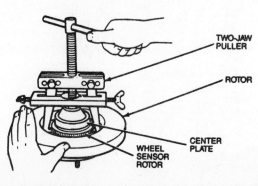

Removing the rear wheel sensor rotor

the caliper from the coil spring with mechanics wire or string.

NOTE: *Do not let the caliper hang by the brake hose.*

4. Remove the disc brake rotor. Refer to the procedure in this Chapter.

5. Remove the sensor rotor from the disc brake rotor, using a 2-jaw puller and center plate.

To install:

6. Position the rotor in a press with the wheel studs facing down.

7. Using sensor ring installer tool T88C–20202–AH or equivalent, press the sensor onto the disc brake rotor.

8. Install the rotor, caliper and anchor bracket.

9. Install the wheel and tire assembly and lower the vehicle.

ABS Relay

REMOVAL AND INSTALLATION

1. Disconnect the negative battery cable.
2. Remove the ABS relay mounting nut.

3. Disconnect the electrical connector and remove the ABS relay.

4. Installation is the reverse of the removal procedure.

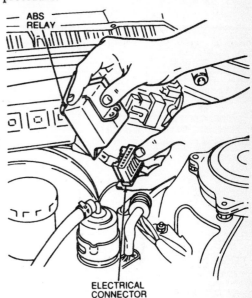

Disconnecting the electrical connector from the ABS relay

BRAKE SPECIFICATIONS
All measurements in inches unless noted

| Year | Model | Master Cylinder Bore | Brake Disc | | | Brake Drum Diameter | | | Minimum Lining Thickness | |
			Original Thickness	Minimum Thickness	Maximum Runout	Original Inside Diameter	Max. Wear Limit	Maximum Machine Diameter	Front	Rear
1989	Probe GL	0.875	0.940	0.860	0.004	9.0	9.060	9.030	0.120	0.040
	Probe LX	0.875	0.940	0.860	0.004	9.0	9.060	9.030	0.120	0.040
	Probe GT	0.875	①	②	0.004	—	—	—	0.120	0.040
1990	Probe GL	0.875	0.940	0.860	0.004	9.0	9.060	9.030	0.120	0.040
	Probe LX	0.875	①	②	0.004	—	—	—	0.120	0.040
	Probe GT	0.875	①	②	0.004	—	—	—	0.120	0.040
1991	Probe GL	0.875	0.940	0.860	0.004	9.0	9.060	9.030	0.120	0.040
	Probe LX	0.875	①	②	0.004	—	—	—	0.120	0.040
	Probe GT	0.875	①	②	0.004	—	—	—	0.120	0.040
1992	Probe GL	0.875	0.940	0.860	0.004	9.0	9.060	9.030	0.120	0.040
	Probe LX	0.875	①	②	0.004	—	—	—	0.120	0.040
	Probe GT	0.875	①	②	0.004	—	—	—	0.120	0.040

① Front—0.940
  Rear—0.390
② Front—0.860
  Rear—0.315

Body

![Door symbol]10

EXTERIOR

Doors

REMOVAL AND INSTALLATION

NOTE: *Two people are needed to remove and install the doors.*

1. Disconnect the negative battery cable.
2. Use a suitable punch to remove the door check pin.
3. Remove the rubber electrical door boot from the body.
4. Disconnect the electrical connector located inside the body.
5. Remove the rubber electrical door boot from the door.
6. With an assistant supporting the door, re-move the bolts from the door hinges and re-move the door.
7. Remove any shims that are found beneath the hinge and, if necessary, remove the hinges from the door.

To install:

8. Feed the electrical wiring through the rubber electrical boot and install the boot to the door.
9. With an assistant positioning the door, in-stall the shims (if used) and bolts to the door hinges.
10. Move the bolts to the necessary position and tighten to 31 ft. lbs. (42 Nm). Check the door fit to be sure there is no bind or interfer-ence with the adjacent panel. Shims can be add-ed beneath the hinges to align the surfaces of the door and front fender.
11. Repeat the operation until the desired fit

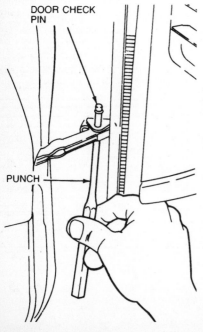

Removing the door check pin

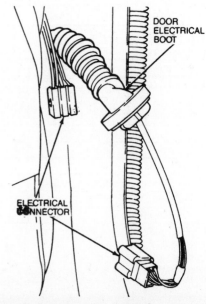

Disconnect the electrical connector

is obtained, then check the striker plate for proper door closing.

12. Connect the electrical connector and install the rubber electrical boot to the body.

13. Install the door check pin.

14. Connect the negative battery cable.

ADJUSTMENT

The door hinges provide enough adjustment to correct most door misalignment conditions. The holes of the hinge and/or the hinge attaching points are enlarged or elongated to allow hinge and door alignment. Do not attempt to correct poor door alignment with a latch striker adjustment

1. Open the door and check the play in the hinges. If play is excessive, replace the hinges.

2. If adjustment is necessary, loosen the hinge bolts just enough to allow movement of the door.

3. Adjust the door to the necessary position and tighten the hinge bolts to 31 ft. lbs. (42 Nm). Check door fit to make sure there is no bind or interference with the adjacent panel.

4. Repeat the operation until the desired fit is obtained, then check the striker plate for proper door closing.

5. If the door doesn't close easily, loosen the striker screws and adjust the striker by moving it up and down or side-to-side.

6. Inspect the rear alignment of the door in relation to the body. If there is a problem, adjust the striker by moving the door lock striker side-to-side.

NOTE: *The latch striker should not be adjusted to correct door sag.*

Hood

REMOVAL AND INSTALLATION

1. Open the hood and support it in the open position. Disconnect the negative battery cable.

2. Install fender covers to protect the paint.

3. Mark the location of the hood on the hinges.

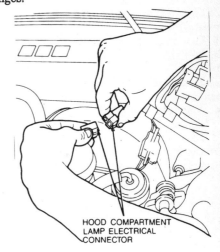

Disconnect the engine compartment light electrical connector

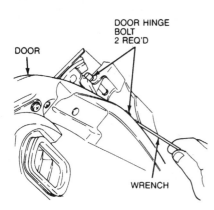

Adjusting door alignment

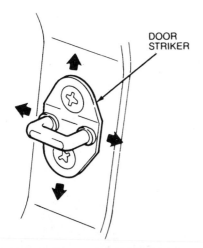

Adjust the striker by moving it in these directions

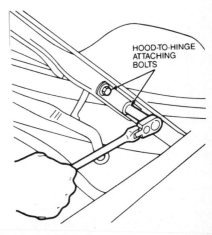

Aligning the hood

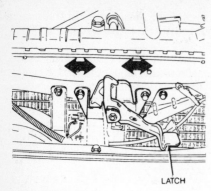

Aligning the hood latch

4. Disconnect the engine compartment light electrical connector.

5. Have assistants support the hood and remove the bolts attaching the hinges to the hood. Be careful not to let the hood slip when the bolts are removed.

6. Remove the hood from the vehicle.

To install:

7. Position the hood on the hinges. Have assistants support the hood and install the attaching bolts. Make sure the marks made during removal are aligned before tightening the bolts.

8. Connect the engine compartment light electrical connector.

9. Connect the negative battery cable and remove the fender covers. Close the hood.

ALIGNMENT

1. The hood can be adjusted front to rear and side to side by loosening the two hood-to-hinge attaching bolts at each hinge. Position the hood as required and tighten the bolts.

2. The hood latch can be moved from side to side to align with the hood opening, and/or up or down to align the hood surface with the fenders. Always align the hood first, then the latch.

3. Loosen the hood latch mounting bolts/nut enough to slide the latch. Move the latch to the position desired and tighten the mounting bolts/nut to 31 ft. lbs. (42 Nm).

4. Open and close the hood several times to check operation.

Liftgate

REMOVAL AND INSTALLATION

NOTE: *Two people are required to remove and install the liftgate.*

1. Disconnect the negative battery cable.

2. Raise the liftgate. Mark the location of the liftgate on the hinges.

3. Remove the liftgate interior trim panels. Refer to the procedure in this Chapter.

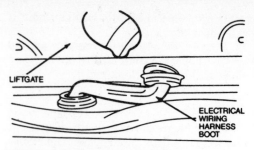

Liftgate wiring harness boot location

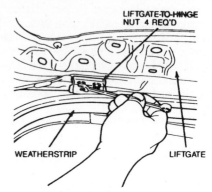

Removing the liftgate-to-hinge nuts

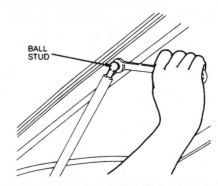

Removing the gas support rod ball stud from the liftgate

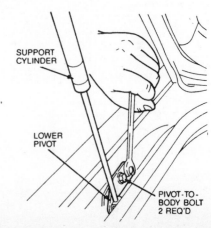

Removing the gas support cylinder from the body

4. Disconnect the rear window defroster, if equipped.

5. Remove the rear window wiper arm and motor, if equipped. Refer to Chapter 6.

6. Remove the wiring harness boot located at the top of the liftgate.

7. Disconnect the liftgate wiring harness from the body wiring harness and remove the connector from the body.

8. While supporting the liftgate, remove the gas support rod ball studs from the liftgate. Remove the support cylinder-to-body bolts and remove the support cylinders.

WARNING: *The ball stud should not be separated from the gas cylinder support rod. If the ball stud separates from the rod, the gas cylinder must be replaced.*

9. While supporting the liftgate, remove the 4 hinge-to-liftgate nuts. With assistance, remove the liftgate.

10. If necessary, remove the headliner to gain access to the hinge-to-body nuts. Remove the 4 nuts and the hinges.

To install:

11. Apply clear silicone rubber sealer to the body side of the hinge. Position the liftgate hinge onto the body and install the 4 mounting nuts.

12. Apply clear silicone rubber sealer to the liftgate side of the hinge. With assistance, position the liftgate onto the hinges and install the 4 hinge-to-liftgate nuts, finger-tight.

13. While supporting the liftgate, install the gas support cylinder mounting bolts to the body and the gas support rod ball studs to the liftgate.

WARNING: *The ball stud should not be separated from the gas cylinder support rod. If the ball stud separates from the rod, the gas cylinder must be replaced.*

14. Align the liftgate hinges with the marks made during removal, then close the liftgate. The liftgate should be adjusted for an even, parallel fit, then tighten the hinge-to-liftgate nuts securely.

15. Route the liftgate wiring harness into the body and connect the harness to the body wiring harness. Install the wiring harness boot.

16. Install the rear window wiper motor and wiper arm, if equipped.

17. Connect the rear window defroster, if equipped.

18. Install the liftgate interior trim panels. Connect the negative battery cable.

ALIGNMENT

The liftgate can be adjusted up and down by the use of shims, or side to side by the use of the elongated holes at the liftgate hinge. The liftgate should be adjusted for an even, parallel fit with liftgate openings and the surrounding panels.

Bumpers

REMOVAL AND INSTALLATION

Front

1. Turn the headlight rotary switch to the 3rd detent to extend the headlights, then disconnect the battery cables. Remove the battery.

2. Remove both headlight assemblies as follows:

   a. Remove the attaching nuts on the retractor hinge unit from the upper bumper assembly cover reinforcement.

   b. Disconnect the headlight electrical connector and remove the motor link assembly from the headlight housing.

   c. Remove the headlight housing from the vehicle.

3. On 1989 vehicles, disconnect the marker and parking light electrical connectors. On 1990–92 vehicles, remove both side marker lenses.

4. Remove the shoulder bolt from the upper corners of the bumper assembly cover.

5. Remove the 2 nuts retaining the bumper cover to the front fender.

6. Remove the bolt from under the inside of the front fender.

7. On 1989 vehicles, remove the bolts securing both of the bumper assembly cover brackets and remove the brackets. Remove the 7 screws securing each fender shield and remove the shields.

8. Remove the 2 bolts securing the bumper assembly cover to each fender from underneath.

9. On 1989 vehicles, remove the 5 plastic screws and clips retaining the bumper assembly cover to the lower front bumper reinforcement. On 1990–92 vehicles, remove the 3 screws and plastic clips retaining the bumper assembly cover to the lower front bumper cover reinforcement.

10. Remove the 6 bolts securing the bumper assembly cover to the upper front bumper cover reinforcement.

11. Remove the fog light assemblies, if equipped. Refer to Chapter 6.

12. Remove the 4 bumper to isolator and bracket retaining nuts and remove the bumper assembly from the vehicle.

13. Remove the 2 nuts retaining each isolator and bracket assembly. Remove the isolator and bracket assembly from the vehicle.

To install:

14. Position the isolator and bracket assem-

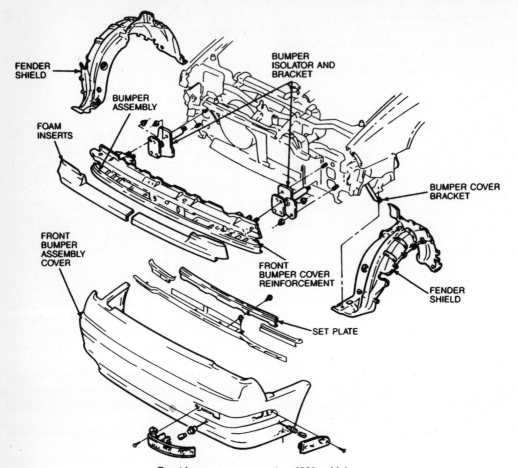

FENDER
SHIELD

BUMPER
ISOLATOR AND
BRACKET

BUMPER
ASSEMBLY

FOAM
INSERTS

BUMPER COVER
BRACKET

FRONT
BUMPER
ASSEMBLY
COVER

FRONT
BUMPER COVER
REINFORCEMENT

FENDER
SHIELD

SET PLATE

Front bumper components—1989 vehicles

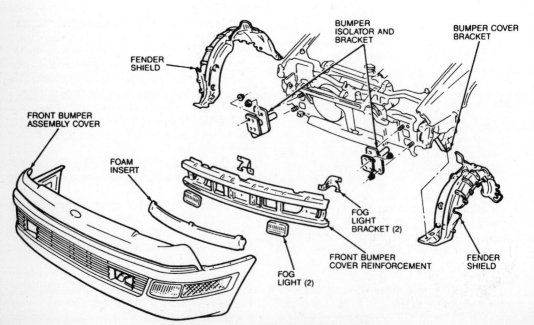

BUMPER
ISOLATOR AND
BRACKET

BUMPER COVER
BRACKET

FENDER
SHIELD

FRONT BUMPER
ASSEMBLY COVER

FOAM
INSERT

FOG
LIGHT
BRACKET (2)

FRONT BUMPER
COVER REINFORCEMENT

FENDER
SHIELD

FOG
LIGHT (2)

Front bumper components—1989–92 vehicles

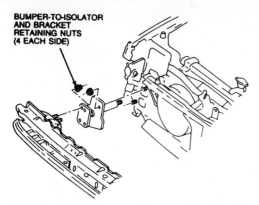

BUMPER-TO-ISOLATOR
AND BRACKET
RETAINING NUTS
(4 EACH SIDE)

Isolator and bracket assembly removal and installation

bly to the vehicle and install the retaining nuts. Tighten to 23–34 ft. lbs. (31–46 Nm).

15. Position the bumper assembly to the isolator and bracket assemblies and install the retaining nuts. Tighten to 23–34 ft. lbs. (31–46 Nm).

16. Install the fog light assemblies, if equipped.

17. Install the front bumper assembly cover and install the 6 bolts securing the cover to the upper front bumper cover reinforcement.

18. Install the screws and clips retaining the bumper assembly cover to the lower front bumper reinforcement.

19. Install the 2 bolts securing the bumper assembly cover to each fender from underneath.

20. On 1989 vehicles, install the fender shields and the bumper assembly cover brackets.

21. Install the bolt to the underside of each front fender and install the nuts retaining the bumper cover to the front fenders.

22. Install the shoulder bolt to each upper corner of the bumper assembly cover.

23. Install the side marker lenses or connect the electrical connectors, as required.

24. Install the headlight assemblies.

25. Install the battery and connect the battery cables.

Rear

1. Disconnect the negative battery cable.

2. Remove the trunk end trim and the lower trunk side trim from inside the vehicle. Refer to the procedures in this Chapter.

3. Remove all of the rear lights from the vehicle. Refer to Chapter 6.

4. Remove both license plate cover retaining screws and remove the cover. Remove the one nut located under the license plate cover.

5. Remove the 8 bumper cover assembly retaining nuts located inside the trunk.

6. On 1989 vehicles, remove the 2 screws under each side of the bumper cover assembly.

7. Remove the 8 plastic screws under the back side of the bumper.

8. On 1990–92 vehicles, remove the splash guard attaching screws and clip and remove the splash guard.

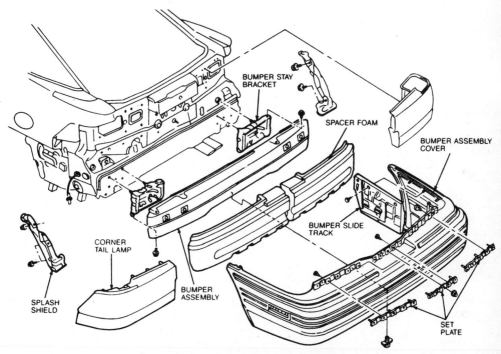

Rear bumper components—1989 vehicles

9. Remove the screw at each upper corner of the bumper.

10. Slide the bumper assembly cover away from the back of the vehicle and remove the cover.

11. Remove the 8 bolts retaining the bumper to both bumper stay brackets and remove the bumper.

12. Remove the 4 top bumper stay retaining nuts, located inside the trunk, and the 4 bottom bumper stay retaining nuts, located underneath the trunk. Remove the bumper stay brackets.

To install:

13. Install the bumper stay brackets and the retaining nuts. Tighten the nuts to 23–34 ft. lbs. (31–46 Nm).

14. Install the bumper to the bumper stay brackets and tighten the 8 retaining bolts.

15. Position the bumper assembly cover and install the screw at each upper corner of the bumper.

16. On 1990–92 vehicles, install the splash guards with the attaching screws.

17. Install the 8 plastic screws under the back side of the bumper.

18. On 1989 vehicles, install the 2 screws under each side of the bumper cover assembly.

19. Install the 8 bumper cover assembly retaining nuts.

20. Install the nut located under the license plate cover and install the cover.

21. Install the rear lights.

22. Install the lower trunk side trim and trunk end trim.

23. Connect the negative battery cable.

Outside Mirrors

REMOVAL AND INSTALLATION

Manual

1. Remove the control knob cover.

2. Remove the retaining screw and knob.

3. Remove the inside mirror trim.

4. Remove the 3 mounting screws and remove the mirror assembly.

5. Installation is the reverse of the removal procedure.

Power

1. Disconnect the negative battery cable.

2. Remove the access cover.

3. Remove the three mirror mounting screws.

4. Remove the mirror from the door and disconnect the electrical connector.

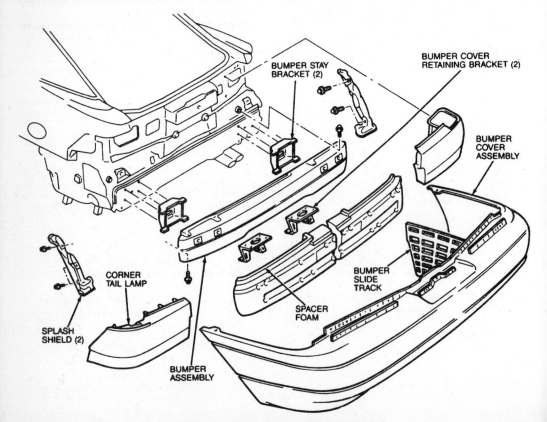

Rear bumper components—1990–92 vehicles

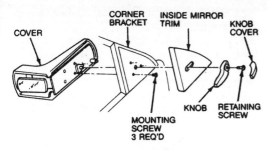

Manual outside mirror removal and installation

5. Installation is the reverse of the removal procedure.

Antenna

REPLACEMENT

Standard Antenna

1. Open the liftgate. Remove the right lower trunk side trim and the upper trunk side garnish. Refer to the procedures in this Chapter.

2. Disconnect the antenna cable and remove the antenna mounting bolt.

3. Remove the antenna tip. Unscrew and remove the bezel, and remove the bezel mount.

4. Note where the drain tube empties, then remove the antenna support and the antenna.

To install:

5. Attach the antenna support and antenna to the bezel mount by lining up the bezel mount tab with the tab slot on the support.

6. Install the antenna bezel and antenna tip. Install the antenna attaching bolt.

7. Connect the antenna cable and position the drain tube.

8. Install the lower trunk side trim and upper trunk side garnish.

Power Antenna

1. Disconnect the negative battery cable.

2. Remove the right lower trunk side trim and upper trunk side garnish. Refer to the procedures in this Chapter.

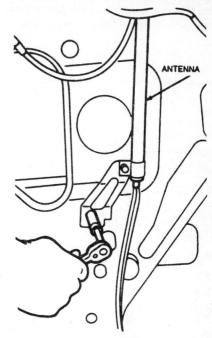

Antenna removal and installation

3. Disconnect the electrical connector and the antenna cable.

4. Remove the power antenna attaching bolts.

5. Unscrew and remove the bezel. Remove the bezel mount.

6. Note the drain tube routing, then remove the antenna support and the power antenna.

To install:

7. Attach the antenna support and antenna to the bezel mount by lining up the bezel mount tab with the tab slot on the support.

8. Install the bezel and the antenna attaching bolts.

9. Connect the electrical connector and connect the antenna cable. Position the drain tube.

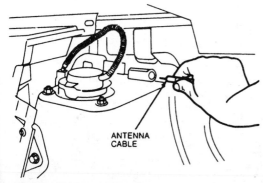

Disconnect the antenna cable

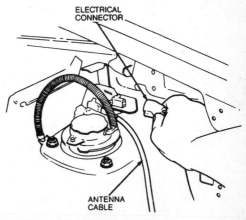

Disconnect the electrical connector

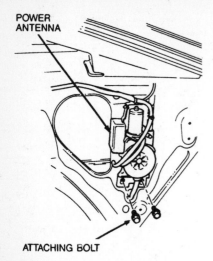

POWER ANTENNA

ATTACHING BOLT

Power antenna removal and installation

10. Install the lower trunk side trim and upper trunk side garnish.

11. Connect the negative battery cable.

INTERIOR

Instrument Panel

REMOVAL AND INSTALLATION

1. Disconnect the negative battery cable.

2. Remove the steering wheel. Refer to Chapter 8.

3. Remove the instrument cluster. Refer to Chapter 6.

4. Remove the lower dash trim.

5. Remove the driver's side sound deadening panel.

6. Remove the instrument panel shake brace.

7. Remove the lower dash ducts.

8. Remove the instrument cluster carrier.

9. Remove the lower steering column bracket retaining screws and lower column.

10. Remove the shift indicator and shift indicator bezel.

11. Remove the ashtray.

12. Remove the shift handle.

13. Remove the floor console. Refer to the procedure on this Chapter.

14. Remove the radio and, if equipped, the compact disc player. Refer to Chapter 6.

15. If equipped, remove the trip computer display as follows:

a. Remove the display cover bezel.

b. Remove the 2 display housing attaching screws and pull the housing straight out of the dash. It may be necessary to gently pry the display free from the instrument panel.

c. Disconnect the electrical connector and remove the display.

16. If not equipped with a trip computer, remove the center mounting nut access cover.

17. Remove the passenger side lower instrument panel panel.

18. Remove the glove box.

19. Remove the left and right console kick panels.

20. Remove the heater control bezel. Disconnect and remove the heater control.

21. Slide the accessory console back far enough to access the mounting bolts at the floor. Remove the bolts.

22. Remove the left and right dash side covers.

23. Remove the bolts from the left and right sides of the dash.

24. Remove the instrument panel center mounting nut.

25. Remove the hood release cable handle.

26. Remove the left and right A to B-pillar trim.

NOTE: *The remaining removal Steps require the help of an assistant.*

27. Lift the instrument panel and tilt it toward the rear of the vehicle.

28. Disconnect all remaining electrical connectors, including the dash harness, the wire connector at the left-hand nain harness, and the shift lock wiring connector.

29. Remove the instrument panel from the vehicle.

To install:

NOTE: *Steps 30 and 31 require the help of an assistant.*

30. Place the instrument panel in the vehicle and connect all electrical connectors, including the dash harness, the wire connector at the left-hand nain harness, and the shift lock wiring connector.

31. Position the instrument panel and install the center mounting nut. Tighten the nut to 3.1–4.6 ft. lbs. (1.2–6.2 Nm).

32. Install the retaining bolts on the left and right sides of the dash.

33. Pull the accessory console back to access the bolt holes and install the bolts.

34. Install the hood release cable handle.

35. Install the glove box.

36. Install the heater control and bezel.

37. Connect and install the radio and, if equipped, the CD player.

38. If equipped with a trip computer, connect and install the diplay. If not equipped with a trip computer, install the center mounting nut access cover.

39. Install the floor console.

40. Install the shift indicator and shift indicator bezel.

41. Install the ashtray.
42. Install the shift handle.
43. Install the passenger side sound deadening panel.
44. Install the console kick panels.
45. Install the left and right dash side covers.
46. Install the instrument cluster carrier and position the steering column. Install the steering column bracket retaining screws.
47. Install the instrument cluster.

48. Install the lower instrument panel shake brace.
49. Install the steering column cover.
50. Install the lower dash ducts and lower dash trim.
51. Install the driver's side sound deadening panel and the driver's side console side panel.
52. Install the steering wheel.
53. Install the right and left A to B-pillar trim.
54. Connect the negative battery cable.

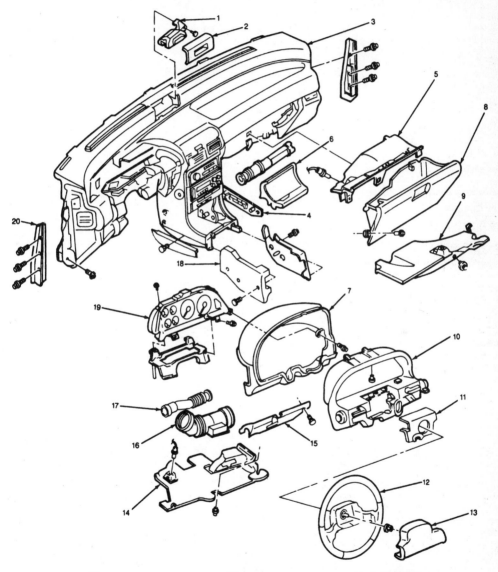

1.	Trip computer display	7.	Cluster cover	14.	Left-hand lower instrument panel
2.	Trip computer display cover	8.	Glove compartment	15.	Shake brace
		9.	Right-hand lower instrument panel	16.	Lap duct
3.	Instrument panel	10.	Switch module	17.	Defrost duct
4.	Dash side cover	11.	Column cover	18.	Dash side wall
5.	Glove compartment panel	12.	Steering wheel	19.	Instrument cluster
6.	Lap duct	13.	Steeering wheel cover	20.	Dash side cover

Instrument panel disassembled view

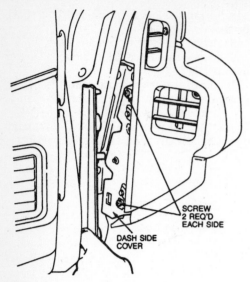

Dash side cover removal and installation

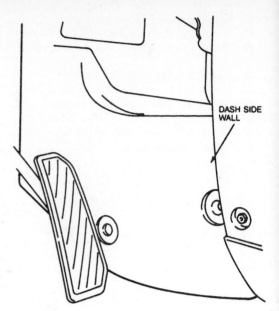

Remove the dash side wall

Console

REMOVAL AND INSTALLATION

Floor Console

AUTOMATIC TRANSAXLE

1. Disconnect the negative battery cable.
2. Remove the 2 selctor lever knob retaining screws and remove the knob.
3. Remove the selector trim piece.
4. Remove the 4 selector bezel mounting screws. Lift the bezel and disconnect the illumination bulb and the shift control switch wiring harness.
5. Remove the selector bezel.
6. Remove the front ashtray and cigar lighter.
7. Remove the 4 retaining screws at the front of the console.

8. Position the front seats to gain access to the console rear access hole covers and remove the covers from each side of the console.
9. If not equipped with a center armrest, remove the retaining screws on each side of the console and position the front seats all the way to the rear.
10. If equipped with a center armrest, remove the 2 retaining screws and the 4 bolts from the lower rear of the center console.
11. Lift the console from the rear and disconnect the power mirror switch and programmed ride control switch electrical connectors.
12. Apply the parking brake and carefully remove the console.
To install:
13. Position the console over the parking

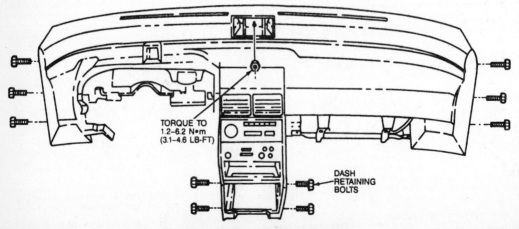

Instrument panel and retaining nut/bolts

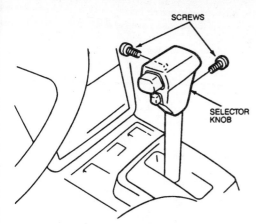

Selector knob removal and installation

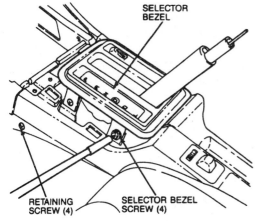

Selector bezel removal and installation

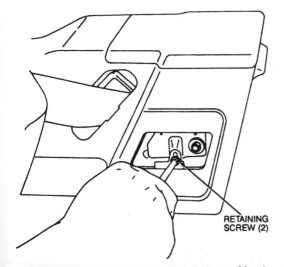

Retaining screw removal and installation—without center armrest

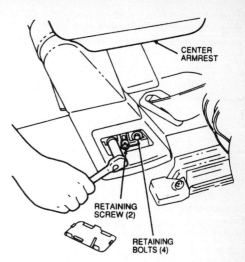

Retaining screw removal and installation—with center armrest

brake lever. Carefully lower the console, front first.

14. Connect the power mirror switch and programmed ride control switch electrical connectors.

15. Position the front seats to gain access to the console rear access holes. Install the retaining screw and bolts on each side of the console and install the access covers.

16. Position the front seats to the rear and install the 4 retaining screws at the front of the console.

17. Install the selector bezel over the selector lever. Install the illumination bulb and connect the shift control switch wiring harness.

18. Install the 4 bezel mounting screws.

19. Install the ashtray and cigar lighter.

20. Install the selector trim piece and the selector knob.

21. Connect the negative battery cable.

MANUAL TRANSAXLE

1. Slide the shifter boot down and remove the shift knob.

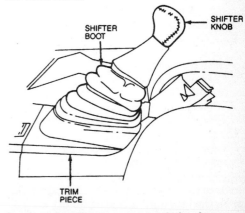

Remove the shifter knob, boot and trim piece

2. Remove the trim piece and boot.

3. Remove the front ashtray and cigar lighter.

4. Remove the 4 retaining screws at the front of the console.

5. Position the front seats to gain access to the console rear access hole covers, and remove the covers from each side of the console.

6. If not equipped with a center armrest, remove the retaining screws on each side of the console and position the front seats all the way to the rear.

7. If equipped with a center armrest, remove the retaining screw and the bolts from the lower rear of the center console.

8. Lift the console from the rear. Disconnect the mirror adjust switch and programmed ride control switch electrical connectors.

9. Apply the parking brake and carefully remove the console.

To install:

10. Position the console over the parking brake lever. Carefully lower the console, front first.

11. Connect the power mirror switch and programmed ride control switch electrical connectors.

12. Position the front seats to gain access to the console rear access holes. Install the retaining screw and bolts on each side of the console and install the access covers.

13. Position the front seats to the rear and install the 4 retaining screws at the front of the console.

14. Install the ashtray and cigar lighter assembly.

15. Install the shifter boot and trim piece. Install the shift knob.

Roof Console

1. Disconnect the negative battery cable.

2. Insert a small prybar in the slot at the rear of the interior light lens. Pry downward and remove the lens.

3. Insert a small prybar at the edge of the roof console trim cover and carefully pry it off.

4. Remove the 4 roof console retaining screws. Lower the console and disconnect the electrical connector.

5. Remove the roof console.

To install:

6. Connect the electrical connector.

7. Install the console with the 4 retaining screws.

8. Carefully snap the roof console trim cover into place.

9. Insert the front tangs of the interior light lens into the slots in the roof console, then push up on the lens until it snaps into place.

10. Connect the negative battery cable.

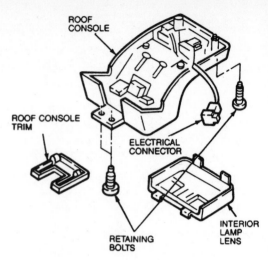

Roof console removal and installation

Door Panels

REMOVAL AND INSTALLATION

WARNING: *Be careful when removing and installing the plastic clips. These clips break very easily and replacements may not be readily available.*

1. Disconnect the negative battery cable.

2. Remove the window regulator handle, if equipped.

3. If equipped, carefully pry the power window switches from the armrest and disconnect the electrical connector.

4. Remove the armrest retaining screws and remove the screw retaining the inner door handle.

5. Disengage the clip attaching the inner door handle to the control rod.

6. Remove the screw retaining the trim panel from the sail panel.

7. Carefully pry outward around the lower

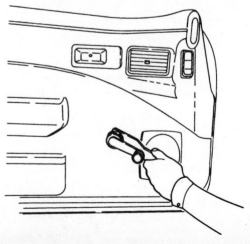

Removing the window regulator handle

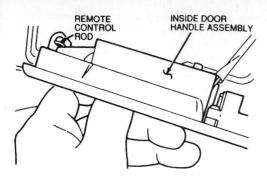

Disengaging the remote control rod from the inner door handle

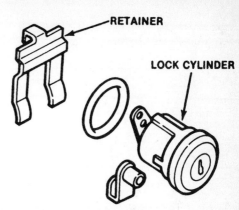

Door lock cylinder and retainer

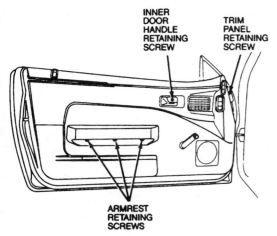

Door panel retaining screw locations

edge of the door panel with a flat tool. Slide the door handle through the door panel and remove the panel from the vehicle.

8. Installation is the reverse of the removal procedure. Replace all broken or damaged panel tabs.

Door Locks

REMOVAL AND INSTALLATION

Door Lock Cylinder

1. Remove the door panel and the plastic door shield.
2. Remove the clip attaching the lock cylinder rod to the lock cylinder.
3. If equipped with illuminated entry, disconnect the electrical connector.
4. Pry the lock cylinder retainer out of the slot in the door.
5. Remove the lock cylinder from the door.
6. Installation is the reverse of the removal procedure.

Power Door Lock Actuator

1. Disconnect the negative battery cable.
2. Remove the door panel and the plastic door shield.

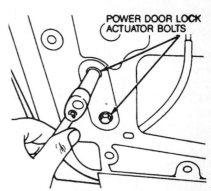

Power door lock actuator removal and installation

3. Disconnect the power door lock actuating rod from the actuator.
4. Remove the 2 nuts retaining the power door lock actuator.
5. Disconnect the poweer door lock actuator electrical connector and remove the actuator.
6. Installation is the reverse of the removal procedure.

Liftgate Lock

REMOVAL AND INSTALLATION

1. Disconnect the negative battery cable.
2. Remove the trunk end trim panel. Refer to the procedure in this Chapter.
3. Remove both tail light assemblies. Refer to Chapter 6.
4. Remove the center lens assembly.
5. Remove the 2 screws and remove the lock cylinder and gasket.
6. Installation is the reverse of the removal procedure.

Door Glass and Regulator

REMOVAL AND INSTALLATION

1. Disconnect the negative battery cable.
2. Remove the door panel and the plastic door shield.

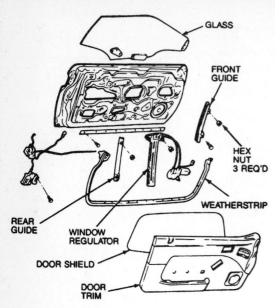

Door window glass and related components

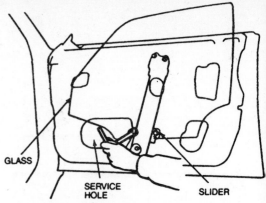

GLASS

Remove the bolts or nuts securing the window glass through the service hole

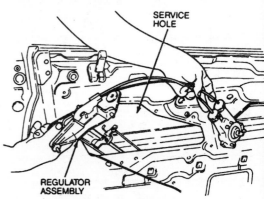

Removing the regulator assembly

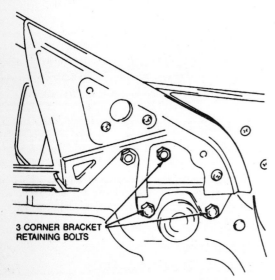

Corner bracket retaining bolts location

3. Remove the door mirror. Refer to the procedure in this Chapter.

4. Remove the upper stop retaining bolts and remove the stops.

5. Remove the 3 bolts retaining the corner bracket and remove the bracket.

6. Position the door glass so the bolts or nuts securing the window glass can be removed through the service hole.

7. Remove the door glass upward along the glass guide.

8. Remove the 6 window regulator-to-door retaining nuts. If equipped with power win-

dows, disconnect the electrical connector from the regulator motor. Remove the regulator through the service hole.

9. Installation is the reverse of the removal procedure.

Stationary Glass

REMOVAL AND INSTALLATION

Liftgate Window

The following tools are recommended to properly remove and install the liftgate window: a sealant dispensing gun, glass adhesive cutter tool 118–00050 or equivalent, shop towels, installation kit D9AZ–19562–A or equivalent, and a knife.

1. Disconnect the negative battery cable.

2. Open the liftgate and remove the package tray.

3. Remove the liftgate interior mouldings. Refer to the procedure in this Chapter.

4. If equipped, remove the wiper arm assembly.

5. Pry off the liftgate upper window mould-

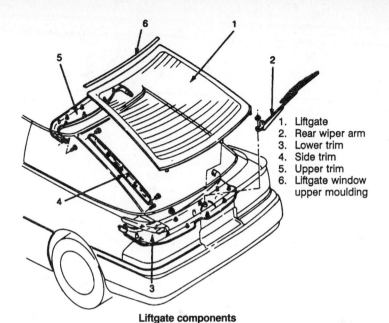

1. Liftgate
2. Rear wiper arm
3. Lower trim
4. Side trim
5. Upper trim
6. Liftgate window upper moulding

Liftgate components

LIFTGATE

GLASS ADHESIVE CUTTER

Separating the glass from the urethane seal

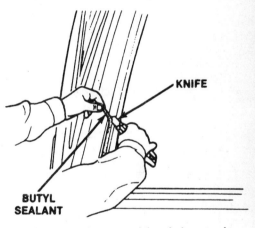

KNIFE

BUTYL SEALANT

Trimming the sealant around the window opening

ing to release the retaining clips and remove the moulding.

6. Remove the 3 nuts retaining the lower liftgate window moulding, from the inside of the liftgate.

7. Disconnect the electrical connectors from the rear window defroster.

WARNING: *Improper use of the glass adhesive cutter tool may damage the vehicle. Use only the blades specified in the procedure. Do not allow the blade to contact the vehicle's glass or sheet metal. Do not apply upward or downward pressure. Repair all damaged*

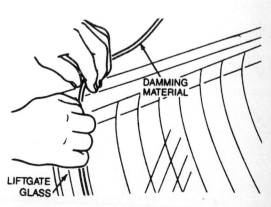

DAMMING MATERIAL

LIFTGATE GLASS

Installing the damming material

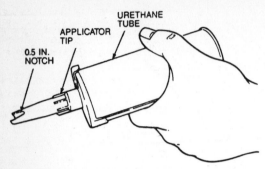

Cut a ½ in. notch in the applicator tip

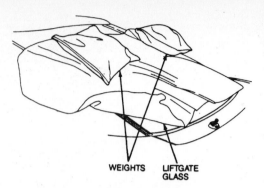

Press the glass with approximately 0 lb. weights

painted surfaces before installing the glass.
CAUTION: *Wear safety glasses and heavy gloves when cutting glass from the vehicle, to prevent glass splinters from entering eyes or cutting hands*
8. Separate the glass from the urethane seal with the glass adhesive cutter, using blade 97 or 98.
NOTE: *If the lower moulding is to be reused, be careful not to damage the 3 retaining studs. If the studs are damaged, replace the lower moulding.*
9. Remove the old sealant from the liftgate window if the window will be reused.
To install:
10. Smoothly trim the sealant around the liftgate window opening to a height less than 0.15 in. (3.8mm).
11. Inspect the sealing surface of the liftgate window opening flange for irregularities, chips, and/or missing paint and repair, if necessary.
12. Using naptha and a lint-free cloth, wipe clean the old urethane remaining on the liftgate flange. Apply urethane metal primer to the painted metal surfaces and allow to dry for 30 minutes.
NOTE: *Keep glass and body surfaces free of dirt, water and oil. Do not touch coated surfaces with your hand.*

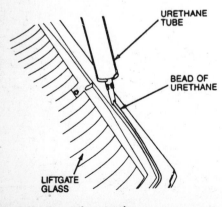

Applying the urethane sealer

13. Thoroughly clean the edge of the glass. Apply urethane glass cleaner to the glass along the edge where the seal will contact and wipe dry with a clean cloth.
14. Apply urethane glass primer, in a 2 in. (51mm) wide strip, around the perimeter of the glass and allow to dry for 3 minutes.
15. Peel the backing tape off the damming material. Install the dam around the perimeter of the glass 10mm from the outside edge.
16. Cut a ½ in. (13mm) notch in the urethane tube applicator tip. Run a bead of urethane sealer between the dam and the outside edge of the glass.
17. With help from an assistant, carefully position the glass in the opening, aligning the studs on the lower trim with the corresponding holes on the lower flange.
18. Press the glass against the urethane with approximately 200 lbs. pressure. Use suitable weights and leave them in place for approximately 30 minutes.
19. Spray water at moderate pressure around the liftgate window and check for water leaks. If a leak is found, wipe the area dry and apply urethane sealant to the affected area.
20. Connect the defroster terminals, if equipped. Be careful not to bend the terminals.
21. Install the 3 nuts on the lower liftgate moulding studs.
22. Install the liftgate interior mouldings.
23. Install the wiper arm assembly, if equipped.
24. Position the upper liftgate window moulding and apply pressure to engage the retaining clips.
25. Install the package tray. Connect the negative battery cable.

Rear Quarter Window

The following tools are recommended to properly remove and install the rear quarter window: a sealant dispensing gun, glass adhesive cutter tool 118–00050 or equivalent, shop

CHILTON'S
AUTO BODY REPAIR TIPS

Tools and Materials • Step-by-Step Illustrated Procedures
How To Repair Dents, Scratches and Rust Holes
Spray Painting and Refinishing Tips

W ith a little practice, basic body repair procedures can be mastered by any do-it-yourself mechanic. The step-by-step repairs shown here can be applied to almost any type of auto body repair.

TOOLS & MATERIALS

Y ou may already have basic tools, such as hammers and electric drills. Other tools unique to body repair — body hammers, grinding attachments, sanding blocks, dent puller, half-round plastic file and plastic spreaders — are relatively inexpensive and can be obtained wherever auto parts or auto body repair parts are sold. Portable air compressors and paint spray guns can be purchased or rented.

Auto Body Repair Kits

T he best and most often used products are available to the do-it-yourselfer in kit form, from major manufacturers of auto body repair products. The same manufacturers also merchandise the individual products for use by pros.

Kits are available to make a wide variety of repairs, including holes, dents and scratches and fiberglass, and offer the advantage of buying the materials you'll need for the job. There is little waste or chance of materials going bad from not being used. Many kits may also contain basic body-working tools such as body files, sanding blocks and spreaders. Check the contents of the kit before buying your tools.

BODY REPAIR TIPS

Safety

M any of the products associated with auto body repair and refinishing contain toxic chemicals. Read all labels before opening containers and store them in a safe place and manner.

• Wear eye protection (safety goggles) when using power tools or when performing any operation that involves the removal of any type of material.

• Wear lung protection (disposable mask or respirator) when grinding, sanding or painting.

Sanding

1 Sand off paint before using a dent puller. When using a non-adhesive sanding disc, cover the back of the disc with an overlapping layer or two of masking tape and trim the edges. The disc will last considerably longer.

2 Use the circular motion of the sanding disc to grind *into* the edge of the repair. Grinding or sanding away from the jagged edge will only tear the sandpaper.

3 Use the palm of your hand flat on the panel to detect high and low spots. Do not use your fingertips. Slide your hand slowly back and forth.

WORKING WITH BODY FILLER

Mixing The Filler

Cleanliness and proper mixing and application are extremely important. Use a clean piece of plastic or glass or a disposable artist's palette to mix body filler.

1 Allow plenty of time and follow directions. No useful purpose will be served by adding more hardener to make it cure (set-up) faster. Less hardener means more curing time, but the mixture dries harder; more hardener means less curing time but a softer mixture.

2 Both the hardener and the filler should be thoroughly kneaded or stirred before mixing. Hardener should be a solid paste and dispense like thin toothpaste. Body filler should be smooth, and free of lumps or thick spots.

Getting the proper amount of hardener in the filler is the trickiest part of preparing the filler. Use the same amount of hardener in cold or warm weather. For contour filler (thick coats), a bead of hardener twice the diameter of the filler is about right. There's about a 15% margin on either side, but, if in doubt use less hardener.

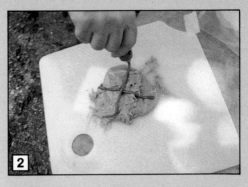

3 Mix the body filler and hardener by wiping across the mixing surface, picking the mixture up and wiping it again. Colder weather requires longer mixing times. Do not mix in a circular motion; this will trap air bubbles which will become holes in the cured filler.

Applying The Filler

1 For best results, filler should not be applied over ¼″ thick.

Apply the filler in several coats. Build it up to above the level of the repair surface so that it can be sanded or grated down.

The first coat of filler must be pressed on with a firm wiping motion.

Apply the filler in one direction only. Working the filler back and forth will either pull it off the metal or trap air bubbles.

REPAIRING DENTS

Before you start, take a few minutes to study the damaged area. Try to visualize the shape of the panel before it was damaged. If the damage is on the left fender, look at the right fender and use it as a guide. If there is access to the panel from behind, you can reshape it with a body hammer. If not, you'll have to use a dent puller. Go slowly and work the metal a little at a time. Get the panel as straight as possible before applying filler.

1 This dent is typical of one that can be pulled out or hammered out from behind. Remove the headlight cover, headlight assembly and turn signal housing.

2 Drill a series of holes ½ the size of the end of the dent puller along the stress line. Make some trial pulls and assess the results. If necessary, drill more holes and try again. Do not hurry.

3 If possible, use a body hammer and block to shape the metal back to its original contours. Get the metal back as close to its original shape as possible. Don't depend on body filler to fill dents.

4 Using an 80-grit grinding disc on an electric drill, grind the paint from the surrounding area down to bare metal. Use a new grinding pad to prevent heat buildup that will warp metal.

5 The area should look like this when you're finished grinding. Knock the drill holes in and tape over small openings to keep plastic filler out.

6 Mix the body filler (see Body Repair Tips). Spread the body filler evenly over the entire area (see Body Repair Tips). Be sure to cover the area completely.

7 Let the body filler dry until the surface can just be scratched with your fingernail. Knock the high spots from the body filler with a body file ("Cheesegrater"). Check frequently with the palm of your hand for high and low spots.

8 Check to be sure that trim pieces that will be installed later will fit exactly. Sand the area with 40-grit paper.

9 If you wind up with low spots, you may have to apply another layer of filler.

10 Knock the high spots off with 40-grit paper. When you are satisfied with the contours of the repair, apply a thin coat of filler to cover pin holes and scratches.

11 Block sand the area with 40-grit paper to a smooth finish. Pay particular attention to body lines and ridges that must be well-defined.

12 Sand the area with 400 paper and then finish with a scuff pad. The finished repair is ready for priming and painting (see Painting Tips).

Materials and photos courtesy of Ritt Jones Auto Body, Prospect Park, PA.

REPAIRING RUST HOLES

There are many ways to repair rust holes. The fiberglass cloth kit shown here is one of the most cost efficient for the owner because it provides a strong repair that resists cracking and moisture and is relatively easy to use. It can be used on large and small holes (with or without backing) and can be applied over contoured areas. Remember, however, that short of replacing an entire panel, no repair is a guarantee that the rust will not return.

1 Remove any trim that will be in the way. Clean away all loose debris. Cut away all the rusted metal. But be sure to leave enough metal to retain the contour or body shape.

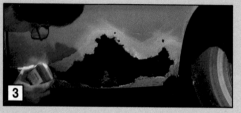

2 Grind away all traces of rust with a 24-grit grinding disc. Be sure to grind back 3-4 inches from the edge of the hole down to bare metal and be sure all traces of paint, primer and rust are removed.

3 Block sand the area with 80 or 100 grit sandpaper to get a clear, shiny surface and feathered paint edge. Tap the edges of the hole inward with a ball peen hammer.

4 If you are going to use release film, cut a piece about 2-3" larger than the area you have sanded. Place the film over the repair and mark the sanded area on the film. Avoid any unnecessary wrinkling of the film.

5 Cut 2 pieces of fiberglass matte to match the shape of the repair. One piece should be about 1" smaller than the sanded area and the second piece should be 1" smaller than the first. Mix enough filler and hardener to saturate the fiberglass material (see Body Repair Tips).

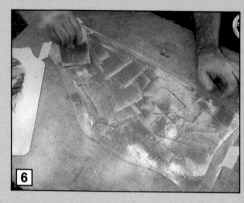

6 Lay the release sheet on a flat surface and spread an even layer of filler, large enough to cover the repair. Lay the smaller piece of fiberglass cloth in the center of the sheet and spread another layer of filler over the fiberglass cloth. Repeat the operation for the larger piece of cloth.

7 Place the repair material over the repair area, with the release film facing outward. Use a spreader and work from the center outward to smooth the material, following the body contours. Be sure to remove all air bubbles.

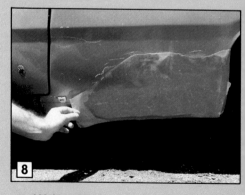

8 Wait until the repair has dried tack-free and peel off the release sheet. The ideal working temperature is 60°-90° F. Cooler or warmer temperatures or high humidity may require additional curing time. Wait longer, if in doubt.

9

9 Sand and feather-edge the entire area. The initial sanding can be done with a sanding disc on an electric drill if care is used. Finish the sanding with a block sander. Low spots can be filled with body filler; this may require several applications.

10

10 When the filler can just be scratched with a fingernail, knock the high spots down with a body file and smooth the entire area with 80-grit. Feather the filled areas into the surrounding areas.

11

11 When the area is sanded smooth, mix some topcoat and hardener and apply it directly with a spreader. This will give a smooth finish and prevent the glass matte from showing through the paint.

12

12 Block sand the topcoat smooth with finishing sandpaper (200 grit), and 400 grit. The repair is ready for masking, priming and painting (see Painting Tips).

Materials and photos courtesy Marson Corporation, Chelsea, Massachusetts

PAINTING TIPS

Preparation

1 SANDING — Use a 400 or 600 grit wet or dry sandpaper. Wet-sand the area with a 1/4 sheet of sandpaper soaked in clean water. Keep the paper wet while sanding. Sand the area until the repaired area tapers into the original finish.

2 CLEANING — Wash the area to be painted thoroughly with water and a clean rag. Rinse it thoroughly and wipe the surface dry until you're sure it's completely free of dirt, dust, fingerprints, wax, detergent or other foreign matter.

3 MASKING — Protect any areas you don't want to overspray by covering them with masking tape and newspaper. Be careful not get fingerprints on the area to be painted.

4 PRIMING — All exposed metal should be primed before painting. Primer protects the metal and provides an excellent surface for paint adhesion. When the primer is dry, wet-sand the area again with 600 grit wet-sandpaper. Clean the area again after sanding.

4

Painting Techniques

P aint applied from either a spray gun or a spray can (for small areas) will provide good results. Experiment on an old piece of metal to get the right combination before you begin painting.

SPRAYING VISCOSITY (SPRAY GUN ONLY) — Paint should be thinned to spraying viscosity according to the directions on the can. Use only the recommended thinner or reducer and the same amount of reduction regardless of temperature.

AIR PRESSURE (SPRAY GUN ONLY) — This is extremely important. Be sure you are using the proper recommended pressure.

TEMPERATURE — The surface to be painted should be approximately the same temperature as the surrounding air. Applying warm paint to a cold surface, or vice versa, will completely upset the paint characteristics.

THICKNESS — Spray with smooth strokes. In general, the thicker the coat of paint, the longer the drying time. Apply several thin coats about 30 seconds apart. The paint should remain wet long enough to flow out and no longer; heavier coats will only produce sags or wrinkles. Spray a light (fog) coat, followed by heavier color coats.

DISTANCE — The ideal spraying distance is 8″-12″ from the gun or can to the surface. Shorter distances will produce ripples, while greater distances will result in orange peel, dry film and poor color match and loss of material due to overspray.

OVERLAPPING — The gun or can should be kept at right angles to the surface at all times. Work to a wet edge at an even speed, using a 50% overlap and direct the center of the spray at the lower or nearest edge of the previous stroke.

RUBBING OUT (BLENDING) FRESH PAINT — Let the paint dry thoroughly. Runs or imperfections can be sanded out, primed and repainted.

Don't be in too big a hurry to remove the masking. This only produces paint ridges. When the finish has dried for at least a week, apply a small amount of fine grade rubbing compound with a clean, wet cloth. Use lots of water and blend the new paint with the surrounding area.

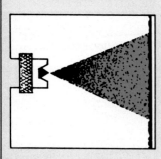

WRONG

Thin coat. Stroke too fast, not enough overlap, gun too far away.

CORRECT

Medium coat. Proper distance, good stroke, proper overlap.

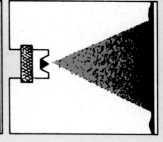

WRONG

Heavy coat. Stroke too slow, too much overlap, gun too close.

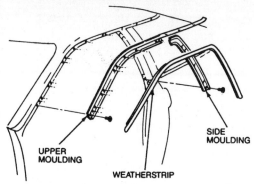

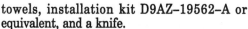

Remove the front window upper and side mouldings

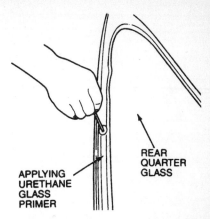

Apply the urethane glass primer in a 2 inch wide strip

towels, installation kit D9AZ–19562–A or
equivalent, and a knife.

1. Remove the front window upper and side
mouldings as follows:

   a. Remove the 3 end clips from the door
jam weatherstrip and pull it off.

   b. Remove the 11 screws from the underside of the upper window moulding.

   c. Release the retaining clips from the rear
portion of the moulding.

   d. Remove the upper window moulding.

   e. Remove the 3 end clips from the door
jam weatherstrip and pull it off.

   f. Remove the 5 retaining screws and remove the side window moulding.

WARNING: *Improper use of the glass adhesive cutter tool may damage the vehicle. Use
only the blades specified in the procedure. Do
not allow the blade to contact the vehicle's
glass or sheet metal. Do not apply upward or
downward pressure. Repair all damaged
painted surfaces before installing the glass.*

CAUTION: *Wear safety glasses and heavy
gloves when cutting glass from the vehicle, to*
*prevent glass splinters from entering eyes or
cutting hands*

2. Open the liftgate and remove the package
tray.

3. Separate the glass from the urethane seal
using the glass adhesive cutter. Use blades 97
and 98 on the top, front and bottom of the window and blade 79 on the rear corner of the
window.

NOTE: *If the rear quarter glass is to be reused, be careful not to damage the locating
stud on the upper right corner.*

4. If the rear quarter glass is to be reused,
place it on a smooth, flat surface and remove
the old urethane.

To install:

5. Smoothly trim the sealant around the rear
quarter window opening to a height of less than
0.15 in. (3.8mm).

6. Inspect the sealing surface of the rear
quarter window opening flange for irregularities, chips, and/or missing paint and repair, if
necessary.

7. Using naptha and a lint-free cloth, wipe
clean the old urethane remaining on the window flange. Apply urethane metal primer to the
painted metal surfaces and allow to dry for 30
minutes.

NOTE: *Keep glass and body surfaces free of
dirt, water and oil. Do not touch coated surfaces with your hand.*

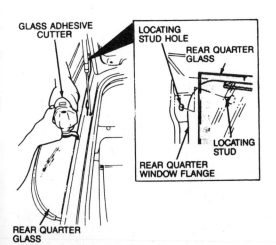

Separating the glass from the urethane seal

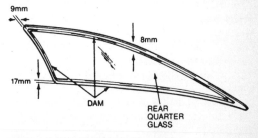

Install the dam around the perimeter

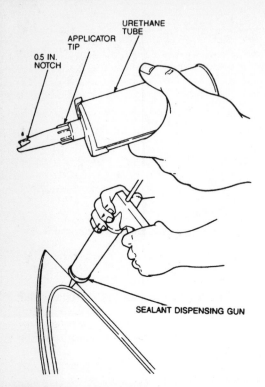

Applying the urethane sealer

8. Thoroughly clean the edge of the glass. Apply urethane glass cleaner to the glass along the edge where the seal will contact and wipe dry with a clean cloth.

9. Apply urethane glass primer, in a 2 in. (51mm) wide strip, around the perimeter of the glass and allow to dry for 3 minutes.

10. Peel the backing tape off the damming material. Install the dam around the perimeter of the glass as shown.

11. Cut a ½ in. (13mm) notch in the urethane tube applicator tip. Run a bead of urethane sealer between the dam and the outside edge of the glass.

12. With help from an assistant, carefully position the glass in the opening, aligning the stud in the upper corner with the corresponding hole.

13. Press the glass against the urethane with approximately 200 lbs. pressure.

14. After the urethane has skinned over, spray water at moderate pressure around the window. Check for water leaks. If a leak is found, wipe the area dry and apply urethane sealant to the affected area.

15. Position the upper window moulding and install the 11 retaining screws. Apply pressure to the rear portion of the moulding to engage the retaining clips. install the weatherstrip and the 3 end clips.

16. Position the side window moulding and install the 5 retaining screws. Install the weatherstrip and secure with the 3 end clips.

17. Install the package tray.

Inside Rear View Mirror
REMOVAL AND INSTALLATION

1. Remove the roof console. Refer to the procedure in this Chapter.

2. Hold the mirror and remove the 2 mounting screws.

3. Remove the mirror.

To install:

4. Position the mirror against the roof. Be sure to install the anti-vibration stopper between the mirror and windshield to prevent excessive vibration.

5. Install the 2 mounting screws.

6. Install the roof console.

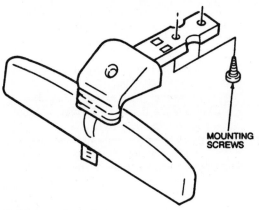

Inside rear view mirror

Seats
REMOVAL AND INSTALLATION
Front Seats

1. Disconnect the negative battery cable.

2. Remove the screws from the seat track access covers secured to the floor at each corner of the seat track.

3. Remove the 3 bolts and 1 nut retaining the seat track to the floor.

4. If equipped with standard seats, lift the seat and disconnect the seat belt switch connector (driver's seat only), then remove the seat assembly.

5. If equipped with power seats, lift the seat and disconnect the seat electrical connector, theen remove the seat assembly.

To install:

5. Position the seat assembly over the floor stud and align the bolt holes.

6. If installing the standard driver's seat, connect the seat belt switch connector. If in-

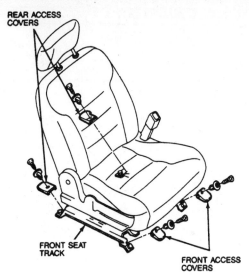

Front seat removal and installation

stalling power seats, connect the electrical connector.

7. Install the front bolts, then install the rear bolt and nut. Tighten to 28–38 ft. lbs. (38–51 Nm).

8. Install the seat track access covers and screws.

Rear Seats

1. Depress the clips on each end of the rear seat cushion and reemove the seat cushion.

2. Fold the seat back down by pulling up on the release knob.

3. Remove the carpet from the rear of the seat back.

4. Remove the 2 bolts from the inside hinge and slide the seat off the outside hinge.

To install:

5. Slide the seat back onto the outside hinge. Install the inside hinge and both retaining bolts.

6. Position the carpet onto the back of the seat and secure it with round plastic button fasteners. Insert the fasteners through the carpet and press them firmly into the hole in the seat back.

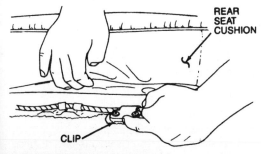

Removing the rear seat cushion

7. Fold the seat back up to the upright position.

8. Position the seat cushion over the floor, making sure to align the retaining pins with the clips.

9. Push down firmly until the 2 retaining pins are locked into the rear seat retaining clips.

Seat Belt System
REMOVAL AND INSTALLATION
Track and Motor Assembly

1. Unbuckle the shoulder belt from the carrier.

2. Cycle the carrier to the B-pillar (retracted) position.

3. Disconnect the negative battery cable.

4. Remove the A-pillar and quarter pillar trim panels. Refer to the procedure in this Chapter.

5. Disconnect the front limit switch electrical connector.

6. Remove the 3 upper track mounting bolts and the upper track mounting screw.

7. Remove the 2 side track mounting bolts.

8. Remove the 4 cable retaining cap screws and the 3 motor mounting bolts.

9. Disconnect the electrical connector and remove the motor and track asseembly.

To install:

10. Position the motor and track assembly and install the 3 upper track mounting bolts. Tighten to 28–58 ft. lbs. (38–78 Nm).

11. Install the upper track mounting screw.

12. Install the 2 side track mounting bolts and tighten to 28–58 ft. lbs. (38–78 Nm).

13. Install the 4 cable retaining cap screws.

14. Install the 3 motor mounting bolts and tighten to 28–58 ft. lbs. (38–78 Nm).

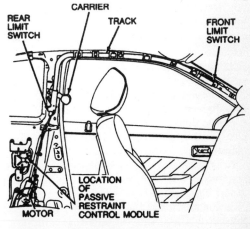

Front seal belt track and motor assembly

15. Connect the front limit switch electrical connector.

16. Install the quarter and A-pillar trim panels.

17. Buckle the shoulder belt to the carrier.

18. Connect the negative battery cable and check the system for proper operation.

Retractor Assembly

1. Disconnect the negative battery cable.

2. Unbuckle both shoulder belts from the carriers.

3. Remove the floor console. Refer to the procedure in this Chapter.

4. Remove the 2 retractor assembly mounting bolts.

5. Disconnect thee electrical connector and remove the retractor assembly.

To install:

6. Connect the electrical connector.

7. Position the retractor assembly and install the 2 mounting bolts.

8. Install the floor console.

9. Buckle the shoulder belts to the carriers.

10. Connect the negative battery cable and check the restraint system for proper operation.

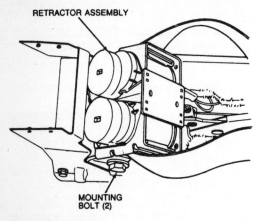

Retractor assembly

Passive Restraint Control Module

1. Disconnect the negative battery cable.

2. Remove the quarter trim panel. Refer to the procedure in this Chapter.

3. Remove the 3 control module mounting plate bolts.

4. Disconnect the 2 control module electrical connectors and remove the module from the mounting plate.

5. Installation is the reverse of the removal procedure. Check the restraint system for proper operation.

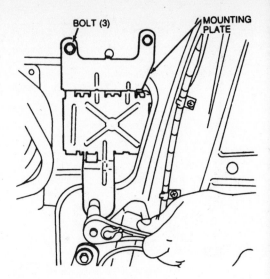

Passive restraint control module removal and installation

Rear Shoulder Belt Retractor

1. Remove the package tray.

2. Remove the upper trunk side garnish. Refer to the procedure in this Chapter.

3. Remove the shoulder belt retractor mounting nut and remove the assembly.

4. Installation is the reverse of the removal procedure.

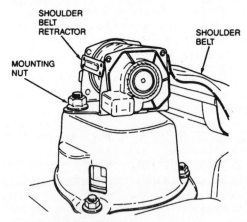

Rear shoulder belt retractor

Rear Shoulder Belt Anchor

1. Remove the upper trunk side garnish. Refer to the procedure in this Chapter.

2. Remove the quarter trim panel. Refer to the procedure in this Chapter.

3. Remove the shoulder belt anchor mounting bolt and remove the anchor.

4. Installation is the reverse of the removal procedure.

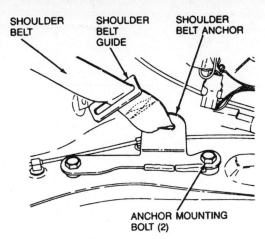

Rear shoulder belt anchor

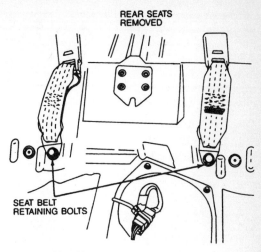

Rear seat buckle

Rear Seat Buckle

1. Remove the rear seat cushion. Refer to the procedure in this Chapter.
2. Remove the bolt securing the rear seat buckle to the floor and remove the rear seat buckle assembly.
3. Installation is the reverse of the removal procedure.

Power Seat Motor

REMOVAL AND INSTALLATION

1. Remove the seat assembly and place it upside down on a clean working surface.
2. Remove the front trim cover. Remove the slide lifter switch handle, the recliner lever handle, and the left side trim cover.
3. Disconnect the slide lifter switch electrical connector.
4. Remove the right side trim cover, and the seat cushion.
5. Remove the four bolts (two per side) retaining the recliner knuckles to the power seat track.
6. Remove the screws that attach each motor to the mounting brackets.
7. Installation is the reverse of the removal procedure.

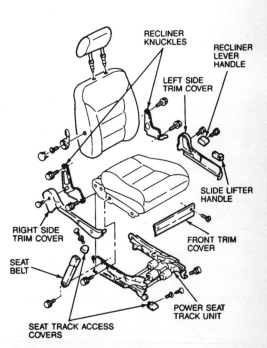

Power seat disassembled view

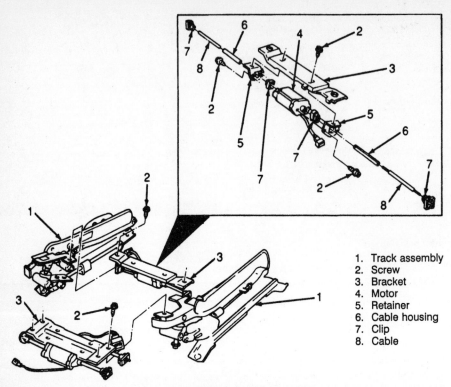

1. Track assembly
2. Screw
3. Bracket
4. Motor
5. Retainer
6. Cable housing
7. Clip
8. Cable

Power seat track and motor assembly

Mechanic's Data

11

General Conversion Table

Multiply By	To Convert	To	
LENGTH			
2.54	Inches	Centimeters	.3937
25.4	Inches	Millimeters	.03937
30.48	Feet	Centimeters	.0328
.304	Feet	Meters	3.28
.914	Yards	Meters	1.094
1.609	Miles	Kilometers	.621
VOLUME			
.473	Pints	Liters	2.11
.946	Quarts	Liters	1.06
3.785	Gallons	Liters	.264
.016	Cubic inches	Liters	61.02
16.39	Cubic inches	Cubic cms.	.061
28.3	Cubic feet	Liters	.0353
MASS (Weight)			
28.35	Ounces	Grams	.035
.4536	Pounds	Kilograms	2.20
—	**To obtain**	**From**	**Multiply by**

Multiply By	To Convert	To	
AREA			
.645	Square inches	Square cms.	.155
.836	Square yds.	Square meters	1.196
FORCE			
4.448	Pounds	Newtons	.225
.138	Ft./lbs.	Kilogram/meters	7.23
1.36	Ft./lbs.	Newton-meters	.737
.112	In./lbs.	Newton-meters	8.844
PRESSURE			
.068	Psi	Atmospheres	14.7
6.89	Psi	Kilopascals	.145
OTHER			
1.104	Horsepower (DIN)	Horsepower (SAE)	.9861
.746	Horsepower (SAE)	Kilowatts (KW)	1.34
1.60	Mph	Km/h	.625
.425	Mpg	Km/1	2.35
—	**To obtain**	**From**	**Multiply by**

Tap Drill Sizes

National Coarse or U.S.S.

Screw & Tap Size	Threads Per Inch	Use Drill Number
No. 5	40	.39
No. 6	32	.36
No. 8	32	.29
No. 10	24	.25
No. 12	24	.17
1/4	20	8
5/16	18	F
3/8	16	5/16
7/16	14	U
1/2	13	27/64
9/16	12	31/64
5/8	11	17/32
3/4	10	21/32
7/8	9	49/64

National Coarse or U.S.S.

Screw & Tap Size	Threads Per Inch	Use Drill Number
1	8	7/8
1 1/8	7	63/64
1 1/4	7	1 7/64
1 1/2	6	1 11/32

National Fine or S.A.E.

Screw & Tap Size	Threads Per Inch	Use Drill Number
No. 5	44	.37
No. 6	40	.33
No. 8	36	.29
No. 10	32	.21

National Fine or S.A.E.

Screw & Tap Size	Threads Per Inch	Use Drill Number
No. 12	28	.15
1/4	28	3
6/16	24	1
3/8	24	Q
7/16	20	W
1/2	20	29/64
9/16	18	33/64
5/8	18	37/64
3/4	16	11/16
7/8	14	13/16
1 1/8	12	1 3/64
1 1/4	12	1 11/64
1 1/2	12	1 27/64

Drill Sizes In Decimal Equivalents

Inch	Decimal	Wire	mm	Inch	Decimal	Wire	mm	Inch	Decimal	Wire & Letter	mm	Inch	Decimal	Letter	mm	Inch	Decimal	mm
1/64	.0156		.39		.0730	49			.1614		4.1		.2717		6.9		.4331	11.0
	.0157		.4		.0748		1.9		.1654		4.2		.2720	I		7/16	.4375	11.11
	.0160	78			.0760	48			.1660	19			.2756		7.0		.4528	11.5
	.0165		.42		.0768		1.95		.1673		4.25		.2770	J		29/64	.4531	11.51
	.0173		.44	5/64	.0781		1.98		.1693		4.3		.2795		7.1	15/32	.4688	11.90
	.0177		.45		.0785	47			.1695	18			.2810	K			.4724	12.0
	.0180	77			.0787		2.0	11/64	.1719		4.36	9/32	.2812		7.14	31/64	.4844	12.30
	.0181		.46		.0807		2.05		.1730	17			.2835		7.2		.4921	12.5
	.0189		.48		.0810	46			.1732		4.4		.2854		7.25	1/2	.5000	12.70
	.0197		.5		.0820	45			.1770	16			.2874		7.3		.5118	13.0
	.0200	76			.0827		2.1		.1772		4.5		.2900	L		33/64	.5156	13.09
	.0210	75			.0846		2.15		.1800	15			.2913		7.4	17/32	.5312	13.49
	.0217		.55		.0860	44			.1811		4.6		.2950	M			.5315	13.5
	.0225	74			.0866		2.2		.1820	14			.2953		7.5	35/64	.5469	13.89
	.0236		.6		.0886		2.25		.1850	13		19/64	.2969		7.54		.5512	14.0
	.0240	73			.0890	43			.1850		4.7		.2992		7.6	9/16	.5625	14.28
	.0250	72			.0906		2.3		.1870		4.75		.3020	N			.5709	14.5
	.0256		.65		.0925		2.35	3/16	.1875		4.76		.3031		7.7	37/64	.5781	14.68
	.0260	71			.0935	42			.1890		4.8		.3051		7.75		.5906	15.0
	.0276		.7	3/32	.0938		2.38		.1890	12			.3071		7.8	19/32	.5938	15.08
	.0280	70			.0945		2.4		.1910	11			.3110		7.9	39/64	.6094	15.47
	.0292	69			.0960	41			.1929		4.9	5/16	.3125		7.93		.6102	15.5
	.0295		.75		.0965		2.45		.1935	10			.3150		8.0	5/8	.6250	15.87
	.0310	68			.0980	40			.1960	9			.3160	O			.6299	16.0
1/32	.0312		.79		.0981		2.5		.1969		5.0		.3189		8.1	41/64	.6406	16.27
	.0315		.8		.0995	39			.1990	8			.3228		8.2		.6496	16.5
	.0320	67			.1015	38			.2008		5.1		.3230	P		21/32	.6562	16.66
	.0330	66			.1024		2.6		.2010	7			.3248		8.25		.6693	17.0
	.0335		.85		.1040	37		13/64	.2031		5.16		.3268		8.3	43/64	.6719	17.06
	.0350	65			.1063		2.7		.2040	6		21/64	.3281		8.33	11/16	.6875	17.46
	.0354		.9		.1065	36			.2047		5.2		.3307		8.4		.6890	17.5
	.0360	64			.1083		2.75		.2055	5			.3320	Q		45/64	.7031	17.85
	.0370	63		7/64	.1094		2.77		.2067		5.25		.3346		8.5		.7087	18.0
	.0374		.95		.1100	35			.2087		5.3		.3386		8.6	23/32	.7188	18.25
	.0380	62			.1102		2.8		.2090	4			.3390	R			.7283	18.5
	.0390	61			.1110	34			.2126		5.4		.3425		8.7	47/64	.7344	18.65
	.0394		1.0		.1130	33			.2130	3		11/32	.3438		8.73		.7480	19.0
	.0400	60			.1142		2.9	7/32	.2165		5.5		.3445		8.75	3/4	.7500	19.05
	.0410	59			.1160	32			.2188		5.55		.3465		8.8	49/64	.7656	19.44
	.0413		1.05		.1181		3.0		.2205		5.6		.3480	S			.7677	19.5
	.0420	58			.1200	31			.2210	2			.3504		8.9	25/32	.7812	19.84
	.0430	57			.1220		3.1		.2244		5.7		.3543		9.0		.7874	20.0
	.0433		1.1	1/8	.1250		3.17		.2264		5.75		.3580	T		51/64	.7969	20.24
	.0453		1.15		.1260		3.2		.2280	1			.3583		9.1		.8071	20.5
	.0465	56			.1280		3.25		.2283		5.8	23/64	.3594		9.12	13/16	.8125	20.63
3/64	.0469		1.19		.1285	30			.2323		5.9		.3622		9.2		.8268	21.0
	.0472		1.2		.1299		3.3		.2340	A			.3642		9.25	53/64	.8281	21.03
	.0492		1.25		.1339		3.4	15/64	.2344		5.95		.3661		9.3	27/32	.8438	21.43
	.0512		1.3		.1360	29			.2362		6.0		.3680	U			.8465	21.5
	.0520	55			.1378		3.5		.2380	B			.3701		9.4	55/64	.8594	21.82
	.0531		1.35		.1405	28			.2402		6.1		.3740		9.5		.8661	22.0
	.0550	54		9/64	.1406		3.57		.2420	C		3/8	.3750		9.52	7/8	.8750	22.22
	.0551		1.4		.1417		3.6		.2441		6.2		.3770	V			.8858	22.5
	.0571		1.45		.1440	27			.2460	D			.3780		9.6	57/64	.8906	22.62
	.0591		1.5		.1457		3.7		.2461		6.25		.3819		9.7		.9055	23.0
	.0595	53			.1470	26			.2480		6.3		.3839		9.75	29/32	.9062	23.01
	.0610		1.55		.1476		3.75	1/4	.2500	E			.3858		9.8	59/64	.9219	23.41
1/16	.0625		1.59		.1495	25			.2520		6.		.3860	W			.9252	23.5
	.0630		1.6		.1496		3.8		.2559		6.5		.3898		9.9	15/16	.9375	23.81
	.0635	52			.1520	24			.2570	F		25/64	.3906		9.92		.9449	24.0
	.0650		1.65		.1535		3.9		.2598		6.6		.3937		10.0	61/64	.9531	24.2
	.0669		1.7		.1540	23			.2610	G			.3970	X			.9646	24.5
	.0670	51		5/32	.1562		3.96		.2638		6.7		.4040	Y		31/32	.9688	24.6
	.0689		1.75		.1570	22		17/64	.2656		6.74	13/32	.4062		10.31		.9843	25.0
	.0700	50			.1575		4.0		.2657		6.75		.4130	Z		63/64	.9844	25.0
	.0709		1.8		.1590	21			.2660	H			.4134		10.5	1	1.0000	25.4
	.0728		1.85		.1610	20			.2677		6.8	27/64	.4219		10.71			

AIR/FUEL RATIO: The ratio of air to gasoline by weight in the fuel mixture drawn into the engine.

AIR INJECTION: One method of reducing harmful exhaust emissions by injecting air into each of the exhaust ports of an engine. The fresh air entering the hot exhaust manifold causes any remaining fuel to be burned before it can exit the tailpipe.

ALTERNATOR: A device used for converting mechanical energy into electrical energy.

AMMETER: An instrument, calibrated in amperes, used to measure the flow of an electrical current in a circuit. Ammeters are always connected in series with the circuit being tested.

AMPERE: The rate of flow of electrical current present when one volt of electrical pressure is applied against one ohm of electrical resistance.

ANALOG COMPUTER: Any microprocessor that uses similar (analogous) electrical signals to make its calculations.

ARMATURE: A laminated, soft iron core wrapped by a wire that converts electrical energy to mechanical energy as in a motor or relay. When rotated in a magnetic field, it changes mechanical energy into electrical energy as in a generator.

ATMOSPHERIC PRESSURE: The pressure on the Earth's surface caused by the weight of the air in the atmosphere. At sea level, this pressure is 14.7 psi at 32°F (101 kPa at 0°C).

ATOMIZATION: The breaking down of a liquid into a fine mist that can be suspended in air.

AXIAL PLAY: Movement parallel to a shaft or bearing bore.

BACKFIRE: The sudden combustion of gases in the intake or exhaust system that results in a loud explosion.

BACKLASH: The clearance or play between two parts, such as meshed gears.

BACKPRESSURE: Restrictions in the exhaust system that slow the exit of exhaust gases from the combustion chamber.

BAKELITE: A heat resistant, plastic insulator material commonly used in printed circuit boards and transistorized components.

BALL BEARING: A bearing made up of hardened inner and outer races between which hardened steel ball roll.

BALLAST RESISTOR: A resistor in the primary ignition circuit that lowers voltage after the engine is started to reduce wear on ignition components.

BEARING: A friction reducing, supportive device usually located between a stationary part and a moving part.

BIMETAL TEMPERATURE SENSOR: Any sensor or switch made of two dissimilar types of metal that bend when heated or cooled due to the different expansion rates of the alloys. These types of sensors usually function as an on/off switch.

BLOWBY: Combustion gases, composed of water vapor and unburned fuel, that leak past the piston rings into the crankcase during normal engine operation. These gases are removed by the PCV system to prevent the buildup of harmful acids in the crankcase.

BRAKE PAD: A brake shoe and lining assembly used with disc brakes.

BRAKE SHOE: The backing for the brake lining. The term is, however, usually applied to the assembly of the brake backing and lining.

BUSHING: A liner, usually removable, for a bearing; an anti-friction liner used in place of a bearing.

BYPASS: System used to bypass ballast resistor during engine cranking to increase voltage supplied to the coil.

CALIPER: A hydraulically activated device in a disc brake system, which is mounted straddling the brake rotor (disc). The caliper contains at least one piston and two brake pads. Hydraulic pressure on the piston(s) forces the pads against the rotor.

CAMSHAFT: A shaft in the engine on which are the lobes (cams) which operate the valves. The camshaft is driven by the crankshaft, via a belt, chain or gears, at one half the crankshaft speed.

CAPACITOR: A device which stores an electrical charge.

CARBON MONOXIDE (CO): a colorless, odorless gas given off as a normal byproduct of combustion. It is poisonous and extremely dangerous in confined areas, building up slowly to toxic levels without warning if adequate ventilation is not available.

CARBURETOR: A device, usually mounted on the intake manifold of an engine, which mixes the air and fuel in the proper proportion to allow even combustion.

CATALYTIC CONVERTER: A device installed in the exhaust system, like a muffler, that converts harmful byproducts of combustion into carbon dioxide and water vapor by means of a heat-producing chemical reaction.

CENTRIFUGAL ADVANCE: A mechanical method of advancing the spark timing by using flyweights in the distributor that react to centrifugal force generated by the distributor shaft rotation.

CHECK VALVE: Any one-way valve installed to permit the flow of air, fuel or vacuum in one direction only.

CHOKE: A device, usually a moveable valve, placed in the intake path of a carburetor to restrict the flow of air.

CIRCUIT: Any unbroken path through which an electrical current can flow. Also used to describe fuel flow in some instances.

CIRCUIT BREAKER: A switch which protects an electrical circuit from overload by opening the circuit when the current flow exceeds a predetermined level. Some circuit breakers must be reset manually, while other reset automatically

COIL (IGNITION): A transformer in the ignition circuit which steps of the voltage provided to the spark plugs.

COMBINATION MANIFOLD: An assembly which includes both the intake and exhaust manifolds in one casting.

COMBINATION VALVE: A device used in some fuel systems that routes fuel vapors to a charcoal storage canister instead of venting them into the atmosphere. The valve relieves fuel tank pressure and allows fresh air into the tank as fuel level drops to prevent a vapor lock situation.

COMPRESSION RATIO: The comparison of the total volume of the cylinder and combustion chamber with the piston at BDC and the piston at TDC.

CONDENSER: 1. An electrical device which acts to store an electrical charge, preventing voltage surges.
2. A radiator-like device in the air conditioning system in which refrigerant gas condenses into a liquid, giving off heat.

CONDUCTOR: Any material through which an electrical current can be transmitted easily.

CONTINUITY: Continuous or complete circuit. Can be checked with an ohmmeter.

COUNTERSHAFT: An intermediate shaft which is rotated by a mainshaft and transmits, in turn, that rotation to a working part.

CRANKCASE: The lower part of an engine in which the crankshaft and related parts operate.

CRANKSHAFT: The main driving shaft of an engine which receives reciprocating motion from the pistons and converts it to rotary motion.

CYLINDER: In an engine, the round hole in the engine block in which the piston(s) ride.

CYLINDER BLOCK: The main structural member of an engine in which is found the cylinders, crankshaft and other principal parts.

CYLINDER HEAD: The detachable portion of the engine, fastened, usually, to the top of the cylinder block, containing all or most of the combustion chambers. On overhead valve engines, it contains the valves and their operating parts. On overhead cam engines, it contains the camshaft as well.

DEAD CENTER: The extreme top or bottom of the piston stroke.

DETONATION: An unwanted explosion of the air fuel mixture in the combustion chamber caused by excess heat and compression, advanced timing, or an overly lean mixture. Also referred to as "ping".

DIAPHRAGM: A thin, flexible wall separating two cavities, such as in a vacuum advance unit.

DIESELING: A condition in which hot spots in the combustion chamber cause the engine to run on after the key is turned off.

DIFFERENTIAL: A geared assembly which allows the transmission of motion between drive axles, giving one axle the ability to turn faster than the other.

DIODE: An electrical device that will allow current to flow in one direction only.

DISC BRAKE: A hydraulic braking assembly consisting of a brake disc, or rotor, mounted on an axle, and a caliper assembly containing, usually two brake pads which are activated by hydraulic pressure. The pads are forced against the sides of the disc, creating friction which slows the vehicle.

DISTRIBUTOR: A mechanically driven device on an engine which is responsible for electrically firing the spark plug at a predetermined point of the piston stroke.

DOWEL PIN: A pin, inserted in mating holes in two different parts allowing those parts to maintain a fixed relationship.

DRUM BRAKE: A braking system which consists of two brake shoes and one or two wheel cylinders, mounted on a fixed backing plate, and a brake drum, mounted on an axle, which revolves around the assembly. Hydraulic action applied to the wheel cylinders forces the shoes outward against the drum, creating friction and slowing the vehicle.

DWELL: The rate, measured in degrees of shaft rotation, at which an electrical circuit cycles on and off.

ELECTRONIC CONTROL UNIT (ECU): Ignition module, module, amplifier or igniter. See Module for definition.

ELECTRONIC IGNITION: A system in which the timing and firing of the spark plugs is controlled by an electronic control unit, usually called a module. These systems have not points or condenser.

ENDPLAY: The measured amount of axial movement in a shaft.

ENGINE: A device that converts heat into mechanical energy.

EXHAUST MANIFOLD: A set of cast passages or pipes which conduct exhaust gases from the engine.

FEELER GAUGE: A blade, usually metal, of precisely predetermined thickness, used to measure the clearance between two parts. These blades usually are available in sets of assorted thicknesses.

F-Head: An engine configuration in which the intake valves are in the cylinder head, while the camshaft and exhaust valves are located in the cylinder block. The camshaft operates the intake valves via lifters and pushrods, while it operates the exhaust valves directly.

FIRING ORDER: The order in which combustion occurs in the cylinders of an engine. Also the order in which spark is distributed to the plugs by the distributor.

FLATHEAD: An engine configuration in which the camshaft and all the valves are located in the cylinder block.

FLOODING: The presence of too much fuel in the intake manifold and combustion chamber which prevents the air/fuel mixture from firing, thereby causing a no-start situation.

FLYWHEEL: A disc shaped part bolted to the rear end of the crankshaft. Around the outer perimeter is affixed the ring gear. The starter drive engages the ring gear, turning the flywheel, which rotates the crankshaft, imparting the initial starting motion to the engine.

FOOT POUND (ft.lb. or sometimes, ft. lbs.): The amount of energy or work needed to raise an item weighing one pound, a distance of one foot.

FUSE: A protective device in a circuit which prevents circuit overload by breaking the circuit when a specific amperage is present. The device is constructed around a strip or wire of a lower amperage rating than the circuit it is designed to protect. When an amperage higher than that stamped on the fuse is present in the circuit, the strip or wire melts, opening the circuit.

GEAR RATIO: The ratio between the number of teeth on meshing gears.

GENERATOR: A device which converts mechanical energy into electrical energy.

HEAT RANGE: The measure of a spark plug's ability to dissipate heat from its firing end. The higher the heat range, the hotter the plug fires.

HUB: The center part of a wheel or gear.

HYDROCARBON (HC): Any chemical compound made up of hydrogen and carbon. A major pollutant formed by the engine as a byproduct of combustion.

HYDROMETER: An instrument used to measure the specific gravity of a solution.

INCH POUND (in.lb. or sometimes, in. lbs.): One twelfth of a foot pound.

INDUCTION: A means of transferring electrical energy in the form of a magnetic field. Principle used in the ignition coil to increase voltage.

INJECTION PUMP: A device, usually mechanically operated, which meters and delivers fuel under pressure to the fuel injector.

INJECTOR: A device which receives metered fuel under relatively low pressure and is activated to inject the fuel into the engine under relatively high pressure at a predetermined time.

INPUT SHAFT: The shaft to which torque is applied, usually carrying the driving gear or gears.

INTAKE MANIFOLD: A casting of passages or pipes used to conduct air or a fuel/air mixture to the cylinders.

JOURNAL: The bearing surface within which a shaft operates.

KEY: A small block usually fitted in a notch between a shaft and a hub to prevent slippage of the two parts.

MANIFOLD: A casting of passages or set of pipes which connect the cylinders to an inlet or outlet source.

MANIFOLD VACUUM: Low pressure in an engine intake manifold formed just below the throttle plates. Manifold vacuum is highest at idle and drops under acceleration.

MASTER CYLINDER: The primary fluid pressurizing device in a hydraulic system. In automotive use, it is found in brake and hydraulic clutch systems and is pedal activated, either directly or, in a power brake system, through the power booster.

MODULE: Electronic control unit, amplifier or igniter of solid state or integrated design which controls the current flow in the ignition primary circuit based on input from the pickup coil. When the module opens the primary circuit, the high secondary voltage is induced in the coil.

NEEDLE BEARING: A bearing which consists of a number (usually a large number) of long, thin rollers.

OHM: (Ω) The unit used to measure the resistance of conductor to electrical flow. One ohm is the amount of resistance that limits current flow to one ampere in a circuit with one volt of pressure.

OHMMETER: An instrument used for measuring the resistance, in ohms, in an electrical circuit.

OUTPUT SHAFT: The shaft which transmits torque from a device, such as a transmission.

OVERDRIVE: A gear assembly which produces more shaft revolutions than that transmitted to it.

OVERHEAD CAMSHAFT (OHC): An engine configuration in which the camshaft is mounted on top of the cylinder head and operates the valve either directly or by means of rocker arms.

OVERHEAD VALVE (OHV): An engine configuration in which all of the valves are located in the cylinder head and the camshaft is located in the cylinder block. The camshaft operates the valves via lifters and pushrods.

OXIDES OF NITROGEN (NOx): Chemical compounds of nitrogen produced as a byproduct of combustion. They combine with hydrocarbons to produce smog.

OXYGEN SENSOR: Used with the feedback system to sense the presence of oxygen in the exhaust gas and signal the computer which can reference the voltage signal to an air/fuel ratio.

PINION: The smaller of two meshing gears.

PISTON RING: An open ended ring which fits into a groove on the outer diameter of the piston. Its chief function is to form a seal between the piston and cylinder wall. Most automotive pistons have three rings: two for compression sealing; one for oil sealing.

PRELOAD: A predetermined load placed on a bearing during assembly or by adjustment.

PRIMARY CIRCUIT: Is the low voltage side of the ignition system which consists of the ignition switch, ballast resistor or resistance wire, bypass, coil, electronic control unit and pick-up coil as well as the connecting wires and harnesses.

PRESS FIT: The mating of two parts under pressure, due to the inner diameter of one being smaller than the outer diameter of the other, or vice versa; an interference fit.

RACE: The surface on the inner or outer ring of a bearing on which the balls, needles or rollers move.

REGULATOR: A device which maintains the amperage and/or voltage levels of a circuit at predetermined values.

RELAY: A switch which automatically opens and/or closes a circuit.

RESISTANCE: The opposition to the flow of current through a circuit or electrical device, and is measured in ohms. Resistance is equal to the voltage divided by the amperage.

RESISTOR: A device, usually made of wire, which offers a preset amount of resistance in an electrical circuit.

RING GEAR: The name given to a ring-shaped gear attached to a differential case, or affixed to a flywheel or as part a planetary gear set.

ROLLER BEARING: A bearing made up of hardened inner and outer races between which hardened steel rollers move.

ROTOR: 1. The disc-shaped part of a disc brake assembly, upon which the brake pads bear; also called, brake disc.
2. The device mounted atop the distributor shaft, which passes current to the distributor cap tower contacts.

SECONDARY CIRCUIT: The high voltage side of the ignition system, usually above 20,000 volts. The secondary includes the ignition coil, coil wire, distributor cap and rotor, spark plug wires and spark plugs.

SENDING UNIT: A mechanical, electrical, hydraulic or electromagnetic device which transmits information to a gauge.

SENSOR: Any device designed to measure engine operating conditions or ambient pressures and temperatures. Usually electronic in nature and designed to send a voltage signal to an on-board computer, some sensors may operate as a simple on/off switch or they may provide a variable voltage signal (like a potentiometer) as conditions or measured parameters change.

SHIM: Spacers of precise, predetermined thickness used between parts to establish a proper working relationship.

SLAVE CYLINDER: In automotive use, a device in the hydraulic clutch system which is activated by hydraulic force, disengaging the clutch.

SOLENOID: A coil used to produce a magnetic field, the effect of which is produce work.

SPARK PLUG: A device screwed into the combustion chamber of a spark ignition engine. The basic construction is a conductive core inside of a ceramic insulator, mounted in an outer conductive base. An electrical charge from the spark plug wire travels along the conductive core and jumps a preset air gap to a grounding point or points at the end of the conductive base. The resultant spark ignites the fuel/air mixture in the combustion chamber.

SPLINES: Ridges machined or cast onto the outer diameter of a shaft or inner diameter of a bore to enable parts to mate without rotation.

TACHOMETER: A device used to measure the rotary speed of an engine, shaft, gear, etc., usually in rotations per minute.

THERMOSTAT: A valve, located in the cooling system of an engine, which is closed when cold and opens gradually in response to engine heating, controlling the temperature of the coolant and rate of coolant flow.

TOP DEAD CENTER (TDC): The point at which the piston reaches the top of its travel on the compression stroke.

TORQUE: The twisting force applied to an object.

TORQUE CONVERTER: A turbine used to transmit power from a driving member to a driven member via hydraulic action, providing changes in drive ratio and torque. In automotive use, it links the driveplate at the rear of the engine to the automatic transmission.

TRANSDUCER: A device used to change a force into an electrical signal.

TRANSISTOR: A semi-conductor component which can be actuated by a small voltage to perform an electrical switching function.

TUNE-UP: A regular maintenance function, usually associated with the replacement and adjustment of parts and components in the electrical and fuel systems of a vehicle for the purpose of attaining optimum performance.

TURBOCHARGER: An exhaust driven pump which compresses intake air and forces it into the combustion chambers at higher than atmospheric pressures. The increased air pressure allows more fuel to be burned and results in increased horsepower being produced.

VACUUM ADVANCE: A device which advances the ignition timing in response to increased engine vacuum.

VACUUM GAUGE: An instrument used to measure the presence of vacuum in a chamber.

VALVE: A device which control the pressure, direction of flow or rate of flow of a liquid or gas.

VALVE CLEARANCE: The measured gap between the end of the valve stem and the rocker arm, cam lobe or follower that activates the valve.

VISCOSITY: The rating of a liquid's internal resistance to flow.

VOLTMETER: An instrument used for measuring electrical force in units called volts. Voltmeters are always connected parallel with the circuit being tested.

WHEEL CYLINDER: Found in the automotive drum brake assembly, it is a device, actuated by hydraulic pressure, which, through internal pistons, pushes the brake shoes outward against the drums.

ABBREVIATIONS AND SYMBOLS

A: Ampere

AC: Alternating current

A/C: Air conditioning

A-h: Ampere hour

AT: Automatic transmission

ATDC: After top dead center

μA: Microampere

bbl: Barrel

BDC: Bottom dead center

bhp: Brake horsepower

BTDC: Before top dead center

BTU: British thermal unit

C: Celsius (Centigrade)

CCA: Cold cranking amps

cd: Candela

cm^2: Square centimeter

cm^3, cc: Cubic centimeter

CO: Carbon monoxide

CO_2: Carbon dioxide

cu.in., in^3: Cubic inch

CV: Constant velocity

Cyl.: Cylinder

DC: Direct current

ECM: Electronic control module

EFE: Early fuel evaporation

EFI: Electronic fuel injection

EGR: Exhaust gas recirculation

Exh.: Exhaust

F: Fahrenheit

F: Farad

pF: Picofarad

μF: Microfarad

FI: Fuel injection

ft.lb., ft. lb., ft. lbs.: foot pound(s)

gal: Gallon

g: Gram

HC: Hydrocarbon

HEI: High energy ignition

HO: High output

hp: Horsepower

Hyd.: Hydraulic

Hz: Hertz

ID: Inside diameter

in.lb.; in. lb.; in. lbs: inch pound(s)

Int.: Intake

K: Kelvin

kg: Kilogram

kHz: Kilohertz

km: Kilometer

km/h: Kilometers per hour

kΩ: Kilohm

kPa: Kilopascal

kV: Kilovolt

kW: Kilowatt

l: Liter

l/s: Liters per second

m: Meter

mA: Milliampere

mg: Milligram

mHz: Megahertz

mm: Millimeter

mm^2: Square millimeter

m^3: Cubic meter

MΩ: Megohm

m/s: Meters per second

MT: Manual transmission

mV: Millivolt

μm: Micrometer

N: Newton

N-m: Newton meter

NOx: Nitrous oxide

OD: Outside diameter

OHC: Over head camshaft

OHV: Over head valve

Ω: Ohm

PCV: Positive crankcase ventilation

psi: Pounds per square inch

pts: Pints

qts: Quarts

rpm: Rotations per minute

rps: Rotations per second

R-12: A refrigerant gas (Freon)

SAE: Society of Automotive Engineers

SO$_2$: Sulfur dioxide

T: Ton

t: Megagram

TBI: Throttle Body Injection

TPS: Throttle Position Sensor

V: 1. Volt; 2. Venturi

μV: Microvolt

W: Watt

∞: Infinity

<: Less than

>: Greater than

Index

CHILTON'S REPAIR MANUAL MODEL INDEX
Car and truck model names are listed in alphabetical and numerical order

Part No.	Model	Repair Manual Title
6980	Accord	Honda 1973-88
7747	Aerostar	Ford Aerostar 1986-90
7165	Alliance	Renault 1975-85
7199	AMX	AMC 1975-86
7163	Aries	Chrysler Front Wheel Drive 1981-88
7041	Arrow	Champ/Arrow/Sapporo 1978-83
7032	Arrow Pick-Ups	D-50/Arrow Pick-Up 1979-81
6637	Aspen	Aspen/Volare 1976-80
6935	Astre	GM Subcompact 1971-80
7750	Astro	Chevrolet Astro/GMC Safari 1985-90
6934	A100, 200, 300	Dodge/Plymouth Vans 1967-88
5807	Barracuda	Barracuda/Challenger 1965-72
6844	Bavaria	BMW 1970-88
5796	Beetle	Volkswagen 1949-71
6837	Beetle	Volkswagen 1970-81
7135	Bel Air	Chevrolet 1968-88
5821	Belvedere	Roadrunner/Satellite/Belvedere/GTX 1968-73
7849	Beretta	Chevrolet Corsica and Beretta 1988
7317	Berlinetta	Camaro 1982-88
7135	Biscayne	Chevrolet 1968-88
6931	Blazer	Blazer/Jimmy 1969-82
7383	Blazer	Chevy S-10 Blazer/GMC S-15 Jimmy 1982-87
7027	Bobcat	Pinto/Bobcat 1971-80
7308	Bonneville	Buick/Olds/Pontiac 1975-87
6982	BRAT	Subaru 1970-88
7042	Brava	Fiat 1969-81
7140	Bronco	Ford Bronco 1966-86
7829	Bronco	Ford Pick-Ups and Bronco 1987-88
7408	Bronco II	Ford Ranger/Bronco II 1983-88
7135	Brookwood	Chevrolet 1968-88
6326	Brougham 1975-75	Valiant/Duster 1968-76
6934	B100, 150, 200, 250, 300, 350	Dodge/Plymouth Vans 1967-88
7197	B210	Datsun 1200/210/Nissan Sentra 1973-88
7659	B1600, 1800, 2000, 2200, 2600	Mazda Trucks 1971-89
6840	Caballero	Chevrolet Mid-Size 1964-88
7657	Calais	Calais, Grand Am, Skylark, Somerset 1985-86
6735	Camaro	Camaro 1967-81
7317	Camaro	Camaro 1982-88
7740	Camry	Toyota Camry 1983-88
6695	Capri, Capri II	Capri 1970-77
6963	Capri	Mustang/Capri/Merkur 1979-88
7135	Caprice	Chevrolet 1968-88
7482	Caravan	Dodge Caravan/Plymouth Voyager 1984-89
7163	Caravelle	Chrysler Front Wheel Drive 1981-88
7036	Carina	Toyota Corolla/Carina/Tercel/Starlet 1970-87
7308	Catalina	Buick/Olds/Pontiac 1975-90
7059	Cavalier	Cavalier, Skyhawk, Cimarron, 2000 1982-88
7309	Celebrity	Celebrity, Century, Ciera, 6000 1982-88
7043	Celica	Toyota Celica/Supra 1971-87
8058	Celica	Toyota Celica/Supra 1986-90
7309	Century FWD	Celebrity, Century, Ciera, 6000 1982-88
7307	Century RWD	Century/Regal 1975-87
5807	Challenger 1965-72	Barracuda/Challenger 1965-72
7037	Challenger 1977-83	Colt/Challenger/Vista/Conquest 1971-88
7041	Champ	Champ/Arrow/Sapporo 1978-83
6486	Charger	Dodge Charger 1967-70
6845	Charger 2.2	Omni/Horizon/Rampage 1978-88

Part No.	Model	Repair Manual Title
6739	Cherokee 1974-83	Jeep Wagoneer, Commando, Cherokee, Truck 1957-86
7939	Cherokee 1984-89	Jeep Wagoneer, Comanche, Cherokee 1984-89
6840	Chevelle	Chevrolet Mid-Size 1964-88
6836	Chevette	Chevette/T-1000 1976-88
6841	Chevy II	Chevy II/Nova 1962-79
7309	Ciera	Celebrity, Century, Ciera, 6000 1982-88
7059	Cimarron	Cavalier, Skyhawk, Cimarron, 2000 1982-88
7049	Citation	GM X-Body 1980-85
6980	Civic	Honda 1973-88
6817	CJ-2A, 3A, 3B, 5, 6, 7	Jeep 1945-87
8034	CJ-5, 6, 7	Jeep 1971-90
6842	Colony Park	Ford/Mercury/Lincoln 1968-88
7037	Colt	Colt/Challenger/Vista/Conquest 1971-88
6634	Comet	Maverick/Comet 1971-77
7939	Comanche	Jeep Wagoneer, Comanche, Cherokee 1984-89
6739	Commando	Jeep Wagoneer, Commando, Cherokee, Truck 1957-86
6842	Commuter	Ford/Mercury/Lincoln 1968-88
7199	Concord	AMC 1975-86
7037	Conquest	Colt/Challenger/Vista/Conquest 1971-88
6696	Continental 1982-85	Ford/Mercury/Lincoln Mid-Size 1971-85
7814	Continental 1982-87	Thunderbird, Cougar, Continental 1980-87
7830	Continental 1988-89	Taurus/Sable/Continental 1986-89
7583	Cordia	Mitsubishi 1983-89
5795	Corolla 1968-70	Toyota 1966-70
7036	Corolla	Toyota Corolla/Carina/Tercel/Starlet 1970-87
5795	Corona	Toyota 1966-70
7004	Corona	Toyota Corona/Crown/Cressida/Mk.II/Van 1970-87
6962	Corrado	VW Front Wheel Drive 1974-90
7849	Corsica	Chevrolet Corsica and Beretta 1988
6576	Corvette	Corvette 1953-62
6843	Corvette	Corvette 1963-86
6542	Cougar	Mustang/Cougar 1965-73
6696	Cougar	Ford/Mercury/Lincoln Mid-Size 1971-85
7814	Cougar	Thunderbird, Cougar, Continental 1980-87
6842	Country Sedan	Ford/Mercury/Lincoln 1968-88
6842	Country Squire	Ford/Mercury/Lincoln 1968-88
6983	Courier	Ford Courier 1972-82
7004	Cressida	Toyota Corona/Crown/Cressida/Mk.II/Van 1970-87
5795	Crown	Toyota 1966-70
7004	Crown	Toyota Corona/Crown/Cressida/Mk.II/Van 1970-87
6842	Crown Victoria	Ford/Mercury/Lincoln 1968-88
6980	CRX	Honda 1973-88
6842	Custom	Ford/Mercury/Lincoln 1968-88
6326	Custom	Valiant/Duster 1968-76
6842	Custom 500	Ford/Mercury/Lincoln 1968-88
7950	Cutlass FWD	Lumina/Grand Prix/Cutlass/Regal 1988-90
6933	Cutlass RWD	Cutlass 1970-87
7309	Cutlass Ciera	Celebrity, Century, Ciera, 6000 1982-88
6936	C-10, 20, 30	Chevrolet/GMC Pick-Ups & Suburban 1970-87

Chilton's Repair Manuals are available at your local retailer or by mailing a check or money order for **$15.95** per book plus **$3.50** for 1st book and **$.50** for each additional book to cover postage and handling to:

Chilton Book Company
Dept. DM
Radnor, PA 19089

NOTE: When ordering be sure to include your name & address, book part No. & title.

CHILTON'S REPAIR MANUAL MODEL INDEX
Car and truck model names are listed in alphabetical and numerical order

Part No.	Model	Repair Manual Title
8055	C-15, 25, 35	Chevrolet/GMC Pick-Ups & Suburban 1988-90
6324	Dart	Dart/Demon 1968-76
6962	Dasher	VW Front Wheel Drive 1974-90
5790	Datsun Pickups	Datsun 1961-72
6816	Datsun Pickups	Datsun Pick-Ups and Pathfinder 1970-89
7163	Daytona	Chrysler Front Wheel Drive 1981-88
6486	Daytona Charger	Dodge Charger 1967-70
6324	Demon	Dart/Demon 1968-76
7462	deVille	Cadillac 1967-89
7587	deVille	GM C-Body 1985
6817	DJ-3B	Jeep 1945-87
7040	DL	Volvo 1970-88
6326	Duster	Valiant/Duster 1968-76
7032	D-50	D-50/Arrow Pick-Ups 1979-81
7459	D100, 150, 200, 250, 300, 350	Dodge/Plymouth Trucks 1967-88
7199	Eagle	AMC 1975-86
7163	E-Class	Chrysler Front Wheel Drive 1981-88
6840	El Camino	Chevrolet Mid-Size 1964-88
7462	Eldorado	Cadillac 1967-89
7308	Electra	Buick/Olds/Pontiac 1975-90
7587	Electra	GM C-Body 1985
6696	Elite	Ford/Mercury/Lincoln Mid-Size 1971-85
7165	Encore	Renault 1975-85
7055	Escort	Ford/Mercury Front Wheel Drive 1981-87
7059	Eurosport	Cavalier, Skyhawk, Cimarron, 2000 1982-88
7760	Excel	Hyundai 1986-90
7163	Executive Sedan	Chrysler Front Wheel Drive 1981-88
7055	EXP	Ford/Mercury Front Wheel Drive 1981-87
6849	E-100, 150, 200, 250, 300, 350	Ford Vans 1961-88
6320	Fairlane	Fairlane/Torino 1962-75
6965	Fairmont	Fairmont/Zephyr 1978-83
5796	Fastback	Volkswagen 1949-71
6837	Fastback	Volkswagen 1970-81
6739	FC-150, 170	Jeep Wagoneer, Commando, Cherokee, Truck 1957-86
6982	FF-1	Subaru 1970-88
7571	Fiero	Pontiac Fiero 1984-88
6846	Fiesta	Fiesta 1978-80
5996	Firebird	Firebird 1967-81
7345	Firebird	Firebird 1982-90
7059	Firenza	Cavalier, Skyhawk, Cimarron, 2000 1982-88
7462	Fleetwood	Cadillac 1967-89
7587	Fleetwood	GM C-Body 1985
7829	F-Super Duty	Ford Pick-Ups and Bronco 1987-88
7165	Fuego	Renault 1975-85
6552	Fury	Plymouth 1968-76
7196	F-10	Datsun/Nissan F-10, 310, Stanza, Pulsar 1976-88
6933	F-85	Cutlass 1970-87
6913	F-100, 150, 200, 250, 300, 350	Ford Pick-Ups 1965-86
7829	F-150, 250, 350	Ford Pick-Ups and Bronco 1987-88
7583	Galant	Mitsubishi 1983-89
6842	Galaxie	Ford/Mercury/Lincoln 1968-88
7040	GL	Volvo 1970-88
6739	Gladiator	Jeep Wagoneer, Commando, Cherokee, Truck 1962-86
6981	GLC	Mazda 1978-89
7040	GLE	Volvo 1970-88
7040	GLT	Volvo 1970-88

Part No.	Model	Repair Manual Title
7593	Golf	VW Front Wheel Drive 1974-90
7165	Gordini	Renault 1975-85
6937	Granada	Granada/Monarch 1975-82
6552	Gran Coupe	Plymouth 1968-76
6552	Gran Fury	Plymouth 1968-76
6842	Gran Marquis	Ford/Mercury/Lincoln 1968-88
6552	Gran Sedan	Plymouth 1968-76
6696	Gran Torino 1972-76	Ford/Mercury/Lincoln Mid-Size 1971-85
7346	Grand Am	Pontiac Mid-Size 1974-83
7657	Grand Am	Calais, Grand Am, Skylark, Somerset 1985-86
7346	Grand LeMans	Pontiac Mid-Size 1974-83
7346	Grand Prix	Pontiac Mid-Size 1974-83
7950	Grand Prix FWD	Lumina/Grand Prix/Cutlass/Regal 1988-90
7308	Grand Safari	Buick/Olds/Pontiac 1975-87
7308	Grand Ville	Buick/Olds/Pontiac 1975-87
6739	Grand Wagoneer	Jeep Wagoneer, Commando, Cherokee, Truck 1957-86
7199	Gremlin	AMC 1975-86
6575	GT	Opel 1971-75
7593	GTI	VW Front Wheel Drive 1974-90
5905	GTO 1968-73	Tempest/GTO/LeMans 1968-73
7346	GTO 1974	Pontiac Mid-Size 1974-83
5821	GTX	Roadrunner/Satellite/Belvedere/GTX 1968-73
5910	GT6	Triumph 1969-73
6542	G.T.350, 500	Mustang/Cougar 1965-73
6930	G-10, 20, 30	Chevy/GMC Vans 1967-86
6930	G-1500, 2500, 3500	Chevy/GMC Vans 1967-86
8040	G-10, 20, 30	Chevy/GMC Vans 1987-90
8040	G-1500, 2500, 3500	Chevy/GMC Vans 1987-90
5795	Hi-Lux	Toyota 1966-70
6845	Horizon	Omni/Horizon/Rampage 1978-88
7199	Hornet	AMC 1975-86
7135	Impala	Chevrolet 1968-88
7317	IROC-Z	Camaro 1982-88
6739	Jeepster	Jeep Wagoneer, Commando, Cherokee, Truck 1957-86
7593	Jetta	VW Front Wheel Drive 1974-90
6931	Jimmy	Blazer/Jimmy 1969-82
7383	Jimmy	Chevy S-10 Blazer/GMC S-15 Jimmy 1982-87
6739	J-10, 20	Jeep Wagoneer, Commando, Cherokee, Truck 1957-86
6739	J-100, 200, 300	Jeep Wagoneer, Commando, Cherokee, Truck 1957-86
6575	Kadett	Opel 1971-75
7199	Kammback	AMC 1975-86
5796	Karmann Ghia	Volkswagen 1949-71
6837	Karmann Ghia	Volkswagen 1970-81
7135	Kingswood	Chevrolet 1968-88
6931	K-5	Blazer/Jimmy 1969-82
6936	K-10, 20, 30	Chevy/GMC Pick-Ups & Suburban 1970-87
6936	K-1500, 2500, 3500	Chevy/GMC Pick-Ups & Suburban 1970-87
8055	K-10, 20, 30	Chevy/GMC Pick-Ups & Suburban 1988-90
8055	K-1500, 2500, 3500	Chevy/GMC Pick-Ups & Suburban 1988-90
6840	Laguna	Chevrolet Mid-Size 1964-88
7041	Lancer	Champ/Arrow/Sapporo 1977-83
5795	Land Cruiser	Toyota 1966-70
7035	Land Cruiser	Toyota Trucks 1970-88
7163	Laser	Chrysler Front Wheel Drive 1981-88
7163	LeBaron	Chrysler Front Wheel Drive 1981-88
7165	LeCar	Renault 1975-85

Chilton's Repair Manuals are available at your local retailer or by mailing a check or money order for **$15.95** per book plus **$3.50** for 1st book and **$.50** for each additional book to cover postage and handling to:

Chilton Book Company
Dept. DM
Radnor, PA 19089

NOTE: When ordering be sure to include your name & address, book part No. & title.

CHILTON'S REPAIR MANUAL MODEL INDEX
Car and truck model names are listed in alphabetical and numerical order

Part No.	Model	Repair Manual Title
5905	LeMans	Tempest/GTO/LeMans 1968-73
7346	LeMans	Pontiac Mid-Size 1974-83
7308	LeSabre	Buick/Olds/Pontiac 1975-87
6842	Lincoln	Ford/Mercury/Lincoln 1968-88
7055	LN-7	Ford/Mercury Front Wheel Drive 1981-87
6842	LTD	Ford/Mercury/Lincoln 1968-88
6696	LTD II	Ford/Mercury/Lincoln Mid-Size 1971-85
7950	Lumina	Lumina/Grand Prix/Cutlass/Regal 1988-90
6815	LUV	Chevrolet LUV 1972-81
6575	Luxus	Opel 1971-75
7055	Lynx	Ford/Mercury Front Wheel Drive 1981-87
6844	L6	BMW 1970-88
6344	L7	BMW 1970-88
6542	Mach I	Mustang/Cougar 1965-73
6812	Mach I Ghia	Mustang II 1974-78
6840	Malibu	Chevrolet Mid-Size 1964-88
6575	Manta	Opel 1971-75
6696	Mark IV, V, VI, VII	Ford/Mercury/Lincoln Mid-Size 1971-85
7814	Mark VII	Thunderbird, Cougar, Continental 1980-87
6842	Marquis	Ford/Mercury/Lincoln 1968-88
6696	Marquis	Ford/Mercury/Lincoln Mid-Size 1971-85
7199	Matador	AMC 1975-86
6634	Maverick	Maverick/Comet 1970-77
6817	Maverick	Jeep 1945-87
7170	Maxima	Nissan 200SX, 240SX, 510, 610, 710, 810, Maxima 1973-88
6842	Mercury	Ford/Mercury/Lincoln 1968-88
6963	Merkur	Mustang/Capri/Merkur 1979-88
6780	MGB, MGB-GT, MGC-GT	MG 1961-81
6780	Midget	MG 1961-81
7583	Mighty Max	Mitsubishi 1983-89
7583	Mirage	Mitsubishi 1983-89
5795	Mk.II 1969-70	Toyota 1966-70
7004	Mk.II 1970-76	Toyota Corona/Crown/Cressida/Mk.II/Van 1970-87
6554	Monaco	Dodge 1968-77
6937	Monarch	Granada/Monarch 1975-82
6840	Monte Carlo	Chevrolet Mid-Size 1964-88
6696	Montego	Ford/Mercury/Lincoln Mid-Size 1971-85
6842	Monterey	Ford/Mercury/Lincoln 1968-88
7583	Montero	Mitsubishi 1983-89
6935	Monza 1975-80	GM Subcompact 1971-80
6981	MPV	Mazda 1978-89
6542	Mustang	Mustang/Cougar 1965-73
6963	Mustang	Mustang/Capri/Merkur 1979-88
6812	Mustang II	Mustang II 1974-78
6981	MX6	Mazda 1978-89
6844	M3, M6	BMW 1970-88
7163	New Yorker	Chrysler Front Wheel Drive 1981-88
6841	Nova	Chevy II/Nova 1962-79
7658	Nova	Chevrolet Nova/GEO Prizm 1985-89
7049	Omega	GM X-Body 1980-85
6845	Omni	Omni/Horizon/Rampage 1978-88
6575	Opel	Opel 1971-75
7199	Pacer	AMC 1975-86
7587	Park Avenue	GM C-Body 1985
6842	Park Lane	Ford/Mercury/Lincoln 1968-88
6962	Passat	VW Front Wheel Drive 1974-90
6816	Pathfinder	Datsun/Nissan Pick-Ups and Pathfinder 1970-89
5790	Patrol	Datsun 1961-72
6934	PB100, 150, 200, 250, 300, 350	Dodge/Plymouth Vans 1967-88
5982	Peugeot	Peugeot 1970-74
7049	Phoenix	GM X-Body 1980-85
7027	Pinto	Pinto/Bobcat 1971-80
6554	Polara	Dodge 1968-77
7583	Precis	Mitsubishi 1983-89
6980	Prelude	Honda 1973-88
7658	Prizm	Chevrolet Nova/GEO Prizm 1985-89
8012	Probe	Ford Probe 1989
7660	Pulsar	Datsun/Nissan F-10, 310, Stanza, Pulsar 1976-88
6529	PV-444	Volvo 1956-69
6529	PV-544	Volvo 1956-69
6529	P-1800	Volvo 1956-69
7593	Quantum	VW Front Wheel Drive 1974-87
7593	Rabbit	VW Front Wheel Drive 1974-87
7593	Rabbit Pickup	VW Front Wheel Drive 1974-87
6575	Rallye	Opel 1971-75
7459	Ramcharger	Dodge/Plymouth Trucks 1967-88
6845	Rampage	Omni/Horizon/Rampage 1978-88
6320	Ranchero	Fairlane/Torino 1962-70
6696	Ranchero	Ford/Mercury/Lincoln Mid-Size 1971-85
6842	Ranch Wagon	Ford/Mercury/Lincoln 1968-88
7338	Ranger Pickup	Ford Ranger/Bronco II 1983-88
7307	Regal RWD	Century/Regal 1975-87
7950	Regal FWD 1988-90	Lumina/Grand Prix/Cutlass/Regal 1988-90
7163	Reliant	Chrysler Front Wheel Drive 1981-88
5821	Roadrunner	Roadrunner/Satellite/Belvedere/GTX 1968-73
7659	Rotary Pick-Up	Mazda Trucks 1971-89
6981	RX-7	Mazda 1978-89
7165	R-12, 15, 17, 18, 18i	Renault 1975-85
7830	Sable	Taurus/Sable/Continental 1986-89
7750	Safari	Chevrolet Astro/GMC Safari 1985-90
7041	Sapporo	Champ/Arrow/Sapporo 1978-83
5821	Satellite	Roadrunner/Satellite/Belvedere/GTX 1968-73
6326	Scamp	Valiant/Duster 1968-76
6845	Scamp	Omni/Horizon/Rampage 1978-88
6962	Scirocco	VW Front Wheel Drive 1974-90
6936	Scottsdale	Chevrolet/GMC Pick-Ups & Suburban 1970-87
8055	Scottsdale	Chevrolet/GMC Pick-Ups & Suburban 1988-90
5912	Scout	International Scout 1967-73
8034	Scrambler	Jeep 1971-90
7197	Sentra	Datsun 1200, 210, Nissan Sentra 1973-88
7462	Seville	Cadillac 1967-89
7163	Shadow	Chrysler Front Wheel Drive 1981-88
6936	Siera	Chevrolet/GMC Pick-Ups & Suburban 1970-87
8055	Siera	Chevrolet/GMC Pick-Ups & Suburban 1988-90
7583	Sigma	Mitsubishi 1983-89
6326	Signet	Valiant/Duster 1968-76
6936	Silverado	Chevrolet/GMC Pick-Ups & Suburban 1970-87
8055	Silverado	Chevrolet/GMC Pick-Ups & Suburban 1988-90
6935	Skyhawk	GM Subcompact 1971-80
7059	Skyhawk	Cavalier, Skyhawk, Cimarron, 2000 1982-88
7049	Skylark	GM X-Body 1980-85

Chilton's Repair Manuals are available at your local retailer or by mailing a check or money order for **$15.95** per book plus **$3.50** for 1st book and **$.50** for each additional book to cover postage and handling to:

Chilton Book Company
Dept. DM
Radnor, PA 19089

NOTE: When ordering be sure to include your name & address, book part No. & title.

CHILTON'S REPAIR MANUAL MODEL INDEX
Car and truck model names are listed in alphabetical and numerical order

Part No.	Model	Repair Manual Title	Part No.	Model	Repair Manual Title
7675	Skylark	Calais, Grand Am, Skylark, Somerset 1985-86	7040	Turbo	Volvo 1970-88
7657	Somerset	Calais, Grand Am, Skylark, Somerset 1985-86	5796	Type 1 Sedan 1949-71	Volkswagen 1949-71
7042	Spider 2000	Fiat 1969-81	6837	Type 1 Sedan 1970-80	Volkswagen 1970-81
7199	Spirit	AMC 1975-86	5796	Type 1 Karmann Ghia 1960-71	Volkswagen 1949-71
6552	Sport Fury	Plymouth 1968–76	6837	Type 1 Karmann Ghia 1970-74	Volkswagen 1970-81
7165	Sport Wagon	Renault 1975-85	5796	Type 1 Convertible 1964-71	Volkswagen 1949-71
5796	Squareback	Volkswagen 1949-71	6837	Type 1 Convertible 1970-80	Volkswagen 1970-81
6837	Squareback	Volkswagen 1970-81	5796	Type 1 Super Beetle 1971	Volkswagen 1949-71
7196	Stanza	Datsun/Nissan F-10, 310, Stanza, Pulsar 1976-88	6837	Type 1 Super Beetle 1971-75	Volkswagen 1970-81
6935	Starfire	GM Subcompact 1971-80	5796	Type 2 Bus 1953-71	Volkswagen 1949-71
7583	Starion	Mitsubishi 1983-89	6837	Type 2 Bus 1970-80	Volkswagen 1970-81
7036	Starlet	Toyota Corolla/Carina/Tercel/Starlet 1970-87	5796	Type 2 Kombi 1954-71	Volkswagen 1949-71
7059	STE	Cavalier, Skyhawk, Cimarron, 2000 1982-88	6837	Type 2 Kombi 1970-73	Volkswagen 1970-81
5795	Stout	Toyota 1966-70	6837	Type 2 Vanagon 1981	Volkswagen 1970-81
7042	Strada	Fiat 1969-81	5796	Type 3 Fastback & Squareback 1961-71	Volkswagen 1949-71
6552	Suburban	Plymouth 1968-76	7081	Type 3 Fastback & Squareback 1970-73	Volkswagen 1970-70
6936	Suburban	Chevy/GMC Pick-Ups & Suburban 1970-87	5796	Type 4 411 1971	Volkswagen 1949-71
8055	Suburban	Chevy/GMC Pick-Ups & Suburban 1988-90	6837	Type 4 411 1971-72	Volkswagen 1970-81
6935	Sunbird	GM Subcompact 1971-80	5796	Type 4 412 1971	Volkswagen 1949-71
7059	Sunbird	Cavalier, Skyhawk, Cimarron, 2000, 1982-88	6845	Turismo	Omni/Horizon/Rampage 1978-88
7163	Sundance	Chrysler Front Wheel Drive 1981-88	5905	T-37	Tempest/GTO/LeMans 1968-73
7043	Supra	Toyota Celica/Supra 1971-87	6836	T-1000	Chevette/T-1000 1976-88
8058	Supra	Toyota Celica/Supra 1986-90	6935	Vega	GM Subcompact 1971-80
6837	Super Beetle	Volkswagen 1970-81	7346	Ventura	Pontiac Mid-Size 1974-83
7199	SX-4	AMC 1975-86	6696	Versailles	Ford/Mercury/Lincoln Mid-Size 1971-85
7383	S-10 Blazer	Chevy S-10 Blazer/GMC S-15 Jimmy 1982-87	6552	VIP	Plymouth 1968-76
7310	S-10 Pick-Up	Chevy S-10/GMC S-15 Pick-Ups 1982-87	7037	Vista	Colt/Challenger/Vista/Conquest 1971-88
7383	S-15 Jimmy	Chevy S-10 Blazer/GMC S-15 Jimmy 1982-87	6933	Vista Cruiser	Cutlass 1970-87
7310	S-15 Pick-Up	Chevy S-10/GMC S-15 Pick-Ups 1982-87	6637	Volare	Aspen/Volare 1976-80
7830	Taurus	Taurus/Sable/Continental 1986-89	7482	Voyager	Dodge Caravan/Plymouth Voyager 1984-88
6845	TC-3	Omni/Horizon/Rampage 1978-88	6326	V-100	Valiant/Duster 1968-76
5905	Tempest	Tempest/GTO/LeMans 1968-73	6739	Wagoneer 1962-83	Jeep Wagoneer, Commando, Cherokee, Truck 1957-86
7055	Tempo	Ford/Mercury Front Wheel Drive 1981-87	7939	Wagoneer 1984-89	Jeep Wagoneer, Comanche, Cherokee 1984-89
7036	Tercel	Toyota Corolla/Carina/Tercel/Starlet 1970-87	8034	Wrangler	Jeep 1971-90
7081	Thing	Volkswagen 1970-81	7459	W100, 150, 200, 250, 300, 350	Dodge/Plymouth Trucks 1967-88
6696	Thunderbird	Ford/Mercury/Lincoln Mid-Size 1971-85	7459	WM300	Dodge/Plymouth Trucks 1967-88
7814	Thunderbird	Thunderbird, Cougar, Continental 1980-87	6842	XL	Ford/Mercury/Lincoln 1968-88
7055	Topaz	Ford/Mercury Front Wheel Drive 1981-87	6963	XR4Ti	Mustang/Capri/Merkur 1979-88
6320	Torino	Fairlane/Torino 1962-75	6696	XR-7	Ford/Mercury/Lincoln Mid-Size 1971-85
6696	Torino	Ford/Mercury/Lincoln Mid-Size 1971-85	6982	XT Coupe	Subaru 1970-88
7163	Town & Country	Chrysler Front Wheel Drive 1981-88	7042	X1/9	Fiat 1969-81
6842	Town Car	Ford/Mercury/Lincoln 1968-88	6965	Zephyr	Fairmont/Zephyr 1978-83
7135	Townsman	Chevrolet 1968-88	7059	Z-24	Cavalier, Skyhawk, Cimarron, 2000 1982-88
5795	Toyota Pickups	Toyota 1966-70	6735	Z-28	Camaro 1967-81
7035	Toyota Pickups	Toyota Trucks 1970-88	7318	Z-28	Camaro 1982-88
7004	Toyota Van	Toyota Corona/Crown/Cressida/Mk.II/Van 1970-87	6845	024	Omni/Horizon/Rampage 1978-88
7459	Trail Duster	Dodge/Plymouth Trucks 1967-88	6844	3.0S, 3.0Si, 3.0CS	BMW 1970-88
7046	Trans Am	Firebird 1967-81	6817	4-63	Jeep 1981-87
7345	Trans Am	Firebird 1982-90			
7583	Tredia	Mitsubishi 1983-89			

Chilton's Repair Manuals are available at your local retailer or by mailing a check or money order for **$15.95** per book plus **$3.50** for 1st book and **$.50** for each additional book to cover postage and handling to:

**Chilton Book Company
Dept. DM
Radnor, PA 19089**

NOTE: When ordering be sure to include your name & address, book part No. & title.

CHILTON'S REPAIR MANUAL MODEL INDEX
Car and truck model names are listed in alphabetical and numerical order

Part No.	Model	Repair Manual Title
6817	4 × 4-63	Jeep 1981-87
6817	4-73	Jeep 1981-87
6817	4 × 4-73	Jeep 1981-87
6817	4-75	Jeep 1981-87
7035	4Runner	Toyota Trucks 1970-88
6982	4wd Wagon	Subaru 1970-88
6982	4wd Coupe	Subaru 1970-88
6933	4-4-2 1970-80	Cutlass 1970-87
6817	6-63	Jeep 1981-87
6809	6.9	Mercedes-Benz 1974-84
7308	88	Buick/Olds/Pontiac 1975-90
7308	98	Buick/Olds/Pontiac 1975-90
7587	98 Regency	GM C-Body 1985
5902	100LS, 100GL	Audi 1970-73
6529	122, 122S	Volvo 1956-69
7042	124	Fiat 1969-81
7042	128	Fiat 1969-81
7042	131	Fiat 1969-81
6529	142	Volvo 1956-69
7040	142	Volvo 1970-88
6529	144	Volvo 1956-69
7040	144	Volvo 1970-88
6529	145	Volvo 1956-69
7040	145	Volvo 1970-88
6529	164	Volvo 1956-69
7040	164	Volvo 1970-88
6065	190C	Mercedes-Benz 1959-70
6809	190D	Mercedes-Benz 1974-84
6065	190DC	Mercedes-Benz 1959-70
6809	190E	Mercedes-Benz 1974-84
6065	200, 200D	Mercedes-Benz 1959-70
7170	200SX	Nissan 200SX, 240SX, 510, 610, 710, 810, Maxima 1973-88
7197	210	Datsun 1200, 210, Nissan Sentra 1971-88
6065	220B, 220D, 220Sb, 220SEb	Mercedes-Benz 1959-70
5907	220/8 1968-73	Mercedes-Benz 1968-73
6809	230 1974-78	Mercedes-Benz 1974-84
6065	230S, 230SL	Mercedes-Benz 1959-70
5907	230/8	Mercedes-Benz 1968-73
6809	240D	Mercedes-Benz 1974-84
7170	240SX	Nissan 200SX, 240SX, 510, 610, 710, 810, Maxima 1973-88
6932	240Z	Datsun Z & ZX 1970-87
7040	242, 244, 245	Volvo 1970-88
5907	250C	Mercedes-Benz 1968-73
6065	250S, 250SE, 250SL	Mercedes-Benz 1959-70
5907	250/8	Mercedes-Benz 1968-73
6932	260Z	Datsun Z & ZX 1970-87
7040	262, 264, 265	Volvo 1970-88
5907	280	Mercedes-Benz 1968-73
6809	280	Mercedes-Benz 1974-84
5907	280C	Mercedes-Benz 1968-73
6809	280C, 280CE, 280E	Mercedes-Benz 1974-84
6065	280S, 280SE	Mercedes-Benz 1959-70
5907	280SE, 280S/8, 280SE/8	Mercedes-Benz 1968-73
6809	280SEL, 280SEL/8, 280SL	Mercedes-Benz 1974-84
6932	280Z, 280ZX	Datsun Z & ZX 1970-87
6065	300CD, 300D, 300SD, 300SE	Mercedes-Benz 1959-70
5907	300SEL 3.5, 300SEL 4.5	Mercedes-Benz 1968-73
5907	300SEL 6.3, 300SEL/8	Mercedes-Benz 1968-73
6809	300TD	Mercedes-Benz 1974-84
6932	300ZX	Datsun Z & ZX 1970-87
5982	304	Peugeot 1970-74
5790	310	Datsun 1961-72
7196	310	Datsun/Nissan F-10, 310, Stanza, Pulsar 1977-88
5790	311	Datsun 1961-72
6844	318i, 320i	BMW 1970-88
6981	323	Mazda 1978-89
6844	325E, 325ES, 325i, 325iS, 325iX	BMW 1970-88
6809	380SEC, 380SEL, 380SL, 380SLC	Mercedes-Benz 1974-84
5907	350SL	Mercedes-Benz 1968-73
7163	400	Chrysler Front Wheel Drive 1981-88
5790	410	Datsun 1961-72
5790	411	Datsun 1961-72
7081	411, 412	Volkswagen 1970-81
6809	450SE, 450SEL, 450 SEL 6.9	Mercedes-Benz 1974-84
6809	450SL, 450SLC	Mercedes-Benz 1974-84
5907	450SLC	Mercedes-Benz 1968-73
6809	500SEC, 500SEL	Mercedes-Benz 1974-84
5982	504	Peugeot 1970-74
5790	510	Datsun 1961-72
7170	510	Nissan 200SX, 240SX, 510, 610, 710, 810, Maxima 1973-88
6816	520	Datsun/Nissan Pick-Ups and Pathfinder 1970-89
6844	524TD	BMW 1970-88
6844	525i	BMW 1970-88
6844	528e	BMW 1970-88
6844	528i	BMW 1970-88
6844	530i	BMW 1970-88
6844	533i	BMW 1970-88
6844	535i, 535iS	BMW 1970-88
6980	600	Honda 1973-88
7163	600	Chrysler Front Wheel Drive 1981-88
7170	610	Nissan 200SX, 240SX, 510, 610, 710, 810, Maxima 1973-88
6816	620	Datsun/Nissan Pick-Ups and Pathfinder 1970-89
6981	626	Mazda 1978-89
6844	630 CSi	BMW 1970-88
6844	633 CSi	BMW 1970-88
6844	635CSi	BMW 1970-88
7170	710	Nissan 200SX, 240SX, 510, 610, 710, 810, Maxima 1973-88
6816	720	Datsun/Nissan Pick-Ups and Pathfinder 1970-89
6844	733i	BMW 1970-88
6844	735i	BMW 1970-88
7040	760, 760GLE	Volvo 1970-88
7040	780	Volvo 1970-88
6981	808	Mazda 1978-89
7170	810	Nissan 200SX, 240SX, 510, 610, 710, 810, Maxima 1973-88
7042	850	Fiat 1969-81
7572	900, 900 Turbo	SAAB 900 1976-85
7048	924	Porsche 924/928 1976-81
7048	928	Porsche 924/928 1976-81
6981	929	Mazda 1978-89
6836	1000	Chevette/1000 1976-88
6780	1100	MG 1961-81
5790	1200	Datsun 1961-72
7197	1200	Datsun 1200, 210, Nissan Sentra 1973-88
6982	1400GL, 1400DL, 1400GF	Subaru 1970-88
5790	1500	Datsun 1961-72

Chilton's Repair Manuals are available at your local retailer or by mailing a check or money order for **$15.95** per book plus **$3.50** for 1st book and **$.50** for each additional book to cover postage and handling to:

Chilton Book Company
Dept. DM
Radnor, PA 19089

NOTE: When ordering be sure to include your name & address, book part No. & title.

CHILTON'S REPAIR MANUAL MODEL INDEX
Car and truck model names are listed in alphabetical and numerical order

Part No.	Model	Repair Manual Title	Part No.	Model	Repair Manual Title
6844	1500	DMW 1970-88	6844	2000	BMW 1970-88
6936	1500	Chevy/GMC Pick-Ups & Suburban 1970-87	6844	2002, 2002Ti, 2002Tii	BMW 1970-88
8055	1500	Chevy/GMC Pick-Ups & Suburban 1988-90	6936	2500	Chevy/GMC Pick-Ups & Suburban 1970-87
6844	1600	BMW 1970-88	8055	2500	Chevy/GMC Pick-Ups & Suburban 1988-90
5790	1600	Datsun 1961-72	6844	2500	BMW 1970-88
6982	1600DL, 1600GL, 1600GLF	Subaru 1970-88	6844	2800	BMW 1970-88
6844	1600-2	BMW 1970-88	6936	3500	Chevy/GMC Pick-Ups & Suburban 1970-87
6844	1800	BMW 1970-88	8055	3500	Chevy/GMC Pick-Ups & Suburban 1988-90
6982	1800DL, 1800GL, 1800GLF	Subaru 1970-88	7028	4000	Audi 4000/5000 1978-81
6529	1800, 1800S	Volvo 1956-69	7028	5000	Audi 4000/5000 1978-81
7040	1800E, 1800ES	Volvo 1970-88	7309	6000	Celebrity, Century, Ciera, 6000 19 88
5790	2000	Datsun 1961-72			
7059	2000	Cavalier, Skyhawk, Cimarron, 2000 1982-88			

Chilton's Repair Manuals are available at your local retailer or by mailing a check or money order for **$15** per book plus **$3.50** for 1st book and **$.50** for each additional book to cover postage and handling to:

Chilton Book Company
Dept. DM
Radnor, PA 19089

NOTE: When ordering be sure to include your name & address, book part No. & title.